38 re-cre: process

Leo Spitzer: Representative Essays

Leo Spitzer

REPRESENTATIVE ESSAYS

EDITED BY
Alban K. Forcione, Herbert Lindenberger, and
Madeline Sutherland

With a Foreword by John Freccero

STANFORD UNIVERSITY PRESS   1988
Stanford, California

Stanford University Press
Stanford, California
© 1988 by the Board of Trustees of the
Leland Stanford Junior University

Printed in the United States of America

CIP data appear at the end of the book

Preface

Any selection of essays from the hundreds that Leo Spitzer (1887–1960) wrote is likely to appear somewhat arbitrary. Although we recognized that many readers would find one or more of their favorite essays by Spitzer missing from this volume, we decided that we could at least select a group to represent the range of his work. Thus we include essays from both his earlier period in Germany as well as his American period, though with emphasis on the latter. We include several essays each on the three national literatures—Italian, Spanish, and French—to which most of his attention over his long career was directed. We have also tried to represent the various genres on which he wrote as well as the range of periods—from medieval to twentieth-century literature—that he commanded. Since Spitzer was highly self-conscious about the critical methods he employed, we include three essays ("Linguistics and Literary History," "Development of a Method," and "The Spanish Baroque") that could be said to constitute his intellectual autobiography. In addition, to demonstrate a critical adventurousness rare during his time, we include his essay on American advertising, which applies the method he was perfecting during his later years to a nonliterary text.

The major editorial decision outside the selection of essays was how to present his footnotes. Spitzer used the footnote for long digressions that are often as important as his "main" text. These footnotes are too unwieldy to go at the bottom of the page; yet to relegate them to the back of the book would not give them the prominence they deserve. We have therefore undertaken a typographical experiment: we have placed Spitzer's notes within our text, but we have marked them with asterisks and set them in a smaller typeface with rules at the beginning and end. Readers who prefer to read the main text of an essay straight through may choose to skip the notes—though they may sometimes find that the digressiveness characterizing the notes is part of Spitzer's essential manner, even in the so-called main text. Insofar as possible, we have removed bibliographical citations from these notes, as well as from the main text, and placed them at the back of the book in the form of numbered endnotes.

Since Spitzer was often casual in recording literary quotations (which he sometimes apparently cited from memory) and in giving their sources, we have tried to retrace his steps and to provide accurate documentation. First names of scholars less familiar to modern readers than to Spitzer himself have been added; in the essays originally given as lectures, these additions have been put in brackets to preserve the tone of the lecture. We have also translated words and quotations from foreign languages; although Spitzer would likely have disapproved of this policy, we recognize that in his own time and place a knowledge of the major European languages could be assumed among scholarly readers to a far greater degree than it can be assumed today.

These translations and other editorial intrusions inserted in Spitzer's text appear in brackets ([ ]), whereas Spitzer's own bracketed comments are within braces ({ }). Published translations have been altered where necessary to reflect the specific details Spitzer is discussing. Quotes from foreign secondary works are given only in English translation. The * indicates a hypothesized linguistic form that has been reconstructed through the methods of historical linguistics.

We are grateful to our colleagues Joseph Frank and William Mills Todd III for joining us as part of an informal committee to choose the essays for this volume. We also thank Claire Burday, corporate librarian for Sunkist, for her efforts—unsuccessful, as it turned out—to find a reproducible copy of the original advertisement that Spitzer analyzed in "American Advertising Explained as Popular Art." We are grateful to Stanford University and Princeton University for providing research funds. In addition, we thank Michelle Amon-Duff, Murphy Halliburton, Eric Miller, and Katherine Trumpener for research help. Translators of essays from foreign languages are cited in the headnotes to these essays.

We are also grateful to our many colleagues at Princeton, Stanford, the University of Texas at Austin, and elsewhere for their valuable assistance: Beverly Allen, Laurie Anderson, Helmut Bonheim, George H. Brown, Brigitte Cazelles, Gregson Davis, Jay Fliegelman, John Freccero, René Girard, the late Donald R. Howard, Alphonse Juilland, David Laurence, John Loftis, Marsh H. McCall, Jr., Richard Meier, Suzanne Nash, Mary Jane Parrine, Thomas Palaima, Pierre Saint-Amand, Cynthia Shelmerdine, Scott Sigel, W. O. S. Sutherland, Edward Timms, Paolo Virno, and Mary Wack.

We would like to thank Wolfgang Spitzer for his encouragement and cooperation in the preparation of this volume. We also thank the following previous publishers of the essays: *Cultura Neolatina*, N. G. Elwert Verlag, *Hispanic Review*, Max Hueber Verlag, *Italica*, *Journal of the History of Ideas*, *Modern Language Notes*, Max Niemeyer Verlag, *Nueva Revista de Filología Hispánica*, Princeton University Press, and *Romanic Review*.

A. F.
H. L.
M. S.

Contents

Foreword

On what may have been the last occasion that they were cordial to each other, Leo Spitzer and Don Cameron Allen were seated at the same large table during the customary coffee break at the Johns Hopkins cafeteria. Allen was saying to a small group of graduate students that he did not believe there was any allegory in Andrew Marvell's "Upon Appleton House." "Put it this way," interrupted Spitzer. "If there is, you'll never find it."

As graduate students, we had learned from Spitzer about the hermeneutic circle and the search for the *Sosein* of the literary work—its being the way it is and not otherwise. We knew too about the "clique" that Spitzer experienced when things fell into place, and we spelled it that way to distinguish it from domestic *daemons* of our own. The theory was not as heady as the "angelism" of Georges Poulet or as rigorous as the history of ideas of Arthur Lovejoy, to mention two other colleagues with whom he disputed in essays reprinted here, but it was not theory that we expected of Spitzer; we turned to him when we wished to know what a word or a poem meant.

Spitzer was, above all, an interpreter of texts. By the time he reached the United States as a refugee from Nazi Germany (via Istanbul, where he taught briefly, along with Erich Auerbach), his earlier interest in style as the expression of "lived experience" (Wilhelm Dilthey's *Erlebnis*) or of the writer's unconscious (Freud) had begun to wane, although examples of such approaches are preserved here. Increasingly, he would read a text as a stylistic and aesthetic artifact, without reference to the "mind" that produced it. Nevertheless, he continued to trace his critical inclinations (they were no more than that) to Schleiermacher and Dilthey, as well as to the philological tradition. He scrupulously acknowledged his indebtedness each time he taught the class that served as our initiation into graduate school: "Introduction to Literary Scholarship." He would begin with a glance at the dusty portraits and photographs hanging on the walls of the seminar room in Gilman Hall and he would identify them one by one: "This is Diez, the founder of our discipline . . . next is Gaston Paris and then Meyer-Lübke, my teacher . . ."

We sometimes wondered if this filial piety toward the continental tradition, contrasting so sharply with his generally polemical relationship to his colleagues, were not simply another way to distance himself from the rest of us, like the opera cape he wore when it rained, or the Homburg set rakishly on a mane of white hair. In those days of crew cuts and white bucks, the figure of the continental virtuoso challenged every canon of male decorum—for years he took his meals in the "Ladies' Wing" of the Faculty Club so that he could talk shop with Anna Granville Hatcher, the only scholar in the department who could come close to his philological learning and whose command of English syntax he trusted for occasional help. To many in the English Department, his dramatic flair sometimes provided a target for "down home" wit. One day, as Raymond Dexter Havens saw Spitzer pacing up and down the corridor in his usual meditation before class, he called out, "Hey, Spitzer! What are you doing there?" Irritated as much by the American pronunciation of his name as by the intrusion, Spitzer replied, "I am preparing my seminar!" With mock sympathy, Havens offered his newly arrived colleague some practical advice: "Gee, most of us finish that the night before."

His aesthetics fit in with the prevailing mood much more readily than his style; he had a profound effect on American critics who were seeking to escape the prevailing orthodoxy of the English Department. His interest in textual interpretation corresponded to what was called "criticism" by dissident modernists and creative writers reacting against the sterility of literary history. For all his classical learning and historical semantics, he seemed to share some of the basic assumptions of the New Criticism: the organic unity of the work, the autonomy of the text, the irrelevance of biography and authorial intention. His "method" (there were many, but he always used the singular) seemed to give philological legitimacy to what was more humbly known as "practical criticism" or, in the Department of Romance Languages, as *explication de texte*. It was one thing to show how a poem "works"; it was quite another to be able to do so in twenty-three languages, even if, as he once told an interviewer for the student newspaper, Latin was the only one he really knew well. It was largely through Spitzer that many American formalists began to use scholarship as an adjunct to the understanding of poetry. In the late 1940's, he and Charles Singleton were so frequently seen together that irreverent students referred to them as "God-the-Father and His Son," alluding both to Spitzer's appearance and to Singleton's natty, Italianate beard. Predictably, the intimacy did not last, but the influence continued to be discernible. Singleton's extraordinary originality consisted in the use of theological traditions to illuminate Dante's poetry, against the prevailing Crocean view of theology as antithetical to *poesia.* In many ways, this was a pragmatic application of Spitzerian scholarship to the explication of a single text, without Spitzer's idealist elaboration. Singleton's reading was "structuralist" in the sense the word used to have when it was applied to some of Spitzer's studies (as, for example, the masterly reading of *Inferno* XIII included here), meaning the explication of broad imaginative patterns in the literary work. In stylistic studies of Dante's text, however, that involve a command of all normative Romance forms in order to evaluate the significance of specific choices, Spitzer was alone. His essay on the farcical elements in the *Inferno* is a philological tour de force.

Spitzer supported the establishment of a program of creative writing at the university and contributed articles to *The Hopkins Review*, founded by Elliot Coleman as an antidote to *English Literary History*. Soon it featured articles by Auerbach and Poulet as well, along with poetry by Karl Shapiro and prose by Louis Rubin and promising undergraduates, such as John Barth. Spitzer's presence precluded any trace of the anti-intellectualism that often surfaces in American departments of creative writing, while vindicating the writer's concern for poetic form rather than literary history. The example was not lost on younger scholars in English. Earl Wasserman, whose faith in poetic coherence was closer to Spitzer's idealism than to Allen's disabused critical skepticism, became one of the most adept users of the *Patrologia Latina* in his interpretation of pre-Romantic English poetry. To the astonishment of the librarians and the consternation of the professors, that dusty and indigestible collection of the writings of the Church Fathers became so popular with graduate students that it had to be brought up from the basement and placed on reserve. A whole generation of "scholar-critics" was thus introduced to interpretive methods that involved wide contextual reading in theological and exegetical materials that, before Spitzer, had been the exclusive preserve of historians.

Yet Spitzer remained inimitable and must have wanted it that way, judging from the reviews and polemical articles he wrote. Under a veneer of urbanity, they were generally caustic, sometimes unfair, and often directed against younger colleagues, like Wasserman, who had learned much from him. In one such review of a younger scholar, Spitzer wrote a condescending but hilarious footnote suggesting a "'negative reading-list' . . . for our younger scholars who deal with older literature: Buber, Bergson, Dilthey, Freud, Heidegger. . . ."[1] In a witty reply, the victim of the attack, Stephen Gilman, defined Spitzer's reviewing technique as "hunting quail with an elephant gun."[2] But when Spitzer went after bigger game, such as Georges Poulet (in "Apropos of *La Vie de Marianne*," reprinted here), he got more than he bargained for; Poulet retaliated with characteristic *noblesse* and no little irony by nominating him for the Legion of Honor.

In retrospect, both Spitzer and the Hopkins formalists might be accused of a certain evasion of their own historicity because of their insistence on the autonomy of the text. It is true that Spitzer seemed relatively unscathed by the cataclysm that had surrounded and nearly engulfed him in prewar Germany, treating it as a ghastly hiatus not connected (as Lovejoy had implied in an article to which Spitzer responds, in "*Geistesgeschichte* vs. History of Ideas," in this volume) with nineteenth-century German ideology. One could not expect a different reaction from a man of his age—in both the chronological and the cultural sense. He once remarked sadly that a lifetime of formal concerns had left him ill-prepared for such a cosmic outbreak of irrationality and violence, just as a whole generation of German academics, nurtured on neo-Kantian myths of culture and the continuity of ancient values, found it impossible to respond to the threat from Hitler. Somehow the interpreter's suspension of disbelief, the effort to understand rather than judge, had a way of extending beyond poetry to the evening newspaper as well. He was not alone in trying to put the past behind him; he quoted with approval the anecdote about Benedetto Croce, who began his first seminar after the war with the single word *Dunque* (roughly, "As I was saying . . ."). Spitzer might have said something like that, had his first class been something other than elementary French. Instead, according to Hopkins folklore, he asked his class of ex-GI's, "How many of you already know Rumanian?"

He soon became acclimatized to his new linguistic surroundings. Expressions of popular taste, however lamentable, entered his world when they acquired appropriate verbal form. The lighter side of this "logocentrism" can be perceived in his essays on American advertising, one of which appears here. He could be equally playful about its more sinister aspects, as, for instance, in his essay on the phrase "Gentiles Only," in which, by an act of the historical imagination, he construes the sign to mean "only heathens and outcasts need apply."[3] Once, after a series on corruption in government, he was moved to write a letter to the editor of the *Baltimore Sun*, not to comment on the issue, but to suggest on etymology for the word "payola." His words, as I recall them, were as follows: "a pseudo-Italian diminutive, on analogy with 'pianola,' trademark coinage to suggest automatic function (compare 'shine-ola,' shoe polish)." For him, the New World, as well as the Old, remained above all a text.

It would be useless to deny that this logocentrism bore with it a trace of what William Empson might term a "pastoral" inauthenticity about immediate human concerns. Today, one can hardly read without wincing Spitzer's telling us that his appreciation for the inherent poetic beauties of the Italian language derived from his service as an Austrian censor in 1915, when he was obliged to read letters written home by Italian prisoners of war. This determination to affirm outmoded aesthetic values in a world that had long since left them behind (if, indeed, it had ever held them) did not endear him to politically engaged intellectuals. Pier Paolo Pasolini was probably thinking of Spitzer's politics, as well as his earlier choice of authors, when he labeled him a "champion of European Decadence," a remark that clearly struck home, as can be inferred from the uneasy allusion to it in the last essay of this volume.[4]

Yet there was a great difference between the evasion of the formalists (or the cry of pain of the decadents) and Spitzer's aestheticism. The "new critical" admonition, "Don't go outside the text," implied a certain reification of the literary artifact (as exemplified by Archibald MacLeish's remark that a poem should *be* and not *mean*) and a pseudo-objectification of the critic, who, as an "ideal reader," was not supposed to have a history.

For Spitzer, the boundaries of the text were far more vast, for the words themselves had independent histories (either semantically or as citations or "sources") that provided the context from which meaning—a single meaning—emerged. It was his conviction that "ambiguity," made fashionable by Empson, was, like "incoherence," the refuge of critical ignorance or impatience. A single word or phrase might be unclear, perhaps an entire sentence ambiguous, but it was precisely the function of an ever-expanding context to delimit the multiple alternative meanings until one sense emerged. Theoretically, the widening gyre of context might include a whole universe of discourse, from the literature of antiquity to Rabelaisian nonsense to the street cries of Parisian vendors, but it was Spitzer's hermeneutic faith that somewhere in its swerving path the particular statement would find its place. He shared this article of faith with Freud; long after he had abandoned Freudian models of interpretation, he cited his compatriot in support of the conviction that language might be unintentional, even mad, but never without significance.

As for the anonymity of the reader, nothing could have been more foreign to Spitzer's individualist sensibility. For him, the cant phrase, "Don't go outside the text," had epistemological resonances never dreamt of by the New Critics, for it recalled the Augustinian injunction, "Noli foras ire; in te ipsum redi" (Do not go outside; enter within yourself). Interpretation was a continual interchange with the text and an interrogation of it, based on the interpreter's full experience and a preconception continually subject to modification by the reading experience. One could lose sight neither of what Hans-Georg Gadamer calls the "otherness" of the text nor of one's own place in time; the interpretive difficulty or "crux" would yield only to the interpreter with the necessary breadth of literary experience and depth of understanding of the entire work, both of which would be altered in the process of reading. Every crux was potentially the totality to which it belonged—"Das Ganze im Fragment"—yet one could never be sure of that totality until every such crux had been resolved.

The "hermeneutic circle" is the name given by Schleiermacher to the paradox that every interpretation implies a pre-understanding, yet any pre-understanding must be changed in the act of understanding. In its methodological application, the paradox implies that each part can be known only in terms of the whole and that the whole can be known only through its parts. It is from this application that Spitzer derived the premise of the coherence of the work and the importance of a textual difficulty—being "pulled up short" by the text, as Gadamer would later say—for modifying our hypothesis concerning that coherence. The initial conception of the work's coherence is purely heuristic, an interpretive paradigm subject to testing, modification, or revision, but the process depends on the initial assumption that the text, like the scientist's "Nature," is intelligible. The assumption may be wrong, of course, but since that would end all discussion, there is always time enough to arrive at such a definitive conclusion.

Analogues of the hermeneutic circle can be traced back to antiquity, possibly as far back as Plato's "star-soul," forever in its rotation "thinking the same thoughts about the same things." Spitzer's figure might more properly be called a hermeneutic spiral, for it is open to broader and broader contexts until a difficulty is resolved in a famous "clique" of understanding, to be then shared with others in a search for the *consensus omnium*, the point of all linguistic communication. In this form, the idea is also strikingly modern, for it is not unlike the principle of "recursivity" as it is described in the fields of cybernetics and artificial intelligence. Spitzer would doubtless be amused to find an analogue of his procedure in the workings of a modern computer, although he would find it barbarous to speak of "inputs" and "nontrivial machines."

The analogy might be put this way: a trivial machine is one that performs certain operations in a mechanical way, such that any determined input will yield a thoroughly predictable result. If the mind were a steam engine or a switchboard (or a thoroughly objective, ideal reader), it would function in this way, and its operations, hermeneutic or otherwise, could be described as a closed (and vicious) circle. A nontrivial machine (sometimes called a "Turing" machine, after Alan Turing, the British mathematician who elaborated the principle), on the other hand, is a machine the "inner state" of which is changed by each successive operation, so that the same information, processed at different times, will yield entirely different results, the prediction of which very rapidly becomes exceedingly complex. However simplistic our analogy, the point is that no modern theorist of artificial intelligence would find it strange to assert that every recursion of the hermeneutic circle might well bring with it new interpretation. Each crux brings a reordering of the interpreter's "inner state," while each new "inner state" subjects that crux to more powerful analysis. This is the essence of what might be called a "constructivist" hermeneutic, directed toward the resolution of textual difficulties.

The term "constructivist" is borrowed from Piaget and cybernetics, but it is especially useful in a critical context, for it describes a process that is the reverse of literary "deconstruction." For Schleiermacher, hermeneutics begins where the textual stumbling block appears. Deconstruction, in its attempt to demystify the claims of Enlightenment rhetoric, follows the opposite interpretive trajectory, beginning from a presumably transparent linguistic structure in order to arrive at the intractable difficulty or *aporia*. One can well understand the pedagogic point made by deconstruction for those who need such a lesson: no literary text can be free of figural language which, more often than not, subverts reference to the point of unintelligibility. Even the most transparent text can be made to seem logically opaque when it is subjected to such an analysis. For students of ancient or medieval literature, however, there is little need to show that intelligibility is fragile and constantly threatened; history has done the work of deconstruction, obscuring and effacing many texts that may once have been clear. Spitzer's interpretive effort in his studies of early texts was to recapture that originary sense, and thus may be thought of as the reverse of demystification. It resembles the process of exegesis that was in fact termed *mystificatio* before the Enlightenment gave that word its modern, pejorative sense. It may be defined as the reestablishment of a coherence in terms of which the otherwise unintelligible fragments of a text can be shown to have their significance.

Perhaps the analogy between his own method and that of the medieval exegete will help us to distinguish more sharply the difference between Spitzer's hermeneutic and modern deconstruction. That he was not unaware of the analogy is perhaps revealed by the fact that he referred to himself as a "philologian," rather than a "philologist," as if it were a calling rather than simply a profession. In fact, much of the interest in hermeneutics has come from theologians, so that Spitzer's almost priestly concern with meaning is consistent with the tradition, even if the aesthetic flair smacks slightly of idolatry. For our purposes, the analogy between modern critical concerns and medieval exegesis is peculiarly apt, since the otherwise crude mechanical imagery suggested by the terms "constructivism" and "deconstruction" finds mythic justification in the biblical story of the Tower of Babel.

The story of the Fall in Eden was always understood as the story of human language as well, or at least as the story of the struggle for linguistic intelligibility. Edenic language was supposed to have been an ideal medium in which the correspondence between language and reality was perfect. The Fall exiled language, as well as our parents, and the myth of the construction of the Tower of Babel remained as a warning against the proud claim of pure intelligibility and the attempt to evade mortality. Virtually every reference to the tower deconstructed it, attacking the naive grammatical realism that would take language and reality to be coextensive.

The leap from the frailty of human discourse to its ultimate unintelligibility is a huge one, however, and it was never taken in the Middle Ages. When a medieval exegete was confronted with a text that seemed to make no sense, he or she was enjoined to search for the *mysterium*, the principle of intelligibility in terms of which disparate elements might be understood. *Mystificatio*, the search for the "mystic" sense, was the same as allegorical interpretation. An interpretive obstacle was called a *crux* ("cross"), as if to suggest the central mystery of their faith, to which Saint Paul had referred as an absurdity and a stumbling block. It does not seem unlikely that Schleiermacher, who was a theologian, was thinking of *mystificatio* when he asserted that sense would reveal itself through textual difficulty.

The process would deserve the negative judgment that semantic history subsequently passed on it were it not for the fact that such interpretations were always tentative; one could never be sure that one had arrived at the *mysterium*, but only that one could do so. It was the ending that gave a sense to history as well as to life and therefore, by analogy, to the text. The openness to interpretive understanding was no different from the openness demanded of the Christian by the virtue of Hope.

Whatever the excesses of the process, it is at least in principle defensible. Since meaning is retrospective even at the level of the syllable, it is arguable that all meaning in time is retrospective from some point of closure. This means privileging the ending of the work, assuming it to be coherent, struggling toward that coherence until it is discovered or one's patience is exhausted. Apart from any critical justification, simple logic suggests that no textual or interpretive problem can be solved unless one admits the possibility of satisfactory solution. Moreover, only a conception of total coherence will permit us to establish relative clarity in a text, so that we may distinguish failures of individual talent from the shortcomings of the human condition: unintelligibility admits of no degrees. If we grant that two verses can be coherent—and perhaps the 14 verses of a sonnet, perhaps even the 140 verses of a canto of the *Divine Comedy*—it is difficult to imagine what form of quantification would allow us with any confidence to establish a priori what the limits of coherence may be. The only way to discover the difference between incoherence and our own limitations is to give the text the benefit of the doubt in our initial assumption. Any other hypothesis proves itself with monotonous regularity, ignoring the difference between a text that makes no sense and an interpreter who doesn't understand.

This was the point of Spitzer's remark to Allen at the coffee break. In a way, it was the point of his whole teaching career. Twenty-five years later, his ideology seems as out-of-date as his polemics and his exuberance. His readings remain exemplary, however, not so much because they are definitive as because they suggest how much there is to know and what a difference it can make to the way we understand.

John Freccero

Leo Spitzer: Representative Essays

LINGUISTICS
AND LITERARY HISTORY

This essay, written as the introduction to a group of studies demonstrating his method of interpretation, constitutes an apologia for
Spitzer's intellectual life. Throughout his career, beginning, as he
tells us, with his negative reaction to the positivistic method practiced by his distinguished teachers, the philologist Wilhelm Meyer-
Lübke and the literary historian Philipp August Becker, Spitzer
proudly maintained his independence from what he saw as the reign-
ing fashions and ideologies in scholarship. Yet as the essay goes on to
show, Spitzer remained strongly committed both to linguistics and to
literary history, each of which, as he points out in discussing his earlier studies of Rabelais and Charles-Louis Philippe, he uses to shed
light on the other. Above all, he refuses to practice any method without grounding his analyses of particular phenomena within the history of culture.

In this essay, as in several others in this volume, Spitzer affirms his
commitment to German *Geistesgeschichte* and to the German tradition of hermeneutics—a tradition that derives from biblical interpretation and that, since Romanticism, had concerned itself with de-
termining the meaning of texts drawn from diverse areas, such as
law, Scripture, and literary tradition. In particular, he here describes
his use of that hermeneutic device known as the "philological circle,"
by means of which he can move at ease between the minute particularities he locates in ordinary linguistic usage or in a literary work
and the larger cultural entities to which these particularities are related. Despite changes of emphasis in his method during the course
of his career, for Spitzer the establishment of these relationships be-

tween concrete details and the culture that they help to articulate and define remained the central task of the humanistic scholar.

Originally an address entitled "Thinking in the Humanities" delivered to the Department of Modern Languages and Literatures of Princeton University, this essay was later published in a slightly expanded form as the title essay in the collection *Linguistics and Literary History: Essays in Stylistics* (Princeton, N.J., 1948), pp. 1–39. It is reprinted by permission of Princeton University Press. Of the four essays to which this one served as introduction, those on Cervantes and Claudel are included in this volume. Spitzer's study of Charles-Louis Philippe's *Bubu de Montparnasse*, which he mentions in this essay, is also included here. His relationship to *Geistesgeschichte* is developed in greater detail in another essay in this volume, "*Geistesgeschichte* vs. History of Ideas as Applied to Hitlerism."

Linguistics and Literary History

It is paradoxical that professors of literature who are too superficial to im-
merse themselves in a text and who are satisfied with stale phrases out of a
manual are precisely those who contend that it is superfluous to teach the
aesthetic value of a text of Racine or Victor Hugo: the student will, in some
way or another, come to grasp its beauty without any direction—or, if he is
incapable of doing so, it is useless to talk about it. But there are hidden
beauties which do not reveal themselves at the first exploratory attempts (as
the apologetic theologians know); in fact, all beauty has some mysterious
quality which does not appear at first glance. But there is no more reason for
dodging the description of the aesthetic phenomenon than of any natural
phenomenon. Those who oppose the aesthetic analysis of poetic works
seem to affect at times the susceptibility of a sensitive plant: if one is to believe them, it is because they cherish so deeply the works of art, it is because
they respect their chastity, that they would not deflower, by means of intellectual formulas, the virginal and ethereal quality of works of art, they
would not brush off the shimmering dust from the wings of these poetic but-
terflies! I would maintain, on the contrary, that to formulate observations
by means of words is not to cause the artistic beauty to evaporate in vain in-
tellectualities; rather, it makes for a widening and a deepening of the aesthetic taste. Love, whether it be love for God, love for one's fellow men, or
the love of art, can only gain by the effort of the human intellect to search for
the reasons of its most sublime emotions, and to formulate them. It is only a
frivolous love that cannot survive intellectual definition; great love prospers
with understanding.

The title of this essay is meant to suggest the ultimate unity of linguistics and literary history. Since my activity, throughout my scholarly life, has been largely devoted to the rapprochement of these two
disciplines, I may be forgiven if I preface my remarks with an auto-

biographic sketch of my first academic experiences: What I propose to do is to tell you only my own story, how I made my way through the maze of linguistics, with which I started, toward the enchanted garden of literary history—and how I discovered that there is as well a paradise in linguistics as a labyrinth in literary history; that the methods and the degree of certainty in both are basically the same; and, that if today the humanities are under attack (and, as I believe, under an unwarranted attack, since it is not the humanities themselves that are at fault but only some so-called humanists who persist in imitating an obsolete approach to the natural sciences, which have themselves evolved toward the humanities)—if, then, the humanities are under attack, it would be pointless to exempt any one of them from the verdict: if it is true that there is no value to be derived from the study of language, we cannot pretend to preserve literary history, cultural history—or history.

I have chosen the autobiographical way because my personal situation in Europe forty years ago was not, I believe, essentially different from the one with which I see the young scholar of today (and in this country) generally faced. I chose to relate to you my own experiences also because the basic approach of the individual scholar, conditioned as it is by his first experiences, by his *Erlebnis*, as the Germans say, determines his method: *Methode ist Erlebnis*, Friedrich Gundolf has said.[1] In fact, I would advise every older scholar to tell his public the basic experiences underlying his methods, his *Mein Kampf*, as it were—without dictatorial connotations, of course.

I had decided, after college had given me a solid foundation in the classical languages, to study the Romance languages and particularly French philology, because, in my native Vienna, the gay and orderly, skeptic and sentimental, Catholic and pagan Vienna of yore was filled with adoration of the French way of life. I had always been surrounded by a French atmosphere and, at that juvenile stage of experience, had acquired a picture, perhaps overgeneralized, of French literature, which seemed to me definable by an Austrian-like mixture of sensuousness and reflection, of vitality and discipline, of sentimentality and critical wit. The moment when the curtain rose on a French play given by a French troupe, and the valet, in a knowing accent of psychological alertness, with his rich, poised voice, pronounced the words "Madame est servie," was a delight to my heart.

But when I attended the classes of French linguistics of my great teacher Wilhelm Meyer-Lübke, no picture was offered us of the

French people, or of the Frenchness of their language: in these classes we saw Latin *a* moving, according to relentless phonetic laws, toward French *e* (*pater* > *père*); there we saw a new system of declension spring up from nothingness, a system in which the six Latin cases came to be reduced to two, and later to one—while we learned that similar violence had been done to the other Romance languages and, in fact, to many modern languages. In all this, there were many facts and much rigor in the establishment of facts, but all was vague in regard to the general ideas underlying these facts. What was the mystery behind the refusal of Latin sounds or cases to stay put and behave themselves? We saw incessant change working in language—but why? I was a long while realizing that Meyer-Lübke was offering only the *pre*history of French (as he established it by a comparison with the other Romance languages), not its history. And we were never allowed to contemplate a phenomenon in its quiet being, to look into its face: we always looked at its neighbors or at its predecessors—we were always looking over our shoulder. There were presented to us the relationships of phenomenon *a* and phenomenon *b*; but phenomenon *a* and phenomenon *b* did not exist in themselves, nor did the historical line *a–b*. In reference to a given French form, Meyer-Lübke would quote Old Portuguese, Modern Bergamesque and Macedo-Rumanian, German, Celtic, and paleo-Latin forms; but where was reflected in this teaching my sensuous, witty, disciplined Frenchman, in his presumably 1,000 years of existence? He was left out in the cold while we talked about his language; indeed, French was not the language of the Frenchman, but an agglomeration of unconnected, separate, anecdotic, senseless evolutions: a French historical grammar, apart from the word-material, could as well have been a Germanic or a Slav grammar: the leveling of paradigms, the phonetic evolutions occur there just as in French.

When I changed over to the classes of the equally great literary historian Philipp August Becker, that ideal Frenchman seemed to show some faint signs of life—in the spirited analyses of the events in the *Pèlerinage de Charlemagne*,[2] or of the plot of a Molière comedy; but it was as if the treatment of the contents were only subsidiary to the really scholarly work, which consisted in fixing the dates and historical data of these works of art, in assessing the amount of autobiographical elements and written sources which the poets had supposedly incorporated into their artistic productions. Had the *Pèlerinage* to do with the tenth crusade? Which was its original dialect? Was there any epic poetry, Merovingian or other, which preceded Old French epic poetry? Had Molière put his own matrimonial disillusionment into the *Ecole des femmes*? (While Becker did not insist on an affirmative conclusion, he considered such a question to be a part of legitimate literary criticism.) Did the medieval farce survive in the Molière comedy? The existing works of art were stepping-stones from which to proceed to other phenomena, contemporary or previous, which were in reality quite heterogeneous. It seemed indiscreet to ask what made them works of art, what was expressed in them, and why these expressions appeared in France, at that particular time. Again, it was prehistory, not history, that we were offered, and a kind of materialistic prehistory, at that. In this attitude of positivism, exterior events were taken thus seriously only to evade the more completely the real question: Why did the phenomena *Pèlerinage* and *Ecole des femmes* happen at all? And, I must admit, in full loyalty to Meyer-Lübke, that he taught more of reality than did Becker: it was unquestionable that Latin *a* had evolved to French *e*; it was untrue that Molière's experience with the possibly faithless Madeleine Béjart had evolved to the work of art *Ecole des femmes*. But, in both fields, that of linguistics as well as that of literary history (which were separated by an enormous gulf: Meyer-Lübke spoke only of language and Becker only of literature), a meaningless industriousness prevailed: not only was this kind of humanities not centered on a particular people in a particular time, but the subject matter itself had got lost: Man.*

---

*The presentation of so great a scholar as Meyer-Lübke from the only angle which concerns us here is necessarily one-sided; for a more complete evaluation of his scholarship, as well as for a picture of his personality, I may refer the reader to my paper "Mes souvenirs sur Meyer-Lübke."[3] As for Philipp August Becker, my few remarks have given no real idea of his exuberant personality—which seldom penetrated into his scholarship; his was an orgiastic nature which somehow did not fit into the traditional pattern of a scholar. A story told me by Walther von Wartburg may illustrate this: Becker, who was rather given to the worship of Bacchus-Dionysus, used to invite his colleagues at Leipzig to a certain popular inn for copious libations. One night, after many hours of merrymaking, he realized that the bourgeois patrons sitting around him were shocked by his exuberance; immediately turning to his colleagues, he remarked: "And now I want to tell you something about early Christian hymns!" For almost an hour he talked, to the delight not only of his colleagues but also of the crowd of *Spiessbürger* [philistines] who had gradually drawn closer to him, enthralled by the eloquence of this greybeard bard who was reviving the spirit of Saint Ambrosius in a tavern.

At the end of my first year of graduate studies, I had come to the conclusion not that the science offered *ex cathedra* was worthless, but that I was not fit for such studies as that of the irrational vowel *-i-* in Eastern French dialects or of the *Subjektivismusstreit* [subjectivism debate] in Molière: never would I get a Ph.D.! It was the benignity of Providence, exploiting my native Teutonic docility toward scholars who knew more than I, which kept me faithful to the study of Romance philology. By not abandoning prematurely this sham science, by seeking, instead, to appropriate it, I came to recognize its true value as well as my own possibilities of work—and to establish my life's goal. By using the tools of science offered me, I came to see under their dustiness the fingerprints of a Friedrich Diez and of the Romantics, who had created these tools; and henceforth they were not dusty any more, but ever radiant and ever new. And I had learned to handle many and manifold facts: training in handling facts, brutal facts, is perhaps the best education for a wavering, youthful mind.

And now let me take you, as I promised to do, on the path that leads from the most routinelike techniques of the linguist toward the work of the literary historian. The different fields will appear here in ascending order, as I see them today, while the concrete examples, drawn from my own activity, will not respect the chronological order of their publication.

Meyer-Lübke, the author of the comprehensive and still final etymological dictionary of Romance languages,[4] had taught me, among many other things, how to find etymologies; I shall now take the liberty of inflicting upon you a concrete example of this procedure— sparing you none of the petty drudgery involved. Since my coming to America, I have been curious about the etymology of two English words, characterized by the same "flavor": *conundrum* "a riddle the answer to which involves a pun; a puzzling question," and *quandary* "a puzzling situation." The *New English Dictionary* (NED) attests *conundrum* first in 1596; early variants are *conimbrum, quonundrum, quadundrum*. The meaning is "whim" or "pun." In the seventeenth century it was known as an Oxford term: preachers were wont to use in their sermons the baroque device of puns and conundrums, for example, "Now all House is turned into an Alehouse, and a pair of dice is made a Paradice; was it thus in the days of Noah? Ah no." This baroque technique of interlarding sermons with puns is well known from the *Kapuziner-Predigt* [Capuchin's sermon], inspired by Abraham a Santa Clara, in Schiller's *Wallensteins Lager*: "Der *Rheinstrom* ist worden zu einem *Peinstrom*" [The river *Rhine* has become a river of *pain*], etc.

The extraordinary instability (reflecting the playfulness of the concept involved) of the phonetic structure: *conundrum–conimbrum–quadundrum*, points to a foreign source, to a word which must have been (playfully) adapted in various ways. Since the English variants include among them a -*b*- and a -*d*-, which are not easily reducible to any one basic sound, I propose to submit a French word-family which, in its different forms, contains both -*b*- and -*d*-: the French *calembour* is exactly synonymous with *conundrum* "pun." This *calembour* is evidently related to *calembredaine* "nonsensical or odd speech," and we can assume that *calembour*, too, had originally this same general reference. This word-family goes back probably to the French *bourde* "tall story" to which has been added the fanciful, semipejorative prefix *cali-*, that can be found in *à califourchon* "straddling" (from Latin *quadrifurcus*, French *carrefour* "crossroads": the *qu-* of the English variants points to this Latin etymon). The French ending -*aine* of *calembredaine* developed to -*um*: *n* becomes *m* as in *ransom* from French *rançon*; *ai* becomes *o* as in *mitten* (older *mitton*) from French *mitaine*. Thus *calembourdaine*, as a result of various assimilations and shortenings which I will spare you, becomes *colundrum, *columbrum and then *conundrum*, *conimbrum*, etc. Unfortunately, the French word-family is attested rather late, occurring for the first time in a comic opera of Jean-Joseph Vadé in 1754. We do find, however, an *équilbourdie* "whim" as early as 1658 in the *Muse normande*, a dialectal text. The fact is that popular words of this sort have, as a rule, little chance of turning up in the (predominantly idealistic) literature of the Middle Ages; it is, therefore, a mere accident that English *conundrum* is attested in 1596 and French *calembour* only in 1757; at least, the chance appearance of *équilbourdie* in the dialectal text of 1658 gives us an earlier attestation of the French word-family. That the evidently popular medieval words emerge so late in literature is a fact explainable by the currents prevalent in literature; the linguist must take his chances with what literature offers him in the way of attestation. In view of the absolute evidence of the equation *conundrum* = *calembredaine*, we need not be intimidated by chronological divergencies—which the older school of etymologists (as represented by the editors of the NED) seem to have overrated.

After *conundrum* had ceased to be a riddle to me, I was emboldened to ask myself whether I could not now solve the etymology of the word *quandary*—which also suggested to me a French origin. And, lo and behold: this word, of unknown origin, which is attested from about 1580 on, revealed itself etymologically identical with *conundrum*! There are English dialect forms such as *quándorum*, *quóndorum* which serve to establish an uninterrupted chain: *calembredaine* becomes *conimbrum, conundrum, quonundrum, quandorum*, and these give us *quandary*.[5]

Now what can be the humanistic, the spiritual value of this (as it may have seemed to you) juggling with word forms? The particular etymology of *conundrum* is an inconsequential fact; that an etymology can be found by man is a miracle. An etymology introduces meaning into the meaningless: in our case, the evolution of two words in time—that is, a piece of linguistic history—has been cleared up. What seemed an agglomeration of mere sounds now appears motivated. We feel the same "inner click" accompanying our comprehension of this evolution in time as when we have grasped the meaning of a sentence or a poem—which then become more than the sum total of their single words or sounds (*poem* and *sentence* are, in fact, the classical examples given by Augustine and Bergson in order to demonstrate the nature of a stretch of *durée réelle*: the parts aggregating to a whole, time filled with contents). In the problem which we chose, two words which seemed erratic and fantastic, with no definite relationships in English, have been unified among themselves and related to a French word-family.

The existence of such a loan-word is another testimony to the well-known cultural situation obtaining when medieval England was in the sway of French influence: the English and French word-families, although attested centuries after the Middle Ages, must have belonged to one Anglo-French word-family during that period, and their previous existence is precisely proved by proving their family relationship. And it is not by chance that English borrows words for "pun" or "whim" from the witty French, who have also given *carriwitchet* "quibble" and (perhaps: see the NED) *pun* itself to English. But, since a loan-word rarely feels completely at home in its new environment, we have the manifold variations of the word, which fell apart into two word-groups (clearly separated, today, by the current

linguistic feeling): *conundrum–quandary*. The instability and dis-
unity of the word-family is symptomatic of its position in the new
environment.

But the instability apparent in our English words had already been
characteristic of *calembredaine–calembour*, even in the home environment: this French word-family, as we have said, was a blend of at
least two word-stems. Thus we must conclude that the instability is
also connected with the semantic content: a word meaning "whim,
pun" easily behaves whimsically—just as, in all languages throughout the world, the words for "butterfly" present a kaleidoscopic instability. The linguist who explains such fluttery words has to juggle,
because the speaking community itself (in our case, the English as
well as the French) has juggled. This juggling in itself is psychologically and culturally motivated: language is not—as the behavioristic,
antimentalistic, mechanistic or materialistic school of linguists, ram-
pant in some universities, would have it—a meaningless agglomeration of corpses: dead word-material, automatic "speech habits" unleashed by a trigger motion. A certain automatism may be predicated
of the use of *conundrum* and *quandary* in contemporary English,
and of *calembour, calembredaine* in contemporary French (though,
even today, this automatism is not absolute, since all these words
have still a connotation of whimsicality or fancifulness and are, accordingly, somewhat motivated). But this is certainly not true for the
history of the words: the linguistic creation is always meaningful
and, yes, clear-minded: it was a feeling for the appositeness of nomenclature which prompted the communities to use, in our case,
two-track words. They gave a playful expression to a playful concept, symbolizing in the word their attitude toward the concept. It
was when the creative, the Renaissance, phase had passed that English let the words congeal, petrify, and split into two. This petrification is, itself, due to a decision of the community which, in
eighteenth-century England, passed from the Renaissance attitude
to the classicistic attitude toward language, which would replace
creativity by standardization and regulation. Another cultural climate, another linguistic style. Out of the infinity of word-histories
which could be imagined we have chosen only one, one which shows
quite individual circumstances, such as the borrowing of a foreign
word by English, the original French blend, the subsequent alterations and restrictions; every word has its own history, not to be confused with that of any other. But what repeats itself in all word-

histories is the possibility of recognizing the signs of a people at work, culturally and psychologically. To speak in the language of the homeland of philology: "Wortwandel ist Kulturwandel und Seelenwandel" [Word change is cultural change and spiritual change]; this little etymological study has been humanistic in purpose.

If we accept the equation, *conundrum* and *quandary* = *calembredaine*, how has this been found? I may say, by quite an orthodox technique which would have been approved by Meyer-Lübke—though he would not, perhaps, have stopped to draw the inferences on which I have insisted. First, by collecting the material evidence about the English words, I was led to seek a French origin. I had also observed that the great portion of the English vocabulary which is derived from French has not been given sufficient attention by etymologists; and, of course, my familiarity with the particular behavior of "butterfly words" in language was such as to encourage a relative boldness in the reconstruction of the etymon. I had first followed the inductive method—or rather a quick intuition—in order to identify *conundrum* with *calembredaine*; later, I had to proceed deductively, to verify whether my assumed etymon concorded with all the known data, whether it really explained all the semantic and phonetic variations; while following this path I was able to see that *quandary* must also be a reflection of *calembredaine*. (This to-and-fro movement is a basic requirement in all humanistic studies, as we shall see later.) For example, since the French word-family is attested later than is the English, it seemed necessary to dismiss the chronological discrepancies; fortunately—or, as I would say, providentially—the Normandian *équilbourdie* of 1658 turned up! In this kind of gentle blending together of the words, of harmonizing them and smoothing out difficulties, the linguist undoubtedly indulges in a propensity to see things as shifting and melting into each other—an attitude to which you may object: I cannot contend more than that this change was *possible* in the way I have indicated, since it contradicts no previous experience; I can say only that two unsolved problems (the one concerning the prehistory of *conundrum*, the other that of *calembredaine*) have, when brought together, shed light on each other, thereby enabling us to see the common solution. I am reminded here of the story of the Pullman porter to whom a passenger complained in the morning that he had got back one black shoe and one tan; the porter replied that, curiously enough, a similar discovery had been made by another passenger. In the field of language, the porter who has mixed up the shoes belonging together is language itself, and the linguist is the passenger who must bring together what was once a historical unit. To place two phenomena within a framework adds something to the knowledge about their common nature. There is no mathematical demonstrability in such an equation, only a feeling of inner evidence; but this feeling, with the trained linguist, is the fruit of observation combined with experience, of precision supplemented by imagination—the dosage of which cannot be fixed a priori, but only in the concrete case. There is underlying such a procedure the belief that this is the way things happened; but there is always a belief underlying the humanist's work (similarly, it cannot be demonstrated that the Romance languages form a unity going back to Vulgar Latin; this basic assumption of the student in Romance languages, first stated by Diez, cannot be proved to the disbeliever).*

---

* In fact, Ernst Lewy would destroy the unity of "Romance languages" by placing French and Spanish, along with Basque and Irish, in an Atlantic group of languages, and Rumanian within the Balkan group.[6] Again, there is the Russian school of "Japhetists," who believe not in "families" but in "systems" of languages, and who make bold to discover in any given language certain primeval, basic "elements" of the prelogical period in human speech.[7]

And who says belief, says suasion: I have, deliberately and tendentiously, grouped the variants of *conundrum* in the most plausible order possible for the purpose of winning your assent. Of course, there are more easily believable etymologies, reached at the cost of less stretching and bending: no one in his senses would doubt that French *père* comes from Latin *pater*, or that this, along with English *father*, goes back to an Indo-European prototype. But we must not forget that these smooth, standard equations are relatively rare—for the reason that such a word as "father" is relatively immune to cultural revolutions or, in other words, that, in regard to the "father," a continuity of feeling, stretching over more than 4,000 years, exists in Indo-European civilization.

Thus our etymological study has illuminated a stretch of linguistic history, which is connected with psychology and history of civilization; it has suggested a web of interrelations between language and the soul of the speaker. This web could have been as well revealed by a study of a syntactical, a morphological evolution—even a phonetic evolution of the type "*a* becomes *e*," wherein Meyer-Lübke had failed to see the *durée réelle*, exclusively concerned as he was with *l'heure de la montre*, his historical "clock time."

Now, since the best document of the soul of a nation is its literature, and since the latter is nothing but its language as this is written down by elect speakers, can we perhaps not hope to grasp the spirit of a nation in the language of its outstanding works of literature? Because it would have been rash to compare the whole of a national literature to the whole of a national language (as Karl Vossler has prematurely tried to do),[8] I started, more modestly, with the question: "Can one distinguish the soul of a particular French writer in his particular language?" It is obvious that literary historians have held this conviction, since, after the inevitable quotation (or misquotation) of Buffon's saying, "Le style est l'homme" [Style constitutes man], they generally include in their monographs a chapter on the style of their author. But I had in mind the more rigorously scientific definition of an individual style, the definition of a linguist which should replace the casual, impressionistic remarks of literary critics. Stylistics, I thought, might bridge the gap between linguistics and literary history. On the other hand, I was warned by the scholastic adage *individuum est ineffabile* [the individual (thing) is ineffable]; could it be that any attempt to define the individual writer by his style is doomed to failure? The individual stylistic deviation from the general norm must represent a historical step taken by the writer, I argued: it must reveal a shift of the soul of the epoch, a shift of which the writer has become conscious and which he would translate into a necessarily new linguistic form; perhaps it would be possible to determine the historical step, psychological as well as linguistic? To determine the beginning of a linguistic innovation would be easier, of course, in the case of contemporary writers, because their linguistic basis is better known to us than is that of past writers.

In my reading of modern French novels, I had acquired the habit of underlining expressions which struck me as aberrant from general usage, and it often happened that the underlined passages, taken together, seemed to offer a certain consistency. I wondered if it would not be possible to establish a common denominator for all or most of these deviations; could not the common spiritual etymon, the psychological root, of several individual "traits of style" in a writer be found, just as we have found an etymon common to various fanciful word-formations?*

---

*Perhaps the transition from a particular historical line in language, traced by an etymology, to the self-contained system of a work of literature, may seem violent to the reader: in the first case the "etymon" is the "soul of the nation" at the moment of the creation of the word; in the second, it is the "soul of one particular author." The difference, as Professor Charles Singleton has pointed out to me, is that between the unconscious will of the nation that creates its language, and the conscious will of one member of the nation who creates wilfully and more or less systematically. But apart from the fact that there are rational elements in popular linguistic creations, and irrational ones in those of the creative artist, what I would point out here is the relationship, common to both, between the linguistic detail and the soul of the speaker(s), and the necessity, in both cases, of the to-and-fro philological movement.

Perhaps a better parallel to the system of a work of art would be the system of a language at a definite moment of its evolution. I attempted just such a characterization of a linguistic system in my article on Spanish.[9]

I had, for example, noticed in the novel *Bubu de Montparnasse* of Charles-Louis Philippe (1905), which moves in the underworld of Parisian pimps and prostitutes, a particular use of *à cause de* [because of], reflecting the spoken, the unliterary language: "Les réveils de midi sont lourds et poisseux. . . . On éprouve un sentiment de déchéance *à cause des* réveils d'autrefois" (p. 80) [These awakenings at midday are heavy and sticky. . . . You feel a sense of degradation *because of* the awakenings of former times]. More academic writers would have said "en se rappelant des réveils d'autrefois . . . ," "à la suite du souvenir . . ." [in remembering the awakenings of former days . . . , following the remembrance . . .]. This at first glance prosaic and commonplace *à cause de* has nevertheless a poetic flavor, because of the unexpected suggestion of a causality, where the average person would see only coincidence: it is, after all, not unanimously accepted that one awakes with a feeling of frustration from a noon siesta *because* other similar awakenings have preceded; we have here an assumed, a poetic reality, but one expressed by a prosaic phrase. We find this *à cause de* again in a description of a popular celebration of the 14th of July: "Le peuple, *à cause de* l'anniversaire de sa délivrance, laisse ses filles danser en liberté" (p. 45) [The people, *because of* the anniversary of their deliverance, let their daughters dance freely in the streets]. Thus, one will not be surprised when the author lets this phrase come from the mouth of one of his characters: "Il y a dans mon cœur deux ou trois cent petites émotions qui brûlent *à cause de toi*" (p. 66) [There are two or three hundred little emotions in my heart that burn *because of you*]. Conventional poetry would have said "qui brûlent pour toi"; "qui brûlent *à cause de toi*" is both less and more: more, since the lover speaks his heart better in this sincere, though factual manner. The causal phrase, with all its semipoetic implications, suggests rather a commonplace speaker, whose speech and whose habits of thought the writer seems to endorse in his own narrative.

Our observation about *à cause de* gains strength if we compare the use, in the same novel, of other causal conjunctions, such as *parce que* [because]: for example, it is said of the pimp's love for his sweetheart Berthe: "{Il aimait} sa volupté particulière, quand elle appliquait son corps contre le sien. . . . Il aimait cela qui la distinguait de toutes les femmes qu'il avait connues *parce que* c'était plus doux, *parce que* c'était plus fin, *parce que* c'était sa femme, à lui, qu'il avait eue vierge. Il l'aimait *parce qu*'elle était bien élevée, *parce qu*'elle était honnête et qu'elle en avait l'air, et pour toutes les raisons qu'ont les bourgeois d'aimer leur femme" (p. 57) [He loved her special voluptuousness when she pressed her body to him. . . . He loved what distinguished her from all the women he had known, *because* it was sweeter, *because* it was more delicate, and *because* this was his woman, his own, whom he had had as a virgin. He loved her *because* she was well-bred, *because* she was honest and looked it, and for all the reasons that the bourgeois love their wives]. Here, the reasons why Maurice loved to embrace his sweetheart (*parce que c'était doux, fin, parce que c'était sa femme, à lui*) are outspokenly classified or censored by the writer as being *bourgeois*; and yet, in Philippe's narrative, the *parce que* is used as if he considered these reasons to be objectively valid.

The same observation holds true for the causal conjunction *car* [for] in the following passage, which describes Maurice as a being naturally loved by women: "Les femmes l'entouraient d'amour comme des oiseaux qui chantent le soleil et la force. Il était un de ceux que nul ne peut assujettir, *car* leur vie, plus noble et plus belle, comporte l'amour du danger" (p. 53) [The women surrounded him with love, like birds singing the praises of the sun and power. He was one of those who cannot be subjugated by anything, *for* their life, more noble and beautiful, includes the love of danger].

Again, it can happen that a causal relationship is implied without the use of a conjunction, a relationship due to the gnomic character adherent, at least in that particular milieu, to a general statement—the truth of which is, perhaps, not so fully accepted elsewhere: "Elle l'embrassa à pleine bouche. *C'est une chose hygiénique* et bonne entre un homme et sa femme, qui vous amuse un petit quart d'heure avant de vous endormir" (p. 39) [She kissed him full on the mouth. *This is a wholesome* and good *thing* for a man and his woman; it amuses you for ten minutes or so before you fall asleep]. (Philippe could as well have written "car . . . ," "parce que c'est une chose hygiénique. . . .") Evidently this is the truth only in that particular world of sensuous realism which he is describing. At the same time, however, the writer, while half-endorsing these bourgeois platitudes of the underworld, is discreetly but surely suggesting his criticism of them.

Now I submit the hypothesis that all these expansions of causal usages in Philippe cannot be due to chance: there must be "something the matter" with his conception of causality. And now we must pass from Philippe's style to the psychological etymon, to the radix in his soul. I have called the phenomenon in question "pseudo-objective motivation": Philippe, when presenting causality as binding for his characters, seems to recognize a rather objective cogency in their sometimes awkward, sometimes platitudinous, sometimes semi-poetic reasonings; his attitude shows a fatalistic, half-critical, half-understanding, humorous sympathy with the necessary errors and thwarted strivings of these underworld beings dwarfed by inexorable social forces. The pseudo-objective motivation, manifest in his style, is the clue to Philippe's *Weltanschauung*; he sees, as has also been observed by literary critics, without revolt but with deep grief and a Christian spirit of contemplativity, the world functioning wrongly with an appearance of rightness, of objective logic. The different word-usages, grouped together (just as was done with the different forms of *conundrum* and *quandary*), lead toward a psychological etymon, which is at the bottom of the linguistic as well as of the literary inspiration of Philippe.

Thus we have made the trip from language or style to the soul. And on this journey we may catch a glimpse into a historical evolution of the French soul in the twentieth century: first we are given insight into the soul of a writer who has become conscious of the fatalism weighing on the masses, then into that of a section of the French nation itself, whose faint protest is voiced by our author. And in this procedure there is, I think, no longer the timeless, placeless philology of the older school, but an explanation of the concrete *hic et nunc* of a historical phenomenon. The to-and-fro movement we found to be basic with the humanist has been followed here, too: first we grouped together certain causal expressions, striking with Philippe, then hunted out their psychological explanation, and finally sought to verify whether the element of "pseudo-objective motivation"* concorded with what we know, from other sources, about the elements of his inspiration.[10]

---

*The method I have been describing in the text is, of course, one that is followed by all of us when we must interpret the correspondence of someone with whom we are not well acquainted. For several years I had been in correspondence with a German emigrant in France whom I did not know personally and whose letters had given me the impression of a rather self-centered person who craved a cozy and congenial environment. When she was finally rescued to another country, she published a book of memoirs, a copy of which was sent me. On the cover of the book I saw pictured the window of the room she had occupied in Paris; behind this window, in the foreground, was a great cat looking out upon the Cathedral of Notre Dame. A great part of the book itself was taken up with this cat, and I had not read far before I found—without great surprise—several sentences such as "blottie dans un fauteuil, j'éprouvai un tel bonheur, je me sentis si bien à mon aise sous ce soleil doux qui me faisait ronronner à la manière des chats" [curled up in an armchair, I experienced such happiness, I felt so much at ease under this gentle sun which made me purr like a cat]. Evidently a catlike existence was the deep-felt aspiration of this emigrant who, in the midst of world catastrophe, had lost the feeling of protectedness and had had to seek protection in herself.

Again, a belief is involved—which is no less daring than is the belief that the Romance languages go back to one invisible, basic pattern manifest in them all—namely, the belief that the mind of an author is a kind of solar system into whose orbit all categories of things are attracted: language, motivation, plot are only satellites of this mythological entity (as my antimentalistic adversaries would call it): *mens Philippina* [Philippe-ine mind]. The linguist as well as his literary colleague must always ascend to the etymon which is behind all those particular so-called literary or stylistic devices which the literary historians are wont to list. And the individual *mens Philippina* is a reflection of the *mens Franco-gallica* of the twentieth century; its ineffability consists precisely in Philippe's anticipatory sensitivity for the spiritual needs of the nation.

Now, it is obvious that a modern writer such as Philippe, faced with the social disintegration of humanity in the twentieth century, must show more patent linguistic deviations, of which the philologist may take stock in order to build up his "psychogram" of the individual artist. But does Philippe, a stranded being broken loose from his moorings, transplanted, as it were, into a world from which he feels estranged—so that he must, perforce, indulge in arbitrary whimsicality—represent only a modern phenomenon? If we go back to writers of more remote times, must it not be that we will always find a balanced language, with no deviations from common usage?

It suffices to mention the names of such dynamic writers of older times as Dante or Quevedo or Rabelais to dispel such a notion. Whoever has thought strongly and felt strongly has innovated in his language; mental creativity immediately inscribes itself into the language, where it becomes linguistic creativity; the trite and petrified in language is never sufficient for the needs of expression felt by a strong personality. In my first publication, "Die Wortbildung als stilistisches Mittel exemplifiziert an Rabelais"[11] (a thesis written in 1910), I dealt with Rabelais's comic word-formations, a subject to which I was attracted because of certain affinities between Rabelaisian and Viennese (Nestroy!) comic writing, and which offered the opportunity of bridging the gap between linguistic and literary history.[12] Be it said to the eternal credit of the scholarly integrity of Meyer-Lübke that he, in contrast to the antimentalists who would suppress all expressions of opposition to their theories, recommended for publication a book with an approach so aberrant from his own. In this work I sought to show, for example, that a neologism such as *pantagruélisme*, the name given by Rabelais to his Stoic-Epicurean philosophy ("certaine gayeté d'esprit conficte en mépris des choses fortuites," prologue to book 4 [a certain lightness of spirit compounded of contempt for the chances of fate]),[13] is not only a playful outburst of a genuine gaiety, but a thrust from the realm of the real into that of the unreal and the unknown—as is true, in fact, of any nonce-word. On the one hand, a form with the suffix *-ism* evokes a school of serious philosophic thought (such as *Aristotelianism, scholasticism,* etc.); on the other, the stem, *Pantagruel,* is the name of a character created by Rabelais, the half-jocular, half-philosophical giant and patriarchal king. The coupling of the learned philosophical suffix with the fanciful name of a fanciful character amounts to positing a half-real, half-unreal entity—"the philosophy of an imaginary being." The contemporaries of Rabelais who first heard this coinage must have experienced the reactions provoked by any nonce-word: a moment of shock followed by a feeling of reassurance: to be swept toward the unknown frightens, but realization of the benignly fanciful result gives relief: laughter, our physiological reaction on such occasions, arises precisely out of a feeling of relief following upon a temporary breakdown of our assurance. Now, in a case such as that of the creation *pantagruélisme*—the designation of a hitherto unknown but, after all, innocuous philosophy—the menacing force of the neologism is relatively subdued. But what of such a list of names as that concocted by Rabelais for the benefit of his hated adversaries, the reactionaries of the Sorbonne: "sophistes, sorbillans, sorbonagres, sorbonigenes, sorbonicoles, sorboniformes, sorboniseques, niborcisans, sorbonisans, saniborsans"? Again, though differently, there is an element of realism present in these coinages: the Sorbonne is an existing reality, and the formations are explainable by well-known formative processes. The edition of Abel Lefranc, imbued with his positivistic approach, goes to the trouble of explaining each one of these formations: *sorboniforme* is after *uniforme*, *sorbonigene* after *homogène*, while *niborcisans*, *saniborsans* offer what, in the jargon of the linguists, is called a metathesis. But by explaining every coinage separately, by dissolving the forest into trees, the commentators lose sight of the whole phenomenon: they no longer see the forest—or rather the jungle which Rabelais must have had before his eyes, teeming with viperlike, hydralike, demonlike shapes.[14] Nor is it enough to say that the scholarly Rabelais indulges in humanistic word-lists with a view to enriching the vocabulary—in the spirit of an Erasmus who prescribed the principle of *copia verborum* [literal copy] to students of Latin—or that Rabelais's rich nature bade him make the French language rich: the aesthetics of richness is, in itself, a problem; and why should richness tend toward the frightening, the bottomless? Perhaps Rabelais's whole attitude toward language rests upon a vision of imaginary richness whose support is the bottomless. He creates word-families, representative of gruesome fantasy-beings, copulating and engendering before our eyes, which have reality only in the world of language, which are established in an intermediate world between reality and irreality, between the nowhere that frightens and the "here" that reassures. The *niborcisans* are as yet an entity vaguely connected with the *sorbonisans*, but at the same time so close to nothingness that we laugh—uneasily; it is *le comique grotesque* which skirts the abyss. And Rabelais will shape grotesque word-families (or families of word-demons) not only by altering what exists: he may leave intact the forms of his word-material and create by juxtaposition, savagely piling epithet upon epithet to an ultimate effect of terror, so that from the well-known emerges the shape of the unknown—a phenomenon the more startling with the French, who are generally considered to inhabit an orderly, clearly regulated, well-policed language. Now, of a sudden, we no longer recognize this French language, which has become a chaotic word-world situated somewhere in the chill of cosmic space. Just listen to the inscription on the *abbaye de Thélème*, that Renaissance convent of his shaping, from which Rabelais excludes the hypocrites:

> Cy n'entrez pas, hypocrites, bigotz,
> Vieux matagotz, marmiteux, borsouflez,
> Torcoulx, badaux, plus que n'estoient les Gotz
> Ny Ostrogotz, précurseurs des magotz
> Haires, cagotz, caffars empantoufléz,
> Gueux mitoufléz, frapars escornifléz,
> Beffléz, enfléz, fagoteurs de tabus;
> Tirez ailleurs pour vendre vos abus. (bk. 1, ch. 54)

> [Enter not here, vile hypocrites and bigots,
> Pious old apes, and puffed-up snivellers,
> Wry-necked creatures sawnier than the Goths,
> Or Ostrogoths, precursors of Gog and Magog,
> Woe-begone scoundrels, mock-godly sandal-wearers,
> Beggars in blankets, flagellating canters,
> Hooted at, pot-bellied, stirrers up of troubles,
> Get along elsewhere to sell your dirty swindles.]

The prosaic commentators of the Lefranc edition would explain that this kind of rather mediocre poetry is derived from the popular genre of the *cry* (the harangue of a barker), and overloaded with devices of the *rhétoriqueur* school.[15] But I can never read these lines without being frightened, and I am shaken in this very moment by the horror emanating from this accumulation of *-fl-* and *-got-* clusters—of sounds which, in themselves, and taken separately, are quite harmless, of words grouped together, bristling with Rabelais's hatred of hypocrisy—that greatest of all crimes against life. A *cry*, yes, but in a more extensive meaning of the word: it is the gigantic voice of Rabelais which cries to us directly across the gulf of the centuries, as shattering now as at the hour when Rabelais begot these word-monsters.

If, then, it is true that Rabelais's word-formation reflects an attitude somewhere between reality and irreality, with its shudders of horror and its comic relief, what of Gustave Lanson's famous statement on Rabelais in general, which is repeated in thousands of French schools and in most of the Lanson-imbued seminars of French throughout the world: "A more copious, more powerful, more triumphant realism has never been seen"?[16] Well, it is simply wrong. I have not time to develop here the conclusions which would round out the utterly antirealistic picture of Rabelais that stands out in his work; it could be shown that the whole plot of Rabelais's epic, the fantastic voyage of fantastic people to the oracle of the priestess Bacbuc (whose ambiguous response: "*Trinc!*" is just a nowhere word), as well as the invention of detail (e.g., Panurge's speech on debtors and lenders, in which the earthy Panurge drives forward, from his astute egoistic refusal to live without debts, to a cosmic, utopian vision of a paradoxical world resting on the universal law of indebtedness)—that everything in Rabelais's work tends toward the creation of a world of irreality.

Thus, what has been disclosed by the study of Rabelais's language, the literary study would corroborate; it could not be otherwise, since language is only one outward crystallization of the "inward form," or, to use another metaphor: the lifeblood of the poetic creation* is everywhere the same, whether we tap the organism at "language" or "ideas," at "plot" or at "composition."

---

* We could here also be reminded of Goethe's simile: "We have learned about a special arrangement of the English Navy: all ropes of the Royal Fleet, from the strongest to the thinnest, have a red thread woven into them in such a way that it cannot be taken out without completely raveling the rope, so that even the smallest particle is stamped as the property of the Crown. Similarly, Ottilia's diary is pervaded by a thread of affection and attachment which connects every part and characterizes the whole of it."[17] In this passage Goethe has formulated the principle of inner cohesion as it exists in a sensitive writer. It is the recognition of this principle which enabled Freud to apply his psychoanalytical finds to works of literature. While I do not wish to disavow the Freudian influence in my earlier attempts at ex-

plaining literary texts, my aim today is to think, not so much in terms of the all-too-human "complexes" which, in Freud's opinion, are supposed to color the writing of the great figures of literature, but of "ideological patterns," as these are present in the history of the human mind.

Mr. Kenneth Burke, in his book *Philosophy of Literary Form*,[18] has worked out a methodology of what he calls the "symbolic" or "strategic" approach to poetry—an approach which comes very close to the Freudian one (and to my own, as far as it was influenced by Freud), and which consists of establishing emotional clusters. When Mr. Burke finds such clusters in Coleridge, for example, and observes their constancy in the writings of this poet, he will claim to have found a factual, observable, irrefutable basis for the analysis of the structure of the work of art in general.

What I would object to in this method is that it can, obviously, be applied only to those poets who do, in fact, reveal such associational clusters—which is to say, only to those poets who do allow their phobias and idiosyncrasies to appear in their writing. But this must exclude all writers before the eighteenth century, the period in which the theory of the "original genius" was discovered and applied. Before this period, it is very difficult to discover, in any writer, "individual" associations, that is to say, associations not prompted by a literary tradition. Dante, Shakespeare, Racine are great literary "individuals," but they did not (or could not) allow their style to be permeated by their personal phobias and idiosyncrasies (even Montaigne, when portraying himself, thought of himself as "l'homme"). When a student of mine, working on the style of Agrippa d'Aubigné, was influenced by Professor Burke's book to apply the method of "emotional clusters" to that sixteenth-century epic poet, and was able, indeed, to find a series of antithetical associations, such as "milk–poison," "mother–serpent," "nature–unnatural" used in reference to pairs represented by the Catholic Catherine de Medici and her Protestant opponents, I had to point out to him that these particular associational patterns (which had reminded him of Joyce) were all given by classical and scriptural tradition: d'Aubigné merely gave powerful expression to age-old ideological motifs that transcended his personal, nervous temperament: the starting point for his "mère non-mère" was, obviously, the Greek μήτηρ ἀμήτωρ [mother not-mother]. Recently, I have had occasion also to point out the same truth in regard to the sixteenth-century poet Antonio de Guevara, whose style has been explained by Freudian frustration.

As regards composition, I could as well have begun with a study of the rather loose literary composition of Rabelais's writings and only later have gone over to his ideas, his plot, his language. Because I happened to be a linguist it was from the linguistic angle that I started, to fight my way to his unity. Obviously, no fellow scholar must be required to do the same. What he must be asked to do, however, is, I believe, to work from the surface to the "inward life-center" of the work of art: first observing details about the superficial appearance of the particular work (and the "ideas" expressed by a poet are, also, only one of the superficial traits in a work of art),* then grouping these details and seeking to integrate them into a creative principle which may have been present in the soul of the artist; and finally making the return trip to all the other groups of observations in order to find whether the "inward form" one has tentatively constructed gives an account of the whole.

---

* Under the noble pretext of introducing "history of ideas" into literary criticism, there have appeared in recent times, with the approval of the departments of literary history, academic theses with such titles as "Money in Seventeenth-Century French (English, Spanish, etc.) Comedy," "Political Tendencies in Nineteenth-Century French (English, Spanish, etc.) Literature." Thus we have come to disregard the philological character of the discipline of literary history, which is concerned with ideas couched in linguistic and literary form, not with ideas in themselves (this is the field of history of philosophy) or with ideas as informing action (this is the field of history and the social sciences). Only in the linguistico-literary field are we philologians competent qua scholars. The type of dissertations cited above reveals an unwarranted extension of the (in itself commendable) tendency toward breaking down departmental barriers, to such a degree that literary history becomes the gay sporting ground of incompetence. Students of the department of literature come to treat the complex subjects of a philosophical, political, or economic nature with the same self-assurance that once characterized those positivists who wrote on "The Horse in Medieval Literature." But while it is possible for the average person to know "what a horse is" (if less so what "a horse in literature" is), it is much more difficult for a student of literature to know "what money is" (and still more so what "money in literature" is). In fact, this new type of thesis is only an avatar of the old positivistic thesis; but, while the original positivism was motivated by a sincere respect for competence, the neo-positivists now would administer the death-blow to scholarly competence.

The scholar will surely be able to state, after three or four of these "fro voyages," whether he has found the life-giving center, the sun of the solar system (by then he will know whether he finds himself in an "excentric" or peripheric position). There is no shadow of truth in the objection raised not long ago by one of the representatives of the mechanist Yale school of linguists against the "circularity of arguments" of the mentalists—against the "explanation of a linguistic fact by an assumed psychological process for which the only evidence is the fact to be explained."[19] I could immediately reply that my school is not satisfied with psychologizing one trait but bases its assumptions on several traits carefully grouped and integrated; one should, in fact, embrace *all* the linguistic traits observable with a given author (I myself have tried to come as close as possible to this requirement of completeness in my studies on Racine, Saint-Simon, Quevedo).[20] And the circle of which the adversary just quoted speaks is not a vicious one; on the contrary, it is the basic operation in the humanities—the *Zirkel im Verstehen* [circle of understanding], as Wilhelm Dilthey has termed the discovery, made by the Romantic scholar and theologian Friedrich Schleiermacher, that cognizance in philology is reached not only by the gradual progression from one detail to another detail, but by the anticipation or divination of the whole—because "the detail can be understood only by the whole and any explanation of detail presupposes the understanding of the whole."*

---

* Schleiermacher distinguishes between the "comparative" and the "divinatory" methods, the combination of which is necessary in "hermeneutics," and since hermeneutics falls into two parts, a "grammatical" and a "psychological" part, both methods must be used in both parts of hermeneutics. Of the two methods, it is the divinatory which requires the *Zirkelschluss* [vicious circle]. We have been dealing here with the *Zirkelschluss* in the "divination" of the psychology of authors; as for "grammatical divination," any college student who attempts to parse a Ciceronian period is constantly using it: he cannot grasp the construction except by passing continuously from the parts to the whole of the sentence and back again to its parts.[21]

Dr. Ludwig Edelstein has called my attention to the Platonic origin of Schleiermacher's discovery: it is in *Phaedo* that Socrates states the importance of the whole for the cognition of the parts. Accordingly, it would appear that I err in adopting Schleiermacher's "theological" approach and that I am undiplomatic in asking for an approach so at variance with that which is traditional in the humanities (when John Dewey reproved the humanists for the residues of theology in their thinking, they made haste to disavow any theological preoccupation—while I take the stand of saying: "Yes, we humanists are theologians!"); would it not, I am asked, be better to show the irrationalism inherent in any rational operation in the humanities, than to demand the overt irrationalism of religion which our secular universities must thoroughly abhor? My answer is that Socrates himself was a religious genius and that, through Plato, he is present in much of Christian thought. As concerns the necessity, for the scholar, of having recourse to religion, compare the conclusive reasoning of Erich Frank in his book *Philosophical Understanding and Religious Truth*.[22]

The traditional view of the "viciousness" of the philological circle is unfortunately held in an otherwise brilliant attack against "the biographical fashion in literary criticism" by Professor Harold Cherniss: in his argument against the philologians of the Stefan George school who, though not dealing with the outward biography of artists, believe that the inner form of the artist's personality can be grasped in his works by a kind of intuition, Cherniss writes: "The intuition which discovers in the writings of an author the 'natural law' and 'inner form' of his personality is proof against all objections, logical and philological; but, while one must admit that a certain native insight, call it direct intelligence or intuition as you please, is required for understanding any text, it is, all the same, a vicious circle to intuit the nature of the author's personality from his writings and then to interpret those writings in accordance with the 'inner necessity' of that intuited personality. Moreover, once the intuition of the individual critic is accepted as the ultimate basis of all interpretation, the comprehension of a literary work becomes a completely private affair, for the intuition of any one interpreter has no more objective validity than that of any other."[23]

I believe that the word "intuition," with its deliberate implication of extraordinary mystic qualities on the part of the critic, vitiates not only the reasoning of the Stefan George school but also that of their opponents. The "circle" is vicious only when an uncontrolled intuition is allowed to exercise itself upon the literary works; the procedure from details to the inner core and back again is not in itself at all vicious; in fact, the "intelligent reading" which Professor Cherniss advocates without defining it (though he is forced to grant rather uncomfortably that it is "a certain native insight, call it direct intelligence or intuition as you please") is based precisely on that very philological circle. To understand a sentence, a work of art, or the inward form of an artistic mind involves, to an increasing degree, irrational moves—which must, also to an increasing degree, be controlled by reason.

Heidegger, in *Sein und Zeit* [Being and Time], I, 32 ("Verstehen und Auslegung" [Understanding and Interpretation]), shows that all "exegesis" is circular, is a catching up with the "understanding," which is nothing else than an anticipation of the whole that is "existentially" given to man:

Zuhandenes wird immer schon aus der Bewandtnisganzheit der verstanden. . . . Die Auslegung gründet jeweils in einer *Vorsicht*, die das in Vorhabe Genommene auf ein bestimmte Auslegbarkeit hin "anschneidet." . . . Auslegung ist nie ein voraussetzungsloses Erfassen eines Vorgegebenen. . . . Alle Auslegung, die Verständnis beistellen soll, muss schon das Auszulegende verstanden haben. . . . *Aber in diesem Zirkel ein vitiosum sehen und nach Wegen Ausschau halten, ihn zu vermeiden, ja ihn auch nur als unvermeidliche Unvollkommenheit "empfinden," heisst das Verstehen von Grund aus missverstehen* {the italics are Heidegger's}. . . . Das Entscheidende ist nicht aus dem Zirkel heraus-, sondern in ihn nach der rechten Weise hineinzukommen. . . . In ihm verbirgt sich eine positive Möglichkeit ursprünglichsten Erkennens, die freilich in echter Weise nur dann ergriffen ist, wenn die Auslegung verstanden hat, dass ihre erste, ständige und letzte Aufgabe bleibt, sich jeweils Vorhabe, Vorsicht und Vorgriff nicht durch Einfälle und Volksbegriffe vorgeben zu lassen, sondern in deren Ausarbeitung aus den Sachen selbst her das wissenschaftliche Thema zu sichern. . . . Der

"Zirkel" im Verstehen gehört zur Struktur des Sinnes, welches Phänomen in der existenzialen Verfassung des Daseins, im auslegenden Verstehen verwurzelt ist.

[The ready-to-hand is always understood in terms of a totality of involvements. . . . In every case interpretation is grounded in *something we see in advance*—in a *fore-sight*. This foresight "takes the first cut" out of what has been taken into our fore-having . . . An interpretation is never a presuppositionless apprehending of something presented to us. . . . Any interpretation which is to contribute understanding must already have understood what is to be interpreted. . . . *But if we see this circle as a vicious one and look out for ways of avoiding it, even if we just "sense" it as an inevitable imperfection, then the act of understanding has been misunderstood from the ground up.* . . . What is decisive is not to get out of the circle but to come into it in the right way. . . . In the circle is hidden a positive possibility of the most primordial kind of knowing. To be sure, we genuinely take hold of this possibility only when, in our interpretation, we have understood that our first, last and constant task is never to allow our fore-having, fore-sight, and fore-conception to be presented to us by fancies and popular conceptions, but rather to make the scientific theme secure by working out these fore-structures in terms of the things themselves. . . . The "circle" in understanding belongs to the structure of meaning, and the latter phenomenon is rooted in the existential constitution of *Dasein*—that is, in the understanding which interprets.][24]

This *Vorsicht*, this anticipation of the whole, is especially necessary for the understanding of philosophical writing. Franz Rosenzweig writes: "The first pages of philosophical books are held by the reader in special respect. . . . He thinks they {such books} ought to be 'especially logical,' and by this he means that each sentence depends on the one that precedes it, so that if the famous one stone is pulled, 'the whole tumbles.' Actually, this is nowhere less the case than in philosophical books. Here a sentence does not follow from its predecessor, but much more probably from its successor. . . . Philosophical books refuse such methodical ancien-régime strategy; they must be conquered à la Napoleon, in a bold thrust against the main body of the enemy; and after the victory at this point, the small fortresses will fall of themselves."[25] (I owe this quotation to Kurt H. Wolff's article "The Sociology of Knowledge." Wolff calls the anticipatory understanding of wholes a "central attitude": "In our everyday social interaction we constantly practice the central-attitude approach without which we could not 'know' how to behave toward other persons, or how to read a book, to see a picture, or to play or listen to a piece of music").[26] What Heidegger, Rosenzweig, and Wolff describe is the method of the humanities which Pascal has called the *esprit de finesse* (as contrasted to the *esprit géométrique*).

For the students in Romance, Gustav Gröber formulated the idea of the philological circle (without mentioning the "circle" itself) in his *Grundriss der romanischen Philologie*: "Unintentional perception, insignificant beginnings provide a goal-oriented search and a comprehensive grasp of the subject. The searcher then strains toward the goal by traversing the space in leaps; he seems, before its nature and its parts are known, to be able to grasp the totality with an overall idea of incompletely formulated views about similar objects. This premature opinion is followed by the recognition of its error. Only slowly, after this, comes the decision to approach the subject in small, in the smallest possible, careful steps, to examine the parts and not to rest until one is convinced that they must be understood in this, and not in any other way."[27]

It is also true of the comparative linguist who establishes his "phonetic laws" on the basis of "evident etymologies," which themselves are based on those "phonetic laws," that he moves in a circle, in the words of Ernst Zupitza: "Our knowledge does not escape a path of circularity. Our knowledge starts with obvious equations, forms from these its laws, and then tests these laws against those equations which form the laws' basics."[28] And even elementary language teaching must move in a circle: Robert A. Hall, advocating the modern "direct method" as preferable to the old "reading method," writes: "When he {the student} has learnt a sufficient number of examples, the linguistic analysis becomes simply a series of obvious deductions from what he has learned; it helps him to perceive the patterns inherent in what he already knows, and tells him how far he can go in extending these patterns to new material."[29] The inference from "patterns" is nothing but an anticipation of a whole deduced from the known examples.

Our to-and-fro voyage from certain outward details to the inner center and back again to other series of details is only an application of the principle of the "philological circle." After all, the concept of the Romance languages as based on one Vulgar Latin substratum, and reflected in them although identical with none—this has been reached by the founder of Romance philology, Diez, the pupil of the Romantics, precisely by means of this "philological circle," which allowed him to sit installed in the center of the phenomenon "Romance Languages," whereas François Juste Marie Raynouard, his predecessor, by identifying one of the Romance varieties, Provençal, with Proto-Romance, found himself in an excentric position, from which point it was impossible to explain satisfactorily all the outward traits of Romance. To proceed from some exterior traits of Philippe's or Rabelais's language to the soul or mental center of Philippe and Rabelais, and back again to the rest of the exterior traits of Philippe's and Rabelais's works of art, is the same *modus operandi* as that which proceeds from some details of the Romance languages to a Vulgar Latin prototype and then, in reverse order, explains other details by this assumed prototype—or even, as that which infers from some of the outward, phonetic and semantic appearances of the English word *conundrum* to its medieval French soul, and thence back to all its phonetic and semantic traits.

To posit a soul of Rabelais which creates from the real in the direction of the unreal is, of course, not yet all that is desirable in order to understand the whole phenomenon: the Rabelaisian entity must be integrated into a greater unit and located somewhere on a historical line, as Diez, in a grandiose way, did with Romance—as we have tried to do, on a minor scale, with *calembredaine–conundrum*. Rabelais may be a solar system which, in its turn, forms part of a transcending system which embraces others as well as himself—others around, before, and after him; we must place him, as the literary historians would say, within the framework of the history of ideas, or *Geistesgeschichte*. The power of wielding the word as though it were a world of its own between reality and irreality, which exists to a unique degree with Rabelais, cannot have sprung out of nothingness, cannot have entirely ebbed after him. Before him there is, for example, Luigi Pulci, who, in his *Morgante Maggiore*, shows a predilection for word-lists, especially when he has his facetious knights indulge in name-calling.[30] And, with Pulci, the Rabelaisian tendency to let language encroach on reality is also to be found: when he retells, in half-facetious vein, the story immortalized by Turoldus of the battle of Roncevaux, we learn that the Saracens fell under the blows of the Christian knights in a trice: they stayed not upon the order of their dying but died at once: not tomorrow, or the day after tomorrow, nor the day after the day after tomorrow, nor the day after the day after the day after tomorrow: not "crai e poscrai, o poscrilla, o posquacchera" (canto XXVII, stanza 55, l. 4). In this sequel of gurgling and guttural sounds, the words *crai* and *poscrai* are genuine Italian reflections of the Latin words *cras* and *posteras* [tomorrow, following]; but *poscrilla, posquacchera* are popular fantasy words.[31] The onomatopoeias with which popular language likes to juggle have here been used by a reflective poet for purposes of grotesque art: we can see here the exact point of transition of popular language into literature. Pulci believes in the ideals of Christian orthodox knighthood less full-heartedly than did Turoldus, for whom the heroic and religious values were real, and who must needs subordinate his language to the expression of these values.[32] The word-world, admitted to a work of art by Pulci, was not yet available to Turoldus, or

even to Dante (the "etymological puns" of the *Vita nuova* are quite
another matter: they are only "illustrations," just as had been true of
the puns of the Church Fathers).*

---

*This is not to say that the puns and repetitions used by Rabelais do not
historically develop from the same devices used by the Fathers and the medieval writers. Rabelais's facetious etymology *Beauce*="{je trouve} beau
ce" [I find this fine] (*Gargantua and Pantagruel*, bk. 1, ch. 16), and his repetition of words, such as "moyne . . . moynant . . . moyna de moynerie"
[monk . . . monking . . . monked . . . monkery] (bk. 1, ch. 27), are scholastic devices—only they are used by him in an antimedieval manner, informed by a worldly spirit and, most important of all, by the consciousness
of the autonomy of a "word-world."

The appearance of this intermediate world is conditioned by a belief
in the reality of words, a belief which would have been condemned
by the "realists" of the Middle Ages. The belief in such vicarious realities as words is possible only in an epoch whose belief in the *univer-
salia realia* has been shaken. It is this phantasmagoric climate, casu-
ally evoked by Pulci, in which Rabelais will move easily and
naturally, with a kind of cosmic independence. It is the belief in the
autonomy of the word which made possible the whole movement of
humanism, in which so much importance was given to the word of
the ancients and of the biblical writers; it is this belief which will in
part explain the extraordinary development of mathematics in the
sixteenth and seventeenth centuries—that is, of the most autonomous language that man has ever devised.

Now, who are the descendants of Rabelais? French classical literature, with its ideal of the *mot juste*, of the *mot mis à sa place*, broke
away from the Renaissance tradition of the autonomy of the word.
But undercurrents persisted, and I would say that Balzac, Flaubert
(in his Letters), Théophile Gautier (in his *grotesqueries*), Victor
Hugo (in his *William Shakespeare*), and Huysmans are, to a certain
extent, descendants of Rabelais in the nineteenth century. In our own
time, with Ferdinand Céline, who can build a whole book out of invectives against the Jews (*Bagatelles pour un massacre*), we may see
language exceed its boundaries: this book, in the words of André
Gide, is a "Don Quijote's ride up in the sky. . . . It's not reality that
Céline paints, it's the hallucination that reality provokes."[33] The fol-

lowing sample of Célinian inspiration makes a pseudo-Rabelaisian effect, and can be compared with the apocalyptic inscription over the portal of Thélème:

Penser "sozial!" cela veut dire dans la pratique, en termes bien crus: "penser juif! pour les juifs! par les juifs, sous les juifs!" Rien d'autre! Tout le surplus immense des mots, le vrombissant verbiage socialitico-humanitaro-scientifique, tout le cosmique carafouillage de l'impératif despotique juif n'est que l'enrobage mirageux, le charabia fatras poussif, la sauce orientale pour ces encoulés d'aryens, la fricassée terminologique pour rire, pour l'adulation des "aveulis blancs," ivrognes rampants, intouchables, qui s'en foutrent, à bite que veux-tu, s'en mystifient, s'en baffrent à crever.[34]

[To think "sozial!" It means, in practical, in real crude terms, "to think Jew! for the Jews! by the Jews, under the Jews!" Nothing else! All the immense surplus of words, the roaring socialitico-humanitaro-scientific verbiage, all the cosmic mumbo-jumbo of the imperative despotic Jew is nothing but the miragelike coating, the jumbled short-winded gibberish, the oriental sauce for these bloat-fucked Aryans, the terminological fricassee just for kicks, for the adulation of the "white blobs," crawling drunks, untouchables, who fuck themselves with it, with dicks or what have you, mystifying themselves with it, stuffing themselves to the bursting point.]

Here, evidently, the verbal creation, itself a *vrombissant verbiage* [roaring verbiage] (to use the alliterative coinage of Céline), has implications more eschatological than cosmic: the word-world is really only a world of noisy words, clanking sounds, like so many engines senselessly hammering away, covering with their noise the fear and rage of man lonely in the doomed modern world. Words and reality fall apart. This is really a "voyage au bout du monde" [journey to the end of the earth]: not to the oracle of Bacbuc but to chaos, to the end of language as an expression of thought.

The historical line we have drawn (we may call it the evolution of an idea: the idea of "language become autonomous"), which is marked by the stages Pulci–Rabelais–Victor Hugo–Céline, is paralleled or crossed by other historical lines with other names located on the historical ladder. Victor Hugo is not Rabelais, although there may be Hugoesque traits in Rabelais, Rabelaisian traits in Hugo. We must not confuse a historical line with a solar system resting in itself: what appeared to us central in Rabelais may be peripheric in Victor Hugo, and the reverse. Every solar system, unique in itself, undefinable (*ineffabile*) to a certain extent, is traversed by different historical lines of "ideas," whose intersection produces the particular climate in which the great literary work matures—just as the system of a language is made up of the intersections of different historical lines of the *calembredaine–conundrum* variety.

Thus we started with a particular historical line, the etymology of a particular word-family, and found therein evidences of a change of historical climate. Then we considered the change of a whole historical climate as expressed in the innovations, linguistic and literary, of writers of two different epochs (the twentieth and the sixteenth centuries), finally to arrive at the point of positing theoretically self-sufficient systems: the great works of art, determined by different historical developments and reflecting in all their outward details, linguistic as well as literary, their respective central "sun." It is obvious that, in this paper, I have been able to give you only scattered samples, the conclusions from which I have loaded, and perhaps overloaded, with an experience resulting from hundreds of such to-and-fro voyages—all directed by the same principles, but each one bound for an unpredictable goal. My personal way has been from the observed detail to ever-broadening units which rest, to an increasing degree, on speculation. It is, I think, the philological, the inductive way, which seeks to show significance in the apparently futile, in contrast to the deductive procedure, which begins with units assumed as given—and which is rather the way followed by the theologians, who start from on high, to take the downward path toward the earthly maze of detail, or by the mathematicians, who treat their axioms as if these were God-given. In philology, which deals with the all-too-human, with the interrelated and the intertwined aspects of human affairs, the deductive method has its place only as a verification of the principle found by induction—which rests on observation.

But, of course, the attempt to discover significance in the detail,* the habit of taking a detail of language as seriously as the meaning of a work of art—or, in other words, the attitude which sees all manifestations of man as equally serious—this is an outgrowth of the pre-established firm conviction, the "axiom," of the philologian, that details are not an inchoate, chance aggregation of dispersed material through which no light shines.

---

*I have often wondered how historians of literature could make such sweeping statements, as they are wont to do, on the whole of the literary work of a poet, or of a period, without descending into the detail of texts (and into the linguistic detail). Goethe speaks pertinently of the *An-*

schauung [observation] necessary for the concrete apperception of works of art: "Um von Kunstwerken eigentlich und mit wahrem Nutzen für sich und andere zu sprechen, sollte es freilich nur in Gegenwart derselben geschehen. Alles kommt aufs Anschauen an; es kommt darauf an, dass bei dem Worte, wodurch man ein Kunstwerk zu erläutern hofft, das Bestimmteste gedacht werde, weil sonst gar nichts gedacht wird. Daher geschieht es so oft, dass derjenige, der über Kunstwerke schreibt, bloss im Allgemeinen verweilt."[35] [If one is to speak of works of art in a precise and useful way to oneself and others, one should do so only in the presence of the works themselves. Everything depends on looking at them; it depends on thinking out the language with which one interprets a work as precisely as possible, for otherwise nothing gets thought. Therefore it often happens that those who write about works of art do not go beyond the level of generalities.]

The same seems to have been felt by Santayana in regard to the field of philosophy; in *The Middle Span*, he has the following to say about the habits of his Harvard students during the last decades of the nineteenth century: "I doubt that the texts were much studied directly in those days at Harvard. The undergraduates were thinking only of examinations and relied on summaries in the histories of philosophy and on lecture notes. . . . Philosophy can be communicated only by being evoked: the pupil's mind must be engaged dialectically in the discussion. Otherwise, all that can be taught is the literary history of philosophy, that is, the *phrases* that various philosophers have rendered famous. To conceive what those phrases meant or could mean would require a philosophical imagination in the public which cannot be demanded. All that usually exists is familiarity with current phrases, and a shock, perhaps of pleased curiosity but more often of alarm and repulsion, due to the heterodoxy of any different phrases."[36] It is needless to add that a "literary history" which is satisfied with enumerating the "phrases" (whether famous or not) used by a writer (philosophical or otherwise), without establishing any connection between them and the mainspring of the writer's inspiration, is sham literary history.

The philologian must believe in the existence of some light from on high, of some *post nubila Phoebus* [sun-god behind the clouds]. If he did not know that at the end of his journey there would be awaiting him a life-giving draught from some *dive bouteille* [divine bottle], he would not have commenced it: "Tu ne me chercherais pas si tu ne m'avais pas déjà trouvé" [You would not search for me if you had not already found me], says Pascal's God. Thus, humanistic thought, in spite of the methodological distinction just made, is not so completely divorced from that of the theologian as is generally believed; it is not by chance that the "philological circle" was discovered by a theologian, who was wont to harmonize the discordant, to retrace the beauty of God in this world. This attitude is reflected in the word coined by Schleiermacher:[37] *Weltanschauung*: "die Weltanschauen":

"to see, to cognize the universe *in its sensuous detail*." The philologian will then continue the pursuit of the microscopic because he sees therein the microcosmic; he will practice that *Andacht zum Kleinen* [meditation on small things] which Jacob Grimm has prescribed; he will go on filling his little cards with dates and examples, in the hope that supernal light will shine over them and bring out the clear lines of truth. The humanist believes in the power bestowed on the human mind of investigating the human mind. When, with scholars whose goal and whose tool are thus identical, the faith in the human mind, as a tool and as a goal, is broken, this can only mean a crisis in the humanities—or, should I say, in the *Divinities*? And this is the situation today. A man without belief in the human mind is a stunted human being—how can he be a humanist? The humanities will be restored only when the humanists shed their agnostic attitudes, when they become human again, and share the belief of Rabelais's humanistic and religious king: "sapience n'entre point en âme malivole; et science sans conscience n'est que ruine de l'âme" [wisdom enters not into the malicious heart, and knowledge without conscience is but the ruin of the soul] (*Gargantua and Pantagruel*, bk. 2, ch. 8)—or, to go back to the Augustinian wording: "Non intratur in veritatem nisi per charitatem" [Nothing enters into truth unless by charity].*

---

* Even with philologians (who are not by nature apt to be insensitive to literary values, as are so many of the so-called linguists), one can discern "unhumanistic" prejudices. For example, Professor William J. Entwistle maintains that the linguistic interpretation of poetry implies the crossing of an intellectual frontier: the philologian has to deal not with "science," which treats of things that can be measured and weighed, not with "unambiguous facts," which can be tested by anyone, but with "knowledge" irreducible to "scientific" treatment—to which belongs hermeneutics, the study of the poet's meaning: this meaning cannot be treated in the "old assertive language" of the positivistic linguist, and still less can be the elusive significance of a poetic text, which transcends the poet's conscious intention.[38] By such distinctions Professor Entwistle is perpetuating the nineteenth-century rift between positivistic science and wisdom. As concerns what Entwistle considers to be the purely scientific part of philology—such as the phonetic laws, which he ranks with the facts testable by everyone—I wonder if the formulation of a phonetic law is not as much of a speculation as is the attempt to discover the significance of a poetic passage; and is it really true that a phonetic law can be tested by anyone who has not had a preparation for this type of study? It can be done only to the same extent, I should think, which would hold true for the establishment of the meaning of a poetic passage. And as for the unconscious intentions of the poet, I simply would not

advise the interpreter to concern himself with them. As a matter of fact, the example of "unconscious poetic intention" offered by Mr. Entwistle seems to me to show how little he has grasped the purpose of philological studies: of the passage from the *Aeneid* [I, 461–63] in which Aeneas sees depicted on the walls of Carthage the Trojan war and his father's deeds:

> En Priamus! Sunt hic etiam sua praemia laudi;
> sunt lacrimae rerum, et mentem mortalia tangunt.
> Solve metus; feret haec aliquam tibi fama salutem.

[See, there is Priam! Here, too, merit finds its reward; here, too, there are tears for misfortunes, and mortal fate touches the mind. Dismiss your fears; this fame will bring you some deliverance.]

Entwistle writes: "The sense of the second last line, in its context, seems to be encouraging {he has translated it: 'tears are shed for his misfortunes and his death moves men's minds to pity'}: it is better to be remembered sorrowfully than to be forgotten altogether. Yet *sunt lacrimae rerum* means something other and more moving than that. There is music and intensity in the line beyond anything Virgil may have consciously meant. . . . 'Nature's tears and the mortal sadness of mankind' has been discovered in that music by posterity, and, I think, justly so."[39] But it can be *proved* by the philologist that Virgil *meant* (and it is only with conscious meaning that the philologian is concerned) the first, the "lesser" of the two meanings mentioned (as is indicated by the two anaphoric *sunt*'s, which suggest a parallelism of arguments leading to the encouraging final line). The second meaning which has been attached to the line by posterity is an error due to its isolated consideration out of context (which led to the misinterpretation of *rerum* as "Nature" instead of "misfortunes," an error comparable to the famous misinterpretation of Buffon's "Le style est l'homme même" [Style constitutes man himself][40]—or even to many witty or punning misinterpretations of certain poetic lines (e.g., when the line of Schiller's Maid of Orleans: "Johanna geht und nimmer kehrt sie wieder" [Johanna goes and will never return] is facetiously interpreted to mean that never again will she sweep the floor [*kehren* can mean either "to turn," so that *wiederkehren* is "to come back," or "to sweep a floor," so that *wiederkehren* is "to sweep once again"]). To the philologian this secondary graft or palimpsest imposed upon the original text may be historically quite interesting, but it has to be discarded from his interpretation of the given work of art. There is no music in Virgil's poetry but that which he put in it—but, by the same token, it is also necessary that this music be retained and not destroyed, as it is by such a translation as "tears are shed for *his* misfortunes and *his* death": the indefinite quality of "misfortune" and "death" should be preserved. Virgil's poetic music consists in the procedure of expanding the particular example of Priam's fate to that of man (and, similarly, *mortalia* should not be concretized to "death" but left as "mortal fate"); it is the general gnome, so indissolubly linked by Virgil with the particular case, that posterity has arbitrarily detached (and, in addition to this antipoetic first move, has misinterpreted—this time poetically, in the manner mentioned above).

In this, as in the following studies, the reader will find me polemizing against the views of fellow scholars. I have sometimes been accused of raising up straw men just to knock them down, instead of being satisfied with offering my own picture of the phenomenon in question. My answer is that, in matters stylistic as well as in factual questions of literary history or linguistics, the *consensus omnium* is a desideratum, the only path to which is the discussion of the pros and cons of theories different from one's own, which enable us to vindicate the relative superiority of our own theory. The greater the objective certainty that a stylistic explanation can claim, the more we will have overcome that impressionism which, until recently, has seemed the only alternative to the positivistic treatment of literature.

———————————— • ————————————

In the essays to follow [that is, in the volume entitled *Linguistics and Literary History*; see headnote], I have made an attempt to apply the principle of the "philological circle" to various authors of different nations and periods, applying it in varying degree and manner and in combination with other methods. But these articles are conceived not only as illustrations of my procedure, but as independent contributions to the understanding of the writers treated therein: contributions which should prove readable for any cultured person interested in the style of works of art.*

*The frequent occurrence, in my text, of quotations in the original foreign language (or languages) may prove a difficulty for the English reader. But since it is my purpose to take the word (and the wording) of the poets seriously, and since the convincingness and rigor of my stylistic conclusions depends entirely upon the minute linguistic detail of the original texts, it was impossible to offer translations. [Since the linguistic range of readers of literary criticism is not always as great as Spitzer's, the editors of this volume decided to provide translations.]

For if my procedure should have any value, this must be revealed in the new results, the scholarly progress, attained by its means: the philological circle should not imply that one moves complacently in the circle of the already known, in a *piétinement sur place* [treading on the spot]. Thus each single essay is intended to form a separate, independent unit: I hope that the repetitions of theoretical and historical statements which are the unavoidable consequence of this manner of presentation will be felt by the reader rather as recurrent *leitmotifs* or *refrains* destined to emphasize a constancy and unity of approach.

Before putting to the test the method of the "philological circle" already delineated, I should like to warn the reader that he must not expect to find, in my demonstration of this method, the systematic step-by-step procedure which my own description of it may have seemed to promise.*

---

*Perhaps I should make it clear that I am using the word "method" in a manner somewhat aberrant from common American use: it is for me much more a "habitual procedure of the mind" than a "program regulating beforehand a series of operations . . . in view of reaching a well-defined result."⁴¹ As used by me it is nearly synonymous with *Erlebnis*, and consequently would correspond relatively to what is called in America "approach," were it not for the volitional and even "strategic" nuance, in this word, of military siege or of tracking down a quarry, by which it may be historically explained.

In this connection I may quote a passage from a letter of Descartes to Mersenne: "Mais ie n'ay sceu bien entendre ce que vous objectez touchant le titre {*Discours de la méthode*}; car ie ne mets pas *Traité de la méthode*, mais *Discours de la méthode*, ce qui est le mesme que *Preface* ou *Advis touchant la méthode*, pour monstrer que ie n'ay pas dessein de l'enseigner, mais seulement d'en parler. Car comme on peut voir de ce que i'en dis, elle consiste plus en Pratique qu'en Theorie, & ie nomme les Traitez suivans des *Essais de cette méthode*, pource que ie pretens que les choses qu'ils contiennent n'ont pû estre trouvées sans elle, & qu'on peut connoistre par eux ce qu'elle vaut."⁴² [But I have not been able to understand what you object to in the title {*Discours de la méthode*}; because I have not called it *Treatise on Method* but *Discourse on Method*, which is the same as *Preface* or *Notice on Method*, to show that I do not intend to teach the method but only to talk about it. As one may see from what I say, it is a practice rather than a theory, and I call the following treatises *Essays in This Method*, because I claim that the things they contain could not have been found without it and that they demonstrate its value].

For, when I spoke in terms of a series of back-and-forth movements (first the detail, then the whole, then another detail, etc.), I was using a linear and temporal figure in an attempt to describe states of apperception which, in the mind of the humanist, only too often coexist. This gift, or vice (for it has its dangers), of seeing part and whole together, at any moment, and which, to some degree, is basic to the operation of the philological mind, is, perhaps, in my own case, developed to a particular degree, and has aroused objections from students and readers—in Germany, where the synthetic capacities of the public are, in general, superior to their analytic capacities, as well as in America, where the opposite obtains. A very understanding but critical ex-student of mine, an American, once wrote me: "To establish a behavioristic technique which would reveal the application of your method is, it seems to me, beyond your possibilities. You know the principles that motivate you, rather than any 'technique' that you rigorously follow. Here, it may be a memory from boyhood, there an inspiration you got from another poem; here, there and everywhere it is an urge in you, an instinct backed up by your experience, that tells you immediately: 'this is not important; this is.' At every second you are making choices, but you hardly know that you make them: what seems right to you must be immediately right. And you can only show by doing; you see the meaning as a whole from the beginning; there are almost no steps in your mental processes; and, writing from the midst of your thoughts you take it for granted that the reader is with you and that what is self-evident to you as the next step (only, it's not the next step, even: it's already included, somehow) will also be so to him."

These words, obviously, offer a picture of the limitations of a particular individual temperament. But much of what my correspondent says is given with the operation of the circle—when this is applied, not to routine reading, on the one hand, or to the deductions of schematic linguistics on the other, but to a work of art: the solution attained by means of the circular operation cannot be subjected to a rigorous rationale because, as its most perfect, this is a negation of steps: once attained, it tends to obliterate the steps leading up to it (one may remember the lion of medieval bestiaries who, at every step forward, wiped out his footprints with his tail, in order to elude his pursuers!).

Why do I insist that it is impossible to offer the reader a step-by-step rationale to be applied to a work of art? For one reason, that the first step, on which all may hinge, can never be planned: it must already have taken place. This first step is the awareness of having been struck by a detail, followed by a conviction that this detail is connected basically with the work of art; it means that one has made an "observation"—which is the starting point of a theory, that one has been prompted to raise a question—which must find an answer. To begin by omitting this first step must doom any attempt at interpretation—as was the case with the dissertation (mentioned in note 1 of my article on Diderot)[43] devoted to the "imagery" of Diderot, in which the concept "imagery" was based on no preliminary observation but on a ready-made category applied from without to the work of art.

Unfortunately, I know of no way to guarantee either the "impression" or the conviction just described: they are the results of talent, experience, and faith. And, even then, the first step is not to be taken at our own volition: how often, with all the theoretical experience of method accumulated in me over the years, have I stared blankly, quite similar to one of my beginning students, at a page that would not yield its magic? The only way leading out of this state of unproductivity is to read and reread,* patiently and confidently, in an endeavor to become, as it were, soaked through and through with the atmosphere of the work.

---

* If I were to give one piece of advice to our students of literary history, it would be substantially the same as that which Lanson, touring the United States forty years ago, gave to the students of his time who were then, as they are now, only too eager to rush to their big libraries to find in the many books of "secondary literature" an alibi for getting away from the "primary" texts they should study: "*Read your texts!*" My "circular method" is, in fact, nothing but an expansion of the common practice of "reading books": reading at its best requires a strange cohabitation in the human mind of two opposite capacities—contemplativity on the one hand and, on the other, a protean mimeticism. That is to say, an undeflected patience that "stays with" a book until the forces latent in it unleash in us the re-creative process.

And suddenly, one word, one line, stands out, and we realize that, now, a relationship has been established between the poem and us. From this point on, I have usually found that, what with other observations adding themselves to the first, and with previous experiences of the circle intervening, and with associations given by previous education building up before me (all of this quickened, in my own case, by a quasi-metaphysical urge toward solution), it does not seem long until the characteristic "click" occurs, which is the indication that detail and whole have found a common denominator—which gives the etymology of the writing.*

---

* Sometimes it may happen that this "etymology" leads simply to a characterization of the author that has been long accepted by literary historians (who have not needed, apparently, to follow the winding path I chose), and which can be summed up in a phrase which smacks of a college handbook.

But, to make our own way to an old truth is not only to enrich our own understanding: it produces inevitably new evidence, of objective value, for this truth—which is thereby renewed. A *comédie-proverbe* of Musset is based, after all, on a commonplace saying: was it a waste of time to illustrate so wittily "il faut qu'une porte soit ouverte ou fermée" [a door must be either open or closed]?[44]

And looking back on this process (whose end, of course, marks only the conclusion of the *preliminary* stage of analysis), how can we say when exactly it began? (Even the "first step" was preconditioned.) We see, indeed, that to read is to have read, to understand is equivalent to having understood.*

---

*The requirement at St. John's [College] for the Hundred Great Books is good, I believe, insofar as it may encourage the "click" to repeat itself in an accelerated manner—if, of course, it has come about in the first experiences: to have read these hundred books "without click" would be equivalent to not having read a single book.

I have just spoken of the importance of past experience in the process of understanding the work of art—but as only one of the intervening factors. For experience with the "circle" is not, itself, enough to enable one to base thereupon a program applicable to all cases. For every poem the critic needs a separate inspiration, a separate light from above (it is this constant need which makes for humility, and it is the accumulation of past enlightenments that encourages a sort of pious confidence). Indeed, a protean mutability is required of the critic, for the device which has proved successful for one work of art cannot be applied mechanically to another: I could not expect that the "trick of the five *grands*" (which I shall apply to an ode of Claudel's) would work for the "récit de Théramène,"[45] or that proper names, which will serve as a point of departure in my article on Cervantes, would play any part in the study on Diderot. It is, indeed, most trying for the experienced teacher to have to watch a beginner re-use, and consequently mis-use, a particular clue that had served the teacher when he was treating a quite different writer—as though a young actor were to use the leer of John Barrymore's Richard III for his performance of Othello. The mutability required of the critic can be gained only by repeated experiences with totally different writers; the "click" will come oftener and more quickly after several experiences of "clicks" have been realized by the critic. And, even then, it is not a foregone conclusion that it will inevitably come; nor can one ever foretell just when and where it will materialize ("The Spirit bloweth . . .").

The reason that the clues to understanding cannot be mechanically transferred from one work of art to another lies in the fact of artistic expressivity itself: the artist lends to an outward phenomenon of language an inner significance (thereby merely continuing and expanding the basic fact of human language: that a meaning is quite arbitrarily—arbitrarily, at least, from the point of view of the current usage of the language—associated with an acoustic phenomenon); just *which* phenomena the literary artist will choose for the embodiment of his meaning is arbitrary from the point of view of the "user" of the work of art. To overcome the impression of an arbitrary association in the work of art, the reader must seek to place himself in the creative center of the artist himself—and re-create the artistic organism. A metaphor, an anaphora, a staccato rhythm may be found anywhere in literature; they may or may not be significant. What tells us that they are important is only the feeling, which we must have already acquired, for the whole of the particular work of art.

And the capacity for this feeling is, again, deeply anchored in the previous life and education of the critic, and not only in his scholarly education: in order to keep his soul ready for his scholarly task he must have already made choices, in ordering his life, of what I would call a moral nature; he must have chosen to cleanse his mind from distraction by the inconsequential, from the obsession of everyday small details—to keep it open to the synthetic apprehension of the "wholes" of life, to the symbolism in nature and art and language. I have sometimes wondered if my *explication de texte* in the university classroom, where I strive to create an atmosphere suitable for the appreciation of the work of art, would not have succeeded much better if that atmosphere had been present at the breakfast table of my students.

PSEUDO-OBJECTIVE MOTIVATION
IN CHARLES-LOUIS PHILIPPE

As the preceding essay indicates, Spitzer took special pride in his study of Charles-Louis Philippe's short novel *Bubu de Montparnasse*. Though little read today, this turn-of-the-century narrative of life among young Bohemians in Paris had a special appeal for those who, like Spitzer and the young T. S. Eliot (images from this novel appear in Eliot's early poetry), had some familiarity with the world that Philippe describes. In its interpretive method, this essay is typical of much of Spitzer's work of the 1920's, for it establishes links between a writer's deviations from a linguistic (or other formal) norm and what Spitzer sees as peculiarities or disturbances in the author's psyche. This approach constitutes a unique use of a Freudian perspective, one that, in its attempt to use a writer's linguistic habits to describe his psychological makeup, is distinctly different from the uses of Freud by later critics.

The essay is also important as a demonstration of the possibilities of close narrative analysis, above all of a writer's use of *style indirect libre* (free indirect speech). This term, coined in 1912 by Ferdinand de Saussure's editor, Charles Bally, refers to past-tense narrative (usually in the third person) that gives the illusion of emanating from a living voice. The concept, which generated considerable excitement at the time, was developed further by two German Romance philologists, Eugen Lerch and Jean Etienne Lorck.[2] The work of these narrative analysts, and of Spitzer in particular, exercised a strong influence on the Russian critic Mikhail Bakhtin, who extended their methods to create his concept of "dialogic" discourse. Bakhtin, in fact, employs and develops Spitzer's term *pseudo-*

objective motivation in his demonstration of the dialogic nature of Dickens's style.[3]

Spitzer's essay, first published in 1923, is notable, among other things, for displaying how a device isolated by linguists can be used to provide a full-range interpretation of a literary work. Spitzer never employs linguistic analysis for purely formal ends, but concerns himself always with the psychological and cultural implications of linguistic forms. In its impersonal, scientific tone and in the copiousness of its examples, this study is typical of German scholarly inquiry of its time. By contrast, Spitzer's later work in English, as though accommodating itself to its American academic environment, is sparser in its use of examples and more personal and essayistic in tone. Readers willing to follow in detail Spitzer's elaborate analysis in this essay will find that he confronts a text with an intensity and an intuitive sympathy that few analysts of narrative since his time have been able to match.

For inclusion in this volume, the essay was translated by Dorothea von Mücke from the German "Pseudoobjektive Motivierung bei Charles-Louis Philippe," in Spitzer's *Stilstudien*, 2 (Munich, 1928), pp. 166–207. It was originally printed in *Zeitschrift für französische Sprache und Literatur*, 46 (1923): 359–85.

Pseudo-objective Motivation
in Charles-Louis Philippe

Certain passages from older literary works present difficulties at first reading even to those readers who are well acquainted with the language of the text, and it is likely that these passages were already a problem for the editor. The reason is partly that the texts existed in several variants (and hence were also puzzling for the copyists), a fact that ultimately drew attention to conspicuous elements in the language of the original. Furthermore, what from a linguistic point of view would be considered conspicuous—works of incompetents who are not fully in command of their own language cannot be considered here—must somehow be explained by the psyche of the artist. Why should the artist feel an urge to leave the solid ground of normal linguistic usage if he were not driven by inner necessity? As a matter of fact, in most cases one can make an emendation by finding parallel instances in standard usage or in an author's own work, since there are consistencies in the way he uses language.

Let us now apply what we have learned from classical philology to stylistic criticism. When we notice something that seems conspicuous in a modern text, we shall, if we search carefully enough, find related phenomena in the same text. Once we have identified the similarities between these passages, we shall be able to draw certain conclusions about the author's psychological makeup. What the "corrupted passages" are to the philologist editing older texts, the "conspicuous passages" are to the modern philologist intent on psychogenetic explications. One might use the Italian term *spie* [spies] for these conspicuous passages, for they allow us to detect psychological traits in language, and they teach us to recognize necessity in individual formulations and to discover originality in conspicuous deviations.*

---

*In fact, the same thing happens in everyday life whenever we hear some unusual formulation coming from someone in our linguistic community. We tend to trace such deviations to their psychological origins: for example, an Austrian living in Germany interjects into his conversation the remark *entschuldigen Sie gütigst* [please accept my most humble apology]. This superlative, which sounds like written German and recalls administrative usage, is almost pointedly courteous; it expresses the attempt not to offend one's fellow creature with a daring assertion, but at the same time it also sounds stiff and formulaic. We naturally assign all these idiosyncrasies to that side of a character which we specifically label "Austrian." To give another example, some professors punctuate almost every statement with a smashing, almost triumphant *nicht wahr?* [isn't that right?]. This phrase obviously represents self-assurance seeking applause, as well as the pleasure the speaker takes in lecturing. While in the first example we are talking about a mixture of national and individual styles, the second example illustrates strictly an individual style. These examples are safely grounded in the here and now, within the context of everyday, contemporary linguistic usage; we need not take our chances speculating about some historically remote era. Our argument is on even safer grounds than was, for instance, that of Karl Vossler when he analyzed certain linguistic innovations in Middle French, or that of Ernst Lewy when he postulated a certain *Altersstil* [late or mature style]. (Contrary to Lewy's assumptions, it is hardly likely that Goethe as an old man would have developed the same stylistic idiosyncrasies as Plato did in old age, for the simple reason that the linguistic norm against which these two styles define themselves is totally different in each of the two cases. Although the German writer's use of the gerund is quite striking, there is nothing special about it for the Greek; surely one cannot find an analogy in Plato for Goethe's avoidance of the article, etc.) These observations that we have at our disposal are due to our present-day sensitivity to language. (Thomas Mann and also Proust like to have their characters use words that express their psychological makeup. Mann, for example, puts the word *mähnschlich* into the mouth of the Russian character Clawdia Chauchat.[1] Hans Castorp says to Clawdia: "Du liebst das Wort, du dehnst es so schwärmerisch, ich habe es immer mit Interesse aus deinem Munde gehört."[2] [You seem to love this word, you draw it out with enthusiasm, I have always listened to you pronouncing it with interest.] Or Hans Castorp, who does not have enough *Format* [size, but also "distinguished character"], uses that word quite frequently when he talks to Mynheer Peeperkorn, unconsciously influenced as he is by Peeperkorn's *Format*, etc.[3]

My present study is based on the theoretical reflections that I developed in *Motiv und Wort*, as well as in my study of Barbusse and elsewhere.[4] This time I shall restrict myself to a single work of a more recent author. I shall attempt to read his lived experience out of his language. I shall try to study the author only as he appears in his work, ignoring all biographical details, which means that a thorough *reading* of his work alone will provide us with the appropriate scholarly criterion for this investigation.

Some time ago I was struck by the sensitive way that Charles-Louis Philippe uses the prepositional phrase *à cause de* [because of, on account of, owing to] in his novel about prostitutes and pimps, *Bubu de Montparnasse*;[5] for instance: "Les réveils de midi sont lourds et poisseux. . . . On éprouve un sentiment de déchéance à cause des réveils d'autrefois" (p. 80). [These awakenings at midday are heavy and sticky. . . . You feel a sense of degradation because of the awakenings of former times.] This does not quite sound like written French, where one would say something on the order of "en comparant les réveils d'autrefois, en se rappelant . . ." [in comparing the awakenings of former days, in remembering . . .]. *A cause de* sounds like spoken language. Its oral, nonacademic character is obviously due to its ascribing a causal function to a fact (*réveils d'autrefois*, awakenings of former days) without giving us any clue to how cause and effect might be related. While spoken language may treat this causal nexus as though it were obvious and state it without any further explanation, written language has to explain the relationship between cause and effect—for instance, with the aid of a clarifying verb, as we have shown above.

My assertion that this *à cause* must be seen as rooted in spoken language can be supported by passages of direct speech from the novel: "Le médecin voulait que j'y aille passer trois mois à cause du bon air" (p. 68). [The doctor wanted me to spend three months there because of the fine air.] "Because of the fine air" is rather imprecise. Written language would require something like "in order to recover in the fine air." The changing of "je souffre à cause de tes souffrances" (p. 121) [I suffer from your suffering] would make it sound highly literary; also, "par tes souffrances" would still sound like written language, whereas *à cause de* has a prosaic, banal, and ordinary ring to it. Nevertheless, the idea itself has a poetic quality, which is heightened by the repetition of the root [*souffr-*].[6]

"Je t'ai vu venir avec ton petit pas. Tu remues tes jambes sous tes jupes, tu te tortilles un peu, tu souris et tu as l'air très doux. On sent que tu as bon charactère. *Je* t'aurais reconnue entre toutes les femmes *à cause de cela"* (p. 64). [I saw you coming with your little steps. You move your legs under your skirts, you wriggle a little, you smile and you look very sweet. One senses that you are of good character. I would have recognized you among all women because of that.] "Je t'aurais reconnue à cela" would mean "I would have recognized you by virtue of that." The emphasis on causality (*à cause*) gives more weight to the possibility of recognition. The moment of recognition seems to be logically connected with the girl's way of walking. While in spoken conversation a mere hint at some causal nexus in very general terms might be sufficient, written speech requires a more detailed explanation, since here the reader should not be surprised by unexplained connections. For this reason the narrative use of *à cause* can assume a conspicuous, bold, almost poetic character, owing to the vague notion of some opaque, causal force that it invokes. *A cause* does not always refer to the actual cause, for sometimes it also refers to the mere occasion that triggered the effect—namely, an even less certain, less tightly defined causality.

Let me add some further examples from narrative descriptions: "Elle vivait dans une boutique d'épicerie une vie sage et encombrée. Elle ne vendait guère que pour deux sous à cause des 'magasins d'approvisionnement' qui prennent tout l'argent des quartiers" (p. 87). [She lived a prudent and busy life in her grocery shop. She hardly sold more than two sous worth of stuff because of the big "supply stores" that take all the money of the quarter.] The *à cause* has been borrowed from the kind of speech we would expect the personality being described to produce: "Je ne vends . . . à cause . . ." [I hardly sell . . . because of . . .]. We find a similar case in these lines: "Les jours d'hôpital étaient encore les jours de Maurice, à cause des jeudis et des dimanches où il venait au parloir" (p. 139). [The days in the hospital were still Maurice's days (for Berthe), because of the Thursdays and Sundays when he came to the visitors' room.] In these cases it is quite obvious that the expression has been taken from spoken language.

Now I should like to present some narrative descriptions that display purely literary intentions, as, for instance, "Elle eut un fond de tristesse les premiers temps à cause des habitudes anciennes" (p. 150). [At first she had this undercurrent of sadness because of old habits.] "Ils n'étaient heureux ni l'un ni l'autre à cause de l'amour qui remue les hommes à vingt ans, et à cause de Paris, qui est dur aux pauvres" (p. 110). [They were not happy, either of them, because of love, which disturbs young men of twenty, and because of Paris, which is hard on the poor.] The translation immediately reveals what is so original about this phrase "because of love . . . and because of Paris." The equation of love and Paris as powers of the same order is as stylistically striking as the idea of a city as an energizing force. It is as though Paris and love must quite naturally have a causal connection. "C'est ainsi que Pierre rencontra Berthe, le soir du quinze juillet. Il souriait à cause de sa gentillesse et de ses bandeaux" (p. 35). [It was like this that Pierre met Berthe on the night of the fifteenth of July. He smiled because of her engaging manner and because of her ribbons.] Again we can see the effect of the equivalence—in this case the author equates an abstract noun with a concrete grooming accessory. The reader must be wondering how the latter can serve as an active force.

Finally, I want to point out some passages using direct speech. In these, the author tries to avoid giving too literary a character to spoken expression: "Il y a par là-bas deux ou trois cents petits nuages rouges. Ça me donne envie de te faire un compliment. Il y a dans mon cœur deux ou trois cents petites émotions qui brûlent à cause de toi" (p. 66). [Over there, there are two or three hundred little red clouds. This makes me want to pay you a compliment. There are two or three hundred little emotions in my heart that burn because of you.] "Qui brûlent pour toi" would mean "my emotions burn for you like candles for a saint," whereas *à cause de toi* [because of you] names the cause without giving a detailed explanation of how this effect is achieved. The image of the burning sentiment is somewhat weakened by the *à cause*, perhaps because of a certain chastity of feeling.

A similar example can be found in the author's apostrophe of a song about the *véralés* [syphilitics]: "tu chantes les remèdes et tu ris des maux, tu danses à cause de nous et tu nous fais croire que nos souffrances sont glorieuses" (pp. 101–2). [You sing of remedies and you laugh at afflictions, you dance because of us and you convince us of the glory of our suffering.] There is no a priori reason to situate dancing within a nexus of causality. Here, too, *à cause* works to key down the Verhaeren-like hymnic lyricism.[7]

A cause indicates not only causality but also a certain general applicability to life that we are to take for granted. The statement "Il souriait à cause de sa gentillesse et de ses bandeaux" [He smiled because of her engaging manner and because of her ribbons] immediately gives the impression that one could not but smile "considering these circumstances"—at least the way it is formulated suggests this inevitability. Although causality in itself, dealing with whatever is vague in rational terms, tends to be quite prosaic, *à cause* can take on a poetic quality because of its appeal to some vaguely defined order that seems to function in an almost automatic way. The less this common prepositional phrase is linked with other words from everyday life, the more poetic it appears to be. Conversely, the more common the phrase used to achieve the new effect, the more successful the stylistic innovation. Because we have been accustomed to the banality of *à cause*, the new usage carries the weight of destiny and strikes us like the egg of Columbus.*

---

*It is not at all surprising that we never find the popular expression *à cause que*, since for (pseudo-)objective motivations a *literary* mode of expression is absolutely essential.

An appeal to a fundamental order, which supposedly regulates the course of events, seems ironical if this order does not make any sense: "Le peuple, à cause de l'anniversaire de sa délivrance, laisse ses filles danser en liberté" (p. 45). [The people, because of the anniversary of their deliverance, let their daughters dance freely in the streets.] It is not at all "logical" that on July 14, in honor of liberty, the prostitutes should be let loose. The *à cause* makes us believe that something is self-evident. And this is how *à cause* assumes the function of caricature; it allows the author to protest against this pseudo-order merely by uttering this prepositional phrase.*

---

*While *à cause de* remains *impassible* [impassive], *grâce à*, originally a term of praise, has more recently been used in an indifferent and objective manner, as Kurt Glaser has shown.[8] I agree with Emile Littré on the mediating irony of *grâce à* in a passage from Flaubert, which Glaser quotes as an example of pseudo-objectivity: "Grâce à ces travaux préparatoires (l'habitude du cabaret, la passion des dominos, etc.), il échoua complètement à son examen d'officier de santé."[9] [Thanks to his preparation (his habit of frequenting bars, his passion for playing dominoes, etc.), he flunked his exam as a health officer.] In the following I want to restrict myself to a cross-section of the psyche and style of a single writer, Charles-Louis Philippe; I do not intend to retrace the history of *impassible* motivations all the way to Flaubert, for instance. Marguerite Lips has shown that the so-called *style indirect libre*, which is closely related to our subject, was indeed discovered by Flaubert.[10] Pseudo-objective motivations suit the pseudo-impersonality of Flaubert's style (and his representation of characters as well).[11] Lips demonstrates how Flaubert very nearly betrays his own principle, "il ne faut pas s'écrire" [the writer should not write himself, i.e., he should not let his own personality be diffused into the text], since he practically "elbows" his way in between the hero and the reader by failing to restrict his characterization to the *erlebten imparfait* [the imperfect of lived experience]. Pseudo-objective motivation stylistically mirrors the pseudo-objectivity of the writer. For instance, the *persona pro re* construction *s'écrire*, as I point out in "Persona pro re,"[12] mirrors the writer's subjectivity and exemplifies the stylistic reflection of his narcissistic attitude toward his art.

After I had recognized the conspicuous use of *à cause*, I told myself that other causal terms used by our author would probably have to show the same expansion of meaning. A second reading of the novel confirmed my expectation. I was able to find that *parce que, puisque, car* [because, since, for] appealed to an order that is not at all normal or self-evident and that appears in an ironical perspective precisely because it is invoked as a matter of course.*

---

*Another example of a pseudo-objective motivation can be found in Friedrich Gundolf's *Goethe*: "ebenso töricht . . . sind die . . . verächtlichen Libertins, die sich auf ihn [Goethe] berufen, wenn sie ein Mädchen sitzen lassen wollen, *weil sie so genial sind und das Mädchen so beschränkt ist*."[13] [Equally foolish . . . are those . . . contemptible libertines who invoke him (Goethe) when they want to abandon a girl, *because they are so talented and the girl is so limited*.]

"C'est un quartier de journaux et de bars, et parce qu'il fait sombre les hommes sont plus faciles" (p. 153). [This is a district of newspaper offices and bars, and because it is dark, men are more free and easy.] In a manner at once ironic and self-evident, it is assumed here that darkness has an influence on morality. And even if the reader, upon some reflection, can find some reasons for the accuracy of the observation, he is still taken aback by the boldness of the generalization.

"Jusqu'à l'âge de seize ans, il resta à l'école parce qu'il vaut mieux avoir un peu plus d'instruction et parce qu'on a le temps d'envoyer les enfants en apprentissage où ils contractent de mauvaises habitudes" (p. 41). [Till his sixteenth year he (Maurice, the pimp) remained in school, because it does no harm to gain a little extra knowledge, and because no one is in a big hurry to send children into

apprenticeship, where they fall into bad habits.] Although author
and reader might agree to that educational program, the mere fact
that these studies have had no effect throws an ironical light on it.
The statement "il resta à l'école" conceals who was responsible for
his remaining in school until the age of sixteen. But since the mode of
expression resembles the banality of oral speech, we are led to assume that we are dealing with reflections of Maurice's mother (who
has been mentioned previously). Only a woman from a simple background would utter a commonplace like "il vaut mieux avoir un peu
plus d'instruction." And only somebody like her would express the
mixture of irritation and disillusionment in a phrase like "on a le
temps. . . ." The author deliberately avoids clarifying the situation,
as he could easily have done with phrases like "Maurice had been
sent to school, because his mother thought that. . . ." Rather, he presents her opinion as valid, necessary, and justified, and in doing so he
ironically identifies himself with his characters (in this case, the
mother). The author completely disappears behind the mother's subjective logic, while we, as readers, are confronted with a passively
perceived, fatalistic, ironical causality. The reader is intimidated, as
he would be by anything that was obviously the manifestation of
some powerful force acting (whether rightly or wrongly) simply
through facts.

In another passage referring back to the one above, we can see that
indeed it is the mother who stands behind the decision, and that her
implied logic is rather an a posteriori justification: "Au temps où sa
mère l'envoyait à l'école par crainte des mauvaises habitudes que l'on
contracte en apprentissage, Bubu fit un certain nombre de connaissances" (p. 42). [In the days when his mother sent him to school for
fear of the bad habits that apprentices fall into, Bubu had made a certain number of acquaintances.] Whereas *par crainte de* [for fear of]
indicates a subjective motivation, *à cause de* [because] and *parce que*
[because] make a subjective way of acting sound as if it were factually justified and objectively valid. By means of these phrases, it remains ambiguous whether we are hearing the author's opinion or
simply the opinion of a fictional character, and the reader thus cannot be certain about the author's attitude: "Il l'annonça avec orgueil
parce qu'on le plaisantait sur sa petite taille et parce que ceci montrait à tous que Bubu était fort comme un déménageur" (pp. 43–44).
[He (Maurice) announced this (i.e., that he would become a furniture mover) with pride, because his shortness laid him open to many

a gibe, and because this demonstrated to everyone that Bubu was as strong as a furniture mover.] Only the second *parce que* is interesting for us: is the fact that one proudly announces one's occupational choice supposed to prove one is strong enough for the job? While the author remains completely *impassible*, it is only our logical reflection, stated above, that makes apparent the irony within the statement. Although the formulation "parce que ceci montrait" [because this would demonstrate] would clearly mark the phrase as a reflection of Maurice's thought, *montrait* [would demonstrate] lends a certain objectivity and necessity to the argument.

Take the following case:

[Il aimait] sa volupté particulière, quand elle appliquait son corps contre le sien et qu'elle se pliait pour qu'il la pénétrât. Il aimait cela qui la distinguait de toutes les femmes qu'il avait connues parce que c'était plus doux, parce que c'était plus fin et parce que c'était sa femme, à lui, qu'il avait eue vierge. Il l'aimait parce qu'elle était bien élevée, parce qu'elle était honnête et qu'elle en avait l'air, et pour toutes les raisons qu'ont les bourgeois d'aimer leur femme. (pp. 57–58)

[He loved her special voluptuousness when she pressed her body to his, bending it so he could penetrate her. He loved what distinguished her from all the women he had known, because it was sweeter, because it was more delicate, and because this was his woman, his own, whom he had had as a virgin. He loved her because she was well-bred, because she was honest and looked it, and for all the reasons that the bourgeois love their wives.]

In these *parce que* phrases we are clearly dealing with reasons that apply to the fictional character: the author, though he evaluates Maurice, in this instance keeps his own opinion separate from that of his character; the formulation *était* [this was] guarantees this separateness. Even the means of expression are chosen with reference to the fictional character. Only Maurice could have chosen this primitive enumeration of reasons for his love of a woman (1, *doux*; 2, *fin*; 3, *sa femme à lui*). And only he would have described her position in lovemaking as *plus fin* [more delicate].

By contrast, the present tense in the following cases is used to refer to commonly accepted truths; it refers—like *parce que*—to unalterable facts: "Elle vit dans leur vie quotidienne les souteneurs et les filous et comprit qu'ils n'aimaient pas le travail parce qu'il vaut bien mieux aimer le plaisir" (p. 52). [She saw the pimps and swindlers in their daily life and understood that they did not care for work because it is far wiser to care for pleasure.] The "pimps and swindlers" said, "il vaut bien mieux . . ." [it is far wiser]; the *parce que* lends a pseudo-generality to the individual motivation. If the author had wanted to make a clear distinction between the motives of a character and a general maxim, he could have written: "parce qu'ils étaient persuadés de la supériorité du plaisir" [because they were convinced that pleasure was far superior to work]. This unphilosophically formulated banality ("il vaut bien mieux") strikes us all the more because it is elevated to the status of a maxim.

The following passage is similar in its effect: "Elle aimait opérer seule parce qu'un travail sérieux a besoin d'une solitude où l'on concentre ses moyens comme un homme qui veut arriver" (p. 153). [She liked to operate on her own because serious work requires solitude in which to concentrate one's powers, like a man determined to succeed in life.] The reader has to ask himself: who thinks so, the writer or "she"? He agrees to the general maxim that serious work requires quiet and concentration. But the application of the general rule to a special case, the "operations" of a prostitute, puts the maxim in an ironical perspective: what, after all, is serious work?

"Elle faisait dans les sentiments chez les jeunes gens et chez les hommes parce qu'il y a beaucoup d'amour sur la Terre, parce que l'Amour coule et nous emmène comme des enfants vers les femmes où l'on voit de l'enfantillage et de la bonté" (p. 155). [She appealed to the feelings of young men, and also to those of the older ones, because there is such a wealth of love here on Earth, and because Love flows and carries us like children toward women who seem childish and kind.] The idea that "the prostitute was very much in demand, because men's need for love makes them dependent on women" would be an objectively causal, almost scientific formulation. The use of personification in the maxim produces the effect of a poetic transfiguration. The literary language in which the maxim is worded indicates that it could reflect only the author's opinion, not that of a fictional character. But one might also think of the statement as a practical justification invented by the prostitute's clientele: "l'Amour . . . nous emmène" [Love carries us . . .]. Yet precisely this uncertainty must have been intended by the author. He could not have chosen a better way to express men's fatal addiction than by leaving open the question whether he as author places himself within this general destiny.

"D'ordinaire, Berthe rentrait parce que les rues n'offrent plus que les quarantes sous du hasard et que les sentiments sont lassés—à deux heures du matin" (pp. 158–59). [Usually Berthe went home, because the streets have nothing to offer except maybe the chance for forty sous and for feelings to go numb—at two o'clock in the morning.] The phrase "à deux heures du matin" must be part of both the main and the subordinate clause, since only then does the use of the present tense, with its implication of a generally accepted truth, make sense.

"L'homme resté seul avec Berthe s'emparait de la minute et commençait l'attaque, parce que Berthe était jolie et parce qu'on n'a jamais trop de moyens" (pp. 159–60). [The man, alone with Berthe, took advantage of the moment and made his move, because Berthe was pretty and because one can never have too many opportunities.] Here we find a juxtaposition of the subjective reason for the man's action (Berthe was pretty) and the pseudo-maxim "on n'a jamais . . ." (one never has enough opportunities for lovemaking).

While we saw earlier that a maxim was invoked by the phrase *il vaut mieux* [it is better, wiser], in the following example we can find an appeal to common morality: "Berthe, en blaguant, se laissa faire, et c'était mal, parce qu'une femme qui se respecte doit choisir un homme qui soit bon à quelque chose" (pp. 165–66). [And jokingly, Berthe let him have his way, and this was bad, because a woman who has any self-respect must choose a man who is good for something.] The question as to who might actually have uttered the phrase "c'était mal, parce qu'une femme qui se respecte" has been deliberately left open. Certainly it is the *communis opinio* that judges here and that separates good and evil. The way this banal judgment is expressed makes it sound comically important.

"Berthe s'essayait à recomposer sa vie . . . avec sa sœur Blanche, avec une petite amie qui s'appelait Adèle, puis avec quelqu'un, avec n'importe qui, parce qu'une femme ne doit pas être seule" (p. 139). [Berthe sought to put her life back together . . . with her sister Blanche, with a little friend called Adele, and then with someone, anyone, because a woman ought not to be alone.] This maxim might reflect the view of Berthe from one of her peers or from the general public.

"Il l'avait juré, comme elle aimait que l'on jurât,—sur la tête de sa mère,—parce qu'alors c'est la vérité" (p. 140). [He had sworn it, as she liked an oath to be sworn—on the head of his mother—because then it is the truth.] "She" probably represents the point of view from which the oath invoking the mother seems binding, though the author may share this view. But the reader immediately notes that in those social circles in which the novel is set, even this kind of oath will not be holy. And this is what again lends an ironical tone to the *parce que* phrase.

The same kind of semiobjective, semisubjective causality that we have observed with regard to *parce que* can also be found in the term *car* [for]: "Les femmes l'entouraient d'amour comme des oiseaux qui chantent le soleil et la force. Il était un de ceux que nul ne peut as-sujettir, *car* leur vie, plus noble et plus belle, comporte l'amour du danger" (p. 53). [The women surrounded him (the burglar and pimp) with love, like birds singing the praises of the sun and power. He was one of those who cannot be subjugated by anything, *for* their life, more noble and beautiful, includes the love of danger.]

And even more so, *puisque* [since]—usually referring to a known fact—can be used ironically: "Il y eut deux ou trois femmes, puis-qu'un homme a besoin de cela" (p. 130). [He had two or three women, since that's what a man needs.] Not everybody would agree as to the content of the *puisque* phrase. "Elle vivait, joyeuse et in-consciente, et puisque l'argent est une fin en ce monde, elle n'avait ni l'idée du bien ni celle de l'honnêteté" (pp. 147–48). [She lived gay and carefree, and since money is an end in itself in this world, she had no idea of virtue or honesty.] *Puisque* here refers to an a priori pes-simistic attitude of disillusionment.

One does not always need causal phrases to invoke a fundamental order that would supposedly determine the course of events: "Elle l'embrassa à pleine bouche. C'est une chose hygiénique et bonne entre un homme et sa femme, qui vous amuse un petit quart d'heure avant de vous endormir" (p. 39). [She kissed him full on the mouth. This is a wholesome and good thing for a man and his woman; it amuses you for ten minutes or so before you fall asleep.] The remark "c'est une chose" sounds like an authorial gloss, but on a more for-mal level it seems as though the two persons kissing are trying to jus-tify what they are doing. Thus we can say that this apologetic nar-rative mode expresses an attitude of ironical resignation. We cannot tell whether Philippe is more ironical or more resigned when he in-vokes the wholesomeness and the "amusement" of the kiss. The *vous* [you] creates a sense of community between mankind, the author, and the fictional characters, in which the fate of the individual is dis-solved. The second sentence is also an imitation of spoken language, in which everything from *c'est* to *endormir* could be uttered unchanged.

Occasionally Philippe uses a sympathetic and generalizing *vous* and *nous* [we], which places the action of an individual character within a larger order and strengthens the individual in the solidarity suggested by *us* or *you*. "Il comprenait bien mieux, à present. Un peu de douleur nous éclaire et nous montre les maux que nous ne savions voir, comme des frères éternels et meilleurs. Il sentait encore que le bonheur est précaire, que notre cœur est une ruine noire [et] branlante" (p. 131). [He understood much better now. A little pain throws light upon the evils that we could not see before, like better and eternal brothers. He felt, too, how precarious happiness is and that the heart is a black, tottering ruin.] The "un peu de douleur" could be the character in the novel speaking of his recent experience, but it could also be the voice of the author abstracting from the individual character.

Car, already latently implied in the passage above, can serve a similar function: "Elle savait de quoi se compose l'amour depuis qu'elle laissait les mâles après elle courir. . . . Elle savait qu'il faut convertir l'amour en espèces, car l'amour est fatigant, et c'est l'argent qui réconforte. Tout cela, Berthe le savait à vingt ans" (pp. 72–73). [She knew what love meant since she had let the men chase after her. . . . She knew that love must be converted into cash, for love is tiring, and money alone comforts and revives. All this Berthe knew at twenty.] Although the maxim is explicitly characterized as derived from Berthe's experience, the use of *savoir* [to know] and the present tense nevertheless suggest acknowledgment of a common truth.

Since all actions of fictional characters have to be made plausible for the reader, how better to accomplish this than against the background of general norms? This is how these actions can be justified, at least on an apparent level. It is quite interesting to note how the description of an isolated situation is turned into something habitual:

Il habitait, dans un hôtel meublé de la rue de l'Arbre-Sec, une chambre au cinquième étage. Ces chambres d'hôtels sont toujours malpropres parce que trop de locataires y ont vécu. Le lit, l'armoire à glace, les deux chaises et la table à roulettes les emplissent. Elles sont si petites que ces quatre meubles semblent encombrants. Ici l'on vit, à raison de vingt-cinq francs par mois, une vie sans dignité. Les matelas du lit sont sales, les rideaux de la fenêtre sont gris. . . . Le garçon de l'hôtel a un passe-partout qui lui permettrait à tout instant d'entrer dans votre chambre. Vos voisins changent tous les quinze jours et vous les entendez à travers la cloison. . . . Les pauvres locataires des hôtels meublés n'ont pas de chez soi. Pierre Hardy ne pouvait pas se dire: "J'ai un refuge où, quand je suis triste, je m'assois parmi des choses qui me plaisent." (pp. 20–21)

[He lived in a small hotel in the rue de l'Arbre Sec, in a room on the fifth floor. These hotel rooms are always dirty because too many people have lived in them. The bed, the wardrobe with its mirror, the two chairs and the table on rollers fill up these rooms. They are so small that the four pieces of furniture seem cumbersome. There, for twenty-five francs a month, you can live a life without dignity. The mattresses are dirty, the window curtains grey. . . . The hotel boy has a pass key that could let him into your room at any time. Your neighbors change once every fortnight and you can hear them through the partition. . . . The poor lodgers in these small hotels have no home, no privacy. Pierre Hardy could not say to himself: "At least I have a refuge where I can go when I feel sad and sit among the things I like."]

The description of Pierre Hardy's hotel blends into the description of a *typical* hotel room. This explains the use of the present tense framed by the narrative past tense. Everything seems self-evident, since "that's the way things are"—for the price of twenty-five francs a month, you cannot ask for more—or since that is just how "we humans" are.

Pierre Hardy lui faisait le récit de toutes ses émotions et de toutes ses aventures et Louis Buisson faisait les mêmes confidences. Une telle amitié nous encourage à vivre, en prolongeant nos plaisirs et en nous consolant de nos chagrins. On se dit: Je raconterai cela à Pierre qui va bien rire—Je raconterai cela à Louis, qui me dira. . . . Mais il y a des soirs où l'amitié ne suffit pas. Les paroles et les spectacles ordinaires de l'amitié nous reposent. Nous avons besoin de nous fatiguer aussi. Pierre Hardy sentait. . . . (pp. 24–25)

[Pierre Hardy confided in him all his emotions and all his adventures, and Louis Buisson did the same. Such a friendship gives us courage for life, prolonging our pleasures and consoling us in our griefs. One says to oneself: I'll tell that to Pierre. He'll have a good laugh—I'll tell that to Louis, and he'll say. . . . But there are evenings when friendship does not suffice. The words and humdrum things of friendship relax us. But we also need to tire ourselves out. Pierre Hardy felt. . . .]

The apologetic narrative invoking what "one does" blends into an account of something particular. After *on se dit* one expects something typical like "Je raconterai cela à mon ami" [I'll tell that to my friend]. The name Pierre seems to be used here like a specific value replacing a variable in an algebraic equation. This leads to an impenetrable fusion of the typical and the particular. Similarly: "Le temps passa. Deux ans passèrent et les cinq mille francs de Maurice passaient aussi. Notre destinée ne se fait pas en un jour, quand nos cinq mille francs sont épuisés, après deux ans de vie commune; elle se décide à . . . chacune de nos fréquentations" (p. 58). [Time went by. Two years passed, and with them went Maurice's five thousand francs. Our fate is not shaped in one day, when our five thousand francs are spent, after two years of communal life; our fate is decided by . . . every person we have met.] Here we can see the transition from the particular case to the maxim, but in the maxim we can find again elements of particular instances that lead to the generalization: "nos cinq mille francs," "deux ans." The "nos cinq mille francs" seems like an example that is supposed to illustrate the general rule: "our money, let's say five thousand francs . . . ."

Frequently the author places his protagonist in a certain category (social class, origin, etc.) that seems to determine his actions:

Pierre Hardy . . . se promenait au milieu des passants du Boulevard Sébastopol. Un jeune homme de vingt ans, qui n'est à Paris que depuis six mois, marche avec incertitude parmi les spectacles parisiens. . . . Tous les provinciaux ont senti ce malaise et sont devenus gauches et tristes en face de cela. Je vous assure que les beaux gars des villages qui paradaient dans les bals font triste figure sur les Grands Boulevards. Un homme qui marche porte toutes les choses de sa vie et les remue dans sa tête. Un spectacle les éveille, un autre les excite. Notre chair a gardé tous nos souvenirs, nous les mêlons à nos désirs. Nous parcourons le temps présent avec notre bagage, nous allons et nous sommes complets à tous les instants. (pp. 15–16)

[Pierre Hardy . . . was strolling among the passers-by on the Boulevard Sebastopol. A young man of twenty, only six months in Paris, walks with little assurance amid the passing Parisian scenes. . . . All the provincials have felt this uneasiness, and, confronted with it, all have turned awkward and sad. I assure you those handsome lads who strutted so jauntily on their village greens cut a sorry figure on the great boulevards. A man walking along carries with him all the parts of his life, and they churn about in his head. Something he sees awakens them, something else excites them. Our flesh has retained all our memories, and we mingle them with our desires. We pass through the present with all our baggage, and as we go on we are complete at every instant.]

"Elle partit dans toutes ses histoires de pauvre petite putain trotteuse. Leur imagination fait bien des pas, et c'est bon de marcher comme cela et de réussir dans toutes ses entreprises" (p. 179). [She launched into all her stories about the poor little whore walking the streets. Their imagination takes great strides, and it is good to go on

walking like this and to be successful in every enterprise.] *Leur imagination* must refer to the cliché of the little whore, which immediately calls to mind all the prostitutes predestined by their professional image of themselves "to be the way they are." This is the only
way we can account for the third-person plural of the possessive pronoun *leur*.[14] And in accordance with their professional ethics, we
also find the conclusion "c'est bon de marcher."

All these actions of the fictional characters are cloaked in a language invoking Christian charity; this leads to the complete identification of an individual's fate and the common destiny. The narrative alternates between particular characters and an all-embracing
one or *you*.

Elle vint sans qu'il l'attendît. Il y avait quelque chose entre eux et chacun,
tout autour de soi-même, sentit qu'il y avait cela. Mais on doit se vaincre et
repousser les points d'honneur quand on est pauvre. Il y eut encore ce qui
sépare les hommes et les femmes: elle pensait qu'elle n'avait pas un sous, il
pensait que cette visite lui coûterait cinq francs. Il faut vivre d'abord, ensuite
on peut avoir des sentiments. Ce ne fut que le lendemain matin, lorsqu'elle
eut quitté Pierre, que Berthe alla chercher des nouvelles chez la mère de
Maurice. (pp. 143–44)

[She came unexpectedly. Something stood between them, and each felt that,
all around them, this thing was there. But you must master yourself and set
aside your principles when you are poor. And there was also that other thing
that stands between men and women: she was thinking that she did not
have one sou, and he was thinking that this visit would cost him five francs.
First you must live, and afterward you may indulge your feelings. It was only
the next morning, after she had left Pierre, that Berthe went for news to
Maurice's mother.]

Whenever possible, psychological motivations are made plausible by
invoking this *you* [*on*]. At the same time one can find in the construc-
tions with *on* fragments of speech that the fictional character might
have said by way of an excuse.

The identification of a fictional character with the general *you* is
particularly conspicuous in those passages where details actually
pertaining to the individual character are attributed to *you*:

Alors, dans ce quartier de Plaisance, il pensa à son ami le Grand Jules et se
sentit renaître à l'espérance. On ne sait pas comment renaît l'espérance. On
marche dans la rue de Vanves, une après-midi d'août, on se souvient que le
Grand Jules a eu la vérole, on se rappelle que Charlot, Paul et d'autres l'ont
encore, et l'on pense qu'à ceux-la jamais la vérole n'a fait de mal. Ensuite on
se dit: Mais rien ne prouve que j'aie moi-même la vérole. Et l'on essaie de se
démontrer qu'on ne peut pas l'avoir, puisque Berthe a parlé dès le premier
symptôme et qu'alors on s'est abstenu. (pp. 89–90)

[Then, in this red-light district, he thought of his friend, Grand Jules, and he felt hope reborn in him. One does not know how hope is suddenly reborn. You are walking along the rue de Vanves on an August afternoon, and you remember that Grand Jules has had the pox, and you remember that Charlot and Paul and others have it still, and you think that the pox has never done them any harm. And then you say to yourself: But there is no proof that I myself have the pox. And then you try to persuade yourself that you couldn't have it, because Berthe spoke up right at the first symptom and since then you haven't touched her.]

The invocation of this *on* raises Maurice's transformation to the level of "general humanity": "that's the way people [*on*] act, that's how things turn out to be." But how is it possible that this *on* has been strolling along the rue de Vanves, of all streets? Here, behind the weary repetition of *on*, we get a glimpse of Maurice's particular situation, though only from an external, not from an internal, psychological point of view.

A similar passage:

Il ne lui [Maurice] venait pas au cœur des poèmes parce qu'il n'en savait pas, mais ils lui revenaient, une à une, toutes les chansons d'amour qu'il avait entendues. Les plus belles et les plus pures étaient les meilleures. Il eut, plus que jamais, le sentiment de la Beauté. Par-dessus tout, la chanson de Lakmé vient en nous et se pose sur la blessure où nous avions mal. Elle lui sortait des lèvres comme un cri, comme une haleine et comme une bonne odeur. (p. 132)

[Poems did not come to him (Maurice) by heart, for he did not know any, but one by one all the love songs he had heard came back to him. The loveliest and purest were the best. More than ever before he was moved by Beauty. Above all, it is the song of Lakmé that comes to our mind and rests on the wound where we were hurt. It sprang from his lips like a cry, like an exhalation, like a good perfume.]

I doubt the assumption that the sentiment of "Beauty" automatically recalls the song from Delibes's opera. Nevertheless, the use of *nous* makes the musical reminiscence seem self-evident.

In the following case, we encounter a particular, unusual event that is narrated by means of *vous*, with the result that it seems perfectly understandable and normal. At the same time, this linguistic usage suggests the inevitability of fate (as though one were interjecting a phrase like "that's how things go"):

Un coup d'œil en arrière, et les deux hommes suivaient sa route. Il entendait leurs souliers comme des bottes, les sentait lourds comme des poings et avec une épaiseur de police qui sait tout. Il essayait de marcher plus vite et plus légèrement. Puis le sang vous rentre au corps, la chose était prévue, deux

poings formidables vous saisissent, deux épaules vous poussent et c'est une
brutalité sans nom, deux voix auxquelles on ne réplique point:—Allez,
ouste! (pp. 136–37)

[He glanced back, and the two men were following him. He heard their
shoes like heavy boots, felt them heavy as fists, with the solidity of the po-
liceman who knows all. He tried to walk faster and more lightly. Then the
blood rushes to your head, the thing was foreseen, two formidable fists seize
you, two shoulders push you, and in this nameless brutality two voices to
which there can be no reply say:—Come on, get going!]

The apologetic *on, nous, vous*—like *à cause* and so on—have been
taken from spoken language.[15] The following passage is quite remarkable in this respect. At first the appeal to a general norm is introduced by *il pensait* (whereby thoughts are—in the novel, as in real
life—rendered in the form of speech), but then, without any mediating transition, the maxim is joined to the narrative in the phrase *il
faut prendre*:

Ce soir-là, Louis Buisson faisait son café. Il pensait: Ce sont ces besognes
simples, faire sa chambre ou préparer son café, qui calment notre esprit et
qui ordonnent nos idées comme des meubles bien en place. . . . D'ailleurs, il
avait ses principes pour la preparation du café. Il n'utilisait pas le marc et
versait l'eau bouillante goutte à goutte sur le café fraîchement moulu. L'operation est un peu plus longue, mais pour avoir de bonnes choses il faut
prendre beaucoup de peine. (p. 108)

[On this night, Louis Buisson was making his coffee. He was thinking: It's
the simple tasks, like fixing one's room or preparing one's coffee, that calm
our mind and arrange our ideas like pieces of furniture in their proper
place. . . . He had, moreover, his own ideas about making coffee. He never
used the old grounds but poured boiling water, drop by drop, over freshly
ground coffee. This operation takes some time, but if you want things to be
good, you must take pains.]

In some cases we encounter a passage that seems to represent actual spoken speech, as in "Au restaurant elle avait des excuses: Je te
demande pardon, je me sers du sel avant toi. Il y a beaucoup de timidité dans nos cœurs et, si l'on est une fille publique avec un cœur en
danse, on est quand même une femme parmi les hommes avec des
douceurs et des hésitations" (pp. 181–82). [In the restaurant she
made apologies: I beg your pardon, I'm helping myself to salt before
you. There is much timidity in our hearts, and even if you are a public
girl with a wanton heart, you are still a woman among men, with all
the delicacy and hesitations.] The line "il y a beaucoup de timidité
dans nos cœurs" certainly sounds like authorial reporting. Yet in the

midst of such reporting we sometimes hear the rhetoric of the characters piercing through, as in the pathetic line "nous qui sommes des femmes" in the following passage:

Tout de suite leurs {Pierre et Berthe} paroles eurent une grande franchise. C'est qu'elle avait besoin de cela parce que dans nos âmes il y a le bon coin qui, du temps où nous ne faisions pas le mal, était plein de sentiments simples et qui reste toujours à sa place et où des voix parfois descendent et viennent crier comme des enfants abandonnés. Elle avait besoin de cela comme nous avons besoin d'une mère, puis d'un époux, nous qui sommes des femmes sans appui, avec des cœurs incertains et qui cherchons la certitude sur les routes. (pp. 170–71)

[All of a sudden they spoke with utter frankness. It was she who needed it, because in our souls there is the pleasant corner, which in the days when we would do no harm was full of simple sentiments, and it remains in its place forever, and at times voices descend into it, and come crying like forsaken children. She needed this as we need a mother, then a husband, we who are women with no support, with uncertain hearts, who seek certainty on the roads.]

In the beginning one thinks that *nous* refers to "we human beings" in general, until, all of a sudden, these women rise out of the dark, full of grief and mourning mysteriously. One could almost talk of an improvised chorus, which, as in ancient tragedy, casts judgment upon the dramatic situation.

———————————— • ————————————

Our discussion of apologetic, fatalistic speech, whether expressed in terms of *à cause de*, *parce que*, *puisque*, *car*, or in a causal clause using *on*, *nous*, *vous*, is closely related to the problems taken up by Jean Etienne Lorck in his excellent stylistic study *Die "Erlebte Rede."*[16] In our case, however, we are mainly concerned with the type of discourse exemplified in the following lines [from Balzac, included in Lorck's analysis]: "Lousteau s'était déjà posé devant ses intimes comme un homme important: *sa vie allait enfin avoir un sens,* le hasard l'avait choyé, *il devenait* sous peu de jours propriétaire." [Lousteau had already presented himself to his intimate friends as a man of importance: *finally his life was going to have a direction,* chance had cherished him, within a couple of days *he would be* a man of property.] The tense of the verb reveals to us the author's dreamlike participation in the experience, as though he were "hearing hallucinations."[17]

Philippe's *parce que* phrases are not, however, transposed into the past tense, since they are to be taken for a pseudo-objective authorial explication, even though they stem from the subjective opinion of fictional characters. They are, as it were, common truths formulated in the atemporal present tense. But these maxims are "experienced" no less deeply than are individual thoughts and expressions rendered in the tense of *style indirect libre*, such as those given in the above example from Balzac. The only difference is in the altered tense, which formally marks the speech more distinctly as lived experience. In all these cases, we are dealing with maxims from the *perspective* of fictional characters, the *mise-en-scène* of their reasons. And whenever we are not dealing with maxims we can quite consistently find the use of the past tense of *style indirect libre*: "Il l'annonça avec orgueil . . . parce que ceci montrait à tous que . . ." (pp. 43–44). [He announced it proudly . . . because this demonstrated to all that. . . .]

An atemporal truth can be phrased not only in the present tense but also in the future, prophesying the regular course of events: "Et c'est auprès de sa sœur, à sa sortie de l'hôpital, que Berthe vécut. Auprès de sa sœur, parce que les idées de famille sont plus fortes que toutes les autres idées et parce qu'une sœur sera notre sœur, quoi qu'il arrive" (p. 149). [It was with her sister that Berthe lived when she came out of the hospital. With her sister because family values are stronger than any other, and because a sister will be our sister whatever happens.]

The reasons that a character attributes to his actions are always most intimately linked to his personality and are therefore least accessible to objective scrutiny. And this is why the *impassible* author renders them quite passively, without pronouncing judgment of his own. For example, Lorck presents a passage from Paul Margueritte in which thoughts drawn from lived experience and rendered in *style indirect libre* are interrupted by a maxim expressed in the present tense of atemporal truth: "Un doute singulier me saisit: avais-je aimé réellement Judith? . . . Aimer: qu'était-ce au juste? . . . La démonstration de l'existence de Dieu . . . *est* impossible à faire. L'amour, pas d'avantage, ne se *prouvait*."[18] [I was seized by a single doubt: Had I really loved Judith? . . . To love: what did it really mean? . . . It *is* impossible to prove the existence of God. Love *would prove* itself even less.] The author does not want to give any further indication as to whether or not he approves of the motivation. Often he even distances himself from his fictional character by means of a latent contextual irony. But sometimes it also seems as though his moralizing has an apologetic intention. And it is exactly this undecidedness that spreads an uncanny atmosphere of resignation over these passages.

An example drawn by Lorck [from Zola] contains a use of *nous/ on* that resembles the passages by Philippe we discussed above: "Morte! ce mot retentit dans la chambre. . . . Morte, mon Dieu, est-ce que c'était leur faute? . . . La sainte Vierge . . . ne savait-elle pas mieux que *nous-mêmes* ce qu'elle devait faire pour le bonheur des vivants et des morts?"[19] [Dead! This word echoed in the room. . . . Dead, my God, was it their fault? . . . The Holy Virgin . . . didn't she know any better than *we ourselves* how to look after the welfare of the living and the dead?] Lorck quite correctly explicates *nous-mêmes* as "we human beings, a term in which the writer, of course, includes himself."[20] Like *à cause*, *parce que*, and *on*, the exclamation *mon Dieu!* in the Zola passage is taken from direct speech. One could easily use quotation marks to distinguish fragments of direct speech, for instance: "Le peuple, 'à cause de l'anniversaire de sa délivrance,' laisse ses filles danser en liberté"—"Jusqu'à l'âge de seize ans, il resta à l'école 'parce qu'il vaut mieux avoir un peu plus d'instruction'"—"Elle l'embrassa à pleine bouche. 'C'est une chose hygiénique . . . qui vous amuse.'" The omission of quotation marks produces an unmediated transition from direct to indirect speech, as if the speech were rendered in a mimetic, almost mimicking fashion. The dividing line between direct and indirect speech has been temporarily removed.*

---

*See also such cases of ironical characterization as the following: "Sa mère n'était pas toujours approbatrice, mais Bubu, dont les convictions étaient fortes, trouva des paroles solides . . . et même lui montra deux ou trois fois qu'il était un homme d'action et n'aimait pas les contradicteurs" (p. 44). [His mother did not always approve, but Bubu, who had strong convictions, found powerful arguments . . . and he even showed her two or three times that he was a man of action who did not like to be contradicted.]—"Maurice, qui était un homme d'action, croyait à la nécessité des châtiments corporels. Il la gifla, persuadé qu'une gifle fortifierait en elle le sentiment de la verité" (pp. 55–56). [Maurice, a man of action, believed in the necessity of corporal punishment. He slapped her, convinced that a slap would strengthen her sense of truth.] The phrase "montra . . . qu'il était" [in the first example] presents the man of action as if he had already proved so by his words. In the second example *un homme d'action* would have to be interpreted as though in quotation marks, as though the author would not take the words of his fictional character at face value.

"Assis sur la chaise, il expliquait la vérole avec des mots égaux, puis, quand il eut parlé, il pensa à autre chose. Ni la prison ni la vérole jamais ne l'avaient gêné parce que sa volonté était plus forte que tous les maux. Il cheminait d'un pas adroit au milieu des dangers et luttait sans colère et sans fièvre quand il avait résolu de lutter. J'ai dit qu'il était plus fort que la vérole" (pp. 92–93). [Seated on his chair, he explained the pox in simple words, and when he had spoken his thoughts went off on something else. Neither prison nor the pox had ever troubled him, for his will was stronger than any affliction. He made his way adroitly through the midst of danger, and he fought without anger and without agitation once he had made up his mind for combat. I've said that he was stronger than the pox.] *J'ai dit que* means "I've said it and that's the way it is." The author seems to take for granted whatever Grand Jules boastingly has to say about himself.

This [combination of direct and indirect speech] can also be observed in the following passages:

Alors Louis Buisson se leva, s'approcha de Pierre et, lui prenant les deux mains, il les pressait. D'ordinaire il était discret dans sa tendresse. Mais j'ai fait mal, Seigneur, avec *mes* discours. Il se révoltait contre lui même, contre ses paroles, contre la vérité, contre l'hôpital Broca. Cela ne peut pas être, puisque cela fait mal et que *mon* cœur est bon. Il se leva, vint à Pierre et dit. . . . (p. 120)

[Then Louis Buisson got up, went over to Pierre and, taking both his hands, pressed them in his own. Usually he was discreet in his tenderness. But I've done wrong, Lord, with *my* talk. He revolted against himself, against his own words, against truth, against the hospital Broca. This cannot be, because it causes pain and *my* heart is good. He rose, went to Pierre and said. . . .]

One could punctuate this passage as follows: "D'ordinaire il était discret. . . . Mais: 'j'ai fait mal, Seigneur, avec mes discours.' Il se révoltait contre lui même. . . . 'Cela ne peut pas être, puisque cela fait mal et que mon cœur est bon.'" This is not *style indirect libre* but the mimetic representation of direct speech. A sententious type of speech that would specifically include the author as well as the audience would substitute *on a fait* [we've done] for *j'ai fait* and *notre cœur* [our heart] for *mon cœur*. We have already noted a similar example in the "poussée de style direct" [thrust of direct speech], as Charles Bally would say, of the passage with *nous les femmes*.

Exactly the same kind of interjected direct speech can also be observed in *style indirect libre*. For instance:

Ils la questionnèrent. . . . —Mais voyons, ma petite, pourquoi faites-vous encore ce métier?
Voilà. Quand Maurice aurait un peu d'argent, elle s'établirait entrepreneuse fleuriste. . . . Elle allait chanter dans un café-concert où elle serait décolletée comme ceci, avec un corsage de soie bleue. . . . Elle aurait bien aimé être serveuse dans un bureau de tabac: "Les demi-londrès, voilà, monsieur!" et l'on sourit en disant ces mots. (pp. 178–79)

[They asked her questions. . . . —But tell us, my child, why do you keep on doing this sort of work?
Here's what she'd do. When Maurice had a little money, she would go into business as a florist. . . . She would sing in a café where she would wear a low-necked dress, like this, with a blue silk blouse. . . . She would have liked to be a salesgirl in a tobacco shop: "Havanas? Here you are, Monsieur!" and you smile while you say these words.]

Fragments of direct speech, the demonstrative ("comme ceci"), and the unmediated mimesis of typical talk ("Les demi-londrès, voilà, monsieur!") ebb into *style indirect libre* ("Voilà. . . . Elle aurait bien aimé").

As Lerch and Lorck have already observed, direct speech seems more vivid than *style indirect libre*, which seems in turn livelier than indirect speech. This means that the phrase *comme ceci* [in the example above] could be described as stepping forth from a dimmer background into a more brightly lit foreground. In modern narrative various ways of reproducing speech are eclectically interspersed. This enables the modern writer to vary the degree of interest or sympathy he expresses toward the reported speeches. He can suddenly change the perspective, he can adjust (often merely for a single phrase) a new lens of the telescope, allowing the object of observation—the speech—to be seen from a closer or greater distance.

We have encountered examples where the boundary separating the invocation of a norm by a fictional character and by the authorial voice completely disappears. Sometimes the maxim borrows details from the particular context ("On marche dans la rue de Vanves," "nos cinq mille francs," "la chanson de Lakmé"), and sometimes the maxim, though supposedly spoken by a fictional character, appears in a form that can only be attributed to the writer. The latter has been called by Lorck *mittelbare B-Rede*[21] [mediated B-speech] in reference to a passage from Thomas Mann's *Buddenbrooks*:

"Hanno Buddenbrook sass vornüber gebeugt und rang unter dem Tische die Hände. Das B, der Buchstabe B war an der Reihe! Gleich würde sein Name ertönen, und er würde aufstehen und nicht eine Zeile wissen, und es würde sein Name ertönen, . . . und es würde einen Skandal geben, eine laute, schreckliche Katastrophe, so guter Laune der Ordinarius auch sein mochte."[22] [Hanno Buddenbrook was sitting in a stooped position and was wringing his hands under the table. The B, it was the letter B coming up! In an instant his name would resound, . . . and there would be a scandal, a loud, awful catastrophe, no matter how good a mood the professor might be in.] None of these—neither the clause "so guter" [no matter how good], nor the explanatory phrase "der Buchstabe B" [the letter B], nor the carefully chosen expression "sein Name würde ertönen" [his name would resound]—could have been uttered by the young pupil Hanno: "Hanno is thinking, but thinking with the brain of somebody else, of the writer; or, what amounts to the same, the writer is thinking Hanno's thoughts."[23]*

---

*Lorck does not present a French example for this *mittlebare erlebte Rede* [mediated speech of lived experience, free indirect speech filtered through the authorial perspective]. However, I happened to find one in a passage he quotes from Mérimée, though it is interpreted differently by Lorck himself: "En vain il parla de la sauvagerie du pays et de la difficulté pour une femme d'y voyager; elle ne craignait rien; elle aimait par-dessus tout à voyager à cheval; elle se faisait une fête de coucher au bivac; elle menaçait d'aller en Asie-Mineure. Bref, elle avait réponse à tout."[24] [He (the colonel) talked in vain about the brutality of the country and how difficult it would be for a woman to travel there: she (Miss Lydia) did not fear anything; above all she loved to travel on horseback; it was a treat for her to sleep in a bivouac; she threatened to go to Asia Minor. In brief, she had an answer for everything.] I agree with Bally about this passage, that here "the author shows the tip of his nose."[25] But the author's narrative and his experience are closely welded. (That is why we find the past tense used everywhere.) Mérimée *interprets* Miss Lydia's utterance as Thomas Mann interprets Hanno's thoughts. By no means can I agree with Lorck, who thinks that an observer of that scene would report the direct speech "if you don't fulfill my wish, I'll go to Asia Minor" to a neighbor in the following words: "She said she would threaten to go to Asia Minor."[26]

Among the examples I have quoted we can find quite similar passages. For instance, we can hardly assume that the prostitute would have expressed herself in terms of the following *parce que* clause:

"Elle faisait dans les sentiments chez les jeunes gens et chez les hommes parce qu'il y a beaucoup d'amour sur la Terre, parce que l'Amour coule et nous emmène comme des enfants vers les femmes où l'on voit de l'enfantillage et de la bonté" (p. 155). [She appealed to the feelings of young men, and also to those of the older ones, because there is such a wealth of love here on Earth, and because Love flows and carries us like children toward women who seem childish and kind.] With his highly cultivated style the writer supports the uneducated prostitute. If the writer wants to render the *thoughts* of his characters, he usually transposes them into speech. And these speeches are tinted by the author's personality. I am going to mark the author's style in italic print: "Et Pierre pensait: Je n'avais pas de femme. J'ai marché la tête basse en répétant: Je n'ai pas de femme. *Il y a dans le malheur une continuité qui nous fait croire au mal de vivre.* C'est fini. Je sens maintenant que tout ce que me manquait va venir et que le monde est bien en place" (p. 215). [And Pierre thought: I had no woman. I walked with bowed head saying to myself: "I have no woman." *There is a continuity in misfortune that makes us believe that life is evil.* It's over now. I feel now that all I lacked is going to come to me, and that everything is as it should be.] This could be called stylized realism. The prostitute's emotional life is expressed in a medium provided by the writer himself. Frequently the literary and the personal modes of the fictional characters are so tightly interwoven in one sentence that they can hardly be kept apart.*

---

* Modern narrative is, on the one hand, completely permeated by linguistic material belonging to the speech of fictional characters and, on the other hand, mixed with the author's lyrical utterances. Frequently a single linguistic element contains certain linguistic traits referring to the author and others referring to a fictional character. For instance:

Il marchait. Des prostituées pirouettaient à des coins de rue, avec de pauvres jupes et des yeux questionneurs: il ne les regardait même pas. Il marchait comme marche l'espérance. Quelque jeune femme à la taille serrée marchait devant lui, alors il ralentissait le pas pour mieux la voir. Voici qu'elle lui adressait un sourire. Alors il allongeait le pas pour mieux la fuir et parce qu'une autre femme à la taille serrée. . . . Il marchait comme marche l'espérance, de femme en femme. Il ne voulait pas des unes parce qu'elles étaient trop faciles. Il n'osait pas parler aux autres parce qu'elles n'avaient pas l'air faciles. Il marchait comme marche l'espérance, de femme en femme, jusqu'à ce qu'il n'y ait plus d'espérance. (p. 27)

[He walked. The prostitutes pirouetted on the street corners in their wretched skirts and with questioning eyes; he did not even look at them. He walked as hope walks. Some young woman with a pinched-in waist walked ahead of him, so he slowed down his steps in order to see her better. And there she turned to him with a smile. So he lengthened his stride in order to escape her better and because another woman with a pinched-in waist. . . . He walked as hope walks, from woman to woman. Some he did not want because they were too easy. Others he dared not approach because they did not look easy enough. He walked as hope walks, from woman to woman, until there was no longer any hope.]

The repeated "il marchait comme marche l'espérance" [he walked as hope walks] is the transposition of the poetical "Je marche comme marche l'espérance" [I walk as hope walks]. But who could have spoken this phrase? The fictional character, the minor civil servant Pierre Hardy? This seems hardly possible. It seems more likely that the writer lent Hardy his own poetic soul. The unfinished sentence "parce qu'une autre femme à la taille serrée . . ." [because another woman with a pinched-in waist . . .] illustrates how Pierre Hardy, in a hurry, might have interrupted his thought in order to follow another beauty. But within the context of a narrative report, the sudden interruption strikes the reader with surprise.

The intermittent narrative itself reflects the lived experience of the fictional characters. The author seems to mimic in his narrative account the intermittent rhythm of lived experience: "Pierre Hardy se disait ces choses avec naïveté et la suivait, bien vite la suivait" (p. 28). [Pierre Hardy naively told himself these things and he followed her, very quickly followed her.]— "Avec sa promptitude de décision, Bubu annonça à l'atelier qu'il quittait le métier d'ébéniste pour celui de déménageur. Il l'annonça avec orgueil parce qu'on le plaisantait. . . ." (p. 43). [Decisive as he was, Bubu announced at the workshop that he was giving up his job as a cabinetmaker to become a furniture mover. He announced this with pride, because he used to be teased. . . .]—"Ce n'était pas vrai, mais il était auprès d'une femme et voulait lui faire connaître des choses sur ses goûts et sur sa vie. Il voulait lui faire connaître son cœur pour qu'elle pensât: Voici un jeune homme au beau cœur. . . . Il voulait l'attirer à lui par toutes ses confidences" (p. 67). [This was not true, but he was near a woman and wished to let her know something about his tastes and his life. He wanted to let her know his heart, so that she would think: Here is a young man with a noble heart. . . . He wanted to draw her to him with all his confidences.]—"On sentait qu'elle avait peu d'idées et peu de courage et l'on sentait encore que la vie est mauvaise" (p. 81). [One could feel that she had few ideas and little courage, and one could feel, too, that life is bad.] By analogy to Lorck's term *erlebte Rede* [speech of lived experience, free indirect speech], we can characterize all of these passages as *erlebter Bericht* [reporting of lived experience, narrative accounts filtered through a personal perspective].

By no means do I intend to give a systematic account of pseudo-objective motivation in *all* of modern French writing, where it has become a frequently employed stylistic device. It will suffice to quote a reflection from

René Benjamin's *Grandgoujon* that has to be understood from the protagonist's perspective, the perspective of someone who is at once a petit bourgeois and a shirker: "Mais la foule qui leur donnait son indulgence, soudain
les couvre de son mépris. Simpliste, elle n'admet pas, la foule, qu'un homme
en paix au coin de son feu souffre aussi rudement qu'un soldat dans la boue.
Et pourtant Grandgoujon était de ces gens qui depuis le 2 août 1914 endu-
raient un martyre moral, incapable de respirer à l'aise dans le même air que
des voisins malheureux."[27] [But the crowd that used to forgive them (the
bon vivants) suddenly despises them. Simplistic, it does not admit, the
crowd, that a man during times of peace can suffer as violently at his hearth
as a soldier in the mud. And, nevertheless, Grandgoujon was one of those
who had been enduring a moral martyrdom since August 2, 1914, unable to
breathe at ease in the same air as their unfortunate neighbors.]

[To return to a passage from Charles-Louis Philippe:] "Il y a beaucoup de timidité dans nos cœurs et, si l'on est une fille publique avec
un cœur en danse, on est quand même une femme parmi les hommes
avec des douceurs et des hésitations" (pp. 181–82). [There is much
timidity in our hearts, and even if you are a public girl with a wanton
heart, you are still a woman among men, with all the delicacy and
hesitations.] Whereas "un cœur en danse" and "avec des douceurs et
des hésitations" belong to the author's language, "si l'on est une fille
publique" and "on est quand même une femme" belong to the prostitute's language. But to whom can we attribute the wonderfully simple "une femme parmi les hommes" or the sententious "il y a beaucoup de timidité . . ."? Probably to both of them, the author and the
prostitute! Particularly those nonliterary phrases that could have
sprung from the naive soul of the character have to be counted
among Philippe's finest stylistic achievements.*

---

*Frequently Philippe's style is marked by a refined simplicity. Note how
he portrays the self-assurance of two pimps: "De chaque côté de l'avenue
large, les maisons semblaient basses, les étalages semblaient mesquins et les
passants semblaient rares. C'est pourquoi Jules et Maurice semblaient gran-
dis" (p. 94). [On either side of the broad avenue, the houses seemed low, the
shop windows seemed shabby, and the passers-by seemed few. For this reason, Jules and Maurice seemed taller.] The monotony of the repeated *semblaient* draws our attention exclusively to the two characters standing in the
landscape.
    Or note the following: "Maurice l'invita à danser une première fois, puis
ils firent une deuxième danse et ensuite une troisième. Ils dansaient admi-
rablement tous les deux, ils étaient à peu près de même taille, il était très
bien élevé, elle était très douce. Il l'invita à prendre quelque chose, mais elle

refusa parce qu'elle était avec ses deux sœurs. Il se fit montrer la grande
sœur. . . ." (p. 46). [Maurice asked her to dance once, then again, and then
a third time. They danced beautifully together, they were about the same
height. He was very well brought up, she was very gentle. He invited her for
a drink, but she refused because she was with her two sisters. He had her
point out her big sister. . . .] The simple and monotonous syntax illustrates
the banality of the polite formulas and the reserve of the first encounter.

Lerch praises *style indirect libre* as an advancement in narrative
technique, for it allows the author to step back and speak through
the personal perspective of his characters.[28] The same technique of
moving inside his characters can also be observed in the examples we
earlier gave of speech with a sententiously moral coloring. Without
taking sides the author merely reports the motives guiding his characters' actions. He does not let us know who is speaking—the author, common opinion, or the protagonists: "Il y a beaucoup de timidité dans nos cœurs"—whose voice is this?*

---

*Although the dividing line between the author and his characters may
occasionally be blurred, in most cases one can locate stylistic features that
clearly belong to the author. This fact allows me to conclude—contrary to
Lorck[29]—that *style indirect libre* will *never* be incorporated in spoken language. Maintaining Lorck's stage imagery we can say that *style indirect
libre* always places the fictional character in the limelight.

Lorck analyzes a passage where the writer is confronted with a
jumble of voices: "He [the writer] registers only those voices that
catch his ear as more articulate and striking. He works by means of
suggestion rather than filling things out. It is an impressionist technique that gives free reign to the reader's imagination. The reader can
add to it as much as he wants, and thus he receives the impression of
an undefined number of speakers."[30]* Similarly, *parce que* or *on* can
convey only a vague idea of the speaker. The actual speaker remains
hidden in an impressionistic dark zone, out of which we can only occasionally (*nous les femmes*) make out some clear-cut characters.

---

*The Spanish language has created a means for expressing anonymous
gossip or a jumble of various voices. It can do so simply by repeating *que*,
the sign for indirect speech. Besides the examples I mentioned in my *Auf-*

sätze,[31] see Padre Apolinar's soliloquy in José Maria de Pereda's *Sotileza*: "Pae Polinar, que este hijo está, fuera del alma, hecho una bestia; pae Polinar, que este otro es una cabra montuna . . . pae Polinar, que esta condenada criatura me quita la vida á disgustos; que yo no puedo cuidar de él; que en la escuela de balde no le hacen maldito el caso . . . que éste, que el otro, que arriba, que abajo; que usté que lo entiende y para eso fué nacido . . . que enséñele, que dómele, que desásnele."[32] [Father Polinar, this child is not himself, has become a beast; Father Polinar, this other one is a mountain goat . . . Father Polinar, this nasty child is ruining my life; I can't take care of him; in the free school they pay no attention to him . . . and this, and the other, and above and below; you who understand it and for that he was born . . . teach him, tame him, show him not to be an ass.]

If a whole complex of stylistic features can be ascribed to an author, we may assume that this complex is paralleled by a particularly strong emotional experience. And this is what links the present study with my research in *Motiv und Wort*. In Philippe's use of *à cause, parce que, on* for pseudo-objective motivations that abstain from any personal comment, we may expect to find mirrored a certain psychological configuration within the author. We have already observed that underlying these expressions one can sometimes see a resigned and sometimes an ironic surrender to fate or to some general norm. Now, since this *fatalistic* mood pervades the novel as a whole, one might conclude that this notion of kismet must also run through the author's blood.

All it takes to prove Philippe's completely deterministic view of his characters' fate is to quote the following passages, which Gundolf would call *Zentralstellen* [key passages]:

Il la battait. . . . La pauvre Berthe, avec son caractère doux, acceptait ces corrections en pleurant. . . . Un peu plus tard elle vit que tous les amis de Maurice battaient aussi leurs femmes et comprit qu'il y avait en ce monde une loi dirigeante qui était la loi du plus fort. (p. 56)

[He would hit her. . . . Poor Berthe, with her gentle nature, accepted these punishments in tears. . . . A little later she saw that all of Maurice's friends hit their women, and she understood that this world was ruled by a law that was the law of the strongest.]

Vraiment, avec ses tempes aplaties, ses pommettes décolorées et ses lèvres lâches, on sentait qu'elle avait peu d'idées et peu de courage, et l'on sentait encore que la vie est mauvaise parce qu'elle frappe à grands coups sur des enfants qui font le mal sans en mésurer l'étendue. (p. 81)

[And in truth, with her hollow temples, her wan cheeks, and her flaccid lips, you felt that she had few ideas and little courage, and you felt, too, that life is bad because it gives such heavy blows to children who do harm without realizing how far it might go.]

Elle partait dans un monde où la bienfaisance individuelle est sans force parce qu'il y a l'amour et l'argent, parce que ceux qui font le mal sont implacables et parce que les filles publiques en sont marquées dès l'origine comme des bêtes passives que l'on mène au pré communal. (pp. 224–25)

[She went into a world where individual benevolence has no power, because there is love and money, and because those who do wrong are implacable, and because prostitutes carry the brand of it from the start, like passive animals that are led to common pasture.]

Connaissez-vous l'odeur du vice qu'une fois l'on respira? Les coups de poing des souteneurs façonnent les filles et laissent leurs marque dans la chair blanche auprès des désirs qu'y mit Dieu. . . . Il y a l'atmosphère des prostituées, qui sent d'abord la liberté de vivre, puis qui descend et qui pue comme mille sexes tout un jour. Et le mal entre sous vos jupes avec des baisers dévorants. Il y a le trottoir, les chambres d'hôtel et les pièces d'argent, tout un commerce où l'on vend son âme pendant que l'on vend sa chair. (pp. 160–61)

[Do you know the smell of vice once it has entered the lungs? The fists of the pimps mould these girls and leave their marks upon the white flesh beside the desires placed there by God. . . . There is this air of prostitution that at first smells of liberty and then sinks and stinks like a thousand crotches all day. And the evil enters under your skirts with its devouring kisses. There are the pavement, the hotel rooms and the coins, an entire trade wherein you sell your soul while you sell your flesh.]

Cela faisait beaucoup de mal, de la voir ainsi. On n'en comprenait pas toutes les causes parce que les causes débordent et suspendent sur nos têtes leurs cent mille poings de fer où les poids se mêlent et pèsent ensemble avec les jours, avec les chagrins, avec les coups reçus, avec le mal que l'on a fait, avec la vadrouille des nuits. Il vient un soir où c'est fini, où tant de gueules nous ont mordues qu'il ne reste plus de force pour nous garder debout et que notre viande pend dans notre corps comme si toutes les gueules l'avaient mâchée. Il vient un soir où l'homme pleure, où la femme est vidée. (pp. 188–89)

[It hurt very much to see her so. You could not understand all the causes, because causes overflow and hang above our heads their thousand little iron fists whose weight mingles and is weighed together with the days, with the sorrows, with the blows received, with the harm one has done, and with the vagabondage of the nights. And an evening comes when all is over, when so many jaws have closed upon us that we no longer have the strength to stand, and our meat hangs upon our bodies, as though it had been masticated by every mouth. An evening comes when man weeps and woman is emptied.]

The sentence "On n'en comprenait pas toutes les causes parce que les causes débordent et suspendent sur nos têtes leurs cent mille poings de fer" illustrates exactly the irony that underlies the *à cause* and *parce que* passages: The reasons we use to account for a certain event are, according to Philippe, only pseudo-causes that can by no means explain our actual actions. In reality there remains for us human beings only the *ignorabimus* [we will never know]. The constant statements about motivation are only a form of verbal intoxication, the self-deception of a man searching for clarity, yet oppressed by the weight of life. Man is, for Philippe, a poor, only apparently proud creature; his actions are inconsistent, illogical, and vain.

Only that kind of irony which considers this illogical way of acting perfectly normal can deal with this empty pseudo-creature. This is precisely the irony that can be found in every *because*, *since*, *one* that is not backed up by any real authority. (That this irony counts for Philippe as a genuinely French reaction to life is evident in the following lines: "à la façon de Paris où l'on met son sourire aux rencontres des rues et où toute chose se passe avec une ironie française" (p. 203) [in the Parisian way where you put on a smile when you meet people in the streets and where everything happens with a French type of irony].) In the passage below one finds, for instance, an ironical *à cause* at the end of a longer ironical narrative to which the reader must add his own corrective commentary. I shall emphasize in italics those crucial terms that are so conspicuous and obtrusive that the author must have intended the reader to examine them critically, and that he might well have set off in quotation marks:

Le Quatorze Juillet arriva. *Bienheureux* jour où les boutiques des marchands de vin sont pleines de drapeaux, où les pétards partent en pleine rue, où les comités socialistes-révolutionnaires célèbrent leurs *victoires*. Le soir, il y a des bals entourés de lampions, les pistons ont des gueules de cuivre et les tables des cafés envahissent la rue *par permission* spéciale du gouvernement. Le peuple, *à cause* de l'anniversaire de sa délivrance, laisse ses filles danser en liberté. (p. 45)

[The Fourteenth of July came. *Blissful* day when the wine shops are filled with flags, when firecrackers go off in the street, and the socialist-revolutionary committees celebrate their *victories*. At night, there is dancing amidst colored lanterns, the cornets open their copper mouths, and the café tables invade the street *by special permission* of the government. The people, *because of* the anniversary of their deliverance, let their daughters dance freely in the streets.]

Or another passage that expresses ironical resignation throughout:

Lorsqu'elle prenait l'omnibus pour aller au travail, elle fermait les yeux, parce qu'elle était un peu lasse, et voyait dans sa pensée Maurice avec les plaisirs. Il lui disait: "Je ne veux pas travailler à mon métier d'ébéniste et je ne veux plus être déménageur," alors elle sentait, qu'il *était* supérieur à tous les métiers. Il parlait de sa mère dont les idées étaient bornées comme deux sous de poivre et quatre sous de café; il en parlait ainsi parce qu'*il avait les idées ouvertes*. Il lui disait: "Quand tu étais chez ton père et que tu t'emmerdais en torchant tes frères," alors elle lui était reconnaissante de l'avoir délivrée. Au bout d'un mois il la battait, mais *non pas par méchanceté*. Voici: Maurice, qui avait le caractère résolu, *classait trop nettement* les connaissances humaines. Comme l'empereur *Charlemagne*, il avait mis d'un côté les idées qui ne lui plaisaient pas et de l'autre celles que lui plaisaient. Il pensait: "Là-bas, c'est l'erreur, mais ici, c'est la vérité." *Comme l'empereur Charlemagne*, il n'avait pas le sentiment des nuances. Il ne comprit jamais, *par exemple*, que l'on se lavât le visage avant de se laver les mains. Il disait à Berthe: "Tu touches ta figure avec tes mains sales." (pp. 54–55)

[When she would take the bus to go to work, she would close her eyes, because she was a little weary, and she would see in her mind Maurice amidst his pleasures. He would say to her: "I don't want to work at cabinet making, and I don't want to move furniture any more," and then she would feel that he *was* superior to any job. He would speak of his mother, whose ideas were limited to two sous worth of pepper and four sous worth of coffee; he would speak of her in this way because *he was open-minded*. He would say to her (Berthe), "When you were with your father you had a hell of a time wiping the filth off your brothers," and then she would be grateful to him for having rescued her. Before the first month was over, he was beating her, but *not from nastiness*. This is how it was: Maurice, who was very decided in his opinions, *would neatly classify* all human things. Like the Emperor *Charlemagne*, he had placed on one side the ideas he did not like, and on the other those he liked. He thought: "Over there, this is false, but here, this is the truth." *Like the Emperor Charlemagne*, he had no feeling for shades of difference. He could never understand, *for example*, how one could wash one's face before washing one's hands. He would say to Berthe: "You touch your face with your dirty hands."]

Philippe chooses a pseudo-objective mode of representation, avoiding judgments and behaving toward his figures like an unmoved reporter who seems able to understand, even to adopt any point of view. This appearance is deceptive, however: There is a critical attitude behind each of his representations, for his mode of representation is only *pseudo-*, not truly objective. Furthermore, one suspects some secret sympathy can be sensed behind his reporting, for his irony takes the form of justification, of a kind of laconic eloquence. Thus he often finds his characters' burdens in life too heavy for him to bear. Then his oppressed heart cries out to God, to the highest being Who would allow all these things he must describe to happen. Beneath this ironical tone we can feel the pulse of some urgent and feverish subjectivity, even if it gives a surface impression of restraint. Sometimes one wonders whether it is the fictional character or the author himself calling out to God:

Cette petite femme mince et maniable était pareille aux femmes que l'on rencontre dans la rue avec des hommes qui leur pressent la taille. Quand le soir tombe et qu'elles sont là, il y a dans le monde un grand désir. *Seigneur*, envoyez-nous des petites femmes comme Berthe pour que nous les baisions et pour que leurs vingt ans ajoutent à nos baisers. Pierre ne se rappelait plus que ce plaisir allait lui coûter cinq francs. (p. 65)

[This petite and pliable little woman was like those women that you see on the streets with men who squeeze their waists. When evening falls and they are there, the world is full of desire. *Lord*, send us little women like Berthe so that we may kiss them, and so that their twenty years may enrich our kisses! Pierre no longer remembered that this pleasure would cost him five francs.]

The cry "Seigneur . . ." might be just the cry of those men, the mere reproduction of direct speech, since the narrative goes on: "Pierre ne se rappelait plus. . . ." But frequently one has no doubt that it is Philippe himself who, confronted with a shocking reality, is addressing God directly:

Ce n'est rien, Seigneur. C'est une femme, sur un trottoir, qui passe et qui gagne sa vie parce qu'il est bien difficile de faire autrement. Un homme s'arrête et lui parle parce que vous nous avez donné la femme comme un plaisir. Et puis cette femme est Berthe, et puis vous savez le reste. Ce n'est rien. C'est un tigre qui a faim. La faim des tigres ressemble à la faim des agneaux. Vous nous avez donné des nourritures. Je pense que ce tigre est bon puisqu'il aime sa femelle et ses enfants et puisqu'il aime à vivre. Mais pourquoi faut-il que la faim des tigres ait du sang, quand la faim des agneaux est si douce? (p. 156)

[(Berthe is knowingly infecting others.) This is nothing, Lord. This is just a woman on the pavement who passes by, making her living because it is very difficult to make do otherwise. A man stops and speaks to her because you have given us woman for our pleasure. And then this woman is Berthe, and then you know the rest. This is nothing. This is a tiger who is hungry. The hunger of tigers resembles the hunger of lambs. You have given us something to eat. I think that this tiger is good, since he loves his female and his cubs, and since he loves to live. But why must there be blood in the hunger of the tiger while the hunger of the lamb is so gentle?]

Philippe is arguing with God—he has taken off the coat of pseudo-objectivity and stands there as a torn man who, as an advocate of mortal creatures, has fallen out with his God.

And his advocacy is becoming more and more urgent. Finally he even dares to name God and the prostitute in one breath, to plead with God to help her:

Et Pierre le {Maurice} voyait. Il vit ces choses à vingt ans et baissait la tête comme Adam lorsqu'il vit qu'il y avait du mal au monde. Seigneur, il y a beaucoup de mal au monde. Il y a des femmes qui sont sous vos yeux et qui sont vos enfants. Vous les avez créées, vous les avez mises à nos côtés pour notre faim comme un joli gâteau. Elles nous semblaient si délicates que nous n'osions pas y mettre la main. Seigneur, Seigneur! Il y a pourtant des femmes sous vos yeux qui portent des croix de fer. Seigneur, Berthe: un homme s'est planté sur ses épaules. (p. 172)

[And Pierre could see him {Maurice}. He saw these things at twenty and bowed his head, like Adam, when he saw there was evil in the world. Lord, there is much evil in the world. There are women before your eyes who are your children. You have created them, and you put them at our side for our hunger, like a pretty cake. They seemed so delicate that we dared not lay our hands upon them. Lord, Lord! And there beneath your eyes are women who wear iron crosses. Lord, Berthe: there is a man astride her shoulders.]

Or the author asks the audience to be his witness, seeking to communicate his own feelings:

Les réveils de midi sont lourds et poisseux. . . . On éprouve un sentiment de déchéance à cause des réveils d'autrefois où les idées étaient si claires qu'on eût dit que le sommeil les avait lavées. Quand tu auras dormi, *mon frère*, tu n'auras rien oublié. Elle ressentit encore ce poids d'angoisse qui, depuis hier, l'empêchait de respirer. . . . *Vraiment*, avec ses temps aplaties . . . on sentait qu'elle avait peu d'idées. (pp. 80–81)

[These awakenings at midday are heavy and sticky. . . . You feel a sense of degradation because of the awakenings of former times, when ideas were so clear you would have said that sleep had washed them. Once you have slept, *my brother*, you will have forgotten nothing. She still felt the weight of anguish, which had, since yesterday, stifled her. . . . *Really*, with her hollow temples . . . you felt that she had few ideas.]

Les voitures qui roulent . . . et le bruit forment une confusion de Babel qui effare et fait danser trop d'idées à la fois. Tous les provinciaux ont senti ce malaise et sont devenus gauches et tristes en face de cela. *Je vous assure* que les beaux gars des villages qui paradaient dans les bals font triste figure sur les Grands Boulevards. (p. 16)

[The cars passing by . . . and the noise create a Babel-like confusion that bewilders and sets too many ideas swirling in the head at the same time. All the provincials have felt this uneasiness, and, confronted with it, all have become awkward and sad. *I assure you* those handsome lads who strutted so jauntily on their village greens cut a sorry figure on the great boulevards.]

The writer becomes so subjectively involved in his narrative that he even addresses a hymn-like apostrophe—in the ancient heroic style—to the scene of the action and to those objects and details that play a significant role: "Vous, rue de Vanves, et vous aussi talus des fortifications, par les beaux soirs sans lune, vous avez vu passer Bubu. Il apprit à connaître la rue" (p. 43). [You, rue de Vanves, and you, slopes of the fortifications, have seen Bubu pass on fine moonless nights. He learned to know the street.]—"Tout à coup il se rappela la chanson. Chanson qui consoles, ô vieille chanson des véroles, qui fais de la musique sur les malades, tu nous rends doux et poétique comme la souffrance des blessés: 'De l'hôpital, vieille pratique. . . .'" (p. 101). [Suddenly he remembered the song. The song of consolation, oh, old song of pox, making music of the afflicted, and rendering us as sweet and poetic as the suffering of the stricken: "De l'hôpital, vieille pratique. . . ."] (The apostrophe to the song is carried on for two more paragraphs.) "Il vit des boîtes de mandarines. Petites mandarines, petits riens avec du jus, vous n'êtes pas faites pour les gueules des marlous" (p. 103). [He saw some boxes of mandarins. Little mandarins, little juicy bits of nothing, you are not made for the coarse mouths of bullies.]

In the following passage we can see the novelist parting from his characters, who have now set out on an enterprise of their own. In this apostrophe it is as if he were cutting the umbilical cord linking the creator with the creatures of his imagination: "Ce fut une histoire simple et décevante. . . . Ils y allèrent, la gorge sèche et du sang dans les poings. *Allez-vous enfin, tous les trois, mes frères,* arrêter vos cœurs et voir ce qu'on voit dans les vols alors que l'on tremble, que l'on cherche et que l'on trouve?" (pp. 134–35). [It was a simple and disappointing story. . . . They went, with a dry throat and blood in their fists. *Are you at last, the three of you, my brothers,* going to make your hearts stop beating, and see what can be seen in robberies when you tremble, when you search, and when you find?] Both the fictional characters and the audience are brothers to him, and this sentiment of fraternity is expressed in the fatalistic *on.*

The author's fatalism results from a struggle with life, a protest against destiny. His language of pseudo-objectivity hides an inwardly glowing subjectivity. Thus we have traced his language to his psychology, his creativity to a *Weltanschauung* [worldview], in Wechssler's terms.[33]

Throughout this analysis we have found two seemingly opposed tendencies—an apologetic and an ironical tone—in pseudo-objective motivations.*

---

* Josef Körner has pointed out to me similar tendencies in Alice Berend's novels. Nevertheless, certain passages I find in *Jungfrau Binchen und die Junggesellen*[34] are quite different [from those in Philippe]. The novel starts with the following words: "Jeder muss sich auf seine Weise mit dem Leben auseinandersetzen. Wie es ihm gelingt ist seine Sache. Auch die besten Familien besitzen kein Rezept dafür. Trotzdem ihr Einfluss nicht abgeleugnet werden kann."[35] [Everybody has to deal with life in his own way. Whatever way he chooses is his own business. Even the best families do not have a recipe. Although their influence cannot be denied.] This is less a pseudo-objective motivation than the *fiction of an average narrator*, who elaborates trivial commonplaces in his everyday moralizing manner. It belongs rather to the type *erzählte Erzählung* [narrated narration], in Oskar Walzel's terms.[36] In this type of narrative the narrator does not hover above the waters as the divine spirit does. Rather, he becomes stylistically involved. This is how we can account for the colloquial beginning of the sentence with *trotzdem* [in spite of the fact that].

But we can find a different passage on the same page: "Sie war überzeugt davon, dass Herr Anton und nicht minder sein Bruder Saphir die Ehe schon als Säugling zu den Erfindungen der Hölle gerechnet. Gleichviel jedoch, woher und wieso, was da ist, muss da sein. Denn nichts ist unnütz im Welthaushalt. Es *gehörten* also auch Junggesellen hinein."[37] [She was convinced that Herr Anton—and his brother Saphir no less than he—had already in his infancy counted marriage among the inventions of hell. No matter whence and why, what is there must be there. For nothing is wasted in the domestic order of the world. There was also a place for bachelors.] As indicated by the imperfect [gehörten], this is *style indirect libre*, as is the following passage: "Wie weit Herrn Antons Erwartungen zu dieser Erfindung des Bruders standen, wusste man nicht. Er liebte es, sich in allen Lebenslagen an das sichere zu halten. Schweigen war auch hier das Unfehlbarste. Jedenfalls hinderte er Saphir nicht in seinem Bemühen. Der Weg zur Ewigkeit ist lang."[38] [One did not know to what extent Herr Anton's expectations were related to his brother's invention. In every situation of life he liked to play it safe. And here, too, silence was undoubtedly right. In any case, he did not obstruct Saphir's efforts. The road to eternity is long.] Here we can find an opposition between *style indirect libre* ("Schweigen *war* . . . ") and pseudo-objective stylization ("Der Weg Zur Ewigkeit *ist* lang").

The following passage illustrates how the boundaries between direct, indirect, pseudo-objective, and free indirect speech can be blurred:

Binchen konnte also Vergleiche anstellen zwischen Eheleben und Junggesellentum. Dienstbotenblicken bleibt nicht weniger verborgen, als dem Auge dessen, der alles sieht {narrator's or Binchen's speech?}. Binchen sagte{!}, dass man nicht vergessen dürfe, dass bei der Ehe alles, was dazu gehöre, vom Priester gesegnet sei. Man musste {not *müsste*!} also sein Nachsehen haben, wenn es nicht so reinlich zugehe{!}, wie in einem Junggesellenheim. . . . Es hatte Binchen überrieselt. Beinah hätte sie gewünscht, dass der hinkende Gehörnte hervorgesprungen wäre. Aber sie war allein geblieben. Niemand war gekommen. Dieser Wunsch erfüllte sich erst in der Nacht darauf. Im Traum. Aber das liess sich {*style indirect libre*} gar nicht weiter erzählen. Obwohl niemand für seine Träume verantwortlich gemacht werden konnte {*style indirect libre*}. Die kamen {*style indirect libre*} aus dem Magen. Nur Böswillige können behaupten {pseudo-objective}, wie die Gedanken am Tage, so die Träume in der Nacht {maliciously ironic punctuation}.[39]

[And so Binchen could compare married and unmarried life. To the eyes of servants there is nothing less concealed than to the eye of him who sees everything {narrator's or Binchen's speech?}. Binchen said{!} that one should not forget that everything that belonged to marriage was blessed by the priest. You had to {not *would have* to!} be lenient if things were{!} not always as clean as in a bachelor's home. . . . Binchen was overwhelmed. She would almost have wished for Satan to jump out of the corner. But she stayed alone. Nobody came. Her wish didn't come true until that night, in a dream. But this was not something she could tell anyone about {*style indirect libre*}. Although nobody could be made responsible {*style indirect libre*} for their dreams. They came {*style indirect libre*} from the stomach. Only malicious people can maintain {pseudo-objective} that like ideas by day, so too are dreams at night {maliciously ironic punctuation}.]

It would also be worth studying mixed styles in those recent German texts in which the writer mimics people lexically and even phonetically, not only in passages that record their speech but also in descriptions *about* them. Texts of this sort would record the linguistic environment of the persons described. For example, in *Die Fackel* Karl Kraus writes of a journalist for the *Deutsche Tageszeitung* who had written "Pfui Deibel!! Ein ganzer Kerrl"[40] [Phwe!! A rreal man]. The *rr*, of course, mimics the pronunciation of that journalist. (But as Körner communicated to me, this could also be an allusion to Alfred Kerr that represents the journalist for the opposite political view as his "stylistic offspring.")

Or, from the same passage: "Sie machen von der Toleranz jenes Königs eben den Gebrauch, der seiner andern Erlaubnis, dass, 'in seinem Staate jeder nach seiner Fasson selig werde,' *directement* widerstreitet."[41] [You are taking advantage of the tolerance of that king to such an extent that it *directly* opposes his consent "for everyone in his state to pursue happiness freely in his own way."] The *directement* merely serves to illustrate the historical landscape of Frederick the Great's language. It is as if the statement were infected by the [francophone] milieu to which it refers.

In describing his travels through Bavaria, Alfred Kerr uses a similar technique. He intersperses his accounts with vernacular, syncopated forms like *g'nug* ['nough]. Occasionally his mimetic eclecticism goes to such extremes that he seems to disdain any purity of language.[42]

This [combination of apology and irony in Philippe's writing] seems contradictory, for irony indicates mastery over life, while apology reveals the need for some support in life. Irony can be attributed mainly to the French, the Jews, and the Levantines, who master life with serenity. The tendency to be on the defensive, constantly to suspect accusations, is common among the Nordic peoples, who characteristically suffer in life. Whoever can write that the people, "à cause de l'anniversaire de sa délivrance, laisse ses filles danser en liberté" [because of the anniversary of their deliverance, let their daughters dance freely in the streets] can free himself from life's oppressive illogicality with the spirit of a serene and skeptical rationality. Whoever can write "Il analysait avec force les événements. . . . L'analyse n'est pas une science froide, elle qui passe par nos cœurs et les trouble" (p. 111) [He forcefully analyzed the events. . . . Analysis is not a cold science, it goes to our hearts and moves them] feels the need to justify the self-analysis of his protagonist, for he is seeking protection from life. Since Philippe, however, is familiar with both perspectives, with an ironical as well as an apologetic mode of presentation, one could conclude that sometimes he is able playfully to master life, while at other times life's tragedy wins the upper hand. And indeed, the amplitude of Philippe's psyche seems to encompass the full range, from a demeaning surrender to fate all the way to mastery of life. In this sense Philippe is a genuinely French writer, one who brings the *post nubila* [once the morning clouds have disappeared] Phoebus of reason in all its brilliance out of the Nordic fog of fate.*

---

*Within his study of François Villon as an autobiographical poet, André Suarès writes in his *Portraits*: "Here [in France] the heart can never be completely the victim of the mind, nor its tyrant. Here the mind is never completely the toy of the heart. In the blackest darkness, in the reddest aberration of the passions, a light awakens: the clear foundation of intelligence. And within the most melancholy ruins of thought, within the most awful debris of analysis, the heart still remains lively, able to play, capable of pleasure and passionate hope."[43]

———————— • ————————

The intentional simplicity, the restrained hope, the submission to an omnipotent and all-determining reality, the willingness to descend to the level of simple life, the closeness to a God directing this world—all these features that we have come to recognize in Philippe's style are themselves mentioned by Philippe as his artistic ideal in some letters he wrote to Max Elskamp. Ernst Robert Curtius quotes from these letters in *Die literarischen Wegbereiter des neuen Frankreich*:[44]

I spent last Monday evening with D. Compared to him I was badly dressed. I wanted to look like a simple person, for my heart is simple, isn't it? I'm writing with tears in my eyes and I'm polishing my sentences, not so they exhibit technical mastery but emotion. And while I found the photographs he showed me beautiful, . . . I was thinking of those things in life which I find even more beautiful. . . . It's not good to know too much. . . . We need barbarians these days. We need to have lived close to God, without having studied Him in books. We need a vision of the natural life to have strength, even rage. The time of mildness and dilettantism is over. Now the time of passion is about to begin. The goal is to become a writer, who tells very simply that which he believes to be good, and to be loved.

And indeed, this visionary realism of the *cœur simple* Charles-Louis Philippe comes from the heart and goes to the heart.

TWO ESSAYS ON GÓNGORA'S 'SOLEDADES'

Spitzer's two most important studies of Góngora's *Las soledades* demonstrate two very different facets of his versatility as a critic. The first is a highly integrated textual analysis, which, as he points out at its beginning, marks an important shift in his critical method. In the years immediately preceding its publication in 1930, Spitzer had become increasingly dissatisfied with the psychologizing directions of his early literary studies, centered as they were on the relations between the work and the murky area of authorial consciousness and experience (*Erlebnis*) that it allegedly manifests. He felt a new approach was necessary, one that focused more rigorously and exclusively on the work as an organic whole and proceeded on the organicist assumption that the unity of the whole can be discerned through the proper analysis of each of its constitutive parts.

Spitzer associated his new "work-immanent" or "structural" method with his own increasing commitment to rationality and clarity of form, and found its most fruitful area of application in the less privatized texts of earlier periods. The *Soledades* of Luis de Góngora, whose legendary obscurity had been frequently dismissed by modern literary historians as an aberrant product of personal idiosyncrasy, provided an interesting challenge for the new critical approach. The revealing metacritical conceits that frame the analysis—the drawing of the blood sample and the examination of the torso—might shock Spitzer's reader, but they are consistent with the mannered style of the entire essay and with the particular kind of stylistic violence that the critic would clarify in Góngora's strange poetic world. As Erich Auerbach has pointed out, not without some misgivings, Spitzer occasionally writes as if he would outdo the work of art through the appropriation of its very style.[1] Starting with the convolutions of Góngora's syntax and their effects on the reading process, the analysis moves through versification, motif, image, and metaphor to show how all the elements of the seemingly centrifugal poem converge in an enactment of the dynamic processes through which the baroque poet brings art into existence and the reader struggles to apprehend that art. Spitzer notes pictorial analogues to Góngora's practices in Velázquez's paintings and suggests that a defining feature of baroque art in general is its interest in celebrating the drama of art's domination of nature.

In the second study, written in collaboration with his students at the Johns Hopkins University some ten years later, Spitzer turns to the most traditional form of literary criticism, the line-by-line textual commentary. In its ongoing polemical strategies and its chaotic speculations concerning etymologies, semantics, sources, literary echoes, mythological allusions, astronomy, geography, etc., it effectively captures the spirit of the Renaissance humanist commentaries, and particularly those that Góngora's controversial poetry inspired in the seventeenth century. Its digressive character, its atomistic approach to the text, and its frequent pedantic skirmishes with other philologists over minute questions of meaning would suggest that Spitzer could work comfortably with the techniques of the academic positivists whom he had earlier repudiated. He was in fact later to acknowledge that his hostility toward their "meaningless industriousness" at the time of his development of a "work-immanent" criticism was too radical in its antihistoricism. Nevertheless, despite its scholarly density, the commentary maintains its focus on the "immanent beauty" of Góngora's text. The philologist's erudition is generally exploited to substantiate and elaborate the critic's imaginative insight into the distinctive forms, meanings, and effects of the poetry. And the kind of vigorous interplay of critical voices which his argumentative commentary on commentary achieves is in one sense ideally suited to the examination of a poetry that, according to Spitzer, would dramatize the struggle to create and construe meaning.

In this most schematic of critical formats, Spitzer is most unrestrained in pursuing his intuitions, frequently drawing attention to their conjectural character and plainly enjoying the free play of his restless mind. His excesses and exaggerations, as well as the oversights resulting from his characteristic insistence on placing the object of his attention within the larger perspectives of European cultural history, as opposed to within its immediate historical and national environment, have been justifiably criticized by specialists.[2] But it is precisely from the long-range perspective that Spitzer offers us some of his most original disclosures—for example, his insight into the complex ways in which Góngora's highly Latinate, classicizing poetry in fact incorporates medieval and popular traditions; his discriminations concerning the relations between the self-conscious artfulness and rationally controlled obscurity of baroque poetry and seemingly comparable features of the modern lyric; and, of course, his revelations of vast, unsuspected imaginative dimensions concealed within numerous arresting moments of Góngora's masterpiece.

For inclusion in this volume, the essay "On Góngora's *Soledades*" was translated by Caroline Wellbery from the German "Zu Góngora's 'Soledades,'" in Spitzer's *Romanische Stil- und Literaturstudien*, 2 (Marburg, 1931), pp. 126–40. It was originally printed in *Volkstum und Kultur der Romanen*, 2 (1930): 244–58. Selections from the essay "Góngora's First *Soledad*: Critical and Explanatory Notes on Dámaso Alonso's New Edition" were translated by Stephen Rupp from the Spanish "La Soledad Primera de Góngora: Notas críticas y explicativas a la nueva edición de Dámaso Alonso," *Revista de filología hispánica*, 2 (1940): 151–76. Stephen Rupp wishes to thank Nancy K. Brown, Frank Ordiway, and Ed Phillips for their assistance.

On Góngora's 'Soledades'

Just as it is possible to evaluate the condition of a whole organism by examining a single blood sample, so must we be able to uncover the inner being of a work of poetry by studying any portion of it, for the order that pulsates through it should be manifest everywhere. This method should yield results similar to those obtained by palpation of the whole body, provided that the site of extraction is well chosen—it should allow the life's blood of the poet to flow out. I used to claim that everything rested on the analysis of the word and the motif, but I have since abandoned the biographical-biological train of thought that I pursued in my youth and have turned instead to a contemplation of the work in itself (without constant reference to the author), which I treat as an organism whose parts provide access to the whole. I would have to call this new approach a study of the word and the work, where the word must be in organic consonance with the work. To penetrate the darkness of Góngora's notoriously obscure poem *Soledades*, I have selected the *Dedicatoria al Duque de Béjar* and have set it next to the modern annotative "translation" provided by Dámaso Alonso's edition:[1]

> Pasos de un peregrino son errante
> cuantos me dictó versos dulce musa:
>   en soledad confusa
> perdidos unos, otros inspirados.
>
> 5 ¡Oh tú, que, de venablos impedido
>   —muros de abeto, almenas de diamante—,
> bates los montes, que, de nieve armados,

gigantes de cristal los teme el cielo;
donde el cuerno, del eco repetido,
10 fieras te expone, que—al teñido suelo,
muertas, pidiendo términos disformes—
espumoso coral le dan al Tormes!:

arrima a un fresno el fresno—cuyo acero,
sangre sudando, en tiempo hará breve
15   purpurear la nieve—
y, en cuanto da el solícito montero
al duro robre, al pino levantado
—émulos vividores de las peñas—
las formidables señas
20 del oso que aun besaba, atravesado,
la asta de tu luciente jabalina,
—o lo sagrado supla de la encina
lo augusto del dosel; o de la fuente
la alta cenefa, lo majestuoso
25 del sitïal a tu deidad debido—,
    ¡oh Duque esclarecido!,
templa en sus ondas tu fatiga ardiente,
y, entregados tus miembros al reposo
sobre el de grama césped no desnudo,
30 déjate un rato hallar del pie acertado
que sus errantes pasos ha votado
a la real cadena de tu escudo.

Honre süave, generoso nudo
libertad, de fortuna perseguida:
35 que, a tu piedad Euterpe agradecida,
su canoro dará dulce instrumento,
cuando la fama no su trompa al viento.

[Dictated by the Muse, these verses, know,
As many footsteps as the pilgrim made;
Though some in solitude confused have strayed
    Others inspired were born.

5 O thou, whom hindering javelins surround
—Diamond battlements, of fir the walls—
Who beatest the high mountains (armed with snow
This crystal giant crew the heavens appals);
Where with repeated echo now the horn
10 Displays wild beasts, that, to the crimson ground,
Dead, for much greater boundaries appeal,
And foaming coral add to Tormes' flood:

Lean by an ash thine ashen spear—whose steel
In few short minutes will, by sweating blood,
15   The snow with purple dye—

And, while the careful beater may apply
To the hard oak and elevated pine
(That living emulate the very stones)
The formidable bones
20 Of bears transfixed before by thy proud shaft
(They even then would kiss the shining haft),
—Either the ilex with its shade divine
A new but regal canopy may bring,
Or let the lofty margin of the spring
25 Supply thy godhead with majestic throne—
O most illustrious peer!
Burning fatigue shall soon sweet coolness find,
And to repose thy limbs delivered here
Upon the turfy ground,
30 Let thyself by the wandering feet be found,
Sure paces offered unto thee alone
And to the royal chains upon thy shield.

And let their soft and generous bond embrace
Him, who when free was dogged by Fortune blind:
35 Euterpe, flattered by thy pitying grace,
Her sweet canorous instrument shall yield
If Fame deny her trumpet to the wind.]

1. Todos estos versos, dictados por una dulce musa, son pasos de un peregrino errante, pasos y versos, perdidos unos en confusa soledad, inspirados otros. ¡Oh tú, noble Duque, que, rodeado del tropel de venablos de tus cazadores (venablos que fingen una muralla de astas de abeto, coronada, como por diamantinas almenas, por los hierros brillantes y puntiagudos), andas dando batida a los montes (a los montes, que, cubiertos con su armadura de nieves, infunden pavor al cielo: porque, recordando éste su antigua lucha con los Gigantes, hijos de la Tierra, teme no sean estos altísimos montes otros nuevos Gigantes, ahora de cristal, a causa de la nieve que los cubre), montes donde el cuerno de caza, repetido por los ecos, va poniendo a tu alcance fieras, que, una vez muertas, tendidas sobre la tierra, tiñen el suelo con su sangre, y, «pidiendo términos disformes al suelo» —siendo tantas en número que apenas caben en él— llegan a manchar de espuma sanguinolenta las aguas del río Tormes, junto al cual estás cazando,

13. ¡oh, noble Duque!: arrima a un fresno el fresno de tu venablo, cuyo hierro irá goteando sangre que al cabo de poco tiempo habrá teñido de rojo la nieve que cubre el suelo, y mientras los cuidadosos monteros van colgando (según antigua costumbre venatoria) de los duros robles y de los eminentes pinos (árboles que casi llegan a competir en longevidad con las peñas), los trofeos de la caza, tal vez la temible cabeza de algún oso, que, atravesado por tu brillante jabalina, parecía, agradecido a tu mano, querer besar el asta del arma misma que le dio muerte,

26. ¡oh esclarecido Duque!, depuestas así las armas, y tomando como dosel augusto una sagrada encina, o, en vez del majestuoso sitial que

corresponde a tu excelsitud, la alta margen de alguna fuente en cuyas aguas
aplaques tu ardorosa fatiga, deja reposar tus miembros sobre el césped
recubierto de grama y déjate hallar por algún tiempo del pie acertado (del
pie acertado —armonioso— de mi verso; de mi mismo pie, acertado pues a
ti se dirige para cantarte; del pie del peregrino, héroe de mi poema, acertado
porque a ti se consagra) —deja que, tendido tú sobre la hierba, llegue yo a
cantarte mis versos—, déjate hallar de este pie que ha dedicado o con-
sagrado sus pasos a la real cadena que orna tu escudo.

33. Que la prisión, o nudo generoso y suave, de esta cadena, honre al
que, siendo libre, fue perseguido de la fortuna, porque así la Musa Euterpe,
mi humilde musa lírica, agradecida a tu protección, dará su dulce y canoro
instrumento, la flauta, a los aires —publicará tus alabanzas con dulces
versos— aunque calle la trompa de la Fama.

[1. All these verses of poetry, dictated by a sweet muse, are the steps of a
wandering pilgrim, steps and verses, some lost in confused solitude, others
inspired. Oh noble Duke! who, surrounded by the multitude of javelins of
your hunters (javelins that simulate a wall of fir shafts, crowned as though by
diamond parapets, by shining and sharp iron tips), you who are beating the
mountains (which, covered with their armament of snow, instill fear in
heaven: because the latter, remembering its ancient battle with the Giants,
sons of the Earth, fears that these very high mountains may be other new
Giants, now of crystal, because of the snow that covers them), mountains
where the hunting horn, repeated by the echoes, keeps putting within your
reach wild beasts that, once dead, stretched out on the earth, tint the ground
with their blood; and asking of the ground monstrous boundaries [in which
to lie]—being so many in number that they hardly fit upon it—they end up
staining with bloody foam the waters of the river Tormes next to which they
[the hunters] are hunting,

13. oh noble Duke! lean against an ash tree the ash of your javelin,
whose point will continue dripping blood, which in a short time will have
stained red the snow covering the ground, and while the careful hunters are
hanging (according to ancient venatic custom) from the sturdy oaks and the
lofty pines (trees that almost manage to compete in height with the cliffs) the
trophies of the hunt, perhaps the frightful head of some bear that, transfixed
by your shining javelin, seemed to want to kiss, grateful to your hand, the
shaft of the very weapon that killed him,

26. oh illustrious Duke! with your arms laid down, taking as a royal
canopy a sacred oak or, instead of the majestic seat that corresponds to your
exalted station, the high edge of some spring in whose waters you placate
your ardent weariness, allow your limbs to rest on the lawn thickly covered
with grass and allow yourself for a while to be found by the sure foot (by the
sure, that is, harmonious foot of my lines; by my own foot, sure because it
is to you to whom I address my song; by the foot of the pilgrim, the hero of
my poem, sure because it is dedicated to you)—allow me to approach you,
to sing my verses to you as you lie upon the grass, allow yourself to be found
by this foot, which has dedicated or consecrated its steps to the royal chain
that decorates your shield.

33. May captivity, oh generous and gentle knot, honor him who, being free, was persecuted by fortune, because thus the Muse Euterpe, my humble lyric muse, grateful for your protection, will sound her sweet and mellifluous instrument, the flute, into the wind—will proclaim your praises with sweet verses—although the trumpet of Fame may remain silent.]

The reader is struck immediately by the difficulty of the grammatical construction, which, like Latin and Greek periodic structure, must be "reconstituted." But this reconstruction does lead somewhere, and we are able to make our way forward to a clear overview of the central syntactical order once the subsidiary branches have been thrust aside: Dámaso Alonso notes the "very complicated, but perfectly orchestrated and intelligible sentence development."[2] I would say that, as we enter this thicket of sentence parts, we are drawn into a tangled net of forces and correspondences that the poet would have us unravel: the enjoyment of his work is not one of serene assimilation, but rather of slow conquest, one that rewards us as we battle difficulties along the way. Presumably the poet did in fact intend to place his reader on this difficult path from synthesis to analysis, from complication to explication, from darkness to clarity, since the dedicatory epistle consists not only of the long and difficult period from "¡Oh tú" to "cadena de tu escudo," but also of two shorter stanzas, the introductory and closing quatrains. Clearly these framing units offer a repose and lucidity, which contrast with the convolution and complexity of the middle section, the long period. Fitted into this transcendent frame, remarkable in its brevity and concision, we discover a convoluted world of mysterious correspondences. A quick check of the subject matter confirms this pattern: lines 1–4 show the *peregrino errante* enter the *soledad confusa*; lines 5–22 describe the "confusion," the impenetrability of a natural world from which a *pie acertado* eventually shows the way out: it is the footstep or the metrical foot of the poet, who in lines 33–37 sings his song into the clear air (*al viento*). The syntactical convolution (with its variety of subordinate clauses, appositions, parentheses) symbolizes the confusion of a world over which poetry achieves mastery. The poet's errant course through his sentence-labyrinth—his disappearance in it, his discovery of the way out, his working his way out before our very eyes, his compelling us to work our way out together with him—reflects the very drama of poetic creation, the process of becoming master over the world and imposing order on it. The waves of the world again and again assault the poet, and one would think they would cause him to lose hold, but he maintains a clear overview and steers with a firm hand. The guiding thread, "¡Oh tú . . . ! arrima a un fresno el fresno . . . ! ¡oh Duque esclarecido! . . . déjate un rato hallar" [Oh lean against an ash tree the ash . . . ! Oh illustrious Duke! . . . Allow yourself to be found], provides an irreproachably clear orientation for the period, signalizing the victory of clarity over sheer abundance. The poet has mastered and tamed confusion. Poetry here becomes a battleground, a dramatic representation of the act of writing poetry, crowned finally by the victory of the poet.*

---

*The creation of poetry as a theme of poetry is a genuine baroque motif. Like the motif of the play within the play, it stems from a "reflected" worldview, according to which all action becomes problematic, and represents the high point of illusionism. The poetic work is supposed to come into existence before our eyes—an improvisation of the moment, as it were, with no interval separating the creation and the reception of the poem. In its illusionistic involvement of the reader, Góngora's difficult poem is thus related to Lope de Vega's sonnet to Violante, which playfully represents its own coming into being (a procedure that Voiture imitates in his rondeau to Isabeau).[3] In both cases the poet seeks to leave a trace of the process that gives rise to his work, as though that work should be the image of its production. The poet strives to loosen the rigid hierarchy of poetic forms and return to the dynamism that created them. Compare with this my comment below on the poem's chapter title, _soledades_.

The poet's choice of the _silva_, with its lines of different length variably arranged, is hardly random. _Silva_, after all, means "medley" [_verworrenes Material_] in Latin. This intrinsically disordered form, here with an odd number of lines (37), several imperfect rhymes (_breve_: _nieve_; _cielo_: _suelo_; _instrumento_: _viento_), and even an occasional absence of rhyme, is nevertheless held tightly in bounds by virtue of its rigorous grammatical structure and the concentrated power of its individual verses.

This battle of the poet with the world can also be found in the poem's motifs. The duke roaming through his vast hunting grounds should let himself be found by the poet (" déjate un rato hallar del pie acertado") and should listen in repose ("entregados tus miembros al reposo") to his words. Poetry disseminates tranquillity and triumphs over intrepid action. Poetry "calms in its waves thirsting toil"; it overtakes and retrieves life in its haste. But poetry is not simply repose: writing poetry also means losing one's way, entering the *soledad confusa*. In the very first lines we hear resonate the inner antinomy that tears at the heart of poetry (which in turn, as I have said, is set in opposition to life). The straying steps of the poet are his verses. What from his point of view are groping, hesitant trials are for the reader or listener completed verses. Hence, for the poet, the composition of poetry is a to-and-fro shuttling between restless wandering and definitive shaping. This dual perspective accounts for the identification of *pasos* with *versos* and for the ambiguous isocolon: "en soledad confusa perdidos unos {pasos?}, otros {versos?} inspirados" [some {steps?} lost in confused solitude, others {verses?} inspired]. By virtue of this syntactic ambiguity, the poet hints at the dual nature of the act of poetic creation. At the same time, through the conflict between the tightly closed verse form ("perdidos unos, otros inspirados," with the chiasmus in the final line) and the open-ended content (*soledad confusa*, i.e., something vague), and that between words that connote contradictory meanings (*dictó versos*—very precise; *pasos de un peregrino son errante*—very vague!), he discloses the inner dialectic involved in the writing of poetry. The ambivalent symbolism of the steps, which are at the same time the verses of the poem, comes across in the "sure foot" (30) taking "wandering steps," where *foot* itself has a double meaning: (1) "metrical foot," in other words, something precise and self-enclosed, and (2) "step," which fits more with *errantes pasos*. And the ambiguity of the poetic act becomes evident once more in the *cadena* [chain] of the duke's coat of arms, to which the poet is chained in his act of homage but which becomes a *süave, generoso nudo* [knot] because the poet is driven by *libertad* [freedom] to dedicate his instrument to the duke's glory. If, earlier, the writing of poetry appeared as a dialectic between errant wandering and the imposition of form, here it reveals itself in both its freedom and lack of freedom. With a word smacking of freedom, *viento* [wind], the poem ends. The dialectical principle that the poet treasures colors the entire poem in two paradoxically separate hues, with the first color neutralizing the second (*pie acertado–errantes pasos*; *cadena–libertad*). But ultimately the poet's apotheosis is complete: the steps of the wanderer in the forest have been transformed into the flight of the song in the wind.

We should note, moreover, how the homage—the poem's theme—is glossed over, forced discreetly into the background and, as it were, "surmounted." As he writes, the poet shows us the process of overcoming not only the difficulties of giving artistic form to matter but also difficulties inherent in his specific subject matter. He loosens the chain that binds him to the emperor's coat of arms and is free (emblematic poetry, the literary perspective of the *blason*, resonates only faintly here). A dedicatory piece must effectively work with exaggeration and extravagant adulation. But while the Duke of Béjar really does loom larger than life—a victorious Nimrod, the tamer of beasts, the subjugator of nature (*bates los montes*)—he, the man of action, is at this point the one to bow down before poetry and the man who creates it. And the grandeur of his figure is revealed, but at the same time hidden or "draped" ("lo augusto del dosel"; "lo majestuoso del sitïal a tu deidad debido—, ¡oh Duque esclarecido!"; "tu piedad"; His Majesty's coat of arms; "fama"; etc.). How cleverly are these exaggerated expressions pressed into a modest corner of the poet's speech! The epithets *majestuoso, augusto, esclarecido* are not entirely in the foreground but are actually only tacked on. *Tu deidad, tu piedad* may be grandiose, but they are also pale abstractions. They are little more than circumlocutions for "you," and are, moreover, embedded in participial clauses. In the phrase "supla . . . lo augusto del dosel" [may the majesty of the canopy be provided by], we are not shown the real heaven of the throne, but rather a substitute, the oak's sheltering branches (similarly with "sitïal a tu deidad" [majestic seat of your divinity], though here, to be sure, "your divinity" exalts the object of the eulogy in a more suggestive and playful manner). The coat of arms, the *cadena*, becomes a freely established "bond"; and ¡oh Duque esclarecido!—the "destination" to which the poem is addressed, following the introductory fragment of line 5 (¡*Oh tú!*)—is fully and clearly revealed only in line 26, which stands out by virtue of its brevity. Certainly we see the duke at the pinnacle of his hunting glory, but this image is embedded in the whole of the homage. He does not stand forth as an independent figure whom one addresses (I am almost tempted to say, colloquially, before whom one "pours it on"). In return for his poetic achievement, the poet demands of his duke an attentive ear (albeit only for *un rato*—the hunting spear was leaned against the oak for only a few moments): the duke owes honor (*honre*) to the poet who, acting on his own free will, has conquered him. And shortly before closing, the poet reminds us that his song will be a tempered, gentle one (*dulce*, l. 36, exactly as before in l. 2; between these two *dulce*s of poetry is harnessed the immeasurable expanse of the world; see the first *Soledad*,

l. 14: "de Arión dulce instrumento"). In the end the sweet tones of the poet's flute sound clearly in the wind above the fanfare trumpeted to the duke's glory. It is a triumph of gentle poetry over harsh noise, a triumph of the poet over worldly grandeur, a triumph, finally, of restraint and of *sosiego* over ostentatious majesty. Witness the muting of the all-too-loud "trompa de la fama"* and the discreet litotes "el de grama césped no desnudo" [the turf not bare of grass].

---

* My interpretation, unlike Dámaso Alonso's, is not "although the trumpet of fame falls silent," but rather "if not the trumpet of fame (as would be appropriate), then at least the flute." It would be impolite of the poet to deny the prince the trumpet of fame. On the contrary, he concedes that he has earned it, but he would offer his humble flute as a poor substitute. What is involved here is one of Góngora's favorite constructs: *if not B, then A*, which Dámaso Alonso has studied masterfully.[4]

A proud modesty adorns this poet, who with his gentle lyre cannot match the trumpet in creating a powerful impression. Aware of such limits, he emphasizes the melodious, insinuating power of his song and calls down the Muse Euterpe to serve him, but only because she is beholden to the duke—a proud way of doing homage! In the end the duke, too, as a listener, is drawn into the *soledad*, into that loneliness of the natural world which the poet seeks and which is to become the central motif of his poetry. Fleeing from the *confusión* of life, the solitary poet creates a solitary hero who confronts nature and natural human beings with his lyrically yearning song. The entire thematic range of the *soledades* is anticipated here. We see the isolated poet surrounded by nature. We see his exalted, solemn listener. And we see a solitary hero who allows nature to pass before him without intervening in her realm and who watches with stoic, "unepical" tranquillity as images dance by his gaze without bringing any "forward movement of the plot." Góngora transforms the *soledad* of nature into *soledad canora* or *sonora*; his poetry sings and rings of solitude. This solitude of nature gives rise to a twofold victory: nature is subdued both through the hunt and through poetry. And the hunt itself yields before poetry—in the very moment that poetry is glorifying it.

To summarize what we have said, the dedicatory poem celebrates and represents in itself the domination of the world through art. Within the reposeful order of his sentence structure, his metrical form, and his distinctive perspectives, the baroque poet holds immense forces imprisoned—forces that are wild, vague, drastic, and obscure. The clarity of poetic form contains within it the "unfermented" plenitude of the world.*

---

* Seen in this light, Góngora's increasing tendency to write obscure poetry as he grew older becomes more understandable; late in life Góngora moved toward a poetry that was against the world. In fact, this growing violence can be observed in the smallest details. Compare, for example, the intensification of a *fatigar la selva* [fatigue the forest] in the very similar *Dedicatoria* of the *Polifemo* to the *bates los montes* [beat the mountains] in our poem; the former is much more *templado* [moderate] (see stanza 2). *Polifemo*'s introductory poem should itself be viewed as an artistically refined rigidification [*Verkrämpfung*] ("culta si aunque bucolica Talia," stanza 1) [cultivated if also bucolic Thalia] of Garcilaso de la Vega's *Egloga primera*. By the same token we can understand how the author of the simple, folkloric *Letrillas* and *Romances* could compose the obscure pieces. The former reflect an achieved mastery of the world; the latter present the difficult struggle for that mastery. Poetry reveals its mastery in the former case *over* nature, in the latter case *against* nature.

In order for us to feel the iron control of this art, the plenitude of the world must swell up in all its violence and in the power and the multitude of its forms; a teeming profusion of shapes, a polymorphic mass of images foam up in the "hunting scene."*

---

* When I interpreted this poem with my students, it turned out that they were at first most powerfully struck by the image of the hunt; only afterward did they recognize the attenuating components that work against its violence. It may be that the dynamic, intoxicating elements have a greater appeal to youth, and especially to German youth. The manner in which we worked our way into the poem seems to me to have been methodologically correct. I began by having the students describe their first impression, and then I asked them to look for elements that might run counter to it. When one student responded immediately after a first reading, "What a very strange hunting scene!" we were actually already involved directly in the process of understanding.

The duke forces the beasts down and masters nature, but nature seems to resist, to rise up hissing and bristling, turning, multiplying, obstructing, and metamorphosing in innumerable forms. It is a thicket of forces which the duke must physically subdue and to which the poet must bring mental clarity. The mountains rise toward the heavens and terrify the gods as the giants once did; the wild dead beasts nestle against the ground in *términos disformes*; oak and pine compete in growth and height (not, as Dámaso Alonso thinks, in longevity; the epithets are *duro* and *levantado*) with the mountainous crags; the bear is bent double over the hunting spear. A multitude of colors play over the scene—the diamond tips of the lances, glistening spears, the mountains "de nieve armados, gigantes de cristal"; the ground tinted red with blood (*teñido*); the river flowing with *espumoso coral*. We even see colors transformed (*purpurear la nieve*); sounds are multiplied (*el cuerno, del eco repetido*). Just as colors can change into their opposites, so can forms be metamorphosed; one form spills over into another, things become interchangeable. In this artificial world, in this world re-created by art, the hunting spears (*venablos*) become walls and battlements; mountains become armed giants; the bleeding prey appears as foaming coral; the trees (*robre, pino*) are high cliffs; the leafy crown of the oak becomes the heaven of the throne; the flower trim is a seat; the footstep becomes the line of poetry; the chain of the coat of arms is liberty, and so on—one form "supplants" the other, takes its place, insinuates itself beneath the one preceding it. A world reshaped (*términos disformes*) submits to the human being (both poet and hunter). The transformation of forms into their opposites, objects in motion into objects at rest ("venablos . . . muros de abeto, almenas de diamante")—one is reminded of the forest of spears in Velázquez's *Surrender at Breda*—and vice versa (mountains into giants, trees into competing warriors, *émulos vividores*; *vividor* [living one] is even more "living," more vibrant than the participle would be), corresponds to the artistic "unfixing" of the world. The movement, the activism, of the human being is transferred to physical objects—"el cuerno, del eco repetido, fieras te expone" [the horn, repeated by the echoes, puts wild beasts within your reach]; "cuyo acero, sangre sudando, en tiempo hará breve purpurear la nieve" [whose point will continue dripping blood, which in a short time will have stained red the snow]—while animals seem to be engaged in an aesthetic performance, carrying out acts of apparent homage that, on closer scrutiny, turn out to be their own executions. Thus we witness a conversion of the horrific and bloody into beauty and serenity: "muertas al suelo . . . pidiendo términos disformes . . . espumoso coral le dan al Tormes" [dead . . . asking of the ground monstrous boundaries . . . they give foamy

coral to the Tormes] (Dámaso Alonso's translation conveys the
suggestiveness of the verb *pedir*); "del oso que aun besaba, atravesado, la asta de tu luciente jabalina" [of the bear that, transfixed, still
was kissing the shaft of your shining javelin]. At the same time human actions are poetically elevated to a higher sphere: "en cuanto da
el solícito montero al duro robre, al pino levantado . . . las formidables señas del oso" [while the solicitous hunter offers the sturdy
oak, the lofty pine . . . the formidable trophy of the bear]; instead of
"hanging the trophies on the trees," the hunter "consecrates them to
the trees." And "su canoro dará dulce instrumento . . . al viento"
(l. 36) [he will offer his sweet, mellifluous instrument . . . to the
wind] is a way of establishing a relationship between himself and
others; to give is more inward, more fully endowed with self, more
solemn than merely to act (compare the first *Soledad*, l. 29: "de la
rota nave aquella parte poca que lo expuso en la playa dió a la roca"
[that small part of the wrecked ship which left him on the beach he
gave to the rock], on which Dámaso Alonso comments: "he offers to
the rock, like a votive offering, this small plank";[5] similarly, l. 10:
"lagrimosas de amor dulces querellas da al mar" [tearful, sweet la-
ments of love he gives the sea]). The individual forms and events are
not unambiguous; rather, they are to be understood as mysterious
correspondences. We are in the midst of a *selva aspera e forte* [rugged
and harsh wood; Dante, *Inferno* I, 5], which might just as well also
be Baudelaire's *forêt de symboles* ["Correspondances," l. 3].*

---

* What we do not yet find, however, is the synaesthesia so popular since
the Renaissance.[6] A study of this phenomenon in the context of sixteenth-
and seventeenth-century Spain still needs to be written.

But this forest of forms that signify more than simply themselves,
of colors that blend into one another, of events that are somehow circumscribed or merely hinted at, is concentrated into a narrow space
of sixteen lines. The storming of the heavens by the giant-mountains
is squeezed into two compact verses. The crowded plenitude offers
an image of the complexity of the world. Greatness becomes, as it
were, even greater in its compression—Michelangelesque gestures in
a narrowly bound space—an essential characteristic of Spanish-
baroque grandeur! Laconic monumentality has something emphati-
cally controlled about it. Góngora's world, "mundo abreviado, re-

novado y puro" [compressed world, renewed and pure],[7] is renewed by virtue of grandiloquence and breviloquence: "Grand and laconic" [*Gross und Knapp!*] is his motto.*

---

*Góngora's art is an art "with closed hands," in contrast to the expansive, worldly manner of the Italian poet Giambattista Marini, from whom he differs not only in questions of sensuality. The restraining of sensuality in Góngora (we never find the word *lascivo*, as often as it appears in the *Soledades*, without some contrasting notion or disclaimer in the very same line) is but one aspect of the more general process of "subduing" that is characteristic of the poet.

Through this compression, the metamorphosis of forms becomes naturally all the more violent and shocking, but all the more convulsive and artificial as well; it becomes a performance in the art of the ingenious combination; for example, "venablos" = "muros de abeto, almenas de diamante" [javelins = walls of fir, battlements of diamonds]; "los montes, que, de nieve armados, gigantes de cristal los teme el cielo" [the mountains, which, armed with snow, giants of crystal, are feared by the heavens] (note the long commentary that Dámaso Alonso is required to give). Apposition is the external syntactic form of density and subordination; it makes possible the collision and purely incidental linkage of ideas that are basically foreign to one another (note especially the apposition, "émulos vividores de las peñas," l. 18 [trees that almost manage to compete in height with the cliffs]). What is important about the metaphors emerging in such juxtapositions is not that they express the essence of the object referred to, but that they reveal its suitability to identification with another object—in other words, not its essential but its accidental character. Hermann Pongs speaks of "fictional metaphors,"[8] and it is hardly by chance that Dámaso Alonso glosses the first image—javelin/walls—with "venablos que fingen una muralla" [javelins that pretend to be a wall]. This fictive, ingenious quality of the metaphorical and metaphor-generating identification produces the effect of an artistically created restlessness, an instability that marks this world and distances it from us (in his introduction, Dámaso Alonso speaks of an "unreal barrier between the mind and its object").[9] Mind inserts itself between us and the world—the mind, that is, of the baroque poet, who enjoys moving about among paradoxes ("purpurear la nieve"; "besaba, atravesado, la asta"; etc.) and who reinterprets chance and circumstance so that these become something spiritually meaningful (the coat of arms becomes symbol, etc.).

Moreover, the effects of unreality and restlessness are heightened through the Latinate word forms (Góngora writes *robre*, which corresponds to the Latin *robar*, and *lilio* instead of *lirio*, etc.) and the inverted Latinate syntax. The poet seems to toss words like dice out of a cup: "sobre el de grama césped no desnudo"; "pasos de un peregrino son errante cuantos me dictó versos dulce musa"; "su canoro dará dulce instrumento," etc. The ordinary syntactic connections are dissolved, new word-bonds are formed, and yet at the same time the energetic verse, with its rhyme, holds the units tightly together, and the ornamental epithet accompanies the nouns in an orderly and regular pace: *duro robre, pino levantado, solícito montero, formidables señas, luciente jabalina.* The appositions alone reduce the number of syntactic conjunctions and thus contribute to the obscuring of the syntactic structure. The absence of "and" makes the bipartite expressions in "muros de abeto, almenas de diamante," "al duro robre, al pino levantado" (in this case, at least, the chiastic symmetry effects closure), and "süave, generoso nudo" seem open-ended, inviting completion and reinterpretation. And the suppression of the article, which necessarily has an even more severe and mysterious effect than in Latin, where this actualizing word-type does not even exist, creates further uncertainty and obscurity. "Honre süave, generoso nudo libertad, de fortuna perseguida" (l. 33): one has to weigh probabilities in order to divide and structure the individual parts of the sentence. And, of course, use of the noun without an article lifts it to the level of the abstract and removes it from contingency, as in line 2: "cuantos me dictó versos dulce musa." The same kind of abstraction is observable when Góngora sets forth the *tertia comparationis* [third terms of comparison] in the neuter: "lo sagrado supla de la encina lo augusto del dosel; o de la fuente la alta cenefa, lo majestuoso del sitïal" [let the sacredness of the oak supply the augustness of the canopy; the high edge of the spring, the majesty of the throne]—one sees how the fictional metaphor establishes equivalences by virtue of abstract similarities and how this poetry, for all its plenitude of forms, does not attempt to grasp objects in their brute presence, but rather in their abstract pallor and distance. It is the same paradoxical scenario that we have already encountered everywhere: richness of forms and materiality on the one hand, abstraction and distance on the other.

One gets the impression from all the antinomies and paradoxes

embedded or mysteriously encoded in the poem that in the case of
Góngora we are dealing with a mystery that has been imposed upon
it (*Geheimnis aus "Drängung"*)—in other words, with an artificial
complication of a form that is in itself quite clear, and not with a
"mystery brought forth by an inner urge (*innerem Drang*)," not with
a creative impulse that is already in and of itself vague or mysterious
and that therefore quite naturally manifests itself in a mysterious external form (at most, one could speak of an urge to impose upon the
poem a particular effect [*Drang zur Drängung*]). Writing poetry is in
itself an antithetical activity, one that has to inject into the created
work its own dynamic rhythm. Oskar Walzel writes, "Opposition is
indeed the experiential mode of the baroque,"[10] a period that gives
artistic form to the problematic in a problematic and agitated way.
According to Victor Klemperer, the same urge to create effects (or,
expressed in other terms, "the will to the unusual and precious
form," "the tendency toward preciosity characteristic of the Romance literatures") can be found in Mallarmé's work.[11] More mys-
tagogy than mystery, more a philologically graspable form than a poetically unanalyzable art of substance, more an accumulation of
murkiness than an organic mystery, the mysteriousness of Góngora's
poetry is not the simple but unfathomable kind that we observe in a
German Romantic (Eichendorff, etc.); it is, on the contrary, a complex but perfectly decipherable kind, one that brings to mind the poetry of the *trobar clus* [hermetic type of Provençal poetry] or *poésie
pure*, these typical Romance forms of arcane poetry with their incorporation of obscurity and their games of concealment.*

---

* As Mallarmé puts it, "ajouter un peu d'inconnu" [add a little bit of the
unknown]. Wilhelm Michels writes of the "compulsion to play hide-and-
seek" in Calderón and Góngora.[12] In a lecture held in Marburg, Georges
Duhamel presented a brief outline of the "history of obscurity" in France,
which, however, ended up being a history of the kind of obscurity that is
achieved by way of clear formulations. Aside from Mallarmé and Valéry, he
mentioned Etienne Jodelle's sonnet "A Luy mesme,"[13] Maurice Scève, and
an eighteenth-century riddle. But in all these cases, it is a question of "forc-
ing obscurity," "obfuscation of clear states of affairs." The riddle conceals a
transparency; Jodelle's sonnet is an artificially complicated circumlocution
of the simple idea: "You, poet, are capable of radiating more glory than the
rising sun," etc.[14]

The concept of *soledad*, which starts from (objective) "solitude"
and encompasses (subjective) "longing,"* is forcibly drawn by Gón-

gora into productive creativity ("the incitement to write verse") and away from the unboundedness of the pilgrim's poetic path.

---

* The meaning "longing"[15] provides an insight into the use of the plural in Góngora's title and the treatment of one *soledad* per chapter. The fact that each chapter contains this word in its title (*soledad primera, segunda*) has parallels, such as those cited by Ludwig Pfandl[16] (Gracián divides his *Criticón* into *crisis* instead of *capítulos*, etc.), but I would not interpret this baroque usage merely as "a drive toward movement and agitation." It is also an effort to draw form into the realm of content. The passages in Góngora and Gracián not only contain longings and judgments; they *are* in their own right longings and judgments—spiritual actions, to return to Pfandl's formulation. From a historical point of view, these titles are related to the medieval dissection of a theme along the lines of *Quinze Joies de mariage* (itself an imitation of the "fifteen joys of Maria"). In these cases, the static retracing of a dogmatic given represents a claim to totality. It is significant that Góngora's worldly *Soledades* can no longer become complete. It is no longer a question of the static mustering of a closed circle of sacred elements, but of a struggling dynamism. The "fifteen joys of Maria" had to be exhaustively enumerated. The poet of solitude in nature struggles with his object, continually opening it up in a sequence of free variations.

The poet strives to emerge from solitude into productivity; he does not languish in yearning and melancholy. It is as though these Romance poets were vying with the mysteriousness of the world, outdoing it through sheer agglomeration and complicating distortion, while the Germans mentioned above pour their feelings of awe into the simplest of forms. In this Romance literary camp we witness the outbreak of explosive "bombast" [*Schwulst*], gigantic forms, strife, and finally victory. For this kind of art, "counter-realism" is essential, a procedure that brings into being a new artificial reality in opposition to ordinary reality and that unleashes unimagined forces but holds them artistically in check, handing over to the human being the reins with which to control them. We discover a parallel in the horse-and-rider portraits of Velázquez, whom one should properly classify not as a realist* but as a "counter-realist."

---

* Ramón Menéndez Pidal compares the *Poema del Cid* and the *Surrender at Breda* ("one looks in vain in Velázquez's paintings for some alteration of his subjects, however slight, whether for the sake of idealizing them or creating an effect: one finds simply a parcel of reality").[17] Eugenio d'Ors emphasizes Velázquez's "simple realism" and "objectivity" (though he con-

cedes a certain lyricism in individual portraits).[18] But a baroque verse, such as line 2801 in the *Poema del Cid*, "los montes son altos, las ramas pujan con las nuoves" [the mountains are high, the branches push against the clouds] (as opposed to the matter-of-fact verse in the *Chanson de Roland* (l. 1830), "halt sunt li pui e tenebrus e grant" [the hills are high and dark and grand]), already shows a relationship with Góngora's "montes . . . gigantes de cristal." José Ortega y Gasset has criticized the "notion, perfectly arbitrary, that as far as art is concerned the Spaniard is a realist," as well as "the conviction, no less arbitrary, that realism is the highest form of art."[19]

The portraits of the Conde-Duque, King Philip IV, and of the child Baltasar Carlos depict a horse—in dimensions larger than life—in several instances leaping toward an abyss and snatched back by the rider holding it in check. (Note Lope de Vega's very similar descriptions of horses, for example in *El castigo sin venganza*, act 3, scene 1, especially the equivalence between the man tamed by the power of marriage and a tamed horse.) The force of nature and human counterforce! "Passion and restraint, freedom and precept," says Dámaso Alonso of Góngora. Or, to put it in Góngora's own words, *cadena y libertad* [chain and freedom].*

---

*Compare with the above remarks Karl Vossler's review,[20] which distinguishes my short essay from the well-planned exegetical analysis by Dámaso Alonso, with its emphasis on the rhetorical-technical aspects of Góngora's poetry, and also from Walther Pabst's comprehensive study,[21] which pleads for a higher aesthetic evaluation of Góngora's "creation." Pabst, too, has recognized the central significance of the *Dedicatoria*, and his interpretation corresponds in several details with mine. My attribution of a new kind of importance to the isolated passage in its symbolic significance for the entire work of art will surely not be difficult to accept as long as we remember that we can easily guess the author of well-chosen passages. Certain types of examinations proceed on the implicit assumption that the whole body is recognizable in its torso. (See Julius Schmidt's suggestion for the revision of the *Reifeprüfung*[22] [examination taken upon the completion of secondary school]; even university examinations have adopted the practice of asking students to "recognize" an author in a particular passage; similarly, students may have to identify a work of art by looking at an archaeological fragment.) See also Ulrich Leo's methodological clarifications in his article on "Historie und Stilmonographie."[23]

Góngora's First 'Soledad':
Critical and Explanatory Notes on
Dámaso Alonso's New Edition

Dámaso Alonso has published a second edition of the *Soledades* of Góngora, notably enriched in relation to the first.[1] One must admire the application of this illustrious Góngora scholar, which has prompted him not to remain content with the results—remarkable in themselves—of his first edition, but to continue refining and deepening the interpretation, intellectual and poetic, of the *Soledades*.

I myself, as well as my students at the Johns Hopkins University, have accompanied him in this spirited task of deepening and perfecting the interpretation of Góngora, in order to contribute to a more accurate resolution of the "surmountable difficulties" and to a possible reduction of the number considered "insurmountable." As a result of our cooperative endeavor, we gather here some observations for the interpretation of the first *Soledad*.

Dedicatoria. Lines 1–4: "Pasos de un peregrino son errante / cuantos me dictó versos dulce musa: / en soledad confusa / perdidos unos, otros inspirados" [Dictated by the Muse, these verses, know, / As many footsteps as the pilgrim made; / Though some in solitude confused have strayed / Others inspired were born].[2] Dámaso Alonso interprets the last two lines in the following way: "footsteps and verses, some lost in confused solitude, others inspired." I adopt here Hermann Brunn's suggestion that "in confused solitude" refers jointly to "some lost and others inspired," and that *confusa* means "wild" (as said of scrub land) inasmuch as it is related to "some lost {footsteps}" and "confused, obscure" inasmuch as it is related to "other inspired {verses}."[3]*

* Karl Vossler's translation in his *Poesie der Einsamkeit in Spanien* seems
to me to represent a step backward:

> Die Schritte hier und Reime eines Pilgers,
> Aus denen freundlich meine Muse flüstert;
>   Von Einsamkeit umdüstert,
> Seelenverlorne sind's und geistgeborne.[4]

> [Here the steps and verses of a pilgrim—
> from which whispers graciously my Muse—
> all shadowed round by solitude,
> are lost in soul, born in spirit.]

The opposition between soul and spirit, which is not present in the original,
is a completely modern idea, and solitude, on the other hand, does not appear in its double role, as a labyrinthine but inspiring confusion.

Line 5: "de venablos impedido" [encircled by javelins]. Dámaso
Alonso translates "surrounded by the multitude of javelins of your
hunters" and, in *La lengua poética de Góngora*, also suggests the
possibility of interpreting *impedido* as "burdened or hindered."[5]
(Compare "de flores impedido" [hindered by flowers]; *Soledad* I,
284.) I would decide in favor of the second supposition, pointing to
one of those semantic borrowings from Latin so favored by Góngora, as in *traducir*, meaning "to lead from one place to another."[6]
Compare "impedire aliquem amplexu, equos frenis" [to bind someone with an embrace, the horses with the bridles] in Ovid (*Metamorphoses* II, 433; *Fasti* II, 736); "impedire caput myrto, crus pel-
libus" [to bind the head with myrtle, the legs with thongs] in Horace
(*Odes* I, 4, 9; *Satires* I, 6, 27).[7] The German poet Stefan George also
translates *umgeben, umwickeln* [to surround, to wind around].

Soledad I. Line 3: "Media luna las armas de su frente, / y el Sol todos los rayos de su pelo" [Whose brow the arms of the half-moon
adorn, / The sun the shining armor of his hide]. Dámaso Alonso explains: "his brow armed by the half-moon of his horns, the bull is
shining and illuminated by the light of the sun, so suffused by the Sun
that the star's beams and the animal's hide fuse with one another."
The image is of Taurus, the constellation of the Zodiac. Without rejecting the editor's interpretation (or that of Walther Pabst, "Seen
head-on, the body of a bull has the roundness and color of a sun, and
his horns form a half-moon"),[8] these demand that we depart from

the traditional pictorial sign with which Taurus is represented in astronomy, which is evidently a half-moon placed above a sun—in this
case, above a circle. This pictorial image is what has given Góngora
the idea of the horns-moon and the body-sun (which can equally be
a body that is *round* like the sun, as Pabst affirms, and a body *bathed*
by the sun, as Dámaso Alonso suggests). Here, as always, Góngora
sees symbolic elements in traditional emblems (as, for example, in
the *chain* within the armorial bearings of the Duke of Béjar, in the
Dedicatoria): since the sun represents the shape of Taurus's body, all
of his hide must shed beams of sunlight.

Line 6: "en campos de zafiro pace estrellas" [in sapphire fields
grazes on stars]. It surprises me that Dámaso Alonso should prefer
the first version, "en dehesas azules pace estrellas" [in blue pastures
grazes on stars], because of *dehesas,* "an immediate image, solid,
Spanish, Andalusian," and *azul,* "a sensation of color, direct, visual."[9] But is he not the first to have shown us that Góngora's world
is an unreal and artificial world in which local taste and style, the
Heimatkunst [regional art], have no part? That celestial landscape,
in which Taurus grazes on stars in fields covered not with flowers but
with precious stones, is something very much in harmony with that
unreality made real, with that "other world" discovered by Góngora
in which everything glitters and blooms. The change from *dehesas* to
campos is almost parallel to the change from *guardianes* [keepers] to
conducidores de cabras [leaders of the herds], as occurs in line 92.

Line 37: "y al sol lo {el vestido} extiende luego, / que, lamiéndolo
apenas / su dulce lengua de templado fuego, / lento lo embiste, y con
süave estilo / la menor onda chupa al menor hilo" [And then the gar-
ments to the sun he spread, / Which, with its mild tongue of temper-
ate fire, / Slowly attacked, and with a gentle style, / The least wave
sipping from the smallest thread]. Dámaso Alonso explains: "and in
such a way, with its gentle heat, attacks them {the garments} bit by
bit." I believe, with the additional support of the first version of line
40 as reestablished by Dámaso Alonso himself ("no sin süave estilo"
[not without a gentle style]), that in this case *estilo* has two meanings: (1) "style," "manner," and (2) "stylus," "graver"; this second
meaning explains the verb *embistir* [to attack, assault]. The *Diccionario* of Alemany y Selfa,[10] so weak in other places, has noted correctly that the lines evoke the absorbent and piercing action of a pen
in relation to ink. The fiery tongue of the sun, as it dries the pilgrim's
rags, is quickly transformed into a graver, into a pen that absorbs liq-

uid: this is one of those transformations of objects "before a drawn curtain," as when the cabin with its light becomes a beacon over a gulf, an animal with a carbuncle (ll. 52–63).

Line 46: "entregado el mísero extranjero / en lo que ya del mar redimió fiero" [The forlorn stranger, clad once again / In what he had redeemed from the wild sea]. Dámaso Alonso interprets the first word as "reinstated." Without abandoning this idea, I believe that it is also necessary to understand *entregado* in the abstract sense of "released to, given to" (compare *Dedicatoria*, l. 28: "entregados tus miembros al reposo" [your limbs given over to repose]). This is probably a legal expression: "to enter into{!} full possession of what he had redeemed{!}." Compare the etymological explanations in *Romanisches etymologisches Wörterbuch*, under *integrare* and *integre*: the original meaning of the corresponding Romance words is "to return in full," and Góngora takes us back to this etymological meaning. Compare also the observation I have recorded above concerning *impedido*. The legal tone also makes itself felt in *restituir* (to return, l. 36) and *redimir* (to redeem, l. 47). On the other hand, *restituir* and *entregar* form a group with the *dar* [to give] that I have already discussed . . . , and alternate with it to avoid more trivial verbs.

Line 48: "entre espinas crepúsculos pisando" [he trod the twilight down 'mid many a thorn]. It is pleasing to see Dámaso Alonso qualify as a "beautiful line" a passage of which L. P. Thomas still could say in 1911, "It would be difficult to find a zeugma harsher and more disagreeable."[11] I will cite, in addition to the line put forward by Dámaso Alonso, "si tinieblas no piso con pie incierto" [if I tread not on twilight with an uncertain foot], the quatrain of the sonnet:

> Descaminado, enfermo, peregrino,
> en tenebrosa noche, con pie incierto,
> la confusión pisando del desierto,
> voces en vano dio, pasos sin tino.

[Lost and sick, a wanderer in the shadowy night, with uncertain foot treading the confusion of the wilds, gave shouts in vain, took aimless steps.][12]

Benedetto Croce, who cites this poem in his article on Góngora, justly rebels against the transformation of Góngora into a Symbolist poet along the lines of Mallarmé (and this from a critic still unfamiliar with the attempt to see in Góngora a poet in the style of Valéry!).[13] I believe that with this verse one can demonstrate the extent to which Góngora's attitude differs from that of the Symbolists:

Góngora has arrived, through a process of gradually intensified refinement, at his paradoxical expression, and probably the paradox is
what has attracted his interest, whereas a modern Symbolist would
express at one stroke, with the same expression, the vague and unreal. Between Góngora and the Symbolists there is the same difference as between "difficult clarity" (this is the formula employed by
Dámaso Alonso, and I would add: clarity *made* difficult) and primordial obscurity.

Line 62: "Rayos—les dice—ya que no de Leda / trémulos hijos,
sed de mi fortuna / término luminoso" ["O rays—if not the wavering
sons," he said, / "Of Leda—then of my ill fortune be / The shining
boundary"]. Dámaso Alonso explains: "since you are not the fires of
Castor and Pollux . . . , stand, at least, as the shining boundary of
my ill fortune, let, at least, my unhappiness find relief in you." I believe it necessary to admit once again that the word *fortuna* has a
double meaning: (1) "fortune, luck" and (2) the nautical meaning of
"a storm at sea,"[14] so that the meaning that is in harmony with all the
nautical nomenclature of the lines that precede (*declina—farol—
ferro—golfo* [descends—beacon—anchor—gulf]) and follow (*norte
de su aguja, el Austro* [his magnetic pole, the South Wind]) suggests
a "second" interpretation: "rays, since you are not St. Elmo's fire
{=since I am not in fact at sea, but on dry land}, stand at least as the
shining boundary of my tempestuous life, of my tormented destiny."
And thus the protagonist would characterize the "nautical" metaphor as purely metaphorical. The spell through which the poet has
made us see the shore in the shape of the sea has dissolved within
itself.*

---

*Has it been noted that Góngora has a fondness for those metaphors
whose progression brings about a metamorphosis before our eyes, thus anticipating the method of Proust? See, for example, the celebrated passage
analyzed by Ernst Robert Curtius in the notable chapter "Study of Lilacs" in
his *Französischer Geist im neuen Europa*: "Le temps des lilas approchait de
sa fin, quelques-un effusaient encore en hauts lustres mauves les bulles délicates de leurs fleurs, mais dans bien de parties du feuillage où déferlait, il y
a seulement une semaine, leur mousse embaumée, se flétrissait, diminuée et
noircie, une écume creuse, sèche et sans perfum."[15] [The season of the lilacs
was approaching its end, some still opened in high purple chandeliers the
delicate bubbles of their flowers, but in many parts of the foliage, where,
only a week ago, their scented spray burst forth, there languished, dimin-
ished and darkened, a hollow spume, dry and without fragrance.] Just as we

witness here the gradual passing of the lilacs into liquid, so we see in Góngora the transformation of the sea into a cabin above the shore—except that Proust defines, through his metaphorical transformation, the inner life of a flower, while Góngora takes pleasure in exchanging the external forms of things. Compare the following lines: 44, "montes de agua y piélagos de montes" [mountains of water, oceans of the height]; 234, "armado a Pan o semicapro a Marte" [satyr of Mars or warrior of Pan]; 829–30, "coronan pámpanos a Alcides / clava empuñe Liëo" [Hercules / By Bacchus crowned, in whose tight grasp the trees / The other's club appear]; 870, "topacios carmesíes y pálidos rubíes" [the pallid rubies and the topaz bright]; compare finally what Brunn calls *Ueberkreuzung* [literally, crossing-over], along with what I say about the *kenning* in Calderón.[16] This instance is somewhat distinct from the type of stanza, marked by a startling ending, that Pabst has noted, and that begins, for example (ll. 952–64), with a young peasant-woman on her way to her wedding, and ends in a vision of the royal tombs of the Egyptians: in that case there is no metamorphosis, but a kind of *psychagogy*.

There is a sharp opposition between *trémulos* [wavering] and *término* [boundary]: the St. Elmo's fire trembles as if it were a ship, the *término* participates in the solidity and firmness of the land. The expression *ya que no . . . sed . . .* coincides essentially with the formula *A if not B* that Dámaso Alonso has analyzed so soundly in a chapter of *La lengua poética de Góngora*. This construction, which proposes as alternatives to the mind of the reader two similar possibilities, of which one seems more removed, is in profound harmony with the poet's ingenious preciosity, which offers his public a choice between several equally viable expressions, because his philosophy of language does not possess (or has abandoned) the idea of a single expression, a particular word that will express a given thought. The metamorphoses to which Góngora submits reality are revealed through a changeable language in which any expression can serve.

Line 151: "la cuchara, / del viejo Alcimedón invención rara" [the spoon, Ancient Alcimedon's invention rare]. Dámaso Alonso observes that the spoon replaces the carved cups in Virgil (*Eclogues* III, 36–37):

. . . pocula ponam
fagina, caelatum divini opus Alcimedontis.

[I will stake two beechen cups, the embossed work of divine Alcimedon.][17]

Just as the cup is of boxwood (l. 145), so the spoon will be made of the same material. Now, the boxwood spoon is a remnant of a primitive Pyrenean civilization. The alteration of the Roman model on Góngora's part is due, then, to a kind of "Hispanization" or "Pyrenization." I have shown that the Spanish *dibujar*, like the Old French *debouissier* and the Old Provençal *de(s) boisar*, "to carve" (then "to paint" and "to draw"), must have meant "to cut in boxwood."[18]

Line 159: "breve de barba y duro no de cuerno" [short of beard and not hard of horn]. Dámaso Alonso has: "{a he-goat}, of a small beard, and of a horn not very hard." The first version of this line was "breve de barba, si novel de cuerno" [short of beard, if new of horn], which was revised because of the idle and mannered *si*. But *duro no de cuerno*—does this perhaps mean the same thing as *no duro de cuerno*? I think that here there is a scabrous allusion to the eroticism of that young he-goat who has supplanted his old predecessor: *duro—no de cuerno* means, according to this view, "hard, surely, but not of horn," that is, "of a hard sexual member." This explication accords well with the condition of *esposo* [spouse] and of *triunfador de celosas lides* [conqueror in jealous strife] that the supplanted rival had enjoyed up until that point. In this stanza there are two motifs that the poet has combined: the sexual potency and the gluttony of the old he-goat browsing on clusters of grapes, both qualities obliterated by his death. The motif of his sexual appetite is subordinated to the motif of the vineyard that frames it. The death of the old he-goat, due in fact to his sexuality, appears as a punishment or vengeance for the damaged vines. Here, brought again up-to-date, is the ancient myth that explains the birth of Greek tragedy through the story of the he-goat punished with death for having eaten from the sacred vineyard of Bacchus. (The detail of the he-goat whose ὕβρις [hubris] extends to eating the clusters of grapes on the god's crown is probably Góngora's own discovery.) Paul Friedländer has drawn my attention to the following passage in Virgil, *Georgics* II, 375–81:

> Pascuntur oves avidaeque iuvencae:
> frigora nec tantum . . .
> quantum illi nocuere greges durique venenum
> dentis et admorso signata in stirpe cicatrix.
> Non aliam ob culpam Baccho caper omnibus aris
> caeditur . . .

[Sheep and greedy heifers feed upon it. No cold . . . has done it such harm as the flocks and the venom of their sharp tooth, and the scar impressed on the deep-gnawed stem. For no other crime is it that a goat is slain to Bacchus at every altar.]

The influence of the *avidae iuvencae* also shows in the "greedy kids" of line 300. In the last line of the stanza, "purpúreos hilos es de grana fina" [the purple threads displayed of scarlet fine], could the word "threads" correspond to the motif of "vines" and "vine shoots," with "purple—scarlet" corresponding symmetrically to the "cluster of grapes," in a synthesis of forms and colors?*

---

* This passage seems to me to indicate, in real terms, the limits of Góngora's art: in short, the "metamorphosis" of the old he-goat into dried meat does not have the poetic force associated with, for example, the mountain-pine transformed into a ship's plank (ll. 15–21) or the light of the cabin's lantern changed into a beacon over a gulf (ll. 58–61), and in this passage the disproportion between the technical display and the content that it expresses is enormous. Here we find a purely intellectual game concerning the relations perceived between flesh and animal, without tasteful intervention from the author or consideration for the possible aversion of the reader, whereas a Baudelaire would extract from precisely such aversion, felt by the poet and assumed in the reader, that *frisson nouveau*, that unexpected thrill of a spiritualization that transfigures the aversive. Góngora's baroque art is content to gild with a fictitious beauty a spectacle that is in itself disillusioning: the accomplished fact of the change from a being full of life to a food-stuff *"now* served in dried meat." Note the technique of the enigma: the essential term *cabrón* or *macho cabrío* [he-goat] does not appear anywhere in the passage (only *cabras* [she-goats]); the expression *el que* [the one who] prompts the reader to suppose that the subject of the sentence is already known; we must reconstruct the enumerated actions ex post, after having read the entire stanza. Brunn has referred to this style of allusion and periphrasis as "distended," in the sense that the words of the language form spheres around the center of gravity, "circumscribing" it, while the center of gravity itself (the word that is the key to the enigma) is not expressed.[19]

Line 281: "Vulgo lascivo erraba / al voto del mancebo, / el yugo de ambos sexos sacudido" [A lusty crowd wandered past, all free—as to the youth it seemed—from the yoke of both sexes]. Dámaso Alonso explains: "There walked from one side to another a happy and playful crowd of highlanders, who, as it seemed to the stranger, had to be all young boys not burdened with the yoke of marriage." I think that the youths who are explicitly male only enter the picture in lines 290–91: "flowery youth—one [of them]" (thirty "strong mountaineers"{!} according to the primitive version), and that in the lines which concern us the youths are of "both sexes"{!} and wander from side to side "lasciviously," that is to say, freely, and allowing one another intimacies. The licentious note is counterbalanced by the phrase "as to the youth it seemed": this is not a fact but a personal opinion held by the protagonist.*

---

*The importance of the *freno* [bridle, curb, restraint] should be noted in this poetry of subjection. See, for example, line 242, "mudo sus ondas, cuando no *enfrenado*" [silenced the ripples it had near *restrained*], and line 442, "temeridades *enfrenar* segundas" [to *restrain* further temerity]. See also the stanzas that are "self-enclosed": line 401, "cuyo famoso estrecho {de Gibraltar} / una y otra de Alcides *llave cierra*" [whose famous strait / Is *pent up* by the twin herculean gate] and, at the end of the *Dedicatoria*, "la real *cadena* de tu escudo" [the royal *chain* upon thy shield]. Compare also line 881: "si la sabrosa oliva / no *serenara* el *bacanal diluvio*" [Only the savoury olives could aspire / To *appease* the *drunken flood*], in which *serenar* constitutes the "curb" of the "drunken flood." There are few stanzas that end with an *opening* of perspective—for example, line 89, "mariposa en cenizas *desatada*" [butterfly in cinders lay *untied*], and perhaps also the stanza comprising lines 602–11, which begins with the "ordered" flight of the cranes and ends with the "winged" characters that they trace "on the diaphanous paper of the sky." Góngora is a poet who *withdraws* into himself, into a *solitude* that rejects this world to construct a new one, like the rosebud in line 727, "rizado verde botón *donde* / *abrevia* su hermosura virgen rosa" [As in its green and frizzled bud the rose / *Abbreviates* its loveliness], or like the young woman who is compared to this bud, "la que *en sí* bella se esconde" [who *in* her beauty had *herself* concealed]. In my view Vossler is wide of the mark when he questions the validity of the definition that I attempted to give some time ago of Góngora's art: *Bändigung des Lebens durch Kunst* (the domination of life through art). It is not merely the "linguist" in me who has perceived this subjection of the thing to the word. The conception of Góngora's *solitude*, exactly as elaborated by Vossler himself—that turning away from life to create another artificial life, simultaneously more ideal and more sensual than actuality—seems to me a triumph of art over life.

Has it already been noted that in Góngora, whose lustful imagination knows how to limit itself, the word *lascivo* is always counterbalanced by an opposing word that, so to speak, "bridles" the imagination? See, moreover, the following examples: lines 256–57, "lasciva el movimiento, mas los ojos honesta" [with lascivious movements but with honest eyes]; line 293, "cuyo *lascivo* esposo vigilante / *doméstico* es del Sol nuncio canoro" [Whose spouse, canorous *domestic* herald to the sun, / Wakeful although *lascivious*]; line 483, "cuyo número—ya que no lascivo— / por lo bello, agradable y por lo vario / la dulce confusión hacer podía" [Whose number, though for no lasciviousness / But for their sweetness and variety, /

The beautiful confusion emulate] (*lascivo* is negated by the formula *A if not B*); line 202 of the primitive version: "hacen sus aguas {las del río} con lascivo juego" [The waters {of the river} make with their lascivious play], which is followed by line 206: "engazando{!} edificios en su plata" [And, linking buildings in its silver force]; line 761, "El *lazo* de ambos cuellos / entre un *lascivo* enjambre iba de amores / Himeneno añudando" [Hymen began straightway, / In a *lascivious* swarm of loves, to tie / On either neck his *band*]; line 803, "*lasciva* abeja al *virginal* acanto / néctar le chupa hibleo" [the *lascivious* bee / From *virginal* acanthus sips the rare / Hyblaean nectar there]. In view of the opposition *moral—honesto*, noted above, I do not believe in a return to the Latin meaning "joyous, playful," as Werner Krauss seems to.[20]

Line 321: "Lo que lloró la Aurora / —si es néctar lo que llora—, / y, antes que el Sol, enjuga / la abeja que madruga / a libar flores y a chupar cristales, / en celdas de oro líquido, en panales / la orza contenía" [That which the Dawn wept—if nectar is what it weeps—and which, acting before the sun, the early bee (who rises to sip the crystals, taste the flowers) dries in cells of liquid gold, in honeycombs—all this the earthen jar contained]. Dámaso Alonso has: "The earthen jar . . . contained (in honeycombs divided into small cells of liquid gold) honey: that nectar which is wept by the eyes of Dawn (if it is true that the Dawn weeps nectar), and which, before it dries in the sun, is wiped up by the early-rising bee." I believe that "that which . . ." signifies "the dew" (which is only compared to nectar in the following line) and that "in cells . . . , in honeycombs" pertains grammatically (ἀπὸ χοινοῦ [in common]) to "dries" and "contained": according to a process of identification that is pleasing to Góngora, the honey is dew dried by the morning bee {and transformed} into shafts of light. "To sip the crystals" is placed very close to "in cells . . . , in honeycombs" to lead the reader's mind through this transformation of dew into honey. I believe that this gradual, expertly executed transition from one phenomenon to another should not be obscured.*

---

* Dámaso Alonso's translation-commentary continuously runs into the difficulty of having to change Góngora's synthetic and Latinizing word order. He thus "explicates" what Góngora implicates and complicates, and even though he aids our comprehension, he destroys the feeling of surprise and of gradual revelation that the poet produces in us. The editor evidently

had no other alternative, given the word order of modern Spanish. By starting with "the earthen jar" and with "another of the highlanders," we destroy from the very beginning the vagueness implied first in the direct object (as we later discover it to be) "that which the Dawn wept," then in the allusion to nectar, and finally in the metamorphosis of this "that which . . ." into something contained in "cells of gold" and in "honeycombs." The same destruction by the commentary of Góngora's enigmatic technique is found in lines 315–17, where the translation reads, "two more peasants carry on their shoulders a long pole from which a hundred partridges are hanging." In contrast, the original shows us (and this has been called, more or less correctly, Góngora's impressionism) first two shoulders, and above them a pole that "displays" a hundred beaks: Góngora's grouping is centered on the "pole," not on the "peasant." In the same way, in the translation of lines 153–62, the enigma disappears when the solution is anticipated: "they also serve him . . . dried goat's meat."

Line 379: The description of the magnet and the compass contains medieval ideas that should be brought out somewhat more in the translation. After having suggested an *amorous* force (that is to say, a psychological one) in the attraction of the compass for iron ("cual abraza yedra escollo" [as ivy embraces rock]), a familiar recourse in Góngora (compare, for example, ll. 221–24, where the ivy that covers the rocks is an "allurement" that time offers to the ruins), it continues along the same path: "y, lisonjera, / solicita el que más brilla diamante" [and, flattering, solicits the most sparkling diamond]. Dámaso Alonso translates: "has . . . the great virtue of turning solicitously toward the star." But *solicitar* is also taken in the sense of "to court a woman," as "flattering" indicates: the compass, a lover courted by iron, turns into the lover of the polestar, which exercises a power, a force (of "attraction" and of "inclination") on it. (In "estrella a nuestro polo más vecina" [the star to our pole most near], Dámaso Alonso does not translate the possessive: the reference is to *our* hemisphere in which the compass turns toward the North Pole.) The image proceeds and becomes explicit through the expression "atractiva, del Norte amante dura" [attractive, hard lover of the North]: the force of attraction (as early as Cassiodorus there is testimony for the phrase *virtus attractiva*) is, in short, love. Dámaso Alonso lessens somewhat the force of the image by translating, "it trusts in the *guidance* of this lover." This is a medieval idea, reinforced in Romance by the phonetic resemblance between the words for "magnet" and "to love" (in French *aimant—aimer—amant*). The pseudoetymological passage of the *Flamenca*, which tells us that the true lover (*amans*) is stronger than a magnet (*azimans*), since the latter is a composite (*ad-imans*), while *amans* is "simple" ("en lati / le premiers cas es *adamas*, / e compo si d'*ad* e d'*amas* [in Latin, the first case is *adamas*, and is composed of *ad* and of *amas*]), has been discussed by Santorre Debenedetti, who recalls the words of Solinus: "ut quasi praedam quandam adamans{!} adamas magneti rapiat atque auferat ferrum"[21] [as if falling in love{!} with a certain prize, the hardest steel seizes and bears away the iron from the magnet]. Guido Guinizelli's famous *canzone* to love locates its subject in the heart, as *adamas* is placed in the "iron mine." Some commentators translate *adamas* as "diamond," others, probably more correctly, as "magnet." But S. Eugene Scalia has demonstrated that as a result of this etymological confusion—as well as of the antimagnetic force of the diamond, recognized from Pliny on—qualities peculiar to the magnet have been attributed to the diamond.[22] For example, "l'aziman, si tot es durs" [the magnet, which is so hard], from the cited passage in the *Flamenca*, which corresponds to Góngora's "hard lover." Albertus Magnus calls the *adamas* "lapis durissimus" [a very hard stone] and says on the other hand that this same stone is also called *diamantus*, which "quidam ferrum attrahere mentiuntur" [some say falsely to attract iron]. It is interesting to note that Góngora, in praising the influence of the compass on the great discoveries of the sixteenth and seventeenth centuries,[23] makes use of metaphorical clichés that stem from the naturalists and metaphysicians of the Middle Ages. On the other hand, according to Eunice Joiner Gates, we may also note here the influence of a passage from Claudianus in which the marriage of Mars and Venus appears in the form of the attraction of iron by the magnet (and Góngora indeed mentions Mars).[24] But the word *atractiva* seems to indicate the medieval topic as well. Perhaps the idea of calling the polestar a "diamond" was also suggested to Góngora by the aforementioned etymological confusion between *adamas* and *diamante*:[25] the diamond-star would then be a lover who attracts the compass.

Line 399: "un mar . . . estanque dejó hecho" [a sea . . . left transformed into a pond]. Note that Góngora opposes "the sea," the Mediterranean, to "the Ocean, father of the waters" (l. 405), just as the ancients (for example Pindar) opposed πόντος or θάλασσα [the Inward Sea, the Mediterranean] to Ὠκεανός [the great Outward Sea]. Everything is ancient in this passage: "father of the waters" reflects both *senex* and *pater*, used among the Romans with reference to the ocean; "de su espuma cano" [white-headed with his foam] reflects the two meanings of *canus* in Latin: (1) "white-haired with age," and (2) "the color of the sea" (*Aeneid* VIII, 672: "fluctu spumabant caerula cano" [the blue water foamed with white billows], with the idea of foam associated with the grey of the sea). Finally, the Mediterranean pond recalls, as Paul Friedländer suggests to me, the passage in Plato (*Phaedo*, 109 AB): καὶ ἡμᾶς οἰκεῖν τοὺς μέχρι Ἡρακλειῶν στελῶν ἀπὸ Φάσιδος ἐν σμικρῷ τινι μορίῳ, ὥσπερ περὶ τέλμα μύρμηκας ἢ βατράχους περὶ τὴν θάλασσαν οἰκοῦντας [and that we who dwell between the pillars of Hercules and the river Phasis live in a small part of it about the sea, like ants or frogs about a pond],[26] which Marsilio Ficino translates "ceu formicas atque ranas circa paludes" [as ants and frogs around ponds]. Góngora has omitted the pejorative note that falls on the ants and frogs, since what the passage attacks is precisely the vanity of navigation. He thus reestablishes, against the device of Charles V, the *non plus ultra* of the ancients and the *non più oltre* [not further beyond] of Dante [*Inferno* XXVI, 109]. It is curious to see the Stoic and solitary Góngora repudiating the new conquests of navigation*—like the old man who raises his voice of disillusion against the Portuguese navigators at the end of the fourth canto of the *Lusiads*—and returning to that classical and measured Greek spirit from the fifth century before Christ, which regarded as ὕβρις [hubris] the attempt to go beyond the pillars of Hercules.[27]

---

* In Camoëns the voice of the venerable old man is lost, and the navigators who represent the "heart of Portugal," deluded by the vision of the Ganges, set sail toward the unknown lands that they are to discover. This voice, which plays the role of the ancient chorus when it dissuades the hero from reckless undertakings, conveys an echo of the Stoic imprecations of a Horace and a Statius (the parallels to Icarus and Prometheus associated with the "vã cobiça d'esta vaidade a quem chamamos fama" [vain covetousness of this vanity that we call fame] indicate clearly that they stem from *Odes* I, 3). Elise Richter, in her article on Camoëns, has noted correctly that the poetry of the sea was unknown in the Middle Ages, whose chivalric exploits were carried out on land.[28] Thinking of Tristan and Brandan, it is perhaps as well to refine this idea, in the sense that the sea was not a functioning character but rather a backdrop; and the Ulysses of Dante, who anticipates Bacon, should not be forgotten: "d'i nostri sensi . . . non vogliate negar l'esperïenza . . . fatti non foste a viver come bruti, ma per seguir virtute e canoscenza" [of our senses . . . choose not to deny experience . . . you were not made to live as brutes, but to pursue virtue and knowledge;

Inferno XXVI, 115–20][29]—an *intellectual* motive that makes Dante more modern than Camoëns and Góngora. It must be said that Góngora is on the one hand more radical than Camoëns, since in his view *all* navigation is in fact covetousness, without excepting (as Portugal's more Christian poet does) even expeditions against infidels. On the other hand, Góngora has synthesized the two possible attitudes—the temerity of the conquistadores and the prudence of the old man in Camoëns—in a description that is *sad* but radiant with beauty, I would say with a sad beauty, which, even as it condemns vanity, glorifies victory. At the same time that he denies the value of the covetousness from which all the glorious exploits are derived, Góngora adorns these deeds with the most dazzling and attractive colors in his palette—an attitude characteristic of the baroque, which gilds with beauty a profound *desengaño* [disillusionment]. The reader comes to understand why the setting of these *Soledades*, in which certain objects and images appear in continuous contrast—the sea and the countryside, the Age of Iron and the Age of Gold, scenes of struggle and of safety, of sadness and joy— lies at the edge of the Ocean. This vast setting is suitable for such retirement to a solitude that denies all exterior things (both the maritime vistas and, in the last analysis, the bucolic ones) and that is free to re-create them entirely as artifice: Góngora's "cultured Thalia" appears to evoke with equal pleasure both the voyages that she rejects and the rural pleasures that she praises.

Line 942: "cuya lámina cifre desengaños, / que en letras pocas lean muchos años" [Your epitaph shall travelers disillusion / Who in few letters many years shall read]. Dámaso Alonso translates: "and may the stone of your grave speak to those who are to come, disillusioning many future generations with the few letters of its inscription." On the other hand, Brunn has: "may the inscription on your gravestone, which will survive for many years and will be visited during that time by many people, awaken, through its humble and praiseworthy brevity, disillusion in its readers, who, before the venerable antiquity of the grave, will feel an involuntary eagerness to know something more about the men of an age that disappeared so long ago."[30] Perhaps "to read" may also convey the sense of "to show," "to give an account of" (= to say): "may your {inevitable} disillusions give an account in a few letters {at least} of the many years {that you will have lived}." This would seem to be a matter, then, of an oath of longevity alluding to the common formula "May you live for many years!" and referring to the oath at the beginning, "Live happy!" On the other hand, we seem to find here an awareness of the dark side of human existence that is similar to what we perceive in the following stanza with the mention of the funeral monuments of the Pharaohs (in a passage dedicated to the description of the bride, a radiant new phoenix),* and also similar to what we note in the mention, in the first epithalamium (l. 815) based on the pair by Catullus, of the scene (so discordant in the optimistic inspiration of the Latin poet) of Niobe transformed into marble and weeping for her numerous children.†

---

*Pabst puts it well: "The stanza begins with a village bride on the way to her wedding and ends with the funeral monuments of the kings of Egypt: truly a long journey."³¹ In opposition to Dámaso Alonso, he attempts to justify the passage by proposing that it is to be enjoyed as a piece of autonomous poetry: the poet surrenders himself to the evocation of the phoenix to the point of following it to its homeland and through the centuries of its legendary past. But I believe that there is much more than a deepening of the *comparatum* in this notably extreme comparison: there is a parallelism between the birds that accompany the phoenix and the peasant-maidens that accompany the bride ("a hundred maidens," ll. 946–50); in addition, the idea of the royalty of the young woman is reinforced successively by the royalty of the phoenix, the Nile, and the Ptolemies. There is, finally, an exact and *visual* analogy—as always, Góngora's parallelisms are born in the visible world—between the green and flowery lists or arena (the "palisade") toward which the bride is bound and that Egypt in which the wind passes through the great "expanses" that were crowned long ago by the pyramids: the great empty expanse serves as a *tertium*; the rural arena (later, in ll. 959 and 961, it is called a "coliseum" and an "Olympic wrestling-ground") is the joyous variant; and the empty land in the place where the ancient pyramids were raised is the melancholy variant (since in Góngora melancholy and darkness are included, on principle, in the outburst of joy, just as the infinite spaces of Africa serve to complete the well-bounded space of the arena). It is my exact belief that this stanza should not be considered as an autonomous passage but as a transitional section: the Egyptian pyramids establish the transition from the maiden-phoenix, on the one hand, and the "coliseum" and "Olympic wrestling-ground," both Greco-Roman, on the other. Of these two structures, the "shadowy coliseum," a massive and somber monument, is closer to the somber pyramids and gives way immediately to the clear, Greek light that floods the "Olympic{!} wrestling-ground"; the mass of the "feigned forest" is cleared away ("they clear the common . . .") and the sovereign light reigns, outlining naked bodies. Mr. Friedländer has drawn my attention to Virgil, *Georgics* II, 530–31: "velocis iaculi certamina ponit in ulmo / corporaque agresti nudant praedura palaestrae" [(the master) sets up a mark on an elm for the contest of the winged javelin, or they bare their hardy limbs for the rustic wrestling-bout]. And in the same way, the word "wrestling-ground" again prepares us for the wrestlers: there is a continuous psychagogy. It will be noted that the maiden reappears once more in line 963 ("Llegó la desposada apenas, cuando / feroz ardiente muestra" [And hardly had the bride arrived there, when / Two sturdy wrestlers showed / Fierce burning sinews]) and fades only gradually before the struggles of the rustic contest, as in line 1069 the pair of lovers reappears while "the prize hangs neutrally." Góngora is a consummate master of this kind of artistic preparation.

It is essential to point out that the entire wedding scene includes pagan and popular elements that had been sustained throughout the Middle Ages, suppressed and nevertheless preserved by the Church, which came to terms with certain pagan customs on the condition of giving them a Christian stamp. Margit Sahlin's book *Etude sur la carole médiévale* gives us a good deal of information about this: for example, the customs of cutting may-boughs, of "adorning with branches" the church, or of carrying the may-boughs in processions (each representing "a kind of wandering wood") were practiced not only on the first of May, but for all the spring festivals.[32] All this calls to mind "feigning a forest" in line 702 and the "trees that had feigned a forest" in line 958. Bear in mind that this "deceit of metamorphosis" or of artistic creation, so pleasing to Góngora (compare l. 2, "el mentido robador de Europa" [the feigned robber of Europa], and l. 680, "los fuegos . . . fingieron día en la tiniebla oscura" [the fires . . . had, feigning, made the obscure darkness day]), is inherited from the ancients (Ovid: "mentiri centum figuras" [to feign a hundred shapes], *Metamorphoses* XI, 253; Virgil: "nec varios discet mentiri lana colores" [wool shall no more learn to counterfeit varied hues], *Eclogues* IV, 42). But the Middle Ages also exploited the idea of nature as creative of forms and therefore "feigning": in Alain de Lille, Johan Huizinga has noted, without referring them to their origin, the expressions: the wood *feigns* the shape of a wall, the lark *feigns* a cithara, the horn strikes the air with a *feigned* wound, the cithara "nunc lacrymas in voce parit *mentite* dolorem, nunc *falsi* risus sonitu *mendacia pingit*" [now feigned grief in its tone and gave rise to tears, now offered a deceptive mimicry of laughter].[33]

The same observance of pagan elements is evident in the dances in front of the church when the wedding is celebrated: the dance with sung accompaniment, performed by the twelve peasant-women (ll. 885–92), is probably a carol or round-dance, according to Sahlin's definition; in Venice, she tells us, the betrothed woman completed a dance step when she appeared for the first time before her parents-in-law, and the Germanic *brautlauf*, like the *choraula* of Vaud, also indicates the essential role of dance in the marriage celebrations. The rites of fertility were performed by the virgins,[34] and Góngora's "hymn," as sung by the young "rustic muse," is permeated by the desire to unite the fertility of nature with that of the recently married couple. It is known that fireworks (l. 1082) replaced the gunshot intended to drive away evil spirits (witches, etc.). Góngora has combined, with all of this pagan-Christian folklore, the openly Grecian element of the "Olympic" peasant-women, the "wrestling-ground," etc., and also the Greco-Roman epithalamium. But I insist on emphasizing the substratum of *popular* elements throughout the scene.

†In the Latin elegiac poets there is found an exhortation to be happy, from the mouth of a character who considers himself estranged from the happy and tranquil life of the rest, which corresponds to the attitude of the hero in the *Soledades* (*Tibullus* III, 5, 31):

> Vivite felices, memores et vivite nostri,
> Sive erimus, *seu nos fata fuisse volent.*[35]

[May ye live happy and with thoughts of me, whether I am here or destiny choose that I be no more.]

Compare Aeneas's words on taking his leave from the Trojans (Virgil, *Aeneid* III, 493): "Vivite felices, quibus est fortuna peracta / iam sua; nos alia et aliis in fata vocamur; / vobis partaquies" [Fare ye well, ye whose destiny is already achieved; we are still summoned from fate to fate. Your rest is won].

These somber notes amid the nuptial happiness are very Spanish, very characteristic of Góngora, and very appropriate to the tone of the disillusioned and melancholy *Soledad*. This is poetry of *desengaño*, whose motto could be the sepulchral inscription (perhaps unknown to Góngora)* cited in the *Thesaurus* under *felix*: "Vivite felices quibus est data vita fruenda, nam mihi non fato datum est felicem morari" [Live happy, you to whom life is given to be enjoyed, for it is not given to me by fate to die happy]. Such is the state of the protagonist's soul.

---

* Compare the polarity of movement and tranquility that Góngora sees in lines 985–91 between the long jumpers and the prize, the dark "smock" which lies, impassive, on the ground and which is an owl with "slothful plumage," while the competitors around it are a "crowd of envious crows" that "swoop down." Slothfulness is confused here with sadness, since the owl Ascalaphus is the Cassandra of the animals. Compare Ovid, *Metamorphoses* V, 548:

> Vixque movet natas per *inertia* bracchia pennas
> *foedaque* fit volucris, venturi nuntia luctus,
> *ignavus* buho, dirum mortalibus omen.

[He scarce moves the feathers that sprout all over his *sluggish* arms. He has become a *loathsome* bird, prophet of woe, the *slothful* screech-owl, a bird of evil omen to men.]

Ovid opposes to the owl Ascalaphus the virginal Sirens with the plumage and feet of birds; Góngora instead opposes to the sluggish owl his envious birds, which pass through the air, modeled perhaps, as Father Owen has indicated to me,[36] on the harpies described by Virgil, *Aeneid* III, 216:

> virginei volucrum voltus, foedissima ventris
> proluvies uncaeque manus et pallida semper
> ora fame,

[maiden faces have these birds, foulest filth they drop, clawed hands are theirs, and faces ever gaunt with hunger]

that (l. 225)

> subite horrifico lapsu *de montibus* adsunt

[suddenly, with fearful swoop *from the mountains*, are upon us]

and (l. 232)

> rursum *ex diverso caeli* caecisque latebris
> turba sonans *praedam* pedibus circumvolat uncis,
> polluit ore dapes,

[once more, *from an opposite quarter of the sky* and from a hidden lair, the noisy crowd with taloned feet hovers around the *prey*, tainting the dishes with their lips]

—words that recall Góngora's expressions "envious" and "from high air," although Góngora, naturally, has had to omit the features that are repellent in order to compare his athletes with the harpies. Finally, it must be remembered that the owl was the favorite decoy of the falconer. The poet's eclectic labor, which combines the owl and the harpies, instead of the owl and the Sirens, is well illustrated by our passage. In lines 886–909 of *Soledad* II, the owl (also called Ascalaphus) attracts birds, which "swooped down" (l. 895), covetous of the gold in his eyes, and a gyrfalcon is called "a boreal harpy" (l. 906), which confirms satisfactorily my interpretation of lines 985–91 of *Soledad* I.

THE SPANISH BAROQUE

When Spitzer proceeds beyond the analytical interpretation of individual works of literature and their authors, he usually attempts to illuminate the large cultural entities of historical period and national civilization which they represent. This essay, a good example of the wide-ranging, speculative character of such writings, reflects Spitzer's lively interest in baroque art and literature and casts a revealing light on his deep personal fascination with Spanish culture. He recalls the intensity of his mid-life encounter with Spanish religious experience—a moment in 1928 when, amid the popular celebrations of Christian mysteries during Holy Week in Seville, he suddenly saw revealed in full clarity "all the abstractness of Judeo-Protestant moral teachings and all the philosophical profundity" of a Mediterranean Catholicism that properly understood the importance of the flesh and was disposed to find "the expression of the transcendent in sensuality itself."

Spitzer was later to express doubts about his enthusiasm and reinterpret his experience as a case of confusion between aesthetic religious sensibility and authentic religious conviction. But he obviously felt very much at home in baroque culture, and some of his most influential monographic studies over the last thirty-five years of his life are dedicated to its masters—Cervantes, Lope de Vega, Góngora, Quevedo, Calderón, and Racine. All of these studies build on the theory that Spitzer elaborates here: the fundamental aspect of baroque culture lies in its drive to conjoin the antithetical demands of flesh and spirit, this world and the transcendental order. The result of this drive is a dualistic art of unresolved tensions and dynamic struggles, an art that displays the splendors of corporeal beauty, love, power, art, and language, while at the same time revealing an insight into their insubstantiality, a vision of *desengaño* (disillusionment). Spitzer supports his argument with a variety of interesting examples from the painting and literature of the period and concludes by proceeding into the larger sphere of European *Geistesgeschichte* (which "untranslatable term" he did "not consider to be properly rendered by 'history of ideas'"; see the essay "*Geistesgeschichte* vs. History of Ideas" in this volume). The baroque should be viewed as "the reworking of two ideas—one medieval, the other Renaissance—into a third idea, which reveals the polarity between the senses and nothingness, beauty and death, the temporal and the eternal."

This essay was originally written in French and translated into Spanish by the poet Pedro Salinas for a lecture that Spitzer delivered at Middlebury College during the summer of 1943. It was first published in Salinas's translation in the *Boletín del Instituto de Investigaciones Históricas* (Buenos Aires, 1944), 28: 12–30, and was republished in *Romanische Literaturstudien, 1936–1956* (Tübingen, 1959), pp. 789–802, as well as in *Estilo y estructura en la literatura española* (Barcelona, 1980), pp. 310–25. For inclusion in this volume, "The Spanish Baroque" was translated from the Spanish "El Barroco español" by Stephen Rupp. To preserve the tone of Spitzer's original lecture, first names have been added in editorial brackets.

The Spanish Baroque

The term "baroque" was a vague word, without exact meaning, until about 1915, when a Swiss art historian, [Heinrich] Wölfflin, arbitrarily and deliberately gave it a new and exact significance.[1] Wölfflin's meaning of the word "baroque" was immediately enveloped in a small magical aura through the efforts of his most enthusiastic acolytes, and simultaneously contradicted by his adversaries. After twenty years of vacillation on the part of scholars, the word has taken on a technical value and is accepted in literary and artistic discussions, but its meaning is neither very exact nor very vague, and thus it must be used with caution. This is what happens with so many abstract words in a language, for example, with the word "evolution." At first they pass through a period of vague use; then there comes an intellectual effort that attempts to stamp them with a fixed and concise meaning, conferring on them a new *vis magica* [magical power]. This effort does not lead to a complete triumph, and what remains from it is a reasonably clear technical term, which men use to designate a limited phenomenon and to allow themselves to continue pursuing new verbal idols, which in their turn will not be slow to lose the splendor of their novelty. The enrichment of the common lexicon seems to run parallel to the impoverishment of the original content of the words. A kind of *desengaño* weighs on any attempt at human knowledge.

The word "baroque" was, at first, in the seventeenth century, a French word that meant *bizarre, fantasque*—strange, fantastic. Its origin is unknown. Does it refer to the baroque or irregular pearl, an expression known from the sixteenth century onward and undoubtedly Iberian in origin, or to the name of one of the Scholastic syllogisms, so much in decline in the seventeenth century? What is certain is that when an art or style was called baroque in French, it was to scorn that art or style. This pejorative was not applied to a historically defined art or style. Such was the state of things toward the middle of the eighteenth century, when a German art critic, [Christoph Friedrich] Nicolai, tells us that the French call the art then in fashion *rocaille, grotesque, arabesque, à la chinoise*, or "of baroque taste." In the nineteenth century the word was applied definitively to the architecture of the Italian masters of the seventeenth century, such as Borromini, in opposition to the classical style. It still implied a pejorative tone, since the baroque art of the seventeenth century appeared to be solely a deformation of the classical ideal, an ideal that was thought at the time to reproduce Greek measure and proportion. It was Wölfflin who, in 1915, in his *Principles of Art History*, removed from the word "baroque," still applied to the art of the seventeenth century, its pejorative tone by demonstrating that baroque art was not marked by a creative faculty inferior to those of other arts but by a different artistic intention, another *Kunstwollen*. Through a series of parallelisms in which he described, by contrasting them one with another, classical and baroque art, he succeeded in defining these two styles, which in his view were equally valid. If the classical painting of a Raphael is tangible, linear, the baroque painting of a Rembrandt is luminous, painterly. If in a Venus by Titian the painter gives equal attention to all the limbs of the body, the figure of the baroque Venus by Velázquez will be subordinated as a whole to an "emphasis," as if unified. The same unifying "emphasis" is seen in other paintings in the depth of the composition's background, toward which all the figures seem to be drawn. Baroque art avoids absolute symmetry and with asymmetry gives an appearance of movement to paintings of groups. For Wölfflin, the Renaissance-baroque sequence is a necessary and irreversible evolution. Not only in the seventeenth century, but at all times, a baroque form of art follows a classical form; linear painting is followed by painterly painting. And Wölfflin sets in place of the old critical appraisal—namely, classical measure, baroque exaggeration—the affirmation of a necessary historical evolution.

Other critics and historians began to expand on Wölfflin's ideas, following three principal directions, all suggested by the master's own work.

It was evident, for example, that the "emphasis" that tended to impose itself on each detail, or the characteristic unification of baroque painting or architecture, corresponded to the unifying emphasis introduced into life in general during that age by the Council of Trent (concluded in 1563), which, in opposition to the Reformation, tended to reorganize Catholicism through an authoritarian Counter Reformation, strongly accentuating the beliefs of the Church that it wished to reimpose. Thus the sense of life of that historical moment was expressed by an art that was exactly congruent to it.

On the other hand, the historians of German literature Fritz Strich and Oskar Walzel, drawing on the idea, so favored by the Romantics, that an art from a given age should cast a new light on another art from the same period (*wechselseitige Erhellung der Künste*), tried to apply Wölfflin's categories to the poetry of the baroque age.[2] And thus they attempted to prove, with greater or lesser success, that works of literature, and especially of drama, seemed to have an architecture analogous to that of a church—that Shakespearean tragedy is baroque and French tragedy classical, in Wölfflin's sense of these two terms. Even lyric poems can be either linear (classical) or painterly (baroque).

The third direction derived from Wölfflin consisted of finding sequences similar to that of the development of sixteenth- and seventeenth-century art in other historical periods. In particular, the art historian [Wilhelm] Worringer found antecedents of baroque art, so full of movement, in medieval gothic, and saw in the Romantics and the postwar Expressionists successors of the baroque artists.[3] Across the centuries the "gothic man"—an expression created by Worringer—joined hands with the baroque man, the *homo romanticus*, the *homo expressionisticus*, etc. Taken together, the history of art and of literature seemed impelled by great ebbs and flows—a classicism and then a baroque, another classicism and after it another baroque, and so on. This was also the point of view of Eugenio d'Ors, who discovered a fifteenth-century Portuguese baroque in the style known as Manueline.[4] In this way the words "classic" and "baroque" lost the narrow meaning that applied them to exact periods and came to be defined in relative terms: one spoke of a fourteenth-century Italian baroque and even of a Greek baroque, all to the grave detriment of a clear delimitation of the particular artistic phenomena.

I have outlined these efforts so that you may witness the birth of a myth, the myth of the "baroque man," which is as glorified now as the art of the same name had previously been reviled. In his theory Wölfflin had begun with stylistic features susceptible to observation and evident to the gaze of someone "for whom the external world exists." He had invented his categories, abstracting them from visual observation, in order to give art history greater objectivity, liberating it from the "sentimental approach." He tried to give art something like a historical grammar, taking art to be something suprapersonal, existing above particular artists. But then the German soul took hold of his *graphic* categories and extracted from them the myth of the "baroque man." I have said "the German soul" because this mentality possesses an innate necessity to take history seriously not only to the extent of believing that any de facto historical development— one that has taken place— was necessary before God (which reaches grotesque proportions in the Germans' acceptance of the *fact* of Hitler), but also to the extent of considering with the greatest seriousness the categories formulated by historians when they wish to fulfill their mission of explaining a historical process. And thus the Germans forget the aspect of human construction and approximation in these categories and deify or exalt to the point of apotheosis what would be for other nations no more than labels. It seems more than chance that words like "Renaissance," "Romanticism," "rococo," "Biedermeier" (the last of these is current solely in Germany) have been transformed in that country into objective entities, to whose definition and description more space is frequently devoted than to the analysis of concrete events. In this, Germany is the opposite pole from the Anglo-Saxon spirit, which distrusts on principle any abstract term. The Dutch historian [Johan] Huizinga has declared that the Germans alone have contributed more explanations than anyone else to the elucidation of the concept of the Renaissance, from [Jakob] Burckhardt to [Konrad] Burdach. This is natural because only the Germans, with the eyes of their soul, see the Renaissance as an allegory. I insist on the German character of this spiritual tendency, on that German necessity to allegorize, to mythologize a historical period. Wölfflin himself, a person of singular purity and austerity of spirit, was somewhat alarmed by the wave of support that he found in his German audience. And my friend [Karl] Vossler told me that he accepted an invitation from a Swiss university solely "to escape from his German students."

I believe, however, that the enthusiastic acceptance of Wölfflin's rehabilitation of baroque art reveals something more than these philosophical and mythological necessities of the German soul. It was a matter, although Wölfflin himself may not have been aware of it, of a change in spirit that occurred in Germany, as in the rest of Europe, after the First World War: religious values, once held in such scorn, recovered their preeminent position. There was in France, as in Germany, a Catholic renewal; in Scandinavia, in Switzerland, in England, and also in Germany, a Protestant renewal. And everywhere the art and literature of the Catholic seventeenth century encountered a more cordial response, because they were imbued with religious feeling. For example, [Josef] Nadler discovered that an entire baroque Catholic literature from southern Germany had been buried beneath a disapproving silence by the Protestant and deist German criticism of the eighteenth century.[5] Spain benefited in a very particular way from this rehabilitation of post-Tridentine Catholicism in Europe. The "Black Legend" invented by the eighteenth-century French Encyclopedists was dispelled, in part through the coincidence—if we can call it a coincidence—that just when Europe was turning an attentive ear to things Spanish, Spain had writers like Unamuno and Ortega y Gasset, who knew how to formulate a Spanish message intelligible to Europeans, advocating the return to a centuries-old tradition but without falling into a blind reaction.

Following art historians like [Julius] Meier-Gräfe, who discovered El Greco, and [Werner] Weisbach, who studied the art of the Counter Reformation, all my fellow scholars of the Romance languages, who had emerged for the most part from Protestant environments of a sober, ethical, and abstract spirit, began to study, around 1924, Spanish literature.[6] Karl Vossler, in his "Spanish Letter to Hugo von Hofmannsthal," studied the Golden Age; Ernst Robert Curtius, in the Catholic journal *Hochland*, the Generation of 1898.[7] That is to say, Spain's literary tradition was studied along with its contemporary rebirth, *Don Quijote* along with Unamuno; and these studies, precisely because they came from Protestant eyes from which the blindfold had suddenly fallen, were more penetrating than the history of Golden Age literature written by a Catholic of apologetic tendencies like Ludwig Pfandl (1929).[8] Before, nothing was seen in Spanish art and poetry but obscurantism, fanaticism, exaggeration, contortions, offenses against taste; now the deep Catholic faith that lay at the heart of that violent dynamism was understood. And thus it can be explained that for an Austrian like myself, brought up beside the ba-

roque architecture of the Karlskirche in Vienna, educated in Grillparzer's studies of Spanish theater and in Hofmannsthal's imitations
of them, it never seemed problematic that Mediterranean Catholicism (Spanish or Italian) should have found in sensuality itself the
expression of the transcendent. Protestants are content to see in the
divine fact something radically different that reaches beyond this
world, and, in accordance with its Old Testament fidelity to Scripture, Protestantism centers, in essence, on the abstract Judaic God,
who manifests Himself only spiritually and on rare occasions,
through thunder, through the burning bush, to Moses, and gives him
the tablets of the Law. Mediterranean Catholicism always understood the place of the flesh in the mystery of Christ's Incarnation, and
it is Spanish art that best expresses the *Verbum caro factum* [Word
made flesh], the Second Person of the Trinity. The divine is not postulated by reason alone, but also by the flesh of man himself. For the
intellectual, the great mystery (and so the French intellectual [Maur-
ice] Barrès understood it on rediscovering Toledo)[9] is not that there
should be above his own limited intellect a universal divine reason,
but that this human intellect should be bound to flesh that is human,
opaque, dense; this would be cause for despair if the divinity had not
entered into it, if the divinity itself had not become flesh. André Gide
has described in his literary works the analogous anguish of the intellectual deprived of his "nourritures terrestres" [fruits of the earth].

Permit me to insert here some personal reminiscences, since the
ones that I am going to cite seem to me very expressive of our age.
When I was a child and listened in the synagogue to the rabbi with
his venerable beard who preached the spiritual mission of Israel, it all
seemed to me too abstract. Why didn't he speak to us, I said to myself, about the hopes and sins of sensuality that must be the great
touchstones for the man of the spirit? He certainly accepted man's
spiritual mission, but he turned the problem of the flesh aside all too
easily. And when, on the contrary, as a professor from a Protestant
German university, I witnessed in 1928 the almost pagan processions
of Holy Week in Seville, when the cathedral spills out into the street,
when the religious confraternities carry through the streets superhuman Virgins dressed in brocade and laden with jewels, Magdalens
with genuine hair, Christs who show in their flesh the abjectness of
suffering, I was shaken to the depths of my soul by something like a
horror at once half mystical and half carnal; here, just two steps
away, I saw the image of the spirit's descent into the flesh. The divin-

ity was no longer to be *heard* in the august clouds of Horeb in Palestine, but to be *seen*, here, now, *hic et nunc*, in the Seville of 1928, within the noisy tumult of the wandering sellers of candy and balloons; and the songs offered to the Virgin from a balcony proclaimed the proximity of the divine to the human; sensual beauty could be put to the service of that divine aspect of Catholicism that embraced the flesh.

I well knew that some of those images that were paraded before me, in a heaven of candles, actually dated from the seventeenth century, or that their style at least was a popularized remnant of that art which had not been shut away in museums. Then, in the museums of that same Seville, I saw the Christ of Murillo who detaches an arm from the cross and almost caresses the head of the kneeling Saint Francis; and the blessed Suso of Zurbarán, with his mystical gaze, who rends with a stiletto the flesh on the right side of his breast to triumph over the demon enclosed in the flask that the blessed one is holding in his left hand. And I saw in Granada the head of John the Baptist modeled in relief, where the decomposition of death is painted and formed with such radiant colors and with such lifelike movement that it recalled for me Baudelaire's "La Charogne"; and that chest with its decorations of silver and of mirrors, which gives us the impression of the dressing table of a *précieuse*, when in reality each compartment is dedicated to saints' relics, to human bones or remains. I understood then all the abstractness of Judeo-Protestant moral teachings and all the profundity found in the religious carnality of Mediterranean Catholicism, in which it is impossible for us ever to forget that phrase "I am made of flesh, of flesh" which Count Keyserling heard a Spanish child crying out, that Spanish Catholicism which mingles the divine with the pleasures and weaknesses of the flesh.[10] Paganism it may be, but a Christianized paganism that extracts spirituality from man's voluptuous flesh, that puts to God's service even flesh itself.

And with this we have come to the center of the problem of the Spanish baroque. How distant Wölfflin's pictorial and architectural categories now appear to us, an abstract grammar of an art that was initially conceived as an abstraction! *The human, concrete, primordial phenomenon of the Spanish baroque is the awareness of the flesh coming together with the awareness of the eternal.* If the Italian Renaissance aroused the gaze of Western man, once benumbed or frightened by medieval transcendentalism, in order to fix it on the sensual beauty of nature and of man—on the Mona Lisa, on Venus, on Pan—the Spanish baroque, also open to the "miracles of the world," never forgot the transience of that beauty, the proximity of the transcendent to the pleasures of the flesh. For the Spanish baroque, there is no more than a brief step from the color of the rose to that of darkness, from flesh to death. Within it, the eternal is combined with the most ephemeral: the banquet of life cannot unfold without having the *memento mori* take its place at the table, and the *memento mori* enters with all the glitter of worldly pageantry. The spiritual fact always appears incarnate, and the flesh always invokes the spiritual. The two elements of this dualist philosophy have always remained separate, each invoking the other. The polarity is never resolved into a complete unity; the rose, although it may stand beside the darkness, is not darkness. The Spanish baroque will recognize neither the subordination of the spirit to the flesh, as in the rococo style of Watteau and Fragonard, nor the subordination of the flesh to the spirit, as in Rembrandt and many other Protestant artists. Nor will it recognize the dissolution of the two elements in a pantheistic spiritualism, in the manner of the Italian masters of the Renaissance, as in Titian, in Leonardo, in Raphael. The dualism is always there, present; the baroque theme par excellence is *desengaño*— dreaming against living, disguise against truth, temporal grandeur against transience. This dualism is present in the two aspirations of Murillo, the so-called realist and the so-called idealist; in the two inspirations of Velázquez, who shows us now the pageantry of worldly grandeur, now the mutilations of the flesh—in his jesters, in his dwarfs, in Christ—and at times the delicate, almost fading flesh of the king adorned with the radiant splendor of the monarch. It is seen especially in the "fetid" realism of Valdés, who paints the decrepitude of the human body weighed down by the magnificent vestments of bishop or sovereign: *sic transit gloria mundi*. In El Greco, the beauty of the body and of dress is impregnated with yellow and livid tones, with the green of ecstatic death and the tempestuous nature of Judgment Day. Zurbarán's delicate, roseate Virgin shelters corpulent, bearded monks beneath her splendid cloak. The spiritual and the physical are not united. That chiaroscuro from which the emaciated but shining bodies of Ribera's hermits emerge leaves no doubt about the irreducibility of the conflicting elements, body and spirit, as if the dazzling light of the Spanish sun demanded as a kind of complement the blackness of the church and the darkness of the monastery. It is beyond doubt that in these paintings there is an "emphasis," as Wölfflin understands the term. This is the spiritual doctrine that evokes the beyond; but that emphasis is imposed on a dualist polarity that is always maintained. Titian could surrender himself to the pleasure of patiently following the delightful physical details of his Venuses. Velázquez, accustomed as he was to giving a final meaning to his productions, had to gather all the different details into one ensemble, even into one painting, as in his Venus, in which no transcendent meaning appears. The spirit triumphs in baroque art, but the artist invites us, the spectators, to make the same effort that he has. That is the interior dynamism that baroque art communicates; one must extract the spiritual element from the mass of the flesh, just as Calderón's Segismundo learns to separate life from dreaming.

On speaking of [Calderón's] *La vida es sueño*, we now return our attention to Spanish baroque literature. Who has described more brilliantly than Calderón the situation of that prince in the world—the attractions of material power and of love, and then the terrible fall of that proud man and his comprehension of the *frenzy* of the worldly dream, of "the dreams that are dreams themselves"?[11] Who has known better than Lope de Vega how to handle the flames of artifice, the illusions, the splendors of beauty and of riches, of the spirit and of poetry, in his so-called autobiography, *La Dorotea*, so as to lead us in the end to the somber lesson that "all pleasure is pain"?[12] I remember that once in Istanbul I read with my students the opening quatrains of the third act of Lope de Vega's *Barlaán y Josafat*, where all the beauties of an exotic nature are enumerated: trees, palms, streams, etc. The enumeration culminates in a conceit about the brooks that reflect the heavens: "Aunque en él no nacéis . . . pasáis por el paraíso, pues entre santos nacéis" [Although you were not born there . . . you pass through paradise, since you were born among saints]. Lope de Vega is alluding to Saint Barlaam, who dwelled in those places. My Turkish students, all young women, had a fine feeling for the poetry, but they regretted that the Spanish poet had not ended with the next-to-last line. What they did not understand was the baroque phenomenon of polarity, nature and saints, man and saint. And Góngora, who multiplies physical beauties and ingenious verbal flourishes in his splendid descriptions, soon encloses himself in a resonant *solitude*, in a world that is surely not religious, but that matches the monasticism of the artist in its austerity.[13] Cervantes, however classical he may be, parades his fantastic hero through an imaginary world, to have him die as a good Christian, after having realized the vanity of his bookish dreams.[14] And finally the two supreme baroque masters of Spanish prose, Gracián and Quevedo, the former leading us to drink at all the sources of worldly beauty, youth, and power, so that he may then administer to us the bitter cup of *desengaño*, erecting before us the elegant facade of the palace in order to destroy it relentlessly:

Sobre él (el delgado filo de una frágil vida) fabrican los hombres grandes casas y grandes quimeras, levantan torres de viento y fundan todas sus esperanzas . . . restriban sobre una no cuerda, sino muy loca confianza, de una hebra de seda. Menos, sobre un cabello. Aún es menos, sobre un hilo de araña. Aún es algo, sobre la vida, que aún es menos.[15]

[On it (the slender edge of a fragile life) men fabricate great houses and great chimeras, they raise towers of wind and found all their hopes . . . they rest on a confidence that is not prudent, but most insane, made of a silken strand. On less, a single hair. On even less, a spider's thread. But even this is something, on life itself, which is even less.]

And the latter, Quevedo, who tortures his delinquent *Buscón*, placing him between two poles, which I referred to in a study with terms that were applied to the German baroque hero of the seventeenth century, Simplicissimus: *Weltsucht* and *Weltflucht*, the hero's irresistible craving for the world and his flight from the world.[16] The author himself (without surrendering to disillusioned railing, like the other baroque writer, Mateo Alemán, in his *Guzmán de Alfarache*) senses this polarity, like his hero, so that in the description of his delinquent's seeming triumphs a macabre irony always slips in, even in the epithets; for example, "prince of the swindling life," "the scoundrels' rabbi"—phrases in which words like "swindling" and "scoundrels" clash with the panegyric scheme usually dedicated to princes and glorious wise men.

How can we account for this Spanish baroque? Why did precisely this country feel in this moment of its history the interior necessity to oppose constantly those two poles, *dream* and *life*, keeping them separate? In the first place, this Spanish phenomenon is not solely Spanish. As [Helmut] Hatzfeld has demonstrated, throughout seventeenth-century Europe, particularly in Catholic countries, a parallel tendency developed, whether under the direct influence of the Spanish spirit or not. Artists like Rubens, Bernini, Barocci, the architects of the Bavarian churches portray, in the same way, the divine taking hold of the sensual; I have already mentioned the German Simplicissimus, derived from the Spanish picaresque.[17] Even in Protestant countries, in a fundamental way, the path of *desengaño* unfolded. I read *Hamlet*, some of Shakespeare's sonnets, the poetry of Donne (one of whose phrases, "For whom the bell tolls," has become popular thanks to Hemingway) as Spanish baroque products. But it is evident that no other nation has maintained with such energy and constancy as Spain the polarity of the sensual and the divine. It used to be said in foreign countries that Spain had no true Renaissance. A German professor, the "malevolent Mr. Klemperer," as Américo Castro calls him, speaks continuously of "that country without a Renaissance" which, in his opinion, is Spain.[18] The facts prove, on the contrary, that the Renaissance as we know it in Italy existed in the same way in Spain. Examples of this are the *Lazarillo*, Garcilaso, the Epistle to Fabio, Luis de León. Castro and [Marcel] Bataillon have shown that all the themes of the Renaissance, even Erasmism, were discussed in Spain, and that Cervantes, the prince of the Spanish Parnassus, was not the "naive genius" that he was thought to have been. But if the themes of the Renaissance all entered into Spain, this country gave them a special character. Vossler's formula is perhaps the one that best conforms to reality: "Spain encountered the Renaissance, but said no to it."[19] We are referring, of course, to the pure Renaissance, Italian and pagan, enamored of sensual beauty. Spain encountered the Renaissance, said no to it, and opposed to it a radical Christian medievalism, so that, although nothing could be more different than Villon and Ronsard in France, or than Dante and Ariosto in Italy, in Spain the road leads directly from Berceo—"Todos somos romeros que camino andamos, cuanto aquí vivimos en ajeno moramos" [We are all pilgrims with a road to travel, as long as we live here we dwell in a foreign land]—through the *Coplas* of Jorge Manrique to *La vida es sueño*.[20] In France there was a split between the Renaissance and the Middle Ages, a split that is observed most visibly in the history of the theater. Performance of the mysteries was prohibited in 1548, and the Pléiade first appears in the history of poetry in 1549. From two different nations two different kinds of art were born. In Spain the sacramental drama lasts throughout the Golden Age, and even far beyond. A persistent medievalism and a recently arrived Renaissance combine and engender a hybrid creature, composed of *Weltsucht* and *Weltflucht*, of beautiful Renaissance dreams and medieval disillusion, of sensory illusions and macabre disillusions. And in the Spanish *comedia* the swords and sumptuous apparel can, at any moment, disappear, giving way to the penitent's scourge and the monk's habit.

The polarity of the baroque is like the conflict of two successive periods transferred to the Spanish national spirit on a plane of contemporaneousness. Baroque art cannot be imagined without medieval transcendentalism, or without the sensual life of the Renaissance, without the macabre dance and the bacchanal. In that way Spain discovered how to relive one of the fundamental aspects of Christianity: the incarnation of the divine and the resignation to the flesh of that divine personage. It must be said that even the stylistic features that we tend to consider most characteristic of Góngora, of Quevedo, and I would say even of Lope de Vega, *conceptismo* and *culteranismo*, are in essence *medieval* features of style. If they display greater brilliance in the Golden Age, it is because of the sensual beauties that the Renaissance has added, inserting them into the old patterns. *Conceptismo* is the more important of the two. Now, the idea of playing with verbal conceits is one of the pleasures assumed by the Christian soul, in its awareness that the reality of this world is infused by another reality, so that the "play on words" is a form of play that the transcendent allows itself to enjoy with the world here below, since it is God alone who knows the true meaning of the words. In the Fathers of the Church, particularly in Tertullian and in Saint Augustine, wordplay abounds. Isidore of Seville, Alcuin, Ramón Llull, and Dante also used the device. In the same way *culteranismo*, which employs words not in frequent usage, is based on the faith placed in Latin as revealing of eternal truths. I do not want, then, to fail to recognize that the abundance of life that the baroque poets invested in the use of these medieval devices is a new element. It corresponds exactly to the Renaissance element that is superimposed on the medieval base.

The French spirit pursues an opposing venture. With the Pléiade, with Rabelais, France encountered the kind of Renaissance associated with the flesh, but it did not come to know the true baroque. The drama of the flesh had less impact there than in Spain, and the Renaissance was soon transformed into a matter of morality and of knowledge, based on reason. (Even Rabelais is more inclined to reason than is generally believed.) In the name of reason Malherbe and Boileau disregard Ronsard; in the name of reason Descartes kills the Middle Ages. The sum of the baroque in seventeenth-century France is defined by the *pathos* of Corneille—who, affecting Spanish ways, transforms a baroque theme into a comedy of reason in his *Illusion comique*, by *préciosité*, with its fashionable and far from metaphysical refinements of language and its aspirations to an exquisite society—and, finally, by the group called the *Grotesques*, a timid group in which we find Saint-Amand and Théophile de Viau. The classicism of 1660 confronted only these three currents of the baroque, all very reduced and refined. This does not mean that seventeenth-century France did not pay its tribute to the baroque spirit. What are Pascal, Racine, and Bossuet, if not cruel unmaskers of the tragedy of the weak flesh? Those who amuse themselves by imagining what this or that great writer from one nation would have been had he lived in another may suppose that in Spain Pascal would produce a Quevedo, Racine a Calderón, Bossuet a Gracián. But those French writers of the seventeenth century dealt with their themes in a way that seemed to them most consistent with reason, although perhaps it was less so than they believed; the famous "roseau pensant" is a conceit in the style of Gracián or Góngora. But the decisive factor is *what they thought*: French classicism can only be viewed on the basis of reason. Bernini, in classical Paris, was a fiasco. The French taste in art, deeply imbued with Jansenism, went by the names of Poussin, Puget, Le Nôtre; it preferred the gardens of Versailles to the facade of the palace.

French classicism is a revolutionary movement—Gallic, in defense of reason, set against the way of Trent—that was established precisely when the Spanish baroque was making its triumph in Europe. It is erroneous to judge the Spanish baroque starting from French classicism, with the eyes of French classicism. This was the general norm before Wölfflin, and Benedetto Croce, who even today defines the baroque as the art that wishes to "astonish" at any cost, perhaps is not aware of how this statement reveals the French classicist within him.[21] It would instead be fitting to evaluate justly the voluntary decision of France, to judge its classicism starting from the Spanish baroque. We now know that two centuries had to pass before the French spirit, which had cut all its ties with the Middle Ages, would allow its romanticism, fairly histrionic in other respects, to reintroduce into its literature Spanish and medieval themes. In the pre-Romantic period it was necessary for the discreet and sensible preachers of the English countryside, bourgeois and moralizing, to supply Europe with the theme of graveyard verse, when in truth the theme of nights and of cemeteries came in a direct line from the macabre dances and pageants of death in the Middle Ages and had been treated with a baroque force of incomparable superiority during the baroque period in Spain and England ("Who is the beggar, who is the king?").[22] The Capuchin caves of Palermo, with their clothed skeletons, in the style of Valdés Leal—evidence of decay, standing from centuries back, for the modern tourist—are remains of the baroque age in which pre-Romantic and Romantic poets from countries radically divorced from the medieval spirit could no longer find inspiration.

We have now come, as I promised at the beginning of this lecture, to circumscribe the crystallized technical term, *baroque*. It signifies a fact of cultural civilization that had its apogee in the seventeenth century in Spain, but that radiated throughout Europe before French classicism set a barrier against it. It consists of the reworking of two ideas—one medieval, the other Renaissance—into a third idea, which reveals the polarity between the senses and nothingness, beauty and death, the temporal and the eternal. This polarity has been sustained, with a tension that is still unresolved, within the contemporary Spanish soul, in popular religion as in the works of poets and essayists—in the "tragic sense of life" of Unamuno, an Unamuno enamored of the style of etymological play, baroque and patristic, and in the metaphysical poetry of my friends Guillén and Salinas. Perhaps there is no "baroque man" but a baroque *attitude*, which is in essence a fundamentally Christian attitude, "to have as if one had not"—an attitude that is better understood today, in this age, uniquely torn and shattered, through which we are passing. Modern civilization, enamored of physical progress, offers surprising analogies with seventeenth-century Spain, whose poets and preachers insisted on the vanity of the temporal riches imported from the Indies, although the Spanish baroque artists did not refuse to employ the attractions of physical and material beauty to give greater splendor to the divine. For example, a modern poet with a Christian soul, an "apocalyptic" like T. S. Eliot, feels the tragic tension of a lost Christian past and an intolerable present. In his view the medieval and the modern are no longer on a level of contemporaneousness, as in the Spanish baroque writers; they are mutually exclusive. No way remains open to his integrity as a poet but to express the irreducibility of what was and what is: hence his dualistic baroque style (an insipid conversion to the twentieth century interrupted by the organ tones of a penitent Christianity); hence his yearning for death in the heart of that wasteland. What we enjoy in T. S. Eliot, in Hemingway, is that strong hold on modern physical reality—that "seeing to the life" beside which any classicism or romanticism impresses us as pallid—combined with the awareness that there is something behind life itself—death, more than anything else, death which is a genuine fact—and that God knows it. Faced with "the dream of life," we can no longer take refuge, as Calderón and Donne did, in an unswerving faith. Lacking something better, with an integrity that wishes "to make the best of it," we seize on that state of unresolved polar tension, we recognize the irremediable division without hiding it from our gaze. And thus we will understand the Spanish baroque, which was never deceitful in its play on the two terms of its central problem.*

---

* This is a lecture that now seems to me to suffer from a certain confusion between a religious creed and an aesthetic creed. Rousset's book has revealed to us a "French baroque" unknown before his work.[23]

THREE ESSAYS ON
DANTE'S 'COMMEDIA'

Although written on different occasions and with different ends in mind, these three essays on Dante are all informed by two central articles of Spitzer's faith—first, his faith in the total coherence of Dante's poem, and second, his faith that he can demonstrate this coherence through his method (that of the so-called philological circle) of moving between and linking the minutest details with the larger ideas informing the poem. In each essay Spitzer shows that supposedly extrinsic elements have been integrated by Dante to suit the purposes of his poem: the Ovidian metamorphosis of the suicide Pier della Vigna into a bush (*Inferno* XIII) achieves a terror and a solemnity alien to ancient literature, yet wholly appropriate to Dante's larger plan; the farcical elements of *Inferno* XXI–XXIII, though seemingly alien to the poem's serious larger purpose, work in fact to reinforce this purpose; the addresses to the reader dispersed throughout the poem must be read not as intrusions from the "outside" but as dramatically integrated examples of Dante's voice in his capacity as narrator.

As often in his work, Spitzer is goaded by the work of earlier scholars who, in locating Dante's sources or placing him within a rhetorical tradition, failed to demonstrate the ways that these sources and traditions function. The first two essays are directed largely against positivistic scholarship—for example, against Charles H. Grandgent's attempt to trace the stylistic devices of the Pier della Vigna episode to the speech habits of the historical personage Pier della Vigna. In the third essay Spitzer takes on his distinguished contemporary, Romance scholar Erich Auerbach, whom he faults for not demonstrating how the poet's addresses to the reader, which Auerbach depicts as a new creation within the history of rhetoric, are also unique for the way they integrate both poet and reader within the confines of the poem.

Similar though these three essays are in their purposes, each is also distinct for the type of scholarly contribution it makes. The first, which Spitzer acknowledged was developed within a seminar context, represents a close and seemingly exhaustive reading of a single canto. The second is a pioneering attempt to show how Dante absorbs elements from popular culture to create a work that is at once learned and popular in character. The third, by tracing the ways that the poet addresses his readers, helps place Dante at the head of a tradition of narrative in which the poet-reader relationship becomes a central component of the text.

These essays are reprinted from Spitzer's *Romanische Literaturstudien: 1936–1956* (Tübingen, 1959), pp. 544–95. "Speech and Language in *Inferno* XIII" originally appeared in *Italica*, 19 (1942): 81–104; "The Farcical Elements in *Inferno* XXI–XXIII," in *Modern Language Notes*, 59 (1944): 83–88; and "The Addresses to the Reader in the *Commedia*," in *Italica*, 32 (1955): 143–65. All quotations from the *Commedia* are taken from Charles H. Grandgent's edition, *La Divina Commedia* (Boston, 1933). This is the edition Spitzer used. Translations of passages from the *Commedia* are from Dante Alighieri, *The Divine Comedy*, trans. Charles S. Singleton (Princeton, N.J., 1970–75).

Speech and Language in 'Inferno' XIII

The most recent commentary on this canto is that of Charles H. Grandgent; below are the lines in which he sums up the episode of Pier delle Vigne and treats of the language of the canto:

The style of this canto abounds in curious conceits, such as the "Cred'io ch'ei credette ch'io credesse" [I believe that he believed that I believed] of line 25, the "infiammati infiammar" [they inflamed, did so inflame] of line 68, the double antitheses of line 69, and the involved paradoxes of the following tercet. It would seem that meditation over Pier delle Vigne, who dominates the canto, had filled our poet with the spirit of the older school, so that, either purposely or unconsciously, he imitated its artistic processes. Pier delle Vigne's epistolary style is highly artificial and flowery.

The suicide uses his freedom of bodily movement only to deprive himself of it, robbing himself, by his own act, of that which corporeally distinguishes him from a plant. Such a sinner, then, his wicked deed eternalized, may aptly be figured as a tree or bush. Dante's self-slaughterers form a thick, wild forest in the second ring of the seventh circle. There, upon hearing their sentence from Minos, they fall at random, in no predestined spot: they have put themselves outside of God's law, rebelling against his eternal plan. On the Day of Judgment they will return, with the rest, for their earthly remains; but, instead of putting on the flesh again, they will drag their corpses through Hell and hang them on their boughs, where the poor bodies will dangle forever, a torment to the souls that slew them. The pent-up agony of these spirits finds no means of expression until they are broken in leaf or branch; then the voice issues forth with tears of blood.

The like had been seen and heard by Aeneas in a Thracian grove, when, to deck an altar, he unwittingly plucked shrubs from the grave of Polydorus: blood trickled from the severed roots, and a voice came forth—not from the tree, as in Dante, but from the mound (*Aeneid* III, 39–43):

> Gemitus lacrimabilis imo
> Auditur tumulo, et vox reddita fertur ad aures:

Quid miserum, Aenea, laceras? Jam parce sepulto,
Parce pias scelerare manus. Non me tibi Troja
Externum tulit. Haud cruor hic de stipite manat.

[A piteous groan is heard from the depth of the mound, and an answering
voice comes to my ears. "Woe is me! Why, Aeneas, dost thou tear me? Spare
me in the tomb at last; spare the pollution of thy pure hands! I, born of Troy,
am no stranger to thee; not from a lifeless stock oozes this blood.]

In the suicides' wood, an outlet for the mournful voice is afforded by Harpies, voracious, filthy birds with maidens' faces, which rend the foliage.
They may well represent misgiving or fear of the hereafter—"triste annunzio
di futuro danno" [dismal announcement of future ill; l. 12].[1]

Thus Grandgent (like other commentators, as we shall see) explains the particular devices of style in this canto as due to an association in the mind of Dante with the speech habits to be found in the
writings of the historical character Pier delle Vigne. While not denying the existence of such an external association, I shall seek to establish a deeper motivation for Dante's choice of language.

First let us consider the treatment of the main motif: the fate of the
suicides who are condemned to assume the shape of plants. As Francesco D'Ovidio points out, Dante has borrowed not only from Virgil
but also from the author of the *Metamorphoses*: the *uomo-pianta*
[plant-man] created by the Christian poet recalls Driope or Lotis or
the Heliads ("Uomini fummo, ed or siam fatti sterpi" [We were men
and now are turned to stocks; l. 37]). This critic, however, points out
the difference between an Ovidian and a Dantean metamorphosis, as
regards the actual process itself through which metamorphosis is
achieved: when, in Ovid, a living person "becomes" a plant (feet
stiffening into roots, hair turning into foliage, etc.), there is a continuous identity between the person-as-a-whole and the plant into
which he is transformed. But in the case of the suicides treated by
Dante, there can, obviously, be no such continuity: it is not the
person-as-a-whole, an indivisible unit of body and soul, that becomes a new kind of being; body and soul have been divorced by the
act of self-murder and it is the soul alone that survives. These souls
bereft of body go to be judged by Minos; wherever they have
chanced to fall, there they put out new roots and grow themselves a
new body—an ersatz body of meaner stuff to replace the human
body from which they have been severed. Thus, in Dante, there is no
"development," properly speaking: the soul itself continues to exist
without change, while the life of the body is utterly destroyed—its
possibility of growth, even into another form, cut off: the second

body, the plantlike body, has no ties with the first, but is the product of a new birth that takes place only after death has severed the first body from the soul. Thus, because Dante is dealing here (as, indeed, throughout the *Inferno*) with the fate meted out to the souls of dead men, there can be none of that delicate tracing of transitory immediate stages in which Ovid delighted, where it is possible to fix that certain moment of perplexity when the living person is no longer human and yet not quite plant or animal; the most famous of all such moments, commemorated by so many artists, is that of Daphne *becoming* a tree (compare also, in the metamorphosis of Actaeon, the lines "Gemit ille, sonumque, / *Etsi non hominis, quem non tamen edere possit / Cervus*" [He groans and makes a sound which, / Though not human, is still one no / Deer could utter]).[2]

So much for the process of which the plant-man is the product: what of the product itself and its behavior? Here too Dante differs from Ovid: his *uomo-pianta*, in fact, is a composite of features drawn from both Ovid and Virgil: from the first, obviously, derives the concept of a person being transformed, though by a different process, into a plant (this is not Virgilian: Polydorus does not *become* the myrtle tree),* from the second derives the incident in which a plant is stripped of a branch, and a voice, though not that of the tree, protests in pain: from Virgil Dante borrowed a segment of epic activity.†

---

* And yet, although no actual metamorphosis is involved in the Polydorus incident, there is a trace of such an idea in the description of the conformation of the myrtle, "densis hastilibus horrida myrtus": this easily suggests a picture of the legendary Polydorus "shot through" with arrows; compare "hic confixum ferrea texit telorum segetes et iaculis increvit acutis" [Myrtles bristling with crowded spear-shafts; here an iron harvest of spears covered my pierced body, and grew up into sharp javelins: *Aeneid* III, 23, 45–46].

†D'Ovidio points out that, in addition to its exterior relationship with the Polydorus episode, this canto reveals an interior association: the guide Virgil, this Dantean character, is at the same time the historic Virgil, author of the *Aeneid*, and it is to his own epic poem that he is referring, when he speaks of *la mia rima* (*Inferno* XIII, 46–49):

> "S'egli avesse potuto creder prima,"
> Rispuose il savio mio, "anima lesa,
> Ciò c'ha veduto pur con la mia rima,
> Non averebbe in te la man distesa."

["If he, O wounded spirit, had been able to believe before," replied my sage, "what he had never seen save in my verses, he would not have stretched forth his hand against you."]

In these lines, which follow upon Dante's act of tearing off the twig, Virgil chides him for his failure to take seriously to heart the account of Polydorus's fate, as found in the *Aeneid*: if only Dante had believed, he would have been forewarned as to the consequences of mutilating the bush. I should add that, in view of the strong medieval tradition concerning the Christian potentialities of the *Aeneid*, we are justified in giving an even deeper meaning to the "lack of faith" for which Virgil upbraids Dante: the latter has failed to realize the implication of the Polydorus incident, that this prefigures the judgment visited upon a sinner by the Christian God (Virgil himself seems, for a moment at least, to have been astounded by the Christian replica of his Polydorus scene—this is the meaning I am tempted to ascribe to the line "la cosa incredibile mi fece / Indurlo . . ." [the incredible thing made me prompt him . . . ; ll. 50–51]).

As to the relationship existing between the pilgrim Dante and his guide, I believe that D'Ovidio puts a false emphasis on the personal vanity which Virgil the author betrays: this is too modernistic an interpretation. Nor am I able to follow this commentator when he would compare Virgil to a professor of medicine who demonstrates to his pupil a "beautiful clinical case" while maintaining a humorous aloofness from the suffering of the patient. Leonard Olschki (see the Appendix below, pp. 165–71) would emphasize the aloofness of Virgil with regard both to Piero and Dante; these last two form a pair (a pair of politicians), according to Olschki, and there takes place between them a "spiritual drama" from which Virgil dissociates himself. I should object that it is rather Virgil and Dante who form a pair—a pair of poets: it is thus that Piero sees them ("E se di voi alcun nel mondo riede, / Conforti la memoria mia . . ." [And if one of you returns to the world, let him comfort my memory . . . ; ll. 76–77]). There is no evidence whatsoever that Virgil feels no interest in his pupil—or that he feels no sympathy for Piero: he shows evident concern for the rehabilitation of Piero's reputation, which Dante shall undertake (thus whatever entente exists between Piero and Dante has been encouraged by Virgil!). In the end, then, there is no strict arrangement of two against one: Virgil, while more intimately connected with his pupil, feels for Piero, and at the same time, would further the association of Piero and Dante. Compare the slightly divergent triangle of poets in the Brunetto Latini episode, where Virgil effaces himself lovingly, but never loses sight of his pupil.

These separate borrowings fuse (in an artistic metamorphosis) to give us something unknown either to Ovid or Virgil: a plant that bleeds and speaks. This creature is "very man and very plant": in its growth from a "seed" it has aped the birth and organic growth of a plant; yet this plant not only bleeds (this in itself and other similar phenomena may be found in Ovid), but reveals the anguished workings of a human mind and heart. It represents, then, something quite different from the creations of Ovid, such as Driope and her like:

with the latter we have to do only with a plant that was once a human being; there is no painful insistence that this creature, after its metamorphosis, is both plant and human. But the plant-man Piero is described as a vegetal body which is capable of physiological manifestations and in which human consciousness survives unabated: this hybrid creation of Dante is more *monstrously* hybrid than anything to be encountered among the ancients.*

---

* It is quite true that ancient literature offers examples of creatures that are just as *unequivocally* hybrid as are Dante's plant-men—namely, the Centaurs, half men and half beasts. But the blend of animal and human is in itself less repugnant than that of plant and human: indeed, the ancients, who did not reject hybridism *in se*, could represent the Centaurs as essentially noble beings (even Dante, who in Canto XII has them, with their "bestial" form, symbolize the sin of bestiality, must speak respectfully of "il gran Chiron, il qual nodrì Achille" [the great Chiron, he who brought up Achilles; l. 71]).

The undoubted loathsomeness of those bird-women, the Harpies, is hardly a case in point: the horror with which these were regarded by the Greeks was due, not to the fact itself of their hybridism, but to the blend of the beautiful (*virginei facies* [maidens' faces]) with the hideous which they offered. To Dante, on the other hand, they probably represented perversions, qua blends: he does not insist on the disturbing beauty of their faces, replacing *virginei* by *umani*: to him the main significance of these creatures lay precisely in their blend of the animal and the *human*.

And this must needs be so, since to the medieval Christian poet the concept of hybridism is, in itself, repellent. The Christian system does not recognize "evolution of species": the species are neatly delimited according to a hierarchic order which purports to know the fixed and once-for-ever established *dignitates, proprietates*, and *virtutes* [ranks, properties, and powers] of man, animal, plant, and mineral. Hybrid creation is outside of the natural plan of God; and, at the hands of Dante, it becomes, according to the law of the *contrappasso* [reciprocal punishment in kind], a symbol of sin and punishment—of punishment for the "anti-natural" sin of suicide by which the God-willed connection between body and soul has been broken. This plant-man, then, is no picture of a happy solidarity between natural man and animated nature but, on the contrary, of a tragic captivity of the soul (*anima incarcerata*) in a minor form of nature; by the creation (after the death of the body) of this monster which combines the human and the nonhuman, the poet succeeds in demonstrating the gulf that exists in nature between the human and the nonhuman. Thus the whole spirit of the Dantean metamorphosis is opposed to that of Ovid: the pagan poet with his pantheistic love for nature (of which man is a part), who could discover a nymph in every fountain, a dryad in every tree, was able to see in metamorphosis only the principle of the eternal change of forms in nature—animating this by the fiction of past human passion and grief, describing the whole "with abundance and charm between the Boccaccio-like and the Ariosto-like."[3] It could be said that in Ovid the (gradual) transformation of a human into a vegetal being seems to take place almost *naturally*; but with Dante the link between nature and man has been broken by a tragic-minded Christianity; where Ovid offers to our view the richness of organic nature, Dante shows the inorganic, the hybrid, the perverted, the sinful, the damned. A metamorphosis at the hands of Dante must be, not graceful, in the way of Boccaccio and Ariosto, but tragic—in the way of Dante.

But while an Ovidian metamorphosis is presented as "natural," it is perhaps less "real" than that of Dante. Ovid is dealing with legendary stories which he retells *as if* he believed; his fabulations play in a remote past and they have the patina of a legend. But the two subjects of Dante's metamorphosis, Pier delle Vigne and the anonymous suicide, were near-contemporaries of the poet: they appear in his poem as belonging to the eternally present and as illustrating the judgment of God that is universally true—"de te fabula narratur" [the story applies to you]. And the fate of these two in the other world is presented by Dante not as legend but as reality*—the real judgment that God has in store for the soul of the sinner "in statu animarum post mortem" [in the state of souls after death]; it is described in terms more graphic and more convincing than those of the ancient tales.

-----

*There is a great gulf between the belief of a Dante in the objective reality of expiation (even though the nature of the manifold punishments be shaped by his imagination) and the almost whimsical attitude of a Hawthorne, who writes romantic novels of expiation. The representations of this novelist (who was acquainted with the punishment-by-*contrappasso* of both Bunyan and Dante) are tempered with an "as if," or an "as it were": he raises questions that invite new possibilities of interpretation, he introduces suggestions meant to anticipate the "smile" of the sophisticated modern reader. There is not with him the firmness of design that characterizes the work of Dante; whereas the medieval poet affirms unhesitatingly always the *one* inevitable consequence of a sin, Hawthorne seems wilfully to attenuate the very correspondence he has established between sin and punishment, offering this as something fortuitous, as something which might have been otherwise: he is an heir to the tradition of deep-rooted belief, but he makes of this a folkloristic quicksand. The two following passages from *The Scarlet Letter* are highly illustrative of this modern vagueness:

"It {the Scarlet Letter} had been intended, there could be no doubt, as an ornamental article of dress; but how it was to be worn, or what rank, honor, and dignity, in by-past times, were signified by it, was a riddle which (so evanescent are the fashions of the world in these particulars) I saw little hope of solving. And yet it strangely interested me. My eyes fastened themselves upon the old scarlet letter, and would not be turned aside. Certainly, there was some deep meaning in it, most worthy of interpretation, and which, as it were, streamed forth from the mystic symbol, subtly communicating itself to my sensibilities, but evading the analysis of my mind.

"While thus perplexed,—and cogitating, among other hypotheses, whether the letter might not have been one of those decorations which the white men used to contrive, in order to take the eyes of Indians,—I happened to place it on my breast. It seemed to me, then, that I experienced a sensation not altogether physical, yet almost so, as of burning heat; and as if the letter were not of red cloth, but red-hot iron. I shuddered, and involuntarily let it fall upon the floor" ["The Custom House"].

"So Roger Chillingworth—a deformed old figure, with a face that haunted men's memories longer than they liked—took leave of Hester Prynne, and went stooping away along the earth. He gathered here and there an herb, or grubbed up a root, and put it into the basket on his arm. His gray beard almost touched the ground as he crept onward. Hester gazed after him a little while, looking with a half-fantastic curiosity to see whether the tender grass of early spring would not be blighted beneath him, and show the wavering track of his footsteps, sere and brown, across its cheerful verdure. She wondered what sort of herbs they were, which the old man was so sedulous to gather. Would not the earth, quickened to an evil purpose by the sympathy of his eye, greet him with poisonous shrubs, of species hitherto unknown, that would start up under his fingers? Or might it suffice him, that every wholesome growth should be converted into something deleterious and malignant at his touch? Did the sun, which shone so brightly everywhere else, really fall upon him? Or was there, as it rather seemed, a circle of ominous shadow moving along with his deformity, whichever way he turned himself? And whither was he now going? Would he not suddenly sink into the earth, leaving a barren and blasted spot, where, in due course of time, would be seen deadly nightshade, dogwood, henbane, and whatever else of vegetable wickedness the climate could produce, all flourishing with hideous luxuriance? Or would he spread bat's wings and flee away, looking so much the uglier the higher he rose towards heaven?" [ch. 15].

Francesco De Sanctis has emphasized the directness of Dante's narration: he eschews the elegant impressionism of Virgilian devices which serve to anticipate, and thus to soften, the impact of events ("Mihi frigidus horror membra quatit / Eloquar an sileam" [A cold shudder shakes my limbs and my chilled blood freezes with terror / Should I speak or be silent? *Aeneid* III, 29–30]); instead the details as sensed by Dante are put squarely before the reader in a manner "so that what is natural is accelerated to the point that it irresistibly creates an impression of the fantastic."[4] The whole paradox of the *Divine Comedy* rests in the procedure of describing as real, and of conceiving as describable with the same precision that might be applied to an object of the outer world, that which, to our secularized imagination today, would seem to be the product of a gratuitous play of fantasy. Indeed, it is when the events are the most "fantastic" that they are presented most realistically: the fact of the plant-man Piero *must* be believed by us because it is accepted so completely by the victim himself: we see how he has adapted himself to his new estate when, in proclaiming his loyalty to his chief, he swears, not as men do, by their heads, but as plant-men (apparently) must do—"per le nove radici d'esto legno" [by the new roots of this tree; *Inferno* XIII, 73].*

---

*Thus I must reject the translation of *nove* by "strange": that Piero could so simply "take over" and modify in accordance with his new status the traditional manner of making oath seems to me evidence that he has ceased to find his condition strange. *Nove* is best translated "new"; thus we are reminded of the genesis of his vegetal body which is the product, not of gradual evolution from the human, but of a "new" birth. Compare the expression *forme novelle* used of the souls in *Purgatorio* XXV, 88.

And not less must we believe that the events that transpire were accepted as real by Dante the pilgrim: Dante the author has filled this canto with details that afford *sense-data* to this character who is the chief witness, details which offer, in particular, an appeal to the eye and the ear. When Dante first comes upon the scene he is told by Virgil to watch out for strange apparitions ("riguarda ben, sì vederai . . ." [look well, and you shall see . . . ; *Inferno* XIII, 20]); Dante's gaze is at first disappointed, for he sees (*vedea*) nothing but rows of plants, but in compensation his ears are assailed by the sound of voices lamenting ("sentia . . . trarre guai" [I heard wailings uttered on every side; l. 22]) that seem to come from unseen sources; it is this conflict between the visual and the auditory that accounts for Dante's initial confusion. But in the manifestations of the plant-man,

Dante is privileged both to hear and to see: as he tears off a leaf, the stump moans and then becomes black with blood ("gridò . . . bruno"; ll. 33–34). And in the single phrase "usciva inseme / Parole e sangue" [came out words and blood together; ll. 43–44], the two sense-data are fused together: there gushes forth a stream of "speech-endowed blood," of "bleeding screams"—a hideous revelation of the hybrid, which we must accept as a unit-manifestation, because of the singular verb *usciva*.*

---

* Here we have to do with a kind of hendiadys, as in "Dirò come colui che piange e dice" in the Francesca episode, or "Parlare e lacrimar vedrai insieme" [I shall tell as one who weeps and tells, V, 126; You shall see me speak and weep together, XXXIII, 9].

And now we have arrived at the point where we may consider the nature of "speech" (I am using this term to mean, not "language," but "the production of language") of the suicides. No commentator, so far as I know, has attempted to analyze this process—though Dante himself has taken pains to give us an elaborate hint of it; compare the famous simile (XIII, 40–44):

> Come d'un stizzo verde, che arso sia
> Da l'un de' capi, che da l'altro geme,
> E cigola per vento che va via;
> Sì de la scheggia rotta usciva inseme
> Parole e sangue . . .

[As from a green brand that is burning at one end, and drips from the other, hissing with the escaping air, so from that broken twig came out words and blood together.]

Tommaso Casini, who notes the effectiveness of such details as the "ensemble" of drops of sap and sound of wind, comments on the graphic quality of this description and cites Giovanni Antonio Venturi, who praises its verisimilitude ("truth of image and rare perspicuity of form").[5] But to consider this simile mainly as a device for enlivening description (an attitude that is a survival of rhetorical aesthetics) is to overlook the explanation which it contains for us of the "origin of language" as this is produced in the plant-men.*

---

* This fact is overlooked by all the commentators I have read on this passage: De Sanctis interprets the simile to mean that Dante does not hear the words spoken by the plant{!}; that his soul is concentrated in his eye. This is

surely not true: Dante is ear as well as eye. Francesco Torraca's contribution is to point out parallel similes in Provençal poetry, in which the "weeping" of a fire-log is compared to the weeping of a poet-lover; he overlooks the fact that this particular simile is meant to throw light on weeping that is precisely *non*-human. He may compare the "dehumanized" weeping of the pope, who "piangeva con la zanca" [was lamenting with his shanks; XIX, 45].

Obviously the ensemble of sap and windy sound which Casini admired is meant to offer a parallel with the ensemble of blood and words that issues from the plants: in both the visual and the acoustic are distinguished and fused by the poet. We have to do with a poetic equation: blood = sap, words = wind; thus the language of the plant-men is mere *flatus vocis*, wind-begotten speech. This is borne out clearly in the lines that introduce the last words of Piero, as he prepares to make answer to a question of Dante's (XIII, 91–92):*

> Allor soffiò il tronco forte, e poi
> *Si convertì quel vento in cotal voce*

[Then the stub puffed hard, and soon *that breath was changed into this voice.*]

---

*D'Ovidio comments on this passage, but only to question the significance of *forte*: why did it blow so *hard*? He answers, correctly enough, that because of the lapse of time since the tearing off of the twig had first given issue to speech, a greater effort was needed for the plant to draw breath enough to last out his words. But D'Ovidio might better have emphasized *soffiò* than *forte*—as well as the entire line "Si convertì quel vento in cotal voce," which describes the transformation of wind into voice or words (both meanings are possible with *voce*).

But apart from delimiting the windy nature of the speech of hybrid beings, the simile serves to assign it to a rank according to a hierarchy of values. The fact Dante chose to describe a hissing, guttering fire-log by way of characterizing the genesis of speech in his *uomini-piante* shows that he conceived this as representing a purely physical process: the issue of blood and cries is on the same low "material" level as is the issue of sap and hissing sound from a fire-log. Indeed, the fact that we have to do with speech of a nonhuman order, with speech that is a matter of bodily discharges, was already suggested by the terrible line "usciva inseme / Parole e sangue"; and that this is speech which is conditioned by physical factors alone is revealed by the incident in which Dante tears off the twig from the plant, thereby providing the channel through which the stream of blood and words could pour forth: only by such a physical gesture could the plant be enabled to "speak"—only by being torn and wounded.

This truth is hammered into our ears again in the latter part of the canto, devoted to the second (anonymous) suicide (ll. 131–32):

> E menommi al cespuglio che piangea,
> Per le rotture sanguinenti, invano.

[and led me to the bush, which was lamenting in vain through its bleeding fractures.]

Again blood and words are coupled, again there is a reference to the tearing of a channel (*per le rotture*) through which the twofold utterance of suffering finds an outlet.*

---

*In this case the mutilation is caused not by Dante but by Giacomo da Sant' Andrea, the spendthrift who hides behind the bush into which the suicide has been transformed; that he chose this particular hiding place may perhaps be explained by the fact that in life Giacomo, after squandering his fortune, had attempted to commit suicide.

A few lines later, after this plant has begun to speak, Virgil refers to its condition in words that echo all the concepts just treated (ll. 137–38):

> Chi fosti, che *per tante punte*
> *Soffi con sangue doloroso sermo?*

[Who were you, that *through so many wounds blow forth with blood your doleful speech?*]

But the most vivid reference to the terrible conditions upon which speech may be released in the plants is to be found in the lines describing the function of the Harpies (ll. 101–2):

> L'Arpíe, pascendo poi de le sue foglie,
> Fanno dolore, e al dolor finestra.

[The Harpies, feeding then upon its leaves, give pain and to the pain an outlet.]

What Dante did once and inadvertently to a particular bush the Harpies do systematically, *in aevum* [forever], to the whole group of plant-men; by feeding on the leaves of the bushes they open wounds and provide an outlet for the grief that they have caused: eternally there must come forth "inseme / Parole e sangue" [words and blood together].*

---

* It must have been noted that, in our attempt to describe the process by which language is achieved for the plant-men, we have drawn from passages which deal with the fate of Piero, of the anonymous suicide, and of the group as a whole. For, though the suicides are individually doomed ("Ciascuno al prun de l'ombra sua molesta" [Each on the thornbush of its nocuous shade; l. 108]), they share a common fate—and each identifies himself with the whole: consider the plural used by Piero, "Uomini *fummo*," and the line "Come l'altre{!} verrem per nostre spoglie" [We were men; Like the rest we shall come, each for his cast-off body; ll. 37, 103]. The story, thrice told, is yet the same story, made terribly explicit: "this is the doom of Piero, this is the doom of any suicide, this is the doom of all." And Dante wants us not only to comprehend his dread truth; he would have us hear the *sounds* of this doom made manifest: the cries uttered by two blood-tinged voices, first that of Piero, finally that of the anonymous suicide, emerge from a chorus to which the whole multitude of plant-voices contribute: "tante voci uscisser tra quei bronchi" [all those voices from amid the trunks; l. 26]; this is the first sound we hear, and it reverberates throughout the canto. But lest our ears grow dull, through constant exposure to the unholy din, Dante allows this chorus to be broken for a moment as the spendthrifts, pursued by hounds (again the *contrappasso*: they are torn and destroyed by ravening beasts because in life they greedily destroyed what should have remained whole), burst upon the centre of the stage: for a moment human screams dominate all others, rising above the chorus of the plant-voices. By this sudden introduction of the normal (framed by the two episodes of individual plant-men), the abnormal is made more frightful.

And with this reference to the Harpies we may note that the problem concerning the "genesis of speech," so important to this particular canto, becomes one with the arch-problem of the whole edifice of the *Inferno*: that of the *contrappasso*. That Dante has transformed the loathsome harbinger-birds of Virgil into instruments of moral punishment is obvious and has been generally recognized (De Sanctis, D'Ovidio, Torraca, Vossler); it also seems clear to me that the eternal laceration wrought by the Harpies upon the suicides is meant to be the punitive counterpart of their own act of self-laceration:* one may note that the words with which the second suicide refers to the mutilation visited upon his plant-body ("lo strazio disonesto / C'ha le mie fronde sì da me *disgiunte*") echo the *disvelta* that is to be found in Piero's description of his act of suicide: "Quando si parte l'anima feroce / Dal corpo ond'ella stessa s'è *disvelta*" [The shameful havoc that has thus *torn* my leaves from me, ll. 140–41; When the fierce body quits the soul from which it has *uprooted* itself, ll. 94–95].

---

*Torraca suggests another variety of *contrappasso*: he would explain the onslaughts of the Harpies as due to the fact that in their life on earth the suicides "had not endured the onslaughts of affliction."[6] Thus to him the great sin of these creatures would lie not so much in the anti-natural act of suicide itself as in their lack of fortitude; somewhat similar is the attitude of Karl Vossler, who states that the suicides were punished because they had not found in life "the liberating word."[7]

(Of course, this before-mentioned bodily mutilation was executed not by the Harpies but by Giacomo, who, like Dante with Piero, became unwittingly an accomplice of the Harpies.) But the function of the Harpies was not alone that of renewing everlastingly the wounds of the suicides, as De Sanctis and D'Ovidio note, but, as Dante himself specifically states, "to cause grief and, by the same token, to provide an outlet for it" (*al dolor finestra*): to make the suicides suffer, at the same time allowing them the cruel consolation of expressing their suffering through the medium of their own ghastly brand of speech.*

---

*This is a consolation doubly cruel in that the expression of their suffering seems only to renew their grief: the tyranny of the need for self-expression by language, the self-mutilating sadistic power of speech which while seeming to give consolation only aggravates the wound—this has never been more powerfully symbolized, nay, more graphically depicted, than in this macabre episode.

Thus Dante, in drawing the logical consequences of the law of *contrappasso*, has created a semi-human plantlike speech for his hybrid plant-souls (just as the devils and Nembrotte are endowed with a speech of their own: "del cul fatto trombetta" [a trumpet of his ass; *Inferno* XXI, 139]; "Raphel may amech zabi almi"; XXXI, 67).

And all this lies implicitly contained in that simple phrase, that

conventional arrangement of subject + predicate: "il tronco suo
gridò" [its stub cried; XIII, 33]!*

---

*Later on we find the much more matter-of-fact verb *dire* used in the
same connection: "Noi eravamo ancora al tronco attesi, / Credendo c'altro
ne volesse dire" [We were still attentive to the shrub, believing it might wish
to say more to us; ll. 109–10].

Such bold sentences, which mould a subject and a predicate not "naturally" belonging together in a sentence which makes this coupling appear as
natural, revives the original polar current which exists in any sentence with
the two members: subject-predicate. According to Hermann Ammann,[8] a
verbal sentence depicts a *Zu-Wort-Kommen* [putting into words] of a living
process: an observation is made by showing us something living (*ein Leben-
diges*), the subject, as displaying its natural activity (*Lebensvorgang*) in the
predicate; in any sentence there is an *Urrythmus* of tension and relaxation
which betrays itself in the musical shadings with which the sentence is
pronounced:

<   >   <   >
The roses flourish, the brook rustles.

In the case of

<   >
Il tronco suo gridò (dice)

the mould of the sentence makes appear as natural a highly paradoxical
statement; in the same manner, the oath "per le nove radici . . ." [by the
new roots . . . ; l. 73] moulds a counter-natural attitude into the frame of a
traditional oath. Both cases reflect the hybridism of plant-speech.

---·---

Now let us turn to the "language" or style of the canto. It is obvious that in discussing this second problem it would not be proper
to limit ourselves to the language of the suicides: though Dante has
devised a peculiar method of speech for these hybrid beings, he could
not do otherwise than to represent their actual words as belonging to
normal, human language, on the same level as that of the other characters—or of the author himself. One distinctive feature of the style
of this canto consists in the use, to an extent unparalleled elsewhere
in the *Inferno*, of onomatopoeic terms: consider, for example, the
following list of harsh-sounding, consonant-ridden words which
(often occurring in the rhyme) appear scattered throughout the canto
for the purpose of evoking the concepts "trunk, bush" and "cripple,
mutilate, dismember":

nodosi [gnarled]	scheggia rotta [broken
'nvolti [warped]	twigs]
stecchi con tosco [thorns	nocchi [knots]
with poison]	tronco [trunk]
aspri sterpi [wild beasts]	disvelta [uprooted]
bronchi [trunks]	disgiunte [disjoined]
tronchi [break]	rosta [tangle]
monchi [mutilated]	cespuglio [bush]
schiante [break]	strazio [havoc]
scerpi [tear]	triste cesto [wretched bush]
sterpi [stubs]	fronde sparte [scattered
stizzo [brand]	twigs]

As we pass in review this bristling array of words, we have almost the impression of being faced with a new language that recalls little of the melody and fluidity of the Italian tongue; these words have much of the quality that is to be found in Provençal, with its tendency toward monosyllabism and its clusters of consonants. Compare, for example:[9]

> Al prim pres dels breus jorns braus
> Quand brand' al brueils l'aura brava,
> E ill branc e ill brondel son nut
> Pel brun tems secs qu'el desnuda . . .

[At the first approach of the brief, harsh day, when the harsh wind shakes the wood, and the branch and bough are made bare by the arid, dark weather that strips them . . .]

> Guillems Fabres nos fai en brau lengage
> Manz braus broncs brenx bravan de brava guia
> E rocs e brocs qe met sen son cantage.

[Guillems Fabres composes for us in harsh languages many harsh knots in a clever way and roads and thorns that he puts into his song.]

In the passage just above there is an interesting allusion to the *brau lengage*: this must refer to the deliberate device on the part of Provençal poets to exploit the effect of harsh strength to which their word-material so easily lent itself. And it is only probable that Dante's procedure, as illustrated in the list above, harks back to this tradition, representing an Italian "softening" of the *brau lengage*.*

---

* The same *brau lengage* is alluded to in such lines as "Così nel mio parlar voglio esser aspro" [Thus in my speech I wish to be harsh] of the *Madonna Pietra* poem (Rime 103) and the first line of *Inferno* XXXII: "S'io avessi le rime aspre e chiocce" [If I had harsh and grating rhymes]. These echo the

"harsh rhymes" of the *sirventes*-technique [a mainly satirical Provençal technique] of the troubadours, which, "strictly conventional and oratorical as they are,"[10] were adapted by Dante to his poetry of wrath.

But it must be observed that, at the hands of Dante, the use of this device is attended with greater refinement and artistic economy; it is only seldom, for instance, that he offers an accumulation of onomatopoeic words within a line (as he does in "stecchi con tosco"; "Ch'ode le bestie e le frasche stormire" [thorns with poison; Who hears the beasts and the branches, we were surprised by an uproar; *Inferno* XIII, 6, 114]): for the most part such elements are scattered, so that the canto is throughout pervaded with sound symbolism. Moreover, while the Provençal poets were apt to resort to this procedure to excess, delighting in sound effects for their own sake,* Dante was careful to limit it to cases where it was suitable to the context, where it would serve best to give a graphic representation of the ideas of moral crippling and laceration: the visual and the aural pictures of moral disease are consonant in their disharmony. In this way Dante was illustrating the medieval (and ultimately ancient) ideas concerning the correspondence between meaning and sound (compare his opinion, expressed in the *Vita nuova*, about the "amorous" sound of the word *amore*).

---

* A more "sincere" stylistic device of the Provençal poets is to be met with in their *descorts*: poems made deliberately discordant by means of a medley of metrics and languages, in order to correspond to the "out of tune-ness" of the soul of the poet. This parallelism of form and content, which may seem naïvely pedantic to us today, is to be explained by the high appreciation which the Middle Ages felt for the symbolic act: it may be applied to anything, whether great or small: symbolism, as used by man, is a consequence of the symbolism everywhere so manifest to human eyes, which God has put into his creation.

The consistent procedure just noted of expressing disharmonious conceptions by means of harsh-sounding words has been passed over by commentators; all, however, have remarked the abundance of rhetorical artifices to be found in this canto. The use of such devices as antithesis, alliteration, repetition of words and word-stems, puns, and etymologies* belongs to a long rhetorical tradition, and, according to Alfredo Schiaffini,[11] the combination of these with the overloaded harshness of sounds was itself a regular procedure of medieval writers (in the passages just cited from the poetry of Provençal troubadours, we may note that the "harsh words" have been coupled with semi-etymological alliterations).

---

* It was a favorite procedure of the times to offer punning etymological interpretations of names. In this canto there is no pun that may compare, for example, with the *de Vinea . . . vinea* "vine-yard" found in the writings of a correspondent of Piero's,[12] and yet the *ambo le chiavi* [both the keys; l. 58], uttered by Dante's Piero, reflects the same tendency to play on names: obviously this contains a historical allusion to the other Peter, guardian of the keys. Indeed, exactly the same allusion is to be found in the writing of the same punning correspondent: "imperii claviger, claudit et nemo aperit, aperit et nemo claudit" [key-bearer of the supreme power closes and no one opens, opens and no one closes].[13] D'Ovidio points to this line as a source of *ambo le chiavi*—but without mentioning the allusion involved in both cases. Compare the underlying pun *Orsini–orsatti* in *Inferno* XIX, 71.[14]

But it is possible to trace the rhetorical devices used by Dante to a more specific source: the majority of them occur in the language of the first suicide, Piero, and Francesco Novati has proved that they are simply echoes of the elegances of style with which the historical personage Pier delle Vigne was wont to embellish his prose writings. Thus it would appear that Dante's choice of these rhetorical artifices was due to a desire on his part for historical characterization; Erich Auerbach has pointed out a consistent tendency in Dante to make the souls in the other world recognizable by having them retain certain distinctive traits of character and physical appearance; here, then, we should have to do with a "linguistic" portrayal, corresponding to the general dogmatic procedure of preserving in the Beyond the earthly features of the various characters. Novati's proof is convincing and his discovery is important in that it offers an objective explanation for the presence of the devices in question; after him, no commentator could resort to such a subjective interpretation as that earlier advanced by De Sanctis, to whom the rhetorical passages in the speech of the suicide Piero were an indication of his (momentary) lack of sincere feeling!

Unfortunately, however, the commentators who have followed Novati have seized upon the "fact" of historical correspondence in order to stress a supposed piece of ironical and malicious caricature offered by Dante. It is remarkable how quick are professors of phi-

lology to gloat over any seeming expression of malice, if this is coupled with verbal skill. The most outspoken member of this guild is
Vossler:

These "grand-style" and heroic bureaucrats, whom we Germans know better than any other people, may become tigerlike and even inhuman toward
themselves. If they are toppled or dismissed from office, they either kill
themselves or become ridiculous. *Even in their ways of expressing them-*
selves privately one can recognize the official style. . . . Deeply and desperately hurt, he {Piero} withdraws and becomes wooden in a literal sense.
. . . Their souls {of these defiant and vain men of violence}, which would
not grow and suffer naturally, harden into thorny brambles.[15]

It is not difficult to see how Vossler has been induced by a purely
German phobia and by the existence of a purely German word association (*ein verknöcherter Bürokrat* [an ossified bureaucrat])[16] to
superimpose a fantastic analogy of his own upon the parallelism
willed by Dante. Having learned from Novati that the language of
Dante's Piero is substantially that of the historical Piero, and that this
represented the "chancellery" or "bureaucratic" style of the times, he
proceeds to identify the Capuan *dittatore* [notary] with the bureaucrats whom he has known and despised in Germany; he even goes so
far as to suggest that, since in life Piero was an "ossified bureaucrat,"
it is only fitting that he must become a crippled thornbush in the Beyond. Moreover, he assumes that Piero was one of those whose style,
in spite of themselves, betrays the bureaucrat even in daily life—a
victim, as it were, of a stylistic *tic*! And we are asked to believe that
it is such a trivial and comical creature that Dante has made the chief
figure of this canto; Vossler's implications about the private nature of
Piero (is the Beyond anything like "private life"?) are entirely without
foundation, as is also his assumption that the style of his writings
was not noble and elegant, but poor fustian, and matter for derision.
We are surely warranted in rejecting the "caricature-theory" (as does
D'Ovidio: "In these stylistic mannerisms Dante scarcely intended
caricature").[17]

Moreover, I believe that the desire to achieve a historical characterization was not the sole, or even the prime, artistic motive behind
the use of these rhetorical devices. At Dante's hand these become
filled with a larger significance; they offer a sort of linguistic, even
onomatopoeic rendition of the ideas of torture, schism, estrangement, which dominate the canto (much as the harsh-sounding words

served to suggest the ideas of "crippled" and "trunk"). Compare, for example, the involved and twisted lines below (ll. 70–72), which bear in themselves the stamp of self-torture and self-estrangement, and ultimately of infructuous paradoxy:

> L'animo mio, per disdegnoso gusto,
> Credendo col morir fuggir disdegno,
> Ingiusto fece me contra me giusto.

[My mind, in scornful temper, thinking by dying to escape from scorn, made me unjust against my just self.]

After this hopeless entanglement in a verbal thicket, the lines become simple and candid (in the limpid tone of Racine's "Le jour n'est pas plus pur que le fond de mon cœur" [The day is not clearer than the depths of my heart]),[18] evoking a clearing: one emerges into the bright open sunshine (ll. 74–75):

> Vi giuro che già mai non ruppi fede
> Al mio signor, che fu d'onor sì degno.

[I swear to you that I never broke faith with my lord, who was so worthy of honor.]

There is here a correspondence between involved sentence and in-volved feeling, between simple sentence and candid feeling—a shift-ing of the shape of the sentences according to the shape of mood. In the line "Ingiusto fece me contra me giusto," I hear sounding above the intricacies of *préciosité* the note *contra*, symbol of the counter-natural: the repetitions of word-stems (*ingiusto–giusto*; *me contra me*) suggest the outrage wrought by one half of the human soul against the other; here we may note, to a certain extent, a parallelism with the *moi dédoublé* [myself doubled], as this is suggested in the most effective line of the second suicide: "Io fei *giubbetto* A ME de le MIE *case*" [I made ME *a gibbet* of MY own *house*; l. 151]. Torture and destruction again form the motif in the lines of Piero (ll. 67–69) that describe the flames of the passion of envy, steadily mounting until all is consumed and honor reduced to strife:

> Infiammò contra me li animi tutti,
> E li 'nfiammati infiammar sì Augusto
> Che' lieti onor tornaro in tristi lutti.

[Inflamed all minds against me; and they, inflamed, did so inflame Augusto that my glad honors were changed to dismal woes.][19]

Again, in the powerfully charged sentence describing the twofold activities of the Harpies, we have to do not only with repetition but with zeugma: "Fanno dolore, e al dolor finestra" [give pain, and to the pain an outlet; l. 102]. The very compression of this line is symbolical of a grief which, although given continual utterance, must endlessly repeat itself and never find release.*

---

*Compare a similar procedure in the famous line "Galeotto fu il libro e chi lo scrisse!" [A Gallehault was the book and he who wrote it; V, 137], where the subject *Galeotto* represents first the title of a book, then a human agent. Again one feels, in such a zeugmatic condensation, an expression of painful, fateful coercion. Compare also *Inferno* XIX, 72: "Che su l'avere, e qui me misi in borsa" [I pursed my gains and here I purse myself].

Finally we may consider the pattern, old as epic poetry, "*a* but not *b*," which occurs three times in as many lines at the beginning of the canto (XIII, 4–6):

> Non fronda verde, ma di color fosco;
> Non rami schietti, ma nodosi e 'nvolti;
> Non pomi v' eran, ma stecchi con tosco.

[No green leaves, but of dusky hue; no smooth boughs, but gnarled and warped; no fruits were there, but thorns with poison.]

D'Ovidio comments on the effect produced by the repetition of the device: he sees therein a deliberate monotony of syntax which "imitates that sort of calm that great stupefaction is wont to produce."[20] But he says nothing about the device itself. To me this negative pattern, with its insistent note of schism, suggests the στέρησις or *privatio* [lack] by which, in ancient as in medieval philosophy, the evil is clearly defined as something characterized by the absence of good; Dante would make us see that this forest is a "wicked" forest.

It must have been observed that the passages above represent not only the language of Piero, but also of the second suicide and of Dante himself. This would clearly invalidate the premise of those who see in the author's use of these rhetorical devices only a program of historical characterization—unless, forsooth, we are to believe that Dante has blundered as an artist and, forgetting his original purpose, has proceeded blindly out of what modern psychologists would call automatism.*

*This would indeed seem to be the attitude of Grandgent, if we may judge by his phrase "either purposely or unconsciously";[21] we are asked to believe that Dante, filled with reminiscences of the chancellery style of writing, allowed the speech habits characteristic of the *dittatore* to encroach upon his own.

But it is difficult to imagine such a lapsus on the part of the conscious artist that Dante was; I should say that Dante has not forgotten but rather transcended his original purpose: granted that this may have been the starting point and may explain the fact that his attention was called to the stylistic features of the civil servant Piero, still, once his poetic imagination had seized upon the devices that characterized this style, they could adapt themselves to a larger design, to play their part in the evocation of that atmosphere of disharmony which pervades the whole canto.*

*One may recall in this connection the scene in Canto XV where Dante, in his intimate conversation with Brunetto Latini, turns to a new and more profound use certain of the rules of *bienséance* [propriety, seemliness] once propounded by Brunetto himself.[22]

From this point of view, the more practical question of historical identification sinks into insignificance; it is right that the second suicide, a crippled being in the image of Piero, should share the crippled style of Piero; or that the pilgrim Dante, so sensitive to the disharmonious atmosphere surrounding the plant-souls, should record his reactions in phrases evocative of this disharmony.

This he does, with most startling effect, in the line to which Grandgent gives especial emphasis and which has proved such a stumbling-block to commentators of the "historical characterization" school: "Cred'io ch'ei credette ch'io credesse . . ." [I believe that he believed that I believed . . . ; *Inferno* XIII, 25].[23] In my opinion this line is the most felicitous possible "psychological characterization," serving to suggest vividly Dante's state of mind at this stage of the narration: that is, the disruption of his mental communication with his master, as a consequence of the *smarrimento* [bewilderment] indicated in the previous line, when Dante's attention is diverted in various directions (advised by Virgil to "look" out for things unheard of, he is able only to recognize sounds); the verse "*Cred'io* . . ." is the "onomatopoeic" rendering of his mental state of estrangement and confusion. Valid in itself, this tortuous mode of expression is also effective in an anticipatory function: before the curtain rises on the main protagonists, before the aweful implications of their fate are unfolded before us, the note is sharply struck which shall pervade the whole canto.*

---

*This same procedure may also be noted in Dante's use of onomatopoeia, as when Virgil, at the beginning of the canto, is made to use the epithet *monchi* (significantly occurring in the rhyme with *tronchi* and *bronchi*) in order to state the simple idea, "your suppositions of the moment will prove to be wrong": "Li pensier c'hai si faran tutti monchi" [The thoughts you have will all be cut short (mutilated); l. 30] (here, "mutilated" [*monchi*] is used of ideas!; in both cases, then, we are offered a shibboleth of mental aberration).

The rhetorical device illustrated by this significant line is simply that of repetition; indeed, this is involved in all the passages discussed above—though often in combination with other devices. That, in nearly every case, the effect achieved is fundamentally the same is due of course to a deliberate artistic intention; the mere repetition of words, no more than any other stylistic device, is not anything formulable in the abstract, but must always be felt and tested against the background of the particular psychic climate. In this canto Dante is mainly interested in evoking the one conception of moral disharmony, whereas, in the Francesca episode, for example, in the line "Amor, ch'a nullo amato amar perdona" [Love, which absolves no loved one from loving; *Inferno* V, 103], he uses the compelling forcefulness of word-repetition in order to offer a verbal equivalent of the coercion toward reciprocation that is inherent in real love. In "caddi, come corpo morto cade" [I fell as a dead body falls; V, 142], this same device serves to reinforce the impression of an inertia imposed by physical laws; in Malherbe's "Rose elle a vécu ce que vivent les roses" [A rose, she had lived a rose's lifetime],[24] it is a symbol of a serene surrendering to the laws of nature; in the Latin sentence which inspired Racine, "Titus reginam Berenicem ab urbe dimisit invitus invitam" [Against his will, Titus sent Queen Berenice from the city, against her will],[25] it suggests the united impulses of the lovers which were dominated by their act of renunciation. The motto of stylistics should be (not "tot capita tot sententiae" [as many opinions as heads] but) "so many sentences, so many meanings": if style must express a psychic content, it can do this only by adapting the given devices to the particular situation: repetition in itself is multivalent; its specific nuance is brought out in the specific situation through a kind of collaboration between the situation and the devices offered by language—through an "adhesion" of language to the psychic content.

In all the passages discussed, Dante has used a stylistic pattern that was familiar in a manner specifically adapted to a particular situation or character: the rhetorical device is never used for its own sake, "in order to use the well-known rhetorical device of . . . ," as philologists like to reason; Dante re-creates the given stylistic patterns by restoring their original strength. The "Amor ch'a nullo amato amar perdona" of the Francesca episode, followed by two other lines with an anaphoric *amor*, inserts itself easily into a well-known medieval pattern used by all preachers and orators (compare "Per me si va" [Through me you enter; III, 1–3], several times repeated, inscribed on the gate of Hell);[26] it is nevertheless an eternal expression of the nature of love—so much so that the modern reader (even the medievalist when he happens to be "just" a reader) does not even sense the presence of an old pattern. Striking examples of that "originality *à partir du connu*" [beyond the known] characteristic of the real genius, who rereads the palimpsest of language!

Appendix: The Anonymous Suicide in *Inferno* XIII

Ever since De Sanctis led the way in his appreciative study of the "personaggi eroici" [heroic personages] who throng the cantos of the *Inferno*, the commentators, stirred by a delight in the strong personalities of "Renaissance" proportions (which the *Inferno* was better able to satisfy than the other two *cantiche*), have, in dealing with this episode, tended too much to concentrate their gaze on the figure of the man Piero; De Sanctis entitles his essay on this canto "Piero delle Vigne," D'Ovidio "Il canto di Piero della Vigne," Olschki *ex professo* deals only with the problem "Dante and Peter de Vinea."[27] By raising him into such high relief one has obscured the fact that Dante intended him to be subordinated to the "law of the circle"; for he is presented, not only as an individual with a story of his own, but as the spokesman of a group with which he shares a common fate (as he himself avows), and as the interpreter of a universal judgment—which, we may suppose, had no little importance for Dante. Moreover, by the process of isolating this figure for purposes of analysis, one destroys the artistic unity of the canto itself,* which, like any great work of art, must be judged from the point of view of its ensemble effect.

---

*Or, better, of the "episode": the episode of the plant-men is really brought to an end only in the opening lines of Canto XIV, where Dante complies with the request of the second suicide to gather together the branches torn from his body: "raünai le fronde sparte" [I gathered up the scattered branches; l. 2].

One must surely question the temerity of Croce's procedure, whereby Dante's work is split into the two parts: "lyrical poetry" (in which are presented the "powerful individualities") and "theological novel."

A particular result of this general attitude, when applied to Canto XIII, is the glorification of Piero at the expense of the second and anonymous suicide. Those who bother to mention him consider him worthy of only a few cursory remarks, and these are usually derogatory: D'Ovidio (who prophesies that this will continue to be "the canto of Piero") decries the "tragicality that is ripe for the gallows and vulgar"[28] of the *mot de la fin* [final words] ("Io fei giubbetto a me de le mie case" [I made me a gibbet of my own house; l. 151]), in which the anonymous suicide refers to a "hanging at home";[29] Vossler echoes the Italian critic, declaring this figure to be a man of no "refined disposition."[30] Such judgments are in my opinion erroneous; they are perhaps to be explained by the fact that the second suicide, overshadowed by the first, has not been considered sufficiently striking to warrant a more careful examination. To my mind he is exceedingly important: not as an individual (for it cannot be denied that, as a "personality," Piero is far more arresting), but as essential to the structure and the ultimate significance of the episode itself.

From the point of view of structure one may note two types of parallelism which indicate that the two figures must be considered together; we have already called attention to parallelism of style, and to the examples cited above others may be added: "*tristo* cesto"—"la

farà *trista*" [*wretched* bush—will make her *sorrowful*; ll. 142, 145];
"al cespuglio che piangea . . . *invano*"—"Que' cittadin . . . Avreb-
ber fatto lavorare *indarno*" [to the bush which was lamenting . . .
in vain—those citizens . . . would have labored *in vain*; ll. 131–32,
148–50]. The second parallelism concerns the "two gestures": it may
be remembered that Dante, held spellbound by the aweful revelations of the plant-souls, finds no words with which to address them
(he speaks only to Virgil, who talks for him to the suicides); the only
overt tokens of his association with the suicides are given when at the
beginning of the episode he tears off the leaf from the plant-man Piero, and at the end, gathers up, in an Antigone-like movement, the
fallen branches (torn off by Giacomo da Sant' Andrea) around the
dismembered plant-body of the second suicide. If we had only the
stylistic parallels, we might be justified in interpreting them as indi-
cating that the episode of the anonymous suicide (though still essential artistically) is merely an echo, a faint reminder of the first and
more elaborate episode dealing with Piero; but in the case of the two
complementary gestures it is unquestionable that the second of them
strikes a note of climax and finality: Dante atones for his unwitting
act of opening wounds by this deliberate and compassionate act of
restoration: the episode is finally rounded out by this gesture, which
would set at rest the troubled condition which the other gesture had
called forth.

The incident of the second suicide, then, is highly essential to the
structure of the poem; it is no less true that this figure is itself important to the *theme* of the canto, which (it must never be forgotten)
concerns the workings of divine justice. And this figure is important
precisely because of its lack of "individuality": Piero is indeed a great
individual (in size he is a *gran pruno* [great thornbush; l. 32],
whereas the other is represented as so small that Virgil must bend
over to speak to him), but, by the same token, this Renaissance-like
figure is *only* an individual. The second suicide, on the other hand,
has a greater role: he is all the Florentines who have slain themselves;
he is Florence herself, who is steadily committing suicide by giving
herself up to intestinal wars: though the Baptist has succeeded Mars
as patron saint of Florence, still the former [Mars] "sempre con l'arte
sua la farà trista" [with his art will ever make her sorrowful; l. 145].
It is with the tragedy of his native city that the anonymous suicide is
concerned—not like Piero, with his personal fate, his personal reputation ("Conforti la memoria mia" [Let him comfort my memory;

l. 77]). And if we think of him as the representative of Florence, his last line in the canto appears as a sublimely terrible evocation of the self-destruction of a city: "Io fei giubbetto a me de le mie case" [I made me a gibbet of my own house; l. 151].*

---

*The implications of the word *case* were overlooked by D'Ovidio, who sees in this line only the trivial theme of a "hanging at home." But in the age of the medieval walled town, *case* inevitably must have suggested a "house among houses"; the use of this word places the anonymous suicide against the background of his city, Florence.

D'Ovidio also points to the vulgarity of the word *giubbetto*. That this was in French a popular, indeed a vulgar, term is stated by Arpad Steiner, who quotes the thirteenth-century William of Auvergne to the effect that it belonged to the "argot des malfaiteurs" [slang of wrongdoers].[31] But the very "vulgarity" of this word succeeds in suggesting most graphically the depth of degradation to which the House of Florence had sunk. A vulgar term is not necessarily anti-poetic: did not Dante, in moments of high poetic exaltation, resort to such terms as *puttana* [whore], *bordello* [brothel], in his poetry of wrath? (And, significantly enough, does not his elegant *dittatore* Piero precisely refrain from using *puttana* of Envy and use *meretrice* [harlot]?)[32]

Little wonder that Dante is moved by "la carità del natio loco" [love of my native place; *Inferno* XIV, 1]; and as he gathers up tenderly the dismembered and scattered branches, he is paying devotion to his native city.

If we compare the relationship between Dante and the (anonymous) Florentine on the one hand, and Dante and the Capuan Piero on the other, a certain parallelism becomes apparent: in each case we have to do with a gesture and a mood. But in the scene with Piero both these manifestations are of lesser significance: indeed, the gesture of breaking off the leaf was directed, not toward Piero himself, but toward what to Dante was still only a bush; thus it could reflect nothing of his attitude toward the suicide. His attitude is of course reflected in the word *pietà*: in "tanta pietà m'accora" [such pity fills my heart; XIII, 84], he tells us that he is moved to pity by the sad story of Piero. But surely in Dante's as in Corneille's scale of values, the feeling of pity for the sufferings of an individual must be less noble than the more comprehensive emotion of patriotic devotion. Thus, by weighing the significance of these parallel manifestations (which offer the only *direct* evidence on which we may rely), one arrives at the conclusion that, of the two suicides, it is with the anonymous figure, despised and rejected by critics, that Dante would identify himself—not with the "powerful individuality," Piero. (Compare a similar diptych, the councilman of Lucca / Ciampolo Navarrese, in Cantos XXI–XXII.)

It is quite another conclusion which Olschki has reached and which he presents in the article entitled "Dante and Peter de Vinea." By omitting all reference to the anonymous suicide, by weighing only the evidence, direct and indirect, contained in the first episode and interpreting this in the light of biographical data, he has succeeded in making a case for the close identification of Dante and Piero: the *pietà* which Dante represents himself as experiencing is to Olschki an indication that the poet has identified his own fate with that of the civil servant Piero, and this sympathetic association explains the fact that Piero is presented as innocent of the crimes with which he had been charged and of which he had been found guilty—according to the only documents which survive today. The fact that Piero is allowed to vindicate himself is obviously proof that Dante was himself convinced of the other's innocence, and it would seem only reasonable to assume that Dante was possessed of other evidence than that which has come down to us. But, according to Olschki, the poet was led to present Piero as an innocent victim of *invidia* [envy] and calumny for no other reason than that he, Dante, once a high official like Piero, had suffered such a fate: to Olschki the self-justifying portrait of Piero is evidence that Dante the man has identified himself with the historical character of Piero:

His {Dante's} sentiment for Peter de Vinea as a fellow-sufferer is confirmed by the similarity of the actual happenings. Both of them . . . were sentenced for malversation in public office and on like charges. Conscious of his own innocence, and convinced that it was easy, and customary, to have a political opponent convicted of malpractice in office in order to dispose of him, Dante transferred his own experience to the chancellor and regarded him as the defenseless victim, like himself, of envious malignity. Thus he rescued the chancellor, whom he revered as highest official of the Empire, as poet and rhetorician, from the ignominy that clouded his posthumous repute. The feeling of companionship in life-experience induced him, again, to pass a self-willed judgment, which might also clear his own self of the suspicions cast upon him by his fellow men. These personal motives gave rise to his conviction, and to the legend, that Peter de Vinea was, blameless, thrown into misery. . . .
    The world-judge adjudicates not according to the public opinion of his day, but according to his own conscience and his political experiences.[33]

What we are really asked to believe, then, is that Dante's favorable judgment of Piero is the result, not of inquiry and weighing of evidence, but of sheer supposition—a judgment motivated largely by his own grievance against an unjust society: he cleared Piero in order to clear himself. I cannot keep from feeling that such an interpretation must cast discredit on the integrity of Dante's reasoning; nor can I understand the practical psychology underlying such a manoeuvre on Dante's part: if his judgment were based on sympathetic intuition alone, if there were at hand in his day no reliable objective evidence of Piero's innocence, how could he expect to convince his readers of this innocence? And, unless they were so convinced, Dante could hope to gain little success in clearing his own name by drawing a parallel between himself and a character so questionable. Moreover, even assuming that he had a fair chance of rehabilitating the reputation of Piero, still this could serve Dante's own aim of self-rehabilitation *only* if a parallel between the two men were clearly established in the poem—and this Dante fails to do. He has not always failed to do this: in the episodes devoted to Brunetto Latini, for example, it is expressly indicated that Dante is identifying his own experience with that of his teacher (since Brunetto prophesies the ingratitude of Florence toward Dante); how is one to explain a lack of any such indication in this case, when, if we accept Olschki's interpretation, so much hangs upon the clear establishment of personal parallel?

In the absence of such an establishment, Olschki is forced to depend upon such hints as Piero's denunciation of *invidia* (from which Dante too had suffered) and the reference to Dante's *pietà* toward Piero—a feeling "which comes over him whenever (and only when) he has before his eyes victims of passions or misfortunes like his own."[34] If this last statement ("and only when") were true, it could only mean that Dante was incapable of distinguishing between pity and self-pity; fortunately, however, it may be easily disproved by a glance at the dictionary of Blanc, under *pietà*, where we are referred to such lines, for example, as "Lamenti . . . Che di pietà ferrati avean gli strali; / Ond'io li orecchi con le man copersi" [Lamentations . . . which had their shafts barbed with pity; at which I covered my ears with my hands; XXIX, 43–45], which describe Dante as pierced by the shafts of pity as he listens to the lamentations of the falsifiers in torment; is Dante here identifying himself as a falsifier? Compare also, in XX, 28, the *pietà* expressed for soothsayers, and the rebuke of Virgil: "Qui vive la pietà quand' è ben morta" [Here pity lives when it is altogether dead]. And as for the evidence supposedly offered by the reference to *invidia* in the following passage (XIII, 64–66),

> La meretrice {*invidia*} che mai da l'ospizio
> Di Cesare non torse li occhi putti,
> Morte commune, *de le corti vizio* . . .

[The harlot {*envy*} that never turned her whorish eyes from Caesar's household—the common death and the *vice of courts* . . .]

it seems to me that Olschki is reversing the emphasis intended by Dante when he says: "The events leading to his condemnation had the same source at the Imperial Court as in Republican Florence, because the 'invidia' that decided the poet's ill fate was *not merely the vice peculiar to princely courts, but the universal undoing of mankind*: "Morte commune, de le corti vizio."[35] Surely the passage as a whole presents *invidia* as characteristic of the court *in particular*; the last line, while conceding this to be a general evil (*morte commune*), labels it, nonetheless, "the court vice" (we should translate then: "not merely the . . . undoing of mankind, but {especially} the court vice"). Piero is here concerned with describing the situation at the court of Sicily, where *invidia* played such a destructive role; if Dante had meant that this description was at the same time and in the same degree applicable to democratic Florence, there is no reason why Piero should not have proceeded to draw such an analogy.

The Farcical Elements in 'Inferno' XXI-XXIII

The atmosphere of these cantos has best been described by Karl Vossler, who characterizes it as "farcical" ("hellish comedy, comic confusion, drastic comedy of situation, farce"):[1] it is an atmosphere in which sinners and guards (the devils) alike, and even the two poet-wanderers, are for the moment on one level—all subjected to the comedy whose setting is a trough of pitch. But Vossler has failed to explain *why* Dante chose to insert this strange interlude, unique of its kind, into his solemn poem, introducing thereby a break in the otherwise grim tone of the *Inferno*; he fails to show the ties which nonetheless bind the farcical episode to the framework of the *cantica*.

As is always the case with Dante's artistic devices, there is an intellectual justification for this respite granted the reader (much akin in tone to the atmosphere of relaxation present in the farcical scenes of the mystery plays—which, too, are built around the escapades of devils): this lies in the nature of the crime itself with which Dante deals in the three cantos. *Baratteria* (which is only approximately rendered by such modern terms as embezzlement, graft, low intrigue, misuse of power and money) is essentially a *petty* crime—one of which any man may be "capable." Therefore do we have this levelling of sinners and their guardians: the delinquents and the authorities are equally unheroic in their reciprocal attempt at cheating: those who punish in the name of the law, as well as those who are punished, form *one* contemptible crew—above whom there stands out no great figure. For Dante (who, by his curiosity, has unleashed the riot* and confusion, the "drastic comedy of situation") goes so far as to include himself in the farce, when for a moment he seems to resign himself humorously to the prevailing atmosphere as he joins the parade of the devils, that parody of knightly corteges: "ma ne la chiesa / Coi santi, ed in taverna co'ghiottoni" [in church with the saints and with guzzlers in the tavern; *Inferno* XXII, 14–15] ("one must howl with the wolves"); nor does Virgil himself escape quite unscathed, since he falls a victim to one of the devils' tricks.

---

* It is perhaps not too bold to assume that the idea of the "riot" was suggested to Dante by a verbal association: *baratta* "riot" (the word used by his Virgil, XXI, 63)—*barattieri* "barators." The pedantry which is so often encouraged by the law of the *contrappasso* [reciprocal punishment in kind] is, in this case, surely not mitigated by the suggestion of a verbal origin. And yet it is still possible perhaps to sense, in the sentence that must have flashed before Dante's mind ("The barattieri must be presented in a baratta!"), a trace of the innate *hatred* against the sin in question. Indeed the whole law of the *contrappasso* or talion is the result of a transformation of hatred against a personal enemy (who has sinned against one) into hatred against the principle of this sin itself; and from this hatred emanate juridical and theological consequences.

Indeed, this overpowering force of an unheroic situation, which stains even the noblest, is precisely the definition of the farce. In the purest examples of the farce (from its beginnings with the Old French *Le Garçon et l'aveugle* to the masterpieces of this genre, *La Farce de maître Pathelin*),² no character is allowed to rise above the standard level of mediocre wickedness; no higher principle of a transcendental, or even of a common moral nature, is allowed to appear on the horizon: with the utter ruthlessness of untranscendental comedy, man is represented as singularly stripped of his suprahuman qualities—wallowing in the pitch and mire of his infrahuman nature. Not only do we see *homo homini lupus* [literally, man is a wolf to man] (everyone cheats the other); man himself is *lupus* [the wolf]: no Divine Grace shines through the farce. It has always appeared to me a great problem that the same Middle Ages which elaborated the highest forms of mystic, religious, and transcendental poetry could also create the most barren and shallow picture of man. But to raise the question is to answer it: in the vast hierarchy of human types more or less illumined by Divine Grace, there must needs be a place for the variant of the entirely God-forsaken.*

* It would seem, then, that our own time, devoid as it is of strong religious belief, harbors a sentimental opposition against the naked harshness of untranscendental farce (this opposition may also explain why commentators are so reserved in their appreciation of these cantos: note the exceptionally cursory "argument" with which Charles H. Grandgent introduces Canto XXII);[3] we can tolerate such a theme only when sugar-coated—that is, alternating with "idealism," as in modern musical comedies and burlesque shows. To the degree that we have lost the fierce resoluteness of faith, we must adopt a sentimentalized approach to what Dante could look upon unveiled in all its God-forsakenness and present without extenuations.

The farce reduces the low nature of man to a hopeless *absurdum* of futile low intrigue and bodily impurity, offering this picture with no relief for the spectator. It is characteristic that Dante, when he quietly reviews (beginning of Canto XXIII: "Io pensava così" [I thought; l. 13], etc.) the confusion of tumbling, sprawling bodies which he had witnessed and in which he had become unwittingly entangled, should have been reminded of the "Aesopian" fable in which a powerful *tertius gaudens* [third one rejoicing] or *troisième larron* [third thief] outwits two small deceitful beasts—one of which kills off the other. In this devil-scene, the parallel to the *tertius gaudens* is ultimately the pitch of Hell (and in the foreground there is parallelism of movements).*

* Grandgent's comment in this connection is as follows: "The fall of the two grappling fiends into the pitch is a reproduction of the plunge of the tethered quadrupeds into the water; and their rescue, as they are hooked out by their mates, is a counterpart of the seizure of the frog and the mouse by the kite."[4]

Here the ultimately triumphant force is that of Evil. It is to be noted, too, that Dante formulates the gist of this scene in terms of a *fable*— that rationally prosaic genre which, like the farce, reduces all illusions about mankind *ad absurdum*; in this the fable differs from the *Tiersage* [beast fable] (e.g., the Renart epic), whose comfortably and naively sinning protagonist, an anticipation of the unheroic Panurge type,[5] is not as "grace-forsaken" as are the characters of a farce.

Dante, well aware of the kinship between farce and fable, knows also the fitting place that should be allotted to these in the hierarchy of genres. In this case, he has woven a farce into the contexture; but we are clearly given to understand that this comic scene, devoted to the debased aspects of human life, is only an interlude: at the beginning of Canto XXI he alludes to incidents "Che la mia commedìa cantar non cura" [of which my Comedy is not concerned to sing; l. 2] (this is slightly reminiscent of the wilful "de cuyo nombre no quiero acordarme" [whose name I do not care to recall; these words are taken from the opening sentence of *Don Quijote*—EDS.] of the great Spanish epic narrator), intimating thereby that the farce scene which is to follow may be considered a whimsical inclusion—a *farcime* (in the literal sense of farce): a "stuffing" for his *Commedia*. Moreover, in spite of their partial involvement in this scene, the two wanderer-poets cannot but stand aloof from the farcical interlude into which they have strayed: Dante's temporary "relaxation" was primarily benevolent; Dante's guilt consisted only of (artistic and moral) curiosity: in itself a noble motive. And from the first moment after he had entered this *bolgia* ("cui paura subita sgagliarda" [who is dismayed by sudden fear; XXI, 27]) to the last ("i'ho pavento" [I dread; XXIII, 22]), he depicts himself as frightened (as would be any righteous man faced with moral impurity); at times his fears are presented comically, but it seems clear that he is experiencing a real terror of the defiling contact of vulgarity. His main attitude seems to be that he, the man, should flee from the vile "l'om cui tarda / Di veder quel che li convien fuggire" [one who is eager to see what he must shun; XXI, 25–26], and this the two poets manage finally to do ("Noi fuggirem l'imaginata caccia" [We shall escape the imagined chase; XXIII, 33]). Here the problem of the artist and moralist who must *see* the gross reality needed for creation, without being caught therein, comes to a solution: flight is the only means for the preservation of his purity.* But in a *pure farce*, escape from the eddies of vulgarity is forever denied to all.

---

*The final escape of Dante from the wiles of the devils suggests to Grandgent's mind "a bit of autobiography": "In reality . . . , as in the Comedy, he had a narrow escape from infernal machinations."⁶ But if Dante had wished to introduce an autobiographical allusion, he could have done so already in Canto XXI, where he describes the crime of barratry—for which he himself had been sentenced to death by the Florentine authorities; here as nowhere else was an opportunity to suggest a personal parallel. Yet Dante failed to take advantage of this opportunity—as an artist he purposely eliminates from his work all elements extraneous thereto. This reticence on

Dante's part, however, does not seem to deter the supporters of the biographical approach.

And when they are so modest as only to include "a bit" of biography in their analysis, I am afraid their attempt will meet with utter defeat. They single out only one aspect of a situation in Dante's life and parallel it with a similar incident in Dante's *Commedia*, without asking themselves how far this parallel applies, or whether an emphasis on the aspect in common between the two may not vitiate the true significance of the situation in the work of art. As for the first: how does the personal experience of the man Dante, who barely escaped seizure by the Florentine authorities, square with this scene in the *Inferno* where the barrators are ridiculed along with the authorities, and where Dante remains aloof both from the sinners and from their persecutors? And to emphasize the "narrow escape from infernal machinations" is to mislead us in regard to the real elements of the conflict to which Dante is given up in this scene: that is, on the one hand, his intellectual and artistic curiosity, on the other, his desire to avoid contact with vulgarity. Not only does the biographical approach fail to help us better to understand the scene: it leads to absolute misunderstanding.

Another element in Dante's peculiar adaptation of the farcical is the theological justification which is introduced. Several times during this interlude Dante has taken care to emphasize the preordained and providential in the devilish horseplay that is enacted: the comical role the devils must play is willed by God. For, unless God so wills it, they have no power on man; Virgil is assured that he is secure from their attacks (XXI, 79–84):

> "Credi tu, Malacoda, qui vedermi
>   Esser venuto," disse il mio maestro,
>   "*Sicuro già da tutti vostri schermi,*
> Sanza *voler divino* e fato destro?
>   Lascian' andar, chè *nel cielo è voluto*
>   Ch'i' mostri altrui questo cammin silvestro."

["Do you think, Malacoda, to see me come here," said my master, "*secure thus far against your defenses*, without *divine will* and propitious fate? Let us pass, for *it is willed in Heaven* that I show another this savage way."]

And in our scene the pride of Malacoda is dashed immediately after he has heard God's will: he is forced to drop his pitchfork. It is well known that in Christian drama, the Devil, the power of Evil, is regularly represented as a comic character, precisely because he is conquered in principle by the Good (it is this optimistic trend of Christian dramatic art which is responsible for its basically undramatic nature).[7] In this epic poem, too, concerned as it is with the fate of hu-

manity, the Devil has his well-allotted place and limit: the lines put
into his mouth (XXI, 112–14):

> Ier, più oltre cinqu' ore che quest' otta,
> Mille dugento con sessanta sei
> Anni compiè, che qui la via fu rotta.

[Yesterday, five hours later than now, completed one thousand two hundred
and sixty-six years since the road was broken here.]

date the advent of Christ's rule with mathematical precision (1,260
years + 1 day + 5 hours have passed since the death of Christ, at
which moment the might of Hell was forever broken). The limit of
the Devil's power is set by Providence (XXIII, 55–57):

> Chè l'alta provedenza, che lor volle
> Porre ministri de la fossa quinta,
> Poder di partirs' indi a tutti tolle.

[For the high Providence which willed to set them as ministers of the fifth
ditch deprives them all of power to leave it.]

Thus the farce introduced by Dante is God-willed, God-limited,
God-judged. It has a definite place of its own in the Holy poem, to
achieve which "Heaven and Earth have collaborated." Dante could
shape the remotest corners of his creation protected by Divine
blessing.[8]

The Addresses to the Reader in the 'Commedia'

Thanks to the studies on medieval poetics by Edmond Faral, Alfredo Schiaffini, Ernst Robert Curtius, and Erich Auerbach, we have been brought to realize more keenly in the last decades the medieval techniques used by Dante in his own masterly manner in order to achieve the poem "to which heaven and earth have collaborated." Far from weakening our artistic appreciation of the *Commedia*, the insight into Dante's conscious (and conscientious) artistry, and into the technical devices used by him in the manifold situations described, has greatly increased our admiration for his poetry: since we have come to know his *maniera* more closely, his choice or rejection of themes and techniques current in his time, we are able to read him more and more (though not entirely, alas) as we would a modern poet whose individual art we may compare with the background, familiar to us, from which he detaches himself. Philology, which insists on close adherence to the text and on comparison of sources, has thus reconquered its due place in Dante studies, which it may keep for a long time unless it should again, as happened at the beginning of our century, deteriorate into narrow pedantry and unartistic positivism.

After Professor Curtius, one of the most emphatic advocates of assiduous philology, had studied Dante's use of the ancient device of the invocation of the Muses and Gods,[1] Professor Hermann Gmelin continued in the same vein, offering us a study of the "addresses to the reader" to be found in the *Commedia*, a device which, contrary to that of the invocation of the Muses, has no true classical (only medieval) antecedents.[2] Whereas Giovanni Andrea Scartazzini (in his commentary to *Paradiso* XXII, 106) had listed sixteen such passages (5, 7, 4 in the three *cantiche*),[3] Gmelin counts 21, according to him evenly divided (7, 7, 7) between *Inferno*, *Purgatorio*, and *Paradiso*, in each of which different nuances may appear: in *Inferno* the "addresses" may be found predominantly in moments of danger or of monstrous appearances; in *Purgatorio* more often in order to bring the transcendental element home to the reader; finally in *Paradiso* the admonishments to the reader to follow Dante's spiritual guidance increase—until the addresses disappear altogether when the poet (as Scartazzini had already seen) becomes exclusively concerned with his own mystic union with God and his salvation (*ultima salute*). Gmelin sees in Dante's "addresses" a new conquest for literature in general, the manifestation of a new relationship between poet and reader, Dante being the "teacher," the "scribe," the "Christian" who wishes by means of his art and knowledge to communicate to his fellow Christians the miracle of his vision of the Beyond.

Professor Auerbach[4] takes up the same subject with his characteristic wide horizon, encyclopedic knowledge, and artistic sensibility: he shows in greater detail than Gmelin had done that, apart from casual "addresses" in Ovid and Martial, there exists no precedent to Dante's procedure in ancient poetry: what may be compared to a certain degree is only the rhetorical figure, found with the ancients, of "apostrophe," which with them has a wider range, since it may be directed to persons present (e.g., the adversaries of Cicero and Demosthenes: Catiline and Aeschines) or to the Gods, to the illustrious dead, to allegorical personifications. In the Middle Ages the "addresses" become more frequent in Latin as well as in the vernaculars, for example, in epic narrative they become endowed with a particular "urgency" anticipating Dante in religious contexts. "If Dante's sublimity {in his addresses} is Virgilian, his urgency is Augustinian." Dante's addresses match the ancient apostrophes in sublimity and at the same time show an urgency which only a Christian prophet may attach to his personal revelations. And when at the end of his article Auerbach contrasts with Dantean "addresses" Demosthenes' apostrophes in the speech on the Crown (μὰ τοὺς Μαραθῶνι προκινδυνεύσαντας [(O you) who were exposed at Marathon]), he points out the difference between the ancient and the medieval climate: Demosthenes appeals only to human values, while Dante interprets divinity and therefore must speak to his readers of his personal visions "with the authority and the urgency of a prophet." The reader, as envisioned by Dante (and, in point of fact, Dante "creates his readers"), is a disciple. "He is not expected to discuss or to judge, but to follow; using his own forces, but the way Dante orders him to do." Auerbach bases himself in this article on Gmelin's list of addresses, whose 21 passages he reduces to 20 (considering as one the two instances occurring in *Paradiso* X in the same situation).

In treating for the third time the same neatly circumscribed philological subject—with the same hope that with Dante consideration of detail will yield insights into his art in general—I am following my conviction that philological questions are indeed susceptible of debate (especially debate among fellow scholars who share with me the feeling of horror at merely impressionistic or verbalistic interpretations, of which we have seen recently too many) and that three philological commentators are not too many in any question concerning Dante, if they sincerely strive to reach the *consensus omnium*.

First a minute detail concerning which this consensus can easily be established: there exist only nineteen "addresses" in the *Commedia*, for one listed by Gmelin and accepted as such by Auerbach (*Paradiso* IX, 10–11) is in truth only an "apostrophe" in the ancient sense:

> Ahi, anime ingannate, e fatture empie,
>   Che da sì fatto ben torcete i cori . . .

[Ah, souls deceived and creatures impious, who from such Good turn away your hearts.]

Here Dante the narrator is under the impression of words spoken by the spirit of Charles Martel (*Paradiso* VIII, 145–47) concerning the all-too-frequent mistakes made by men in their choice of profession, who thereby are prevented from following their natural inclination:

> Ma voi torcete a la religïone
>   Tal che fia nato a cingersi la spada, . . .
>   Onde la traccia vostra è fuor di strada.

[But you wrest to religion one born to gird on the sword, . . . so that your track is off the road.]

(notice the repetition by the narrator of the *torcete* "you twist the right way" of the king's speech) and breaks out into one of his well-known invectives against foolish or sinful men. Dante is surely here not addressing his reader (whom it would be singularly tactless to identify with "anime ingannate e fatture empie"), rather is he using an apostrophe directed against persons who become "present" only by his castigation. We may compare a similar invective of Dante's against earthly sinners, uttered at the moment when he sees the punishment of the Proud in Purgatory (*Purgatorio* X, 121–25):

> O superbi Cristian miseri lassi,
> Che, de la vista de la mente infermi,
> Fidanza avete ne'retrosi passi,
> Non v'accorgete voi che noi siam vermi
> Nati a formar l'angelica farfalla . . . ?

[O proud Christians, wretched and weary, who, sick in mental vision, put trust in backward steps: are you not aware that we are worms, born to form the angelic butterfly . . . ?]

Surely no one in his senses would advocate the identification of Dante's readers with the *superbi*! The most famous invective or apostrophe of the *Commedia* is, of course, the passage "Ahi serva Italia, di dolore ostello . . ." [Ah, servile Italy, hostel of grief . . . ; *Purgatorio* VI, 76], which again no one will list as an address to Dante's Italian readers.*

---

*The poetic value of such apostrophes lies in our realization that to Dante's sudden outburst there must correspond a latent, somehow stored-up emotion in him—which by repercussion increases the impression of reality of the scenes in the Beyond described by him. For instance, the invective against *serva Italia*, torn by strife, comes after the friendly embrace, so to speak above the centuries, of the two Mantuan poets Sordello and Virgil—a fantastic episode, obviously contrived by Dante, which, however, by the contrast with the undoubtable reality of the Italy torn by strife of Dante's time and the reality of his wrath, acquires an equal reality of its own. For our later discussion we shall need to remember Dante's concern for establishing the reality of his vision by certain devices.

If then we have to count with only nineteen "addresses," we shall explain their distribution over the three *cantiche* (7,7,5) in the way of Scartazzini, with Dante's concern in *Paradiso* with his own salvation. On his lonely road he leaves the reader behind. And the last "address" (*Paradiso* XXII, 106–8), his "leave-taking from the reader,"[5] as Scartazzini says,

> S'io torni mai, lettore, a quel divoto
> Trïunfo, per lo quale io piango spesso
> Le mie peccata, e 'l petto mi percuoto . . .

[So may I return, reader, to that devout triumph for the sake of which I often bewail my sins and beat my breast . . .]

shows indeed, in the adjuration of the conditional desiderative, a deeply moving final manifestation of solidarity with the reader, who is, as though quite naturally, assumed to sympathize with Dante's urge to expiate his sins and with his hope to return forever to that Paradise which it was given to him to see once in his vision: "S'io torni mai, lettore . . ." = "if it be your wish, o reader, as it is mine, that I return . . ."—surely this passage denotes an abiding Christian humility on the part of a Dante who had already in poetry won access to Heaven.

From my last remark the reader may judge that I doubt the generalization of Auerbach as to the "authoritative" character of Dante's addresses, but, before taking up this particular question, let us simply analyze our nineteen sure examples from a most factual point of view: into what types do they fall according to literal context?

A first type, which is unique in the *Commedia* and which has no consequences for our discussion of other types, is "O tu che leggi, udirai nuovo ludo!" [Now reader, you shall hear new sport; *Inferno* XXII, 118]. The situation in which this "address," also conspicuous by its brevity, occurs is the slapstick comedy or farce in the *bolgia* of the *barattieri*, in which the damned souls in the lake of burning pitch and their guardians, the grotesque devils, attempt to outwit each other. Dante is here exploiting comic effects of the lowest type in order to represent the low level of the crime (*baratteria*) to which the punishment, according to the system of the *contrappasso* prevalent in *Inferno*, must correspond. It is therefore no chance that Dante uses here ironically—witness the ironical use of the Latin word *ludus* in a sense akin to that of modern terms such as "comedy" or "interlude"—a short formula reminiscent of the technique of the performers in medieval "oral literature," of the *jongleurs* who, wishing to be heard, attempt to attract audiences by stressing the "novelty" of their entertainment (compare the type of *exordia* [beginnings]: "Eo, sinjuri, s'eo fabello, / lo bostru *audire* compello" [If I speak, O Lord, I call forth your attention (literally, *hearing*)]; "Je vous en diray deux, les plus *nouvelles* que vous ouystes oncques" [I will tell you two of the most *unusual* things you have ever heard]).[6] Only in this "address" does Dante ask his public to "listen" using the verb *udire* (as we shall see later, his general use in this connection is *pensa, imma-*

gina, *lettor*), counteracting its impact of vulgarity, as it were, by the
stylized vocative "O tu che leggi" [literally, O you who read]. Even
when Dante seems to transgress the boundaries of the *poema sacro*,
he does not allow us to forget that his is not a work to be listened to
in the marketplace, but read on our respective *banchi* [benches] (as
he suggests in a passage to be discussed later).

A second type of address is represented by the three cases in which
Dante takes his reader into his confidence as to his own poetic technique, a type which shows much affinity with other rhetorical devices similarly used by the poet: at the door of Purgatory (*Purgatorio*
IX, 70–72) Dante pauses to announce to the reader the necessity of
proceeding on a higher stylistic level, which is only meet for the sublimity of the scenes he must describe—a thought which he could also
have rendered in the form of an invocation to the Muses:

> Lettor, tu vedi ben com'io innalzo
> La mia matera, e però con più arte
> Non ti maravigliar s'io la rincalzo.

[You see well, reader, that I uplift my theme: do not wonder, therefore, if I
sustain it with greater art.]

Again, when describing, within the allegorical "procession of the
Church" (*Purgatorio* XXIX, 97–105), the six wings of the four animals representing the Gospels, Dante couples the device of *praeteritio* [by which an author pretends to bypass material] with the indication of his procedure of *contaminatio* [conflation of elements from
separate works] of two sources in this passage and attracts the attention of the reader to these devices:

> A descriver lor forme più non spargo
> Rime, lettor; ch'altra spesa mi strigne
> Tanto che a questa non posso esser largo.
> Ma leggi *Ezechïel* . . .
> E quali i troverai ne le sue carte
> Tali eran quivi, salvo ch' a le penne
> *Giovanni* è meco, e da lui si diparte.

[To describe their forms, reader, I do not lay out more rhymes, for other
spending constrains me so that I cannot be lavish in this. But read *Ezekiel*
. . . and such as you shall find them on his pages, such were they here, except
that, as to the wings, *John* is with me, and differs from him.]

Finally, at the end of *Purgatorio* (XXXIII, 139–41), in another
praeteritio, Dante explains to the reader that he will not be able to

describe the "sweet drink" from the spring Eunoë in *più lungo spa-zio* [greater space] because he has already reached the limit of lines that must be set if artistic symmetry between the three *cantiche* is to be maintained:

> . . . piene son tutte le carte
> Ordite a questa Cantica seconda,
> Non mi lascia più ir lo fren de l'arte.

[(But since) all the pages ordained for this second canticle are filled, the curb of art lets me go no further.]

(an artistic stylization of a medieval "formula of ending" a poem or a part of a poem). In all three cases we see Dante concerned with the reader's artistic appreciation of his work, which he is composing, so to speak, before his eyes; it is this artistic communion with the reader that centuries later a Cervantes will exploit with a new sense of irony. Surely there is in Dante's, as it were, leisurely explanations to the reader none of that authoritative attitude which Auerbach has found in them: the reader is made aware by Dante of the necessities and jus-tifications of his work of art: "tu vedi ben, lettor" = "you, my reader, doubtless understand my motives."*

---

*Needless to say, there are many cases in which Dante, without formally addressing the reader as such, nevertheless speaks (and it can only be to the reader that he speaks) of certain artistic necessities imposed upon him at this particular moment, for example (*Inferno* XX, 1–3):

> Di nova pena mi conven far versi,
> E dar matera al ventesimo canto
> De la prima canzon, ch'è de'sommersi.

[Of new punishment I must make verses, and give matter to the twentieth canto of the first canzone, which is of the submerged.]

We are thus made to see Dante at the moment of the composition of his poem, to participate in its *status nascendi* [being born].

A third category of addresses is concerned, not with the correct ar-tistic, but with the correct dogmatic interpretation of certain pas-sages, and here indeed Dante would seem to do something of what Auerbach attributes to him throughout: he appears as the guide who leads the reader along the paths on which he wishes him to move. Two passages of this category deal clearly with the necessary allegor-ical interpretation of the literal sense in the narrative, in terms reminiscent of the *Convivio*, where this theory is exposed in greater detail: *Inferno* IX, 61–63 (in the moment of the appearance of Medusa):

> O voi c'avete li 'ntelletti sani,
> Mirate la dottrina che s'asconde
> *Sotto il velame* de li versi strani.

[O you who have sound understanding, mark the doctrine that is hidden *under the veil* of the strange verses!]

Purgatorio VIII, 19–21 (before the appearance, in the valley of the Princes, of the two angels who drive the serpent away):

> Aguzza qui, lettor, ben li occhi al vero,
> Chè *'l velo* è *ora ben tanto sottile,*
> Certo, che'l trapassar dentro è leggiero.

[Reader, here sharpen well your eyes to the truth, for *the veil* is *now indeed so thin* that certainly to pass within is easy.]

Nevertheless, it should be noted that the interpretation ("der Dichtung Schleier aus der Hand der Wahrheit" [the veil of poetry out of the hand of truth], in Goethean terms), offered by Dante here as the only one conceivable, is presented simply as that which would normally occur to any (we would add: medieval) reader of sound judgment ("O voi c'avete li 'ntelletti sani—'l trapassar dentro è leggiero"). Just as in the last passage, where Dante's admonition to the reader precedes the description of the scene to be interpreted, so in *Purgatorio* X, 106–11, a scene which deals with the punishment of the Proud by backbreaking loads, the reader is asked beforehand to concentrate, not so much on the form of punishment itself, as on its consequences for the Proud (for the expiation of their sin will lead them to their salvation at the last judgment):

> Non vo'però, lettor, che tu ti smaghi
> Di buon proponimento. . . .
> Non attender la forma del martire:
> Pensa la succession; pensa ch'al peggio
> Oltre la gran sentenza non può ire.

[But, reader, I would not have you turned from good resolution. . . . Heed not the form of the pain: think what follows, think that at the worst beyond the great Judgment it cannot go.]

It is hope, not contrition, fear, or despair, that we should see at the center of *Purgatorio*.

Only in one, probably the most solemnly poetic passage, does

Dante give his readers to understand that they need an extraordinary preparation or natural inclination, in order to follow him: in the beginning of *Paradiso* II, when he marshals his own forces for the attempt to sing of a theme never sung before him ("L'acqua ch'io prendo già mai non si corse" [The water which I take was never coursed before; l. 7]), he combines in his address to the readers ("O voi che siete in piccioletta barca" [O you that are in your little bark; l. 1]) what Curtius has called the *Schiffahrtsmetapher* [sea-journey metaphor] (the comparison found with the ancients of a poem with a sea-journey; in this case the journey of poetry will be itself the poetic description of an unheard-of journey), the appeal to the Gods and the Muses, and, finally, an appeal to the relatively small public to which alone this part of the poem will be understandable (and even these "happy few"* will, as we have said above, be lost sight of in the last third of the cantica).

---

* This line of thinking ultimately goes back in Dante's literary evolution, as Auerbach has seen, to the exclusivism that underlies the *Vita nuova*, in which it is the *fedeli d'amore* [believers in love] who are addressed by lines such as: "O voi che per la via d'Amore passate" [O you who pass along the way of Love].

Dante foresees here, in his self-conscious artistic awareness, what many readers in later centuries have confirmed: that *Paradiso* is food only for those who have already developed the taste for this *pan de li angeli* (II, 10–11):

> Voi altri pochi, che drizzaste il collo
> Per tempo al pan de li angeli . . .

[You other few who lifted up your necks betimes for bread of angels.]

With this passage we are already on the brink of another category of addresses, frequently found in the *Commedia*, the group that shows concern with the *imaginative* capacities of the reader as to the feelings that Dante, that human being that alone had access to the Beyond, must have felt in actual situations never experienced before by a mortal. This group is characterized by the imperative *pensa (per te, lettor)* which is found in six passages listed but not discussed by Auerbach, in all of which Dante pleads to the reader to plunge deep into the memory of his own experiences in order better to approximate those of Dante. This device creates a feeling of intimacy between author and reader: for obviously the reporter-on-the Beyond must be closer to the latter than the pilgrim-to-the-Beyond.

1. *Inferno* VIII, 94–96 (Dante has heard the refusal of a thousand demons of Hell to let him enter):

> *Pensa, Lettor.* se io mi sconfortai
>   Nel suon de le parole maladette;
>   Chè io non credetti ritornarci mai.

[*Judge, reader*, if I did not lose heart at the sound of the accursed words, for I did not think I should ever return here.]

Here the reader is asked to represent to himself Dante's feelings when his life was in danger and his mission close to failure.

2. *Inferno* XX, 19–25 (the false soothsayers must go backward with their necks craned and their gaze directed toward their posteriors):

> Se Dio ti lasci, lettor, prender frutto
>   Di tua lezione, or *pensa per te stesso*,
>   Com'io potea tener lo viso asciutto,
> Quando la nostra imagine di presso
>   Vidi sì torta, che 'l pianto de li occhi
>   Le natiche bagnava per lo fesso.
> Certo io piangea . . .

[Reader, so God grant you to take profit of your reading, *think now for yourself* how I could keep my cheeks dry when near at hand I saw our image so contorted that the tears from the eyes bathed the buttocks at the cleft. Truly I wept.]

Here the reader should realize Dante's tears of pity before the defacement of the human body which those sinners brought upon themselves. By means of the possessive pronoun in the phrase *la nostra imagine* (=the image of God in which man was made), Dante includes the readers and himself in one community, an attitude which was indeed already indicated in the first line of the *Commedia*: "Nel mezzo del cammin di nostra vita" [Midway in the journey of our life; *Inferno* I, 1]—it would not be entirely wrong to include all the passages containing the "possessive of human solidarity" among the addresses to the reader.

3. *Inferno* XXXIV, 22–27 (Dante in the presence of Lucifer petrified, more dead than alive):

Com'io divenni allor gelato e fioco,
Nol *dimandar, lettor,* ch'i' non lo scrivo,
Però ch'ogni parlar sarebbe poco.
Io non mori', e non rimasi vivo!
Pensa oggimai per te, s'hai fior d'ingegno,
Qual io divenni, d'uno e d'altro privo.

[How frozen and faint I then became, *ask it not, reader,* for I do not write it, because all words would fail. I did not die and I did not remain alive: *now think for yourself,* if you have an ounce of wit, what I became, deprived alike of death and life!]

(The tie of intimacy between author and reader is made closer by the rather colloquial phrase "if you, reader, have an ounce of wit," which also offers a slight "comic relief" from the terrifying vision of Lucifer: Lucifer is a grotesque figure which arouses fear tempered by laughter.)

4. *Purgatorio* XXXI, 124–26 (Dante sees that the eyes of Beatrice reflect those of the Gryphon {=Christ} in their double nature, human and divine):

Pensa, lettor, s'io mi maravigliava,
Quando vedea la cosa {=the Gryphon} in sè star queta,
E ne l'idolo suo {=its reflection} si trasmutava.

[*Think, reader,* if I marveled when I saw the thing stand still in itself, and in its image changing.]

Here it is Dante's elation about the miracle that the reader is invited to share.

5. *Paradiso* V, 109–13 (Dante's curiosity has been aroused by seeing in the heaven of Mercury the souls of the great men of action that radiate light and joy):

Pensa, lettor, se quel che qui s'inizia
Non procedesse, come tu avresti
Di più savere angosciosa carizia,
E per te vederai come da questi
M'era in disio d'udir lor condizioni . . .

[*Think, reader,* if this beginning went no further, how you would feel an anguished craving to know more, *and by yourself you will see* what my desire was, to hear of their conditions from them.]

Here Dante, almost roguishly* calling upon the reader to imagine what he would have felt had Dante the narrator stopped at this point, is thereby able to suggest his own, Dante's, at this point almost anguished feeling of curiosity that must be satisfied. By supposing suspense in his reader he has, of course, created it in him.

---

*In my opinion, the earlier (see ll. 100ff.) comparison of these men of action with fishes, a comparison that perplexed Auerbach as to its possible connotations of "playful humor" (which he, however, in the end refuses to admit in Dante), is only a detail in a larger and sublime context. As Dante and Beatrice enter the heaven of Mercury, they are suddenly and swiftly surrounded by the spirits of those who in life were ever active in aiding their fellowmen. If Dante is reminded by them of the fish who suddenly swim toward food suddenly thrown into their midst, it is because he would compare their craving for an opportunity of helpful action to physical hunger (compare their words about Dante, l. 105: "Ecco chi crescerà li nostri amori" [Lo one who shall increase our loves!]; and to Dante, ll. 119–20: "se disii / Da noi chiarirti, a tuo piacer ti sazia" [If you desire to draw light from us, sate yourself at your own pleasure]). And these "fish" are souls that radiate light and joy that come from their inner being (the lines immediately preceding the simile are: "Vedeasi l'ombra piena di letizia / Nel fulgor chiaro che di lei uscia" [The shade was seen full of joy, by the bright effulgence that issued from it; ll. 107–8])—their hunger consists in craving to give, they radiate the joy of activity in the service of others. And it is this paradox of apparent, "comical" greed (=ardent desire to give) which in Dante's mind must stimulate the curiosity of the reader, the more so that Dante, impressionable as he is (l. 99), has fallen himself under the spell of the men of action: Dante sees that while their radiance seems to bathe Beatrice (he says to her, l. 125: "de li occhi il traggi" "from their eyes do you derive your light"), they themselves bathe in her smile. Beatrice is indeed "active," too, in leading Dante toward salvation. We must remember Dante's fierce hatred of moral sluggishness in order to understand the enthusiasm displayed by him here for men of action—on the other hand, he was not blind to the comic side of their craving for action.

---

6. *Paradiso* X, 22–27 (Dante has contemplated in the heaven of the Sun the beauty of the cosmic order):

> Or ti riman, lettor, sovra 'l tuo banco,
>> Dietro pensando a ciò che si preliba,
>> S'esser vuoi lieto assai prima che stanco.
> Messo t'ho innanzi: omai per te ti ciba!
>> Chè a sè torce tutta la mia cura
>> Quella materia ond'io son fatto scriba.

[Now remain, reader, upon your bench, reflecting on this of which you have a foretaste, if you would be glad far sooner than weary. I have set before

you; now feed yourself, because that matter of which I am made the scribe
wrests to itself all my care.]

Here, where Dante seems to indicate to the reader that henceforth, as
in this scene, it will be up to him to fully understand what Dante has
only been able to suggest, we see for the first time the *figure* of the
reader: he has a body (whereas before he had only a mind or eye or
ear) and he sits at his desk, reading contemplatively. Here Dante
truly has "created his reader"—in the moment in which he must
leave him behind.

The device represented in the six passages just quoted, colloquial
in origin, of *pensa per te stesso, lettor* [think for yourself, reader] is,
of course, a clever diversion on the part of Dante, who influences the
reader without giving the appearance of doing so: also in everyday
conversations, in the moment in which the partner follows the suggestion "Imagine how I felt!" he has already accepted the truthfulness of "what" was narrated and concentrates only on "how" it acted
on his partner. To give the reader "something to do" about a matter
difficult to imagine is a psychological inducement to make him accept this subject matter.

And now we come to the last category of addresses, those concerned with the reader's ability or inclination to represent to himself
visually what Dante saw. Some general observations, not new in
themselves, are here in order. If Dante made his vision of the Beyond
credible to a degree matched by no predecessor (as one may easily infer from Karl Vossler's comparison of the *Mönchsvisionen* [monks'
visions], usual before him, with the *Commedia*), it was because he
presented the Beyond with a logically coherent precision of detail,
anticipating thereby the realism of Defoe, who similarly chose elaborate descriptions of detail in order to make plausible his—for the
eighteenth-century reader—fantastic tale. "Dante's is a visual imagination. . . . Dante's attempt is to make us see what he saw," writes
T. S. Eliot,[7] who points out also the importance for "the clarity of the
vision" of graphic comparisons such as the one that already Mat-
thew Arnold had praised: *Inferno* XV, 20–21 (Dante "is speaking of
the crowd in Hell that peered at him and his guide under a dim
light"):

> E sì ver noi aguzzavan le ciglia
> Come 'l vecchio sartor fa nella cruna.

[And they knit (literally, sharpen) their brows at us as the old tailor does at
the eye of his needle.]

"The purpose of this type of simile is solely to make us *see more definitely* the scene which Dante has put before us in the preceding lines."[8] (What strikes me particularly in this passage is the phrase itself, *aguzzavan le ciglia*, which describes most graphically the act of seeing sharply, scrutinizingly, that was Dante's own main capacity; we shall speak later about the same verb, *aguzzare* "sharpen one's sight," to which Auerbach has called our attention in a footnote.)[9] It may be noted that Dante's favorite device is, not the metaphor in which *A* becomes *B*, but the simile in which *A* remains *A* and *B* remains *B*; indeed the whole *Commedia* could be said to be *one* great simile in which *A* (the Beyond) is explained in terms of *B* (this earth). Among Dante's similes that achieve "clarity of vision," we should particularly mention those of geographical reference by which localities and happenings in the Beyond are defined in terms familiar to the reader of Dante's homeland, Italy. One example for many in which again the pronoun *nostro* establishes the solidarity between the poet and his readers (*Paradiso* XIII, 22–24):

> Poi ch'è tanto di là da nostra usanza
> Quanto di là dal mover de la Chiana
> Si move il ciel che tutti li altri avanza.

[For it is as far beyond our experience as motion of the heaven that outspeeds all the rest is beyond the motion of the Chiana.]

(The slow dancing movement of the 24 saints forming two groups is as superior to human movement as is the movement of the Primum Mobile in comparison with the slow movement of the Tuscan river Chiana.) All such similes, in which visualization is induced by an appeal to the reader's memories, could be considered as containing a hidden address to the reader. Thus we will not be astonished to find "true" addresses (seven cases) whenever Dante would insist on the exact shapes or movements that he has witnessed in the Beyond.

We may first mention the relatively simple cases in which the address to the reader is added to, or grows out of, a simile which in itself would be sufficient for visualization: in *Paradiso* II, 19–21:

> La concrëata e perpetüa sete
> Del deïforme regno cen portava
> Veloci quasi *come 'l ciel vedete*.

[The inborn and perpetual thirst for the deiform realm bore us away, swift almost *as you see the heavens*.]

The last line containing the address is nothing but an amplification of
veloci quasi come la rotazione del cielo. More complicated is the second example, in the lines immediately preceding the last passage
quoted:

> Quei glorïosi che passaro al Colco
> Non s'ammiraron, *come voi farete,*
> Quando Jason vider fatto bifolco.

[Those glorious ones who crossed the sea to Colchis, when they saw Jason
turned plowman, were not as amazed *as you shall be.*]

Here Dante anticipates the astonishment of the reader at the swiftness and ease of his upward movement in the Heavens by his reference to the astonishment, in the well-known ancient myth, of the Ar-
gonauts when they saw that the hero Jason's desire for the Golden
Fleece was so great that he even agreed to till the soil: in the same
manner Dante's thirst for God ("la concrëata e perpetüa sete Del deï-
forme regno") has enabled him to reach his goal.

Again, *Paradiso* XXII, 109–11 (Dante has voiced his hope to return to Paradise after his death):

> *Tu non avresti in tanto tratto e messo*
> *Nel foco il dito,* in quant 'io vidi 'l segno
> Che segue il Tauro, e fui dentro da esso.

[*You would not have drawn out and put your finger into the fire so quickly*
as I saw the sign which follows the Bull, and was within it.]

Here Dante's miraculous upward flight has been brought closer to
the reader by this brief mention of the most common, even trivial
daily experience. Note the personal *tu* instead of the indefinite pronoun "one" (perhaps this was at Dante's time the only indefinite pronoun available in popular speech, the type represented in modern
English by *you:* "you can't take it with you"). In similar references to
the swiftness of Dante's passage from one heavenly location to another, Dante uses a simple simile alone; for example, *Paradiso* II,
23–25:

> E forse in tanto in *quanto un quadrel posa*
> *E vola e da la noce si dischiava,*
> *Giunto mi vidi* {to the heaven of the Moon} . . .

[And perhaps in that time *that a bolt strikes, flies, and from the catch is released, I saw myself arrived.*]

To the pattern "simile + address" belong also certain of the most
solemn and elaborate examples in *Purgatorio* and *Paradiso*, those

cantiche in which the poet seems to expect from the reader a greater ability to share his experiences, so that greater solemnity is attuned to greater understanding; for example, *Purgatorio* XVII, 1–9:

> Ricorditi, lettor, se mai ne l'alpe
>   Ti colse nebbia . . .
> Come, quando i vapori umidi e spessi
>   A diradar cominciansi, la spera
>   Del sol debilemente entra per essi;
> E fia la tua imagine leggiera
>   In giugnere a veder com'io rividi
>   Lo sole in pria, che già nel corcar era.

[*Recall, reader*, if ever in the mountains a mist has caught you, . . . how, when the moist dense vapors begin to dissipate, the sphere of the sun enters feebly through them, *and your fancy will easily* come to see how, at first, I saw the sun again, which was now at its setting.]

While in this case a "geographical simile" is recalled to the *memory* of the reader (*ricorditi*) so that his visual apperception of Dante's imaginary landscape will become "easy" (*leggiera*), in the solemn passage *Paradiso* XIII, 7–27, it is not to memory, but to *imagination* that the poet is appealing; here the reader must try to imagine forms which, though well known singly, are not to be found in combination on this earth—a pseudo-astronomic simile is here developed in 21 lines, the dance of two groups of *santi lumi* [holy lights] (each of which comprehends twelve spirits) being compared to a hypothetic garland that would be formed by 24 stars assembled in two constellations and moving in concentric circles round Dante. The activity of representing to oneself such an extraordinary pattern of movement is called repeatedly *imaginare* ("Imagini chi bene intender cupe / Quel ch'i' or vidi . . . Imagini . . . Imagini . . . E avrà quasi l'ombra de la vera / Costellazione e de la doppia danza" [Let him imagine, who would rightly grasp what I now beheld, . . . let him imagine, . . . let him imagine . . . and he will have as it were a shadow of the true constellation, and of the double dance; *Paradiso* XIII, 1–20]). By the repetition of this verb and also by the poet's suggestion that his reader (or rather that type of refined reader of the *Paradiso* who wishes to understand Dante thoroughly: "chi bene intender cupe") should keep the astronomic simile in his mind "firm like a rock," and by his reminder that with all this the ideal reader would still see only a "shadow" of that fantastic reality, we are brought to realize how conscious Dante was of the burden which he imposes on the reader's "imagination." The simile, so far removed from the latter's experience, requires here, as it were, an appeal on Dante's part to the utmost of the imaginative power in the reader.

Another rather simple basic pattern of "addresses in the service of visualization" is twice represented in the *Commedia* by an insistence on the *truth* of what was seen—indeed, Dante goes to the extent of swearing to this truth: *Inferno* XVI, 127–31 (Dante sees Geryon, the "sozza imagine di froda" [foul image of fraud; XVII, 7], appear above the water like a diver, half animal, half human):

> E per le note
> Di questa comedìa, *lettor, ti giuro,*
> S'elle non sien di lunga grazia vote,
> Ch'i' vidi per quell'aere grosso e scuro
> Venir notando una figura in suso . . .

[And, *reader, I swear to you* by the notes of this Comedy—so may they not fail of lasting favor—that I saw, through that thick and murky air, come swimming upward a figure.]

Dante introduces his oath by the admission (XVI, 124–29) that there may exist cases of "truths that seem lies" which, because of their very incredibility, it is useless to state, but he immediately points out that the scene he is about to describe is not in this category ("Ma qui tacer nol posso" [but here I cannot be silent; l. 127]): all will depend here on the belief of the reader, which he secures by swearing in the name of the completion of the *Commedia*, which in turn depends on divine grace: in other words, grace from above and, at the other end of the chain, belief of the reader are of equal importance for Dante's poem, a thought to which we shall come back in our conclusions. In this passage we note, coupled with the oath *ti giuro*, the desiderative *se* "if" in an asseverative context: "if it is true that (just as truly as) . . . I wish that my *Commedia*. . . ." The same rather sophisticated and solemn asseverative construction also occurs alone, without the outright oath, in the passage *Paradiso* XXII, 106–9, discussed above, "S'io torni mai, lettore, a quel divoto / Trïunfo. . . . Tu non avresti . . ." [So may I return, reader, to that devout triumph. . . . You would not have drawn out . . .]; in both cases a personal wish of Dante is placed on the same level as a universal truth ("just as true as God exists" becoming "just as truly as I may . . .").*

* A complete list of Dante passages containing this construction in its asseverative as well as adjurative function is given by Giuliano Bonfante.[10]
There occur in the *Commedia* 19 examples (exactly as many as "addresses"), in decreasing number in the three *cantiche* (as with the addresses): 11 in *Inferno*, 7 in *Purgatorio*, 1 in *Paradiso*—obviously, Dante
feels asseveration and adjuration increasingly less necessary toward the end
of his work.

As to the origin of the Old Romance construction (Old French *se Dieus
m'aït* [if God aids me], Old Italian *se Dio m'aiuti*), which is more sophisticated than the parallel, equally old construction *si m'aït Dieus, sì m'aiuti Dio*,
I still persist in spite of the new treatment of the problem by Thomas B. W.
Reid[11] in my old explanation of Old French, Old Italian—*se*=Latin *sī* (conjunction), Old French, Old Italian *si*=Latin *sīc* (asseverative particle).[12] Mr.
Reid's explanation to the effect that in a possible formula of Christian Latin,
sic te Deus adjutet, "its structure ceased to be analysed by the speaker, the
stress came to fall entirely on the meaningful elements and the atonic *sic* was
reduced . . . to *se*"[13] is entirely speculative and contrary to linguistic experience. If I find, in Romance languages that distinguish *sī* > *se* [if] from *sīc*
> *si* [so] (Italian, French, Portuguese), the two types *se Dieus m'aït* and *si
m'aït Dieus*, I feel it the duty of the linguist to explain them in terms of the
usual meaning of *se* and *si* respectively. Mr. Reid's further assumption that
"this now unanalysable formula {*se Dieus m'aït*} did not, however, prevent
the 're-thinking' of its basic idea in more living terms"[14] {with the result that
se Dieus m'aït, which goes back according to Reid to *sic* . . . , was reinter-
preted as *si m'aït Dieus*, with *sic* > *si*} is hardly corroborated by the "re-
thinking" process that indeed has taken place in the later type *ainsi m'aït
Dieus*: for a *si* < *sīc* here could be very well strengthened into an *ainsi* of the
same meaning, whereas one does not easily understand how an "unanalysable" *se* could be replaced by a *si* of entirely different meaning. Phonetic juggling seems to be still an acceptable procedure, while the assumption of the
semantic expansion of a syntactic type (in this case of the type "if God
exists" > "if I wish that I may . . .") is met with doubts.

In the next example Dante's concern for the credibility of his report takes the form of a pretended incredulity on the part of the poet
himself, who, unable to count on the reader's immediate belief, appeals to his lack of belief as the common bond, for Dante himself at
first could not believe what he saw: *Inferno* XXV, 46–48 (the thief
Cianfa will be shown transforming himself into a serpent):

> Se tu se'or, lettore, a creder lento
> Ciò ch'io dirò, non sarà maraviglia,
> Chè io che 'l vidi appena il mi consento.

[If, reader, you are now slow to credit that which I shall tell, it will be no wonder, for I who saw it do scarcely admit it to myself.]

Still another device for the visualization is that in which the poet would insist on "exact measurement by the reader"—of that which cannot be measured: in *Inferno* XXXIV, 30–33 (in the same description of Lucifer in which he had already asked the reader: "Pensa oggimai per te, s'hai fior d'ingegno" [Now think for yourself, if you have an ounce of wit; l. 26]) the poet offers himself—obviously in a humorous intention—as a yardstick for the size of the devil:

> E più con un gigante io mi convegno,
> Che i giganti non fan con le sue braccia:
> Vedi oggimai quant'esser dee quel tutto
> Ch'a così fatta parte si confaccia.

[And I in size compare better with a giant than giants with (Lucifer's) arms: see now how huge that whole must be to correspond to such a part.]

From these proportions the reader may infer the size of the whole body of Lucifer. It must be noted that the same procedure is used sometimes by Dante's guide, who has him infer consequences from words proffered: *Purgatorio* XVII, 138–39 (Virgil speaking of the *three* circles of Purgatory in which foolish love is being expiated): "Ma come tripartito si ragiona, / Tacciolo, acciò che tu per te ne cerchi" (*tu per te ne cerchi=pensa per te stesso*) [But how it is distinguished as threefold I do not say, that you may search it out for yourself].

Just as Dante in his own visualization of the Beyond enjoys the help of his guide, who directs his vision beyond earthly limits, so Dante as guide to the reader enjoins him, in one of the most solemn passages (*Paradiso* X, 7–22, modelled on Boethius, *De Consolatione* III, v. 9, ll. 22–25) to lift his eyes level with Dante's in order to contemplate "along with him" the beauty of cosmic order. Whereas with the ancient writer, Lady Philosophy prayed to God for Boethius's enlightenment:

> Da pater augustam menti conscendere sedem,
> Da fontem lustrare boni, da luce reperta
> In te conspicuos animi defigere visus—

[Grant, Father, that our minds Thy august seat may scan, Grant us the sight of true good's source, and grant us light That we may fix on Thee our mind's unblinded eye.][15]

Dante presupposes an understanding potentially equal to his own (*Paradiso* X, 7–22):

> Leva dunque, lettor, a l'alte ruote
>   Meco la vista . . .
> E lì comincia a vagheggiar ne l'arte
>   Di quel maëstro . . .
> Vedi come da indi si dirama . . .
> Or ti riman, lettor, sovra 'l tuo banco . . .

[Lift then your sight with me, reader, to the lofty wheels . . . and amorously there begin to gaze upon that Master's art. . . . See how from there (the oblique circle) . . . branches off. Now remain, reader, upon your bench.]

If we look back now at the variety of Dantean addresses in their combination with other rhetorical devices and their different shades of mood, we will realize that the overwhelming majority of the passages are concerned with the reader's visualization of what Dante felt or of what he "saw" in the Beyond. In no single case do we find Dante associating the reader with his personal judgments or prophecies (especially not with his political prophecies, which Auerbach emphasizes so much because of the role of the "prophet," which seems to him all-important in Dante). Consequently we will perhaps be reluctant to accept Auerbach's emphasis on the authoritative nuance in this "new prophet's addresses" to the reader. Have we not seen him always remaining close to the latter (up to the point in *Paradiso* where, after having declared him to be sufficiently experienced in visualization, he is forced to leave him to his own resources)? It would seem strange to me that Professor Auerbach, the author of such excellent works as *Dante: Poet of the Secular World* and *Mimesis*,[16] did not think (or not primarily think) of the possibility that Dante's addresses are meant to be in the service of—precisely!—mimesis, of the description of the other world carried out with the vividness, or realism, with which things of this world may be described, and I can attribute Auerbach's failure to draw the consequences of mimesis for our particular problem only to that understandable tendency of the scholar to tire of those very categories he has most superbly developed in other works of his.*

---

*Speaking in terms of my personal method of the "philological circle," I would say that Mr. Auerbach has taken his point of departure from his un-

surpassed encyclopedic knowledge of the whole of the *Commedia*, neglect-
ing the exact analysis of the detail chosen in this article to represent the
whole, while I would prefer to start with the analysis of a detail, assuming,
at least in the beginning of my investigation, that the whole of the work is
still unknown to me, and finally approximating that whole in terms of the
previous analysis of detail. I have the impression that Mr. Auerbach, having
a genuine vision of the whole, looked only secondarily for a detail that could
symbolize it.

"The authority and the urgency of a prophet"—this interpretation
smacks more of the arrogantly hieratic solemnity of Stefan George or
of certain would-be religious poses applied to Dante by certain
American critics than of the urbane this-worldliness and the subtle
flair for artistry and its techniques that have ever characterized Erich
Auerbach's writings.

I have also the impression that the final contrast between Demosthenes and Dante which is the culmination of the article is both over-
strained and out of place: Auerbach compares, as to "sublimity and
urgency," with the Dantean addresses to the reader the following
"apostrophe linked with an address to the hearer" in the oration on
the Crown:

But it cannot be, no, men of Athens, it cannot be that you have acted wrong,
in encountering danger bravely, for the liberty and the safety of all Greece.
No! by those generous souls of ancient times who were exposed at Mara-
thon (μὰ τοὺς Μαραθῶνι προκινδυνεύσαντας), by those who stood arrayed
at Plateae, by those who encountered the Persian fleet at Salamis, who
fought at Artemisium, by all the brave men whose remains lie deposited in
the public monuments. All of whom received the same honorable interment
from their country, Aeschines.[17]

The point Mr. Auerbach seems to be making here is that while the
Demosthenian passage and Dante's "addresses" are equal "in solemnity and urgency," no relationship comparable to the one established
by Dante with his readers obtains between Demosthenes and his listeners—an obvious truism: Demosthenes *spoke* on a rostrum before
the community of his fellow Athenians; Dante addresses himself to
isolated individual *readers*, sitting behind their respective *banchi*,
out of whom he must, by his art, make companions and create a
community. As to the "apostrophe linked with the address of the
hearer," this is an oath (an oath in this case secularized by Demosthenes, the religious type "by Zeus, by the Styx" having been re-

placed by the evocation of the Athenian heroes who died in the Persian wars and who died in vain as little as the victims of the Macedonian war), and an oath of Demosthenes' can be compared, not to Dantean addresses to the reader, but only to Dantean oaths, for example, to our well-known passage (*Inferno* XVI, 127–30):

> per le note
> Di questa comedìa, lettor, ti giuro,
> S'elle non sien di lunga grazia vote,
> Ch'i' vidi . . .

[reader, I swear to you by the notes of this Comedy—so may they not fail of lasting favor—that I saw . . .]

in which the traditional formula of the oath has been filled, in a manner remotely similar to Demosthenes, with a content pertinent to the particular situation—but Dante's is still a religious oath, Demosthenes' is not, and thus in the end the two apostrophes are hardly comparable.

As to the contrast between the worldliness of Demosthenes, who recognizes only human values, and the religion of Dante, who recognizes only the will of the divinity, the alfresco diptych offered us by Auerbach can teach us no new insight into the differences between the ancient and the Christian cultural climate. Again, only commensurable phenomena lend themselves to comparison: two "poets of the supernatural" such as Plato and Dante could indeed be compared (as has been done by George Santayana). But what common ground is there between a political orator who addresses a group of specific fellow citizens in order to justify a specific well-known program of action of his before the polis (this was an ancient genre anticipating our modern autobiographies, according to Werner Jaeger)[18] and a religious writer who addresses potential individual readers to whom he hopes to reveal impersonal universal truths and in whom he wishes to strengthen the desire for moral regeneration? Would we compare a speech over the radio by Churchill with a religious ode by Claudel?

In my opinion, Dante's discovery of a new auctorial relationship with the reader was the consequence of the nature of his *vision*, in which the presence of the reader for whom it is told is required. Although Dante presents himself as having actually been in the Beyond ("Nel ciel . . . / Fu'io" [I have been in the heaven; *Paradiso* I, 4–5]) and giving an accurate factual account of his travel, and although he was well aware of the originality of his treatment of his subject, he surely thought no more of himself as belonging to a superhuman category of prophets than did any truly religious poet in other ages, and his *licentia poetica* was recognized as such by any sensible contemporary reader;* his "I" is indeed, as I attempted to show, a poetic-didactic "I" that stands vicariously for any other Christian (compare again the first lines of the *Commedia*: "Nel mezzo del cammin di nostra vita / Mi ritrovai" [Midway in the journey of our life I found myself; *Inferno* I, 1–2]) for whom, just as for Dante, a sudden illumination is possible thanks to the nature of the Christian God.[19]

---

* I have never understood why critics dealing with Dante's religious art consider him to have less poetic invention than other artists (such as Rabelais or Baudelaire) whose rich visual imagination is immediately recognized. It is as though Dante's subject matter intimidated the critics more than it did Dante himself. In the episode of Minos (*Inferno* V, 10), who is represented signalling, in the manner of a busy hotel desk-clerk, by the number of circumvolutions of his tail the particular circle of Hell reserved for the particular sinner, can any reader in his senses think that Dante expected from his public more than *poetic* belief, or that Dante himself would believe in Minos as an administrator of the Christian God's justice? This is grotesque art, nothing but art!

As I wrote in *Traditio*: "Dante attempts to show us a human being actually experiencing the truths of the Beyond. And this personality which Dante the beholder, the experiencer, retains, is in direct correspondence with the personal character of divinity: according to Augustine, it is the personality of God which determines the personal soul of man: only through God's personality has man a personal soul—whose characteristic is its God-seeking quality. Thus Dante in his report of his quest performs artistically the basic endeavor of the Christian: to seek a personal relationship with divinity."[20] Thus when Dante mentions in the *Commedia* autobiographical detail, he does this not out of any inner urge for self-expression, but in order to establish the contours of his Christian individuality representative of other Christian individualities. This presentation rests on the assumption of a special concern of divinity for Dante the pilgrim-to-the-Beyond. It is the Virgin, that main intercessor for mankind, who will use Lucia as intermediary between herself and Beatrice, who, although seated in the Celestial Rose next to Rachel, will descend to the limbo to find Virgil, who will guide Dante to her. Beatrice is an allegory of revelation, or rather of the *personal* revelation that comes to Dante because she alone, as the object of his youthful love, has in herself the miraculous potentialities for that role.*

---

*That Beatrice is the allegory, not only of revelation, but of *personal* revelation, is proved both by the autobiographical origin of this figure and by her status in the Beyond: she is not an angel, but the blessed soul of a human being that, just as it influenced Dante's life on this earth, is called to perform for Dante in the course of his pilgrimage services of which she alone is capable; she is not a saint, but a *Beatrice*, not a martyr, but one who died young and was allowed to stay on earth only in order to show Dante the possibility of miracles (*miracol mostrare*; Vita nuova, 1st poem, XXVI). The dogmatic license here taken by Dante appears less daring if we consider the fact that revelation may come to the Christian in an individual form, suited to him personally. But the Beatrice of the *Commedia* is in addition to an allegory, as Auerbach has shown, a *figura impleta* [fulfilled figure], an earthly figure in her human concreteness that, somehow like the "historical" figures Virgil and Cato, has reached in the Beyond her transcendental fulness. In my opinion, Beatrice has even a third role, hitherto not clearly formulated by critics who may not have been fully aware of the many-faceted aspects of this composite, "unhistorical figure" of Dante's own making: the role of an *imitatrix* (or *imago*) *Christi*. She is in this respect the exact counterpart of the *figurae* (or *praefigurationes*) *Christi*, those historical persons born before the Redeemer who foreshadow him. In a history of mankind whose central point is the birth of Christ, *praefiguratio* must be the role of the good Christian before Christ, *imitatio* that of the good Christian after Christ. Without establishing clearly this point, Auerbach has listed passages both from the *Vita nuova* and the *Commedia* in which Beatrice is described with details characteristic of Christ, passages that were used again by Charles Singleton[21] in order to prove that in the episode of the Procession of the Church (in *Purgatorio*), "Beatrice *comes as Christ*" (in order to judge Dante). Faced with this latter rather vague definition, one wonders how Christ could be represented twice in the same episode: both as the Gryphon harnessed to the chariot of the Church (according to the traditional explanation, which is not outspokenly rejected by Professor Singleton) and as Beatrice. It seems more satisfactory to me to assume that Beatrice comes not as Christ, but as *imago Christi*, that she shares, that is, certain features with the Redeemer, as do certain saints (e.g., Saint Alexius, in the Old French poem [*Vie de Saint Alexis*], has the same life span as Christ, etc.)—that, in other words, she is, if not a saint, a saintlike being representing the personal element in Dante's redemption (while Virgil and Saint Bernard are only objective tools of Providence who could theoretically just as well serve as guides to other pilgrims to the Beyond).

Now obviously, just as Dante is guided by Virgil (who is inspired by Beatrice who is inspired by Lucia, etc.), so he must guide the reader, so that there may be established the final link in that uninterrupted chain that binds humanity to heaven—that Great Chain of Revelation. Again, just as Dante is receiving in the Beyond continuous instructions from his mentors (to an extent that made Vossler, with his protestantic point of view, wonder why Dante is never shown us alone in meditation, solving a problem without help or intercession from above), so Dante must pass on to his reader what he himself has been taught. Dante is indeed the poetic guide to worlds described for the sake of the reader's edification. Never has any writer studied the visible world or stored up an equal treasure of concrete forms for the purpose of presenting this hoard of images as so many images of a transmundane world.*

---

*Isaiah Berlin, in his recent book on Tolstoy, *The Hedgehog and the Fox*,[22] distinguishes among famous writers the "fox type" that deals with manifold unrelated subject matter and the "hedgehog type" that brings all subject matter together under one principle: Dante and Lucretius are listed under the second, Goethe and Herodotus under the first type. Tolstoy is explained by Mr. Berlin as a born "fox" who unsuccessfully attempted to make himself over into a "hedgehog." In my opinion, if I may use such a trivial comparison, Dante was born a fox type of writer and became a *successful* hedgehog.

Since Dante will ask his reader to see exactly what he saw, the same will be true of the visualization of the allegories, which for him partake of the visible. T. S. Eliot, whose remark on Dante's visual imagination we have quoted, also points out that his "allegorical method makes for simplicity and intelligibility"[23]—in other words (in words, that is, of Jakob Burckhardt), Dante lived in an age that was able *to see abstractions* (which we today can do only in the realism of politics, whose artist is the cartoonist).*

---

*Santayana sees in Dante the perfect conclusion of a Socratic task to understand the world in terms of good and evil: "So earnestly and exclusively did they {the Christian philosophers} speculate about moral distinctions that they saw them *in almost visible shapes, as Plato had seen his ideas.* They materialized the terms of their moral philosophy into existing objects and power" (emphasis added).[24]

We will then not be astonished if Dante (*Purgatorio* VIII, 19–20), when enjoining his reader to see the abstractions behind his visual report (which will be punctuated by verbs of seeing: "Io vidi quello esercito gentile; E vidi uscir de l'alto e scender giue / Due angeli; Ben discernea in lor la testa bionda; Ma ne la faccia l'occhio si smarria" [Then I saw that noble army; And I saw come forth from above and descend two angels; I clearly discerned their blond heads, but in their faces my sight was dazzled; ll. 22, 25–26, 34–35]), uses the very word *aguzzare* which, as we saw, served him for intense sensual seeing:

> Agguzza qui, lettor, ben li occhi al vero,
> Chè 'l velo è ora ben tanto sottile . . .

[Reader, here sharpen well your eyes to the truth, for the veil is now indeed so thin.]

In another passage, too, Dante makes it clear that the task of understanding is ultimately the same for himself and the reader—and this he indicates by applying the same verb to his own endeavors and those of the reader: in Canto II of *Paradiso*, which, Dante tells us, is only for "Voi altri pochi, che drizzaste il collo / Per tempo al pan de li angeli" [You other few who lifted up your necks betimes for bread of angels; ll. 10–11], he himself is told by Beatrice at their arrival in the heaven of the Moon, "Drizza la mente in Dio grata . . . / Che n'ha congiunti con la prima stella" [Direct (literally, lift up) your mind to God in gratitude . . . who has united us with the first star: ll. 29–30] (and the same verb *drizzare* had earlier been used by Virgil, *Purgatorio* XVIII, 16–17, in his explanation to Dante of the various levels of love: "Drizza . . . ver me l'agute luci / De lo 'ntelletto" [Direct on me the keen eyes of your understanding]; compare Isaiah 40:26, "Levate in excelsum oculos vestros et videte . . ." [Lift up your eyes on high and see . . .], a passage that in turn has influenced the passage in *Paradiso* X, 7–8: "Leva dunque, lettor, a l'alte ruote / Meco la vista" [Lift then your sight with me, reader, to the lofty wheels]). Even in this small detail of word-repetition we see an indication of Dante's friendly closeness to his truly "beloved reader."

————————— • —————————

In his posthumously published book, *Literary Language and Its Public in Late Latin Antiquity and in the Middle Ages*, Auerbach has reformulated and revised his ideas about the "addresses to the reader" in view of my criticisms.[25]

'GEISTESGESCHICHTE' VS.
HISTORY OF IDEAS
AS APPLIED TO HITLERISM

Some of Spitzer's most important pronouncements during his American years resulted from strong reactions to the work of his colleagues at the Johns Hopkins University. Among the essays included in this volume, this one and the study of Marivaux ("Apropos of *La Vie de Marianne*") take the form of debates with, respectively, the philosopher Arthur O. Lovejoy, founder of that discipline known as the history of ideas, and the phenomenological critic Georges Poulet. In his argument with Lovejoy, Spitzer affirms his essential commitment to the German tradition of *Geistesgeschichte*, which, diverse though the views of its practitioners have been, posits the notion that a historian can synthesize the various activities—philosophical, political, aesthetic—of a particular period into a composite concept to which we attach a name such as Renaissance or Romanticism. By contrast, Lovejoy's history of ideas tends to blur the distinctions between periods and to speak instead of "unit ideas" such as *plenitude* and the *scale of being*, whose continuity Lovejoy, in his classic work *The Great Chain of Being* (1936), traced from Plato until recent times.

For Spitzer the history of ideas is not, properly speaking, history at all, for in its analytical and often skeptical attitude toward the conceptualizing of earlier historians, it stresses continuity and similarity over many periods, and as a result robs individual historical moments of their uniqueness. The present essay replies specifically to an essay by Lovejoy that asserts a continuity between German Romanticism and the ideas guiding Nazism. By implication Spitzer is also replying to an influential earlier essay by Lovejoy, "On the Discrim-

ination of Romanticisms" (1924),[1] which took an extreme nominal-
ist view on whether a concept such as Romanticism has any meaning
in the first place. By arguing for the notion from *Geistesgeschichte*
that each period retains its uniqueness, Spitzer attempts to restore
the integrity of German Romanticism, which during World War II,
when this essay was written, was often blamed—by serious historians as well as journalists—for the atrocities being committed in Germany at the time.

This essay was first published in the *Journal of the History of
Ideas*, 5, no. 2 (Apr. 1944): 191–203 (and followed by Arthur O.
Lovejoy's "Reply to Professor Spitzer"), and is reprinted by permis-
sion of the Executive Editor of that journal.

'Geistesgeschichte' vs. History of Ideas
as Applied to Hitlerism

> No es la idea la que apasiona, sino la pasión que idealiza.
> [It is not the idea that empassions, but the passion that idealizes.]
> *José Bergamín*

Professor Arthur O. Lovejoy, in a provocative article entitled "The Meaning of Romanticism for the Historian of Ideas,"[1] considers the particular combination of three "separate," "ruling ideas" of "the Romantic period" (1780–1800) in Germany, and sees therein an important factor "in the production of the state of mind upon which the totalitarian ideologies depend for their appeal" and, consequently, of "the tragic spectacle of Europe in 1940"; these three ideas, as excogitated in the 1780's and 1790's, are *Ganzheit, Streben*, and *Eigentümlichkeit* (holism or organicism, dynamism or voluntarism, diversificationism).

While recognizing the presence and the importance of these three ideas in Hitlerism, I cannot see in them, or in their "combination," an important factor in the production of this system; I do not believe in their historical continuity, nor can I accept the assumption that any historical movement may be explained by that analytical kind of "History of Ideas" of which Professor Lovejoy is the most outspoken and the most illustrious advocate. I submit that not analytical History of Ideas but only synthetic *Geistesgeschichte* (which untranslatable term I do not consider to be properly rendered by "History of Ideas," with its plural unintegrated into a unity)* can explain historical events.

---

* I do not use the English expression "*intellectual* history," because of the over-intellectual connotation of this term, which does not include, as does the German word *Geist*, *all* the creative impulses of the human mind (e.g., feelings): the *Histoire littéraire du sentiment religieux en France* of Abbé Bremond is *Geistesgeschichte*, not intellectual history.

It is as a criticism of his general methodology that this paper is primarily intended; but I have chosen to concentrate on this particular article of Professor Lovejoy's because the contemporary significance of the conclusions drawn therein offers a singular opportunity to test the soundness of his method.

The first step taken by Professor Lovejoy is to disavow the title of his article "The Meaning of Romanticism . . . ," for to him "Romanticism" has no meaning ("signification")—that is, it defies definition. Because the term cannot be straightforwardly defined he proceeds as though the phenomenon did not exist; since the whole is ungraspable he clings to individual facts of thought; instead of considering Romanticism he chooses a side-path by considering instead certain ideas, to him distinctive of "the Romantic period." But it is just such an analytical procedure that destroys the organic entity and makes the understanding of the whole no longer possible.

"Romanticism" is of course a very complicated "thing," since it is a "thing" hypostatized by the student of history in order to represent as a unit many traits concurring in different and not always precisely measurable doses in this particular movement. But so is any other classificatory term introduced by historians, as, for example, its opposite, "classicism" (Romanticism is of course *more* complicated, for a certain anarchy is an inherent feature of this phenomenon born of revolt). There is, of course, a certain violence done in cutting out of the flow of time a particular period, marked by various traits, and subsuming these under a label. But such violence is in the nature of the classifying function of language. If Professor Lovejoy's terminological punctiliousness were to be generally adopted by historians, they would be thereby deprived of the linguistic symbols which spare them the trouble of redescribing each time a given series of events which have been integrated into a unit, held together by a certain *Geist*, by the scholar who hopes to have grasped historic reality. And this would tend to encourage indulgence in the easy scepticism of that professor of history who, faced with the different conceptions of the French Revolution entertained by different historians (and by the revolutionaries themselves), asks cynically: "*Was* there ever a French Revolution?" And why stop at this stage of scepticism? Why not ask "Was there any Goethe?"—since we know that no parcel of Goethe's mind or body remained the same during the whole course of his life, marked by the manifold utterances of so self-contradictory a genius. By coining nouns in -*ism* and -*ist* the historian is simply following the natural trend of any linguistic community; indeed science in general does nothing but carry forward and perfect the work of language, as Condillac and Lichtenberg have said. Thus Romanticism is an appropriate symbol, coined by language, which suggests an emphasis on emotion, on the irrational, the mysterious, the metaphysical, the Christian, the fatalistic, the historical, a reaction against classicism (that *romantisme dompté* [tamed Romanticism]), etc., etc.—all of which features have in reality been found together in a definite period.

But since Professor Lovejoy does not recognize the factual existence of this compound phenomenon, he eschews the term "Romanticism." He uses the adjective "Romantic," but only with strictly temporal limitations ("the Romantic decades," "the Romantic period") or else in expressions which exempt him from responsibility ("writers traditionally labeled 'Romantic,'" "the German writers who . . . first introduced the term 'Romantic'"). He does not hesitate to use the personal substantive, since historians are agreed on the specific individuals to whom this term in -*ist* applies—but who can these be save the well-known representatives of German "Romanticism"? It is as if one should speak of Protestants while denying that such a thing as "Protestantism" exists (there are at least two features common to both Romanticism and Protestantism: rebellion against previous beliefs, and the supposition, for each one, of a creed of its own). Professor Lovejoy refuses to take the step which the Romanticists of whom he writes took, and which has been endorsed by common speech after them: the positing of an -*ism* as a—more or less hypothetical—unit. We may, qua philosophers of language, welcome the *Sprachkritik* [critique of language] which Lovejoy applies to language as a human institution, in regard to an -*ism* (Fritz Mautner, the coiner of this term, has spoken of the *Schlangenbetrug der Sprache* [snakelike betrayal of language]). But why should we, qua historians, shun a generally accepted term—and, in fact, a generally understood term? For the cultured public reacts to this word with the correct associations of connotations; not everyone is led by "his own associations of ideas with the word": there is a *communis opinio* concerning the descriptive elements implied by "Romanticism." It is only when analysts seek to replace the synthetic and descriptive implications of such a term by clear-cut definition (an attempt in which they must inevitably fail) that anarchy results; the unity which was understood by everyone is destroyed. It is a bias to believe that understanding must always wait on definition. To define even the word *table* is more difficult than to use the word correctly. And to distinguish all the different senses of *nature*, as Lovejoy has sought to do in other papers, does not release us from the obligation to see all these senses as a unit—since common use has posited this unit. In fact, the *-ism* "Romanticism," offered to us by language, can be, *pace* Lovejoy, a proper object of scientific research.

Having renounced an investigation of the phenomenon of Romanticism (i.e., denied "signification" to the term) he turns toward the "significance," the historic results, of some Romantic ideas: he limits himself to an examination of three separate ruling ideas which he has isolated by analysis out of the bulk of the German writings of the 1780's and 1790's. Professor Lovejoy outlines the next procedure incumbent upon the historian of ideas: to inquire into (1) the "logical," (2) the "psychological," (3) the "historical" relations of the ideas so discriminated. The first two inquiries the historian of ideas is admonished to carry out in his own mind "before he goes on to confront their results with the historical evidence to be found in his sources." That is, one should ask oneself: "What are the logical implications of such an idea as *Streben*?"; then, "What psychological relationships, what elective affinities, what emotional concomitants are theoretically possible to such an idea?"; and finally, "What actually *were* the implications of this idea, as found with a given thinker, in a given period?" According to Lovejoy the first two steps correspond to "the phase of constructing tentative hypotheses in the work of the natural scientist."

This obsession with the methods of natural science I shall discuss later; here I should like to stress the a priori approach advocated by Lovejoy as proper for the analyst of historical events. The analyst is not to seek to understand the given historical event in its complexity; he must analyze the compound offered to him (before really having understood its entirety), then close his eyes to the real event as it has taken place in history, and proceed to the combination, in his alembic, of the supposedly "pure chemical elements"—only later to compare with the *homunculus* of his breeding what history really has done with the same elements. But this last, properly "historical" operation is the *only one* which history itself, in its concreteness, has carried out: the operations (1) and (2) are useless games *in abstracto*. It is as if before contemplating a picture called "Spring" the student of art, after having read simply the inscription, should close his eyes and attempt to figure out the various logical possibilities of depicting Spring—only later to discover that he has not reckoned with the possibility (or possibilities) actually chosen by the painter. Why not first look at the actual picture?

Underlying the whole reasoning of Professor Lovejoy's scientific program is the assumption of the possibility of an "unemotional idea": an idea detachable from the soul of the man who begot or received the idea, from the spiritual climate which nourished it; an abstract idea that survives in history from generation to generation; a separate idea, always identifiable to the eye of the historian, in whatever period. *Eigentümlichkeit, Streben, Ganzes* may be discriminated in Romanticism; *Eigentümlichkeit, Streben, Ganzes* are just as easily to be discriminated in Hitlerism. I must object to that divorce between thought and feeling which Lovejoy seems to think possible: according to his phrase "affective *concomitants*" he would imply that it is only in a secondary way, as a result of a kind of adulteration, that the abstract idea is given a new slant by emotional factors. I should say rather that important ideas are from the start a *passionate* response to problems which agitate their period. Even the rationalism of Descartes was conceived, by him and by his contemporary followers, as a passionate destruction of an ageing order (Victor Klemperer, the German philologian, has spoken of the *heiße Vernunft*, "rationalism hot with passion," of Corneille the Cartesian). And the three Romantic "ideas" which Professor Lovejoy has singled out, organicism, dynamism, and diversificationism, seem to me to spring from *feelings*: basically, from the bodily or vital feelings of a healthy organism which enjoys the full display of its forces, and takes pride in its individuality. Indeed it is precisely this "healthiness" of Romantic thought which distinguishes it from the unhealthy, hectic fanaticism of the Hitlerites.

The assumption that an idea in history is a completely separate element is inconceivable to me: in any movement, with any individual, one idea is ever ready to merge with another. Nor may the living idea be considered apart from the movement, from the individual. *Streben* with the Schlegels [Friedrich and August Wilhelm] cannot be the same as with Goethe or Nietzsche—and the idea of any philosopher must be *toto coelo* different from an "idea" of a Hitler.*

---

*The great truth on this subject is implicitly stated in a quotation from Karl Mannheim which turns up in a review: "All the ideas that must be described as historical, since they are essentially embedded in the cultural setting of the age, change with the changing conception of human nature, and with the ethics and psychology which go with it."[2]

Professor Lovejoy will not permit himself the use of the "label" *Romanticism*, but he does not hesitate to employ the three labels *organicism, dynamism, diversificationism*. The first label, it is true, has been applied to a phenomenon composed of elements which, taken singly, may appear disparate and even antithetical. But surely not as disparate, not as antithetical, as are the three main tendencies of Romantic idealism to those of Hitlerian barbarism, to which Lovejoy would apply the same labels.

To a large extent Lovejoy admits this disparity. He does not suggest for a moment that the Nazis have an organic attitude toward life and nature and art. Obviously, the ideal of a personal striving toward the Infinite, as an aim for the German individual, has no place in the Nazi system. Nor does the New Order foster that tolerance, that joy in diversificationism, which the Romantics knew. How then, one may wonder, can he say that the Romantic ideas of *Ganzheit, Streben ins Unendliche* [dynamism toward the infinite],[3] and *Eigentümlichkeit* have survived?

He is enabled to say this, without the slightest difficulty, because he is dealing, not with the Romantic ideas themselves (i.e., *the ideas as conceived and as applied by the Romantics*), but with three abstract entities which he has chosen to name with the same names. As for the disparity between the *actual* Romantic ideas and those of Hitlerism, this is to be explained by reference either to (1) shift of application of the abstraction, or (2) a change in the nature of the "affective concomitants" attached thereto. *Eigentümlichkeit*, he says, has remained *Eigentümlichkeit*. It is true that, in utter opposition to the Romantic ideal of diversification, the New Order depends upon a system of standardization, of *Gleichschaltung*, which aims to obliterate all individuality. But this involves factor (1): shift of application: *Eigentümlichkeit* has shifted from the individual to the State. Or again, whereas to the Romantics *Eigentümlichkeit* inspired an essentially tolerant attitude, which encouraged each thing's growing in its kind, in Hitlerism it manifests itself in an essentially *in*tolerant insistence on one's own particular kind as supreme. To explain this we need only turn to factor (2): there has been an alteration in the "affective concomitants." Thus we need not be surprised that Lovejoy is able to find organicism with the Nazis: *das Ganze* has been applied to the political sphere, emerging from this operation as Totalitarianism, even though in this New Order the organic attitude may not endure, and in this Whole, which is the State, the individual functions, not organically, as a living member, but as a machine. Shift of application likewise explains how *Streben ins Unendliche* may be destroyed and yet survive: now it is the State that strives. In such enormous shifts as this lies precisely the subject-matter which should properly concern the historian of ideas: Which historical forces are responsible for the alterations? There is no driving force in any historical "line" *itself*!

After comparing the three Romantic ideas with their travestied counterparts in Hitlerism, one may well ask the reason why ideas potential of such good have borne such bitter fruit. This reason Lovejoy finds, not in any abrupt sociological change, not in the slow development of various trends deep-rooted in German civilization; he is able to solve the problem without stepping beyond the limits of the three ideas themselves. He insists that it is the *combination* of the three elements which is such an important factor in the establishment of Hitlerism. Any one or two of the ideas alone, he states, might have had beneficial results; it is in the compound formed by the three elements that the source of the evil must be sought. One is tempted to ask why the "culminating joint-effect" of which he speaks did not materialize until a century and a half after the teachings of the Romantic decades, and why the period immediately following upon Romanticism was attended with such a marvelous expansion in all fields of the humanities. It was then that modern philology, linguistics, history of art, folklore, etc., were brought to birth; and in these fields it is clear how the self-same "combination of elements" culminated in a quite different joint-effect. Here the diabolic trinity *Ganzheit–Streben–Eigentümlichkeit* did not work to the hurt of science and art. And, in opposition to Professor Lovejoy, I submit the thesis that it could just as well have brought about a beneficial German and international situation. It might have led to an introspective, mystic way of life, as advocated by Rilke after the First World War, which would have consisted in an individual striving toward the goal of developing the particular richness of the German spirit, by incorporating the whole of the world in itself. It is just such an ideal that Hitler would erase forever from the minds of his subjects.

But perhaps Professor Lovejoy does not mean to imply that his three elements must *necessarily* have combined to such a pernicious effect. At one point he indicates that it was because *das Ganze* had come to represent the State (a development apparently harmful per se) that *Streben* and *Eigentümlichkeit* were perforce modified and accommodated to this new nationalistic implication. But how is one entitled to assume that, within this combination, it was *das Ganze*, as the State, which represented the controlling idea, behind which the other two must needs fall in line? Moreover, the influence of the concern with the State is a variable factor, and the question of "dosage," disregarded by Professor Lovejoy, is highly important; the application of this combination of ideas to the State could, theoretically, have produced an ideal situation.

And one may even question the legitimacy of positing a combination of a, b, and c. Professor Lovejoy recognizes that other ideas are present in Hitlerism; he would probably admit the presence of an indeterminate number of ideas, d, e, f, . . . x. How then, in a discussion purporting to deal with Hitlerism, which is all of these things and all of these things at once, can one assume that any three of these elements have joined together to form a compound, and produce a joint-effect? Or, even assuming such a combination, $a + b + c$, since a given idea has now this implication and now that (a_1, a_2, a_3, . . . a_x), the actual number of combinations and permutations is virtually endless. Is it $a_2 + b_5 + c_{12}$ that have formed a compound? If so, the result may very well be quite different from that produced by $a_3 + b_7 + c_{16}$, etc.

The development suggested by Professor Lovejoy could perhaps be illustrated by the following diagram:

$$a + b + c + . . . x \qquad \text{Romanticism ("ideas of the Romantic}$$
$$\downarrow \quad \downarrow \quad \downarrow \qquad\qquad \text{critics of the 1780's–1790's")}$$
$$a_1 + b_1 + c_1 + . . . x_1 \qquad \text{Hitlerism}$$

a is continued in a_1, etc.; $a + b + c$ form a compound; this compound "helps to explain" Hitlerism; therefore Romanticism helps to explain Hitlerism.

In contrast I submit a different diagram:

$(a_{\alpha\text{-}\varrho}, b_{\alpha\text{-}\varrho}, c_{\alpha\text{-}\varrho}, \ldots x)$ Romanticism

$(a_{\nu\text{-}\omega}, b_{\nu\text{-}\omega}, c_{\nu\text{-}\omega}, \ldots x)$ Hitlerism

I draw no lines to indicate a continuity between the separate ideas in the first and second series; such a line might suggest an identity between, for example, a_η and a_π, and would give no indication of the differences that might exist between the subscripts. There has been no continuity, nor are the ideas separate entities. The subscripts $\alpha\text{-}\varrho$ and $\nu\text{-}\omega$ make allowance for the possibility of really identical variants in the two systems, although the likelihood of their occurrence is not too great; thus the "ideas" ν, ξ, o, π, ϱ may be common to both. Nor are the combinations of the three ideas separate entities. The only two entities involved are Romanticism and Hitlerism, each conceived as a whole. These form "climates," here indicated, for convenience in printing, by parentheses; there should really be an ellipse enclosing each polynome. There are no connecting threads; the two entities are disparate and incommensurable.

It must be stated that at no point does Professor Lovejoy declare his belief in the inevitable efficacy of the combination he posits; nowhere does he speak in terms of rigorous laws. Indeed, he is continually introducing qualifications lest any statement seem over-bold or too rigorously scientific. But I maintain that the very appeal of his article rests precisely upon the bold *implications* of his study, upon the scientific attitude *underlying* all his propositions. A scholarly text, as well as a poem, may have overtones; and listening to them is an essential part of reading. And it is to these implications, to this underlying attitude, that I am opposed.

For I do not doubt that like most readers I should find myself mainly in agreement with Professor Lovejoy's conceptions of both Romanticism and of Hitlerism. He must feel as keenly as I the vast differences between the two climates; it is evident that he recognizes that the *Eigentümlichkeit* of Hitlerism is a far cry from the *Eigentümlichkeit* of the Schlegels. And if I have insisted so strongly upon these differences of climate it is because, in my opinion, it is the two climates which must first be grasped; it is the differences which strike me as far more significant than any single details which might be said to exist in common. If Professor Lovejoy, faced with the same two climates, chooses to emphasize continuity, to deal with separate ideas abstracted from their wholes, it is because he has adopted the analytic method of the chemist, who isolates elements from their compounds.

Now the chemist claims for each element certain constant properties, a certain determinable efficacy; he establishes rigorous laws—otherwise he could not convince. Professor Lovejoy makes no such claim for his "element-ideas." But in spite of his own caution the very method he has chosen is one which must depend for its cogency upon scientific rigor. An article entitled "The Meaning of Romanticism," which rejects the possibility of ascertaining the "signification" of this term and seeks, in its stead, the "significance" of the historical phenomenon—and finds it in Hitlerism—such an article, orientated from the start to such a goal, can reach it only by establishing clearcut, uncontrovertible relationships. Otherwise, Hitlerism has no place in this article on Romanticism. *Tertium non datur* [There is no third alternative].

To a reader who has made up his mind to follow the scientific method in the history of ideas, it must be disappointing that Lovejoy's method, while not flexible enough to cope with the complexity of the problems envisaged, is, at the same time, not rigorous enough—not as rigorous as a "scientific" approach should be.

But now let us step beyond the limits of the narrow system of *a*, *b*, and *c* and examine the second "climate." As with Romanticism, Lovejoy does not discuss Hitlerism-as-a-whole or seek to define it. Nor shall I hazard a clear-cut definition or a lengthy discussion; instead I shall try to "describe" it, simply by jotting down a list of catch-words, *-isms*—a list which does not pretend to be exhaustive. This description will be as little original as any description must be of a phenomenon which has become familiar to all thinking contemporaries:

Nationalism + socialism { = national socialism} in domestic as in foreign policy; collectivism (*Volksnähe*); messianism (*Führerprinzip*); anti-intellectualism; *Realpolitik* and worship of technology (the German word *Gleichschaltung*, originally applied to electrical contrivances, is significant!); paganism (this-worldliness); acceptance of death and dangerous life; racism ("diversificationism"); *étatisme* [state control] (*das Ganze*); Machiavellianism (force + ruse); emphasis on a simple, austere private life (in contrast with the sumptuous "life of the State"); politicism (everything must be considered from the political angle—especially the power of words); dynamism (called *Dezisionismus* by Karl Schmidt, the theoretician of the Reich); an (officially stated) hierarchy of values and of individuals—subject to change.

To this list of the component parts of Hitlerism it may be objected that some are only the methods purporting to carry out the "ideas"—as, for example, Machiavellianism and the worship of technology. But who could truly claim that in Hitler's system Machiavelli's story of the lion and the fox serves merely the subordinate purpose of suggesting a means for the carrying out of certain ideas, and has not itself come to represent an idea, an ideal of a new type of mankind? And as for technology, this is surely an "idea," an *idée fixe* with Hitler. Again, one may object that my descriptive terms are often contradictory: socialism of the Hitler brand is not egalitarian but tinged with diversificationism (as much so in the international as in the national field); and the anti-intellectualistic creed of "soil and blood," "back to nature and hearth" should inspire a hatred of technicism. But such is the reality of Hitlerism and to iron out contradictions would be to falsify this reality.

It is the totality of just such heterogeneous features that gives us the moral climate of Hitlerism—which tinges each of the single features. Embedded in this whole one may discern Lovejoy's three elements. But with a picture, however roughly sketched, of this whole before our eyes, how arbitrary now it seems to single out any given three component parts and marshal them into a combination! Indeed, I wonder if a study of Hitlerism would ever lead one to single out, even for emphasis, these particular three (unless, of course, one had begun his inquiry with these ideas already in mind). That Professor Lovejoy found these ideas in Romanticism is one matter, and everyone must agree that they are indeed highly characteristic of the German Romantics. But what student of Nazi philosophy, concerned immediately with the "tragic spectacle of Europe today" considered in all its complexity, would think of characterizing it in terms of *Ganzheit–Streben ins Unendliche–Eigentümlichkeit*? This is only another way of saying that the "Romantic" elements *a*, *b*, *c* found in Hitlerism occupy a different position in relation to other elements and possess a different degree of relevance for the Hitlerian system.

Now the question of the relative importance of these three ideas in the Hitlerian system has, if considered merely as a difference of opinion about the present-day political situation in Germany, no particular significance for the debate in question. But I am not objecting that Professor Lovejoy, after studying Hitlerism, has chosen to assign more importance to certain aspects than I should. My objection is that he found these ideas first, not in Hitlerism, but in Romantic idealism, and then sought to find them in Hitlerism by the procedure of tracing the career of individual, abstract ideas as isolated units. This method seems to me erroneous, and bound to lead to erroneous conclusions; and as a corollary to my objections to his method, I must object also to its results—which consist not only of a questionable characterization of Hitlerism, but, what is far more important, of the conclusion that present events can be blamed on the great Romantic thinkers.

This is a startling opinion to ascribe to Professor Lovejoy, and I do not make the statement lightly. I find this assumption implied throughout the article in his insistence on *continuity*; if I believed, as does Professor Lovejoy, that the main ideas of Romanticism had survived until today and that they represented the main ideas of Hitlerism, then I should *have* to believe that Romanticism has been responsible for Hitlerism. To this argument, based on his paper as a whole, it might be objected that, since Professor Lovejoy is dealing with abstract ideas the nature of which I fail to grasp and the existence of which I doubt, it is possible that he has not drawn the logical deductions which appear to me inevitable, given, for example, such a statement as "*Eigentümlichkeit* has survived." But how, then, is the following positive statement to be explained?

"For a particular group of these {Romantic} ideas, *continuously at work on the minds of the educated and reading public*, for fifteen decades, have produced in our time a sort of culminating joint-effect, which is at least an essential and conspicuous part of the monstrous scene presented by Germany and by Europe today."[4] What meaning does this sentence possess, if not that Romanticism has been influential in the production of Hitlerism? For while it is one thing to say that the Nazi leaders have seized upon certain Romantic ideas, distorting them to serve their purpose, it is quite another to say that these ideas worked continuously upon the people, making it easier for them to accept Hitlerism.

But it is hardly accurate to speak of the continuous influence of these or any other Romantic ideas on the "educated and reading public." In German secondary schools and universities, the teaching of the humanities was, until the unhappy day when Hitler came to power, based upon the German *classics* of the eighteenth century: Goethe and Schiller were given three times more space and importance in the literature classes than the Romanticists, who in Germany at least produced few lasting and perfect works of art. Indeed, it was the humanistic spirit of the classics and of Kant which managed to counterbalance the strong nationalistic tendencies which betrayed themselves in the *Gymnasien*. In the second place—perhaps this is primary—it was precisely *not* the educated and reading public which had become conditioned for Nazism: it was from quite other ranks of society that Hitler recruited his followers. Thomas Mann, who is after all the typical representative of humanistic tendencies in the higher German bourgeoisie, in his *Deutsche Ansprache* called the Hitlerites "truants from school" (*entlaufene Schuljungen*).[5] And this is the true analysis: Hitlerism arose not among those who formed the backbone of German culture, but from the masses of the uneducated (ever a more ready prey for slogans), who had increased in number under the impact of war and post-war conditions. Thus there is no continuity of teaching from the Schlegels to Hitler; between them there is a cultural break caused by social upheaval. To the intellectuals of the Reich, the seizure of power by the Nazis appeared, as Eric Vögelin has phrased it, "an invasion by a foreign nation."[6]

Hitlerism is pagano-collectivism, the German variant of a worldwide development—the ancestry of which is certainly not to be sought in the German Romantics of the eighteenth century, but, as Vögelin correctly states, in Marx and Lenin, to whom the *Führer* has avowed his debt (or rather, to the vulgarized decoctions of their philosophies as he understood them). Naturally, if one wanted to "analyze" Hitler's "ideas" and trace them back to Marx, and from Marx to Hegel and from Hegel to the Romantics, one could say that, in a way, Hitler's thinking goes back to the Romantics; but then one would arrive at the truism that Europe in general has gone through Romanticism, a conclusion which would not lead to any specific reduction of this or that Hitlerian thought to Romantic ideas.

It is not the letter of any idea, or of any set of ideas, but the "spirit" in which the ideas are carried out and allowed to associate with each other—it is the total system of ideas charged with emotion that explains a historical movement. Professor Lovejoy's analytic "History of Ideas" fits easily into the pattern which, according to his own description, was superseded by the new scientific ideas which germinated in the 1780's and 1790's:

The whole was just the aggregate of its parts, and apart from them was nothing; and the dominant conception of scientific method . . . proceeded, in its investigation of any complex thing, by an "analysis" or "resolution" of it into its ultimate component parts. To understand *it*, you had but to take it to pieces, to know the parts and *their* characteristics and the laws of their action, and how many of them there were in the given complex—and your problem was solved.[7]

This is exactly what Professor Lovejoy is doing in his History of Ideas and what, according to my way of thinking, has made him miss the right explanation of Hitlerism. In fact, this atomistic kind of History of Ideas is derived, via the immediate French models (Gustave Lanson's history of the idea of progress, etc.), from the analytical philosophy of history of the French Encyclopedists, more specifically from Voltaire's *Dictionnaire philosophique*, which obviously rests on the assumption that, just as words may be listed in a dictionary detached from the whole of the linguistic system in question (and, supposedly, may exist as detached items), so ideas are detachable from their "climate" (Voltaire would say *mœurs*).

But we are only now beginning to realize how little justified is the linguistic analogy itself: the boundaries between words are never fixed; and it is impossible to trace the history of a single word without taking into account the whole conceptual field (*Begriffsfeld*). One cannot outline the history of *wit*, for example, without taking into account *wisdom, cleverness, intelligence, humor, sage, wizard,* etc. And it is even more true that the linear histories of ideas, in order to correspond to reality, must fit into larger histories of spiritual aggregates. Even Voltaire occasionally recognizes this; it is true of his French followers, and it is especially true of Professor Lovejoy himself, whose masterpiece, *The Great Chain of Being*,[8] the history of "three ideas which have . . . been so closely and constantly associated that they have often operated as a unit," turns out to be a kind of universal *Geistesgeschichte*, a world history of spiritual climates focused on these several ideas. The most brilliant chapters, those dealing with the cosmography of the Renaissance, the philosophy of the Enlightenment and of Romanticism, really belong to universal history—and are only incidentally connected with Plato's "chain of being." It could not happen otherwise; it happened fortunately (*felix culpa!*), and this in spite of the program, outlined in the introduction, for an analytic history of ideas comparable to analytic chemistry— the program carried out, if somewhat hesitatingly, in the article under discussion.

I do not deny the possibility of writing a history of one idea; but in that case the idea must remain in its proper climate—that is, within the limits of one definite science or field of activity. Obviously one may write the history of the idea of evolution *in biology*, the idea of inhibitions *in psychology*, the idea of ideology *in political science*. It is also possible to study horizontally the influence of the idea of biological evolution on other fields of human thought and activity, the influence of the idea of psychic inhibitions on other fields, etc. But to reduce artificially the history of a historical event or movement, which rests on the whole human climate of an epoch, to two or three components, and to make this match a similar "reduction" of another epoch arrived at with equal artificiality, seems to me to involve an encroachment of the analytic capacities of the inquirer on the human reality that is the object of his research. Moreover, to shift continuously from an "idea" in the realm of thought to an "idea" in the realm of action, and to assume their basic identity, seems to me to be based upon an illicit generalization which in our case blurs the clear lines of demarcation between thinking and action.

In opposition to such an *histoire des idées*, with its bias for naturalistic and atomistic methods applied to the history of the human mind, I propose a *Geistesgeschichte*, in which *Geist* represents nothing ominously mystical or mythological, but simply the totality of the features of a given period or movement, which the historian tries to *see as a unity*—and the impact of which, the philosophy of the Encyclopedists and positivistic mathematicians to the contrary, does in fact amount to more than that of the aggregate of the parts. There have been, God knows, many *Fabrikate* [manufactured goods] of more or less recent German make, in which the pursuit of the integration of features of detail into one whole has served as an excuse for confusion and muddled thinking—so rightly condemned by Professor Lovejoy. But such writings should not be allowed to discredit the legitimate endeavors of a Burckhardt, a Dilthey, a Simmel, a Max Weber, a Tröltsch. There is nothing fraudulent or even revolutionary in a procedure which seeks to see wholes, to put one whole into relation with another, instead of making combinations of parts detached from their wholes. This is simply the *factual*, the more accurate approach toward the historical problem in question.

And so it seems to me tragic that, in inorganically detaching certain features from the whole of Romanticism in order to draw lines of continuity with our times, the historian of ideas has discarded the very method, discovered by the Romantics, which is indispensable for the understanding of the alternation of historical or cultural climates.

LINGUISTIC PERSPECTIVISM
IN THE 'DON QUIJOTE'

This essay appeared as the first of four studies presented by Spitzer as demonstrations of the method of interpretation that he outlined in "Linguistics and Literary History" (the first essay in this volume). It is in fact one of the most perfectly realized examples of the "philological circle." From beginning to end its argument follows the "pendulum movement, to-and-fro" between minute details of the periphery of the literary work and its "life-giving center" in the *Weltanschauung* of the author, integrating more and more textual elements and disclosing wider and wider ranges of significance concerning the unified structure of the work, its place in cultural and literary history, and the nature of its author's vision. The analysis demonstrates how brilliantly Spitzer can exploit his great experience in linguistics to clarify literary texts. The initial intuition through which he grasps the work's inner ordering principle is the result of his observation of the numerous name changes in Cervantes's characters and the varying etymological explanations that are attached to them. Such linguistic phenomena and numerous others that Spitzer goes on to analyze—puns, hybrid word-formations, the interplay of different levels of speech and dialects, the perspectivistic refraction of things and actions through inconclusive dialogue—reveal the "multivalence which words possess for different human minds" and reflect Cervantes's relativist vision of the complexities and ambiguities of man's life on earth. Spitzer's concluding remarks concerning Cervantes's revolutionary creation of a new literary form that would integrate the critical and the imaginative, and his striking portrait of the artist as the hero of the work—standing godlike above the uncertainties of his created universe, endowing his characters with autonomy, and manifesting his presence and total control by numerous illusionistic narrative techniques—place his interpretation firmly in the critical traditions descending from the German Romantics' unprecedented insights into Cervantes's irony.

It might be pointed out that, although Spitzer is widely known for his polemical dialogues with other scholars, this essay shows how fruitfully he can utilize their interpretations. In a discussion of his method shortly before his death in 1960 (see "Development of a Method," the last essay in this volume), he even acknowledged that many of his studies take as their point of departure not the textual detail but rather the insight of a critic, which is then subjected to the proof of stylistic analysis. In this case Spitzer points out that his general interpretation of *Don Quijote* confirms the conclusions of Américo Castro's influential study of Cervantes's perspectivism within the philosophical milieu of the European Renaissance. Spitzer's essay has endured as one of the most important of the numerous studies written under the impact of *El pensamiento de Cervantes*, and, in its relentless focus on the details of Cervantes's text, it can be said to be a refinement on Castro's more positivisitic and atomistic approach to *Don Quijote* as a manifestation of intellectual backgrounds.

This article was first published in Spitzer's *Linguistics and Literary History: Essays in Stylistics* (Princeton, N.J., 1948), pp. 41–85. It is reprinted by permission of Princeton University Press.

Linguistic Perspectivism in the 'Don Quijote'

Argumentum: Here, the procedure will be to start from a particular feature of Cervantes's novel which must strike any reader: the instability and variety of the names given to certain characters (and the variety of etymological explanations offered for these names), in order to find out what may be Cervantes's psychological motive behind this polyonomasia (and polyetymologia). I see this as a deliberate refusal on the part of the author to make a final choice of one name (and one etymology): in other words, a desire to show the different aspects under which the character in question may appear to others. If this be true, then such a relativistic attitude must tinge other linguistic details in the novel; and, indeed, it is surely such an attitude that is behind the frequent debates (particularly between Quijote and Sancho), which never end conclusively, over the relative superiority of this or that word or phrase. It is as if language in general was seen by Cervantes from the angle of perspectivism. With this much settled, it will not be difficult to see (what, in fact, has been recognized by Américo Castro) that perspectivism informs the structure of the novel as a whole: we find it in Cervantes's treatment of the plot, of ideological themes, as well as in his attitude of distantiation toward the reader.

And yet, beyond this perspectivism, we may sense the presence of something which is not subject to fluctuation: the immovable, immutable principle of the divine—which, perhaps, to some extent, is reflected in the earthly *artifex* himself: the novelist who assumes a near-divine power in his mastery of the material, in his own unshaken attitude toward the phenomena of his world (and even in his aloofness from the reader). And it is in this glorification of the artist that the main historical significance of the Spanish masterpiece is to be seen.

Much, though not too much, has been written about Cervantes's master novel. Yet, we are still far from understanding it in its general plan and in its details as well as we do, for instance, Dante's *Commedia* or Goethe's *Faust*—and we are relatively further from an understanding of the whole than of the details. The main critical works of recent years, which represent gigantic strides forward toward the understanding of the whole, are, in my opinion, Américo Castro's *El pensamiento de Cervantes*,[1] in which the themes of Cervantes's poetry of ideas are stated, and Joaquín Casalduero's article "La composición de 'El ingenioso hidalgo Don Quijote de la Mancha,'"[2] in which the artistic architecture of the novel, as based on the themes recognized by Castro, is pointed out. As for the style of the novel, Helmut Hatzfeld, in his book *Don Quijote als Wortkunstwerk*,[3] has attempted to distinguish different "styles" determined by previous literary traditions (the pastoral or chivalric styles, the style of Boccaccio, etc.)—without, however, achieving what I should call an integration of the historical styles into one Cervantine style in which the personality of the writer would manifest itself. Perhaps it is better not to break up the unity of a work of art into historical units which, in any case, are extraneous to Cervantes and, instead, to proceed according to a method by which one would seek to move from the periphery toward the center of the artistic globe—thus remaining within the work of art. Any one outward feature, when sufficiently followed up to the center, must yield us insight into the artistic whole, whose unity will thus have been respected. The choice of the particular phenomenon, then, would appear to be of secondary importance: any single one must, according to my ideology, give final results.

Accordingly, I shall choose certain linguistic phenomena (of, at first glance, slight importance for Cervantes's artistic cosmos) which I shall attempt to reduce to a common denominator, later to bring this into relationship with the "pensamiento," the *Weltanschauung* of Cervantes.

Any reader of the *Quijote* is struck by the instability of the names of the main characters of the novel: in the first chapter we are told by

Cervantes that the protagonist has been called, by the sources of "this so truthful story," alternatively Quijada, Quesada, or Quijana (this last, according to Cervantes, being the best "conjecture"); from this assortment the *ingenioso hidalgo* [ingenious gentleman] chose, before starting his knightly career, the name that he was to bear in the whole book: Quijote. When, at the end, he is cured of the fever of quixotism and repudiates *Amadís de Gaula* and the rest of the novels of chivalry, he recovers his unpretentious prosaic original name (bk. II, ch. 74): "ya no soy don Quijote de la Mancha, sino Alonso Quijano, a quien mis costumbres me dieron renombre de *Bueno*" [I am Don Quijote of la Mancha no longer, but Alonso Quijano, called for my way of life *the Good*];[4] and the final scene of his Christian death and regeneration seems rounded out by a kind of re-baptism, as this *loco* [madman] becomes a *cuerdo* [sane man] (the change of name is thrice mentioned in this final chapter, as if the author wanted to din it into our heads that the old Adam is dead); in his will, "Quijano" calls his niece Antonia by the name "Quijana," as if to emphasize that he is now a *bourgeois rangé* to the extent of having a family bearing his own (everyday) name. The first-mentioned name, Quijada, is also used in recognition of the reasonable side of the protagonist's nature: earlier (I, 5) he was referred to, by an acquaintance who knew him in the days before his madness, as "Señor Quijada." Again, just as Quesada, Quijada, or Quijana became a Quijote when he fancied himself a knight, so, when his chivalric dreams seemed about to give way to those of pastoral life, he imagines himself to be called "el pastor Quijotiz" [the shepherd Quijotiz] (and his companion, Sancho Panza, "el pastor Pancino").*

---

* And in that same pastoral game (II, 67) Sansón Carrasco would become "el pastor Sansonino" or "el pastor Carrascón" (two names!), the barber > "Nicolás Miculoso" (after *Nemoroso*, as Quijote explains), *el Cura* [the priest] > "el pastor Curiambro" (reminiscence of the giant Caraculiambro?); as for the name of Sancho's wife, however, the squire, who always pays heed to the *convenientia* of words and objects, agrees only to "Teresona" as the pastoral name for his fat Teresa. We see why he cannot agree to "Teresaina": this name, proposed by Sansón Carrasco (II, 73), is so evocative of the ethereal music of the flute (*dulzaina*) that Don Quijote must laugh at "la aplicación del nombre."

In another episode, Dorotea, who plays the role of Princess Micomicona (I, 30), feigns that her presumptive rescuer is called "{si mal no me acuerdo,} don Azote o don Jigote" [{if I remember rightly,} Don Azote or Don Gigote]. And the Countess Trifaldi jocundly endows him with the superlative for which she seems to have a predilection: "Quijotísimo." As for his epithet "de la Mancha," this is coined (I, 1) after Amadís de Gaula. Later, he will be called by the name, first given him by Sancho, "el Caballero de la Triste Figura" [the Knight of the Sad Countenance], still later by "el Caballero de los Leones" [the Knight of the Lions] (in II, 27–29, this change is strongly emphasized, and a certain character is rebuked by Sancho for having disregarded the distinction).*

---

* A pendant to Quijote, the believer in an unreal order of virtue, is Cardenio, the lover who cannot face that injustice which so often obtains in the reality of love. Thus we will not be astonished to find that the onomastic pattern, dear to the romances of chivalry, represented by "Caballero de la Triste Figura" is also applied to Cardenio: he is alternatively called (by the shepherds who tell his story) "Roto de la Mala Figura," "Caballero de la Sierra," "Caballero del Bosque" [Ragged Knight of the Sorry Countenance, Knight of the Mountains, Knight of the Wood]—before he himself is allowed to state his simple, real name: "Mi nombre es Cardenio" [My name is Cardenio].

The importance of the *name* for the Middle Ages appears here most clearly; any knight of romance, Amadis or Perceval or Yvain, is presented as undergoing an inner evolution, whose outward manifestations are the different "adventures" which mark his career; and it is by virtue of these adventures that he acquires different names, each of which is revelatory of the particular stage attained; in this way, the evolution is clearly labeled for the reader. Yvain acquires a new dignity, so to speak, when he becomes the "Chevalier au Lion"; "Orlando innamorato" is a different person from "Orlando furioso." Consequently, a mistake in names is no slight mistake: it is a sin against the law of inner evolution which presides over the events of a heroic life. It is significant that Don Quijote speaks (I, 18) of "la ventura aquella de Amadís {de Grecia}, *cuando se llamaba el Caballero de la Ardiente Espada, que fué una de las mejores espadas que tuvo caballero en el mundo*" [It is even possible that my fortune may procure me the sword Amadis wore *when he was called the Knight of the Burning Sword*. It was one of the best ever worn by any knight in all the world]. It is precisely because this extraordinary sword distinguishes objectively one of the exemplary phases of the evolution of the knight that the name under which he appears has a somewhat objective, temporally definable validity.

It is obviously required by chivalric decorum that whoever enters the sphere of the knight Don Quijote must also change his or her name: Aldonza Lorenza > Dulcinea ("nombre a su parecer músico y peregrino y significativo" [a name that seemed to him musical, strange, and significant]), Tolosa > doña Tolosa, la Molinera > doña Molinera (I, 3), and the anonymous nag receives the name of Rocinante ("nombre a su parecer alto, sonoro y significativo" [a name that seemed to him grand and sonorous]: note the parallel wording appearing in the justifications for the names given to Dulcinea and to the nag); incidentally, the ass from which Sancho is inseparable is not deemed worthy of a change of name that would be indicative of a change of rank. Although Sancho Panza, the peasant squire, undergoes no change of name similar to that of his master,* and is resolved always to remain (governor or no governor) plain Sancho without the addition of "don" (II, 4), there is some uncertainty in regard to his name, too, since, in the text of Cide Hamete Benengeli, the Arabian chronicler whose manuscript Cervantes purports to have found at the moment when other sources gave out (I, 9), there is a picture of thick-set Sancho with "la barriga grande, el talle corto, y las zancas largas" [a big belly, a short body, and long shanks], bearing the inscription: "Sancho Zancas."

---

* In II, 2, Sancho reports with pride that, though Don Quijote and his beloved are being celebrated by the historiographer Cide Hamete Berengena {*sic*} under their fanciful names ("El ingenioso hidalgo," "Dulcinea del Toboso"), his name has suffered no such treatment: "que me mientan . . . *con mi mesmo nombre de Sancho Panza*" [I'm mentioned, too, . . . *under my own name of Sancho Panza*].

It is, however, in regard to the name of Sancho's wife that the greatest confusion obtains: Sancho calls her first "Juana Gutiérrez mi oíslo" [Juana Gutiérrez, my poppet] (I, 7); a few lines later, he ponders whether a crown would fit "la cabeza de Mari Gutiérrez" [Mary Gutiérrez's head]—which change the more intelligent commentators, seeking to avoid bringing the charge of inconsistency against Cervantes, rightly explain by the fact that *Mari* had come to represent simply a generic and interchangeable name for women. But in II, 5, Sancho's wife calls herself Teresa Cascajo; from then on she is either Teresa Panza or Teresa Sancho, "mujer de Sancho Panza" [wife of Sancho Panza]; of the name Teresa itself she says (II, 5): "Teresa me pusieron en el bautismo, nombre mondo y escueto" [Teresa they wrote me down at my baptism, pure and simple]. Evidently we have to do with a woman named Juana Teresa Gutiérrez, who becomes a Juana Panza, or Teresa Panza when called after her husband, or . . . Cascajo when called after her father. Occasionally, however, according to the mood of the situation, she may be called "Teresaina" (II, 73) or "Teresona" (II, 67: because of her "gordura" [fatness]).*

---

* Again, we have evidence of the importance of nomenclature: a change of suffix, in itself, may be equivalent to a change of linguistic perspective.

In another incident (I, 22), from one of the secondary episodes, we are told that, when the guard speaks of his prisoner, Ginés de Pasamonte, as "el famoso Ginés de Pasamonte, que por otro nombre llaman Ginesillo de Parapilla" [the famous Ginés de Pasamonte, alias Ginesillo de Parapilla], the other retorts: "Señor Comisario, . . . no andemos ahora a deslindar nombres y sobrenombres. Ginés me llamo, y no Ginesillo, y Pasamonte es mi alcurnia, y no Parapilla, como voacé dice . . . algún día sabrá alguno si me llamo Ginesillo de Parapilla o no. . . . Yo haré que no me lo llamen" [Sargeant, . . . don't let us be settling names and surnames now. I am called Ginés, not Ginesillo, and Pasamonte is my surname, not Parapilla as you say . . . but one day somebody may learn whether my name is Ginesillo de Parapilla or not. . . . I'll stop them calling me that]. Again, just as in the case of Sancho's rebuke to the one who had altered Quijote's title, Cervantes takes occasion to show the natural indignation aroused by a violation of the "perspective" which the bearer of the name has chosen and under which he has a right to appear.

There are other cases, slightly different from those enumerated so far, in which the ignorance and weak memory of Sancho seem to create a "polyonomasia": here we can hardly think in terms of different traditions offered by chroniclers (as in the case of the names of Quijote), or of popular variation (as in that of the names of Sancho's wife): Sancho must multiply names simply because all the forms of names that he retains are only approximations to the real ones; they are variable because he cannot take a firm hold on them; he indulges in what linguists call "popular etymologies"—that is, he alters names according to the associations most convenient to his intellectual horizon. Sometimes he offers several variations, but even when only one alteration is involved, the effect of polyonomasia still remains because of the fact that the real name is also present in the reader's mind. Mambrino (I, 19–21), of whose helmet he speaks, becomes "Malandrino" (a "moro" [Moor]), "Malino" (=the Evil One), or "Martino" (a common first name); Fortinbras>feo Blas [ugly Blas] (I, 15), Cide Hamete Benengeli>". . . Berengena" [eggplant or aubergine] (II, 2; this Sancho justifies with the remark: "los moros son amigos de berenjenas" [Moors, for the most part, are very fond of aubergines]*), Señora Rodriguez de Grijalva > Señora González (II, 31), Magalona > "la señora Magellanes o Magalona" (II, 41).

---

* The same type of justification of a mispronunciation by the invention ad hoc of a (secondary) relationship is found in II, 3, when Sancho, in order to explain his version of the Arabic name *Benengeli* (i.e., Berengena), refers to the Moors' predilection for *berenjenas*.

A similar alteration of names is practiced by the *ama* [housekeeper], who (I, 7) contends that the books which we know to have fallen prey to the *auto-da-fé* (I, 6) had been ravished by the sorcerer Muñatón: Don Quijote corrects this to "Frestón." "Never mind Frestón or Fritón," answers the *ama*, "provided it is a name ending in -*ton*": word forms that are unalterable for the learned Don Quijote are quite exchangeable in the mind of the uncultured *ama*.

The names of the Countess Trifaldi are in a class by themselves since, in addition to the instability of names conditioned by a masquerade, there are involved the alterations to which Sancho is prone: here there coexist polyonomasias of the first and second degrees. The Countess is first (II, 36) introduced to us (by her messenger Trifaldín de la Blanca Barba [Trifaldín of the White Beard]) as "la condesa Trifaldi, por otro nombre llamada la Dueña Dolorida" [the countess Trifaldi, otherwise called the Afflicted Waiting-Woman]; one of the two names is her authentic one, the other, her "name within the world of romance" (just as Don Quijote is also the "Caballero de la Triste Figura"). When she appears in the pageant (II, 38) of the *carro triunfal* [triumphal car],[5] her name "Trifaldi" is given the following explanation: "la cola, o falda, o como llamarla quisieren, era de tres puntas" [her tail or skirt, or whatever they call it, fell in three trains]; the "mathematical" (geometrical) figure of her skirt with three flounces (or trains?) is so striking that every spectator must interpret her name as "la Condesa de las Tres Faldas" [the Countess with the Three Skirts]. But the scrupulous chronicler Benengeli, who, like Cervantes, seems to care about even the minor details of the fiction-within-the-fiction, is said by Cervantes to have stated that the character was really called "la Condesa *Lobuna*"—allegedly because of the presence of wolves [*lobos*] in her domain (he adds that, according to onomastic traditions in princely houses, she would have been called "la Condesa Zorruna" if foxes [*zorros*] had been prevalent in her domain)—but that she had dropped this name in favor of the more novel one derived from the form of her skirt. Now, this etymology of the name "Trifaldi," as stated by the chronicler (and as made evident to the eye of the spectators who see the masquerade skirt), had been somewhat anticipated by Sancho's popular etymology in II, 37: "esta condesa Tres Faldas o Tres Colas (que en mi tierra faldas y colas, colas y faldas todo es uno)" [this Countess Three Skirts or Three Tails (in my country skirts and tails, tails and skirts, are all the same)]. Ultimately we are presented with an array of (possible) names for the same character: la Condesa Trifaldi, de Tres Faldas, de Tres Colas (the latter name would be due to what the modern linguist in his jargon calls "synonymic derivation"), Lobuna ("Zorruna" again being a "synonymic derivate"),* Dueña Dolorida—a list as impressive as that of the names of Don Quijote.

---

* Sancho offers us another example of popular "synonymic derivation": *rata* "rate, installment of payment" has been understood by him as "rat," which, with him, must lead to *gata* "cat." As a matter of fact, the procedure by which developments take place in argot is not basically different from this: *dauphin* "dolphin" > "pimp" in French argot was interpreted as *dos fin* so that a *dos vert* could follow. The modern linguist would say that Sancho has the makings of an excellent subject for an inquirer such as Jules Gilliéron, who wanted to seize, on the spot, the working of the popular imagination. When faced with the problem of language, Sancho is not lazy and passive, as he is in general (and in this incessant linguistic criticism and linguistic activity, side by side with inactivity in other realms of life, he is typically Spanish): he asks himself why the Spanish battle cry is ¡*Santiago y cierra España!* [St. James and close Spain!]: "¿Está, por ventura, España abierta, y de modo, que es menester cerrarla, o qué ceremonia es esta?" [Is Spain perhaps open, that she has to be closed? Or what is this ceremony?] Erroneously he seeks to interpret, by contemporary patterns, a way of speech obscured by historic development. While he does not know as much historical grammar as does Antonio Rodríguez Marín, the modern commentator of the *Don Quijote*, he shows himself to be aware of the basic problem of linguistics: the opaqueness of certain ways of speech.

Now those commentators who, in general, take the line of emphasizing the satiric intent of Cervantes will point out that the variety of names attributed to the protagonist by Cervantes is simply an imitation of the pseudo-historical tendencies of the authors of chivalric novels who, in order to show their accurateness as historians, pretend to have resorted to different sources.*

---

*Accordingly, this variety of names would be on one level with such pseudo-historical interruptions of the narrative as we have seen in I, 2, when Cervantes pretends to hesitate about which particular adventure of his protagonist to narrate first: it seems that there are some *autores* ("authors" or "authorities") who say that the adventure of Puerto Lápice was the first; others contend the same about that of the windmills, while Cervantes, himself, has ascertained, from the annals of La Mancha . . . etc.

We shall see later, however, that the pseudo-historical device has implications much more important than the parodying of chronicles.

In the case of the names of Sancho's wife, some commentators point out, as we have seen, that the polyonomasia is due to the onomastic habits of the period; in the alterations of the name "Mambrino" they usually see a satire on Sancho's ignorance; in the case of the Condesa Trifaldi I have seen no explanation (Rodríguez Marín's edition points out possible "historical" sources for the costume itself of "tres colas o faldas").[6] But, evidently, there must be a common pattern of thought behind all these cases, which would explain (1) the importance given to a name or change of name, (2) the etymological concern with names, (3) the polyonomasia in itself.

Now it happens that just these three features are well known to the medievalist (less, perhaps, to students of Renaissance literature): they ultimately derive from biblical studies and from ancient philology: one need only think of Saint Jerome's explanation of Hebrew names or of Isidore's "Etymologies"—and of the etymologizing habits of all great medieval poets. The names in the Bible were treated with seriousness; in the Old Testament the name, or rather the names, of God were all-important (Exodus 6:2–3: "I am *Iahve*, and I have appeared to Abraham, Isaak and Jacob as *El Schaddai*, under the name of *Jahve* I was not known to them"; compare Exodus 3:14); the many *nomina sacra* [holy names] revealed the many aspects through which the divine might make itself felt.[7] Nor does the importance of the name decrease with the New Testamentary divinity (Christ is Immanuel). And, in the New Testament, a tendency appears which will have great influence on medieval chivalry: the change of name subsequent to baptism will be imitated by the change of name undergone by the newly dubbed knight. In all these sacred (or sacramental) names or changes of names, etymology plays a large part, because the true meaning (the etymon) may reveal eternal verities latent in the words—indeed, it was possible for many etymologies to be proposed for the same word, since God may have deposited different meanings in a single term: polyonomasia and polyetymology. Both these techniques are generally applied to a greater degree to proper names than to common nouns—because the former, "untranslatable" as they are by their nature, participate more in the mysterious aspect of human language: they are less motivated. In proper names the medieval mind could see reflected more of the multivalence of the world full of arcana. The Middle Ages were characterized by an admiration as well for the correspondence between word and thing as for the mystery which makes this correspondence unstable.

By all this I do not mean to deny that Cervantes followed the models pointed out to us by the commentators: what I do say is that, in doing so, he was also following certain accepted medieval patterns (which, however, he submitted to a new interpretation: that of his critical intelligence). It is possible, for example, in the case of the name "Trifaldi," to see on the surface a medieval imagination at work: the name is given an interpretation (*Trifaldi=tres faldas*) which, from our modern linguistic or historical point of view, is evidently wrong but which would have delighted a medieval mind, ever ready to accept any interpretation offering a clarification of the mystery of words.*

---

* It is in the medieval vein that Cervantes, in the Trifaldi episode (II, 40), has the name of the horse *Clavileño el Alígero* [Clavileño the Swift] explained as follows: "cuyo nombre conviene con el ser de leño y con la clavija que trae en la frente y con la ligereza con que camina" [which name fits him because he is wooden, because of the peg he has in his forehead, and because of the speed at which he travels]: *convenir, conveniencia* are the medieval (originally Ciceronian) expressions for "harmony"—as well as "grammatical accord," harmony between word and meaning, etc.

The ancient and medieval etymologies are indeed rarely those a modern linguist would offer, trained as he is to respect the formational procedures current in human language; the aim of those etymologies was to establish the connection between a given word and other existing words as a homage to God whose wisdom may have ordained these very relationships. The etymological connections that the medieval etymologist sees are direct relationships established between words vaguely associated because of their homonymic ring—not the relationships established by "historical grammar" or those obtained by decomposition of the word into its morphological elements.*

---

*A characteristic trait of the ancient and medieval etymological procedures was to explain by compounds where the modern linguist would assume derivation: Thus English *dismal* was explained by *dies mali* instead of as a derivative from Old French *disme* "dime."[8] In the same vein is the decomposition of the derivative *Truff-ald-{ino}* into the two parts *tri + fald-*. Compare also Sancho's decomposition (II, 3) of *gramática* into *grama* (the herb) + *tica* (the meaning of the latter word has not yet been elucidated by commentators).

In other words, we are offered edifying ideal possibilities, not deterministic historical realities; Isidore will connect *sol* [sun] and *solus* [alone] because of the ideological beauty of this relationship, not *sol* and ἥλιος [helios] as the comparative grammarian of today must do.

But, if the equation *Trifaldi = tres faldas* represents a "medieval" etymology, Cervantes himself did not take too seriously his own etymologizing: he must have been perfectly well aware of the historically real explanation—that which prompted him to coin the word. *Trifaldi* is evidently a regressive form from *Trifaldín*, which name, in turn, is the farcical Italian *Truffaldino*, "the name of a low and ridiculous character of comedy";[9] the reference to *truffare* "to cheat" is apposite, in our story, given the farcical episode intended to delude Don Quijote and Sancho. Thus the name of the messenger *Trifaldín* is (historically) not a diminutive of *Trifaldi*, as it might seem but, on the contrary, was preexistent, in Cervantes's mind, to the name of the mistress. The etymology of *tres faldas* is, historically speaking, entirely out of place. We have to face here the same para-etymological vein in which Rabelais (facetiously imitating medieval practice, while exemplifying the joyous freedom with which the Renaissance writer could play with words) explained the name *Gargantua* by *que grand tu as* {sc. *le gosier*}! [what a big one you've got {namely, the gullet}!] and *Beauce* by {*je trouve*} *beau ce* {sc. *pays*} [I find this fine {namely, the country}].[10] In this story, the para-etymological play with names serves to underline the deceitfulness of outward evidence; what for Quijote and Sancho are wondrous events are, in reality, only *burlas* [jests] in a baroque world of histrionics and disingenuity.*

---

* The trick intended for the protagonists is revealed in the midst of the pageant, when the majordomo, who plays the countess, corrects himself: "a este su criado, *digo, a esta su criada*" [this is your waiting-man—*I should say, waiting-woman*].

It may be stated that such baroque effects are on the increase in the second part of the *Quijote*, where pageants, *burlas*, and *truffe* flourish (compare "Las bodas de Camacho" [Camacho's wedding, II, 20 and II, 21]). In Part I we are shown the aggressive Don Quijote and his grumbling but faithful follower Sancho challenging the outward world—meeting, in their adventures, with a flux of humanity in a series of chance encounters against the fluid background of roadsides and inns. In Part II, however, the couple appear rather as being challenged than as challenging the world—and this world, the world of the big city, the world of the aristocracy, is now more formidable, more firmly constituted. The resistance of the first environment was not sufficient to bring about the necessary cure of the knight: Quijote must be brought to face the criticism of the higher spheres of society, where he is victimized with sophisticated *burlas*. The aristocrats play theater for Don Quijote and Sancho (in a way that may remind us of Shakespeare's Sly—and the "governorship" of Sancho resembles Sly's temporary courtship). And theater, like *sueño* [dream], is bound to end with an awakening from illusion. This is a baroque theme.

If Mr. Stephen Gilman is right in claiming for Avellaneda's continuation of the *Quijote* a baroque style, it might be apposite to add that Cervantes himself, whether prompted by his competitor or not (and I personally think, rather not), went the same path of "baroquization" in his own continuation of the story.[11]

The disingenuous procedure of offering such "medieval" etymologies as would occur to his characters (for the simpleton Sancho as well as the learned Arab Benengeli are medieval primitives) is also exemplified in the case of the nag Rocinante, whose name is interpreted by Don Quijote* in the style of Isidore: the horse was a *rocín antes*—which may mean either "a nag before" ("previously a nag," "an erstwhile nag") or "a nag before all others": "antes de todos los rocines del mundo."

---

* Don Quijote himself explains words according to an Isidorian scheme: for example, when he takes it upon himself to explain *albogues* (II, 67), he

begins by describing the *res* designated by the word ("albogues son unas chapas . . ." [*albogues* are thin brass plates . . .]), and follows this with the etymon: it is originally Arabic, he says, as the prefix *al-* suggests. Don Quijote cannot stop here, however; giving full rein to his associative imagination, he goes on to mention other Arabic words in Spanish likewise characterized by *al-*, and ends by including certain loan-words with a termination in *-í*.

Two explanations are given of one word, as was the general medieval practice—not the *one* historically true significance according to which the name was actually coined: namely, *rocín* + the noble and "literary" participial ending *-ante*. Cervantes was perfectly aware of the correct etymology but he allowed his medieval Don Quijote to offer a more "significant" one. He knew also the explanation of the name *Quijote* (= *quij-*"jaw" + the comic suffix *-ote*, derived from *jigote*, etc.), while his protagonist, who adopted this name, thought of it as patterned on *Lanzarote* [Lancelot].*

---

*The same "twofold pattern" is followed for the etymology of the (legendary, medieval) island of which Sancho is to become the ruler (II, 45): "la ínsula Barataria, o ya porque el lugar se llamaba Baratario o ya por el *barato* con que se le había dado el gobierno" [this was called the Isle Barataria, either because the town's name was *Baratario*, or because of the *barato*, or low price, at which he had got the government]; here, the first etymology is the formal or tautological one which Cervantes slyly proposes (in order to remain faithful to the dichotomy) as an alternative to the second—which is the historically "real" etymology.

My reason for believing that the *hidalgo* had *Lanzarote* in mind when he changed his name is found in the episode of I, 2, where Don Quijote adapts the text of the old *romance* [ballad] to his own situation, substituting his own name for that of the protagonist: "Nunca fuera caballero / De damas tan bien servido / Como fuera don Quijote / Cuando de su aldea vino" [Never was there knight / By ladies so attended / As was Don Quixote / When he left his village]. The suffix *-ote* (as in *monigote, machacote* [dunce, bore]) has a comic ring for the reader but not, evidently, for the coiner of the name.

We have a somewhat similar bivalence in the case of the name *Rocinante*—though here, of course, it is not the suffix but the radical which provides the comic effect. The noble connotation of *-ante*, that participial ending which had dropped out of current use in Old Romance languages, is to be found, with a nuance of high distinction, in such epic names as Old French *Baligant, Tervagant,* and in common nouns such as Old French *aumirant* (Spanish *almirante* [admiral]) and Spanish *emperante* [emperor] (found along with *emperador* in the *Libro de buen amor*). Thus, our learned knight, with his "epic imagination," came naturally by his predilection for such a pattern of nomenclature.

As for the factual etymology of the word *quijote* (<Old French *cuissot*, "cuissart"), this has been established by Yakov Malkiel. Mr. Malkiel, however, confuses historical linguistics with the study of a work of art when he writes: "The etymology of this word naturally aroused the curiosity of Cervantes."[12] In reality, Cervantes has not shown himself interested in the etymology of the common noun *quijote*, but in that of the proper name *Quijote*; and the latter was not, for him, derived from Old French *cuissot*, but from *Lanzarote*, and from the group *Quijada*, *Quijano* (whatever the origin of these may be).

Thus we may conclude that, while, for the medieval world, the procedures of polyonomasia and polyetymologia amounted to a recognition of the working of the divine in the world, Cervantes used the same devices in order to reveal the multivalence which words possess for different human minds: he who has coined the names put into them other meanings than those conceived of by the characters themselves: a *Trifaldín* who is for Cervantes a *truffatore*, a cheater or practical joker, is understood by Don Quijote and Sancho to be the servant of a Countess *Trifaldi* who wears a three-flounce skirt.

Perhaps this procedure is symptomatic of something basic to the texture of our novel; perhaps a linguistic analysis of the names can carry us further toward the center, allowing us to catch a glimpse of the general attitude of the creator of the novel toward his characters. This creator must see that the world, as it is offered to man, is susceptible of many explanations, just as names are susceptible of many etymologies; individuals may be deluded by the perspectives according to which they see the world as well as by the etymological connections which they establish. Consequently, we may assume that the linguistic perspectivism of Cervantes is reflected in his invention of plot and characters; and, just as, by means of polyonomasia and polyetymologia, Cervantes makes the world of words appear different to his different characters, while he himself may have his own, the coiner's, view of these names, similarly he watches the story he narrates from his own private vantage point: the way in which the characters conceive of the situations in which they are involved may be not at all the way in which Cervantes sees them—though this latter way is not always made clear to the reader. In other words, Cervantes's perspectivism, linguistic and otherwise,* would allow him qua artist to stand above, and sometimes aloof from, the misconceptions of his characters. Later we will have more to say about what lies behind this attitude of Cervantes; suffice it for us here, where we are given the first opportunity to look into the working of the (linguistic) imagination of the novelist, to have summarily indicated the relationship between his linguistic ambivalences and his general perspectivism.†

---

*As a nonlinguistic example of such perspectivism, we may point to the passage made famous by Hume: two kinsmen of Sancho, called upon to give their opinion of a hogshead of wine, find it excellent, in the main, except for a peculiar flavor—on which they disagree. The one insists it has a leathery taste, the other, a metallic taste. When they have finally drunk their way to the bottom of the cask, they find a rusty iron key with a leather strap attached.

†It is not astonishing that Dostoevsky, that great absolutist who delighted in showing up the relativity in human affairs, should have imitated the polyonomasia of Cervantes: In *Crime and Punishment*, the monomaniac Raskolnikov (whose name, related to *raskolnik* "heretic," suggests his monomania) has a friend named *Razumichin* (related to *razum* "reason"), who is the flexible, optimistic, helpful, and loquacious defender of reason: his flexibility of mind is mirrored in the alterations to which his name is subjected by other characters in the novel: *Vrazumichin* (to *vrazumlyaty* "to explain") and *Rassudkin* (to *rassudok* "judgment").

If, now, we turn back for a moment to Sancho's mispronunciations of names—which, as we have seen, was one of the contributing factors to the polyonomasia of the novel—we will recognize a particular application of Cervantes's linguistic perspectivism at work: to Sancho's uncultured mind, "Mambrino" must appear now as "Malino," now as "Martino," etc. In this, there is no suggestion of smugness on the part of Cervantes, as there might be with modern intellectual writers who would mock the linguistic "abuses" of ignorant characters; Cervantes presents "Malino," "Martino," etc., simply as the "linguistic appearances" of what, for Don Quijote, for example, can evidently be only Mambrino.*

---

*Sancho, who appears so often as the representative of that Catholic positivism which takes the world, as it is, as God-given, without envisaging the possibility of a more ideal order, expresses his linguistic doubts about the mysterious, significant, and musical names of Quijote's making, just as he usually (though not always) suspects the *arcana* of the world of enchant-

ment that his master visualizes: (I, 18): "no eran fantasmas ni hombres en-
cantados, como vuestra merced dice, sino hombres de carne y de hueso
como nosotros, y todos, según los oí nombrar . . . tenían sus nombres: que
el uno se llamaba Pedro Martínez y el otro Tenorio Hernández, y el Ventero
oí que se llamaba Juan Palomeque el Zurdo" [they were not phantoms or
enchanted, as Your Worship says, but flesh-and-blood men *like ourselves*.
And they had all got names, for I heard them . . . one of them was called
Pedro Martinez, another Tenorio Hernandez, and I heard them call the
innkeeper Juan Palomeque, the left-handed]. When he hears from Quijote's
lips the fantastic names of beings from a world he does not believe to exist,
he tries to bring these names down to earth, to adapt them to his homely environment. And in I, 29, when it is explained to him that the princess Micomicona is called so after her estate Micomicón in Guiney, Sancho is
happy only when he can find a parallel in the names of the common people
he knows, such as Pedro de Alcalá, Juan de Úbeda, Diego de Valladolid,
who are named after their birthplaces.

Evidently, the names in the world of Don Quijote must be, in opposition
to the homespun names of Sancho's world, the more grandiloquent the less
they cover of reality: they are of the grotesque, that is, the comically frightening kind, that distinguishes the names of Pulci's and Rabelais's giants: we
find (I, 18) Caraculiambro de Malindranía; el gran emperador Alifanfarón,
señor de la grande isla Trapobana [the great Emperor Alifanfaron, lord of
the great island of Trapobana]; Pentapolín del Arremangado Brazo [Penta-
polin of the Naked Arm]; Espartafilardo del Bosque, duque de Nerbia [Es-
partafilardo of the Wood, Duke of Nerbia]; and (I, 30) Pandafilando de la
Fosca Vista [Pandafilando of the Frowning Eye]—which last is transposed
by Sancho (in accord with the feeling he has acquired for linguistic correspondences between his master's speech and his own: $f > h$, *-ando* > *-ado*)
into *Pandahilado*; similarly, the poetic name *Fili* becomes, with Sancho,
hilo [thread] (I, 23): Sancho's capacity of transposition is the linguistic
equivalent of his capacity for adopting the fanciful schemes of Don Quijote.
Another aspect of Sancho's positivistic approach is his lack of that symbolic
feeling so characteristic of his master. He gauges symbolic actions according
to their "positive" or pragmatic value in actual life: when Don Quijote invites him, in order to symbolize the Christian democracy of men, to sit at his
table with him and the shepherds, Sancho refuses because of the inconve-
nience of having to be on his best behavior at the master's table. On the
other hand (for Cervantes knows always an "on-the-other-hand"), Sancho's
unmystical attitude is capable of producing good results: he is, during his
governorship, able to uncover the swindle involving the money concealed in
the staff, precisely because he disregards the symbolic value of the staff.

This lack of auctorial criticism in the face of so much linguistic relativity tends to shake the reader's confidence in established word-
usage. Of course, we are apt to rely on the correctness of Don Quijote's use of words and names; but who knows whether the knight,
who is so often mistaken in his attempts to define reality (as he is pre-

cisely in his identification of the helmet of Mambrino), has hit this time upon the right name, whether this name is not as much of a dream as are the fantastic adventures he envisions? (We are reminded of the baroque theme par excellence, "los sueños sueños son" [dreams are dreams].) Why should, then, "Mambrino" and not "Malino" or "Martino" be the name representing *reality*? The same insistence on "correctness" of word-usage, as applied to the non-existent, occurs in the scene where Quijote listens to the *ama*'s cock-and-bull story of the theft of the books by "the sorcerer Muñatón," and finds nothing to correct therein but the name: not "Muñatón" but "Frestón": Frestón and Mambrino are names correct in irreality (in books), representing naught in reality. Evidently we are offered in Don Quijote a caricature of the humanist* who is versed in books and bookish names but is unconcerned as to their valid relationship to reality (he has a pendant in the *licenciado* [licentiate] to whom Don Quijote tells the fantastic story of his descent to the *cueva de Montesinos* [cave of Montesinos] and who is outspokenly qualified by Cervantes as a *humanista*).†

---

*For us to apply this label to the knight striving to revive a medieval chivalric world, in the midst of his contemporary world of mass armies employing firearms, may seem surprising to the reader. But the humanistic world was a continuation of the medieval world: and what Don Quijote seeks to revive and reenact are humanistic dreams of antiquarians. The humanist tends to revive, by the strength of his imagination, a more beautiful past, regardless of how it may fit into his time; this is the ideal strength and the weakness of any humanist, and Cervantes has described both aspects.

†It has not been sufficiently emphasized that Cervantes, as so often happens (e.g., in the case of the diptychs Marcela–Don Quijote, Cardenio–Don Quijote, *el Cautivo–el Oidor* [the Captive–the Judge]; or in Don Quijote's speech on *armas y letras*), is proceeding by offering pendant pictures when he opposes to Don Quijote's vision in *la cueva de Montesinos* the speech of the *licenciado* on the humanistic books which he intends to write. Both turn to the past: the one seeks to relive it in the present, the other, to exhume it and transmit it through his books; both attempts, illustrating the same pattern of thought, are equally futile. Don Quijote's account of his visions is welcomed by the *licenciado* as a new "source" for his compilation of fanciful lore—while these same visions have been inspired by that same sort of lore.

In these two incidents we have a suggestion of a theme which informs our whole novel: the problem of the reality of literature. I belong with those critics who take seriously Cervantes's statement of

purpose: "derribar la máquina mal fundada de los libros de caballe-
ría" [overthrowing the ill-based fabric of these books of chivalry];
this statement, which indicts a particular literary genre, is, in fact, a
recognition of the potential danger of "the book." And, in its larger
sense, the *Quijote* is an indictment of the bookish side of humanism,* a creed in which, seventy years earlier, Rabelais had so firmly
believed, and an indictment of the "word-world" in which the Renaissance had delighted without qualms. Whereas the writers of the
Renaissance were able to build up their word-worlds out of sheer exuberance, free to "play" linguistically because of their basic confidence in life, with the baroque artist *desengaño* "disillusionment" is
allowed to color all things of the world, including books and their
words, which possess only the reality of a *sueño*. Words are no
longer, as they had been in the Middle Ages, depositories of truths
nor, as they had been in the Renaissance, an expansion of life: they
are, like the books in which they are contained, sources of hesitation,
error, deception—"dreams."

---

*Cervantes himself must have been vulnerable to the humanistic "book-
virus": he tells us that he used to pick up every printed scrap of paper—
surely not, like Saint Francis, because some sacred words might be on it, but
in order to live through the printed words a vicarious existence, in the fashion of his Don Quijote, that is, as a "novel-reader."

Cervantes must also, like any humanist, have delighted in the deciphering
of old documents: he tells us of the adventure of having Benengeli's Arabic
deciphered for his benefit; in the story of the *Cautivo*, the Arabic letter of
Lela Zoraida is puzzled out; and, in II, 39, a Syriac text is referred to: "es-
critas en lengua siríaca unas letras, que habiéndose declarado en la canda-
yesca, y ahora en la castellana, encierran esta sentencia" [some characters
written in the Syriac tongue, which, translated into Candayesque and then
into Castilian, make up this sentence]. To be polyglot is to delight in many
perspectives.

The same linguistic perspectivism is present in Cervantes's treatment of common nouns. For the most part we have to do with the
confusion, or the criticism, engendered by the clash of two linguistic
standards determined mainly by social status.*

---

*It could be said, of nearly every character in the *Quijote*, that he appears
located at his own particular linguistic level, somewhere along a hierarchic
ladder. The duchess, for example, who is quite conscious of her social and
linguistic superiority over Sancho, and who takes care to distinguish her

speech from his (II, 32: "la flor de las ceremonias, o cirimonias, *como vos decís*" [the flower of ceremonies, or "cirimonies," *as you call them*]) must be shown her inferiority, at least in matters linguistic, to Don Quijote: when the latter has occasion to speak of "la retórica ciceroniana y *demostina*" [Ciceronian and *Demosthenian* rhetoric], the duchess asks about the significance of the last word, remarking "que es vocablo que no le he oído en todos los días de mi vida" [it is a word I have never heard in all the days of my life], and is taunted by her husband: "habéis andado deslumbrada en la tal pregunta" [you have shown your ignorance by asking such a question]. Thus the same character has a chance to snub and be snubbed linguistically—as well as otherwise.

On the other hand we may ask ourselves: does Cervantes the super-humanist smile here at the reader over the head of the humanistic character Don Quijote? For the adjective *demostino* (an evidently popular haplology for *demostenino* "of Demosthenes") is incorrectly formed. Is Cervantes here revindicating again for himself a position above his protagonist by having Quijote the scholar make elementary mistakes?

Even when the characters lapse into a foreign language, there is a difference according to social classes—the standard "second language" in Cervantes's time being Italian. Don Quijote, being a Spanish humanist, must, of course, know Italian: he expressly states (II, 52) that he knows "somewhat" of Tuscan and can sing some stanzas of Ariosto; he examines a printer as to his knowledge of Italian vocabulary ("does he know that *pignatta* corresponds to the Spanish *olla* [stew]?"); and he occasionally inserts Italian forms into his facetious speeches: II, 24: "Notable *espilorchería*, como dice el italiano" [A notable *spilorceria*, as the Italians say]; II, 25: "Dígame vuestra merced, señor adivino: ¿qué peje pillamo?" [Tell me, you, Master Fortune-teller, *what fish do we catch?*]. Here we have rather farfetched idioms by which the humanist Quijote shows how conversant he is with the nuances that are better expressed in Italian than in Spanish.

We also find, in our novel, Italianisms used in the speech of the lower strata of society, where they seem to suggest the language of conviviality: the Ventero says of Maese Pedro (II, 25): "es hombre galante (como dicen en Italia) y bon compaño" [he's a gallant man, as they say in Italy, and a boon companion]; in the drinking scene between Sancho, his ex-companion Ricote, and the other pseudo-pilgrims, a *lingua franca* version of Italian is used at the height of their merriment (II, 54): "Español y tudesqui tuto uno: bon compaño"—(Sancho:) "Bon compaño, jura Di" ["Spaniard and Dutchman all one—goot gombanion," and Sancho would reply, "Goot Gombanion, I swear by Gott"]. Clemencín and Rodríguez Marín are therefore wrong when they object to a *caro patrón mío* [dear master] in the mouth of Sancho (II, 23); this is not humanistic Italian but the language of plain people indulging in exuberant gaiety.

Thus we have two types of Italianate Spanish, according to social strata.

Here, too, in this continuous give-and-take between cultured and uncultured speakers, there is given a suggestion of linguistic relativism that is willed by Cervantes. The opposition between two different ways of speech takes different forms: it may be Sancho who is interrupted and corrected by Don Quijote: in I, 32, {*hereje o*} *flemático* [heretical or phlegmatic] is corrected to *cismático* [schismatic]; in II, 7, *relucido > reducido* [concerted > converted]; II, 8, *sorbiese > asolviese* [resorb > resolve]; II, 10, *cananeas > hacaneas* [nackneys > hackneys]; II, 19, *friscal > fiscal* [cricket > critic].*

---

* Compare, for other mispronunciations of Sancho (II, 68): *trogloditas > tortolitas, bárbaros > harberos, antropófagos > astropajos, scitas > perritas a quien dicen cita cita* [troglodytes > ortolans, barbarians > barbers, Anthropophagi > Andrew popinjays, scythians > silly 'uns].[13]

Particularly interesting are the cases in which the term used by Sancho and the correction offered by Quijote are in the relationship of etymological doublets (popular and learned developments of the same root): (I, 12): *cris–eclipse, estil–estéril* [clipse–eclipse, stale–sterile] (how admirably has Cervantes anticipated the discoveries of nineteenth-century linguistics!). Again, it may be a question of Sancho's reaction to the language of the knight which the squire either misunderstands (in I, 8, Quijote's *homicidios* "murders" is transposed by Sancho into the more familiar, semipopular doublet *omecillos* "feuds") or fails to understand (in II, 29, Quijote must explain the meaning of *longincuos* {"por longincuos caminos" [longinquous ways]}, which he "translates" by *apartados* [remote]). In general, Don Quijote shows more tolerance for linguistic ignorance (in regard to the *longincuos* just mentioned, he excuses Sancho with the words: "y no es maravilla que no lo entiendes, que no estás tú obligado a saber latín" [and it is no wonder you do not understand it, for you are not obliged to know Latin]) than his uncultured associates (who seem more concerned with things than with words) do for linguistic pedantry: they often blame the knight for his *jerigonza* [gibberish] (I, 2), for his *griego* [Greek] (I, 16). And, when Don Quijote reproves Sancho for his use of *abernuncio* [bernounce] instead of *abrenuncio* [renounce], the squire retorts: "Déjeme vuestra grandeza, que no estoy agora para mirar en sotilezas ni en letras más o menos" [Let me alone, Your Highness, I'm in no state now to consider a letter or two more or less] (similarly, in II, 3, when the *bachiller* [bachelor] Sansón Carrasco corrects *presonajes* [presonages] to *personajes* [personages], Sancho remarks: "¿Otro reprochador de voquibles tenemos? Pues ándense a eso y no acabaremos en toda la vida" [So we have another vocabulary-corrector! If it goes on like this we shall never be done in this life]). Sancho adopts the attitude of a Mathurin Régnier, opposing the *éplucheurs de mots* [hairsplitters]! It may happen that the same Sancho, the advocate of naturalness in language, turns purist for the moment* for the edification of his wife, and corrects her *revuelto* [revolved] to *resuelto* [resolved] (II, 5); but then he must hear from her lips—oh, relativity of human things!—the same reproach he was wont to administer to his master: "No os pongáis a disputar, marido, conmigo. Yo hablo como Dios es servido, y no me meto en más dibujos!" [Don't start arguing with me, husband. I speak as God would have me speak, and I don't meddle with grand words!] (here, she is referring to the language of God, Who, as Sancho himself had already claimed, is the great *Entendedor* [Understander] of all kinds of speech).†

---

*It was to be expected that when Sancho became governor he would establish a linguistic level of his own, above that of his subjects. And, in fact, he once satirizes the way of speaking of a peasant by ironically carrying further a grammatical mistake of the latter; the scene in question could not be better analyzed than in the words of Alfred Morel-Fatio: "When the peasant comes to relate his case to the governor of Barataria, he searches his memory for the juridical word which expresses decently the act he has committed [that is, *yacer*, 'to lie, to sleep with'], and instead of 'hizo que *yoguié-semos*' [(the devil) made us lie together], the imperfect subjunctive, a form of which he has only a vague memory, he says *yogásemos . . .* as if the infinitive were *yogar*. Sancho, who, since he has become governor, has made an effort to speak correctly, gleefully seizes the occasion to underscore a blatant grammatical error by one of his fellow peasants: 'See to it, my good man, that you never again *yogar* [couple] with anyone,' he says with a patronizing smile, lingering as he does so on the word. Here one observes a finesse which the majority of readers of *Don Quijote* must have noted."[14] Sancho, the perpetrator of so many linguistic sins, is not insensitive to those committed by his subjects; his linguistic personality varies according to his interlocutor.

†This idea, which is a medieval one, is clearly expressed by Sancho when his wife contends that, since the time he became a member of the knight-errantry, she is no longer able to understand him (II, 5): "Basta que me entienda Dios, mujer, que el es el entendedor de todas cosas" [It's enough that God understands me, wife, for He's the understander of all things]. The same reliance on God appears in II, 7, when Sancho, whose remark, "yo soy tan *fócil*" [I am so *focile*] (*fócil* evidently representing a combination of *dócil* [docile] + *fácil* [simple]) has not been understood by Quijote, explains:

"soy tan así" [I am so-so!]; when this does not help, he exclaims: "Pues si no me puede entender, no sé cómo lo diga; no sé más, y Dios sea conmigo" [Well, if you can't understand me, I don't know how to say it, I can't say any more, God help me]. The coinage *fócil*, however nonexistent it may be in common language, covers the reality of Sancho's inner being, which is defined simply as "being as he is," and which he trusts God may recognize.

(Don Quijote, himself, must admit (II, 20) that Sancho, in spite of his *rústicos términos* [country language], would make a good preacher; and Sancho concurs boastfully, immediately introducing a solecism: "Bien predica quien bien vive, y no sé otras *tologías*" [He preaches well that lives well, and I know no other *thologies*].)

Another example of the linguistic intolerance of the common people is the retort of the shepherd who has been corrected for having said *más años que sarna* [live longer than Sarna] instead of *que Sarra* [than Sarah]: "Harto vive la sarna," he answers, "y si es, señor, que me habéis de andar zaheriendo {='éplucher'} a cada paso los vocablos no acabaremos en un año" [*Sarna* (the itch) lives long enough, too. If you make me correct my words at every turn, sir, we shan't be done in a twelvemonth]. In this case Don Quijote apologizes, and admits that there is as much sense to the one as to the other expression (in other words, he is brought to recognize the wisdom of "popular etymology"). Indeed, Don Quijote the humanist is made to learn new words, popular graphic expressions unknown to him—such as terms descriptive of *naturalia turpia* [natural matters to be ashamed of] which the high-minded knight was wont to eschew in his conversation (I, 48: *hacer aguas* "to urinate"; Sancho is triumphant: "¿Es posible que no entienda vuestra merced hacer aguas mayores o menores?" [Is it possible that Your Worship doesn't understand what making big or little waters is?]), or low argot expressions (I, 22: *gurapas* [galleys], *canario* [canary], from the language of galley-slaves). And—the acme of shame for a humanist!—it may even happen that he has to be instructed in Latinisms by Sancho (with whom they appear, of course, in garbled form), as when he fails to understand his squire's remark: "quien infierno tiene *nula es retencio*" [for him that's in hell, there is no holding back] (I, 25): it is significant that Sancho the Catholic Positivist is more familiar with ecclesiastical Latin terms than is his master, the idealistic humanist. Thus, Don Quijote is shown not only as a teacher but also as a student of language; his word-usage is by no means accepted as an ideal. And the reader is allowed to suppose that, to Cervantes himself, the language of the knight was not above reproach: when, in his solemn challenges or declarations of love, Quijote indulges in archaic phonetics (*f*- instead of *h*-) and morphology (uncontracted verb forms), this is not so different from the *a Dios prazca* [may it please God] of Sancho, or the *voacé* of one of the captives.

It seems to me that Cervantes means to present the problem of the Good Language in all its possibilities, without finally establishing an absolute: on the one hand, Sancho is allowed to state his ideal of linguistic tolerance (II, 19): "Pues sabe que no me he criado en la corte ni he estudiado en Salamanca para saber si añado o quito alguna letra a mis vocablos, no hay para qué obligar al sayagués a que hable como el toledano, y toledanos puede haber que no las corten en el aire en esto del hablar polido" [You know I wasn't brought up at the Court, and never studied at Salamanca to learn whether I'm putting a letter too many or too few into my words. You mustn't expect a Sayagan to speak like a chap from Toledo, and there may be Toledans who aren't so slick at this business of speaking pretty either]. On the other, Don Quijote may assert his ideal of an "illustrated language" (in the sense of Du Bellay): when Sancho fails to understand the Latinism *erutar* [eruct] (II, 43), Don Quijote remarks: "*Erutar*, Sancho, quiere decir 'regoldar,' y este es uno de los más torpes vocablos que tiene la lengua castellana, aunque es muy significativo. La gente curiosa se ha acogido al latín, y al *regoldar* dice *erutar*, y a los *regüeldos*, *erutaciones*; y cuando algunos no entienden estos términos, importa poco, que el uso los irá introduciendo con el tiempo, que con facilidad se entiendan; y esto es enriquecer la lengua, sobre quien tiene poder el vulgo y el uso" [*Eruct*, Sancho, means belch, and that is one of the coarsest words in the Castilian language, though it is very expressive; and so refined people have resorted to Latin, and instead of *belch* say *eruct* and for *belches*, *eructations*; and if some people do not understand these terms it is of little consequence, for they will come into use in time, and they will be generally understood; for that is the way to enrich the language, which depends on custom and the common people]. Thus, Don Quijote would create a more refined word-usage—though, at the same time, he realizes that the ultimate decision as to the enrichment of the language rests with the people; and he does not deny the expressivity of the popular expressions. Sancho's principle of linguistic expressivity, which is in line with his advocacy of the natural, of that which is inborn in man, must be seen *together* with Quijote's principle of linguistic refinement—which is a reflection of his consistent advocacy of the ideal: by positing the two points of view, the one problem in question is dialectically developed. It is obvious that in the passage on *erutar* we have a plea for a cultured language—though ratification by the common people is urged. But this is not the same as saying that Cervantes himself is here pleading for linguistic refinement: rather, I believe, he takes no final stand but is mainly interested in a dialectical play, in bringing out the manifold facets of the problem involved. Sancho has a way of deciding problems trenchantly; Don Quijote is more aware of complexities; Cervantes stands above them both: to him, the two expressions *regoldar* and *erutar* serve to reveal so many perspectives of language.*

---

*The attitude of Cervantes toward the popular adages is no different from that toward popular words: Sancho is given to piling up such stereotyped word material indiscriminately; Don Quijote, who is himself prone to quote adages, admires Sancho's spontaneity and fluency in this regard, as well as the original and natural wisdom which they reveal—though he advocates more restraint in their use; Cervantes does not commit himself one way or the other.

Within the framework of linguistic perspectivism fits also Cervantes's attitude toward dialects and jargons. Whereas, to Dante, all dialects appeared as inferior (though inferior in different degrees) realizations of a Platonic-Christian ideal pattern of language, as embodied in the *vulgare illustre*, Cervantes saw them as ways of speech which exist as individual realities and which have their justification in themselves. The basic Cervantine conception of perspectivism did not allow for the Platonic or Christian ideal of language: according to the creator of Don Quijote, dialects are simply the different reflections of reality (they are "styles," as the equally tolerant linguist of today would say), among which no one can take precedence over the other. Giuseppe Antonio Borgese, in "Il senso della letteratura italiana," speaks definitively of Dante's conception of the *vulgare illustre*: "Look at how, in the *De vulgari eloquentia*, Dante constructs an Italian language which has the character of divine perfection, which is, so to speak, a celestial language, a language of angels, of religion, of reason; so much that this language—illustrious, ancient, essential, and courtly—is not to be found anywhere by nature, and the native speech of this or that place, the dialect of this or that city, is more or less noble to the extent that it approaches that ideal, just as a color is more or less visible, more or less luminous, to the extent that it resembles white or contrasts with white. The white, the pure, the 'all-light,' the abstract . . . is considered by Dante . . . the supreme type of the beautiful."[15] Cervantes, on the contrary, delights in the different shades, in the particular gradations and nuances, in the gamut of colors between white and black, in the transitions between the abstract and the concrete. Hence we may explain the frequent excursions of Cervantes into what today we would call "dialectal geography" (I, 2): "un pescado que en Castilla llaman *abadejo* y en Andalucía *bacallao* y en otras partes *curadillo,* y en otras *truchuela*" [a fish that is called *pollack* in Castile and *cod* in Andalusia, in some parts *ling* and in others *troutlet*] (in fact, a modern Catalonian linguist, Manuel de Montoliu, has been able to base his study of the synonyms for "mackerel" on this passage); I, 41: "*Tagarinos* llaman en Berbería a los moros de Aragón, y a los de Granada *mudéjares,* y en el reino de Fez llaman a los mudéjares *elches*" [In Barbary they call the Moors of Aragon *Tagarines,* and those of Granada *Mudejares,* and in the Kingdom of Fez they call the Mudejares *Elches*].*

---

*In the *entremés* "Los habladores" a character is made to accumulate synonyms in different languages: "Una criada se llama en Valencia *fadrina,* en Italia *masara,* en Francia *gaspirria,* en Alemania *filomiquia,* en la corte *sirvienta,* en Vizcaya *moscorra,* y entre pícaros *daifa*" [In Valencia a servant is called *fadrina,* in Italy *masara,* in France *gaspirria,* in Germany *filomiquia,* in the court *sirvienta,* in Vizcaya *moscorra,* and among *pícaros daifa*]. Here we have the raw material (*copia verborum*) on which Cervantes will draw in the *Quijote.*

In these lexicological variants, Cervantes must have seen not a striving toward the approximation of an ideal, but only the variegated phantasmagoria of human approaches to reality: each variant has its own justification, but all of them alike reflect no more than human "dreams." Don Quijote is allowed to expose the inadequacy of such chance designations, as appear in any one dialect, by punning on the word *truchuela* "mackerel": "Como hay muchas truchuelas, podrán servir de una trucha" [so long as there are plenty of troutlet they may serve me for one trout], where he interprets (or pretends to interpret) *truchuela* as "little trout." What, ultimately, is offered here is a criticism of the arbitrariness of any fixed expression in human language

(*Sprachkritik*): the criticism which underlies the unspoken question, "Why should a mackerel be called a small trout?" Again, when Don Quijote hears the expression *cantor* used in reference to the galley-slaves, he asks the candid question (I, 22): "¿Por músicos y cantores van también a galeras?" [Do men go the galleys for being musicians and singers?]. Thus the literal interpretation of the expression serves to put into relief the macabre and ironic flavor of its metaphorical use {*cantar = cantar en el ansia*, "to 'sing' under torture"}. Here we witness the bewilderment of Don Quijote, who tries to hold words to a strict account; we may, perhaps, sense a criticism of Quijote's too-literal approach toward language—but this, in itself, would amount to a criticism of the ambiguity of human speech. Cervantes is satisfied, however, merely to suggest the linguistic problem, without any didactic expansion.

A masterpiece of linguistic perspectivism is offered in the transposition, by Sancho, of the high-flown jargon of love contained in Don Quijote's letter to Dulcinea, of which the squire has remembered the spirit, if not the exact words. Sancho, like most primitive persons, has an excellent acoustic memory—"toma de memoria" [he commits to memory] and "tiene en su memoria" [he holds in his memory] (in line with medieval practice, he does not "memorize")[16]—but, in attempting to cope with Don Quijote's florid language, he must necessarily "transpose," remembering what he *thinks* Quijote has said. In this way, "soberana y alta señora" [sovereign and sublime lady] becomes "alta y sobajada señora" [sublime and suppressed lady]—which the barber corrects to "sobrehumana o soberana" [superhuman or sovereign]: for this single term of address we are presented with three versions, resulting in a polyonomasia, as in the case of the proper names. Again, "de punto de ausencia y el llagado de las telas del corazón" [the dart of absence and pierced to the heart's core] > "el llagado y falto de sueño y el ferido" [he that is oppressed with sleep and wakeful and wounded] (it is as though Sancho, while indulging in Isidorian etymologies, is shrewdly diagnosing his master). In such linguistic exchanges we have a parallel to the numerous dialogues between the knight and the squire which, as is well known, are inserted into the novel in order to show the different perspectives under which the same events must appear to two persons of such different backgrounds. This means that, in our novel, things are represented not for what they are in themselves, but only as things spoken about or thought about; and this involves breaking the narrative presentation into two points of view. There can be no certainty about the "unbroken" reality of the events; the only unquestionable truth on which the reader may depend is the will of the artist who chose to break up a multivalent reality into different perspectives. In other words, perspectivism suggests an Archimedean principle outside of the plot—and the Archimedes must be Cervantes himself.

In another chapter [II, 25], the nickname *los del rebuzno* [the brayers] is loaded with a double entendre: the Spanish variants of Gothamites draw on the doubtful art of braying for their proud war slogan: their banner bears the verse "no rebuznaron en balde / el uno y otro alcalde" [They did not bray in vain, / Our worthy bailiffs twain] (the *regidores* [aldermen] have been promoted to *alcaldes* [bailiffs] in the course of history and—evidently—thanks to the compulsion of rhyme). Here, Don Quijote is entrusted by Cervantes with exploding the vanity of such sectional patriotism: the humanistic knight, in a masterful speech which includes a series of Spanish ethnic nicknames (which take the modern philologian, Rodríguez Marín, over four full pages to explain)—"los de la Reloja, los cazoleros, berenjeneros, ballenatos, jaboneros" [the people of the Clock Town, the Heretics, the Aubergine-eaters, the Whalers, the Soap-boilers]—shows the excessive vanity, originating in the flesh, not in the spirit, in the devil, not in true Catholicism, that is underlying the townspeople's attitude of resenting nicknames, that is, of investing such trifling expressions of the language with disproportionate symbolic value. The Don Quijote who, on other occasions, is only too apt to introduce symbolism and general principles into everyday life is here inspired by Cervantes to expose the vanity of misplaced symbolizing and generalization. The epithet *los del rebuzno* is thus made to shine with the double light of a stupidity that wants to be taken seriously, of a local peculiarity that aspires to "national" importance. The reader is free to go ahead and extend this criticism to other national slogans. That here Cervantes is endorsing Don Quijote seems beyond doubt since, when the novelist introduces this incident, he, speaking in his own right, attributes the adoption of the communal slogan to the activity of "the devil who never sleeps" and who is forever building "quimeras de no nada" [chimaeras out of nothing]— we might say, to a baroque devil who delights in deluding man. The chimeric and self-deluding quality of human vanity could hardly be illustrated more effectively than in this story, where the art of braying is first inflated and then deflated before our eyes, appearing as a "special language of human vanity."* And we may see in Cervantes's two-fold treatment of the problem of nicknames another example of his baroque attitude (what is true, what is dream?)—this time, toward language. Is not human language, also, *vanitas vanitatum* [the vanity of vanities], is it not sometimes a "braying" of a sort? Cervantes does not outspokenly say so.

---

* The raw material from which Cervantes drew the first episode is, according to Rodríguez Marín, a folktale (I would say, of the *Schildbürger*-tale variety). But, obviously, the introduction therein of the baroque element is a Cervantine touch. It is also in line with this element that the chimeric expedition of the townspeople, who are bent on conquering the whole country-side, should end in the beating administered to Sancho—a victory which, if they had been familiar with the ancient Greek custom, says Cervantes, they would have celebrated by raising a monument, a *trofeo*.

The double point of view into which Cervantes is wont to break up the reality he describes may also appear in connection with one key word, recurring throughout a given episode, upon which Cervantes casts two different lighting effects. We have a most successful example of this in the two chapters II, 25 and 27, where our interest is focused on the motif "braying like an ass." The connecting link between the two chapters is evidently "vanity": it is vanity that prompts the two *regidores* of the Mancha de Aragón to try to out-bray each other, as they search for the lost animal which they want to decoy and whose answering bray each seems to hear—only to learn, at the end, that the braying he heard was that of the other *regidor* (the ass, meanwhile, having died). It is vanity, again, that induces the townspeople—who, after this adventure, were called *los del rebuzno* by the inhabitants of neighboring villages—to sally forth to do battle with their deriders. And it is also due to vanity, on Sancho's part, that he, while deprecating, along with Don Quijote, the gift of imitating an ass, cannot refrain from showing off his own prowess in this regard before the townspeople—who straightway turn upon him in anger and beat him.

The vanity of "braying" shares with all other vanities the one characteristic that an inconsequential feature is invested with a symbolic value which it cannot, in the light of reason, deserve. Thus a duality (sham value vs. real value) offers itself to the artist for exploitation.

In the first chapter, Cervantes has the two *regidores* address each other with doubtful compliments: "de vos a un asno, compadre, no hay alguna diferencia en cuanto toca al rebuznar" [in the matter of braying there's nothing to choose between you and an ass], or "{you are the} más perito rebuznador del mundo" [the most skilled brayer in the world]. In the word *rebuznador*, there is a striving after the noble ring of *campeador, emperador*—which is drowned out by the blatant voice of the unregenerate animal: an ambivalence which exposes the hollow pretense.

There is one case in which Cervantes's perspectivism has crystallized into a bifocal word-formation; in Don Quijote's remark: "eso que a ti te parece bacía de barbero me parece a mí el yelmo de Mambrino, y a otro le parecerá otra cosa" [what seems to you to be a barber's basin appears to me to be Mambrino's helmet, and to another as something else] (I, 25),* there is contained a *Weltanschauung* which Américo Castro has, in a masterly fashion, recognized as a philosophical criticism (typical of the Renaissance) of the senses ("el engaño a los ojos" [the deceit of the eyes]); and this vision finds its linguistic expression, highly daring for Cervantes's time, in the coinage *baciyelmo* [basin-helmet], with which the tolerant Sancho concludes the debate about the identity of the shining object—as if he were reasoning: "if a thing appears to me as *a*, to you as *b*, it may be, in reality, neither *a* nor *b*, but *a + b*" (a similar tolerance is shown by Don Quijote a little later in the same episode, when he remarks, in the argument about the hypothetical nature of the hypothetical Mambrino: "Así que, Sancho, deja ese caballo, o asno, o lo que quisieras que sea" [Therefore, Sancho, leave the horse, or ass, or whatever you would have it be] (I, 21); Quijote, however, does not go so far as to coin a *caballiasno*). Now, it is evident to any linguist that, when shaping *baciyelmo*, Cervantes must have had in mind an existing formation of the same type; and his pattern must have been that which furnished designations of hybrid animals—that is, of a fantastic deviation from Nature—so that this quality of the fantastic and the grotesque is automatically transferred to the coinage *baciyelmo*; such a form does not guarantee the "actual" existence of any such entity *a + b*. In most cases, Cervantes must obey language, though he questions it: a basin he can only call *bacía*, a helmet, only *yelmo*; with the creation of *baciyelmo*, however, he frees himself from linguistic limitations.† Here, as elsewhere, I would emphasize, more than Castro (whose task it was to show us the conformity to

Renaissance thinking of what Cervantes himself has called his *espíritu lego* [secular spirit]), the artistic freedom conquered by Cervantes. In the predicament indicated by (the paradigmatic) ". . . o lo que quisieras que sea," the artist has asserted his own free will.

---

*The same pattern is evident in other passages: what is the *cueva de Montesinos* for Quijote is a "pit of hell" for Sancho: "'¿Infierno le llamáis?' dijo Don Quijote" ["Hell, you call it?" said Don Quijote] (II, 22).

†Linguistically speaking, *baciyelmo* fits into the group of *dvandva* formations [copulative compounds] designating hybrids in Spanish: *marimacho* [mannish woman], *serpihombre* [serpentman] (Góngora); an object, like an animate being, may present a hybrid aspect, and be represented by the same pattern: *arquibanco* [a bench or seat with drawers], *catricofre* [a folding bed] (and *baciyelmo*). As Anna Granville Hatcher will show, in a forthcoming article, this Renaissance type in Spanish word-formation goes ultimately back to Greek: ἀνδρογύνης-τραγέλαφος [androgynes-tragelaphos; man-woman–goat-deer], in Latinized form: *masculo-femina* [man-woman], *hircocervus* [goat-deer], and *tunico-pallium* [tunic-cloak]. Thus Cervantes has expressed his perspectivistic vision in a word-formational pattern of the Renaissance reserved for hybrids.

Now, from what has been said it would appear that the artist Cervantes uses linguistic perspectivism only in order to assert his own creative freedom; and this linguistic perspectivism, as I have already suggested, is only one facet of the general spirit of relativism which has been recognized by most critics as characteristic of our novel.*

---

*Interesting, in connection with Cervantes's linguistic perspectivism, are the many puns that appear in the *Quijote*: (I, 2) Don Quijote calls the innkeeper a *castellano* [Castilian-castellan] because the inn appears to him as a *castillo* [castle] in which he will be dubbed knight, but the innkeeper thinks that he has been called a "Castilian" "por haberle parecido de los sanos {the toughs} de Castilla" [because he took him for a "worthy tough" of Castile]; (I, 3) "No se curó {'did not care'} el harriero destas razones (y fuese mejor que se curara porque fuera curarse {'be cured'} en salud)" [The carrier did not care for his speech—it would have been better if he had cared for it, for he would have been caring for his own health]; (II, 26) {someone takes money} "no para tomar el mono sino la mona" [not in order to catch the monkey but to get tipsy (literally, to catch the she-ape—EDS.)]; (II, 66) when the lackey says to Sancho, "tu amo debe de ser un loco" [this master of yours ought to be counted a madman] the squire answers: "¿Cómo debe? No debe nada a nadie; que todo lo paga, y más cuando la moneda es locura" [Why "ought"? He owes nothing to anyone, for he pays his debts, especially where madness passes for coin].

The pun is a bifocal manner of expression which relaxes and relativizes the firmness with which language usually appears to speaking man.

Sometimes the "word-world," in Renaissance fashion, encroaches on outward reality. The word *donas* in the phrase *ni dones ni donas* is an entirely fantastic formation, without any reality behind it (since the feminine of *don* is *doña* or *dueña*): it is to be explained as an extraction from *don(es)* and susceptible of usage in connection with this word alone—just as *ínsulos* is possible only in the phrase *ni ínsulas ni ínsulos*. Such formations are intended to exclude from consideration all possible varieties of the species denoted by the radical—a tendency to be found in many languages: compare the Turkish *šapka yok mapka yok* "{I have} no cap no nothing" (*mapka* being a nonce-word patterned on *šapka*). But by the very creation of a name for that which exists only at the moment it is denied, the nonexistent entity is endowed with a certain (fantastic) reality.

Such perspectivism, however, had, in the age of Cervantes, to acknowledge ultimately a realm of the absolute—which was, in his case, that of Spanish Catholicism. Cervantes, while glorying in his role of the artist who can stay aloof from the *engaños a los ojos*, the *sueños* of this world, and create his own, always sees himself as overshadowed by supernal forces: the artist Cervantes never denies God, or His institutions, the King and the State. God, then, cannot be attracted into the artist's linguistic perspectivism; rather is Cervantes's God placed above the perspectives of language, He is said to be, as we have seen, the supreme *Entendedor* [Understander] of the language He has created—just as Cervantes, from his lower vantage point, seeks to be. Perhaps we may assume with Cervantes the old Neoplatonic belief in an artistic Maker who is enthroned above the manifold facets and perspectives of the world.

The story of the *Cautivo* (I, 37–42), one of the many tales interpolated into the main plot, exemplifies linguistic perspectivism made subservient to the divine. The maiden betrothed to the ex-captive, who enters the stage dressed and veiled in Moorish fashion and who, without speaking a word, bows to the company in Moorish fashion, gives from the beginning the impression "que . . . debía de ser mora y que no sabía hablar cristiano" [that . . . she must certainly be a Moor and not know the Christian tongue] (note the expression *hablar cristiano* instead of *hablar castellano* [Castilian tongue] which, with its identification of "Spanish" and "Christian," anticipates the religious motif basic to the story). Dorotea is the one to ask the all-important question: "¿esta señora es cristiana o mora?" [is this lady a Christian or a Moor?]—to which the *Cautivo* answers that she is a Moor in her costume and in her body, but in her soul, a great Christian, although not yet baptized—but "Dios será servido que presto se bautice" [please God, she will soon be baptized] (again, we may see in this mention of God not only a conventional form but a suggestion of the main problem, which is the working of Divine Grace). The *Cautivo*, speaking in Arabic, asks his betrothed to lift her veil in order to show forth her enchanting beauty; when asked about her name, he gives it in the Arabic form: *lela Zoraida*. And now the Moorish girl herself speaks for the first time: "No, no Zoraida: María, María"—repeating this statement twice more (the last time half in Arabic, half in Spanish: "Sí, sí, María: Zoraida *macange* {'not at all'}"). The change of name which she claims—evidently in anticipation of the change of name which will accompany her baptism—is of deep significance; it is a profession of faith, of conversion. We will learn later that she must become a María because, since her early childhood, she had been taken under the mantle of the Virgin.

After this first appearance of "Zoraida-María," whose two names are nothing but the linguistic reflection of her double nature, the episode is interrupted by Don Quijote's speech on *armas y letras* [I, 38]; thus, after the briefest of introductions, we must lose sight for a while of Zoraida-María, the puzzle of whose twofold name and Janus-like personality remains suspended in midair. The interruption is significant: Cervantes, in the episodic short stories, follows for the most part a technique opposed to that of the main plot: in the latter we are always shown first the objective reality of events, so that when they later become distorted after having passed through the alembic of Don Quijote's mind (Sancho, in general, remains more true to the reality he has experienced) we, from the knowledge we have previously gained, are proof against the knight's folly. But, in the short stories, on the contrary, Cervantes's technique is to tantalize us with glimpses into what seems an incredible situation, worthy of Quijote's own imagination (in our own story there suddenly appears before the group of Don Quijote's friends assembled in an inn an exotic-looking woman, dressed in outlandish gear, with her companion who has to talk for her) and with all the connotations of the unreal; the author is careful to protract our suspense to the utmost before giving us the solution of the initial puzzle. Thus the interpolations of these episodic short stories, whose reality is at least as fantastic as the most daring dreams of the mad knight, offer another revelation of the perspectivism of Cervantes; we have to do not only with the opposition between prosaic reality and fantastic dreams: reality itself can be both prosaic and fantastic. If, in the main plot, Cervantes has carried out his program of "derribar la máquina mal fundada" of the fantastic, he has taken care to rebuild this machinery in the by-stories. And our tale of the Captive is an excellent illustration of this rule.

When, after Don Quijote's speech, the Captive tells his story *ab ovo* [from the beginning], explaining how the startling fact of a "Zoraida-María" came to pass, we are allowed a glimpse into the historic reality of that hybrid world of Mohammedans and Christians which was the equivalent in Cervantes's times of the *fronterizo* [frontier] milieu of the *romances*—only a more complicated variant because of the two different groups representative of the Mohammedan faith then facing the Spaniards: the Turks and the Arabs, the former the more ruthless type, the latter (to which Lela Marién and her father belong) the type more amenable to the Christian way of life. Indeed, the Arabs themselves seem to feel more akin to the Christian civilization than to the Turkish (the girl's father calls the Turks *canes* [dogs]; it is ironic that later, after he has been deeply wronged by the Christians, he must call them *perros* [dogs]).

As the Captive tells the story of the tragic events that took place against the background of the warring Turkish Empire, he embellishes his (Spanish-language) narrative with words from Turkish and Arabic, offering a linguistic mosaic that adds to the local color of his story. If we compare the Turkish words with the Arabic, we will note the sharpest of contrasts: the former are of a factual reference, narrowly descriptive, with no transcendental connotations (for the Turks are excluded from the possibility of Enlightenment by Grace): *leventes* [Turkish soldiers], *bagarinos* [Bagarine Moorish oarsmen], *baño* (wrongly offered as a Turkish word for "prison"), *pasamaques* [shoes], *zoltanís* [a type of coin], *gilecuelco* [jacket or slave's coat]; we find also the pejorative epithet *Uchalí Fartax* "que quiere decir en lengua turquesca *el renegado tiñoso*, porque lo era" [which means in Turkish "the scabby renegade," which he was] (again, the *convenientia* between names and objects!). The Arabic words, on the contrary, are nearly always connected with things religious and, more specifically, with things Christian—so that a kind of transposition (or perspectivism) is achieved: "Lela Marién" instead of "Nuestra Señora la Vírgen María"; "Alá" for the Christian God, and also the interjection *quelá* in the same reference; *nizarani* for "Christians"; *la zalá cristianesca* for "the Christian prayer," in which the adjective *cristianesco* (instead of *cristiano*), formed after *morisco* [Moorish], *turquesco* [Turkish], has something of the same transposed character, as if the Christian rites were seen from the outside. And, in addition to the linguistic medley offered the reader directly, there is a reference to the polyglot habits among the protagonists of the story. Zoraida, for example, chooses Arabic as the private language in which to talk and write to the Captive, but converses with the Christians (as also does her father) in the *lingua franca*—which language is characterized by the Captive as "lengua que en toda la Berbería, y aun en Constantinopla se habla entre cautivos y moros, que ni es morisca ni castellana ni de otra nación alguna, sino una mezcla de todas las lenguas, con la cual todos nos entendemos" [the language that is spoken between slaves and Moors all over Barbary, and even in Constantinople: it is neither Moorish nor Castilian, nor the tongue of any other country, but a mixture of every language, in which we can all understand one another], or "la bastarda lengua que . . . allí se usa" [the bastard language which . . . is in use there]: a characterization, it may be noted, which is not basically different from that offered in our times by Hugo Schuchardt ("Mischsprache," "Verkehrssprache"), the student of *lingua franca*, of the Creole languages etc., and the advocate of an international artificial language. Castilian, Turkish, Arabic, with reminiscences of *lingua franca*: why this Babelic confusion of tongues in our story? It does not suffice to appeal to the historical fact that these languages were actually spoken at the time in the Ottoman Empire, where Cervantes himself had lived as a captive: for, in addition to the foreign phrases that might serve simply for local color, we have to do evidently with an express concern for each individual language as such—to the extent that we are always informed in which language a certain speech, letter, or dialogue was couched. It seems to me that Cervantes would point out that differences of language do not, by principle, hinder the working of Christian Grace—though he evidently grades the languages according to their penetrability by things Christian: Turkish is presented as on a lower level than Arabic, which lends itself so easily to the transposition of Christian concepts.*

* In the story of Ana Félix, the Christian daughter of the Morisco Ricote, we see again how closely connected are language and faith: she explains (II, 63): "Tuve una madre cristiana . . . mamé la Fé católica con la leche; criéme con buenas costumbres; ni en la lengua ni en ellas jamás, a mi parecer, di señales de ser morisca" [I had a Christian mother . . . I sucked the Catholic faith with my mother's milk. I was brought up with good principles, and neither in my language nor in my customs, I think, did I show any signs that I was a Moor]. The reader should note the expression *mamar la fé con la leche*: the same expression is used in Cervantes (II, 16) of the mother tongue: "todos los poetas antiguos escribieron en la lengua que mamaron con la leche" [all of the ancients wrote in the tongues they sucked with their mother's milk]; and Castro has pointed out the origin of this metaphor (Bembo, *Della volgar lingua* (1525): "nella latina {sc. *lingua*} essi {the Romans} tutti nascevano et quella insieme col latte dalle nutriei loro beeano" [they {the Romans} were all born in Latin, and they all drank it {Latin} together with their wet nurses' milk]). Here, we are at the bottom of the concept of *Muttersprache, langue maternelle, mother tongue*, which ultimately goes back to an Augustinian concept: the Christian learns the name of God from his mother ("hoc nomen salvatoris mei . . . in ipso adhuc lacte matris tenerum cor meum biberat" [this name of my savior . . . my tender heart drank in the very milk of my mother]): the "name of God" is the most important and the most intimate linguistic knowledge the mother can impart to her child; thus (and this is in harmony with Christianity, which, in general, tends to present spiritual truths behind a human veil), the concept of "mother tongue" is vitally connected with that of maternal religion.[17]

And this linguistic transposition of things Christian into things Moorish reflects only the transposed situation of a Moor who becomes a Christian; the story of the Captive and of Zoraida-María shows Grace working toward the salvation of a disbeliever and toward the sacramental union, by a Christian marriage, of two beings of different races: above the divergence of race and language* God understands the Christian longing of Zoraida for the *Alá cristiano*. It was the Virgin Mary, of whom she had learned from a Christian nurse, who inspired her to rescue the Christian soldier and to flee with him to a Christian country in order there to be baptized and married. When Zoraida speaks of Alá, everyone knows that the Christian God is meant—whose true nature shines through the linguistic disguise. The same symbol is carried out on another plane: when, from her window, Zoraida's white hand is seen, adorned with Moorish jewels (*ajorcas*), waving a Christian cross, the *ajorcas* are naturally overshadowed by the cross.† Again, in the case of Zoraida's letters to the prisoners, written in Arabic but adorned with the sign of the cross, it is clear that these indications of different cultural climates clearly express only one thing: her will to be a Christian. It is not the language, the gesture, the costume, or the body that matter to Him, but the meaning behind all the exterior manifestations: the soul. God, Cervantes is telling us, can recognize, behind the "perspective" of a disbeliever, His true faithful follower.

In the other Moorish story in our novel, that of the expelled Ricote who, having fled to Germany, comes back in the disguise of a German pilgrim to Spain (II, 54), the exile mixes German (¡Guelte! ¡Guelte!* [Geld! Geld!]) into his Spanish—a language which he knows as well as does Sancho, whose "neighborhood shopkeeper" he had been. Cervantes describes Sancho's inability to understand the Germanate jargon of Ricote, whose identity he fails at first to recognize. Later, the pilgrim throws aside his incognito and hails Sancho "en voz alta y muy castellana" [loudly in Castilian]; "Ricote, sin tropezar nada en su lengua morisca, en la pura castellana le {to Sancho} dijo las siguientes razones" [Without once stumbling into his Moorish jargon, Ricote spoke as follows in pure Castilian]. In the ensuing drinking scene, Sancho, in his mellow tipsiness, finally ends up by speaking the esperanto of *lingua franca*. In this episode we must infer that the difficulties of linguistic understanding are all artificially contrived: here are *Ricote el morisco* and *Sancho el bueno*, who have lived side by side for many years and who are quite able to understand each other perfectly, who have the same habits of living, eating, and drinking—and who are separated from each other only by the (arbitrary) fact of the Morisco's exile.

Ricote is as good a Spaniard as is Sancho (perhaps also a more gifted one: this comes out in his ironic question, so natural with emigrants who, returning to their mother country, see themselves in a position inferior to their merits: "¿Faltaban hombres en el mundo más hábiles para gobernadores que tú eres?" [Was the world short of men more capable of being governors than you?]), and his daughter is a perfect Christian; nevertheless, as exiles, they have been the victims of an arbitrary death-blow. But, by his exile, Ricote has not only learned to say *guelte* instead of *limosna* [alms]: he has come to know religious tolerance as he saw it practiced in Augsburg, in the heart of Protestantism. No bolder words could have been written, in Counter-Reformation Spain, about religious freedom, than are expressed here by Ricote. Nevertheless, the same Ricote bows submissively before the expulsion of the Moors by the Spanish king and his minister, which has plunged him and his family into despair and misery. Cervantes seems here more interested in the dialectic play of arguments, in the facets and perspectives of the problem, than in giving a decision on the moral issue. To the Spanish subject matter of the novel, the stories of Moorish emigrants, renegades, and converts add a new perspective, that of Spain seen from the outside—a perspective of "spiritual geography."

†The same double light is cast on the *caña*, that angling rod dropped by Zoraida to the captives, which is first only a utensil, an astute device, and then becomes a symbol of the miracle (*milagro*) of a twofold salvation.

I cannot quite agree with Castro, who seems to see mainly the human side of the episode, when he says: "Love and religion (the latter as a kind of swathe of the former) bear Zoraida after her captive," and considers the story to be one of "harmony between human beings in perfect accord."[18] Rather, I should say that religion is the kernel, love the envelopment; we have here a drama of Divine Grace working against all possible handicaps and using the love between Moor and Christian as a means to an end: the conversion of Zoraida (and, incidentally, the return of a renegade* to the bosom of the Church); therefore Cervantes has devised his story against the background of the Spanish-Turkish wars, which ended with the victory of the Spaniards at Lepanto and in which, as Titian has represented it, Spain succors Christian faith.

---

*In this tale, the "renegade" develops before our eyes and gradually comes to take on stature; he shows his eagerness to help in the escape of the prisoners: after his repentance, when he swears by the cross to change from a "foul" member of the Church to a true member, the Christian fugitives put themselves "en las manos de Dios y en las del renegado" [in the hands of God and the renegade] (as though God's hands used those of the renegade for His purposes). Later, it is true, his plan is abandoned for another one ("Dios, que lo ordenaba de otra manera, no dio lugar al buen deseo que nuestro Renegado tenía" [God decreed otherwise, and did not give this fellow a chance of carrying out his plans]) but, nevertheless, he is saved along with the whole party and succeeds in his desire "a reducirse por medio de la Santa Inquisición al gremio santísimo de la Iglesia" [to be reconciled to the bosom of Mother Church by means of the Holy Inquisition].

I concur absolutely with Castro, however, when he goes on to say that this story of abduction is the most violent and the most tragic of all the episodes in the novel: Zoraida, in her zeal to receive holy baptism and the sacrament of Christian marriage, must cheat her father, must see him subjected by her doings to the violence of the Christians who truss him up and finally leave him marooned on a desert island, where he cries out to his daughter, alternately cursing and beseeching her. Here is a good Arab, meek and truthful to Christians, who is thrown back to the Mohammedan god by the ruthless deed of his Christian daughter. That such sins may be committed for the rescue of a soul can only be explained, Cervantes seems to tell us, by the incalculable will of Providence. Why should these sins be made corollary to the salvation of the particular soul of Zoraida—while the soul of her father becomes thereby utterly lost to salvation? What whimsicality of God! I should say that this scene exhibits not so much the "abysses of the human,"[19] as Castro has it, but rather the "abysses of the divine." No harmonious earthly marriage could be concluded on the basis of such a terrifying violation of the Fourth Commandment; but God is able to put the laws of morality out of function in order to reach His own goal.

In our story, which is the story of a great deceit, the words referring to "deceit" take on a particularly subtle double entendre. When, for example, Zoraida, in one of her letters to the Captive, says: "no te fíes de ningún moro, porque son todos *marfuzes*" [do not trust any Moor, they are all *deceitful*] of her Moslem coreligionists, she is using an originally Arabic word for "treacherous" which had come to be borrowed by the Spaniards, probably to refer, primarily, to the treachery of the Mohammedans (meaning something like "false as a Moor"); the choice of this word, which sounds rather strange when used by an Arab, must mean that Zoraida is judging the Arabs according to Christian prejudices (it is ironical that, in this story, it is the Arabs who are faithful and kind, and the Christians who are *marfuzes*—although working toward a goal presumably willed by Providence). Again, the accusation of cheating is reversed when Zoraida, speaking as a Moor to the Christian captive, in the presence of her father, remarks: "vosotros cristianos siempre mentís en cuanto decís, y os hacéis pobres por engañar a los moros" [you Christians always lie and make yourselves out poor to cheat us Moors]; here, where her judgment is, indeed, factually justified, she is actually speaking disingenuously—in order to further the stratagem planned by the Christians. The discrepancy between words and meaning, between judgment and behavior, has reached such proportions that we can view only with perplexity the "abyss of the divine" which makes it possible that such evil means are accepted to further a noble purpose; the story offers us no way out but to try to share Zoraida's belief in the beneficent intervention of Lela Marién, who has prompted the good-wicked enterprise ("¡Plega a Alá, padre mío, que Lela Ma-rién, que ha sido la causa de que yo sea cristiana, ella te consuele en tu tristeza!" [May it please Allah, dear father, that Lela Marién, who has been the cause of my becoming a Christian, may console you in your grief]). When Zoraida, speaking to her father, states of her deed "que parece tan buena como tú, padre amado, la juzgas por mala" [which I know to be good, beloved father, though it appears wicked to you], we are offered basically the same perspectivistic pattern that we have noted in the case of the *baciyelmo*: it is implied, evidently, that Lela Marién knows of no perspectivism. There can be no doubt that what Cervantes is dealing with here is the tortuous and Jesuitic divinity that he was able to see in his time—whose decisions he ac-cepts, while bringing out all the complications involved. Along with the submission to the divine there is instituted a tragic trial against it, a trial on moral grounds, and, on these grounds, the condemnation is unmitigated; the sacramental force of a father's curse is not entirely counterbalanced by the sacramental force of the Christian rites, the desire for which on Zoraida's part brought about the father's plight. Perhaps no writer, remaining within the boundaries of orthodox re-ligion, has revealed more of the perplexities inherent in the theocratic order (a Nietzsche might have called this story an example of the im-morality of God and have advocated the overthrow of such a God— whereas Cervantes quietly stays within the boundaries of the Chris-tian fold). And this acme of submissive daring has been achieved by placing the divine beyond the perspectives which appear to the hu-man eye.

Zoraida herself, for all her religious fervor, innocence, and super-natural beauty is, at the same time, capable of great wickedness. And again linguistic perspectivism is invoked in order to bring this side of her nature into relief. There is a moment when the band of fugitives passes the promontory called, after the mistress of Roderick, the last of the Gothic kings, *cabo de la Cava Rumía*, "la mala mujer cris-tiana" [*the Cape of the Cava Rumía*, the wicked Christian woman]; they insist, however, that to them it is not the "abrigo de mala mujer, sino puerto seguro de nuestro remedio" [wicked woman's shelter, but a secure haven of refuge]. Now, when the name of this infamous woman, who sinned for love, is brought before the reader, he cannot fail to think of Zoraida—though, in the comparison with the Arabic prostitute "por quien se perdió España" [through whom Spain was lost], the betrothed of the Captive must appear as a pure woman,

who refused to live in a state of sin before her marriage. At the same
time, however, Cervantes may wish us to realize how close was Zoraida to the abyss, and to see the ward of the Virgin, for a moment,
under the perspective of la Cava.[20]

———————————— • ————————————

If we look back now over the development of this essay, we will see
that we have been led from a plethora of names, words, languages—
from polyonomasia, polyetymologia, and polyglottism—to the linguistic perspectivism of the artist Cervantes, who knows that the
transparence of language is a fact for God alone. And, at this point,
I may be allowed to repeat, as a kind of epitomizing epilogue, the final passages of a lecture on the *Quijote* which I have given at several
universities—which, I trust, will serve to round out the linguistic details I have pointed out earlier and to put them into relationship with
the whole of the novel: a relationship which, in the course of our linguistic discussion, has already been tentatively indicated. After explaining that the *Quijote* appeals as well to children as to adults because of its combination of imagination and criticism, and that the
modern genre of the critical novel, which started with a criticism of
books and of a bookish culture (a criticism of the romances of chivalry) and came to be expanded to a new integration of the critical
and the imaginative, was the discovery of Cervantes, I continued
thus:

It is one of the great miracles of history (which is generally regarded deterministically by professional historians, who present individual phenomena as enclosed within tight compartments) that
the greatest deeds sometimes occur at a place and a time when the
historian would least expect them. It is a historical miracle that, in
the Spain of the Counter-Reformation, when the trend was toward
the reestablishment of authoritarian discipline, an artist should have
arisen who, thirty-two years before Descartes's *Discours de la méthode* (that autobiography of an independent philosophical thought,
as Gustave Lanson has called it), was to give us a narrative which is
simply one exaltation of the independent mind of man—and of a
particularly powerful type of man: of the artist. It is not Italy, with its
Ariosto and Tasso, not France with its Rabelais and Ronsard, but
Spain that gave us a narrative which is a monument to the narrator
qua narrator, qua artist. For, let us not be mistaken: the real protagonist of this novel is not Quijote, with his continual misrepresenta-

tion of reality, or Sancho with his skeptical half-endorsement of quixotism—and surely not any of the central figures of the illusionistic by-stories: the hero is Cervantes, the artist himself, who combines a critical and illusionistic art according to his free will. From the moment we open the book* to the moment we put it down, we are given to understand that an almighty overlord is directing us, who leads us where he pleases.

---

* In this connection, we should consider the famous opening sentence of the novel: "En un lugar de la Mancha de cuyo nombre no quiero acordarme" [In a certain village in La Mancha, which I do not wish to name]. All the explanations hitherto offered—the silly autobiographical one (Cervantes had personal reasons for not wanting to remember the name); that based on literary history, proposed by Casalduero (Cervantes opposes his novel to the romances of chivalry, which claimed to know exactly wherefrom their heroes hailed); the folkloristic one of María Rosa Lida (the sentence is in line with the beginning of folktales)—fail to take into sufficient consideration the functional value, for the novel, of the attitude of the author expressed therein—which, in my opinion, is the glorification of the freedom of the artist. Even if, for example, Mme Lida should be right, the transfer of a sentence traditional in folktales into this particular novel of Cervantes could give the transferred sentence a new meaning, just as certain folklorisms adopted by Goethe or Heine become more than folklorisms in the lyrical poetry of these poets. By the deliberate assertion of his free will to choose the motifs of his plot, to emphasize or disregard what detail he pleases (and *no quiero* expresses deliberate disregard), Cervantes has founded that genre of "subjective storytelling" which, before him, is found at its incipient stage with Boccaccio and which, later, was to inspire Goethe (in the beginning of the *Wahlverwandtschaften* [Elective Affinities]: "Eduard—so nennen wir einen reichen Baron im besten Mannesalter—Eduard hatte . . ." [Edward—so we shall call a wealthy baron in the prime of life—Edward had . . .]), Laurence Sterne, Fielding, Melville ("Call me Ishmael"!).

In an address to the Baltimore Goethe Society, entitled "Laurence Sterne's *Tristram Shandy* and Thomas Mann's *Joseph the Provider*," Professor Oskar Seidlin pointed out the presence, in both these modern works, of some of the same comic devices (change of names, assumption of fictional sources, introduction of "relativizing dialogues," etc.) which I have been discussing as characteristic of Cervantine perspectivism.[21] Since Thomas Mann himself had stated in 1942 that during the composition of his *Joseph* he had had two books as his steady companions, *Tristram Shandy* and *Faust*, the stylistic congruences between the German and the English novel are easily explained.[22] On the other hand, the devices of Sterne which reappear with Mann were, in turn, borrowed from Cervantes; and, in this connection, it is relevant to note that, in 1935, Thomas Mann had published his essay on the *Don Quijote*:[23] thus the Cervantine climate may have acted doubly upon him: directly as well as indirectly. And, though the idea expressed in *Joseph the Provider* that the world is "Jehovah's Jest" would not have occurred to Cervantes, who glorified the "artist beneath the dome of God," the great *Entendedor*, the Spanish poet could have subscribed to Mann's idea of "artistic lightness" as man's consolation: "For lightness, my friend, flippancy, the artful jest, that is God's very best gift to man, the profoundest knowledge we have of that complex, questionable thing we call life. God gave it to humanity, that life's terribly serious face might be forced to wear a smile. . . . Only in lightness can the spirit of man rise above them {the questions put to us by life}: with a laugh at being faced with the unanswerable, perhaps he can make even God Himself, the great Unanswering, to laugh."[24]

It is interesting that Thomas Mann, who, in his *Buddenbrooks*, was still the pure representative of what Oskar Walzel has called "objective narration" (in the Spielhagen style), has from the time of his *Magic Mountain* developed consistently in the direction of Cervantine "storytelling" technique; this evolution must be due not only to the general change in literary trends that has been taking place, but also to Mann's growing consciousness of the triumphant part the artist is called upon to play in modern society.

In this connection I may cite also the opening line of E. M. Forster's novel *Howards End*: "One may as well begin with Helen's letters to her sister,"[25] on which Lionel Trilling remarks: "Guiding his stories according to his serious whim . . . Forster takes full and conscious responsibility for his novels, refusing to share in the increasingly dull assumption of the contemporary novelist, that the writer has nothing to do with the story he tells, and that, *mirabile dictu*, through no intention of his own, the story has chosen to tell itself through him. Like Fielding, he shapes his prose for comment and explanation. He summarizes what he is going to show, introduces new themes when and as it suits him."[26]

The prologue of the whole work shows us Cervantes in the perplexity of an author putting the final touches to his work, and we understand that the "friend" who seemingly came to his aid with a solution was only one voice within the freely fabricating poet. And, on the last page of the book when, after Quijote's Christian death, Cervantes has that Arabian historian Cide Hamete Benengeli lay away his pen, to rest forever, on the top of the cupboard in order to forestall any further spurious continuation (after the manner of Avellaneda) of the novel, we know that the reference to the Arabian pseudo-historian is only a pretext for Cervantes to reclaim for himself the relationship of real father (no longer the "stepfather," as in the prologue) to his book. Then the pen delivers itself of a long speech, culminating in the words: "For me alone Don Quijote was born and I for him; his task was to act, mine to write. For we alone are made for each other" ("Para mí sola nació Don Quijote, y yo para él; él supo obrar, y yo escribir; solos los dos somos para en uno"). An imperious *alone* (*solo*[*s*]), which only Cervantes could have said and in which all the Renaissance pride of the poet asserts itself: the poet who was the traditional immortalizer of the great deeds of historical heroes and princes. An Ariosto could have said the same words about the Duke of Ferrara.

The function of eulogizing princes was, as is well known, the basis of the economic situation of the Renaissance artist: he was given sustenance by the prince in return for the immortal glory which he bestowed upon his benefactor.[27] But Don Quijote is no prince from whom Cervantes could expect to receive a pension, no doer of great deeds in the outer world (his greatness lay only in his warm heart), and not even a being who could be attested in any historical source—however much Cervantes might pretend to such sources. Don Quijote acquired his immortality exclusively at the hands of Cervantes—as the latter well knows and admits. Obviously, Quijote wrought only what Cervantes wrote, and he was born for Cervantes as much as Cervantes was born for him! In the speech of the pen of the pseudo-chronicler we have the most discreet and the most powerful self-glorification of the artist which has ever been written. The artist Cervantes grows by the glory which his characters have attained; and in the novel we see the process by which the figures of Don Quijote and Sancho become living persons, stepping out of the novel, so to speak, to take their places in real life—finally to become immortal historical figures. Thomas Mann, in a recent essay on the *Quijote*, has said: "This is quite unique. I know of no other hero of a novel in world literature who would equally, so to speak, live off the glory of his own glorification" ("ein Held, . . . [der] von dem Ruhm seines Ruhmes, von seiner Besungenheit lebte").[28] In the second part of the novel, when the Duke and Duchess ask to see the by now historical figures of Quijote and Panza, the latter says to the Duchess: "I am Don Quijote's squire who is to be found also *in the story* and who is called Sancho Panza—unless they have changed me in the cradle—I mean to say, at the printer's." In such passages, Cervantes willingly destroys the artistic illusion: he, the puppeteer, lets us see the strings of his puppet show: "see, reader, this is not life, but a stage, a book: art; recognize the life-giving power of the artist as a thing distinct from life!"*

---

*I realize that this is an opinion contrary to that of the writers of the Enlightenment who, in their treatment of the *Don Quijote*, made much of

Cervantes's own classicistic pronouncement that art imitates nature. Locke, for example, has written: "Of all the books of fiction, I know none that equals Cervantes's 'History of Don Quijote,' in usefulness{!}, pleasantry, and a constant decorum. And indeed no writings can be pleasant, which have not nature at the bottom, and are not drawn after copy." And Thomas Sydenham, the English Hippocrates and founder of modern clinical treatment, is reported to have advised young medical students to read the *Don Quijote* instead of books on medicine—because (as Professor Ludwig Edelstein shows)[29] he evidently thought the Spanish novel offered a deterrent example of a person who views the world in the light of his preconceived ideas instead of that of facts—with which alone Dr. Sydenham was concerned.

Needless to say, my historical interpretation is also at the other pole from the poetic vision of an Unamuno, who believes that this story was dictated to Cervantes's pen by the suprapersonal and perennial Spanish character, by the innate Spanish will to immortality by suffering and the "sentimiento trágico de la vida" [tragic sense of life] as embodied in the figures of the quasi-saint Nuestro Señor Don Quijote de la Mancha [our Lord Don Quijote de la Mancha] and his evangelical squire. In my opinion, it is Cervantes the "artistic dictator" who dictated the story to his pen, and Cervantes, no half-Christian like Unamuno, knew how to distinguish the earthly plane from the transcendental. On the former plane he obeyed his own *sovereign reason.* He does not, then, belong to the family of Pascal and Kierkegaard, but to that of Descartes and Goethe.

By multiplying his masks (the friend of the prologue, the Arabian historian, sometimes the characters who serve as his mouthpiece), Cervantes seems to strengthen his grip on that whole artistic cosmos. And the strength of the grip is enhanced by the very nature of the protagonists: Quijote is what we would call today a split personality, sometimes rational, sometimes foolish; Sancho, too, at times no less quixotic than his master, is at other times incalculably rational. In this way, the author makes it possible for himself to decide when his characters will act reasonably, when foolishly (no one is more unpredictable than a fool who pretends to wisdom). At the start of his journey with Sancho, Don Quijote promises his squire an island kingdom to be ruled over by him, just as was done in the case of numerous squires in literature. But, acting on his critical judgment (of which he is not devoid), Don Quijote promises to give it to him immediately after their conquest—instead of waiting until the squire has reached old age, as is the custom in the books of chivalry. The quixotic side of Sancho accepts this prospective kingship without questioning its possibility, but his more earthly nature visualizes— and criticizes—the actual scene of the coronation: how would his rustic spouse Juana Gutiérrez look with a crown on her head? Two examples of foolishness, two critical attitudes: none of them is the attitude of the writer, who remains above the two split personalities and the four attitudes.

With the Machiavellian principle "divide and conquer" applied to his characters, the author succeeds in making himself indispensable to the reader: while, in his prologue, Cervantes calls for a critical attitude on our part, he makes us depend all the more on his guidance through the psychological intricacies of the narrative: here, at least, he leaves us no free will. We may even infer that Cervantes rules imperiously over his own self: it was he who felt this self to be split into a critical and an illusionistic part (*desengaño* and *engaño* [disillusionment and illusion]); but in this baroque ego he made order, a precarious order, it is true, which was reached only once by Cervantes in all his works—and which was reached in Spain only by Cervantes (for Calderón, Lope, Quevedo, Gracián decided that the world is only illusion and dreams, "los sueños sueños son"). And indeed, only once in world literature has this precarious order come into being: later thinkers and artists did not stop at proclaiming the inanity of the world: they went so far as to doubt the existence of any universal order and to deny a Creator, or at least, when imitating Cervantes's perspectivism (Gide, Proust, Conrad, Joyce, Virginia Woolf, Pirandello),* they have failed to sense the unity behind perspectivism—so that, in their hands, the personality of the author is allowed to disintegrate.

---

* Pirandello's perspectivism is in this respect different from that of Cervantes: with the latter, it is the *author* who looks for his characters, not the reverse.

I beg also to disagree with those critics who compare Cervantes with El Greco because of the novelist's "modern impressionism." We must be clear about the meaning of the term "impressionism." Cervantes never offers *his own* impressions of outward reality, as does the modern artist of the impressionistic school; he presents simply the impressions which his characters may have had—and, by juxtaposing these different impressions, he implicitly criticizes them all. The program of the modern impressionist, on the other hand, makes impossible the intervention of the critical sense into what he sees. As for the impressionism of El Greco, while this involves no criticism of reality, as does that of Cervantes (since the ultimate reality he portrays is the divine), it does offer the evanescent reflections of the divine—which may, of course, have prepared the public for the perception of the evanescent in this world, that is, for modern "impressionistic" perception.

Cervantes stands at the other pole from that modern dissolution of the personality of the narrator: what grandeur there is in his attempt—made in the last moment before the unified Christian vision of the world was to fall asunder—to restore this vision on the artistic plane, to hold before our eyes a cosmos split into two separate halves: disenchantment and illusion, which, nevertheless, by a miracle, do not fall apart! Modern anarchy checked by a classical will to equipoise (the baroque attitude)! We recognize now that it is not so much that Cervantes's nature is split in two (critic and narrator) because this is required by the nature of Don Quijote, but rather that Don Quijote is a split character because his creator was a critic-poet who felt with almost equal strength the urge of illusionary beauty and of pellucid clarity.

To modern readers the "schizophrenic" Don Quijote might seem to be a typical case of social frustration: a person whose madness is conditioned by the social insignificance into which the caste of the knights had fallen, with the beginnings of modern warfare—just as, in Flaubert's *Un Cœur simple*, we are meant to see as socially conditioned the frustrations of Félicité, the domestic servant, which lead to the aberration of her imagination. I would, however, warn the reader against interpreting Cervantes in terms of Flaubert, since Cervantes himself has done nothing to encourage such a sociological approach. Don Quijote is able to recover his sanity, if only on his deathbed; and his erstwhile madness is but one reflection of that generally human lack of reason—above which the author has chosen to take his stand.*

---

*Professor Erich Auerbach, in his book *Mimesis*, states the lack in the *Don Quijote* (as in the whole literature of the *siglo de oro* [Golden Age]) of any "problematic study of contemporary reality," of any "movement in the depths of life," of any search into the social motivations of Don Quijote's madness, and of the life of his age[30]—the underlying idea being that the "real" motivations of life are those of sociology, not of morality, on which Cervantes has based his novel (though, as we have said, he offers us the conflict between different moral standards). The attitude of this critic, which seems to abound in the sense of Carl Becker ("the historian has become the successor of the theologian"), is, in my opinion, contingent on the presupposition that moral values are obsolete in a modern world given to the sociological explanation of history.

High above this worldwide cosmos of his making, in which hundreds of characters, situations, vistas, themes, plots and subplots are merged, Cervantes's artistic self is enthroned, an all-embracing creative self, Nature-like, God-like, almighty, all-wise, all-good—and benign: this visibly omnipresent Maker reveals to us the secrets of his creation, he shows us the work of art in the making and the laws to which it is necessarily subjected. For this artist is God-like but not deified; far be it from us to conceive of Cervantes as attempting to dethrone God, replacing Him by the artist as a superman. On the contrary, Cervantes always bows before the supernal wisdom of God, as embodied in the teachings of the Catholic Church and the established order of the state and of society. Qua moralist, Cervantes is not at all "perspectivistic."*

---

* It should perhaps be pointed out here that "perspectivism" is inherent in Christian thought itself. The pair Don Quijote–Sancho Panza is, after all, a Cervantine replica of the medieval characters Solomon and Marcolf, in whom the wisdom of the sage and that of the common man are contrasted (we may also see in Sancho Panza's *refranes* [sayings] a later version of the *proverbes au vilain* [simple proverbs]). Such an exemplary contrast is derived from the evangelic truth that the common man has access to wisdom, as well as the learned man; that the spirit, if not the letter, of the law can be understood by anyone. Here, we have an example of "medieval gradualism," according to which the social or mental level of Christ's followers is ultimately irrelevant. It is for this reason that, in medieval mystery plays, lofty scenes treating the life of Christ may alternate with scurrilous scenes in which shepherds or clowns are allowed to express their "point of view" on the august events in question, in their own unregenerate rustic speech. In this "gradualism," perspectivism is implied; and, to the perspectivism which Cervantes found in the medieval tradition, he added only the artistic aloofness of a Renaissance thinker.

Nor can we expect to find in Cervantes any of that romantic revolt of the artist against society. But, on the other hand, the artist Cervantes has extended, by the mere art of his narrative, the Demiurge-like, almost cosmic independence of the artist. His humor, which admits of many strata, perspectives, masks—of relativization and dialectics—bears testimony to his high position above the world. His humor is the freedom of the heights, no fate-bound Dionysiac dissolution of the individual into nothingness and night, as with Schopenhauer and Wagner, but a freedom beneath the dome of that religion which affirms the freedom of the will. There is, in the world of his creation, the bracing air with which we may fill our lungs and by which our individual senses and judgment are sharpened; and the crystalline lucidity of an artistic Maker in its manifold reflections and refractions.

INTERPRETATION OF AN ODE
BY PAUL CLAUDEL

Spitzer considered his study of Claudel's ode "La Muse qui est la Grâce" (The Muse that is Grace) a particularly revealing example of his hermeneutic method and its distinctive interpretive movement from an intuitive response to a small textual detail to the illumination of the entire work and the authorial consciousness it manifests. The point of departure is Spitzer's perception of the importance of certain "word motifs" in organizing the structure of Claudel's initial strophe, punctuating the surging rhythms of its free verses, and articulating a thematic conflict that "rages" through the entire poem. The study is a striking example of the way in which Spitzer uses the essayistic footnote to situate a tightly focused textual analysis in the various contexts necessary for its proper elucidation: the nature of the ode and the history of its classical and Christian manifestations; the Thomist philosophical doctrines concerning the relations between mind, sense, and nature; the Catholic revival in modern cultural history; and, of course, the larger artistic unit in which the fragment appears, the entire sequence of the five *Grandes Odes* and processional.

In a characteristic appropriation of his subject's style, Spitzer elaborates Claudel's own admonition to his reader, "Ne cherche point le chemin, cherche le centre!" [Do not seek the road, seek the center!] into a metacritical conceit justifying his "thickets of notes" as necessary if one is to penetrate the labyrinth that Claudel has in fact constructed around his poem's imaginative center. The empathy that marks nearly all of Spitzer's studies is particularly visible in his treatment of this poet, who transformed the classical ode into a universal

poem, a *Weltgedicht* (world-ode) in the tradition of Dante and
Goethe, reflecting all the strivings of his epoch and singing of a reconciliation of man and nature, reason and faith, science and religion.
Whether a reflection of that love which Spitzer sees as the professional obligation of the philologist or an expression of personal affinities with the French poet, Spitzer's enthusiasm for Claudel's harmonious vision clearly points to a major area of his own work in
criticism and historical semantics: his studies of the origins, development, and survival of the motifs in which the idea of world harmony has taken shape in Europe and, specifically, their continuing
presence in the seemingly endless catalogues of objects in the works
of such modern lyric poets as Walt Whitman, Rubén Darío, and
Franz Werfel.[1] As Spitzer argues, Claudel's "chaotic enumeration" of
trivial and transcendental objects, assembled indiscriminately but
bound together through the biblical patterns of anaphoric repetition
and parallelism, reveals in its apparent disorder a glimpse of the
plenitude and unity of a higher order and re-creates a world concert
of love and harmony in which the attentive listener might distinguish
a distant echo of the Ambrosian hymns.

This essay was first published in Spitzer's *Linguistics and Literary
History: Essays in Stylistics* (Princeton, N.J., 1948), pp. 193–236. It
is reprinted by permission of Princeton University Press.

Interpretation of an Ode by Paul Claudel

Argumentum: One stanza (the first) from one poem ("La Muse qui est la Grâce"), belonging to a series of six *Grandes Odes*, is singled out from the whole work of Claudel for stylistic interpretation—a stanza of unusual length (covering several pages) in which the author seems to set forth the purpose of the ode(s), and which, at first sight, appears oppressively dense and opaque. The linguistic detail which, here, served as the point of departure was the repetition of the epithet *grand* [great], found five times in the selection. The five lines in which it occurs were found, when analyzed logically, to offer a skeleton outline of the author's program; when observed from the lyrical point of view, they revealed an ever-increasing intensity and breadth. This suggested that theme and rhythm must be considered together: the theme is that of gradual ascension and triumph (a twofold triumph: that of man over Nature, and that of the poet struggling to conquer his subject), and this forward and onward movement is incarnated in the ever-ascending waves of the rhythm—as in the verbal motif-work. But, as one begins to follow the course of the poem, one sees that this ascending movement makes its way against an adverse current: the poet's expressions of determination and confidence in his solemn purpose are counterbalanced in the first part of the poem: we find successive outbursts (gradually diminishing) of petulance, which reveal a conflict in the poet (such devices as the repetition of *Laisse-moi* . . . [Let me . . .]!), as well as occasional shifts of tone from the lofty to the trivial and jocular. Both of these are due to the influence (from which the poet has not yet been able quite to free himself) of the pagan Muse, to whom he had formerly paid allegiance. Thus the whole stanza reveals itself as expressing a struggle between pagan and Christian forces in the breast of the poet—a struggle which informs also the other odes of the collection, and which is inherent in any attempt on the part of a modern Christian poet who would write in the form of an ancient ode. And, with this, we are brought to a comparison of Claudel's Christian ode with the paganistic ode of Ronsard: where the latter failed, Claudel has succeeded in resolving the ever-present paradox underlying the reception by a modern artist of an ancient form. Whereas a literary historian, interested in his categories, may easily speak of "Christian versus pagan poetry," this *versus*, this sign of a historical struggle of cultures, is reenacted in Claudel's soul and is embodied in the linguistic form of his poem.

> O grammarien dans mes vers!
> Ne cherche point le chemin, cherche le centre!
> [O grammarian within my verses!
> Do not seek the road, seek the center!]
>
> *Cinq Grandes Odes*, I

The passage below is taken from the fourth ode in the collection *Cinq Grandes Odes suivies d'un processional pour saluer le siècle nouveau* [Five Great Odes followed by a Processional to Greet the New Century],[1] which deals, with variations, with the task of the Catholic poet in our modern world. Ode IV, "La Muse qui est la Grâce," was written at Tientsin in 1907. The passage we shall consider is Strophe I of the ode, which is constructed according to a Ronsardian or Pindaric scheme: after an introduction there follow three "strophes" with their respective "antistrophes" (the first containing the words of the poet, the latter those of the Muse), and the poem ends with an "epode" which, like the introduction, reveals to us the feelings of the poet.*

---

* It must be borne in mind that, in our ode, Claudel changes the tripartite scheme of the Pindaric-Ronsardian form in two ways: he replaces the sequence, repeatable at will, of strophe, antistrophe, and epode (the first two of which are equal in structure) by three sequences of strophe and antistrophe of unequal length and structure, followed, only at the end, by an epode and preceded by an introductory stanza; in addition, only in the dialogue between the Muse and the poet is there any alternation of strophe and

antistrophe (in this way, the dialogue finds a form reflecting the to-and-fro movement of dialectics). This tight cohesive pattern may be contrasted with the leisurely air of Ronsard's "Ode à Michel de l'Hôpital"—at the end of which the author confesses that "the law of the song" bids him stop: he could have continued indefinitely with his system of loosely connected stanzas.

In the other odes the tripartite scheme is completely abandoned in all its original length, thereby improving the error of Ronsard who, misled by the contemporary editions of Pindar, thought to respect the Pindaric scheme by using shorter lines.

To this ode Claudel has prefixed the following *argument* (in which I have introduced references to the metrical divisions): "{introduction} Invasion de l'ivresse poétique. {strophes and antistrophes I–III} Dialogue du poète avec la Muse qui devient peu à peu la Grâce. Il essaye de la refouler, il lui demande de la laisser à son devoir humain, à la place de son âme il lui offre l'univers entier qu'il va recréer par l'intelligence et la parole. En vain, c'est à lui personnellement que la Muse qui est la Grâce ne cesse de s'adresser! C'est la joie divine qu'elle lui rappelle et son devoir de sanctification personnelle.— {epode} Mais le poète se bouche les oreilles et se retourne vers la terre. Suprême évocation de l'amour charnel et humain." [Inrush of poetic inspiration. Dialogue between the poet and the Muse who little by little becomes Grace. He tries to drive her back, commanding her to leave him to his human duties; he offers to give her, instead of his soul, the whole universe which he is about to re-create through intelligence and the word. In vain. The Muse who is Grace will address herself to him alone. She reminds him of divine joy, and of his duty of personal sanctification.—But the poet will not listen, and turns back toward the earth. Supreme evocation of fleshly and human love.] Here follows the text of Strophe I:

> —O Muse, il sera temps de dormir un autre jour! Mais puisque
>   cette grande nuit tout entière est à nous,
> Et que je suis un peu ivre en sorte qu'un autre mot parfois
> Vient à la place du vrai, à la façon que tu aimes,
> Laisse-moi avoir explication avec toi,
> 5 Laisse-moi te refouler dans cette strophe, avant que tu ne reviennes
>   sur moi comme une vague avec un cri félin!
> Va-t-en de moi un peu! laisse-moi faire ce que je veux un peu!
> Car, quoique je fasse et si que je le fasse de mon mieux,
> Bientôt je vois un œil se lever sur moi en silence comme vers
>   quelqu'un qui feint.

Laisse-moi être nécessaire! laisse-moi remplir fortement une place
    reconnue et approuvée,
10 Comme un constructeur de chemin de fer, on sait qu'il ne sert pas à
    rien, comme un fondateur de syndicats!
Qu'un jeune homme avec son menton orné d'un flocon jaunâtre,
Fasse des vers, on sourit seulement.
J'attendais que l'âge me délivrât des fureurs de cet esprit bachique.
Mais, loin que j'immole le bouc, à ce rire qui gagne des couches plus
    profondes
15 Il me faut trouver que je ne fais plus sa part.
Du moins laisse-moi faire de ce papier ce que je veux et le remplir
    avec un art studieux,
Ma tâche, comme ceux-là qui en ont une.
Ainsi le scribe égyptien recensait de sa pointe minutieuse les tributs,
    et les parts de butin, et les files de dix captifs attachés,
Et les mesures de blé que l'on porte à la meule banale, et les barques
    à la douane.
20 Ainsi l'antique sculpteur avec sa tignasse rougie à la chaux attrapé à
    sa borne de basalte noir avec la massette et le ciseau,
Et de temps en temps il souffle sur ses caractères pareils à des clous
    entrecroisés pour ôter la poussière et se recule avec contentement.
Et je voudrais compasser un grand poème plus clair que la lune qui
    brille avec sérénité sur la campagne dans la semaine de la
    moisson,
Et tracer une grande Voie triomphale au travers de la Terre,
Au lieu de courir comme je peux la main sur l'échine de ce
    quadrupède ailé qui m'entraîne, dans sa course cassée qui est à
    moitié aile et bond!
25 Laisse-moi chanter les œuvres des hommes et que chacun retrouve
    dans mes vers ces choses qui lui sont connues,
Comme de haut on a plaisir à reconnaître sa maison, et la gare, et la
    mairie, et ce bonhomme avec son chapeau de paille, mais l'espace
    autour de soi est immense!
Car à quoi sert l'écrivain, si ce n'est à tenir des comptes?
Que ce soit les siens ou d'un magasin de chaussures, ou de
    l'humanité tout entière.
Ne t'indigne pas! ô sœur de la noire Pythie qui broie la feuille de
    laurier entre ses mâchoires resserrées par le trisme prophétique et
    un filet de salive verte coule du coin de sa bouche!
30 Ne me blesse point avec ce trait de tes yeux!
O géante! ne te lève pas avec cet air de liberté sublime!
O vent sur le désert! ô ma bien-aimée pareille aux quadriges de
    Pharaon!
Comme l'antique poète parlait de la part des dieux privés de
    présence,
Et moi je dis qu'il n'est rien dans la nature qui soit fait sans dessein
    et propos à l'homme adressé,

35 Et comme lumière pour l'œil et le son pour l'oreille, ainsi toute chose
   pour l'analyse de l'intelligence,
   Continuée avec l'intelligence qui la
   Refait de l'élément qu'elle récupère,
   Que ce soit la pioche qui le dégage, ou le pan du prospecteur et
   l'amalgame de mercure,
   Ou le savant, la plume à la main, ou le tricot des métiers, ou la
   charrue.
40 Et je puis parler, continu avec toute chose muette,
   Parole qui est à sa place intelligence et volonté.
   Je chanterai le grand poème de l'homme soustrait au hasard!
   Ce que les gens ont fait autour de moi avec le canon qui ouvre les
   vieux Empires,
   Avec le canot démontable qui remonte l'Aruwhimi, avec l'expédition
   polaire qui prend des observations magnétiques,
45 Avec les batteries de hauts fourneaux qui digèrent le minerai, avec
   les frénétiques villes haletantes et tricotantes, (et ça et là une anse
   bleue de la rivière dans la campagne solennelle),
   Avec les ports tout bordés intérieurement de pinces et d'antennes et
   le transatlantique qui signale au loin dans le brouillard,
   Avec la locomotive qu'on attelle à son convoi, et le canal qui se
   remplit quand la fille de l'Ingénieur en chef du bout de son doigt
   sur le coup-de-poing fait sauter à la fois la double digue,
   Je le ferai avec un poème qui ne sera plus l'aventure d'Ulysse parmi
   les Lestrygons et les Cyclopes, mais la connaissance de la Terre,
   Le grand poème de l'homme enfin par delà les causes secondes
   réconcilié aux forces éternelles,
50 La grande Voie triomphale au travers de la Terre réconciliée pour
   que l'homme soustrait au hasard s'y avance!

   Muse, there will be time to sleep another day! And because this
   whole great night is ours,
   And because I am a little drunk, so that sometimes another word
   comes,
   In the way that you like, instead of the right one,
   Let me have it out with you,
5 Let me drive you back in this strophe before, with a feline cry, you
   spring on me again like a wave.
   Go a little away from me! Let me do what I want a little!
   For, whatever I do and though I do my best at it,
   I soon see your eye turned silently upon me, as if I wasn't trying.
   Let me be necessary! Let me fill, vigorously, a place that is
   recognized and approved,
10 Like a builder of railways, known to be good for nothing, like a
   trade-union organizer!
   When a young man with yellow down on his chin
   Writes verses, people only smile at him.

I waited for age to deliver me from the furies of that Bacchic spirit,
And, far from making my sacrifice to the laughter which seizes the depths of us,

15 I must make sure that his role is not mine.
At least let me do what I want with my piece of paper, and accomplish with studious art
My task, like those who have one.
Like the scribe in Egypt, meticulously checking the tribute with the point of his stylus, and the shares of booty, and the files of captives, roped in groups of ten,
And the measures of wheat brought to the common mill, and the ships at the customs.

20 Like the ancient sculptor, his rough wig colored by the lime-dust clinging to the pillar of black basalt under his mallet and chisel.
And now and again he blows the dust away from these signs that look like crossed nails, and steps contentedly back.
I would like to chart out a great poem, brighter than the moon that shines serenely over the land in the week of harvest,
And to trace on the Earth a great triumphal Way,
Instead of racing along as best I can, my hand on the back of this winged quadruped that carries me off with its broken gait, half flying, half leaping.

25 Let me sing the works of men, so that each man finds in my verses the things that are known to him,
As it gives us pleasure to see our homes from on high, and the station, and the town-hall, and that fellow there in his straw hat, though a vast space is around us.
What is the writer good for, if not to keep the accounts?
Whether these are his own, or those of a shoe-shop, or those of all humanity?
Do not be angry, sister of the dark Pythia who crushes the laurel leaf between jaws clenched in the spasm of prophecy, so that a thread of green spittle runs from the corner of her mouth!

30 Do not wound me with that dart from your eyes!
Giantess! Do not rise with that air of sublime freedom!
Wind over the desert! Beloved, you are like the chariots of Pharaoh!
As the ancient poet spoke on behalf of gods without presence,
I say in my turn that nothing is made in Nature without design and purpose toward man,

35 And, as the light is made for his eyes, and sound for his ears, so all things are made for analysis by his intelligence,
Which is continuous with the intelligence that
Remakes them from the recovered element,
Freeing it with the pick, or the prospector's sieve, or with amalgam of mercury,
Through the scholar, pen in hand, with the plough, or the looms weaving.

40 And I can speak, being continuous with all silent things,

Words which in their place are intelligence and will.
I shall sing the great song of man set free from chance.
What men have accomplished around me with the cannon that open
    the old empires,
With collapsible boats ascending the Aruwhimi, with polar
    expeditions observing the effects of magnetism,
45 With groups of tall furnaces smelting the ore, with frenetic cities,
    breathless, hurrying along (and here and there a blue loop of the
    river in the peaceful countryside),
With ports, fringed within by pincers and antennae, and the
    transatlantic liner hooting far off in the fog,
With the locomotive coupled to its wagons, and the canal, filling
    when the daughter of the Chief Engineer puts her finger on the
    lever, and both the dams fall at once,
I will do it with a poem; no longer the adventures of Ulysses among
    Laestrygonians and Cyclops, but a poem acquainted with the
    Earth,
A great poem where man is at last beyond secondary things,
    reconciled to eternal powers,
50 A great triumphal Way over the reconciled Earth, where man goes
    forward, freed from the tyranny of chance![2]

Strophe I opens after the poet has already been invaded by the poetic frenzy, and when he is ready to formulate the task he feels to be
incumbent upon him; this strophe, in which this formulation is developed, is addressed to the Muse, whose answer, given only in Antistrophe I, sets up a conflict which rages throughout the poem—
namely, the question of the estrangement of the poet from the earth.
Though we isolate this one strophe of one ode, the notes will provide
the connections with the other parts of the ode and the other odes of
the collection.

An artistic unit such as this, startling as it must have appeared
when first printed, is hardly less baffling to us today: it offers the
form of a sphere, whose unbroken surface seems to yield no likely
point of attack. For, whatever particular part we may choose to concentrate upon, we are intimidated from the start by the thought that
this will always be only a particular part, and that such concentration may impair our understanding of the unity and cohesiveness of
the work of art. But, if we think of this globe as a sun-ball, and of the
particular points as sunbeams, we may be sure that, just as from any
particular sunbeam we may infer the live force which sends forth all
the sunbeams, so we will be able to penetrate from any peripheral
point of the work of art to its core. It is my firm belief, corroborated
by the experience of many exercises practiced in seminars with my

students, where I chose to start from any particular point suggested by one of the group, that any one good observation will, when sufficiently deepened, infallibly lead to the center of the work of art. There are no preferential vantage points (such as the "ideas," the structure, of the poem, etc.) with which we are obliged to start: any well-observed item can become a vantage point and, however arbitrarily chosen, must, if rightly developed, ultimately lose its arbitrariness.

Let us decide to start with the language of the poem—which, in itself, offers various aspects: the poet's syntactical license, his blend of popular and learned words,* etc.

---

*This was the starting-point I took in my explanation of Claudel's *Ballade*, the subject of an address at the convention of the Modern Language Association in 1937, which could not be published in its *Publications*—although the secretary had asked to have the manuscript submitted for publication—because the editorial committee deemed it "schoolroom work," not "scholarship." As though schoolroom work should not imply scholarship, and as though "scholars" are not tempted to err often in delimiting scholarship arbitrarily! The article ultimately appeared in the December 1942 issue of *The French Review*.[3]

I shall deal with Claudel's technique of "word-motifs," where the possibilities are still greater: I could start from any single one of the leading words indicated in the title of this collection, or in the title of our ode (*Muse, Grâce, odes, saluer, siècle nouveau*)—all of which are repeated or paraphrased in our strophe. I choose to start with the epithet *grand* in the title *Cinq Grandes Odes . . .* , an epithet which suggests that level of poetic sublimity which is traditionally associated with the ode, and which distinguishes Claudel's ode from the lighter Anacreontic variety with which in France the genre has traditionally been confused since the time of the Pléiade. The epithet *grand* occurs six times:*

---

*The epithet *grand* appears, in fact (together with the initial reference in Strophe I), in the introductory lines (before Strophe I): "Ah, ce soir est à moi! ah, cette *grande* nuit est à moi! . . . Voici le dépliement de la *grande* aile poétique!" [The evening is mine! this whole *great* night is mine! . . . The *great* wings of poetry unfold!] (the last line suggests an allusion to the Greek Nike of the Louvre).

(1) O Muse, . . . puisque cette grande nuit tout entière est à nous
(22) Et je voudrai compasser un grand poème
(23) Et tracer une grande Voie triomphale au travers de la Terre
(42) Je chanterai le grand poème de l'homme soustrait au hasard!
(49) Le grand poème de l'homme enfin par delà les causes secondes
  réconcilié aux forces éternelles
(50) La grande Voie triomphale au travers de la Terre réconciliée
  pour que l'homme soustrait au hasard s'y avance!

[(1) Muse, . . . because this whole great night is ours
(22) I would like to chart out a great poem
(23) And to trace on the Earth a great triumphal Way
(42) I shall sing the great song of man set free from chance!
(49) A great poem where man is at last beyond secondary things,
  reconciled to eternal powers
(50) A great triumphal Way over the reconciled Earth, where man
  goes forward, freed from the tyranny of chance!]

Three things are great: the night of inspiration (l. 1), the poem envisaged (ll. 22, 42, 49), and the progress of man (ll. 23, 49, 50)—which shall be the subject of this poem. The purposefulness and precision of Claudel's use of *grand*, as illustrated by these six passages,* is evident and could suggest that the passages themselves have prominence in the architecture of our strophe; and, upon examination, this turns out to be the case.

---

*The epithet *grand* applied to our poem will, in later strophes, be expanded to *entier* [whole] (in Strophe III we find: "Et cependant quand tu m'appelles ce n'est pas avec moi seulement qu'il faut répondre, mais avec tous les êtres qui m'entourent, / Un poème tout entier comme un seul mot tel qu'une cité dans son enceinte pareille au rond de la bouche. / . . . Et moi c'est le monde tout entier qu'il me faut conduire à sa fin avec une hécatombe de paroles!" [And yet when you call me I cannot answer with myself alone, but with all the beings that surround me, / A whole poem like a single word, a city within its walls which are like the round "O" of the mouth. / . . . I must lead the whole world to its end with an hecatomb of words]), and, in Ode V (as well as in the "Processional"), to *catholique* in the two meanings of the word: "Je vois devant moi l'Eglise catholique qui est de tout l'univers! . . . Tout est à moi, catholique, et je ne suis privé d'aucun de vous" and "Voici l'immensité de tous mes frères vivants et morts, l'unanimité du peuple catholique, / Les douze tribus d'Israël réunies et les trois Eglises en une seule basilique" [I see before me the Catholic Church which is the whole universe! . . . I am catholic, all relates to me, I am cut off from none of you; Here is the measureless throng of all my brothers, living and dead, the unanimity of catholics, / The Twelve Tribes of Israel reunited and the Three Churches within one basilica].
  The progression "great" > "complete" > "catholic" is a progression, to

some extent, from dimension to integration and finally to the signification informing the integrated whole: Claudel considers himself a husbander of this vast, finite universe (Ode V: "Mon désir est d'être le rassembleur de la terre de Dieu! Comme Christophe Colomb quand il mit à la voile, / Sa pensée n'était pas de trouver une terre nouvelle, / Mais dans ce cœur plein de sagesse la passion de la limite et de la sphère calculée de parfaire l'éternel horizon" [I want to create the world of God again. Like Christopher Columbus, who hoisted sail / Not to discover new lands / But holding within his own wise heart the desire for limits, the passion for the determinate sphere, the completion of the eternal horizon]. This is also the main idea of Claudel's Spanish Catholic world-drama, *Le Soulier de satin* [The Satin Slipper]. Claudel subjects this plenary universe to the limits of Catholicity. The *grande ode* is thus an annunciation of the Catholic Ode. There is a willful violence in this procedure of setting limits to the boundless universe and of making it Catholic in the narrower sense of the word: it is inspired by that same *passion de la limite* which the poet recognizes in Columbus (and which explains better, perhaps, than do the epithets "stubborn and obstinate" of the modern historian Samuel Eliot Morison, the reason for Columbus's misinterpretation of his own discovery).

The first passage sets the background of the composition of our strophe (while also connected with the Introduction descriptive of the invasion of poetic frenzy); in the last (which is the final line of the strophe) we are offered the program of Claudel's poem—his *arma virumque cano* [Arms and the man I sing; these are the opening words of *The Aeneid*—EDS.], which he builds up for us piecemeal in the preceding four lines: we see first a triumphal way traversing the earth, then man freed from the accidental and, finally, the convergence of both motifs in a triumphant apotheosis.*

---

* Here we could use as well the metaphor of the path hewn through the forest: "une grande Voie triomphale au travers de la Terre" [a great triumphal Way over the Earth] comes to view only after the reader has fought his way through the underbrush of wildly luxuriant verse-vegetation.

We could also speak of five motifs contained in this program and which are basic to the strophe: *homme* (l. 11), *Voie triomphale, terre* (l. 23), *l'homme, soustrait au hasard* [freed from chance](l. 42)— several of which we find repeated or paraphrased in these same six passages.

These six lines can be immediately reduced to four (ll. 1, 22–23,

42, 49–50), giving us three subdivisions of the strophe which we may be allowed to call "stanzas"—although no such indication is given by the printed arrangement. In the upward progression of this strophe the lines we have isolated represent plateaus breaking our climb toward the peak whence we can envisage the final panorama of Claudel's vision. Or if, remembering the surging flow of our poem, which from the start engulfs us like an ocean, we may be allowed to change our metaphor, these high ridges which loom above the rest of the lines are so many crests of onrushing waves, the last of which seems to prolong itself beyond the limits of our strophe—whose final word is *avance!* [forward!].*

---

* Anyone who has watched the energetic consistency with which, at high tide, the assault on the beaches is carried forward by the irregular succession of master-waves, while the weaker and less far-reaching currents provide *intermezzi* of relaxation, will realize how well this simile fits the rhythm of our poem, with its bold forward dashes, alternating with spells of calm, during which the poem rests for a moment, before undertaking a new attack.

We may, perhaps, conjecture that by this rolling upward and onward of word-floods and word-waves, Claudel means to figure the progression and ascension of man in his conquest of Nature; not only will the poem tell of progress, it will, itself, vibrate with the rhythm of a progress which carries us along in its forward movement—an idea become poetic activity. Here we are reminded of the poetry of Péguy in which we find the same process of gradual expansion toward a climax (though with Péguy each climax leads immediately, without recession, to a new height). What Claudel and Péguy have in common is the Bergsonian sensitivity to the *élan vital* and to the flow of time; the theme of Progress is essentially a theme of Time. By both poets the work of art is offered not as something *tout fait* [finished], but as *se faisant* [developing], before our eyes.*

---

* In fact, we may state here that Claudel's collection of odes constitutes an *ars poetica* dramatically enacted. It is no didactic work like those of Boileau and Verlaine—or like Claudel's own treatise *Art poétique*—but an *art poétique se faisant*, which develops before our eyes while the poet is wrestling with all the contradictory strivings which he feels in himself.

Who says rhythm says metrics. We will not find in Claudel any regular system of rhyme or meter. Language, with him, is not subjected to the coercion from without of preordained metrics, as is the case with orthodox French poetry; it is conditioned by an inner motivation and impulsion whose intensity and direction may vary at any moment. And the divisions which the poet usually indicates by metrical devices are here suggested by the recurrence of word-motifs—what we have called the flood-and-wave technique. Within the expanse of the strophe, which is like a sea sending forth its floods, there cannot be the sharp division of fixed stanzas—only the tenuous limits we have been able to discern by following the wave-movement to its crest: indeed, it is possible to find double or triple crests, as in lines 22–23 and 48–49–50. As for the "stanzas" so discerned, we may observe the diminishing size of the three units: the poem starts slowly, with a gradual acceleration of its course until the end is reached—which prolongs itself into the infinite. The corresponding efforts of understanding called for from the reader must be given a chance to gain sufficient strength for the final synthesis or apotheosis. And, to the progressive intensification of the reader's effort corresponds a growing firmness on the part of the poet; the stiffening of his will is reflected in the variation of tenses suggestive of three stages of decision: (l. 1) "Et je voudrais compasser un grand poème" [I would like to chart out a great poem] (still wavering); (l. 42) "Je chanterai le grand poème . . ." [I shall sing the great song . . .] (prediction of a firm decision); (l. 48) "Je le ferai avec un poème" [I will do it with a poem] (*faire* emphasizes the practical realization of this purpose).

Up to now we have followed the verbal-metrical scheme of the strophe only insofar as it throws light upon the ideological purpose of this proem. But in a proem there is generally present a second topos: in order to fulfill his purpose the poet calls upon the Muse for inspiration. In our strophe the Muse is mentioned in the title and in the opening line (as in Homer's Ἄνδρα μοι ἔννεπε, Μοῦσα, πολύτροπον [Tell me, Muse, of the man of many ways; this is the opening line of *The Odyssey*—EDS.]) but, as the poem proceeds, her influence seems to fade; she is mentioned for the last time in lines 31–32, where the vocatives and imperatives addressed to her come to an end. It is as though the "flood" of the Muse-motif had completely receded at this point. But in our strophe Claudel's Muse is a force, not invoked for his help but, on the contrary, rejected by him; this attitude, strange enough on the part of a poet, takes definite shape as early as the fifth line: "Laisse-moi te refouler dans cette strophe; avant que tu ne reviennes sur moi comme une vague"* [Let me drive you back in this strophe, before you spring on me again like a wave] (here Claudel himself uses the "wave" metaphor—which, I may say, was not suggested to me by this line but occurred to me independently when I was attempting to define his technique).

---

*This *refouler* in Strophe I must not be confused with the *refouler* of the *argument*—though there may be a relationship of motif between the two cases: in Strophe I Claudel rejects the pagan Muse; in Strophe II (which is resumed in the *argument*) he rejects the poetic Muse as such because she distracts him from his earthly communion with human beings.

The "wave" motif has been prepared by numerous references, in the introductory lines, to the "sea," with which the poetic frenzy was compared: "Encore! encore la mer qui revient me rechercher comme une barque" [Once more! once more the sea seeking me as if I were a ship], etc. And it is, as we have said, an oceanic impression that we receive from the opening lines of the poem.

And the recession of the Muse-flood forms a movement contrary to the movement by which the program of the poet gradually takes shape: she is an antagonistic power in whom is incarnated all that he would shun, that he fears or loathes; the inebriation caused by the gods of pleasure, of licentiousness, of casualness (her animality is emphasized by *cri félin* [feline cry],* l. 5, and *le bouc* [the goat], l. 14).

---

*This motif recurs in Strophe II, where the poet rejects the inspiration of the pagan Muse who receives no light from the Gospel: "les ténèbres et le Chaos qui n'a point reçu l'Evangile. / . . . Ténèbres de la privation de Dieu! ténèbres actives qui *sautent sur vous comme la panthère*" [darkness, and the Chaos unblessed by the Gospels. / . . . Darkness and the privation of God! Active darkness that *leaps upon me like a panther*] (= the *incursiones daemonum* of the Scriptures).

Now, if we seek to discover a "Muse" word-motif comparable to that descriptive of the poetic program, we shall find signs of this only in the series of vocatives and imperatives (which suggest the presence of an influenceable being and which must cease when the poet's new-found determination releases him from dependence on the Muse);

this being, who must be *refoulée*, is distinguished by no motif as graphic as that which was used in allusion to the positive purpose of the poet. The presence of the Muse as it acts on the poet is indicated only indirectly by allusions to his attitude toward her, and this attitude expresses itself in words with a climate of their own. First, we find humorously slighting expressions and a particularly flippant tone, as though the poet, in a gesture of withdrawal, sought to taunt her, and make light of his previous inclination toward her.*

---

* If we were to state a literary model for the inclusion of the teasing tone into a serious poem, we could think of Victor Hugo's "Le Satyre" (in *La Légende des siècles*)—especially of its first part where the satyr, who later is to become Pan and thus mightier than the Gods, is facetiously introduced as though seen from the point of view of the Gods before they have realized his power.

But nothing could be further from Claudel than the state of mind of a Hugo who seems to suggest (though without full conviction or convincingness) that a satyrlike animality is the source of art, science, political freedom. *Pace* Thibaudet, Victor Hugo was not as "intelligent" a poet as is Claudel: his vague humanitarianism and his pantheism did not integrate. To use Claudel's terminology, Victor Hugo did not create the "necessary" poem.

The particular flavor of this vocabulary, fickle, wavering, unprecise, is, perhaps, primarily due to the poet's state of mild intoxication inspired by the capricious pagan Muse—against whose influence he is on guard ("en sorte qu'un autre mot parfois / Vient à la place du vrai, à la façon que tu aimes" [so that sometimes another word comes, / In the way that you like, instead of the right one]).*

---

* Distrust of "enthusiasm" does not imply a lack of those qualities normally associated with enthusiasm: exuberance, power of expression, revolutionary striving for new forms. In Ode I Claudel declines to follow in the footsteps of Homer, Virgil (and Dante), when he says: "Rien de tout cela! *toute route à suivre nous ennuie!* toute échelle à escalader! /. . . O mon âme, il *ne faut concerter aucun plan!* ô mon âme sauvage, il faut nous tenir libres et prêts, /. . . O mon âme impatiente, pareille à l'aigle sans art! . . . / Que mon vers ne soit rien d'esclave! mais tel que l'aigle marin qui s'est jeté sur un grand poisson, / Et l'on ne voit rien qu'un éclatant tourbillon d'ailes et l'éclaboussement de l'écume!" [Away with all this! *every known road wearies us!* every ladder which is there to be climbed! /. . . O my soul, *let us plan nothing!* o my untamed soul, let us be free and ready, /. . . O my im-

patient soul, without guile like the eagle! . . . / Let there be nothing slavish about my verses! let them be like the sea-eagle that swoops on a great fish, / Nothing visible but a shining flurry of wings and the leaping spray!]. He hastens, however, to add: "Mais vous ne m'abandonnerez point, ô Muses modératrices" [But you will never desert me, mediating Muses]; that is to say, Claudel's poetic revolution amounts not to anarchy but to a new order. It is a revolution, nonetheless: Boileau's precept concerning the ode—"Son style impétueux souvent marche au hasard, / Chez elle un beau désordre est un effet de l'art" [Its bold style often advances as if by chance / In the ode a beautiful disorder is an effect of art] (which is concerned only with an "*effect* of disorder" given by a poem which should be, in reality, most well-ordered)—is timid in comparison.

The poet is only *un peu ivre* [a little drunk], not drunken (as he must have been earlier, since he fears being invaded again by the Muse: "que tu ne reviennes sur moi" [before you spring on me again])—not drunken, that is, with the heavenly enthusiasm and sweet frenzy celebrated by the pagan poets from Plato to Ronsard.*

---

* With this stipulation Claudel shows himself opposed to the *furor poeticus*—and this in an ode, the very genre for which poetic frenzy had been held indispensable ever since the rediscovery of Pindar by the humanists. We can see in these lines a direct rebuke intended for Ronsard (who has his Jupiter tell the Muse: "Votre métier, race gentille, / *Les autres métiers passera* / D'autant qu'esclave il ne sera / De l'art {=technical skill}, aux Muses inutile. / Par art le navigateur / En la mer manie et vire /. . . Par art se font les ouvriers; /. . . Sans plus, ma sainte fureur / Polira votre science" [Your trade, genteel race, *will surpass other trades* because it will not be a slave of art {=technical skill}, useless to the Muses. By art the navigator plies and tacks in the sea . . . by art workers make themselves; . . . without more, my holy furor will refine your knowledge]) and ultimately a criticism of Plato, who had put enthusiasm above *sophia* and *techne*. Claudel, by his theory (so at variance with his own practice and with the law of the genre of the ode he cultivates) that the poet should strive to be comprehensible to the average man, dissociates himself from the aristocratic poets of humanism who despised the common people for their failure to grasp poetic enthusiasm (compare also Strophe XV of Ronsard's "Ode à Michel de l'Hôpital").

One of the first of the expressions used about the Muse has a popular, even a vulgar ring: "Laisse-moi avoir explication avec toi" ("Let me thrash things out with you"), as if tipsiness encouraged vulgarity, freeing the poet from the obligation of using the vocabulary of a cultured man. The teasing tone continues: "Va-t-en de moi *un peu*!"

[Go *a little* away from me!] "Laisse-moi faire ce que je veux *un peu!*"
[Let me do what I want *a little!*]; a pouting child that wants to be left
alone would indulge in such stubborn, monotonous phrases.* Again,
"quoique je fasse et *si que* je le fasse de mon mieux" [for whatever I
do and *though* I do my best at it] has the deranged syntax that is to
be heard in any French bistro. These humorous† expressions may
seem at first glance strangely aberrant from the sublime tone characteristic of the ode.

---

*In Strophe II, where the poet rejects the Muse still more violently, the
same childish *un peu* is repeated: "Ah! quoique mon cœur se brise, non! /
Je ne veux point! va-t-en de moi un peu! ne me tente pas ainsi cruellement!"
[No, though my heart break! / I wish none of this! go a little away from me!
do not tempt me so cruelly!]; and in the epode, where the poet finally turns
away from the Muse, the *va-t-en* appears without the childish *un peu*: "Va-
t-en! Je me retourne désespérément vers la terre! / Va-t-en! tu ne m'ôteras
point ce froid goût de la terre . . ." [Away with you! Desperately I turn back
to the earth! / Away with you! You will not take from me this chill taste of
the earth . . .].
†In other words, humor, with Claudel as with the medieval poets, appears subordinated to the sacred, whereas the paganistic Ronsard was able
to introduce burlesque among the Olympians: in the "Ode à Michel de
l'Hôpital" he shows us an assembly of the Gods listening to the song of the
Muses, with Jupiter laughing at Mars "qui tenait l'œil fermé, / Ronflant sur
sa lance guerrière, / Tant la chanson l'avait charmé" [who held an eye closed,
snoring on his war lance, so charmed by the song].

And indeed, the very fact that they are transplanted into an exalted
environment serves to bring out in strong relief the lack of harmony
and poise in the poet's attitude at this point: not yet having attained
finality of decision, he can show his aversion only through (a humorous assumption of) childish petulance.

But humor recedes as a more serious guide makes an appearance—an anonymous force which bans the casual: "Bientôt je vois
un œil se lever *sur moi en silence* comme vers quelqu'un qui feint.
Laisse-moi être nécessaire . . ." [I soon see your eye turned *silently
upon me,* as if I wasn't trying. Let me be necessary . . .] (as opposed
to "avant que tu ne reviennes *sur moi . . . avec un cri félin*" [before,
with a feline cry, you spring on me again]). This silent being whose
gaze he feels—and which may remind us of Hugo's silent eye of conscience—is evidently Christian Grace, which will ultimately assume
the role of the poet's true Muse and which now, mutely, within his

conscience, rebukes him for his infidelity with the pagan Muse. And, with *nécessaire*, the motif of *l'homme soustrait au hasard* appears for the first time; the poem, which will sing of man freeing himself from the casual, must not be casual. For what Claudel censures most in the pagan Muse is not sensuality itself so much as the arbitrariness of a spirit not oriented on Christian, on "necessary" principles. It would be a betrayal of his own nature to indulge in the irrelevancy of Bacchic frenzy or Dionysiac corybantism (ll. 13–14); there is an insidious danger to the Christian soul in the laughter of Bacchus, "ce rire qui gagne des couches plus profondes" [the laughter which seizes the depths of us]; laughter per se is, for Claudel, not *le propre de l'homme* [man's proper lot] (as Rabelais has declared); it is not *nécessaire*, it is juvenile, worthy of a "jeune homme, avec son menton orné de . . ." [young man with yellow down on his chin].*

---

*We can sense here the paraphrase of a colloquial word (such as *béjaune* [novice], *blanc-bec* [greenhorn], for example) as well as a transposition into Homeric style (*orné de . . . !*). We remember Claudel's words: "Pas aucune de vos phrases que je ne sache reprendre!" [Not one of your phrases I cannot turn to good use!].

The motif of the *jeune homme* recurs in Strophe II: "Alors ne permettez point {ô Seigneur} à celle-ci {à la Muse} qu'elle vienne me tenter comme un jeune homme . . ." [Do not permit this Muse to come, and to tempt me as if I were a young man] (here, without the epithet equivalent to *béjaune*); compare the parallel sublimation *va-t-en un peu > va-t-en*.

And now that the poet feels more free to follow his true and necessary nature, we will find again that technique associated with his positive purpose: word-repetition; *nécessaire* is the first wave which will ultimately lead to the "crests" of "Et je voudrais compasser un grand poème" [I would like to chart out a great poem], "Je chanterai le grand poème de l'homme soustrait au hasard" [I shall sing the great song of man set free from chance]—which can be achieved only after pagan enthusiasm has completely subsided. It is only gradually that this intoxication recedes: even after the poet has expressed his desire to write "un grand poème plus clair que la lune" [a great poem, brighter than the moon], the frivolous note reappears (though here, as always, he uses frivolity to exorcise the pagan world of frivolity): in line 24 he describes Pegasus in words which limp, as if to mimic the erratic gait of this absurd beast (for, with Claudel, the heavenly courser of the Greeks limps): "dans sa course cassée qui est à moitié aile et bond" [with its broken gait, half flying, half leaping].*

---

*This motif of the "hybrid" nature of the paganistic poet is emphasized again in Antistrophe II, when the Muse, encouraging the poet to follow his path with the pride of a god, says:

> Afin que je te regarde et rie, et que j'imite, moi, la déesse, ton
>   avancement mutilé!
> Je ne t'ai point permis de marcher comme les autres hommes d'un
>   pied plan,
> Car tu es trop lourd pour voler
> Et le pied que tu poses à terre est blessé!

> [I want to look at you and laugh, and copy (I who am a goddess)
>   your crippled progress.
> I have not allowed you to walk like other men, with an even pace,
> For you are too heavy to fly
> And the foot you put to earth is wounded.]

Here the whimsicality of pagan poetry appears in the form of hybridism. And Claudel spurns the hybrid, which had been exalted in pagan poetry; like the medieval poets in their treatment of classical demigods, he (cynically) pretends to see in such blends only the imperfect and incongruous.

Now, after following the poet in his excursion into frivolity and animality, let us return to line 9, where the motif *nécessaire* first appears. This impressive line is followed by a hemistich which may astonish many readers: after the poet has proclaimed inner necessity to be his moving force, we hear the request: "laisse-moi remplir fortement une place reconnue et approuvée, / Comme un constructeur de chemin de fer, on sait qu'il ne sert pas à rien, comme un fondateur de syndicats!" [Let me fill, vigorously, a place that is recognized and approved, / Like a builder of railways, known to be good for nothing, like a trade-union organizer!]. The poet asks to play a role in society! This premium placed on *fama*, this acceptance of the *ut in pluribus* [as in many] principle is evidence of the Thomist trend in Claudel; the inner necessity which guides him in his poetic activity asks for the complement of a necessary role among his fellowmen. In Claudel's opinion, the poet should not be a peripheral phenomenon: he should occupy a place in society,* he should be necessary as a modern railroad executive is necessary, or a trade-union leader.

*Here, Claudel is in accord with Péguy, the son of the *rempailleuse de chaises* [woman who replaces the straw in chairs], who always expressed pride in the craftsmanship of the *homme de lettres* [man of letters; Spitzer translates it as "writing-man"—EDS.] and who saw in Christ, the carpenter's son who did *de la bonne ouvrage* [good work], the patron of the intellectual.

And, since Claudel would like to join the ranks of the workingmen (to be himself a "writing-man"), he must adopt their language; his words have the bluff, hearty flavor of the speech of a Parisian workingman who talks straight from the shoulder ("on sait qu'il ne sert pas à rien" [known to be good for nothing])*—as "one sensible person to another."

*It must also be remarked that the inclusion, in large periods, of such brief main clauses as though they were incidental clauses (a sentence-unification made possible by the breath), belongs to oral speech: this is one of the cases in which a great writer is able to conquer new areas of oral speech for artistic writing—which has a tendency to drift away from the spoken form. This incorporation of the spoken into the written is the great secret of innovation in writing. Compare in Antistrophe II, "Jusque tu aies appris la mesure que je veux, à quoi ne sert point de compter un et deux, *tu l'apprendras*, serait-ce avec le hoquet de l'agonie!" [Until you have learnt the measure that I wish to teach, and for that it's no good your counting one and then two; *you will learn it*, though it be with sobs of anguish!], where the interpolation is one of those benignly consoling sentences with which the Muse mocks the poet.

With this shift into the practical, commercial, and political world of today, we are given the first indication in this strophe of the complex of ideas represented by the *siècle nouveau** mentioned in the title of the collection: it is the material progress of our world which Claudel hails.

*Claudel is writing a twentieth-century *carmen saeculare* [secular song], as he will state later:

Salut aurore de ce siècle qui commence!
Que d'autres te maudissent, mais moi je te consacre sans frayeur ce
  chant pareil à celui qu'Horace confia à des chœurs de jeunes
  garçons et de jeunes filles quand Auguste fonda Rome pour la
  seconde fois.

[Welcome, dawn of the new century!
Let others speak ill of you, I will fearlessly dedicate this song to you,
    like the song Horace made for the chorus of boys and girls when
    Augustus founded Rome for the second time.]

Claudel's *carmen saeculare* will, of course, be a Christian and a Catholic
one, in which progress and religion are reconciled: *un temple nouveau* [a
new temple] will rise in the place of the French sanctuaries destroyed by "la
pioche qui ne sait ce qu'elle fait" [the pick which does not know what it is
doing]; "Je vois devant moi l'Eglise catholique qui est de tout l'univers" [I
see before me the Catholic Church which is the whole universe] (to entertain
such a hope in 1907, only two years after the laws separating Church and
State had been enacted and when venerable sanctuaries were being dese-
crated, was most courageous). And he states in the "Processional":

Je crois que Dieu est ici bien qu'il me soit caché.
Comme il est au ciel avec tous ses anges et dans le cœur de la Vierge
    sans péché,
Il est mêmement ici, dans la gare de chemin de fer et l'usine, dans la
    crèche, dans l'aire et dans le chais.

[I believe that God is here even though he is hidden from me.
Just as he is in heaven with all his angels, and in the heart of the
    Virgin without sin,
Present even in the railway station and the factory, in the manger,
    upon the threshing-floor, in the wine-shed.]

The poet must not despise the world of his day, as Alfred de Vigny
did in "La Maison du Berger," as Georges Duhamel does in *Scènes
de la vie future.**

-----

* If, for a moment, I may step out of my role of linguistic-literary commentator of poetry, I may venture to say that this seems to me the most sensible view for a critic of our epoch to take. I have never understood the attitude of those critics of the mechanization of our world and of supposedly
mechanized America, who see an unbridgeable gap between faith and technics. Duhamel, for example, in his *Scènes de la vie future*, speaks with derision of the church he saw in Chicago which was located on the top floor of
a skyscraper. What matters is that people preserve their faith and that they
are not swallowed up by the machines; if the community *can* pray in that
Chicago church, it is of little importance that they must use an elevator to
enter the church instead of walking in through the front door. The moral
significance of technics depends entirely on the moral purpose to which it is
put: war or peace, irreligion or faith.

But this gigantic program is not presented in one piece, a manifesto
tout fait; it emerges only gradually out of conflicting tendencies; and

the solemn resolve is first expressed childishly, almost petulantly ("laisse-moi *du moins*" [*at least* let me])—though it is immediately recast in accents of dignity: "remplir fortement une place reconnue et approuvée" [fill vigorously a place that is recognized and approved]. The expression *art studieux* joins the ideological complex of *nécessaire* in its reminder of that laboriousness necessary to one who would be a workingman. The best examples which Claudel gives of the *art studieux* are drawn not from ancient Greece and Rome but from Egypt and Assyria: the Egyptian "scribe"* (which word is an etymological pun on *écrivain*, l. 27),† who was a tabulator, and the Assyrian engraver of cuneiform, bring to mind not the reverie of a poet withdrawn from the world but a technical skill which is socially useful (Claudel would share the professional pride of the Assyrian workman who rejoices in his skill), as well as precision of craftsmanship; from "pointe minutieuse" [point of his stylus], "attrapé avec la massette et le ciseau" [under his mallet and chisel]‡ there is a smooth transition to "compasser (un grand poème plus clair que la lune)" [chart out (a poem brighter than the moon)]§ and "tracer (une grande Voie triomphale au travers de la Terre)" [trace (on the Earth a great triumphal Way)]—which brings us to that main artery we have distinguished before. This vastest of enterprises which the poet envisages must be worked out with the greatest minuteness of detail, and this he proposes in lines which themselves have been chiseled with a painstaking precision that retards for the moment the oceanic sweep of the verse. The poet, then, must be an *écrivain*, a scribe—a simple "writing-man." What Dante-like modesty (coupled with Dante's ambition) on the part of one of the greatest poets of all times!‖

---

* It may be noted that the two anaphoric *ainsi*'s [like's] in lines 18 and 20, introducing carefully developed "Homeric similes," correspond to the usage of ancient poets who compare (by means of sentences introduced, e.g., by *sic . . . sic . . .*) the situation they are describing with parallels from the mythic or the historic past. But Claudel takes care also to vary the expression of the parallels by devices more modern: the "census" taken by the Egyptian scribe assumes the form of a Claudelian "chaotic enumeration" (*vide* [empty] later in our text); the picture of the Assyrian engraver is given in a *raccourci* [abridgement] by a participial construction ("l'antique sculpteur . . . attrapé" [the ancient sculptor . . . clinging]) followed by an anacoluthon ("Et de temps en temps il souffle . . ." [And now and again he blows]) with the biblical ring which will be described below.

One would expect Claudel to mention the Greek and Roman epigraphists, who certainly did not lack a *pointe minutieuse*, instead of the Egyptians and Assyrians; but we must face the fact that, in this context, the poet was forced to exclude a positive appraisal of the Greco-Roman civilization.

†This is a medieval device, amply represented in Saint Bernard and in Dante,[4] which Claudel has revived most felicitously. His equation *connaître* = *co-naître* is well known.

We may think that in this passage Claudel had another etymological pun in his mind: Latin *ratio* means "accountancy" and "reason," hence French *raisonable* "accountant" and "reasonable." Thus *tenir des comptes* can also evoke the ideas of "being rational, reasonable, using reason."

One may be reminded here of the words of the French historian Gabriel Hanotaux, who asked to be no more than "le greffier de l'histoire" [the accountant of history]. In Ode I Claudel defines the Muse of history as "Clio, le greffier de l'âme, pareille à celle qui tient les comptes" [Clio, the registrar of the soul, its accountant]. We may see in this idea the explanation for the outward biography of the poet: he can reconcile a bureaucratic job with his poetic métier. I, personally, am of the conviction that the idea was preexistent to his outward biography: "celle-ci s'est mise à imiter celle-là . . ." [this one started to imitate that one].

‡The motif of *massette et ciseau* [mallet and chisel], a suggestion of technical precision, recurs in the following strophe containing the rejection by the Muse of Claudel's poetic program:

> Que m'importent toutes vos machines et toutes vos œuvres
> d'esclaves et vos livres et vos écritures? . . .
> Ce n'est point avec *le tour et le ciseau* que l'on fait un homme
> vivant . . .
>
> [What do they mean to me—all your machines, and these things
> made by slaves, and your books and your writings? . . .
> A living man is not made with *the lathe or the chisel*.]

And, in Antistrophe III:

> Ce n'est point *l'auge et la truelle* qui rassemble et qui construit,
> C'est le feu pur et simple qui fait de plusieurs choses une seule.
>
> [It is not *the hod and the trowel* that assemble and construct,
> But the fire, pure and simple, that makes several things into one.]

In Ode V ("La Maison fermée"), the idea of the "necessity" of the poet, as well as the theme of the "accountant," recurs:

> Je sais que c'est moi qui vous {i.e., aux grandes forces célestes} suis
> nécessaire . . .
>
> [I know it is I who am necessary to you {i.e., to the great heavenly
> beings}.]
>
> Et toutes vous êtes en ma possession, *comme un banquier* qui de son
> bureau de Paris fait argent avec l'écriture des gommes de la
> Sénégambie . . .
>
> [And all of you are owned by me, *as by a banker* who makes money,
> as he writes in his office in Paris, from the gums of Senegambia.]

(Note the colloquialism *faire argent* and the bureaucratic flavor of *écriture*!) In *Positions et propositions*, Claudel explains the French aversion to excess and superfluity, as "le besoin de la nécessité," deeply rooted in the French national character: "Le Français a horreur du hasard, de l'accidentel et de l'imprévu. . . . Il a besoin de justifier devant lui-même chacun de ces actes, et, avisé d'ailleurs des regards acérés que chacun de ses voisins dirige sur lui, il s'arrange comme s'il avait à répondre à une accusation continuelle de détournement et de gaspillage. . . . Le Français s'est toujours senti actionnaire d'une société dont chaque membre *doit des comptes* à tous les autres. Il ne veut rien laisser perdre. Un bien inutile et gâché, un agrément qu'on se donne, lui paraissent de mauvaises actions" [The Frenchman abhors chance, what is accidental, and unpredictable. . . . Constantly aware of the piercing look that each of his neighbors directs at him, he behaves as if he had to answer continuous accusations of misappropriation and squandering. . . . The Frenchman has always felt himself to be a stockholder in a company in which each member *is accountable to* all the others. He does not want to lose anything. A useless and wasted good, a pleasure paid to oneself, appear to him to be immoral actions].[5] What he is describing here is the Jansenist streak in the French national character.

§Why should Claudel's poem be "clear like the moon," not "like the sun"? Evidently, not only because the Muse traditionally appears at night (a fact which troubled so greatly Alfred de Musset, who wished us to visualize in his *Nuits* the rebirth of Nature and his own Nature-like spiritual rebirth—at night!), but mainly because the moonlight is clearly defined, cool and calm, not diffused, and not dazzling like that of the sun; and because the *via triumphalis* Claudel wants to draw must be coolly, calmly designed, must be clear-cut and sharply visible in the midst of the maze of the earth.

The simile of the "scribe" may have been prompted by scriptural passages such as Psalms 44: "Lingua mea calamus scribae, velociter scribentis" [My tongue (language) is the reed of the scribe writing quickly], which is interpreted by Saint Jerome in Ephesians 45: "Debeo ergo et linguam meam quasi stilum et calamum preparare, ut per illam in corde et auribus audientium scribat Spiritus Sanctus" [Therefore I should prepare my tongue as though it were a pen and my reed so that through it the Holy Spirit may write in the heart and ears of those listening].[6] Claudel, however, with his aversion to enthusiasm, will not be the "stenographer writing {*velociter*!} under the dictation of the Holy Spirit": he will adopt only the skill and meticulousness of the scribe.

Claudel's poetry admits of no ambiguity behind which the poet may hide: he addresses himself to the whole of the nation and of humanity, and takes pride in being understood. His is not the "Mes-vers-ont-le-sens-qu'on-leur-prête" [My words have the meaning that is given to them] attitude of the esoteric Valéry, who could smile as he sat in the balcony of that Sorbonne amphitheater listening to Gustave Cohen explaining one of his poems. Claudel's poetry can be clearly, unambiguously explained—as we are trying to do here.

‖Similarly, Claudel's contemporary, Valéry, also insists on the ideal of "craftsmanship" for the modern artist, as opposed to the ideals of the enthusiastic romantic poetry of yore. And, today, one hears that the great and

original Stravinsky asks to be considered as a "craftsman," to the indignation of the lesser and more conventional Gian Francesco Malipiero, who retains the name of "musician."

With line 25, which is situated exactly in the middle of the poem,
man makes his first appearance, in the phrase *les œuvres des
hommes* [works of men] (anticipatory of *l'homme*, in l. 42)—as if to
imply that man is the center of a universe created for him; this idea
(which, for all of Claudel's disregard of serious pagan thought, is a
Thomist derivate of the ancient πάντων μέτρον ἄνθρωπος [Man is
the measure of all things]) will be outspokenly stated in line 34. In
this same line (l. 25), where the program motif *chanter* [sing] appears, we also find the last of Claudel's defensive *laisse-moi*'s [let
me's] addressed to the Muse—whose "wave" must recede as his assurance gains in strength. His *chanter* is immediately followed by "et
que chacun retrouve dans mes vers ces choses qui lui sont connues"
[so that each man finds in my verses the things that are known to
him];* this is an echo of the motif *une place reconnue* [a place that is
recognized], wherein was suggested the poet's association with the
practical things of modern everyday life—of which he will act as tabulator: *tenir des comptes* (l. 27) may remind us of the duties of the
Egyptian scribe.

---

* In the introductory lines (before Strophe I) Claudel himself says:

> Les mots que j'emploie, ce sont les mots de tous les jours, et ce
> ne sont point les mêmes!
> Vous ne trouverez point de rimes dans mes vers ni aucun
> sortilège. Ce sont vos phrases mêmes. Pas aucune de vos
> phrases que je ne sache reprendre! {note the vulgarism *pas
> aucune*!}
> Ces fleurs sont vos fleurs et vous dites que vous ne les
> reconnaissez pas.

> [The words I use are everyday words—and yet they are not the
> same!
> You will find no rhymes in my verses, nor any trickery. Just your
> own phrases. Not one of your phrases I cannot turn to good
> use!
> These flowers are your flowers, and you say you do not
> recognize them.]

In Antistrophe I the public is shown in its incapacity to understand, that is,
to recognize the things presented by the poet who is, at the moment of writing, under the impact of enthusiastic frenzy: he sees "Les choses à la fois

comme elles sont et comme elles ne sont pas et les gens commencent à ne pas comprendre ce qu'il dit" [Things both as they are and as they are not, and people no longer understand what he says]. In Ode V the public, recalcitrant to Claudel's esoteric poetry, is presented as saying: "Est-ce langage d'un homme ou de quelque bête? Car nous ne reconnaissons plus avec toi, ces choses que nous t'avons apportées" [Is this the speech of a man, or that of some beast? Now they are yours, we no longer recognize the things that we brought you].

If we should attempt to define, in terms of the Roman tradition, the position claimed by Claudel for the poet, it would be neither that of the poets in archaic Rome (of whom it was said "in quibus nulla solida utilitas omnisque puerilis delectatio" [in whom there is no solid benefit and all childish pleasure]), nor that of the *vates* [poet as prophet or seer], who is above society, claimed by Horace ("odi profanum vulgus et arceo" [I hate the profane mob and keep them out]). Claudel looks upon his poetic activity as a *negotium* [profession], exercised in the interests of the people.[7] Thus the words of Claudel's poems will be those of Everyman.

One could also define Claudel's intention in Christian terms, if we remember the Church Fathers who ascribed to the Scriptures a style that "condescendat . . . ad eorum inscitiam qui non intelligunt, et *simplici et planiore atque usitato sermone* utatur, ut possit intelligi" [might come down . . . to the level of those who do not understand, and uses a *simpler and plainer and more common level of speech* in order that it can be understood] (Ambrose); this is a language which, because of its clarity, wields all the more authority the more widely it is read: "et omnibus ad legendum esset in promptu . . . *verbis apertissimis et humillimo genere loquendi* se cunctis praebens . . . *ut exciperet omnes populari sinu* . . . multo . . . plures quam si nec tanto apice auctoritatis emineret nec turbas gremio sanctae humilitatis hauriret" [it was at once a book that all could read and read easily . . . for it offers itself to all *in the plainest words and the simplest expressions* . . . *it receives all within its welcoming arms* . . . (it brings a few direct to You by narrow ways: yet these few would be fewer still) but for this twofold quality by which it stands so lofty in authority yet draws the multitude to its bosom by its holy lowliness] (Augustine)[8]—terms which have been echoed by hundreds of medieval poets (e.g., Berceo: "Quiero fer una prosa en roman paladino, / en cual suele el pueblo hablar con su vecino"; "quiero fer la pasion de Sant Laurent / en romanz, que la pueda saber toda la gent" [I want to write a story in the simple language which the people speak with each other; I want to write the martyrdom of Saint Lawrence in the common tongue so all the people may know of it]).

Thus in Claudel's modest-ambitious definition of the role of the modern poet, there is no suggestion of a *poeta vates* on the scale of a Tyrtaeus or a Victor Hugo. Because the universe God has created is finite, the task of the poet can be only to re-create what has been created—or, better, to "take stock of" (*recenser*) things already existing. The ποιητής of Claudel is no divine artifex or Maker, but an artisan or recording-clerk, gathering together the work of God (drawing up a *summa* in medieval fashion); his public should not seek for novelty in his poetry but should recognize therein old familiar things.

But, though a tabulator rather than a creator, the modern poet must not abandon his lofty vantage point, his eyrie, from which his gaze embraces infinite space, within which he can descry the single points. The poet is equally at home in the micro- and in the macrocosmos (ll. 26–28). In order to express this fusion of the macro- and the microcosmic, which is basic to Claudel's vision of the world, he uses a particular stylistic device discovered by Walt Whitman (after the way had been prepared by Gautier and Balzac): this is a presentative device which I have called "chaotic enumeration,"[9] and which bespeaks the same inspiration, on another plane, as the modern department-store with its agglomeration of wares brought from the four corners of the globe. While the exuberant enumerations, the lists, the "catalogues" to be found with Rabelais or Quevedo still respected the distinctions between the different realms of Nature, the post-Whitmanian writer can enumerate things and thoughts detached from their frames, in order to evoke the plenitude of the world. Thus Claudel will list, among "ces choses qui lui sont connues" [the things that are known to him] (note this pleonastic demonstrative, incorrect according to school grammars, which takes for granted our close association with "these" familiar objects): "la maison," "la gare," "la mairie," "ce bonhomme avec son chapeau de paille," "l'espace" [the house, the station, the town hall, that fellow there in his straw hat, space], for he must keep "les comptes" [the accounts] (and here again there is an indiscriminate listing: "les siens," ". . . d'un magasin de chaussures," ". . . de l'humanité tout entière" [his own, (those) of a shoe shop, (those) of all humanity]). The whole and the part, the far and the near, the concrete and the abstract, the important and the inconsequential can all appear side by side because they are fused in Claudel's vision. The more confusing and inchoate our civilization appears, the firmer seems to become the poet's grip on the essentials. But Claudel does not meet the confusion of our world by imposing thereupon a rigid orderliness of his own making: he is able to *accept* it without letting himself be distracted from the essentials: he can calmly depict the apparent disorder, for he sees it in a higher order. His faith remains unshaken. Evidences of this same faith that can so easily accept the juxtaposition of part and whole can be found in any Catholic church, where a painting presenting a single scene from the life of Christ, or of one of his saints, may hang side by side with one which represents the totality of God (the Trinity). And the juxtaposition of the sublime and the trivial ("ce bonhomme avec son chapeau de paille") is paralleled by the arrangement of those medieval towns in which, from out the midst of booths and shops and sheds, there emerges the Gothic spire—or perhaps by the medieval mysteries in which comic and solemn scenes are made to alternate. By adducing such parallels I would seem to be assuming a religious inspiration for a passage which speaks only of the *choses connues* [known things] of everyday life and where the "Gothic spire" is missing. But I contend that it is indeed Claudel's religious nature which has enabled him to see together the trivial and the transcendental.*

---

*Evidence that the chaotic enumeration is in Claudel a development of the conception of the omnipresence of God in creation can easily be seen from this stanza of the "Processional":

Je crois que Dieu est *ici* bien qu'il me soit caché,
Comme il est au ciel avec tous ses anges et dans le cœur de la Vierge sans péché,
Il est mêmement ici, dans la gare de chemin de fer et l'usine, dans la crèche, dans l'aire et le chais.

[I believe that God is *here* even though he is hidden from me.
Just as he is in heaven with all his angels, and in the heart of the Virgin without sin,
Present even in the railway station and the factory, in the manger, upon the threshing-floor, in the wine-shed.]

It is significant that here the manger is referred to, not together with heaven or the heart of the Virgin, but with the railway station and the wine-cellar. And the *ici* is most striking, which conjures up a momentary proximity, here, now, of all these disparate things which are inhabited by God.
Again, we find, in the "Processional," an enumeration of the saints:

Voici tous les Saints du calendrier, répartis sur les quatres Saisons,
Les saints de glace et de braise, et ceux qui annoncent la sortie des bêtes et la fenaison,
Saint Médard et Saint Barnabé, Saints Crépin et Crépinien de Soissons,
Saint Martin et Saint Vincent des vignerons, Sainte Macre de Fère-en-Tardenois où est la fête de ce bourg,
Et Sainte Luce en décembre où le jour est plus court.

[Here are all the Saints of the calendar, divided among the four
     seasons,
The saints of ice and fire, those who announce the coming forth of
     the beasts and the hay-harvest,
Saint Medard and Saint Barnabas, Saints Crespin and Crespinian of
     Soissons,
Saint Martin and Saint Vincent patron of vine-growers, Saint
     Macrius of Fère-en-Tardenois whose day is the feast-day of that
     town,
And Saint Lucy in December, hers is the shortest day.]

Though the choice of these saints is evidently determined by a definite pattern (the four seasons are represented, and the saints named are all patrons
of labor), still the immediate impression is one of disorder and arbitrary selection—which serves impressively to evoke the richness of the Catholic calendar, able to furnish every day of the year with its saint, so that the menial
can be continuously pervaded by the transcendental. (The patriotic note is
inescapable in this list of exclusively French saints; we may also discern a
parochial sentiment in "Sainte Macre de Fère-en-Tardenois où est la fête de
ce bourg": Claudel, writing these words in China, visualizes, in immediate
proximity, the annual feast-day in "ce bourg.")

For Claudel, no barrier between the two realms of the transcendental and
the trivial is allowed to stand; the most daring example of barriers annihilated may be seen in the lines below from Ode V, in which he is depicting the
solitary and silent immersion of his soul in Christ: "Moi tout seul, tout en
bas, éclairant la face du grand Christ de bronze *avec un cierge de 25 cen-
times*" [I stood alone and lowly, lighting the face of the great bronze Christ
with a 25-centime candle].

It is true that in our strophe the religious note is greatly subdued; but,
later, it will sound forth gloriously in the poem.

But there is still another justification for the device of "chaotic
enumerations" in our poem. According to the pattern fixed by Pindar, an ode must be rhapsodic, since this genre in contrast to others
calls for the perpetuation, by the work of art, of the poet's original
fervor: that "first fine careless rapture." In order to achieve this effect
of enthusiasm, Ronsard, in his Pindaric odes, went to great pains to
introduce drastic breaks (change of thought or of scenery) within his
balanced stanzas; Claudel, having banned prophetic frenzy and
Pythian obscurity from his poem, could not follow the Pindaric trend
which Ronsard tried to imitate. It is the "disorderliness" of the chaotic enumerations, reflecting the diversity and fullness of the world,
which offered the best approximation to the rhapsodic style of the
ode. Thus Claudel does not, in the manner of the classicist André

Chénier, seek to make new poetry with ancient devices but, rather, to reach the effects of ancient poetry by means of new devices. His attempt is comparable with that of the modernist architect [Gaudí] who designed the Catholic cathedral in Barcelona.

But now that he has defined the activity of the modern poet by inclusion of the trivial and the practical, Claudel cannot but think back to the idealism and sublimity of the ancient art which he has left behind him. In his last address to the pagan Muse (ll. 29–32), a new note informs his imperatives: behind him are the half-hearted, nervously joking maneuverings of self-defense (*laisse-moi, laisse-moi*); now that he has decided to cut old ties, he is free squarely to appraise the totality of the being he abandons; for the first time he forces himself to contemplate her bitter beauty and sublimity; now he can call the Greek Muse his *bien-aimée* [beloved], of whom he has loved the prophetic spirit ("ô sœur de la noire Pythie!" [sister of the dark Pythia])*—though admitting the bodily ugliness which must accompany prophetic frenzy ("et un filet de salive verte coule du coin de sa bouche" [a thread of green spittle runs from the corner of her mouth]),† the great Nike-like wings of freedom ("ô géante!" [Giantess!]); and the winds of spaciousness that blow about her ("O vent sur le désert!" [Wind over the desert!])—though he extends the background of the Greek goddess to include Egypt ("les quadriges de Pharaon" [the chariots of Pharaoh]).

---

*In this allusion Claudel has coupled the prophetic with the poetic enthusiasm. Plato, in addition to these, speaks of two other enthusiasms, those of the *mystes* [initiate in the mysteries] and of the lover (and the same four are to be found, listed rather inorganically by Ronsard in his "Ode à Michel de l'Hôpital"). The enthusiasm of the *mystes* is also found in our strophe where it is represented by the dionysiac element—which Claudel wishes to repress. And the enthusiasm of love is embodied in the Muse who tempts the poet as a woman (Antistrophe I: "Et moi, je suis une femme entre les femmes" [And I am a woman among women]). "La Muse" in our strophe (i.e., the pagan Muse) is evidently Erato, the muse of love songs, who had earlier (Ode I) abducted the poet to her ship.

†The anacoluthon in "ô sœur de la noire Pythie qui broie . . ." et un filet de salive verte coule . . ." [sister of the dark Pythia in the spasm . . . *and* a thread of green spittle runs . . .] is figurative of disharmony; it is as though, in the phenomenon of prophetic enthusiasm, the bodily declares itself anarchically independent. Again, in the anacoluthon of line 26—"Comme de haut on a plaisir à reconnaître sa maison, . . . mais l'espace autour de soi est immense!" [It gives us pleasure to see our homes from on high, . . . though

a vast space is around us]—the syntactical yoke is shaken off by the exclamatory phrase: it is as though there is no easy transition from the pettiness of small-town existence to the immensity of space. Thus intellectual objections are figuratively mirrored by an anarchic syntax.

The most remarkable case of anacoluthon is offered by "Comme l'antique poète parlait de la part des dieux privés de présence, / Et moi je dis qu'il n'est rien dans la nature . . ." [As the ancient poet spoke on behalf of gods without presence, / I say in my turn that nothing is made in Nature] (ll. 33–34), where the flow of the sentence alluding to Lucretius is broken up by the impact of the phraseology of Jesus ("but I say unto you"). The anacoluthon, as found in Claudel, usually represents the deliberate introduction of the oral style into the written—though, at the same time, Claudel exploits the patterns hallowed by biblical and Homeric traditions.

But now the poet finds the strength and clarity of vision to oppose to the majesty, the enthusiasm, the propheticism, the freedom and spaciousness of Greek art, the fundamental objection of the Christian poet: Greek poetry cannot be ours because the Greek gods it praises have no "presence" (similarly, Lucretius had imagined the pagan gods as envious of man's reality)—they have, that is, no action on man.*

---

* Compare Lucretius III, 18–20: "apparet divum numen sedesque quietae, / quas neque concutiunt venti nec nubila nimbis / aspergunt . . ." [before me appear the gods in their majesty, and their peaceful abodes, which no winds ever shake nor clouds besprinkle with rain]; II, 1093–94: "nam pro sancta deum tranquilla pectora pace, / quae placidum degunt aevom vitamque serenam"[for I appeal to the holy hearts of the gods, which in tranquil peace pass untroubled days and a life serene][10]—it is well known that Lucretius, like his teacher Epicurus, sought not "to put the Greek gods into retirement as ex-service rulers, but to establish them as the images and prototypes of the Epicurean sage."[11] This very life of the gods in the *intermundia*, without influence on the universe, but also without its griefs, must evidently have appeared to Claudel, who is conversant with the Judeo-Christian omnipresent God in whose "face" (=presence) everything on earth and in heaven happens, as a "lack of presence." (Paradoxically enough, Claudel uses, in denying real, spiritual presence to the pagan gods, the very word which for the ancients denoted their helpfulness: cf. such Latin phrases as *numina praesentia* [divinities who are present], *praesentes divi* [present gods], etc.)

The reference to Lucretius as to a pagan poet superseded by Christianity, is quite outspoken in the following lines of Ode V:

> Maintenant je puis dire, mieux que le vieux Lucrèce: "Vous n'êtes plus, ô terreurs de la nuit!"

Ou plutôt comme votre saint Prophète: "*Et la nuit est mon
exaltation dans mes délices!*"
Réjouis-toi, mon âme, dans ces vers ambrosiens!
Je ne vous crains point, ô grandes créatures célestes! Je sais que c'est
moi qui vous suis nécessaire . . .

[And now, with more right than Lucretius of old, I can say: "You
exist no more for me, terrors of the night!"
Or, better still, with your holy Prophet: "*The night is my exultation
in my delight!*"
Rejoice, my soul, in these words of Saint Ambrose!
Great heavenly beings, I do not fear you. I know it is I who am
necessary to you.]

This idea of a Nature who needs Man complements that of Nature addressed to Man.

But in the Christian conception of *natura rerum* [the nature of
things], all things are addressed to man's intelligence. And at this
point the word-floods "man" and "earth" ("earth" = "Nature,"
"things") again coalesce; "les œuvres des hommes," "au travers de la
terre" [the works of men; on the earth] are revealed in their full dimensions: it is to man that the works of Nature have been addressed* (we remember the biblical account of Adam completing
creation by giving things created their names). Nature, that is, is as
purposeful in her workings ("rien . . . qui soit fait sans dessein et
propos" [nothing is made . . . without design and purpose]) as is
man in his—and as the poet, a simple workingman, must be, according to Claudel, who opposes the Dionysiac and the enthusiastic. Nature addresses herself to man through the mediation of the senses
(Claudel shares the Thomist, the non-Kantian {originally Greek}
trust in the senses, the belief that "nihil est in intellectu quod non
fuerit in sensu" [there is nothing in the intellect which was not in the
senses]); the observations carried out by means of the senses contain
the results of an intellectual admixture of a "continued" intelligence,
and penetrate to the elements of Nature.†

---

*The wording "il n'est rien dans la nature qui soit fait sans dessein et pro-
pos à l'homme adressé" [I say in my turn that nothing is made in Nature
without design and purpose toward man] is resumed in Antistrophe III
when the Muse who has become Grace says: "Entre tous les êtres qui vivent,
je suis la parole de grâce qui est adressée à toi seul" [I am the word of grace,
addressed to you alone among all living beings] (and in the *argument*: "c'est

à lui {au poète} personnellement que la Muse qui est la Grâce ne cesse de s'adresser!" [The Muse who is Grace will address herself to him {the poet} alone!]). It is significant that what was the action of Nature has, in the progress of the poem, become that of Grace.

†When Claudel presents the visual and acoustic senses as "intelligent" senses, he must have had in mind the Thomist hierarchy of senses in which the highest are those which involve material alteration of the sensing organ by the things sensed, the accuracy of the eye being the closest to the operation of the intellect.[12]

It may be assumed that here Claudel offers a paraphrase of the Thomist *vis cogitativa* [the thinking force], an "internal sense" (on one level with imagination, memory, etc.), and therefore superior to the external senses, but still a sense and, accordingly, inferior to the operations of the intellect and separated therefrom by an unbridgeable gulf because it is directed toward the individual and the material, whereas the intellect is directed toward the universal and the immaterial. In the following lines, we see how a modern psychologist versed in Thomism defines one of the activities of the *vis cogitativa*: "Whenever the value-aspect of a thing is emphasized it is the *vis cogitativa* which is operative. To act upon something, the psychological power must have got hold of this value-content . . . {Saint Thomas} frequently refers to the *vis cogitativa* as a *ratio particularis* [individual reason] and assigns it the task of co-operating with the rational faculties in the formation of judgments pertaining to action. Action by its very nature is destined to realize some value and, accordingly, presupposes an awareness of the value as well as a capacity of referring the will to the particular good in question."[13] Thus man, acting with his will upon material and individual sensorial reality (that is, isolating and regrouping the elements thereof, as Claudel speaks of doing in our strophe), is still operating on the level of the senses, with his *ratio particularis* or *vis cogitativa*: he has not yet lifted himself up to the spheres of intellectual cognition of the immaterial and the universal. And Claudel, in our collection, reaches only in Ode V the stage of cognizing the universal and the immaterial. In our strophe the most important words are "at their place"—where we have to do with the pattern of medieval gradualism which stabilizes things at the "right place." The "word of the poet," on one level with the element isolated by the scientist, is the field for the *vis cogitativa* which, as Rudolf Allers has said, "co-operates" with reason, but is not identical therewith.

It is characteristic of the Thomist Claudel that he sees religious belief as based not on emotional and mystical fervor, not on a feeling of union with the divine which is realized in moments of rapture, but on the workings of human intelligence in the practical everyday world—progress promoted by intelligence is seen by Claudel as working to the glory of God. In the line "pour l'analyse de l'intelligence continuée avec l'intelligence qui la / Refait de l'élément qu'elle récupère" [which is continuous with the intelligence that / Remakes them from the recovered element], Claudel means to emphasize the motif of the continuity of the exercise of intelligence by his anaphoric repetition of *re-* in *refait* and *récupère*; the *re-* suggests the re-creation by man of what God has first created.*

---

*It is time for us to recapitulate what the prefix *re-* means to our poet, who is so "prefix-conscious" (compare his well-known puns on *connaître–co-naître*, on *com-poser*, etc.). The words with *re-* which Claudel uses are apt to be words quite current in French but, by repetition or groupment and by semantic expansion, he is able to create a *re*-cluster which reflects a group of ideas dear to him. Any single formation may be unobtrusive but, when all are taken together, they have an impressive power.

First, the poet declares himself to be simply a *recenseur* (similar to the Egyptian scribe, l. 18), a garnerer of things existing and already created in a finite world. In Ode II he will say: "J'ai recensé l'armée des Cieux et j'en ai dressé l'état, /. . . J'ai tendu l'immense rets de ma connaissance" [I have numbered the Army of Heaven, and drawn up the muster, /. . . I stretched the huge net of my awareness] (note the reference to a net, which, with its clear lines, delimits the catch). When he speaks of the martyrs of whom he will sing (in "Processional"), it is of those "dont les noms sont recensés au ciel et sur nos diptyques" [whose names are recorded in Heaven and upon our diptychs].

Second, since the poet is not a creator but a re-creator, the public that listens to him must "recognize" the things already created: "et que chacun retrouve dans mes vers ces choses qui lui sont connues" [so that each man finds in my verses the things that are known to him] (l. 25)—a variant of the passage, in the Introduction of our ode: "Pas aucune de vos phrases que je ne sache *reprendre*! / Ces fleurs sont vos fleurs et vous dites que vous ne les *reconnaissez* pas." [Not one of your phrases I cannot *turn to* good use! / These flowers are your flowers, and you say you do not *recognize* them!].

Third, the "recognition" as a procedure that repeats the process of original creation is in the nature of our human intelligence, which only continues the "intelligence of the senses" (ll. 36–37): "{l'intelligence} continuée avec l'intelligence qui la / *Refait* de l'élément qu'elle *récupère*" [{his intelligence} which is continuous with the intelligence that / *Remakes* the *re*covered element]. God's creation was the creation of the intelligent senses.

Fourth, poetic activity is nothing but the continuation and repetition of the God-given human intelligence: to integrate, in the catholic manner, things garnered and catalogued (*recensées*) brings unity into the poet's own mind and into the universe as cognized by it: contrary to Corneille's Auguste ("Je suis maître de moi comme de l'univers; / Je le suis, je veux l'être . . ." [I am master of myself as of the universe; / This I am, this I want to be]), the poet Claudel gives freedom, the freedom of cognition, to himself and to the universe. In Ode V he announces his intention "De connaître Dieu dans sa fixité d'acquérir la vérité par l'attention et chaque chose qui est toutes les autres en la *recréant* avec son nom intelligible dans ma pensée" [To know

God in his fixity, and to find truth by attention and each thing that is all the others by *re-creating* it with its intelligible name in my thought]; and he glorifies "cette énergie divine de l'esprit qui ouvre les yeux, / *Recommençant* sa journée et qui trouve chaque chose à sa place dans l'immense atelier de la connaissance" [this divine energy of the spirit, / *Beginning* a new day, which opens its eyes and finds all things in their place, in the huge workshop of consciousness]. He wants to be "le *rassembleur* de la terre de Dieu" [the *one who groups* the world of God] (this is the theme of Claudel's baroque drama, *Le Soulier de satin*, in which he portrays the conquest, at the hands of the Spanish conquistadores, of the whole world by the Catholic God); "et moi aussi, toutes les figures de la nature m'ont été données, . . . pour que je les *rassemble* dans mon esprit" [and me, too, all the forms of Nature were given to me, . . . so that I *group* them in my spirit]. Thus the poet is only a copyist (another variant of the accountant or the surveyor), comparable to the monk (of whom Claudel tells us in Ode V) whose task it was to copy the Gospel and who, returning to his devastated monastery, takes up once more his work where he had stopped: "*Recommence* l'initiale d'or sur le diplôme de pourpre" [And *begins once again* the golden initial upon the purple diploma].

And finally, since all activity of human (and poetic) intelligence consists in continuing, repeating, retracing God's creation, the poet is a "reconciliator" of what seems discordant ("le grand poème de l'homme . . . réconcilié"). "*Re-*" is, so to speak, the principle by which, in the medieval system of thought of an Alanus ab Insulis, the God-created universe is kept functioning by Nature.

As for the metrical break: "qui la / Refait de l'élément qu'elle récupère," this is introduced to make us draw breath before the important word *refait*, which stands out before us in relief; in "qui la / refait" Claudel would have us pronounce *re-fait* with a distinct separation of the two syllables, the stress being laid on the first—as is the practice of a Frenchman in oral speech when special emphasis is called for. Thus, by means of this metrical break, Claudel is able to indicate the intonation of oral speech (in a way that is generally impossible with the usual system of printing): oral speech and a technique of breathing. Here, indeed, metrics does reflect the measure of human breathing, but the modulation here indicated is due, not to the limitations of human nature but to its "intelligence et volonté."

Compare the separation of the versets in the lines of the Introduction to Ode IV: "Ce n'est pas pour eux {les hommes} que je suis fait, mais pour le / Transport de cette mesure sacrée" [It was not for them {the men} I was made, but for the / Transport of this holy measure]. The words of the last verset are isolated from the rest and are held up above earthly contamination like a pyx. Again, the poet must pause for breath—which is a pause of reverence before the transcendental revelation. Compare also the lines in Ode V: "Faites que je sois entre les hommes comme une personne sans visage et ma / Parole sur eux sans aucun son comme un semeur de silence . . ." [Make me faceless among mankind, and soundless my / Word among men, like a sower of darkness]—the phrase *parole sur eux* seems to hover aloft over the believers. In Ode I, when Claudel imagines himself on the bark with the Muse Erato, he exclaims: "Toujours / Plus avant, jusqu'au cœur de la mer luisante" [Forward / Always forward, into the heart of the shining sea!], whose quest *plus ultra!* adapted here to his own state of mind, must detach itself from the rest; it is "quoted" reverently.

The continuity which, according to Christian belief, is established between the sense-data (Nature), the senses, and the intelligence of man, is precisely the opposite of the pagan presencelessness of the gods. Nature's presence is manifested in her continuous "address" to man's mind. The lines "Et je puis parler, continu avec toute chose, / Parole qui est à sa place intelligence et volonté" [And I can speak, being continuous with all silent things, / Words which in their place are intelligence and will] follow up the motif of *lumière continuée* (i.e., the poet continues the work of Nature), of *moi je dis . . .* [I say] (a motif which is soon to reappear in the "crest" line 42: "Je chanterai le grand poème de l'homme soustrait au hasard" [I shall sing the great song of man set free from chance]: when Claudel says "je puis parler" we realize how completely he has become disenthralled from the pagan Muse), of *nécessaire* ("à sa place": this anticipates "l'homme soustrait au hasard"), and of *natura rerum* ("toute chose muette" [all things silent]: this, taken together with "moi je dis," "je puis parler," suggests that the poet is the voice of silent Nature). Nowhere in our strophe is there any word of the Christian divinity; apparently we are offered only the operation of Nature (as in Lucretius's poem). But when Claudel opposes to the presencelessness of pagan gods the workings of a Nature present at every moment to man's intelligence, the Christian reader knows that this Nature is the creation of the omnipresent God. We realize that there has been taking place in the strophe a psychomachy in which silent, intelligence-directed Nature has calmly defeated the winged, majestic, and prophetic pagan Muse.

The crest line 42 is surrounded on both sides by new chaotic enumerations of the achievements of modern progress, wherein the plan of Nature is revealed. We shall not be surprised to find that in these lists man-made instruments, rather than man himself, occupy the foreground: the pen of the scholar is on the same level as the prospector's instrument; the Ingénieur-en-chef is dwarfed by "le canal qui remplit" [the canal filling]: indeed, he is made superfluous by the automatism of his creation which can be released at the touch of a child. Man can retire from the stage which he has set, to allow the

drama to unfold: the drama between the stage-properties themselves. And this "play" is, in fact, that of Nature: we do not find in
Claudel's poetry, as so often in modern indictments of the machine
age, engines opposed to *natura rerum*: rather, engines, which are the
creations of man's intelligence, represent the continuation of *natura
rerum* which addresses itself to man's intelligence.

The first of the two enumerations is concerned with the rudimen-
tary tools with which man first learned to extend his range of influence over Nature; in the second are mentioned the more complicated
modern machines, along with the vast achievements which are due
to these instruments and which serve, in their turn, to produce new
achievements. And just as, in Claudel's vision, *rerum natura* and machines are reconciled so, too, are man and Nature: it is Nature who
encourages man to regroup its elements into new combinations,
whereby he is enabled to free himself from the given in Nature—
while remaining true to her essential designs. Claudel can sing, not
only ἔργα καὶ ἡμέραι [works and days], as did Hesiod in primitive
times, not only "Georgica," as did Virgil in a primitivistic mood:
with his face turned toward the future he joyfully hails the progress
of industry, and is able to see in the industrial achievements of our
age the modern variant of the primitive industries hallowed by traditional poetry: all human industry, all "industriousness" bespeaks
the continuous communion between man and Nature. And so Claudel, by regrouping the elements and the fabricants of Nature, is
working in accord with this great design. He need have no fear of scientific positivism since man, as he sees him, has never lost contact
with the supernal forces.

It is in the second "chaotic enumeration" (ll. 43–47) that Claudel's imagination is given fullest expansion: his eye roves near and
far* ("ce que les gens ont fait autour de moi . . ."—"le canot démontable qui remonte l'Aruwhimi"; "les ports tout bordés intérieurement . . ."—"le transatlantique qui signale au loin . . ." [what
men have accomplished around me . . . —the collapsible boats ascending the Aruwhimi; with ports fringed within . . . —the transatlantic liner hooting far off . . .]), embracing panoramas and single
concrete details ("les frénétiques villes haletantes et tricotantes"—
"quand la fille de l'Ingénieur en chef du bout de son doigt . . ." [fre-
netic cities, breathless, hurrying along—when the daughter of the
Chief Engineer puts her finger . . .]), the perennial or archaic, and the
modern which invades them ("le canon qui ouvre les vieux empires"

[the cannon that opens the old empires] or again "le canot démontable qui remonte l'Aruwhimi" [the collapsible boats ascending the
Aruwhimi]), technical civilization and Nature ("avec les frénétiques
villes . . . et ça et là une anse bleue de la rivière dans la campagne solennelle" [frenetic cities . . . and here and there a blue loop of the
river in the peaceful countryside]: a blue patch of river glimpsed in
the midst of the industrialized area),† the prosaic and the poetic ("le
transatlantique qui signale—au loin dans le brouillard") [the transatlantic liner hooting far off—in the fog]).

---

* We may note here a variant of the chaotic enumeration which is particularly Claudelian and, at the same time, characteristic of our time, in which
distances are annihilated: the device of the "geographically chaotic enumeration": "le canon qui ouvre les vieux Empires" is evidently the artillery of
Admiral Perry in Japan, the "Aruwhimi" represents Africa, the blast-
furnaces are Pittsburgh, while, in the transatlantic steamboat we have an allusion to the ocean separating continents. Compare, in Ode V:

> Et toutes {choses} vous êtes en ma possession, comme un banquier
> qui de son bureau de *Paris* fait argent avec l'écriture des gommes
> de la *Sénégambie*,
> Et de la pelletée de minerai sur le carreau de la mine *antarctique*, et
> de la perle des *Pomotou*, et du grand tas de laine *Mongol*.

> [And all of you {things} are owned by me, as by a banker who
> makes money, as he writes in his office in *Paris*, from the gums of
> *Senegambia*,
> From a shovelful of ore in the depths of an antarctic mine, from the
> pearls of *Pomoto*, and a great stack of *Mongol* wool.]

(Here Claudel adopts the capitalization of the ethnic adjective as in English,
in order to make the geographic entities stand out more independently.)
And, in Ode II:

> Je tire, j'appelle sur toutes mes racines, le Gange, le Mississippi,
> L'épaisse touffe de l'Orénoque, le long fil du Rhin, le Nil avec sa
> double vessie . . .

> [I would draw to me, summon through my roots, the Ganges, the
> Mississippi,
> The thick tuft of the Orinoco, the long thread of the Rhine, the Nile
> with its double bladder.]

Again, from his *Art poétique*: "Cependant à toute heure de la Terre il est
toutes les heures à la fois; à chaque saison, toutes les saisons ensemble. Pendant que l'ouvrière en plumes voit qu'il est Midi au cadran de la Pointe-
Saint-Eustache, le soleil de son premier rayon ras troue la feuille virginienne,
l'escadre des cachalots se joue sous la lune australe. Il pleut à Londres, il

neige sur la Poméranie, pendant que le Paraguay n'est que roses, pendant
que Melbourne grille" [At each hour of the Earth, however, all hours exist
at once; no matter what the season, all seasons live at once. While the seam-
stress sees noon on the dial of the Tower of Saint Eustache, the first low rays
of the sun pierce the Virginian leaf; squadrons of cachalots frolic under the
southern moon. It rains in London, it snows over Pomerania, while Paraguay is all roses, while Melbourne roasts].[14] (This passage is probably influenced by *Purgatorio* XXVII, 1–6, where Dante states that when it is sunset
in Purgatory it is sunrise at Jerusalem, midnight in Spain, noon in India; but
Dante admits of no chaotic disorder; he merely points out the synchronic relationships of the four fixed cardinal points.)

†How touching is this parenthesis which suggests a "parenthetical interpolation" of Nature and which seems somehow related to the main effect of
the poem intended by Claudel; we were told that this poem should be "plus
clair que la lune qui brille avec sérénité sur la campagne dans la semaine de
la moisson" [brighter than the moon that shines serenely over the land in the
week of harvest]—the moonlight and the patch of blue river combine to the
same color sensation of clarity and linearity, serenity and solemnity. Claudel
sees the cities framed by Nature: in his vision the two are not opposed to
each other, but are fused—a fusion which is so characteristic of our modern
landscape (I think I shall never forget the impression made on me by the
noisy streets of Istanbul teeming with gesticulating and screaming South-
erners and the solemn quiet of the Bosporus and the mountains of Asia—
boundless beyond man's gaze). A still further step would be to see the landscape character of our modern cities themselves: for example, the "canyon"
of Wall Street.

Should "et ça et là une anse bleue" be constructed grammatically together
with "avec les frénétiques villes"? That is, should we understand: "ce que les
gens ont fait avec les villes . . . et avec . . . une anse bleue"? Evidently not.
We have here to do with a quite independent expression "et ça et là une
anse . . . !" and this syntactical break is indicative of the cleavage man has
forced between civilization and Nature. The brusqueness of the break, however, is mitigated by the inclusion of the exclamation within the sentence
structure.

Claudel dominates the chaos of the modern world, not by reducing
its confusing manifoldness and concreteness to a regularized, abstract, skeletal design (which has been attempted with greater success in painting than in poetry) but by subordinating this confusion
to established poetic patterns—which, precisely because of their
modern content, are difficult to recognize at first glance. But we may
recognize in his chaotic or rhapsodic enumeration of modern industrial achievements, the old, the biblical patterns of anaphoric repetition (*avec . . . , avec . . .*) and of *parallelismus membrorum* [paral-
lelism of parts] (ll. 44–47); and, grafted thereupon, the more

modern device of successive expansion of versets: in lines 43–47 the versets grow in size in proportion to the increase of the achievements of modern technics.

This whole enumeration is contained within the framework of the simple statement: "ce que les gens ont fait autour de moi avec le canon . . . je le ferai avec un poème" [what men have accomplished around me with the cannon . . . I will do it with a poem]. How revelatory is the phrase: "je le ferai avec un poème": by means of the preposition *avec* a parallel is offered between the poem Claudel is to write and the cannon, the collapsible boat, the blast-furnaces, the harbors, the ocean liner, the locomotive. We have already accepted that these industrial achievements are "necessary" fulfillments; now the full measure of their sublime and grandiose nature is brought out. How great, then, will have to be the poem which shall equal these achievements of modern civilization! And indeed, in the closing versets of this tremendous sentence, Claudel reveals in its final form a poetic program fit for a Conquistador.

And Claudel the Conquistador aims at nothing less than a poem of a Lucretian scope: he will treat "la connaissance de la terre" [knowledge of the earth]—in which phrase we recognize the combined motifs of intelligence (cognizance) and of things (Earth, Nature). He spurns the Homeric model of "unnecessary" adventurings in exotic lands; he will not celebrate a hero in his casual rovings over the earth: indeed, he will praise not a single man, but man himself and his cognizance of Nature.* The temporal indication given in his rejection of the Odyssean theme (*ne sera plus* . . . [no longer]) is followed up in line 49 by the *enfin* (conspicuous by its unexpected position in the verse): "finally" is said from the point of view of the poet's inner struggle with the Muse which has come to an end, and also from the point of view of world history: Claudel feels strongly that the reconciliation of man with the laws of Nature has, in our day at least, become possible—and his affective *enfin* bespeaks the intensity of his desire to ally himself with this great cause.†

---

*It must be noted that Claudel's *carmen saeculare* is a glorification of his century, not of any one august personality of the times, as was the case with the poem of Horace, and with those of the court poets of the baroque age (Ronsard and Boileau) who had accepted this limitation. It is true that Claudel, in more recent times, seems to have descended to the obsequious level in his "Ode to Marshal Pétain" (which I have not seen).

†Grammatically speaking, *enfin* is an ἀπὸ κοινοῦ [apokoinou; the use of a common word in two clauses to create a deliberate ambiguity]: you may construct "le grand poème de l'homme enfin" (*finally* the great poem comes into being) or "le grand poème de l'homme / enfin . . . réconcilié" (of mankind finally reconciled . . .). Sometimes Claudel places an ἀπὸ κοινοῦ in a clause to which it would not seem to belong naturally, thereby suggesting two contrasting forces which draw, as it were, the adverbial phrase toward themselves with equal force—compare the *dans mes vers* [within my verses] in the motto of this chapter.

Claudel does not use the expression "{réconcilié avec} les lois de la nature" [{reconciled to} the laws of Nature]; he speaks instead of *les forces éternelles* [eternal powers], which, of course, stand for Nature. But at the same time, these are more than Nature. For the eternal forces are "above" the *causae secundae* [second causes]: they can be only the *causa primaria* [main cause], or God. And again, just as we have noticed in the passage above dealing with the pagan gods *privés de présence* [without presence], the Christian divinity has been evoked indirectly: simply by mentioning one member of a binomial he forces us to think in terms of the other: *force éternelle* in itself could be interpreted in a purely naturalistic manner, but once it is opposed to *causes secondes*,* it serves inevitably to suggest the supernatural. By using a term so suggestive of medieval Scholasticism, Claudel has been able to evoke the atmosphere of centuries of Christian philosophy.

---

*In order to realize the full impact of this line, we must remember that Thomist philosophy, while centering all activity of creation in God, recognizes, at the same time, that things created act out of their own impulse: this is the so-called efficacy of the *causae secundae*; it is a gift of God's love just as creation is the act of His power. Etienne Gilson represents the convergence of God's activity (that is, the activity of the *causa principalis*) and the activity of things created, by the simile of a hatchet swung by a carpenter: although the hatchet has been made and is wielded by the carpenter, it is undeniably true that the hatchet, the *causa secunda*, does the chopping.[15] Claudel, faithful to Thomism, seems to share the belief that "detrahere actiones proprias rebus est divinae bonitati derogare" [to take away their own actions from things is to deprive them of divine goodness]. And, accordingly, he puts the *causae secundae* in the foreground; he feels, nevertheless, the estrangement which has taken place in the modern world between the *causae secundae* (our material civilization) and the Prime Cause. Claudel offers no complaint against the "evil" modern world; he simply works by means of his harmonizing poetry toward the necessary "reconciliation":

"oportet omnes causas inferiores agentes *reduci* in causas superiores sicut instrumentales in primarias" [all inferior acting causes can be *reduced* to superior causes, just as instrumental ones into primary ones].

And only now, "finally," does the full implication of the title of our ode "La Muse qui est la Grâce" stand revealed: the poem, which treats of man's secular progress, is a polemic against heathendom and an apologia of Christianity—the poem of glorification of Christian Grace has assumed the form of a Greek proem only in order to reject the core of pagan poetry—an apologia which points to the reconciliation of science and religion.*

---

* At the celebration of the 400th anniversary of the University of Marburg in 1929, I heard a Catholic delegate quote a sentence he had heard from the mouth of the Pope: "Gaudet ecclesia studio veritatis" [The Church rejoices in the pursuit of truth]. Or, as Claudel would say: "Gaudet Deus studio veritatis" [God rejoices in the pursuit of truth].

The progress of the twentieth century is welcomed in this new *carmen saeculare* which traces the *via triumphalis* of man who is about to enter upon a new Augustan age of *pax christiana* (we remember that our poem was written in 1907!). "Reconciliation" is the final word-wave lifted up in the surge of the last crest line (l. 50), in which, as we have seen, all the motifs of the strophe have been integrated. And the working of Christian Grace has been shown as well in the liberation of cognizant mankind from chance as in the poet's inner liberation from pagan seduction: the "Muse qui est la Grâce" has worked within the poem without ever having been mentioned by name (though from the ninth line on her silent gaze has rested on the poet). She can have worked only through the inner development of the poet who was brought from the petulant *laisse-moi*'s addressed to the pagan goddess, through *je voudrais, je puis parler,* to the confident *je chanterai,* and finally to {ce que les gens ont fait . . .} *je le ferai,* in which his poetic activity is aligned with the good works of his fellow men.

This strophe, which reveals the activity of Grace, is entirely given up to praise of man's activity; and this can be so because, to Claudel, human achievements (of which poetic achievements form only one branch) represent the intramundane workings of Grace. It is as if Claudel would have us recognize the divine in what is close at hand, familiar to us all; he will not encourage us to look away from the things of the earth toward heaven. The very fact that Grace is here not explicitly mentioned can be taken as proof of Claudel's deep belief that man is the field in which Grace silently and efficaciously works—this Grace who is Claudel's true Muse.*

---

* It is worthy of note that Claudel does not use the Ovidian technique of metamorphosis: he states suddenly the achieved transformation of "la Muse qui est la Grâce." In the *argument* Claudel speaks of (a gradual) *devenir* [becoming], but in the poem there is only stage *a* followed by stage *b*—and declared identical therewith. A Christian miracle does not admit of gradual transformation: Segismundo, in *La vida es sueño* [Life is a Dream] *is*, suddenly, from a particular scene on, enlightened.

Has not the idea of "la Muse qui est la Grâce" been suggested to Claudel by Ronsard's "Ode à Michel de l'Hôpital," which opens with the line: "Errant par les champs de la grâce" [wandering through the fields of grace] (where the particular "grace, or gift of poetry" is meant), and which contains such passages as: "C'est lui {Michel de l'Hôpital} dont les grâces infuses / Ont ramené par l'univers / Le chœur des Piérides Muses" [It is he {Michel de l'Hôpital} whose innate graces / Brought back into the universe / The chorus of the Pierian Muses] (where the wording seems to suggest the fusion of "grace-gift" and Divine Grace)? But with Ronsard there is rather an unconscious shift from the pagan to the Christian meaning, whereas Claudel maintains the opposition between the two extremes.

(Thus, in contrast to the procedure of conventional poetry, according to which the Muse is invoked at the beginning, our poem opens with a rejection of the traditional pagan Muse—without, however, following this up by an invocation of the Muse which is Grace. For Grace does not come at our bidding; we must abide the miracle of its coming.)*

---

* One could doubt whether I have not overstated the facts as far as our strophe is concerned; is Christian Grace really the Muse of the poet, *by the end of the first strophe*? It is true that, in the answer given by the Muse in Antistrophe I, we find only ideas which are quite at variance with Christianity and which can only be intended as a temptation to the poet—a temptation to which he almost succumbs (Strophe II); again, in Antistrophe II, the Muse presents creation as an amoral fire and appeals to the flamelike in the poet's nature. In Strophe III, where the poet reaffirms the inner necessity he feels of representing the whole world in his limited poetic activity, there is no word to indicate that he appeals to the Muse as to Grace. Only in Antistrophe III do we find the words, spoken by the Muse: "Tu m'appelles la

Muse et mon autre nom est la Grâce" [You call me Muse and my other name is Grace], and later she explains her personal message to him: "je suis la parole de grâce qui est adressée à toi seul" [I am the word of grace, addressed to you alone among all living beings]. And yet it is this envoy of heaven that the poet, in the epode, rejects in his desire to cling to the earth and to his sainted earthly love: "Va-t-en! Je me retourne désespérément vers la terre!" [Away with you! Desperately I turn back to the earth!]. And we are asked to suppose that in the interval between the composition of Odes IV and V the poet has found happiness with his love, the *épouse nocturne* [nocturnal wife]. It is only in Ode V that the poet is fully ready to reconcile his private and circumscribed family-life (*la maison fermée* [the closed house]) with the task of "collecting" the whole world for God. Thus it would appear that the moment when he was able to formulate his program in Strophe I of Ode IV was only an anticipation of that state of Grace-given inner freedom reached in Ode V. "La Muse qui devient peu à peu la Grâce" (as she is called in the *argument*) has only in Ode V truly become "la Muse qui est la Grâce." Ode IV ends on a desperate note: the poet had already understood, in our strophe, his superhuman task, but could not reconcile it with his earthly love; only in Ode V does he gain the strength necessary both for his superhuman and his earthly task. Still, our strophe remains a first and interimistic stage on the long and wavering road toward the final conquest of Grace. The miracle of the revelation of his task to the poet takes place, in fact, in our strophe, but it finds him yet not quite prepared to accept it. Grace is a gift coming to those who are not yet great enough fully to deserve it.

And now we are in a position to recognize the development of form, and the inner connection, in the sequence of the odes. Whereas, in Ode I, the Muses (and particularly the Muse Erato) are invoked without any response on their part, we have, in Ode IV, a dialogue between the poet and the Muse. Such a dialogue is meant, with all modern poets (we may remember Musset) to symbolize the conflict between the creative forces of the poet and the rest of his being. This comes to an end in our ode: in Ode V the dialogue takes place only with the public. From this we may infer that the poet no longer has need of communication with his creative forces, since the latter have been integrated into his being. We can also understand now the alternation, in our collection, between paganistic and Christian odes: Ode I, "Les Muses"; II, "L'Esprit et l'eau"; III, "Magnificat"; IV, "La Muse qui est la Grâce"; V, "La Maison fermée"; VI, "Processional"—of which III and VI, the liturgical pieces, show two fairly clear stages in the gradual process by which the pagan element in the poet's soul is absorbed into Christianity. Ode III ends in the meditative serenity and confident peace of a vesper service, at a time of day when sharp contours are blurred "avant que la nuit ne commence et la pluie, avant que la longue pluie dans la nuit sur la terre ensemencée ne commence!" [before night begins with its rain, before the long rain falls in the night upon the sown earth!]. The setting of our Ode IV is the night—a night in which the poet, after his triumphant wrestling with the pagan Muse is, at the end, brought to a temporary defection from poetry altogether, and seeks happiness with his wife. In V, he is able to reconcile his avocation of poet with earthly happiness in "La Maison fermée," where he

finds the ultimate peace which sets the tone of the "Processional": "Proce-
damus in pace in nomine Domini" [Let us go forth in peace in the name
of God]. Thus our collection of six odes embodies the whole drama of
the separation and reintegration of the spiritual forces of the poet—a
psychomachy.

There is still another development underlying the sequence of odes: the
unfolding of the autobiographical element. It is as if the development by
which the Muse becomes Grace is paralleled by the settlement of the practical existence of the poet in his house and his family—as if the abstract suffering due to his position between earth and heaven gave way in proportion
as he took firmer roots in the concrete and necessarily narrower life: the
more protected by God he is, the more *la maison fermée* comes into its own,
and the more concrete becomes "la Muse qui est la Grâce." Whereas the *je*
of the Introduction and of Strophe I of Ode IV is a quite general "poetic I,"
it tends, in the following stanzas, to become more and more the particular
"Claudelian I" who identifies himself not only with the universe but with his
family. In Strophe II of Ode IV Claudel will still complain to God: "Mais
vous m'avez placé dans la terre, afin que j'endure la gêne et l'étroitesse et
l'obscurité" [But you have put me on earth, to suffer constraint and constric-
tion and darkness]; in Strophe III he will formulate his own situation in this
narrow world in general terms: "Celui qui a acheté une femme à l'âge juste,
ayant mis l'argent de côté peu à peu, / Il est avec elle comme un cercle fermé
et comme une cité indissoluble, . . . / Et leurs enfants entre eux deux comme
de tendres grains mûrissants" [The man who buys himself a woman at the
right age, having put aside the money little by little, / Lives with her like a
closed circle, like an indissoluble city, . . . / And their children are between
the two of them like tender, ripening seed]—the motif of the *maison fermée*
appears here for the first time, but the biblical *acheter une femme* still veils
the existence of his particular wife. In Ode V, however, she appears as *la
gardienne du poète* [the poet's guardian], to explain to the public (in the
words of the *argument*): "Je sais que la clôture lui est nécessaire; il est temps
que toute sa vie soit ordonnée vers l'intérieur; et par moi il a cet intérieur"
[I know that being shut off is necessary to him; it is time his life was directed
toward interior things; and through me he obtains his innerness]. Claudel
includes the autobiographical element not at all moments but *chemin faisant* [as he goes along], as his being is allowed to affirm itself in life: the autobiographical matter is not a fixed quantity, and nothing would be more
contrary to the spirit of this poetry than for pragmatistic literary critics to
operate with that matter as if it were something primordially given. Much
earlier, Claudel had disclosed that he was writing from exile; only after he
has, helped by Grace, made his peace with the world and heaven does he
write the lines (reminiscent of Ovid's *Tristia ex Ponto*): "Mon Dieu qui
m'avez conduit à cette extrémité du monde . . . , / Ne permettez point que
parmi ce peuple dont je n'entends point la langue, / Je perde mémoire de mes
frères qui sont *tous les hommes, pareils à ma femme et à mon enfant* [Lord
God, you who have led me to this far end of the world . . . , / Do not let me
forget, among this people whose tongue I cannot comprehend, / My broth-

ers who are *all of them human, like my own wife and my child*]. When the biographical makes its appearance, it is fused with the ecumenic or Catholic concern of the poet; it has no exhibitionist purpose, as with some of the Romantic poets.

Our remarks about the gradual recession of the pagan theme and the final enthronement of the intramundane Christian element, as embedded in the practical biography of the poet, lead to another observation: the extension of the "poetic I." Claudel has beautifully exploited the wide range that is inherent in the personal pronoun. This type of pronoun is a kind of proper name that stands for a human person in his unquestionable evidence: "I" speaks of a human being as *existing*, as imposing his evidence on the interlocutor; we may use it before being "introduced" to someone: by means of "I" we introduce ourselves sufficiently without giving our name, presenting ourselves as "this human being before you, whatever his name." When the interlocutor becomes better acquainted with the person calling himself "I," he is in a position to fill out the empty framework of the being indicated only as "I," without sensing any interruption of continuity: "I" becomes not only an unquestionable existence as such, but a filled-out (*étoffée*) existence. In Odes I–IV Claudel furnished us only the "poetic I," accepted in its vagueness by the reader; in Ode V, the "poetic I" has truly become that "Paul Claudel, the French ambassador who is living in China with his family." The autobiographical filling-out of the pronoun is meant for the reader (the interlocutor of the poet) and surely gives him the feeling of having come closer to the poet; at the same time, however, the poet has gained confidence in his "I"—that is, in the relevance of his autobiography—ever since the moment when Grace has affirmed him in life. The struggles whereby the "poetic I" is enabled to take root in life are the content of this sequence of odes. We have here a paradigmatic example of the poet's capacity of widening and deepening, in an individual manner, the meaning of a simple grammatical tool which is given to any individual speaker, quite matter-of-factly, by his mother-tongue. Or, in other words, the poet shows us the inner, the human struggle hidden behind the screen of the word "I"—that word on which rests all poetic and all human activity.

A last question remains to be solved: Why does Claudel write *five* odes ("followed by a processional")? And why are there 50 versets in the strophe we have here selected? The symbolism of numbers is in line with medieval practice (Dante), but why is Claudel's symbolism based on the number 5 (or 6)? One may think immediately of Alessandro Manzoni's five *Inni sacri* (though these five odes simply happen to be the only ones preserved of the greater number Manzoni originally intended to write). But such literary parallels are less instructive than are Claudel's own words: in Ode V, on the cardinal virtues, we find the following lines on "Justice":

> Elle considère la terminaison de toutes choses et le jour quand il se
>   consomme . . . ,
> Ce jour qui est le sixième, celui qui précède le sabbat et qui suit les
>   cinq premiers.

Elle acquitte mes comptes; elle règle pour moi ce qui est dû; . . .
D'autre part je sais que toute chose est bénie en elle-même et que je
suis béni en elle.
Car l'homme, héritier des cinq jours qui l'ont précédé, reçoit sur sa
tête leurs bénédictions accumulées.

[She meditates on the end of all things, and day consuming
itself . . . ,
Upon this, the sixth day, which precedes the Sabbath and follows
the other five.
She discharges my debts; she pays for me whatever is due; . . .
On the other hand, I know that each thing is blessed in itself, and
that I am blessed within it.
For man, the heir of the five days that came before him, receives
upon his head their accumulated benedictions.]

In this passage which shows the workings of Providence-in-Time (or, Justice), a Providence which was at work in the creation of man at an ap-
pointed time (the sixth day) and which still works in bringing things to their
just ends and in settling human accounts, Claudel figures the week (as a division of time) as divided into the Sabbath, the day before the Sabbath, and
the remaining five, relatively undistinguished workdays. Perhaps this division can serve as a clue to the arrangement and the theme of the collection
as a whole: the block of the five odes corresponds to the block of five days
(the five working days); the sixth ode ("Processional") corresponds to the
day preceding the Sabbath, and treats of the ritual of purification in view of
the heavenly Sabbath—a theme which Claudel (unlike Dante) makes no attempt to treat: his poem takes us only to the threshold of Heaven (Ode V
ends with the lines: "Le custode seulement et non point la coupe, car nous
ne goûterons point de ce fruit de la vigne avant que nous le buvions nouveau
dans le Royaume de Dieu" [The pyx alone and not the chalice, for we shall
not taste that fruit of the vine before we drink the new wine in the Kingdom
of God]). The idea of the whole collection, then, is to prepare us for the
heavenly Sabbath and to lead us, by way of everyday chores, through the
particular purification of the Sabbath, to the threshold of eternal joy.

This poem, which is so strongly opposed to ancient enthusiasm, is
intellectual rather than mystical—it has, that is, the orthodox-
Catholic approach to the divine. To Claudel, whose motto seems to
be *intellige ut credas* [understand in order to believe], science and
technics are intramundane *ancillae theologiae* [handmaidens of the-
ology]. It is possible to speak here of a miracle: the miracle by which
Claudel becomes more and more aware of the necessity and nature of
the poem that asks to be written. But the "miraculous" revelation
that unfolds before our eyes implies no deviation from the intellec-

tual, consisting as it does in the very working of intelligence for the glorification of intelligence.

Among the attempts made in the last century to reconcile aspects of modern civilization with values of the past, we may remember Ernest Renan's "Prière sur l'Acropole," in which he offers the tortured image of modern man wavering between a Christian faith sentimentally retained and Greek clarity which his reason affirms, and the "Invocation à Minerva" of Charles Maurras, who harmonizes French classical *raison* with Greco-Roman *ratio* and order—while Jean Giraudoux, in his "Prière sur la Tour Eiffel,"[16] simply ignores any such conflict and speaks only in terms of the general preeminence of *French* reason and taste. Claudel, for his part, without any similar symbolical localization, spreads before us the panorama of a pan-Christian harmony of reason and belief, offering us, in this panorama, the most "total" vision of our modern civilization I know of. Indeed, this is Claudel's *summa*, it ranks with such poems as the *Commedia*, as *Faust* and *Lear*; it is a *Weltgedicht*, a world-ode. Such a *summa* must contain all the main strivings of the epoch it reflects and, if we survey the whole range of our strophe, we will see that no essential is missing here: we find references to art, to religion, technics, science, nature, society (and the relationship of these with art); the professions are fully represented, including that of the poet; the wide sweep and intricate nature of our civilization is revealed, its history and that of mankind (Egypt, Assyria, Greece, Japan; Rome is mentioned later in the ode); the spirit of Christianity blends with that of the Enlightenment, of the Industrial Revolution, and of imperialism. This strophe, which purports to offer the prospectus of a poem to be written, is in itself "le grand poème de l'homme enfin par delà les causes secondes réconcilié aux forces éternelles" [a great poem where man is beyond secondary things, reconciled to eternal powers]. A complete factual commentary would have to extend over many pages if it were to clarify all the allusions to historical and technical details which the strophe furnishes; this poetry rivals in factual density that of Dante, while the French poet loses sight as little as the Italian of things eternal. One might say that it is just because these poets have their eyes calmly fixed on eternity that they can portray so well the "man of the world" and the things of their own century; for them (as Auerbach has pointed out in regard to Dante) the fullness of God radiates through the manifoldness of this earth. Dante, and

Claudel, too (in spite of his polemics against the Greeks), cast a Greek eye on this world; in fact, it seems to me that Catholicism has been the most faithful continuator of things Greek, particularly that vivid pictorial sensitivity of the ancients to things seen in our world. This continuation is really symbolized, as George Santayana has suggested, in the significant name of that Roman church *Santa Maria sopra Minerva* (and perhaps Claudel cannot be exempted from blame for his failure to see fully his indebtedness, as a Catholic thinker, to the θεία κόρη [divine maiden] Pallas Athene-Minerva).*

---

*As an exception I venture here to voice criticism and not to apply only the *critique des beautés* [aesthetic critique]. I feel justified in so doing because I have tried to understand Claudel's world of thought from within, and only after my apperception of his art was (in a manner of speaking) completed have I found a flaw which is inherent to the very conception of his poem. This "historical" flaw is conditioned by the basic idea of having Grace replace the Muse, or of having pious rationality replace secular enthusiasm: since there had to be the Muse (who was also made necessary by the invocation in the proem), she had to become the *repoussoir* [foil]: the personification of the Greek culture which had to be rejected. Claudel could then not admit in his poem a Pallas Athene as a prefiguration of the numerous Catholic patron saints of skills and technics.

My objection cannot be met by the argument that a poet is free to alter historical facts in accord with the laws of poetry: since Claudel's poem implies a historical picture of our civilization, this picture must be in harmony with at least that historical picture which our civilization calls its own, and which forms a part of it. When Dante alters history he is in accord with what his civilization taught him about history: Virgil could be his *duca e maestro* [leader and master]. When Villon makes of the Greek Alcibiades a lovely woman Archipiada, this is in accordance with what his civilization thought of Alcibiades. But when Claudel willingly shuts his eyes to *his own knowledge* that Greek philosophy and religion anticipate Christian philosophy and religion, he puts himself in opposition to himself, and the rift makes itself felt within the poem (the Egyptians and the Assyrians must replace the Greeks and Romans!).

In this poem Claudel has offered Frenchmen an example of the "Christian Ode," a genre which, properly speaking, was only to be found in England with Milton, in Germany with Klopstock, in Italy with Manzoni. In France, Ronsard had succeeded in re-creating the antique ode characterized necessarily by "enthusiasm" (Claudel suggests his opposition to the Pléiade in the words "loin d'immoler le bouc" [literally, far from sacrificing the goat—EDS.]), while Victor

Hugo had shown his complete misunderstanding of the nature of the ode by mixing this with the ballad. Claudel has been able to renew an ancient genre* and to retain its main ingredient, mythology, by substituting a Christian mythology concerned with the intramundane working of Grace.

---

* According to Karl Viëtor,[17] who seeks to define the ode on the basis of all the examples of this genre from antiquity to our day, the ode is characterized by its position between the *lied* and the hymn: its style ends toward the sublime and the elaborately poetic, its mood is that of heightened feeling coupled with reflection—Herder's definition "die poetische Ausbildung eines lebhaften Gedankens" [the poetic shaping of a living thought] can, according to Viëtor, be maintained if we grant to the terms used their full range of significance (*poetisch*—"elaborately poetic"; *lebhaft*—"animated by heightened feeling"; *Gedanken*—"mood of reflection"). From these basic characteristics Professor Viëtor derives other features: the mythical element must be in evidence and there must be that *beau désordre* which Boileau posited; the poem must have been inspired by a solemn occasion; rhyme must be absent (according to the Horatian model). Professor Viëtor states that the pure type of the ode which would contain all those elements together in perfect harmony is rarely to be found in the actually existing historical representatives of the genre; I would venture to claim for Claudel's odes the harmonious presence of *all* these essential features (in spite of the fact that the French poet was not able to read Viëtor's treatise!). And, when we read Viëtor's lament over the inability of contemporary German poets to breathe into their odes a new spirit uniting *Freiheit und Gesetz* (the freedom of artistic creativity and the law of form), we Romance philologists can point with pride to Claudel.

And, what is still more important, he has (as certain critics have stated) made poetry sing of Christian subjects more than one hundred years after Chateaubriand had made the same attempt in his poetic prose. The difference between the two procedures is that between pious speech and pious work: Claudel's ποίησις [poiesis; root sense, making] is a doing, the doing of a workingman (perhaps he had in mind this revelatory etymological pun when he made the comparison between the poet and the worker); and its pious incentive is blessed by Grace, whose presence we feel in the poem. Chateaubriand, with much documentation couched in aesthetic language, is forever advocating piety, but his pages of magic and sweetness cannot achieve the simple evidence of the presence of Grace. It is interesting to inquire into the reasons why the two apologists of Christianity had to come so late, and why it was necessary that their two undertakings were separated from each other by a century. We must remember that, since the time of classical Humanism, French poetry had teemed with pagan themes; this was possible, in a Catholic country, precisely because it represented simply a literary practice which subsisted quite apart from religious belief—and this tolerance of pagan themes could continue so long as faith remained unshaken (even today, in a Jesuit school, the inclusion of classical studies in the curriculum—though they are rigidly separated from Christian studies—is held to be without danger to religion, just as, in Catholic circles, there has never been any fear of scientific positivism: "render unto Caesar those things which are Caesar's, and unto God those things which are God's"). But, with the period of the Enlightenment and the development of positivistic science, Christian beliefs were shattered: it was against this background that Chateaubriand reacted, as, later, Claudel had to react against the period of laicism in which the state (and its schools) was separated from the Church (our ode was written two years after the laws of separation were enacted): both poets voiced a reaction and helped bring about a *renouveau catholique*. Claudel had to revive the program of Chateaubriand one hundred years later, because the Romantics had deflected poetry from the path laid out by Chateaubriand and had continued certain eighteenth-century (scientific or pantheistic) trends, which they endowed with a new poetic halo. Claudel sings of Christian values to a laicized world, but his attack on laicism disarms the opposing forces by declaring them ultimately God-willed: this lay-science, which had been so proudly hailed ever since the Enlightenment as an arm against religion, is accepted by Claudel as the preordained instrument of Christian divinity! Instead of impugning the scientific tendencies of our age, he suggests another inspiration behind them; he does not, like Chateaubriand, preach the aesthetic values of Catholicism as offering a supererogatory beauty to earthly life: he discloses to us the continuous presence of the "cathedral" in the midst of the secular beauty of the workshops. What the lay institutions of the state have purported to protect—the labor of the common man—is now revealed as under the protection of divine powers. Thus, that scientific positivism in whose name the cudgels had been taken up against religion is revealed to be an intramundane form of religion: science and faith are reconciled.

Turning from the aspect of practical policy which must have been underlying Claudel's poem to its purely literary significance, it may be observed that Claudel has restored in our time that "poetry of ideas" once practiced by Lucretius, Dante, and Rabelais; in this, he joins forces with Valéry, who considers the true subject matter of poetry to be not the "poetic" or the emotional but the "intellectual": that which offers most resistance to the alchemy of poetry. Claudel, however, while endorsing Valéry's program of extracting poetry from the shock and integration of ideas ("faire chanter les idées" [make ideas sing]), opposes the arrant agnosticism of Valéry by stressing the harmony of intelligence and faith.

A world-poem of today must evidently find a new form, evenly balanced between the conservative and the progressive, reflecting our own time while reminding us of the past. The old alexandrine* and the old stanza-forms were inadequate for this task; the first, Claudel replaced by the biblical and Whitmanian verset which offered the possibility of retaining the parallelism of biblical style and the caesura characteristic of the alexandrine; the second was replaced by the "flood and wave" technique, a system of metrics in which the fixed forms of earlier literature give way to a Bergsonian flow: the language of such a poem must find a place somewhere between prose and poetry, since it is to show the integration of the prosaic and the poetic of modern life. The hymnic and the sublime characteristic of our ode had to emerge from the trivial; the totality of the vista implies the representation of a diversity of styles within the poem.

---

* As if out of a feeling of pique against the alexandrine—which he has criticized in his treatise on French versification[18]—Claudel carefully avoids giving his shorter lines (generally descriptive of energetic decision, of concentration of forces, etc.) the correct form of an alexandrine:

line 3: $7 + 7$ (with two hiatuses)
    4: 12 (without a caesura; one hiatus)
 15: $5 + 7$
 17: $3 + 9$ (one hiatus)
 27: $7 + 8$
         etc.

In our analysis we have sought to show the ascending movement in language; the network of the forces which determine the "waves and floods" was the task of this study*—which becomes superfluous once we have performed the mental activity imposed on us by the poet's words.

---

*The reader may have noticed that, from the moment I had pointed out, with the help of the word-motif, the main structure of the poem, my study shifted more and more away from Claudel's words.

I have sought to obey the Claudelian motto of this study by first disobeying it: by starting with the attempt to cut a path through the poetic labyrinth in order to reach the "center." In clearing my path, it was necessary to brush away, for the moment, much of the underbrush—which later on had to be properly accounted for: hence the thicket of notes which could not be avoided if we were to respect the labyrinthine aspect of the poem willed by the poet. Thus it was necessary, for the purpose of exposition, to split into two (text and notes) what appears in the poem as a unit.

Once the architecture of the work of art has been laid bare, the scaffolding, which the critic had to erect provisionally for this purpose, can be scrapped. Stylistics, as I conceive it, is an exclusively auxiliary science. Just as, according to Pascal, for him who knows truth no style, no *art de persuader* is needed, so stylistics (and the devices of suasion) must abdicate once the true nature of the work of art has been apperceived. A study of the kind we have attempted could have been made entirely unnecessary from the start by a simple recital of the poem, if the performer were able, by various pauses and intonations, to suggest the main motifs we have taken pains to distinguish, and to show, within the crystalline ball of the work of art, the play of the conflicting forces in the equilibrium which Claudel has been able to establish. For Claudel's poetry is, above all, an invitation to the listener to "reconcile," to harmonize its *idées-forces*—and to rest harmoniously in contemplation of harmony.

AMERICAN ADVERTISING
EXPLAINED AS POPULAR ART

Spitzer presents this essay as an experiment, an attempt to see what might result from the application of his philological method to the nonliterary, everyday art of the American advertisement. In case his readers are uneasy about his decision to exclude all "snobbish feelings" and explicate the text of the *Sunkist* orange ad as if it were a mystical poem by Saint John of the Cross, Spitzer emphasizes at the outset the rewards that such an unprecedented exercise might bring. The popular art form exists as a genre with its own coherent system of laws and devices and its own historical tradition. The proper study of individual texts sheds light on what is evidently an important area in the aesthetic experience of modern man, while at the same time furnishing insights into the larger "unwritten text" of the culture that contains them. In a striking formulation of his belief in cultural unity, he describes the study as "a step toward the understanding of the well-motivated, coherent, and consistent organism which our civilization is."

The structural analysis of the text is a fine example of Spitzer's brilliant wit, his critical acumen, and his mastery of the kind of art of the astonishing juxtaposition that he admired in the great writers of the baroque. With an exegetical virtuosity grounded in immense knowledge, he reveals that the business art of selling orange juice utilizes pastoral devices found in the esoteric *Soledades* of Góngora, perspectivistic shifts analogous to those of *Don Quijote*, and, most astonishingly of all—in its description of a glass of orange juice towering toward the summits of California mountains—the method of "naive" stylization that enabled medieval artists to paint Christ as much larger than his disciples. Spitzer's intentional playfulness with his reader is well suited to his argument, for its conclusion is that the American art of the advertisement is itself an elaborate game played by writer and public in full awareness of required rules and conventions. The ironies, the capriciousness, and the exaggerations of the advertiser, as well as the audience's willingness to adopt a complicitous, "as if" stance toward the deceitful manipulation of language, might recall the refined word games (*préciosité*) of baroque society and the skeptical view of language that characterized that period.

Spitzer's consideration of the important role of the reader in the construction of this utilitarian art form leads him into the larger areas of his study. The advertisement is in fact a revealing manifestation of the two fundamental, seemingly antithetical traditions at the heart of American civilization—Calvinism, with its divine sanction of labor and business success, and deism, with its promise that each individual can achieve and enjoy a condition of material happiness in this world. In the crowning conceit of his virtuoso performance, Spitzer suggests that the ad should be seen as a kind of secularized sermon of a "laicized civilization, where human activity in pursuit of material welfare is not shunned but accepted as a blessing from God." If Spitzer's analytical approach to the texts of advertisements looks forward to the practices of structuralism and semiotics of the following decades, his provocative speculations concerning the reader's participation anticipate the directions of recent reception theory and its fruitful exploitation of sociological research. Although Spitzer would propose a strikingly "sunny" interpretation of the civilized advertising game in the face of the "biased" approaches prevailing among sociologists and semanticists, several of his observations suggest that he shared some of their pessimism concerning its adverse effects on American moral values, life-style, and language. Ten years later he would speak of the "highly destructive" cultural experience of advertising and political slogans as contributing decisively to the rise of a disturbing critical movement, inspired by William Empson, which focused on the indeterminate, polysemous aspects of language and aimed at breaking down textual coherence.

This essay was first published in Spitzer's *A Method of Interpreting Literature* (Northampton, Mass., 1949), pp. 102–49. It was reprinted in Leo Spitzer, *Essays on English and American Literature*, ed. Anna Hatcher (Princeton, N.J., 1962), pp. 248–77; and it appears here by permission of Princeton University Press.

American Advertising Explained
as Popular Art

The philological method of *explication de texte* is usually applied to works of art and works of great art. But, at all times, there has existed, side by side with great art, that everyday art which the Germans have called *Gebrauchskunst* ("applied practical art"): that art which has become a part of the daily routine and which adorns the practical and the utilitarian with beauty. At no time has this type of art played so compensatory a role as is the case today, in the age of machinism, of rationalization, and of the subjection of man to the impersonal necessities of social, economic, and political life. An emphasis on the beautiful has penetrated all levels of fabrication, down to mucilage bottles and matchbooks, and to the packaging of goods; it has also penetrated to the forms of propaganda used to advertise these goods. And the success of such attempts at aesthetic appeal achieved by modern advertising is borne out by the many exhibits of original commercial designs which have attracted a large public. It is also true that particularly novel and clever devices of advertising find an appreciative echo among sophisticated journalists, and there exists today a whole literature devoted to the requirements of effective advertisements.[1] In such treatments, however, the emphasis is generally placed on the psychological element and on the utilitarian efficacy of the propaganda, while little or no attention is paid to the aesthetic as such,* to the artistic tradition in which the particular advertisement has its place, to the satisfaction which advertising may offer of contemporary extra-commercial needs, or, finally, to the historical explanation of the phenomenon of advertising, which must, somehow, be related to the American national character and cultural history.†

---

*The psychologists of advertising recognize the influence of advertising on the aesthetic taste of their public only insofar as they admit that public taste may be educated by the display of artistic objects;[2] they acknowledge also that it is sometimes possible for the advertisement to provide for the beholder "a vicarious fulfillment of desires."[3] I would say that it is possible to see these two facts together, and to state that advertising as such may offer a fulfillment of the *aesthetic* desires of modern humanity.

†Such a study presupposes that type of "symbolizing" thinking which has been advocated in the introduction to my book *Linguistics and Literary History;*[4] to see the relationship between an everyday detail which is, all too often, simply taken for granted, and a spiritual entity in itself not unknown, but only vaguely and separately conceived—this is, I believe, to take a step toward the understanding of the well-motivated, coherent, and consistent organism which our civilization is. It is not enough, in the case of American advertising, to admire or savor a new coinage, psychological trick, or strategy, as this may develop in the technique in question: one must try to see the manifold cross-relationships between the detail (the advertisement) and the whole (our civilization) in order that our capacity for feeling at home in this civilization and of enjoying it will be increased. I may say that, in the matter of understanding one's civilization, the French (incidentally, the inventors of the *explication de texte*) have a great advantage over Americans, who, as it seems to me, are less given to probing into the motivation behind the products of their civilization; the French are past masters in establishing (sometimes to excess) relationships between specific aspects of their civilization (French literature or French cuisine) and this civilization itself; they are able to recognize even in the most trivial detail the expression of an implicit national profession of faith. The present writer must confess that it was by applying *explication de texte* to American advertising that he was given the first avenue (a "philological" avenue) leading toward the understanding of the unwritten text of the American way of life.

Can the linguistically minded literary historian, who harbors no snobbish feelings toward this genre of applied art, give an *explication de texte* of a good sample of modern advertising, in which he would proceed from the exterior features to the "spirit of the text" (and to the spirit of the genre), just as he is accustomed to do with literary texts? Let us try the experiment.

In undertaking this study, I shall be attempting to apply my method to things American, with which my listeners will be much more familiar than I—a circumstance which, in itself, can only provide a better test of the method. It is needless to state that, in line with this method, I shall here carefully avoid the biographical or pragmatically historical approach: I know nothing about the genesis of the particular advertisement to be discussed, about the persons involved in the choice of the name of the particular product, or about the history of the business firm in question. I shall seek to analyze a given advertisement in the same unbiased manner as I have attempted to do in the case of a poem of Saint John of the Cross or a letter of Voltaire, believing, as I do, that this kind of art, if not comparable in greatness to the texts usually analyzed by the scholar, offers nevertheless a "text" in which we can read, as well in its words as in its literary and pictorial devices, the spirit of our time and of our nation—which are, surely, in their way, *unmittelbar zu Gott* [next to God]. To adopt a resentful or patronizing attitude toward our time is, obviously, the worst way to understand it.*

---

* My distinguished friend and colleague, the Spanish poet Pedro Salinas, has said in regard to the language of advertising: "Capitalist society has in this century produced a new kind of rhetoric, the rhetoric of advertisement. Effective linguistic means, delicate shadings, which have been tested and proven in literary language, where they were used to provoke pure and disinterested emotion, are combined to form a most cunning verbal mechanism, which arouses minor passions in the reader, violent possessive desires, which are relatively easy to satisfy without tragedy—for this or that price, at this or that business establishment. In this case utilitarianism has gone so far as to dare to assault language not simply in its exterior creations—current spoken speech—but in its very citadel, literary language, which up to now has been the exclusive servant of pure feelings."[5]

I must protest against the sentiments expressed in this paragraph: it is surely not true that the literary language has always served "exclusively" the expression of pure, disinterested feelings; I would say that the prose of Cicero, the attorney, which has influenced European writing (and not oratory alone) for 1,800 years, was "utilitarian," that is, was used for definite practical purposes. Thus, the use of refined literary devices in the "rhetoric of advertisement" is not necessarily reprehensible on the grounds of its purely utilitarian nature. It is precisely the purpose of this article to show that art can arise within the realm of the utilitarian.

A view somewhat similar to that of Salinas is expressed by S. I. Hayakawa in *Etc.: A Review of General Semantics*.[6] According to the aim of this journal, which is to teach us how to distinguish words from facts and how to learn what the words "really" mean, Hayakawa would see in advertising (which he defines as "venal poetry") the enemy of true poetry (which he calls "disinterested poetry"); according to him, one of the main reasons why poets in our time have become esoteric, obscure, pessimistic, "unpoetic," is that any genuine and hearty expression of common feeling is suspected of being salesman's poetry—that is, advertising. Of course, he is forced to admit that venal poetry is as old as the world; and I would add, for my part, that the esotericism of poets did not start as a counteraction to advertising; Maurice Scève and Góngora were esoteric poets, and esotericism has only become more conspicuous in the democratic age: the *sottisier* [collection of foolish sayings] of Voltaire, the *dictionnaire des idées reçues* [dictionary of received ideas] of Flaubert testify to the existence of the misuse of word symbols by the masses, long before advertising, as we know it, was invented. I think it only fair to replace the pejorative label "venal poetry" applied to advertising by my term *Gebrauchspoesie* [applied poetry], which takes into account the unquestionable fact that the masses have come to absorb the standard poetry of the ads. Great poets find probably no more difficulty in writing today than they have at any other time: the pre-emption of words for common utilitarian purposes has to be undone at all times by any great poet, who must always react against trivial poetry.

Meditation is needed in the face of things modern as of things ancient. Finally, since the following study is intended as an *explication de texte*, it is hardly necessary to warn the reader that the discussion will be mainly limited to one "text," to one example of one particular type of advertising; there is no intention on my part of offering a general survey of advertising trends.

In the drugstores throughout our country, the brand of oranges known as *Sunkist* was advertised some years ago by the following picture-with-text:* on a high mountain range, covered with snow that glistens in the bright sunshine, furrowed by vertical gullies, towering over a white village with its neat, straight rows of orange trees, there rests a huge orange-colored sun, inscribed with the word "Sunkist."

---

*The genre of picture-with-text is, obviously, a development of the "cartoon"—which, itself, can be traced back to the emblem literature of the sixteenth and seventeenth centuries.

In front of this vista, set squarely in the midst of the groves, is a glass of orange-juice which rises to the exact height of the mountain range and whose color exactly matches that of the sun ball. Next to this gigantic glass of juice is a smaller one of the same color, and next to that, a fruit-squeezer on which lies the orange to be squeezed. In the left corner of the advertisement we read, as the only inscription:

> From the sunkist groves of California
> Fresh for you

The first feature we will observe is that in advertising its *Sunkist* oranges, the firm did not expatiate on the goodness, juiciness, flavor, etc., of this particular "ready-made" type of product, but chose to trace the origin of the product back to the groves which yielded it, so that we may concentrate our attention on the natural beauty of California. From the fruit, our glance is allowed to pass to the countryside, to the soil, to Nature that grows the fruit—and only to Nature, not to the orange-growers or those who pick the fruit, not to the packers who prepare its distribution, not to any human factor. It is Nature that, as by a miracle, brings forth these "sunkist" oranges, brings them "fresh for you," from California. The commercial product (those millions of oranges packed methodically in thousands of cases and transported by the railroads) is shown against the background of its natural environment—indeed, the glass of orange-juice, as we have seen, is set down right in the midst of Nature. In the inscription, there is not even the verbal form "brought," which would suggest human activity: the oranges kissed by the sun are there as an accomplished fact; their transportation over miles and miles of territory is passed over in silence. The elimination of man from this pictorial representation, the concentration on productive Nature and on the miracle of the final appearance of the juice, as we have it before us in our drugstores, represents a highly poetic procedure, since, thereby, our everyday causality (the laws of supply and demand, of mass production and lowered prices) is replaced by other laws (the laws of Nature—and of the miracle); and on our routine reality there is superimposed another, dream-like reality: the consumer may have the illusion, for a moment, of drinking nectar at the source.*

---

*In radio advertising, the transposition of the utilitarian into art must necessarily tend toward the acoustic; when, in the advertisement of *Rinso*, the notes of the bird bob-white are introduced as an accompaniment to a lyric boasting of the accomplishments of the soap in question, this is intended to provide the housewife with an ingratiating domestic song ("happy little wash-day song"), so that the drudgery of her household tasks may be lightened by an association of her work with bird life, with outdoor life, and Nature. The creators of this tune have taken into account the nostalgia for Nature which is part of our urban civilization.

And the public accepts willingly the hypocrisy of the artist. It is as though this manifestation of commercial self-expression were denying its essential purpose, that of selling and of profit-making; as though the business world were engrossed only in harvesting what Nature gives and in bringing her gifts to the individual enjoyer—in an Arcadian life harmonious with Nature. In the city drugstore, over whose counter this sunny picture shines, the wall opens up before us like a window on Nature.* Business becomes poetic because it recognizes the great grip which poetry has on this modern, unpoetic world. It is true that the subtle device of eliminating man is calculated only to bring man back again into the picture, for what, the spectator must ask himself upon reflection, has made possible the miracle of transportation and of transformation, if not the skill, indeed, the magic, of modern industry? And the modest way in which the business firm hides its own tremendous activity behind anonymous Nature will impress us favorably.†

---

*Unwittingly{?}, the advertisers of *Sunkist* oranges have acted in agreement with the associational psychology of Gustav Theodor Fechner, who in his *Vorschule der Aesthetik* gives as an example of such associations precisely an orange—which would suggest to him the whole of Italy: whoever finds an orange beautiful "sees in it, so to speak, the whole of Italy, the country to which a romantic yearning has drawn us from time immemorial."[7] The advertisers have caused "the whole of California" (the "romantic" equivalent, for Americans, of Italy) to be associated with the orange.

†It may occasionally be true that the industrial process would be painful to visualize; in such a case the procedure of advertising will consist in evoking the beauty of the natural origin without insisting on the necessary subsequent stages. I remember seeing a pictorial advertisement of *Jones' Country Sausage*, in which there is shown only the diptych of the beginnings in Nature and of the final industrial product: above, there is pictured the deep green of mountain pastures in which cattle graze idyllically among the trees and flowers; below, we see the small cones of the processed meat. Hypocrisy? Yes, but the hypocrisy inherent in any poetizing of our animal instincts. After all, we wish to enjoy the meat we eat, and this enjoyment is not furthered by a realization that we are carnivorous animals.

Now, when business becomes poetic, for whatever reasons, it must subject itself to the ancient laws of poetry, which remain unshaken by the technical developments of the modern world. We can, then, expect to find in this business art the old, time-honored poetic devices. And, indeed, is the poetically achieved evocation of the natural state of the product of human industry anything but the repetition of a device known to the ancient and the Renaissance poets? We may remember the anonymous inscription (listed in Bartlett's *Famil-*

iar Quotations, 11th edition) discovered on an old violin: "Arbor
viva, tacui; mortua, cano" [When I was part of a living tree, I was silent; now dead, I sing]. Or again—why not?—we might think of the
lines in Góngora's *Soledades* in which the drowning protagonist res-
cues himself by means of a floating spar—which is described in terms
of the original living pine tree, that once resisted the blasts of the
north wind and now resists the floods:

> Del siempre en la montaña opuesto pino
>   al enemigo Noto
>   piadoso miembro roto
> —breve tabla. . . .

> [A pitying broken limb
> of the mountain pine, which always opposed
>   its enemy Notus
> —a brief plank. . . .]

Similarly, the poet who devised the *Sunkist* advertisement reminds
us, when we put a dime down on the counter for a glass of orange-
juice, of all the sunshine that went into this refreshing drink: as if we
should be able to buy for so small a sum the inexhaustible source of
warmth and fecundity, the Sun. We came to the counter for reasons
of practical necessity; we walk away, having seen the picture and enjoyed the juice, with an insight into the generosity of Nature and the
persistence of its goodness in its smallest yields.

Recourse was had to another ancient poetic and pictorial device
when our poet chose to point out a continuous line between the
orange-juice and California Nature: he wished to trace a consistent
link between the *Sunkist* orange and the orange-juice by use of a motif which shows how Nature plans and man carries out her will: this
fusion of man's and Nature's activities manifests itself in the repetition of one motif which has a central part in these activities—the
motif of the orange, pictorially represented by means of the unifying
orange color. In all, we have the one orange-color motif repeated
four times:* a natural orange, two glasses of orange-juice, and the
"sun" itself (which bears the inscription "Sunkist"); in this representation is offered the symbol of the unity, of the harmony of Nature's
and man's concern with the fruit. And, here, modern advertising is
returning to a medieval form. On the eleventh-century portal of the
Hildesheim cathedral, in a bas-relief representing the scene of the Fall
of Man, we may see four apples which traverse the sculpture in one
horizontal line: one is in the mouth of the dragon in the tree, one is in

Eve's hand, one is figured as the apple of her breast, and one is in the hand of Adam.†

---

* We have here the principle of "repetition," so basic to all forms of propaganda, except that here it is no word, no slogan, which is repeated, but a single feature abstracted from the objects pictured; namely, their orange color.

†There'll always be an ad-man: this very biblical scene in its medieval presentation has been adapted to an advertisement of Countess Mara's ties: the four apples are replaced by four ties, and Eve, acting as always under the command of the serpent, is luring the reluctant Adam, who has already taken one tie, into acceptance of a second, and perhaps a third (a fourth being also visible in the background, guarded by the serpent in the tree). While, in the medieval sculpture, the forbidden fruit was multiplied only for didactic reasons, in the modern advertisement the device of multiplication is exploited as an excuse to display a variety of wares, presented as forbidden fruit.

The central motif in the medieval work of art, the apple, is, of course, the symbol of the forbidden fruit, whereas the central motif in our modern work of *Gebrauchskunst* serves to praise the natural fruit accessible to all; again, the momentous event of Man's Fall is presented in slow motion, broken up into stages, whereas man's progress in the exploitation of Nature comes to us with an acceleration provided by the technique of the "accomplished fact." Nevertheless, the basic technique, that of the didactically repeated central motif, is the same; modern pantheism has espoused forms of art devised in the religious climate of the Middle Ages.

There may be discerned in this device a subsidiary feature which might appear incongruous with the realism supposedly required in a genre devoted to such practical ends: the "sun-orange" which figures in our picture, and which borrows the *exact* shade of coloring from the fruit on which it shines, is a quite violent, surrealistic misrepresentation of reality, apparently symbolical of the powerful attraction exerted by business, which draws all things into its orbit—which puts even the sun to work. Or, perhaps, may we not have to do with the myth of an orange-sun (figured by a sun-orange) which would have the particular function of nurturing orange groves—just as there were ancient *Sondergötter*, particular gods devoted to the growing of wine, of cereals, etc.; just as there are Catholic saints devoted to particular industries and particular natural processes? (A black Madonna caring especially for Negro worshippers is no more startling than is the orange-sun which takes its color from the thing it grows.)

As for the gross misrepresentation of size which appears in the gigantic glass of orange-juice in the foreground, which is equal in height to the California mountain range and, despising all laws of proportion, completely overshadows the orange-squeezer, this focuses our attention on the protagonist of the scene, on that glass of juice you will order at the counter—with the same "naive" technique of the medieval paintings, in which Christ is presented taller than his disciples, and these taller than common folk (and which is reflected also in the Nuremberg tin soldiers, whose captain is twice as tall as the common soldier); the significance of a figure is translated into material size. One could, perhaps, think that the huge size of the glass in the foreground is due to a naive application of the law of the perspective—if it were not for the presence, also in the foreground, of the smaller glass and the fruit-squeezer of normal proportions.

But why does the glass appear twice, as giant and as dwarf, when there is no difference of technical stages between them? Is the glass of normal size a concession to the realism of the beholder, an apology for the colossal glass, which had to be honored and magnified as the protagonist? According to this, we should have, along with the fantastic, the criticism thereof—as in the *Don Quijote*, with its double perspective. Thus the element of naïveté would be far from absolute, the naive and the critical attitudes being juxtaposed. And this twin presentation serves also the more practical aim of attracting "consumer interest": we see first the sun, then the groves of California, then the picked fruit, then the finished product (the glass of orange-juice)—and, finally, in the glass of normal size (the size of the glass to be had at the drugstore counter), we are shown the customer's own personal glass of *Sunkist* orange-juice: by this reduplication in small, the line beginning at the sun is prolonged out from the picture, in the direction of the customer—who, in taking up the glass of orange-juice, puts himself into direct contact with the California sun.* In the glass-that-is-the-customer's-glass there is the suggestion to the prospective customer: "*Have* a glass {of this juice}." The imperative which was carefully avoided in the text is insinuated by the picture.†

---

*It may be noted that the invitation to drink offered by our advertisement stops short of guaranteeing either the virtue of the product or the happiness in store for the consumer.

If Philip Wylie, in his diatribe *Generation of Vipers*, is right in indicting

"90 percent" of commercial advertising on the grounds that it promotes a general feeling in the public that material goods can add to their personal happiness and social worth ("Cars are, after all, mechanical objects, and nothing else. The rest of the qualities that are attributed to them in the ads . . . belong to *people*. Purchase and possession does not, in itself, do *anything* to an individual"), then our *Sunkist* advertisement, which promises no transformation of character, would belong to the unimpeached 10 percent.[8]

†This technique of extension, by which you, the consumer, are drawn into the orbit of the picture, is the main feature of a certain advertisement of Campbell's soups (highly praised by critics of advertising), in which we see, seated at an elegant table, partaking of a certain Campbell's soup, three persons: a couple and a single lady—the suggestion being that you, the (masculine) prospective customer, should join the group and retrieve the single lady from her loneliness (and also, enjoy with her some soup of the brand in question).

It is not blasphemous, in this regard, to call to mind the magic intention underlying many religious paintings and sculptures of late Greek and Christian times, in which the imperious look of a frontally represented deity with "starry" eyes draws the beholder into its orbit or in which the tympana, representing peoples from all corners of the earth obeying the call of Christ, are located above the entrance of Romanic and Gothic churches so as to force the Christian believer to enter the church.[9] Classical Greek or Renaissance art shuns such drastic devices of stepping out of the frame of the work of art—but then, the art of advertising is not classical.

The imperative implied in the repetition of the "glass motif" has been overstressed in a recent advertisement of *Valliant California Burgundy*: at the left we see a couple dining happily and drinking the Burgundy in question, while, at the right, there opens up before us the wide expanse of Burgundian landscape, out of which grows the magnified hand of the lady which holds the (also magnified) glass of Burgundy: the correspondence of the "actual" hand of the lady with the hand coming out of the Burgundian vineyards is surprisingly exact—even to the manicuring. The imperative suggestion seems to be that the hand of a real lady (outside of the picture) should meet the magnified hand of the picture which holds the glass of Burgundy. But the *avis au lecteur* is marred by the quite inorganic and rather ghastly conceit of a hand coming out of a vineyard. Moreover, in the *Sunkist* advertisement, the source of the bliss prepared by Nature for man (the sun) was at the left, and the "life-sized" glass which appealed to the customer, at the right (closer to the right hand, the active hand, of the customer), while in the *Valliant Burgundy* advertisement it is Nature which has been presented at the right—so that the appeal to the customer's right hand must be artificially engineered by the weird figure of a lady's manicured hand in the midst of Nature.

If we now analyze our own analysis, we see that the first general impression was that of a tribute to the fertility of Nature; after reflection, we are made aware of the necessary intervention of man himself (not only the enterprise of the business firm but also the participation of the consumer). We are left, then, with the realization that the advertiser has fooled neither us nor himself as to the real purpose of his propaganda. That glass of orange-juice as tall as the mountains of California is a clear testimonial to the businessman's subjective estimation of the comparative importance of business interests. Indeed, when we review the violence done to Nature in our picture (displacement of proportions, surrealistic use of a motif, change of the natural color of objects), we see how, in a very artistic manner, this procedure has served to illustrate, in a spirit, ultimately, of candid self-criticism, the very nature of business which, while associating itself with Nature, subordinates her to its purpose—and to ours. Our picture has used all the attractions of living Nature in order to advertise her commercialized form.

Before concluding the analysis of the pictorial elements of our advertisement, we must note the failure to present graphically the metaphor indicated by the trademark: we do not see the oranges being kissed by the sun. No trace of solar activity is suggested—even in the traditional, schematic form of rays. For this sun is no living entity, it is an emblem, an ideogram created by the advertisers to bear their label. Emblematic poetry uses stereotyped symbols; just as in sixteenth- and seventeenth-century imagery, the arrow of Cupid or the scythe of Death represented ready-made ingredients, the modern industrial labels are (or at least anticipate being) permanent: the *Sunkist* business firm is more interested in propagating its label than in reenacting the original metaphor. (We are far from the atmosphere of the Greek world, where personal gods embrace and beget.) On the other hand, we do not find in the caption of our advertisement the label as such, only a reference to *sunkist groves*. In this way, the reader is cleverly led to retrace the origin of the label. Many years ago the label *Sunkist* had been coined and it had become generally accepted, its pristine freshness lost. With the reference to *sunkist groves* (notice that *sunkist* is not capitalized!) it is as though we were presented with the original situation that inspired the name, with the "pre-proper-name state" or etymology of the trademark.

Now, if we consider the phrase *sunkist groves* from a philological point of view, it is to be noted that this was intended as a poetic expression:* it is to be doubted whether millions of Americans have ever read or heard the word "sun-kissed"—except as the denomination of a brand of oranges. At the same time, however, it does not have the flavor of distinguished poetry; the expression "sun-kissed" itself is rather stalely poetic,[10] and the particular form "-kist" is, in addition, a sentimental pastiche of Shakespearian style.†

---

*I do not know the exact date of the coinage of the *Sunkist* trademark, but I assume that it preceded the expansion of the "vitamin myth" as we have this today in America (the word *vitamin* itself was first used by Casimir Funk in 1912). Nevertheless, it is possible that the originally "poetic" term *Sunkist* may have become secondarily attracted into the orbit of that "poetry of science" which has developed from the vision of a world in which longevity and undiminished vigor will be the result of a diet of correctly balanced vitamins. Since oranges, like other citrus fruits, contain the (antiscorbutic) vitamin C, and since the development of the (anti-rachitic) vitamin D is promoted by the sun (particularly by its ultra-violet rays), and since, too, there is a general tendency on the part of the public to associate loosely all the various vitamins, it would be in line with that poetry of science espoused by the salesman to present the oranges as actually containing the vitamins fostered by the sun: in the advertisement of another firm of orange-growers their fruit-juice is presented as "canned liquid sun." Again, we find, in one of Katherine Anne Porter's short stories, the picture of a travelling salesman of cooking utensils who praises a particular vegetable cooker for its vitamin-preserving qualities, and uses the phrase "those precious sun-lit vitamins"—as if assuming that wherever there are vitamins there the sun must be also. I cannot, of course, be sure how much this secondary flow of scientific poetry has colored, for the mind of the average person who sees the *Sunkist* advertisement, the traditional associations of the all-embracing and all-nurturing sun.

†It is obvious that "the poetry of advertising" can never be vanguard poetry: in the period of a Frost it can never be "Frostian," but only Emersonian, Tennysonian, Swinburnian, Elizabethan; it must have a familiar ring, must reproduce the stock poetic devices which the average reader of advertising has been taught to accept as poetic—the folklore of poetry, as it were.

Miss Anna Hatcher has shown that the style of advertising, in borrowing from stock poetic devices, may succeed so completely in acclimatizing these that they are henceforth ruined for poetry. Shakespeare could coin *maiden blushes*, and Keats, *maiden blooms*, but this type is apt to be eschewed in poetry today, when *Maidenform* is the trademark of a brassiere.[11]

Incidentally, advertising may set its mark not only on "poetic" patterns but also on phrases common in everyday use: for example, when I wished to conclude a scholarly article with the statement "The reader must be the judge {in this moot question}," I was warned against using a formula current in advertising ("The consumer must be the judge").

One might also mention, in this connection, the verb "to offend," which has become a euphemism for "to smell of perspiration."

It is very interesting to note, however, that this would-be poetic spelling is also reminiscent of the tendency illustrated, for example, by the use of *nite* for *night*, or *u* for *you* (*Uneeda Biscuit*), which is to be found only in arrantly commercial language (and which is due, I have been told, to an economical desire to save space;* for myself, however, I am inclined to believe that it is inspired by the more positive desire to create an energetic, streamlined impression of efficiency).†

---

*The eccentric spelling of trademarks is, of course, one of the devices intended to facilitate their registration (or the copyrighting of the labels): *Sunkist* can be legally protected as "intellectual property" much more easily than would *Sun-kissed*. The spelling gives to the trademark that exclusive right to which the "generic use" of the words of the language cannot pretend.

It could be said in general that the law on trademarks and copyrights is a powerful promoter of linguistic change—and linguistic sham-originality—and, with each registration, forces upon the language a new "proper name" which, as is the function of proper names, presents things as unique, irrespective of their actual status in this regard. Are not *all* oranges "kissed by the Sun"? Is the shampoo called *Tallulah* truly as outstanding among shampoos as Tallulah Bankhead among actresses? The protection given by the law to such "ad hoc proper names"—in which the usual process of name-giving (first an emotion concentrated so intensely on an object that it appears unique—then the actual word-coinage) has been reversed (since it is taken for granted by the manufacturer that a proper name *must* be coined)—is the ultimate consequence of the concept of "intellectual property," a concept, unknown to antiquity and to the Middle Ages, which has developed as a result of modern man's decreasing consciousness of a common human heritage and of the increasing insistence on the rights of the individual. The author of that truly unique poem "to which heaven and earth have collaborated" was satisfied with the quite generic name *Commedia*!

But linguistic standardization, as active in our times as before, sets certain limits to the individualism of the trademarks. Not only is their proper-name character gradually weakened as the product and its name become familiar to the buying public, not only is their phonetic form not respected (*Coca Cola* > *coke*); it may even happen that the individual trademark, precisely because it has become so familiar to the public, is used in a quite generic sense: in spite of repeated warnings ("A camera is not a Kodak unless it is an Eastman Kodak"), that most original coinage *Kodak*, which, because it had no connection with any word of the language, seemed to enjoy the privileges of an *Urwort* (comparable in this respect to *gas*), has acquired in common speech the generic meaning of "small, portable camera"; and similarly *Victrola* has become the synonym of "phonograph."

†How the idea of efficiency and easy functioning may influence the syntax of advertising ("This car parks easily," "This paint applies easily") and,

subsequently (if ironically), common speech, has been shown in an article by Professor Hatcher.[12]

We have, that is, to do with a hybrid form, suggestive of two mutually exclusive stylistic environments. And something of this same duality obtains with the compound form consisting of "ablative" + participle: unlike so many compounds, this particular type (*God-given, heaven-blest, man-made, wind-tossed, rain-swept,* etc.) was originally highly literary, and even today it is excluded from colloquial speech. When first introduced into advertising, it represented a literary effort on the part of the writer—though this may no longer be true of all advertising writers, just as it is probably not true of most of their readers, who perhaps are acquainted only with the commercial flavor of the type *oven-baked beans,* etc.*

---

* The psychologists of advertising are agreed as to the pleasant atmosphere created by the trademark *Sunkist,* but they seem to lack the linguistic categories in which to place it: Burtt groups *Sunkist* along with *Holeproof, Wearever,* and *Slipnot* (probably only because of the compound character of all these coinages);[13] Brewster and Palmer with *Sun-Maid* (where a pun is involved—as is also the case with *Slipnot*), and with *Sealdsweet* (where we have a spelling-pronunciation—with none of the connotations of *Sunkist*).[14]

As for the particular expression *sunkist,* we are probably justified in assuming a "poetic" intention on the part of the creator of the coinage because of the poetic nature of the concept involved ("kissed by the sun"); at the same time, however, he must have been conscious of its commercial by-flavor; he has been able to play on two chessboards, to appeal to two types of consumers: those who admire a brisk, efficient, businesslike style, and those who think that "the sun of Homer, it shineth still on us." Thus our hybrid word, which is without roots in normal speech, is doomed to a homeless existence: *sunkist* is possible only in that No Man's Land where the prosaic is shunned—but the poetic is taken not quite seriously.*

---

* There is also contained in this half-serious poetry of advertising, a consolation of a sort, an assurance for the average reader, to whose self-confidence and vanity advertisements are always addressed: truly perfect

form, truly ideal beauty is crushing; it leaves the beholder breathless, humiliated; "there is nothing one can say" when looking upon the Venus of Milo or a painting of Raphael. I would paraphrase Keats: "A thing of beauty is a *grief* forever"; its seriousness and self-contained disregard for all other things of this world allow for nothing but a mystic self-absorption in the thing of beauty. Nothing could be less congenial to the American public, which prefers not to be reminded of self-annihilation and which is more active than contemplative. It is true that many advertisers resort to the reproduction of classical works of art; but by the very fact that they are used in a subordinate function, that they are "only advertisements," which the beholder is free to accept or reject, they can be better enjoyed by the average public than when they are seen in a serious exhibit.

And this last fact explains, perhaps, why it can be that businessmen should be so eager to coin, as a technical, commercial term, such a word as *sunkist*, which appeals to poetic imagination in a manner and to a degree quite at variance with their own and their public's speech, and in utter contradiction to what we are supposed to accept as the essential characteristic of business. Psychologists would answer with the concept of "affective appeal," the tendency by which feelings that are aroused by one stimulus will spread and attach themselves to other stimuli.[15]*

*The "affective appeal" envisaged by advertising is not, of course, limited to the (semi-)artistic form given to the advertisement itself: we also find works of pure art put to the service of advertising—as when, for example, symphony programs are sponsored by commercial firms. Thus it is calculated that the pathos and tenderness aroused in us by Rodzinsky's performance of the *Eroica* will inspire us with tender feelings for the "service through science" of the U.S. Rubber Co.

And yet, we should not, I think, be too quick to deny the vein of idealism underlying the artistic programs sponsored by industrial firms. Quite aside from, and above, all their calculating and budgeting, they begin by generous giving (knowing quite well that many who listen to the *Eroica* will not buy one ounce the more of rubber goods). And this giving without immediate returns is capable of awakening a certain loyalty in the listener: I know of one young businessman who reproved his wife for turning off the radio immediately after a concert; to his mind, she should return the courtesy she had received at least to the extent of listening to the advertiser's words.

But I fear that the psychologists of advertising oversimplify the psychology of the advertiser, who is not only a businessman but a human being—one who is endowed with all the normal potentialities of emotion and who finds expression of these in the exercise of his profession. In his private life, in his social relations, he has been taught to minimize or even to ridicule the poetic apperception of life; the idea of whiling away his leisure time by composing sonnet sequences, as is quite common with his counterpart in South America, would be almost unthinkable to him. But his copywriter feels free to indulge in that poetic fancy from which his superior, the business executive, ordinarily shies away (let us not forget that many a copywriter is a thwarted poet whose college dreams have not quite come true). And why does the advertiser, whose mouthpiece is the copywriter, allow himself to be presented before the public as a poet *malgré lui*? Surely it is because he feels himself protected, he feels the fanciful words of the advertisement protected, by invisible "quotation marks" which can ward off the possible ridicule of the public and which exculpate him, in his own eyes, for his daring.

By "quotation marks" I mean to characterize an attitude toward language which is shared by the speaker and his public, and according to which he may use words with the implication: "I have good reasons for saying this—but don't pin me down!" The public, for its part, reacts accordingly: there is on both sides a tacit understanding of the rules of the game (a game which also involves the necessary embellishment by the seller of his products and a corresponding attitude of sales-resistance on the part of the prospect). Thus the word *sunkist* comes to us with its range calculated and delimited, with its impact of reality reduced; this word is noncommittal of reality: it transports the listener into a world of Arcadian beauty, but with no insistence that this world really exists. Of course, the beautiful groves of California which produce excellent oranges do exist, but a world in which they may really be called "sunkist" does not. And everyone knows that, while the advertised goods may be quite first-rate, the better world which the advertiser evokes is a never-never land.*

---

*The world of optimism and idealism which advertising unfolds before us is reflected in its predilection for the superlative; each of the goods praised is supposedly the finest of its kind, from the tastiest bread in America to the most perfect low-priced car in America. This superlative, which rules supreme, and which is not challenged by any factual comparison (since disparaging statements about goods of competitors are prohibited by law),[16] tends to destroy the difference between the superlative and the elative: "the finest . . ." becomes equal to "a very fine . . . ," somewhat equivalent to the Italian elative *buonissimo* (not *il migliore*). The abolition of true comparison (good–better–best) is easily understandable in a world containing only "best" things.

As another variety of the advertising elative, we may mention the use of the comparative, which *The New Yorker* has recently defined as the "agency comparative" or the "comparative without comparison": an item is called "better" without any further qualification: "Better than what?" asks *The New Yorker*. (A parallel case is the absolute use in advertising of "different" {even a laxative medicament is called simply "different"}, patterned on the popular usage with its slightly snobbish overtones.)[17]

Incidentally, it is interesting that in a satirical magazine such as *The New Yorker*, where the stories as well as the illustrations and cartoons are intended as a criticism of the easily beautiful and of conventional standards, the advertisements are allowed to provide, unquestioned, the illusory beauty and the snobbism typical of their genre.

Nonetheless, the idealizations of advertising are not wasted upon the listener: though he cannot take up forthwith his dwelling in the paradisiac world filled with fragrant groves where golden fruit slowly ripens under the caress of the sun,* his imagination has made the detour through this *word-paradise* and carries back the poetic flavor, which will season the physical enjoyment of the orange-juice he will drink for breakfast the next morning.

---

* Often, he is portrayed by the advertiser as already dwelling in (a rather bourgeois and mechanized) El Dorado: if a historian of American civilization were to base himself exclusively on the representation of daily life which is offered in advertisements, he would reach the conclusion that this country is now an Arcady of material prosperity and social ease (and of questionable moral worth); but the spectator, we may be sure, is equipped with his own criteria, and subtracts automatically from the pictures of felicity and luxury which smile at him from the billboards. Nevertheless, while making this subtraction, he is able to gaze at the beauty portrayed, with disinterested enjoyment, *in abstracto*.

The tendency toward over-glamorization in advertising must constantly be counterbalanced by the "as-if" attitude, in order to avoid becoming ridiculous and ineffective. When, occasionally, one advertisement oversteps the mark, rival advertisers are quick to exploit this excess by excessively discreet understatement in regard to their own products: the sensational picture of the passionate havoc which perfume may wreak, in an advertisement circulated several years ago to publicize *Tabu*, has resulted in such mock-modest claims, by other advertisers, as "We do not guarantee that this perfume will make of you a *femme fatale*: we only say it smells nice."

Here, in an unexpected corner of our technologically organized age, and in the service of the most highly rationalized interests, poetry has developed its most miraculous quality: that of establishing a realm of pure, gratuitous, disinterested beauty, which has existence only in the imagination. And the poetic achievement is presented to the public with all sincerity—and with all cautiousness: with overtones of irony which preclude any too-serious commitment.

If we ask ourselves with which historical literary climate we should associate this playful language of advertisement, which is satisfied with feigning gratuitously an ideal *word-world* in empty space, the kinship with certain baroque or *précieux* ways of speech becomes evident: *sunkist* for "oranges" belongs to a poetic "as-if" speech, no different essentially from *conseiller des grâces* for *miroir*.

Préciosité and the parallel baroque styles of euphuism, *Schwulst*, *marinismo*, and *gongorismo* (it was not unadvisedly that we quoted above a passage from Góngora) have their cultural roots in a polar tension between life as it is and life as it should be: reality appears on the one hand with all the attractions of beautiful sensuousness and, on the other, beclouded by our consciousness of the futility of these attractions, by the feeling of *desengaño* [disillusionment]—a feeling which prevailed even in France, where only the most "reasonable" variant of the baroque existed. One knows quite well that the mirror cannot always counsel graceful behavior, but one lends it this role in order to create an illusion absolutely unwarranted by reality. The *précieuse* dwells in that borderland of poetry which could "perhaps" be true, but, as she knows, is not true—this is an example of the same mild form of wishful thinking which is at the bottom of American advertising. The American public, exposed at every moment to the impact of advertising propaganda, easily applies its grain of salt; it does not condemn outright the excesses of *préciosité*, as did Molière's Gorgibus; it can afford to let itself be seduced to a certain point, for it is fully aware of the matter-of-fact reality of the product advertised. Thus, an attitude of *desengaño* would seem to be present here, too. Does this represent a general disillusionment, due to particular unfortunate experiences in American history, to the disenchantment of pioneers who had left the Old World in search of a better one—or who, already in this country, had turned to the West in search of gold—and have often seen their hopes frustrated? In view of the ingrained optimism which still today enables the American to meet each calamity with his hopes of a better deal just around the corner,* this hypothesis can hardly endure. Nor can we assume, in the case of the situation of advertising, any actual distrust of the merits of any particular product; there is, undoubtedly, in America an attitude of confidence (supported, it is true, by a whole framework of supervisory regulations) in the factual truthfulness of the claims made by manufacturers.†

---

*It could be said that the American's optimism is also reflected in the abundance of neologisms in advertising: by coining new words one suggests a picture of new and therefore better things to come. This tendency also reveals a special attitude toward language itself as something continuously in flux (as H. L. Mencken has repeatedly emphasized)—an attitude which shares with the first a basic "future-mindedness."

Any neologism, however, in the course of time, tends to lose its freshness once it has been accepted by the community—in which case the linguists must speak of "lexicological petrification." The advertisers themselves eventually recognize that the inevitable stage of lexicalization has set in, and are careful thereafter not to stir the ashes of the dead—for any insistence on the symbolic value once possessed by the label would be tedious to the public.

And our *Sunkist* had, obviously, to go the way of all linguistic creations: at a certain moment it stopped being a living expression to become a label used glibly and matter-of-factly by the community. That this has been recognized by the advertisers is indicated by the fact that the *Sunkist* advertisement we have been describing, and which I had seen for four summers in the same drugstore, was replaced, in 1945, by one of a quite different type, and one which did not go to the length of "explaining" (verbally or pictorially) the choice of the label. The new advertisement was of a schematic or ideographic character: it showed a frieze with an ornamental arrangement of bunches of flowers and fruits (oranges and lemons), underneath which were seen two glasses (of orange-juice and lemonade, respectively) forming a cross-bar and bearing the label *Sunkist*. Sun and Nature had disappeared, except for the slight and stereotyped reminder of the latter offered by the fruits.

†The confidence of the public in the honesty of advertisers is an established fact in this country; there seems to be little or no suspicion that the advertiser is advancing false claims. In a country where moral integrity in business life is not taken for granted by principle, advertising can develop no gratuitous poetry; such an attempt would invite the question, fatal to poetry: "Are your words true or false?"

I should say that, in the skeptical, or half-skeptical, attitude of the American public* in regard to advertising, we may see that basic mistrust of language itself which is one of the most genuine features of the Anglo-Saxon character,† as opposed to the trust in words by which the Romance peoples are animated—those *Wortmenschen* [word-people], as Hugo Schuchardt has called them, whose aesthetics Benedetto Croce has formulated in the postulate: "Quello che non è espresso non esiste!" [That which is not expressed does not exist!]

---

* In no language, so far as I know, are there so many prefixes which tend to unmask false values: *pseudo-, sham-, make-believe-, makeshift-, mock-, would-be-, fake-, phony-, semi-, near-*{beer}, *baloney-*{dollars}, *synthetic-*, etc.; it is as though the Anglo-Saxon attitude of distrust of the pretentious would find for itself a grammatically fixed pattern of expression in the language. Americans delight in their impermeability to "bunk" (as is shown by the fertility of the "buncombe" word-family).

†It would seem that there is a difference in this regard between the two Anglo-Saxon nations themselves, if we are to believe Dennis William Brogan, who has been struck by the American love for oratory: "In Chambers of Commerce, at Rotary Club meetings, at college commencements, in legislatures, in Congress, speech is treated seriously, according to the skill and taste of the user. There is no fear of boss words or of eloquence, no fear of clichés, no fear of bathos. . . . The British listener, above all the English listener, is surprised and embarrassed by being asked to applaud statements whose truth he has no reason to doubt, but whose expression seems to him remarkably abstract and adorned with flowers of old-fashioned rhetoric."[18] Mr. Brogan gives himself the explanation that Americans "like slogans, like words. They like absolutes in ethics."[19] And the English critic might have brought up the contrast between the American Constitution and the unwritten British Constitution.

On the other hand, I would suggest that there is an English brand of oratory which is slightly alien to the American—for example, the prose of Churchill, which, with its archaisms and periphrastic turns of speech, weaves poetry round the casual concrete happenings of history; by the Americans the "word" is considered less as an artistic than as a moral tool, as abstractly purposeful as the flag. But, even in the realm of absolute morals, the distrust of language is not entirely lacking with Americans; Mr. Brogan himself cannot overlook the fact that many slogans are greeted by Americans with an ironical "Oh, yeah?" or "However you slice it, it's still baloney." How else save by mistrust of the word could one explain the fact that after the exchange of wild abuse indulged in on both sides during an election campaign, Americans, once the election is over, are able to go quietly to work the next day, no attempt being made by the defeated party to start a revolution. The word in itself is not "sacred" and final to the Americans. The difference between the American and the German concepts of the word can be seen in the absence of free speech in Germany: freedom of speech involves a concept of nonfinality of speech. In America the human word is thought of only as having a provisional value. One word can be undone, and outdone, by another.

For the Anglo-Saxon, on the contrary, reality remains ultimately inexpressible. Such a people will, obviously, have a mistrust of poetry because of its too easy, too felicitous finds, which cannot be made to square with the complexity of reality. Now since, in the game continually going on between the advertiser and the public, the customer is expected to take the role of skeptic, it is possible for poetry to be given full play; the advertiser does not ask that his words be taken completely at face value, and he must not be held to literal account for the truth of every syllable. Thus the poetry of advertisement can be truly enjoyed because it makes none of the solemn claims of literary poetry. It is precisely because Americans know reality so well, because they ask to face it, and do not like to be hoodwinked, because they are not easily made victims of metaphysical word-clouds as are the Germans, or of word-fulgurations, as are the French, that they can indulge in the *acte gratuit* of the human word in its poetical nowhereness. So fully aware is the advertiser of this discounting attitude on the part of his public that, not infrequently, he anticipates the forthcoming skepticism by the feint of self-indictment—as when Macy's apologizes prettily for its many entrances, but insists, for the reassurance of harassed husbands shopping for their wives, that not *all* subway exits lead to their store. And, in a more pedantic, statistical vein, the well-known claim of "99 $^{44}/_{100}$ percent" of purity uses a screen of scrupulous precision and self-criticism to advance the claim of what is, after all, an extraordinary degree of near-perfection.

Every work of art is addressed to a public, whether outspokenly or implicitly. A painting on the wall, for example, is an invitation to the beholder to engage in a relationship with it; there are always involved in the painting $n + 1$ elements, with n elements included from the beginning in the work of art itself; and $n + 1$ remains the formula even when there are several beholders. In the case of three persons, for example, the relationships between them and the picture of n elements would be $n + 1^a$, $n + 1^b$, $n + 1^c$, respectively—and in the case of x persons, $n + 1^x$. Now, we have seen how, in the case of our advertising picture, there has been established, by means of that second glass of normal proportions, a relationship between the groves of California and the ultimate individual consumer. At the same time, this personal relationship is underscored (in a manner unknown to other works of art) by the phrase "fresh *for you*," which every customer must understand as a personal address to himself (incidentally these three words of personal address are printed in script). In this *you* we have, obviously, a device which is not peculiar to the picture in question but is highly representative of the genre itself, and is a quite common feature to be found in every page of the daily newspaper.*

---

* This "for you" is not limited, of course, to advertising, but is a generally characteristic feature of the language of the tradesman when addressing his customer: "Shall I wrap it *for you*?" "I'll fix it *for you* by tomorrow." We may see here the influence of the idea of service to one's fellowman, which has permeated so many of the formulae of commercial life: "May I help you?" "What can I do for you?" said by clerks in shops and offices; or "Have you been taken care of?" a question of waiters—which may be contrasted with French "Madame désire?" Italian "Commandi?" and German "Sie wünschen?"

If we would ask ourselves what is involved in the use of this advertising "you," we must first inquire, superfluous and far-fetched as the procedure may seem, into the meaning of this second personal pronoun, according to the philosophy of grammar. "You" is a startling word: it calls up the dormant ego in every human being;* "you" is in fact nothing but the ego seen by another; it addresses itself to our feeling that we are a unified person recognizable from the outside; it also suggests someone outside of us who is able to say "you" and who feels akin to "us" as a fellow man.†

---

* This personal susceptibility of the individual to any address which is intended generally, has been, perhaps, nowhere more effectively exploited than in the famous cartoon of James Montgomery Flagg which was used as an enlistment poster in the First World War (and was revived in the Second): "Uncle Sam Needs YOU for the United States Army" is written beneath a picture of the stern-eyed old gentleman who fixes with his gaze, and singles out with an accusing finger, whoever steps within the range of the picture. (Needless to say, such a drastic method of attracting the attention of the individual is not recommended for advertising.)

The constant "you see" of the radio announcers is a characteristic insertion in an otherwise impersonal broadcast—motivated only by an initial vocative such as "Men," "Ladies." It simulates a conversation with a "you," instead of a one-sided harangue; "you see" (which is equal to a "let me explain it to you") seems intended to counteract an observation or a resistance on the part of the partner in the conversation. *The New Yorker* once remarked that this device is coming to be used as a means of introducing the most startling contentions of the advertiser, in order to make them appear as something quite evident on closer investigation.

†Coming from an anonymous being, as does the "fresh for you" of our advertising picture, the effect is perhaps more startling than when a radio announcer (who has a human voice and may be known to us by name and voice) addresses "you." Nor, as often is the case in written advertisement, has the firm in question presented itself first as "we": suddenly, an appeal is made by an undefined agency to "me personally." By the elimination of the human element at work, by the retreat behind things, by the assumption of a miracle, to which is due, for example, the arrival of the oranges from California—it is as if we were told: "*Nature* has brought fresh for you . . . ," "*God* has brought fresh for you . . ."; the identity of the fruit-packing firm disappears within the greater connection of a helpful universe, mindful of each man and woman dwelling therein.

Now, in English, the pronoun "you" enjoys an ambiguity to a degree unknown in the main European languages, which are characterized by greater inflection; it is equally applicable to a singular or a plural audience, and, in advertising, this double reference is fully exploited: the advertiser, while preparing his copy for the general public, thinks of the "you" as an "all of you"—but intends it to be interpreted as a "you personally," applicable to the individual *A*, *B*, or *C*. In the case of our advertisement, *A* translates the algebraic *X* of the "you" as "fresh for *me* has the orange been brought here from California"; and *B* and *C* do the same. Though he is only one of millions, every single individual is individually addressed and flattered.*

---

*Compare also "I have arranged this sale with you in mind. You, Mrs. America, are the best buyer and the best-dressed woman in the world" (from an advertisement of furs); "For you, Madame, I have done the utmost to bring you more valuable things than ever. For you, Madame, I have traveled to Europe. Your taste is to us all we do, think, plan." (It is obvious that the "for you" pattern, while appealing to the vanity of the buyer, also implies self-praise of the services rendered by the merchant.)

It is also true that he has come to accept this flattery as no more than his due. Of all the peoples among whom I have lived, the Americans seem to me most jealously insistent on the right of being addressed as individuals. It is an interesting paradox that the same civilization that has perfected standardization to such a degree is also characterized by this intense need for the recognition of one's personal existence. And this need, which is most acutely in evidence when individuals deal with each other (the relationship between teacher and pupil in America, for example, must impress any European) can, evidently, not be ignored even when both parties are anonymous. The concern shown in American advertising for the individual psychology, in spite of the impersonal relationship which is given with such a setup, must have deep roots in the American soul. And with this, we reach out for a historical explanation of the genesis of American advertising itself (for, so far as chronological priority and degree of development and intensity are concerned, advertising must be considered as an Americanism).

And here I would take into account what Max Weber and Ernst Tröltsch have called *Religionssoziologie*: the discipline which sees in economic and social developments ultimately the workings of the "only powerful lever of all civilization, religion" (as the Romantic philosopher Johann Jakob Bachofen has expressed it). Thus it was possible for these scholars* to explain modern capitalism from the religious background of Calvinism: this religion, which preaches a God far removed from man and his earthly doings, and, in spite of the inscrutability of Providence, still insists on the sanctity of work, with the implication of its possible influence on the decisions of Providence: this has encouraged a program of work for work's sake (and of capital for capital's sake), according to which the individual must work as if God had selected his soul for salvation—in the hope that, perhaps, the resultant increase in worldly goods may be a sign of this selection.

----

* Among the later exponents of this doctrine may be mentioned Herbert Schöffler, who has explained certain typical features of Anglo-Saxon civilization (such as sports, freedom of parliamentary debate, etc.) from the "religious-sociological" basis of English life.

Thus the most transcendent of religions has, paradoxically enough, served to encourage the pursuit of the most secular of interests. Now, in America, as is well known, the Calvinism of the early English immigrants was overlaid by deistic teachings, which proved more congenial to the Americans than did the Genevan doctrines, because of an even greater emphasis on human values at the expense of concern with the divine, and an even more optimistic picture of the universe.

As far as the field of advertising itself is concerned, I would say (and I do not know whether or not this point has been made before) that the *Reklame-Gesinnung*, as the Germans would call it, the "advertising mentality," is not alone due to the Calvinistic-deistic business-mindedness which encourages the increase of goods for the sake of increase. In order to explain the tremendous development of advertising, which today is an industry in itself, we must take into account a second factor, itself related to religious Protestant impulses: this is the "preaching mentality" which has impressed so many observers of American life (one thinks immediately of certain observations of André Siegfried), and which is based on the conviction that every man, possessed as he is of the divine spark of reason (in this connection we may remember the words of de Tocqueville, who observed that the Americans are the most Cartesian of peoples), has only to be taught what is the good in order to accept it and to pursue it to the ever-increasing perfection of his nature. There is no doubt that, to a great extent, present-day advertising has taken over the role of the teacher of morals who, by an appeal to their reason, points out the good to his pupils, confident, like Socrates, that man needs only to be shown the good in order to do it—though, given the weakness of human nature, he must constantly be reminded of his real advantage, lest he slip back into apathy; the advertiser, like the preacher, must "create the demand" for the better. This belief in the teachability of man and in his readiness, if duly and regularly aroused, to improve his condition (here, of course, his material condition) is everywhere evident in advertising: "You can have what you want if you save for it"* and "Do not look back. Past is past. You are over the dam. Look forward!" are exhortations appearing in banking advertisements; "I can resist no temptation!" are the opening words of an advertisement for a digestion aid. Not always, of course, is the didactic note so strongly in evidence, but it would not, perhaps, be wrong to see a sermon in all advertising:† the advertiser is one who preaches the material good with confidence in the ever-possible increase of material welfare and in the ever-possible self-perfectibility of man in his rational pursuit thereof.

---

* It is to be noted that, in this example, we have to do with the "gnomic *you*." Here, then, is still one more possibility of the English pronoun, which

is equivalent, not only to French *tu* and *vous*, but also to *on*—though, even in its gnomic use, the personal overtones are not entirely lacking.

†A particularly interesting example of the directly moralizing note is offered by a series of advertisements for Seagram's whiskies which preach the virtues of moderate drinking! It was, perhaps, shrewdly calculated by the firm that such admonitions would do nothing to decrease the sales of their products; the result might, indeed, be to increase them, because of the tacit flattering assumption that consumers of this particular brand are persons of decorum (if not of distinction).

And, true to Protestant sectarian tradition, every advertiser preaches a gospel of his own. Voltaire has said: "Tout protestant est un pape, une bible à la main" [Every Protestant is a pope, with a Bible in his hand]. Similarly, every advertiser points you to his product as the only way to salvation.

And, in his preaching, the advertiser must always envisage the individual listener, just as the Protestant pastor seeks to press his truths home to each individual member of his congregation. Indeed, in our "for you," we have a phrase which can, perhaps, be traced back directly to statements of dogma made from the pulpit. When the pastor declares that "Christ has suffered death for *you*, for the liberation of *your* soul from sin," he is presenting this divine intervention as working for each individual separately, and his "you" is interpreted by each of his listeners as "for me personally."*

---

*The reader may recall having heard in his youth the evangelical hymn "Whosoever will may come" with the final line: "*Whosoever* meaneth *me*."

Here we have not so much an exhortation as a promise. And a comparable note of promise is present in our advertisement—which, obviously, does not belong to the didactic type noted above; here, the command to buy is present only in the sublimated form of the "second glass" inviting to drink; the emphasis is on the riches of the earth waiting to be enjoyed by man. In a secularized, laicized civilization, where human activity in pursuit of material welfare is not shunned but accepted as a blessing from God, it was easily possible for the mysticism of the pastor's "for you" to become diluted: material welfare, too, could be seen as something willed by God "for you," "for me," personally; there is only a small step from the optimistic preaching of the boundless, the paradisiac possibilities of divine goodness which man must only be ready to accept, to the optimistic preaching of the boundless, the paradisiac possibilities of earthly well-being which, likewise, man must simply allow himself to enjoy.*

---

*It may be noted that the first advertisements to appear regularly in American newspapers (in the middle of the nineteenth century) were those of patent medicines, with their claims of miraculous efficacy. It is highly significant that the industry of advertising had its inception in an appeal to the age-old craving to be saved by magic from the ills and shortcomings of the flesh.

With its insistence on the *you*, advertising is closer to deism than to Calvinism: whereas (Calvinistic) capitalism, with its sternness and austerity, tends to ignore the consumer, bent as it is toward what Weber has called an *innerweltliche Askese*—that is, toward production for production's sake, for the sake of the morality of the producer and for the glory of God ("Work in order to acquire riches for God!" as Richard Baxter said)—advertising, the byproduct of capitalism, takes into account the consumer's right: his right to happiness; it is "for him," for his enjoyment of earthly pleasure, that the effort of production has been made. Advertising appeals to the eudaemonism of the consumer.*

---

*The two tendencies, Calvinistic austerity and eudaemonistic deism, are often met side by side within the individual American—who can be at one moment the *Pflicht- und Arbeitsmensch* [the man of duty and work] and at another the pagan enjoyer of earthly goods. In the features of the American man and woman there is often revealed a sternness of purpose—which is given a lie by their (Arcadian) happy smile. Historical conditions have made of the American a somewhat "relaxed pioneer": a pioneer who manages also to "take it easy."

Professor Alexander Rüstow, in a witty article,[20] characterizes the mentality of the modern capitalist by ascribing to him the implicit attitude: "To produce and to sell belong to the elect, to buy and to consume, to the damned." (He also brings out the fact that the capitalist is unable to enjoy the fruits of his own labor, and compares him to the cormorant which is used by the Chinese fishermen to catch fish, the bird being prevented from swallowing them by means of an iron band around its throat.) Advertising, on the other hand, seems to scream from all the billboards and posters: "To the buyer and consumer belongs the paradise!" This eudaemonistic deism with which advertising is informed is the same philosophy underlying the faith of Adam Smith, who believed that, by the "invisible hand" of Providence, the private egotisms of all human individuals are welded together into the common good. While, in the offices and factories, the *Pflicht- und Arbeitsmensch* may fulfill his relentlessly austere duties, in the shops and on the streets advertising proclaims the right of man to the "pursuit of happiness." It is this basic right of the American which is pictorially emblazoned in the many pictures, lining the highways and byways, of man enjoying the goods of life. American advertising thus becomes one of the greatest forces working to perpetuate a national ideal: in their own way the pictures of happy family life or of private enjoyment have a conservative function comparable to that of the statues in the old Greek Polis; though the American images are not embodiments of gods and heroes, they preach an exemplary well-being as an ideal accessible to every man in the American community.

While I do not claim that, in "From the sunkist groves of California / Fresh for you," which contains the impersonal-personal "you" of the preacher, the religious implications are still present to the mind of the public (or were present to that of the advertiser), there is nevertheless to be found in the sentence, it seems to me, the deistic, optimistic confidence in a world-order in which Nature works for the good of the individual man and in which helpful, busy mankind joins with Nature in creating, without stint and with the modesty that comes from acting in harmony with the universal laws of Nature, all possibilities of relaxation for the fellow individual who is asked only to follow the precepts of reason by taking unto himself the gifts of Nature. We have, it is true, shown also that the utopian hopes for mankind which are suggested are somewhat toned down by a feeling of *desengaño*, but, in the interstices between paradisiac dreams and harsh reality, the gracious and gratuitous flowers of poetry, aware of their own unreality, spring up here and there, offering glimpses of an oasis in the aridity of a modern mechanized and pragmatic world. Thus our advertisement, designed to promote the retail sale of oranges, offers a colorful image of quiet Nature to refresh the city dwellers in their environment of hustle and drabness.

APROPOS OF
'LA VIE DE MARIANNE'

Written in the form of an open letter to the distinguished phenomenological critic Georges Poulet, this essay pits Spitzer's interpretive
method, based as it is on both historical and formal analysis, against
the atemporal and antiformalist philosophical approach for which
Poulet achieved considerable fame as a critic during the early 1950's.
Although Spitzer here treats his colleague Poulet a good bit more politely than he did those other colleagues at Johns Hopkins with
whom he debated in print, he attempts to refute the very premises
that guide Poulet's work. To do so, he concentrates on a single essay
by Poulet—the chapter on Marivaux from *La Distance intérieure*.
As in most of his criticism, Poulet in this chapter isolates what he sees
as a generative philosophical experience from which all the writing
of a particular author supposedly springs.

Spitzer's own critical stance is so far removed from Poulet's that
this confrontation between the two helps define the method, the
biases, and the purposes of each critic in a particularly striking way.
Whereas Poulet establishes his perspective a priori and then moves to
particular texts, Spitzer claims to be empirical and to move from
particularities to larger generalizations. Whereas Poulet treats the
consciousness of the writer under consideration as his object of inquiry and draws his evidence from brief passages drawn from this
writer's whole œuvre, Spitzer respects the individuality of particular
texts and concentrates here wholly on Marivaux's major novel, *La
Vie de Marianne*. Whereas Poulet views writing as emanating from
deep, individual existential experiences, Spitzer views literature as
rooted in the thick of history. Whereas Poulet removes a writer's

philosophical statements from their fictional and dramatic contexts
to create a coherent system of thought, Spitzer refuses to systematize
such statements and instead shows that they must be interpreted by
means of a close examination of their contexts. Whereas Poulet
stresses universals, finding in Marivaux an attitude toward time that
can manifest itself in diverse periods, Spitzer concentrates on vari-
ables and particularities contingent upon specific historical moments; in rebutting Poulet, he sees in Marivaux's novel a particular
stance toward time that is rooted in the historical conditions of early
eighteenth-century France and in the specific genre, the adventure
novel, that Marivaux is reworking.

A contemporary critic would show considerably more skepticism
than either Poulet or Spitzer does about how reliably one can interpret the larger generalizations that a first-person narrative such as
Marivaux's novel seeks to express. Yet Spitzer's argument against
Poulet remains an eloquent defense both of his interpretive method
and of his faith that this method can reveal to the modern reader
both the meaning of a literary work and its relationship to its historical milieu and its literary tradition.

This essay was first published under the title "A propos de *La Vie
de Marianne* (Lettre à M. Georges Poulet)" in *Romanic Review*, 44
(1953): 102–26; it was reprinted in Spitzer's *Romanische Literaturstudien: 1936–1956* (Tübingen, 1959), pp. 248–76. It was translated by Nancy Ruttenburg for inclusion in this volume.

Apropos of 'La Vie de Marianne'
(Letter to Georges Poulet)

My dear new friend and colleague:

In the course of your first semester at Johns Hopkins University (and our first semester of close and enthusiastic collaboration), you expressed the desire on several occasions to attempt the integration and cross-fertilization of our two "methods"—a desire that in itself bears witness to the modesty and integrity of the true scholar. In effect, you said that you thought you had "found a method" but that it seemed to you "to destroy the work of art," whereas you acknowledged that mine had the advantage of avoiding this pitfall (I suppose that I owe your silence concerning my lack of philosophical culture or philosophical affiliation to your great courtesy). Therefore, in the following lines I will undertake to discuss—with the utmost goodwill, but not without that passion that can only reaffirm the bonds already uniting us—one of your articles, that which you devoted to Marivaux in your volume *La Distance intérieure*.[1] To the subject which you treat according to the "existentialist" or "a priori" method (since you seek the a priori that is your author's point of departure), I shall apply my own method, which I like to call the critique "immanent in the text" [*critique immanente à l'œuvre*].

First, however, let me say that our two methods seem to me to have this common characteristic, that they see the object—even the literary object—directly and not in the oblique manner of the biographers, the seekers of origins, the historians of ideas and of civilizations, in a word, of the entire historical school. Of all the critical literature on Marivaux, your study—so concise, so enriched with quotations from the text—eliminates most thoroughly the *allotria* despised by Benedetto Croce[2] and speaks Marivaux's language, and not merely about him. Since we both tend to describe "things" before dealing with their "causes"—you by examining the feeling of existence [*le sentiment de l'existence*] that informs Marivaux's writings, and I by examining a particular work of his—our two methods might indeed serve as controls to each other, and I am indebted to you for that suggestion whose cogency I am sure to encounter again and again as I proceed.

I begin with a brief résumé of your article: Mind in Marivaux is primarily a vacancy—"a nothing," inertia (*ID*, pp. 3–5), in which only astonishment provoked by an event external to it creates movement, the movement of the consciousness of a feeling (*sentio, ergo sum*) [I feel, therefore I am]. It is love, the result of chance, that is the great surprise for the being rising up out of nonexistence (*ID*, pp. 5–8). "Without a past to sustain them, without identity, without temporality, Marivaudian beings know neither who they are nor where they are" (*ID*, pp. 8–11). "The actual being seems less a being than a plurality, a *mêlée* of beings, . . . a mixture *in which* one is and *which* one is, a state in which one can neither isolate anything nor embrace anything. Pure confusion" (*ID*, pp. 11–13). Marivaux recapitulates himself in the profundity and intensity that he gives to the instant (*ID*, pp. 13–17). There is no knowledge of oneself outside of that which gives instantaneous feeling (*ID*, pp. 17–20). The instant includes neither the past nor the future: "I know not where I am" corresponds to "I know where I am going" (*ID*, pp. 20–23). For that reason, in Marivaux there is no "temporal perspective." However, if in Marivaux the being is at each point different from himself, yet "there is no hiatus whatever between these different moments. It is like a continuous slope." Time in Marivaux is, in the manner of Bergson, made of a continuous surge which in new moments incessantly prolongs its inventive duration. And by a singular turn, does not the writer who had appeared to us the writer of the instantaneous par excellence now appear to us the least instantaneous that could be, whose work consists only in the tracing of a temporal line in which the point of the instant disappears? But Marivaux is precisely both this and that, the point and the line—a point which extends itself and prolongs itself, becoming a line; an instant which overtakes itself and continues itself and which is transformed into time—time which risks remaining perpetually that of pure succession, for between the events which take place within it, no connection is discovered, and one loses oneself then in an indefinite movement in which, when all is said and done, nothing survives except a sort of vaporous memory of all that has happened. And it is that sort of time along which the novels of Marivaux end by evaporating. Marivaux can best render the limited duration of love, capable of sustaining a relative unity, in his drama. His style perfectly reflects an "instantaneous plurality" that shifts to a "continuous plurality": spontaneous, naive language, the "play of time and of chance," becoming a "play of words" (*ID*, pp. 23–28).

First an objection, suggested by your text itself. How is it that the writer of the instantaneous, of the interrupted line and the broken curve, of the staccato and the stippled—the writer whose style I would readily describe as rococo—is suddenly transformed into a Bergsonian writer whose *élan vital* necessarily translates itself into creative, uninterrupted curves, and precisely because there must be continuity? (You recall the Bergsonian image, which goes back to Saint Augustine, of a verse or a melody comprehensible only in its unity, in its *élan*.) By your saying "a singular turn," I suspect you suffer some doubt here, a twinge of intellectual conscience. You seemed to sense that a point cannot by definition become a line, or the discontinuous become the continuous; the being that has neither past nor future and for whom nothing relates to anything else cannot be the hero of a novel, that is to say, of a genre which functions as "a mirror carried along a high road" [*miroir le long d'une route*].[3] Your assertion concerning the Bergsonism of Marivaux ("So soon?" said a character of Offenbach's) somewhat veils the reality. "A continuous flow which in new moments incessantly prolongs its inventive duration" (*ID*, p. 26)—doesn't this acknowledge that, in addition to the instantaneous which you have so subtly observed, there exists at times for the Marivaudian being a creative and continuous element that, while perhaps not connecting one moment to another, still represents a steady force directing that being at every moment of his life? In like manner, from the humus of many different species of plant there arises a number of creatures—creatures who, without any connection one to the other, still bear witness to that single power of nature animating them all. In addition to the alternative "continuous-discontinuous," then, we should consider the "watering-can" paradigm: the individual streams of water, each separate from the other, nevertheless constitute a single stream or flow of water.

It is at this juncture that the "immanentist" method [*la méthode "immanentiste"*] must enter the lists—the method that respects the integrity and the unity of particular works and does not "destroy" them through reflections on the writer's work as a whole. As a basis for discussion, then, I will select a single book of Marivaux, a masterpiece from which you extract a number of compelling quotations, one of those novels about which you claim that the temporality seems "to vanish": *La Vie de Marianne; ou, Les Aventures de Madame la Comtesse de . . .* [*The Life of Marianne, or the Adventures of the Countess of . . .*].[4] If your analysis of Marivaudian existence as preexisting Marivaux's œuvre is correct, it will apply to this particular work as well. And, since you have deliberately limited your study to "human time" and to "interior distance" in Marivaux, your observations on those subjects should be rigorously applicable to *Marianne*. It is understood that the "a priori" and "immanentist" methods should account for the same facts and follow the same course (from the detail to the whole and vice versa), even if in the formal presentations of our analyses we adopt very different procedures (you moving from the whole to the detail, I from the detail to the whole). In the investigations that preceded our presentations, we made use of the same "hermeneutic circle" (detail to whole to detail) characteristic of every philological or historical study. You examined Marivaux's œuvre and I am expounding a particular work of this author: the œuvre should reflect the particular work and the latter elucidate the former.

Now, the contradiction that struck me in your examination of Marivaudian existence renders *Marianne* inexplicable. That is, how can a central character like Marianne support a novel of such length if Marivaudian existence consists only of discontinuous moments? While remaining within the parameters of this particular work, I will here suggest a *detail*, a consistent stylistic detail, that might throw new light on this work (and perhaps on the œuvre as well), for according to my experience, such consistent stylistic details correspond to an element of the soul [*âme*] of the work and of the writer. In rereading *Marianne*, I was surprised by the frequency of terms such as *heart* [*cœur*] and *soul* used in ways akin to "courage, bravery, valor, magnanimity, virtue, steadfastness, energy, constancy, strength, pride, resoluteness"—implications that these terms no longer have and that the linguist-historian must take into consideration. Permit me to present an extensively abridged list of significant passages, omitting, naturally, those passages in which *heart* is used to signify "that organ that feels love" or "kindheartedness":

{Marianne expresses her unwillingness to become a servant. M. de Climal responds:} Eh! mon enfant, . . . je vous loue de penser comme cela, c'est une marque que vous avez *du cœur*, et cette *fierté-là* est permise. . . . {Marianne adds:} Et il est bon de vous dire que, toute jeune que j'étais, j'avais *l'âme un peu fière*. (pp. 44–45)

[Ah! my child, . . . I praise you for your way of thinking. It is a sign that you *have spirit*, and this kind of *pride* is permissible. . . . And I should tell you that, as young as I was, I did have *a rather proud spirit*.]

{Marianne, throwing money Climal has given her on the table:} Le voici, ajoutai-je en le jetant sur une table avec une action vive et rapide qui exprimait bien les mouvements d'un *jeune petit cœur fier, vertueux* et insulté. (p. 128)

["There it is," I added, throwing it on the table in an ardent and hasty manner that well expressed the sentiments of a *young, proud heart, virtuous* and insulted.]

Cette idée d'être véritablement aimée de Valville eut tant de charmes, m'inspira des *sentiments si désintéressés et si raisonnables*, me fit penser si *noblement*; enfin, *le cœur* est de si bonne composition quand il est content en pareil cas, que vous allez être édifiée du parti que je pris. Oui, vous allez voir une action qui prouva que Valville avait eu raison de me respecter.

Je n'étais rien, je n'avais rien qui pût me faire considérer; mais à ceux qui n'ont ni rang ni richesses, qui en imposent, il leur reste *une âme*, et c'est beaucoup; c'est quelquefois plus que le rang et la richesse, elle peut faire face à tout. (p. 176)

[The idea of being truly loved by Valville was so utterly delightful, inspired me with *such selfless and proper sentiments*, made me think so *nobly*; in short, *the heart* is of such a pleasing disposition when thus delighted that you will be satisfied with the side I have taken. Yes, you will witness an action that proved Valville was right to respect me.

I was nothing, and possessed nothing that might render me significant; but to those who have neither rank nor riches thrust upon them, *a soul* remains, and that is a great deal; it is sometimes more than rank and wealth, and it can stand up against anything.]

Je venais de m'engager à quelque chose de si *généreux*, je venais de montrer . . . tant de franchise, tant de reconnaissance, de donner une si grande idée de *mon cœur*, que ces deux dames en avaient pleuré d'admiration pour moi. Oh! voyez avec quelle complaisance, je devais regarder *ma belle âme*. (p. 188)

[I had just acted with *such generosity*, I had shown . . . so much sincerity, so much gratitude, so much pride in *my heart*, so that the two ladies had wept in admiration of me. Oh! see with what satisfaction I was entitled to look upon *my beautiful soul*.]

J'allais soutenir une terrible scène: je craignais de manquer de *courage*; je me craignais moi-même; j'avais peur que *mon cœur* ne servît lâchement ma bienfaitrice. (p. 189)

[I was about to endure a dreadful scene: I feared I would lack *courage*; I was frightened of myself and was afraid that *my heart* might poorly serve my benefactress.]

{Mme de Miran says of Marianne:} C'est *un cœur*, c'est *une âme*, une façon de penser qui vous étonnerait . . . *noble, généreuse et désintéressée* . . . j'ai vu d'elle des traits *de caractère* qui m'ont touchée jusqu'au fond du cœur. (pp. 311–12)

[She has *a heart, a soul*, a manner of thinking that would astonish you . . . *noble, generous, selfless* . . . I have seen in her traits *of character* that moved me to the very depths of my heart.]

{The same:} par son bon esprit, par les *qualités de l'âme*, et par la *noblesse* des procédés, elle est demoiselle autant qu'aucune fille, de quelque rang qu'elle soit, puisse l'être. . . . Il faut que cela soit dans le sang. (p. 317)

[by her good spirit, by her *soulful qualities*, and by her *noble* behavior, she is as much a lady as any other, whatever her rank is or may be. . . . It must be in the blood.]

{The minister judges Marianne thus:} La *noblesse* de vos parents est incertaine, mais celle de votre *cœur* est incontestable et je la préférerais, s'il fallait opter. (p. 325)

[The *nobility* of your parents is uncertain, but that of your *heart* is incontestable and this I would prefer, if I had to choose.]

We are not surprised to discover Mme Dorsin, in one of those episodic "portraits" that Marivaux inserted in his work as a counterpart to the unchanging portrait of the heroine painted throughout the novel, endowed with similar qualities, particularly of *heart* and of *soul*:

Mme Dorsin, à cet excellent *cœur* que je lui ai donné, à cet esprit si distingué qu'elle avait, joignait une *âme forte, courageuse et résolue*; de ces *âmes supérieures* à tout événement, dont la *hauteur* et la *dignité* ne plient sous aucun accident humain. (p. 221)

[Mme Dorsin, in addition to the excellent *heart* that I have attributed to her and to her distinguished mind, had a *powerful, courageous and resolute soul*, one of those *souls superior* in any circumstance whose *loftiness* and *dignity* yielded to no human accident.]

Here, character, nobleness, virtue, and courage are synonymous with stability, continuity, ethical standards, behavior consistent with itself and renewing itself at every moment, inner resources to which the individual can address himself at any moment of danger or distress. Marianne, at least, is therefore not the evanescent being that you represent as typically Marivaudian. She acknowledges a temporal line from which she will not deviate, despite the calculations, the faintheartedness, the coquetries, and the coyness of certain moments—a line, moreover, indicated first by her social advancement (for there can be no doubt that this nameless and originless Marianne will one day become the "Countess of . . . ," as the novel's title indicates), and second by her morality (it is the aged Marianne, full of the wisdom of maturity, who writes her life). Marianne becomes in the course of the novel what she already is by "blood," an aristocrat of the heart [*une aristocrate du cœur*]. Although she finds herself in situations throughout the novel that can have no connection with one another, Marianne nevertheless draws constantly on inner resources that, in the manner of the watering can, cultivate a way of acting "instantaneously," of handling these momentary situations. She becomes that which she is—she succeeds in realizing herself like the *Paysan parvenu*, except that, unlike this sort of fellow, she is no *parvenue*, no *arriviste*. She is, rather, a woman who truly arrives, who attains her real point of departure—that is, her nature as a born aristocrat. The continuity of admirable character, at once completely Spanish ("I am who I am" was a device of chivalric characters of Spanish drama that a Stendhal would have appreciated) and yet reminiscent of Corneille, reveals its existence within the "chance" events (scenes of surprise, of recognition, etc.) coming from without.*

---

*Actually, Marivaux's usage of such terms as *cœur* (heart) and *âme* (soul) associated with "noble birth" is exactly like Corneille's:

Rodrigue, as-tu *du cœur*? (*Le Cid*, act 1, sc. 6)

[Rodrigue, are you *courageous*?]

[Il] soutient *avec cœur et magnanimité*
L'honneur de sa *naissance* et de sa dignité. (*Pompée*, act 3, sc. 1)

[He sustains *with heart and magnanimity*
The honor of his *birth* and of his dignity.]

Je suis jeune, il est vrai; mais aux *âmes bien nées*
Le valeur n'attend pas le nombre des années. (*Le Cid*, act 2, sc. 2)

[I am young, yes; but for *souls of noble lineage*
Valor is not based on the number of years.]

That is, it reveals itself in the character of the *resisting* woman, active by virtue of her resistance (Marianne puts herself forward less than the picaresque Jacob [hero of Marivaux's novel *Le Paysan parvenu*]), at times to the point of stoicism: Marianne's "activity" is to say *no* in essential situations. She will say no to the position as servant that is offered her, no to the dubious propositions of M. de Climal, no to an impossible husband that Valville's relations offer her, no to marriage with her beloved when she envisions its consequences for her benefactress, no to the hasty marriage proposed by the officer, no to the convent. These are the negative responses to the temptations of chance that constitute the steps of the labyrinthine path she imperturbably follows, as if guided by Ariadne's thread or some mystical inner star.*

---

* This is precisely the metaphor that you chose, only you use it to withhold Ariadne's thread from the Marivaudian character: "He has lost the thread of his very existence. He wants to recover it, to renew it; he feels he must regain his vital continuity. He cannot. Ariadne's clue (and that of the Fates) is broken. He is no longer a habitual being; he is nothing more now than an actual being, lost among the turnings of the labyrinth" (*ID*, p. 10). But Marianne never loses the thread of her existence! You also put forward certain of Marianne's expressions: "Quand je serais *tombée des nues*, je n'aurais pas été plus étourdie que je l'étais" [Had I *fallen from the skies*, I could not have been more giddy], or "C'était pour moi *l'Empire de la Lune*; je n'étais plus à moi" (*DI*, p. 12) [For me it (Paris) was *the Empire of the Moon*; I was no longer myself] in order to comment as follows: "Without identity, without memory, without origin, fallen from the skies, the Marivaudian being lands upon an indescribable world. Nothing in it is recognizable; consequently nothing in it is intelligible. Nothing within it is related to anything else. It is the Empire of the Moon and the Kingdom of the Actual" (*ID*, p. 12).
But surely one can permit a little provincial of fifteen-and-a-half, disembarking alone in Paris, to be momentarily disoriented. She will not be for long. Do we not also have her testimony that the *beau monde* in the Parisian church seemed to her not in the least unfamiliar, and that, on the contrary, she felt on familiar ground there? You treat the following scene (the quarrel between Marianne and Dutour, which the latter initiates) in a similar fashion. Marianne says:

Je sentais tant de mouvements, tant de confusion, tant de dépit, que je ne sa-
vais par où commencer pour parler; c'était d'ailleurs une situation bien
neuve pour moi que *la mêlée* où je me trouvais. Je n'en avais jamais tant vu.
(*La Vie de Marianne*, pp. 59–60)

[I felt so much agitation, so much confusion, so much spite, that I knew not
where to begin to speak; it was moreover a situation quite new to me, *the
confusion* in which I found myself. I have never seen anything like it.]

You comment: "movements of all sorts immediately spring forth from all
sides to entangle their threads within a mind which they stun with their agitation and their number. . . . All these elements come together at the same
time and yet do not form an ensemble. They fill up the whole, without ever
becoming a whole. A staggering mixture that invades the mind. . . . Pure
confusion" (*ID*, p. 13). Here, I would ask you to observe that the paragraph
of Marivaux which you cite continues thus:

A *la fin*, quand mes mouvements furent un peu *éclaircis*, la colère se déclara
la plus forte; mais ce fut une colère si franche et si étourdie, qu'il n'y avait
qu'une fille innocente de ce dont on l'accusait qui pût l'avoir. (p. 60)

[*Finally*, when my feelings were somewhat *clarified*, anger triumphed over
all; but this was an anger so frank and so thoughtless that only a girl innocent of that of which she had been accused could have felt it.]

And the good Mme Dutour, baffled, begins to appease the young hothead,
and the scene ends in tears and benevolence. That is, Marianne succeeds;
she wins a victory. Marianne by definition is a character who leaves the fray
invincible. I still maintain that the "Où suis-je?" "Laissez-moi me reconnaître," "Je ne me reconnais plus" (*DI*, pp. 9–11) [Where am I? Let me find
my bearings. I no longer know myself] that seem to you so characteristic of
Marivaux, if it is Marianne who uses them, act as a prelude to the moment
when she will know how to clarify the situation and will know where and
who she is.

Marianne, the secular heroine, "sustains a dreadful scene" like the
martyr Eulalie of the venerable Old French poem "sustains" torture.[5]
Her "actions" (refusals, renouncements) prove the noble texture of
which her being is made. *La Vie de Marianne* is beautiful and certainly the first French novel to feature the secular heroism of the
proud and virtuous woman (in Spanish literature, one could cite as a
predecessor the *Gitanilla* of Cervantes) left to herself in the midst of
the torrent of life, stronger than the men who surround her or pursue
her because strong within herself; she is the ancestor of a long literary
line in France and elsewhere, of which a late offshoot is the heroine
of *Gone with the Wind*.*

*Preciosa is, in fact, fifteen years old like Marianne, and "aunque de quince años . . . soy ya vieja en los pensamientos"[6] [although fifteen years old . . . (I) am already old in my thoughts]—that is to say, a perfect example of the *topos* that Ernst Robert Curtius called *puer senex* [boy as old man].[7] Again, like Preciosa, and in this regard unlike Richardson's Pamela, who was conceived in a more democratic fashion, Marianne *becomes* before our eyes what she also *is*, in the sense that her high birth determines her noble character. I interpret this respect for the literary convention (Cervantian) on Marivaux's part as a sign that the medieval idea of a preexisting harmony between the social state and moral value, the image of divine harmony, is not yet weakened for our author, who manifests no revolutionary impulses. We find the same preestablished harmony between state and value in Marivaux's comedy, for example in *Le Jeu de l'amour et du hasard* [The Game of Love and Chance], whose title should not mislead us: at bottom this is a play of love and of the natural elective affinity of souls *born* noble that overcome the hazards of disguise. By the fourth scene of the first act, the problem of the play is posed: "Voyons si *leurs cœurs* ne les avertiraient pas de ce qu'ils valent" [Let us see if *their hearts* would not tell them what they are worth]. We find here the characteristic term *cœur* in the sense of "innate nobleness"; and when Dorante reveals his noble identity to Silvia, who loved him as a manservant, she cries out: "Ah! je vois *clair* dans mon *cœur*" (act 2, sc. 12) [Ah! I see *clearly* in my *heart*].

Let us now examine a bit more closely the history of this heart and this soul. Where does this inner strength of Marianne's, her "romantic" pride, come from? The answer is that she is *born* with it, and the author, a democrat at heart, leaves no doubt that though Marianne is "highborn," she would nevertheless have been what she is without this "birthright" (see the passages quoted from pp. 176 and 325 above). *La Vie de Marianne* is therefore not a novel of development or of education (a *Bildungsroman* of the type of *Wilhelm Meister*, attributable in the last analysis to the Pietist movement, which exalted inner perfection) but a novel of "explication," if I may invent the term, a novel in which an innate inner strength is explicated: Marianne is "née coiffée" [born under a lucky star] as two lower-class women, Mme Dutour (on p. 58) and the maid who had abducted her from the convent (on p. 296), vulgarly express it. Marivaux attaches more importance to "nature" than to "nurture" (education). According to him, we are born (and particularly women are born) arrogant, proud, and vain, a birthright that conjoins with our character as well as with virtue. Marivaux stands with moralists like La Rochefoucauld and Nietzsche in this pessimistic psychology:

Le plus pressé pour nous, c'est nous-même, c'est-à-dire, *notre orgueil*; car notre orgueil et nous, ce n'est qu'un, au lieu que nous et notre vertu, c'est deux. N'est-ce pas, Madame? (p. 96)

[The most important thing for us is our own self, that is to say, *our pride*; for our pride and our self are one thing, whereas our self and our virtue are two. Isn't that so, Madame?]

Marianne in particular, "toute jeune qu'[elle] était, . . . avait l'âme un peu fière" (p. 45) [young as she was, . . . had a rather proud spirit]. And the aged Marianne who recounts her adventures is well aware that at bottom the inherent character of woman's mind is vanity:

{Marianne at the church contemplating the *beau monde* in the upper part of the choir, where she had escaped in order to prepare her appearance:} Et moi, je devinais la pensée de toutes ces personnes-là sans aucun effort; mon instinct ne voyait rien là qui ne fût de sa connaissance, et n'en était pas plus délié pour cela; car il ne faut pas s'y méprendre, ni estimer ma pénétration plus qu'elle ne vaut.

Nous avons deux sortes d'esprits, nous autres femmes. Nous avons d'abord le nôtre, qui est celui que nous recevons de la nature, celui qui nous sert à raisonner, suivant le degré qu'il a, qui devient ce qu'il peut, et qui ne sait rien qu'avec le temps.

Et puis nous en avons encore un autre, qui est à part du nôtre, et qui peut se trouver dans les femmes les plus sottes. C'est *l'esprit que la vanité de plaire nous donne*, et qu'on appelle, autrement dit, *la coquetterie*.

Oh! celui-là, pour être instruit, n'attend pas le nombre des années, il est fin dès qu'il est venu; dans les choses de son ressort il a toujours la théorie de ce qu'il voit mettre en pratique. C'est *un enfant de l'orgueil qui naît tout élevé*, qui manque d'abord d'audace, mais qui n'en pense pas moins. Je crois qu'on peut lui enseigner des grâces et de l'aisance; mais il n'apprend que la forme, et jamais le fond. Voilà mon avis. (pp. 70–71)

[As for myself, I guessed the thoughts of all those people there without any effort; my instinct perceived nothing that wasn't already familiar to me and wasn't any finer for it; for one must not be mistaken, nor estimate my insight at more than it is worth.

We have two sorts of minds, we women. We have first our own, the one that we receive from nature and that allows us to reason to whatever degree, that becomes whatever it can, and that can know nothing except through time.

And then we have yet another, apart from our own, that is found even in the most foolish women. This is the *mind that the desire to please gives us* and that, in a word, we call *coquetry*.

Oh! This mind does not require many years to be instructed, for it is complete as soon as it arrives; in the things within its province it always has the theory of what it seeks to put into practice. It is a *child of pride born full-*

grown, who at first lacks audacity but does not think less of it. I believe that one can teach the mind grace and elegance, but it learns only the form and never the substance. That is my opinion.]

This is a text remarkable for its undeceived psychological lucidity (pride has a mind, a mind that "thinks," "guesses," "perceives," has "insight," has a "theory"), but also decisive for what concerns us here: the problem of inner continuity, human time. The mind behind woman's vanity "does not require many years to be instructed, for it is complete as soon as it arrives," "is born full-grown," has a "substance" that does not need to be learned. It is an inherent given—the immediate fact of continuity—a line of thought and of straightforward, unalterable behavior. Marianne is a woman and therefore vain, therefore possessing the inherent mind that vanity provides as well as the psychological insight that penetrates the *beau monde* in which she, though never having seen it, feels "on familiar ground." This same spirit of pride becomes confounded with the proud redressing of virtue. We see it at work when Marianne is returning to her room after two terrible scenes, that in which her lover, Valville, had seen M. de Climal kneeling before her ("Voilà qui est fort joli, mademoiselle!" (p. 125) [This is mighty pretty, Mademoiselle!], and the other scene, following the first, in which she had sharply refused all of M. de Climal's "charities" and had thrown on the table his money and his cap, which she had in her possession:

L'objet qui m'occupa d'abord, vous allez croire que ce fut la malheureuse situation où je restais; non, cette situation ne regardait que ma vie; et ce qui m'occupa me regardait, moi.

Vous direz que je rêve de distinguer cela; point du tout: notre vie, pour ainsi dire, nous est moins chère que nous, que nos passions. A voir quelquefois ce qui se passe dans notre instinct là-dessus, on dirait que, pour être, il n'est pas nécessaire de vivre; que ce n'est que par accident que nous vivons, mais que c'est naturellement que nous sommes. On dirait que, lorsqu'un homme se tue par exemple, il ne quitte la vie que pour se sauver, que pour se débarrasser d'une chose incommode; ce n'est pas lui dont il ne veut plus, mais bien du fardeau qu'il porte. (p. 133)

[The thing that first occupied me was the unhappy situation in which I remained; no, that situation concerned only my life; and what occupied me concerned me, myself.

You will say that I dream in making such a distinction. Not at all: our life, so to speak, is less dear to us than ourselves or our passions. To sometimes see what happens in our instinct, one would say that in order to be, it is not necessary to live; that it is only by accident that we live, but that it is by nature that we are. One would say that when a man kills himself, for example, he leaves life only in order to save himself, in order to get rid of something bothersome. It is not himself that he is weary of, but rather the burden he bears.]

You yourself cited this essential text, but in a context that seems to me not to address the author's intention, at the end of your section 5, which deals with Marivaudian existence "in the instant." You preface this passage with these words: "Our being is a rapid sketch, an immediate gesture, a cry of astonishment that mounts to our lips. . . . At the same time a thousand thoughts traverse the troubled waters of our soul. All that is us; and it is only that which could be true and could be us. Let us receive it, let us live it in the instant in which one can live it. . . . Let us concern ourselves first of all with the moment in which we are; for man never is, except in the moment; he is never in time" (*ID*, p. 16). And you underscore in Marivaux's passage, between other passages, the phrase "pour être, il n'est pas nécessaire de vivre" (*DI*, p. 19) [in order to be, it is not necessary to live], which evidently is to link Marivaux's passage to your preamble. But it seems to me that here it is not a question of the opposition "moment"–"life," but of "life"–"passion," which is also the opposition between "to live" and "to be," as the passage on suicide, which you omitted, demonstrates: the man who kills himself cherishes his self (which he identifies with his passion to free himself from the burden of life) more than his life. Likewise, Marianne, concerned not with her exterior situation but with the attack on her pride in the form of Valville's disdainful remark, attaches more importance to her passion, her pride, than to the necessity of material subsistence. She says further on:

Il me méprise donc actuellement, il m'accuse de tout ce qu'il y a de plus affreux. . . . Et je pourrais excuser cet homme-là! J'aurais encore le *courage* de le voir! il faudrait que je fusse bien lâche, que j'eusse bien peu de *cœur*. (p. 134)

[And now he despises me, he accuses me of all that is most terrible. . . . And could I pardon such a man! Should I still have the *courage* to see him! I would have had to have been very cowardly, to have had very little *heart*.]

Courage, heart—pride, the eternal backbone of Marianne's character! If the passage gives us information about the author's intentions, it is certainly not the lived moment that he exalts but, as you say elsewhere, this "inventive duration" that the passion of pride

points to, consubstantial with and inherent in the woman "of genius." "We are naturally thus"—this (antievolutionary) linking of
being with nature is, moreover, a motif that recurs often in Marianne's story: it is due to her nature, to what is innate in her [*son in-
néité*], that she has the psychological perspicacity, the taste, the *politesse du cœur*, the *savoir faire*, the ability to keep her head in
unforeseen situations.

Psychological perspicacity: we have already read the passage (p.
70) that shows how Marianne comprehends instinctively, without
surprise, the *beau monde* that she had never before seen. Here is another where we see Marianne, a young woman on the threshold of
life, already distinguishing the difference between a lover and a
friend, and her perspicacity is attributed by the author himself to the
lessons of "nature" (Marianne is no Emma Bovary, a victim of
novels):

Il se pourrait bien faire que cet homme-là {M. de Climal} m'aimât comme
un amant aime une maîtresse; car, enfin, j'en avais vu, des amants, dans
mon village, j'avais entendu parler d'amour, j'avais même déjà lu quelques
romans à la dérobée; et tout cela, *joint aux leçons que la nature nous donne,*
m'avait du moins fait sentir qu'un amant était bien différent d'un ami. (p.
52)

[It could well have been that that man {M. de Climal} loved me as a lover
loves a mistress; because I had seen lovers in my village, and I had heard talk
of love, I had even read some novels surreptitiously; and all this, *together
with the lessons that nature gives us,* made me at least sense that a lover was
very different from a friend.]

Taste is another gift of nature with which time has nothing to do—
a type of platonic *anamnesis* where the soul recaptures its pre-
individual past:

{Marianne is repelled by the vulgarity of Mme Dutour:} Dites-moi *d'où cela
venait?* Où est-ce que j'avais pris mes délicatesses? Etaient-elles *dans mon
sang?* cela se pourrait bien; venaient-elles du séjour que j'avais fait à Paris?
cela se pourrait encore: il y a *des âmes perçantes à qui il n'en faut pas beaucoup montrer pour les instruire,* et qui, sur le peu qu'elles voient, soupçon-
nent *tout d'un coup* tout ce qu'elles pourraient voir.
   La mienne avait le sentiment subtil, je vous assure, surtout dans les
choses de sa vocation, comme était le monde. Je ne connaissais personne à
Paris, je n'en avais vu que les rues, mais dans ces rues il y avait des personnes
de toutes espèces, il y avait des carrosses, et dans ces carrosses un monde qui
m'était très nouveau, mais point étranger. Et sans doute, il y avait en moi un
goût naturel, qui n'attendait que ces objets-là pour s'y pendre, de sorte que,

quand je les voyais, *c'était comme si j'avais rencontré ce que je cherchais*. (p. 48)

[Tell me *where it came from*? Where did I acquire my delicacy? Was it *in my blood*? That could very well have been. Did it come from the trip I took to Paris? That again might have been the case. There are *insightful souls to whom it is not necessary to show much in order to instruct them*, and who, on the basis of the little that they do see, *suddenly* surmise all that they could see.

Mine had this subtlety of feeling, I assure you, especially for things that concerned it, as did the world. I knew no one in Paris, I had only seen the streets, but in those streets there were people of all kinds, there were coaches, and in these coaches a world that was very new to me, yet not at all foreign. And without doubt, there was in me a *natural taste* that awaited only those particular things in order to make itself known, such that when I saw them, *it was as if I had found what I was looking for*.]

Politesse du cœur is only an avatar of taste; it is, in effect, the aesthetic aspect of morality:

{"Those secret depths of feeling" of which Mme de Miran boasts:} Pour moi, *je fus au fait*; les gens qui ont eux-mêmes un peu de *noblesse de cœur* se connaissent en égards de cette espèce, et remarquent bien ce qu'on fait pour eux. . . . C'est que *notre âme est haute*, et que tout ce qui a un air de respect pour *sa dignité* la pénètre et l'enchante. (p. 158)

[For my part, *I came to understand*; the people who themselves have a little *nobleness of heart* are quick-sighted in observing it in others, and notice what one does for them. . . . *For our soul is lofty*, and everything that has an air of respect for *its dignity* penetrates and enchants it.]

Savoir faire in strange surroundings results from "natural taste," which encourages you to feel at ease and to demonstrate your worth:

Quelque inusité que fût pour moi le service qu'elle {la femme de chambre de Mme de Fare qui vient habiller Marianne} allait me rendre, je m'y prêtai, je pense, d'aussi bonne grâce que *s'il m'avait été familier*. Il fallait bien soutenir mon rang, et c'étaient là de ces *choses que je saisissais on ne peut pas plus vite*; j'avais *un goût naturel*, ou, si vous voulez, je ne sais quelle *vanité délicate* qui *me les apprenait tout d'un coup*, et ma femme de chambre ne me sentit point novice. (p. 255) {You will notice the "atemporal" continuity of this natural taste and its relationship with vanity.}

[However obsolete this service that she {Mme de Fare's maid who is coming to dress Marianne} rendered was for me, I lent myself to it, I think, with as good a grace *as if it had been familiar to me*. I had to uphold my rank and behave consistently with my present circumstances; *these things I was instantly sensible of*; I had a *natural taste* or, if you will, some sort of *delicate pride*, that *taught me at once how to behave*, and my maid did not think me at all a novice.]

{M. de Climal kisses Marianne's hand:} Façon de faire qui . . . me parut singulière, mais toujours de cette singularité qui *m'étonnait sans rien m'apprendre* . . . *mon imagination avait fait son plan* sur cet homme-là . . . tous les motifs de simple tendresse qu'un bienfaiteur peut avoir dans ces cas-là, une fille de plus de quinze ans et demi, quoiqu'elle n'ait rien vu, les sent et les devine confusément. (pp. 50–51)

[His behavior . . . seemed to me peculiar, but it was a peculiarity that *surprised me without shocking me* . . . *my imagination had divined her purposes* toward this man . . . a girl of more than fifteen-and-a-half, although she has seen nothing, feels and guesses confusedly at all the motives for tenderness that a benefactor can have in these cases.]

Quelque novice et quelque ignorante que je fusse en cette occasion-ci, comme l'avait dit Mme de Miran, j'étais née pour avoir *du goût*, et je sentis bien avec quelles gens je dînais. Ce ne fut point à force de leur trouver de l'esprit que j'appris à les distinguer. . . . Si je n'avais pas eu un peu de *goût naturel*, un peu *de sentiment*, j'aurais pu m'y méprendre, et je ne me serais aperçue de rien. . . . Il n'y avait rien ici qui . . . n'encourageât ma petite raison. (pp. 206–7)

[However inexperienced and ignorant I was on this occasion, as Mme de Miran had said, I was born to have *taste* and I felt comfortable with those I was dining with. It was not at all because I found them lively that I learned to tell them apart. . . . If I had not had some *natural taste*, a little *feeling*, I could have been misled, and I would not have noticed anything. . . . There was nothing here that . . . did not encourage my reason.]

Marianne, with that detestable vanity of the young girl of fifteen-and-a-half for which she reproaches herself, refused to let herself be escorted to the Dutour shop and to reveal her name, but is mortified by the impression that her attitude must make on her beloved. What to do? She abandons herself to tears—and that is wisdom itself:

Je pleurais donc, et il n'y avait peut-être pas de meilleur expédient. . . . *Notre âme sait bien ce qu'elle fait*, ou du moins *son instinct le sait pour elle*. Vous croyez que mon découragement est malentendu, qu'il ne peut tourner qu'à ma confusion; et c'est le contraire. Il va remédier à tout. . . . C'est que cet abattement et ces pleurs me donnèrent, aux yeux de ce jeune homme, je ne sais quel air de *dignité romanesque* qui lui en imposa . . . laissez faire aux pleurs que je répands: ils viennent *d'ennoblir* Marianne dans l'imagination de son amant; ils font foi d'une *fierté de cœur* qui empêchera bien qu'il ne la dédaigne. . . . Il y a de certaines infortunes qui embellissent la beauté même, qui lui préparent de la *majesté*. . . . Si une femme pouvait être prise pour une *divinité*, ce serait en pareil cas que son amant l'en croirait une. (pp. 89—90)

[So I cried, and there was perhaps no better expedient. . . . *The soul knows well what she does*, or at least *her instinct knows it for her.* You believe that my despondency is misplaced, and that it can work only to confuse me, but to the contrary. It is going to remedy everything. . . . That is, this dejection and these tears gave me, in the eyes of this young man, an inexpressible air of *romantic dignity* that impressed itself upon him . . . do not mind the tears that I shed: they just *ennobled* Marianne in the imagination of her lover; they attest to a *pride of heart* that will well prevent him from ever disdaining her. . . . There are certain misfortunes that embellish beauty itself, that lend it an air of *majesty.* . . . If a woman could be taken for a *divinity*, it would also be true that her lover would believe her to be one.]

We read this supporting phrase: "Voyez si mes pleurs m'avaient bien servie" (p. 93) [See for yourself if my tears have served me well].

It was the wisdom of innate instinct [*l'instinct inné*] that counseled tears, which in themselves might be considered proof of weakness but which in the event produced an effect that even the shrewdest calculation could not have produced: that which makes visible to her lover the *heart*, the *dignity*, the *romantic aura*, the *majesty*, even the *divinity* of Marianne. Natural instinct acted in her as if she had made use of an "expedient." The sincerity of her emotional outburst resulted in, as a sort of "by-product," a divine vainglory. She was a good actress at the same time that she was acting on her feeling. Sincerity or feminine ruse? The two coalesce in divine natural instinct. And now we come face to face with one of the directing principles of the Marivaudian work: natural spontaneity, in his system of ideas, is intuitive, creative, artistic, and refined to a degree that the mind, reflection, calculation, education, science, or philosophy can never attain. Nature makes "plans" and has "theories," all the while mocking science or philosophy. *The heart is a sort of natural genius.* The passages where Marivaux shows that natural genius contains art without resorting to artifice are innumerable. The nun says to Marianne, "Vous êtes née avec un bon cœur, avec un cœur simple et *sans artifice*" (p. 366) [You were born with a good heart, with a simple heart *without artifice*]—a singular phrase if we reflect on all the feminine ruses employed by Marianne, and explicable only if we consider that simplicity contains complications, subtle ruses, "natural" stratagems. Marivaux does not, like a disillusioned philosopher, disdain coquetry, sister to vanity, because coquetry has recourse to intelligence, to taste, to art, and because, in the end, virtue turns all to account:

> Si on savait ce qui se passe dans la tête d'une coquette en pareil cas, combien *son âme est déliée et pénétrante*; si on voyait la *finesse des jugements* qu'elle fait sur les goûts qu'elle essaye, et puis qu'elle rebute, et puis ce qu'elle hésite à choisir, et qu'elle choisit enfin par pure lassitude; car souvent elle n'est pas contente, et *son idée* va toujours plus loin sur son exécution; si on savait ce que je dis là, cela ferait peur, cela humilierait les plus forts esprits, et *Aristote* ne paraîtrait plus qu'un petit garçon. (p. 64)

[If one knew what happens in a coquette's head on such occasions and how *delicate* and *penetrating* is her *soul*; if one saw the *fineness of the judgments* she makes on the fashions she tries, and then rejects, and then what she hesitates to choose, and that she chooses at last from pure weariness; for she is seldom content, and *her idea* always goes farther upon its execution; if one knew the significance of what I am saying here, it would frighten and humiliate the most powerful minds, and *Aristotle* would seem nothing more than a young boy.]

Why reject nature if it ends in art? Marianne keeps the beautiful dress given to her by M. de Climal:

> Sans scrupule, j'y étais autorisée par la raison même: *l'art imperceptible de mes petits raisonnements* m'avait conduite jusque-là. (p. 137)

[Without scruples, I was authorized to act by reason itself: *the imperceptible art of my little reasonings* had led me thus far.]

Nature contains "imperceptible art." The natural is refined, if unreflecting:

> Ce raisonnement *coula de source*; au reste, il paraît fin, et ne l'est pas; il n'y a rien de *si simple*, on ne s'aperçoit pas seulement qu'on le fait. (p. 52)

[This reasoning *flowed from the source*; it seems refined, and yet is not. There is nothing *so simple*. One is not aware one is doing it.]

Marianne, up against the entreaties of M. de Climal, instinctively tries to stall for time:

> Je consultais donc en moi-même ce que j'avais à faire {au sujet de Climal}; et, à présent que j'y pense, je crois que je ne consultais que pour perdre du temps: *j'assemblais je ne sais combien de réflexions dans mon esprit*; je me taillais de la besogne, afin que, dans la confusion de mes pensées, j'eusse plus de peine à prendre mon parti, et que mon indétermination en fût plus excusable. (p. 54)

[I consulted myself then as to what I had to do {in regard to Climal}; and, now that I think of it, I believe that I did so only to waste my time; *I assem-*

bled I don't know how many reflections in my mind; I cut out my work so that in the confusion of my thoughts, I had more trouble taking a side, and my indetermination was thereby the more excusable.]

Natural genius gives itself "instructions":

Je ne pleurais pourtant point alors {Marianne se sent comme dans un désert dans ce Paris dans lequel elle est abandonnée}, et je n'en étais pas mieux; je recueillais de quoi pleurer; *mon âme s'instruisait* de tout ce qui pouvait l'affliger, elle se mettait *au fait* de ses malheurs. (p. 139)

[I wasn't crying at all then {Marianne feels as if she is in a desert in this Paris where she is abandoned}, and I was none the better for it. I collected something for my sorrow; *my soul instructed itself* in everything that could afflict it, and applied itself to *the fact* of its misfortunes.]

The process of feeling includes a way of thinking, an orientation (Marivaux's *sentio, ergo sum* [I feel, therefore I am] includes a *cogito* [I think]) that instinctively puts one in step with reality.

And now I feel myself prepared to take up your commentary on this key phrase of our novel, whose importance you have readily seen: "Je pense, pour moi, qu'il n'y a que le sentiment qui nous puisse donner des nouvelles un peu sûres de nous" (p. 38) [As for me, I think that feeling alone can give us a reasonably sure understanding of ourselves]. You write:

For Marivaux then, as for Pascal, true knowledge is a knowledge of the heart. . . . Intelligence, therefore, is not something superimposed upon the heart. It does not analyze the passions in order to extract from them, by no one knows what operation, some essence. Strictly speaking, there is no possible rational knowledge of being. At least for ourselves. . . . Existing only in the instant, the Marivaudian personage comes upon himself, so to speak, on the wing and by chance. He catches himself by the same motion that makes him live. . . . It is a question of a being who is simply his own passions, and a thought that is not different from the movements of the heart. Consequently this instinctive thought, immediate and fortuitous, triumphantly completes the actuality of the Marivaudian being. (*ID*, pp. 19–20)

Given that Marianne herself is not at all a colorless being or a puppet, living at the moment and for the moment without scruple and without reflection (if she were, she would be a Manon Lescaut, a woman of the genre "of Manons and of Cathos," a *grisette*, an "adventuress," from which Marivaux always distinguishes her), and that, to the contrary, we see her navigate through life, when all is said and done, guided by a marvelously steady compass—what shocks me in your passage is that an *exemplary* being like Marianne, whom

Marivaux presents to us as the ideal personification of natural genius (and of the natural genius of Woman), seems to you to fit the description of the average human being ("at least for ourselves"—that is, humanity as we know it). What a pessimistic tone! According to Marivaux, for man in general—such is he made, you seem to say— there is no difference between feeling and thinking, there is no knowledge except "on the wing and by chance," etc. To read you, the novel of Marianne should have been a work impressed with a profound melancholy, that of the disintegration of the whole rational order and of moral nihilism, whereas in reality he proclaims the optimism of the eighteenth century (of Goethe and Defoe), his belief in the resources given to man, his cult of genius, of the natural and the spontaneous. Moreover, how can you in the same breath invoke the "heart" of Pascal, which in reality is intuition, the instrument of supreme knowledge if ever there was one (which the humanist, the philologist, the historian, the theologian, and particularly the "scientist" have always employed), and which is not exempt from thought, but to the contrary, contains and produces it? Evidently, you have every reason in the world to identify the natural genius of exemplary, noble, and disinterested beings with intuition, the "heart" of Pascal. And in effect, Marianne, whose vocation is "life" (see above), miraculously enjoys the same gift of ingenious intuition in the situations which confront her that distinguishes the philosophers and the men of professional science to whom Marivaux seems to attach so little importance.

Indeed, Marivaux's idea is precisely that the natural genius that a Marianne reveals in the situations of her turbulent life *equals* that of the men of science and of the philosophers, that it contains or implies a science and a philosophy, that it itself is and results in thought— thought, it is true, that one does not acquire through long preparation and "long patience," but that is innate in certain "geniuses of life." It seems to me, therefore, that here you are somewhat the victim of a semantic fallacy if you identify "feeling," the sole organ of knowledge for Marivaux, with the vulgar and chaotic passions that we commonly call "sentimental," instead of acknowledging here "intuition"—that thought which flashes out of the unconscious and is creative, but which is thought all the same: the "heart" of Marivaux is, in effect, the "heart" of Pascal's celebrated phrase. Is Marivaux Pascalian? Surely, but a Pascal who would apply *l'esprit de finesse* to the art of living.

And note well that the entire *Vie de Marianne* is inspired by this Marivaudian belief in innate genius triumphant over the vicissitudes of life. The story of the nun, which occupies the last books of the novel, is a counterpart to Marianne's own—a fact that the majority of critics do not seem to have recognized. Her being is defined by the author in the same terms (now familiar to us) that he employs for Marianne, who almost became a nun herself: the nun (a Marianne become, in effect, religious), "du meilleur *cœur* du monde, en même temps du plus singulier" (p. 210) [with the best and, at the same time, the most remarkable *heart* in the world], had been persecuted in a similar manner by destiny since early youth but, thanks to her gifts of mind and heart, she possesses Marianne's "courage" and holds her own in situations analogous to those that threaten Marianne. She, too, knows how to say no to what fails to satisfy her noble nature; she has the same inherent flair for nobleness of heart. But—gentler, chastened by sorrow, retired to the depths of her soul (p. 428)—she reveals her genius, true Christian that she is, not so much for self-defense as for the defense of others: witness her, with all of Marianne's capability, repeatedly intervening for others. Marianne knows how to plead her own case ingeniously; the nun uses the same genius (not exempt from vanity) to aid others. Note that this genius is also as precocious as Marianne's, that it consists of seizing the opportune moment with rapid intuition: "Il y a de ces instants-là qui n'ont qu'un point qu'il faut saisir; et ce point, nous l'avions manqué, *je le sentis*" (p. 504) [There are those instants in which one had to seize the moment, and we had missed it, *I felt it*]—here feeling = intuition—and of taking into account a multitude of facts in order to obtain a decisive result: remember the nun skillfully "setting the stage" to bring about that complicated intrigue, the coup, with which she planned to reconcile the aunt with her family ("J'avais tout *disposé* moi-même pour arriver à ce terme . . . ; le coup qui devait la frapper était *mon ouvrage*," p. 504 [I had *done* my utmost to gain this end . . . ; the blow that was to fall was *my work*]). Thus we see in our novel two parallel heroines—the one a genius of self-defense, the other of self-abnegation and altruism—both following their own "predestination" and triumphing by their natural genius, their "heart." Marianne, with a little less vanity, could have become someone like the nun, and the nun, with a little more feminine vitality, a Marianne. Marianne is a martyr to life who becomes a heroine by saying no to that which fails to conform to her nature; the nun is a martyr who says no to life itself. The nun's story is related to us by Marianne—who is not a nun but "retired from life"—in a more pragmatic and direct manner and with less reflection than usual, first because the "counterpart" requires less explanation, and also because the nun's life must impress us as the tableau of a simple life leading to sainthood. It is certain that our novel, far from being unbalanced (as so many of the critics think) by the story of the nun, can only gain in scope and seriousness through the parallelism suggested between secular and pious heroism.*

---

* We must consider that since the *Vie de Marianne* was left to us a fragment, the nun's story is situated in Marianne's as one egg might be situated inside another: if one cut the crown of the containing egg, one would also by necessity cut the crown of the contained egg. Marcel Arland was mistaken in telling us that the nun's story "forms a second novel, very different from the first, a novel that remains incomplete."[8] There is only a single—incomplete—novel.

But Marianne finds her counterpart not only in a being devoted to saintliness but also in certain characters of the *beau monde* that she decides not to renounce. You will observe what the critics still seem to pass over in silence: that all the "good" characters in our history are in some manner allied to Marianne via the "heart," spontaneous genius. In those portraits of ladies—to which Marivaux dedicated all the exquisiteness of his style—conducing to the glorification of the mind (Mme Dorsin) and of the kind heart (Mme de Miran), what emerges as essential is the naturalness of their gifts. Mme Dorsin, one of those "âmes supérieurs à tout événement" (p. 221) [souls superior at all events], has all of Marianne's qualities but is conspicuous in society by virtue of this particular union of "wit" [*esprit*] and goodness, with wit predominating, while Mme de Miran is the genius of goodness to which wit is subordinated ("C'était son cœur, et non pas son esprit qui philosophait là-dessus," p. 170 [It was her heart and not her mind that philosophized about that]—*heart* here = good heart). One feels Marivaux's sympathy gravitating more toward Mme Dorsin, whereas it is Mme de Miran who proves herself more efficacious, more Christian. We sense here the same preference accorded by Marivaux to grace (in comparison with goodness) that we found in his treatment of Marianne (vis-à-vis that of the nun): as a thinker, he appreciates grace and goodness equally, but the artist in him makes him favor the former. The two portraits of ladies are therefore linked to that of Marianne by the spontaneity that animates them: everything for these three "hearts" flows from the source, where neither affectation nor ostentation is to be found. Their nature is a work of art.

The same confluence of the natural and the artistic is found in this portrait of the abbess:

Cette abbesse était âgée, d'une grande naissance. . . . Je viens de vous dire qu'elle était âgée; mais on ne remarquait pas cela tout d'un coup. C'était de ces visages qui ont l'air plus ancien que vieux; on dirait que le temps les ménage. . . . Imaginez-vous quelque chose de *simple*, mais d'extrêmement net et *arrangé*, qui rejaillit sur l'âme, et qui est comme une image de sa pureté. (p. 286)

[This abbess was elderly and of noble birth. . . . I have just told you that she was elderly, but one did not notice that right away, for she had one of those faces that appear more ancient than old. One might say that time spares them. . . . Imagine something *simple*, extremely neat and *arranged*, which reflects on the soul, and which is like an image of its purity.]

You will not be at all surprised if I find parallel features in Monseigneur the minister, the impartial judge before whom Marianne pleads her case with so much success. Marivaux tells us that unlike former rulers who surrounded themselves with mystery to show off their own skillfulness, this minister

gouvernait à la manière des sages, dont la conduite est douce, *simple, sans faste*, et désintéressée pour eux-mêmes. . . . Ils n'avertissent point qu'ils seront habiles. {One readily translates into English here, modernizing the phrase: "They do not advertise. . . ."} C'est un génie sans ostentation qui les {leurs opérations} a conduites. (p. 304)

[governed in the manner of the wise, whose conduct is mild, *simple, without pomp*, and, disinterested with respect to themselves. . . . They do not at all show off their own abilities. A genius without ostentation guides their operations.]

Natural genius, I said—innate heart [*cœur inné*]. We note finally that the spirit of good conversation is described in almost the same terms as good conduct: "Ce n'étaient point eux qui y mettaient de la finesse, c'était de la finesse qui s'y rencontrait" (p. 207) [It was not at all they who put an effort into refinement, it was refinement that came to them]. The genius of conversation is, like that of government, like that of the conduct of life, "without ostentation," because *innate*.

On the other hand, let us compare Marianne's adversaries (who find their exact counterpart in the nun's adversaries). They have in common a lack of continuity, an interrupted line of life, a contradiction between exterior and interior, the absence of feeling, of innate *heart*. First there is the Tartuffe-type M. de Climal, whose hypocrisy is not completely foreign to Marianne's thought (she also wants to hunt with the hare and run with the hounds, to win material profit while sustaining a pure conscience—the parallel between her and the hypocrites is explicitly mentioned on p. 78) and whose principal error is one of *aesthetic* order, in that his charitable deeds are pompous and ostentatious, gracelessly carried out. There is the prioress of "pious portliness," of the "affable exterior" and the "indifferent interior." There is Mlle de Fare, the young woman who from goddess (Flora, Hebe) evolves into a female Tartuffe. There is Valville, who from faithful lover becomes traitor, the typical representative of the average Frenchman and of contemporary love (one recalls p. 352), without constancy or heart. One notices the refinement of Marivaux's invention: he has Valville fall in love twice, and on the heels of two similar spectacles carried out before his eyes—a fainting woman, first Marianne and then Mlle de Fare. He is thus twice the victim of his own visual sensuality, and is related in this manner to M. de Climal, who, "born with a sensitive heart," also falls in love with Marianne "haplessly," "unexpectedly." Finally, there is the good Dutour, representative of the common people who lack principled conduct, who can change her friendship to hostility from moment to moment, her anger to kindness, all the while subordinating both to curiosity (p. 56); who doesn't know how to distinguish between affection and coarseness; for whom morality is as vacillant as taste.*

---

* One is surprised at Gustave Larroumet's list of errors in judgment, from Marivaux's time to that of Sainte-Beuve, concerning the scene of the hackney coachman and the linen-draper—errors that culminate in the unabashed condemnation of Marivaux's realism by the university pedant who is Larroumet himself.[9] It is evident that this scene functions in contrast with the well-balanced conduct of Marianne, who corrects Mme Dutour's error. Mme Dutour, an incarnation of "bons gens {du peuple} de peu d'esprit" (p. 107) [good people {common people} of little intellect], has a false idea of human dignity: "C'est qu'elle s'imaginait que plus on se fâchait, plus on faisait figure; . . . son ton, quand il était brusque, engageait son esprit à l'être aussi" (p. 107) [She imagined that the more angry she became, the finer a figure she cut; . . . her tone of voice, when it was brusque, bound her mind to be so as well]. We note the lack of coordination in the movements of her sensibility, the lack of "heart" in Marianne's sense (although she is equipped with the good heart of the common people). Her mind cannot go beyond her measuring device, the symbolic object in this scene.

At the bottom of the ladder is the gawking commoner of Paris, neither good nor mean but always curious, that is to say, "amoral" and abandoned to contingency: witnessing a quarrel, "Il va voir, il va ouvrir des yeux stupidement avides. . . . Cela remue son âme qui ne sait jamais rien, qui n'a jamais rien vu, qui est toujours toute neuve" (p. 104) [He will see, and he will open stupid, eager eyes. . . . This stirs his soul, which never knows anything, which has never seen anything, and which is always completely new]. A lady of rank equal to that of Mme de Fare is depicted as essentially vulgar and "of the people": note the similarities of expression in the passage just cited and in this, which characterizes Mme de Fare:

Il y a de certaines gens dont l'esprit n'est en mouvement que par pure disette d'idées; c'est ce qui les rend si affamés d'objets étrangers, d'autant plus qu'il ne leur reste rien, que tout passe en eux, que tout en sort; gens toujours regardants, toujours écoutants, jamais pensants. Je les compare à un homme qui passerait sa vie à se tenir à sa fenêtre. (p. 246)

[There are certain people whose minds are stirred only by pure famine of ideas; it is this which renders them so starved for foreign things, especially as they retain nothing, as everything passes through their minds, then leaves; people always looking, always listening, never thinking. I compare them to a man who would spend his life standing at his window.]

By this arrangement of characters in two contrasting groups, the beings of genius and the mediocre, Marivaux seems to me to have made his intention clear: his "hearts" detach themselves from the apathy of the average man. Can one say henceforth that "Marivaudian existence" contains only "the instantaneous" (which, "by a singular turn," could become a temporal line)? On the contrary, is not his novel the novel of the "line"? Has one the right to exclude from human "existence," according to Marivaux, the spiritual principle that organizes brute matter and to accept as a constitutive element only this last, on which our author turns his back with contempt?

If I were to write on "time" in Marivaux, I would treat the *two* types of time that this author knows: on the one hand, *the instants* where Marivaux's pessimistic psychology, which you have investi-

gated so thoroughly, gives itself free reign (he had a presentiment of
Valéry's maxim that every great sentiment can maintain itself only by
virtue of hypocrisy, and demonstrated the weakness and the apathy
of which the human instant is composed); and, on the other hand,
the continuity above the instants, the vital, total spirit that can be noble and good despite the humiliating lapses of the moment. It is here
that the idealist optimism of the eighteenth century is most evident:
a perfect whole (a perfect life) can be composed of imperfect parts,
the whole is more moral than the part (the economic theory of
laissez-faire is inspired precisely by the same belief). Thus we find in
Marivaux a double structure: idealism placed above pessimism. By
means of the idealist superstructure it connects itself to the past; by
means of the pessimistic substructure, to the realists of the nineteenth century, Stendhal, Balzac, Flaubert—this last knowing only
the pessimistic substructure, what Erich Auerbach calls the "tragic
everyday."[10]

The two types of Marivaudian time are revealed by a character in
our novel of whom we have not yet spoken: the aged Marianne who
is the narrator. This character says "I," thereby suggesting unity of
character, whereas at bottom there is a doubling—narrated events
are split in two: into the brute matter of events as the young Marianne lived them, and into their interpretation by the old woman.
Marivaux was careful to warn us that the numerous "reflections," or
moral digressions, must be attributed to the narrator. And the great
majority of critics jeer at these reflections as superfluous or boring!
But who can fail to see that the narrative process chosen by the author is in admirable harmony with the structure of Marianne's character? The young Marianne, with her natural and spontaneous genius, who knew how to keep her head from earliest adolescence in
the face of the most disconcerting events, would neither have known
how to explain the precise line of conduct she happened to choose at
a given moment, nor have been able to see clearly in the continuous
"Where am I?" that destiny inflicts on her. It is the old Marianne, retired from the world but benevolently contemplating it still, who sees
clearly into the troubled mind of the young girl, who knows how to
separate the very distinct components of the alloy (noble, less noble)
that produced this decision or that refusal. In sum, the narrator reveals to us the multiple reflections, unconscious or subconscious, the
hesitations, the contradictions, the compromises with unarticulated
principles that preceded or inspired the decisions and the refusals of

the acting character. It is she who is able to discover formulas and psychological categories that the young girl in the process of living could not have elaborated. The narrator is an "esprit sérieux et *philosophe*" (p. 24) [serious and *philosophical* mind], despite the sallies against the philosophers that Marivaux puts in her mouth. On another occasion, Marivaux himself defines his role as author in terms relevant to his Marianne-author: speaking of young people in the theater whose discourse he is giving an account of, he says: "Je ne fais que débrouiller le chaos de leurs idées: j'expose en détail ce qu'ils sentent en gros"[11] [I only sort out the chaos of their ideas: I explain in detail what they crudely feel].

The innate genius of the young Marianne, in contrast to that of Emma Bovary, is manifested in reasonable actions forming the "straight line" of her behavior. Marianne the narrator will show us all the complicated interior cogs (intellectual, sentimental, moral) that condition this innateness. The superimposition of the two Mariannes serves to deconstruct the apparently simple act of genius; it reflects the "two times" of Marivaux. How colorless a unilinear and idealistic novel, such as the *Gitanilla* of Cervantes, would have been in the middle of the eighteenth century after La Rochefoucauld and La Bruyère, in an epoch when the need for the ideal was being nuanced by a pessimistic and realistic psychology! But on the contrary, what fascination a novel constructed on dual temporal planes ("two times") must have generated—the simple naturalness of Marianne in action revealing itself, in the light of her mature self's reflections, as a continuous and complicated work of art on which her emotions and her intellect, her nobleness and her baseness, have collaborated. Genius in the fullness of its powers marches straight ahead, on a course in some sense nontemporal or atemporal—but, paradoxically, to explain this, one needs "time."

Yet the character of the narrator not only functions as a mirror carried along Marianne's high road, it also has its own part to play, that of the storyteller herself, for although the character who says "I" refuses to be an "author," it is undeniable that in reality Marianne is writing a novel. Let us examine two passages that inform us of the scruples of Marianne, woman-author of the novel:

Je ne sais point philosopher, et je ne m'en soucie guère, car je crois que cela n'apprend rien qu'à discourir; les gens que j'ai entendus raisonner là-dessus ont bien de l'esprit assurément; mais je crois que sur certaine matière ils ressemblent à ces nouvellistes qui font des nouvelles quand ils n'en ont point, ou qui corrigent celles qu'ils reçoivent quand elles ne leur plaisent pas. Je pense, pour moi, qu'il n'y a que le sentiment qui nous puisse donner des nouvelles un peu sûres de nous, et qu'il ne faut pas trop se fier à celles que notre esprit veut faire à sa guise, car je le crois un grand visionnaire. . . .

Eh! pourquoi n'y reviendrais-je pas? Est-ce à cause que je ne suis qu'une femme, et que je ne sais rien? Le bon sens est de tout sexe, je ne veux instruire personne; j'ai cinquante ans passés; et un honnête homme très savant me disait l'autre jour que, quoique je ne susse rien, je n'étais pas plus ignorante que ceux qui en savaient plus que moi. Oui, c'est un savant du premier ordre qui a parlé comme cela; car ces hommes, tout fiers qu'ils sont de leur science, ont quelquefois des moments où la vérité leur échappe d'abondance de cœur, et où ils se sentent si las de leur présomption, qu'ils la quittent pour respirer en francs ignorants comme ils sont. (p. 38)

[I do not know at all how to philosophize, and care not the slightest, for I believe it can teach us nothing but to declaim. The people that I have heard reason in this way surely have intellect; but I believe that on certain matters they resemble those tale-tellers who have no tales to tell or who attempt to improve on any tale they may hear when it fails to please them. As for me, I think that feeling alone can give us slightly more reliable stories of ourselves, and that we should not trust too much the stories that our intellect would devise in its way, for I believe our mind is a great visionary. . . .

Ah! why would I not return to the subject? Is it because I am only a woman, and know nothing? Good sense is common to both sexes, I do not want to instruct anyone; I had passed my fiftieth year; and a very wise man told me the other day that, although I knew nothing, I was no more ignorant than those who know more. Yes, it was a wise man of the first order who spoke thus, for these men, as proud as they are of their learning, have times when the truth escapes them from fullness of heart, and when they feel so weary from their presumption that they abandon it to breathe freely in a frank ignorance such as they are.]

Quand je dis que je vais vous faire le portrait de ces deux dames {Mme de Miran et Mme Dorsin}, j'entends que je vous en donnerai quelques traits. On ne saurait rendre en entier ce que sont les personnes; du moins cela ne me serait pas possible; je connais bien mieux celles avec qui je vis que je ne les définirais; il y a des choses en elles que je ne saisis point assez pour les dire, et que je n'aperçois que pour moi, et non pas pour les autres; ou, si je les disais, je les dirais mal. Ce sont des objets de sentiment si compliqués et d'une netteté si délicate qu'ils se brouillent dès que ma réflexion s'en mêle; je ne sais plus par où les prendre pour les exprimer: de sorte qu'ils sont en moi, et non pas à moi.

. . . il me semble que mon âme, en mille occasions, en sait plus qu'elle n'en peut dire, et qu'elle a un esprit à part, qui est bien supérieur à celui que j'ai d'ordinaire. Je crois aussi que les hommes sont bien au-dessus de tous les livres qu'ils font. Mais cette pensée me mènerait trop loin. (p. 166)

[When I say I am going to paint you a portrait of these two ladies {Mme de Miran and Mme Dorsin}, I mean to give you a rough sketch. It is impossible to render them entirely as they are—or at least it would be impossible for me. I know those with whom I live far better than I would be able to describe them in words. There is something in them that I cannot grasp well enough to talk adequately about it, and which I understand only for myself, but not for others. If I were to explain it, I would say it badly. These are objects of feeling so complex and delicate that they confuse me even as I reflect upon them. I do not know how to express them such that they are in me and not mine.

. . . It seems to me that my soul, on a thousand occasions, knows more than it can say, and that it has a mind apart, quite superior to what I ordinarily have. I also believe that men are far beyond all their books. But this thought will carry me too far.]

I will return only briefly to the principal passage in the first citation ("feeling alone can give us unfailing intelligence of ourselves"), which you extracted from the author's monologue and which you interpreted as a blank check given to fugitive passions. In reality, as the phrase from the second citation proves ("these {the portraits of a living person} are objects of feelings so complex . . . that they confuse me even as I reflect upon them"), it is a question of *intuitive* knowledge (as opposed to the logical, discursive thought of the scholar and the philosopher), which is necessary either to elaborate a novel or a portrait. The human material in both cases is too complex to be rendered by *l'esprit géométrique*—what is required is *l'esprit de finesse*. Marianne the author refuses to be an author because every author in principle betrays this intuitive genius which the accurate representation of men requires; but she is a woman and consequently closer by nature to this intuition. She will therefore attempt to remain a woman even while becoming an author and to remind herself how inferior what she describes (this "barbouiller . . . du papier," p. 33 [scribbling on paper]) must be compared to what she knows inwardly, and in effect she doesn't "write" her descriptions: her "novel" will be "spoken" rather than written ("Où voulez-vous que je prenne un style? Il est vrai que dans le monde on m'a trouvé de l'esprit; mais, ma chère, je crois que cet esprit-là n'est bon qu'à être dit, et ne vaut rien à être lu," p. 26 [Where do you want me to find a style? It is true that in the world I was thought witty, but, my dear, I think that this wit is good only to be spoken, and is not worth reading]). Marianne, the author of *La Vie de Marianne*, is still the "optimal" case of an author—being a woman, she is intuitive, she knows how to chat, and her narrative will attempt to distance itself as much as possible from the scientific and philosophical as well as from the stylistically self-conscious. Moreover, Marianne the author of the novel is biologically consubstantial with Marianne the protagonist, also a woman of intuitive genius and an adroit manipulator of the word, which means that the author found a subject in marvelous accord with her own nature—or should we say that the subject "Marianne" chose an excellent author? And going still further, is it Marivaux who chose an excellent subject, *La Vie de Marianne*, or is it the subject "Marianne" who chose her author, Marivaux? Marivaux in effect is looking at himself in looking at Marianne look at herself. There is a mirror carried along the high road that reflects another mirror (but not a mirror that reflects "nothing," as you seem to think). Whatever the case may be, by remaining in the frame of the novel we can judge that Marianne the narrator, character of *La Vie de Marianne*, completes and fleshes out the characters of the novel even while accentuating its subject: *the glorification of feminine intuition as an organ of knowledge*, duplicated in two characters. Marivaux, the singer of that intuition peculiar to the feminine genius, salutes the other author of the eighteenth century who excelled, as Bismarck said, in the portrayal of women as well as men: Goethe, the singer of woman as the redeemer of man. Who would expect to find Marivaux more on the intellectual side than on the moral side? For him, man is more obtuse than woman, while for Goethe he is more depraved. If one describes Marivaux as possessing "a feminine soul" (Marcel Arland),[12] one must still acknowledge that he celebrated *knowledge*, a "masculine" theme, under the aspect of the Eternal Feminine. Consider this text:

Marianne n'a aucune forme d'ouvrage présente à l'esprit. Ce n'est point un auteur, *c'est une femme qui pense* . . . enfin, dont la vie est un tissu d'événements qui lui ont donné une certaine *connaissance* du cœur et du caractère des hommes . . . et, dans cet esprit-là, mêle indistinctement les faits qu'elle raconte aux réflexions qui lui viennent à propos de ces faits: voilà sur quel ton le prend Marianne. Ce n'est, si vous voulez, ni celui du roman, ni celui de l'histoire, mais c'est le sien: ne lui en demandez pas d'autre. (p. 68)

[Marianne has no specific form of work in mind. This is not an author, *this is a woman who thinks* . . . for whom life is a tissue of events that have given her a certain *knowledge* of the heart and of the character of men . . . and, in this spirit, she mixes up the facts that she narrates with the reflections that come to her with respect to these facts: this is the tone that Marianne assumes. This tone is not, if you will, that of the novel, nor that of history, but it is her own: do not expect any other of her.]*

---

*You comment on this metaphor [of the "tissue of events"] as follows: "... a moving tapestry. A tapestry of points so serrated that one ends by renouncing any desire to count them" (*ID*, p. 27). But in this context the tissue of life is precisely such that Marianne, "the woman who thinks," succeeds in unraveling it and in drawing wisdom from it.

A *woman who thinks*—whereas, from Michelangelo to Rodin, the Thinker has always been a man! According to Marivaux the woman's mind has a greater chance of being without sex, or above sex, than that of man: witness his Mme Dorsin, whose mind unites virility and feminine grace.

We note, finally, that the nonchalant (almost affectedly so) manner of Marianne the author coincides admirably with the definition of the spirit of conversation, of right conduct—in short, with everything which to Marivaux signifies culture: lack of ostentation and of pomp, natural and spontaneous *savoir faire*. The reflections of Marianne the author are naturally sagacious, dispensed with the ease characteristic of all true culture; while not compromised by the immateriality of an old woman's chatter, they still retain something of its lightness. The literary theory that Marivaux develops through the mouth of his "character-author" is therefore not at all an hors d'oeuvre but a necessary element in the contexture of the novel. Moreover, the attitude of Marianne the author must be that of Marivaux himself—that of "an author in spite of himself," since he would prefer to have "the mind of woman," more complete than his own.*

---

*I think that the passage of Marivaux with which you open your essay— "An author is a man who in his idleness feels within himself a vague desire to think about something; and this could be called reflecting on nothing"— and on which you comment thus—"A mere nothing reflected in a mind which also is nothing: a reflection in a mirror, such is Marivaudian literature" (*ID*, p. 3)—must be taken as a statement of literary-theoretical and literary-polemical import, rather than of existential philosophical significance. Far from those authors who take themselves very seriously and consider themselves as solemnly fulfilling some national or humanitarian obligation, Marivaux demands the Horatian liberty of the writer to do as he pleases, even to trivialize, since for Marivaux as well as for Pascal, to be a man and to do nothing at all is still more important than to be an author. That is what Voltaire, conscious of his role as advocate of humanity, must have felt: "C'est un homme qui passe sa vie à peser des œufs de mouche dans des balances de toile d'araignée"[13] [This is a man who spends his life weighing the eggs of a fly in the scales of a spider web]. At bottom, Marivaux, with his ideal of man, is as serious as Voltaire in his defense of humanity.

I am not far from thinking that the subject of *La Vie de Marianne* is not so much the narrative of an intrepid young woman's life as the glorification *of the feminine principle in human thought* revealing itself both in life and in literature.

One question—of biographical import—remains to be answered. Why didn't Marivaux finish *La Vie de Marianne*?*

---

* Arland thinks that Marivaux was on the verge of abandoning *La Vie de Marianne* well before the eleventh book (his last): after the seventh book the novel seems complete, but continues after a fashion (and Arland misses the point in denying the beauty scattered throughout the second part of Marianne's story).[14] I think that once again the critic is wrong, absolutely wrong. He has not understood the structure of the medieval and renaissance adventure novel, of which *La Vie de Marianne; ou, Les Aventures de Madame la Comtesse de . . .* is only a late offshoot and which typically shows us a steadfast character exposed to different adventures that "happen to him" (*veniunt ad eum—adventura*) and that come to test him without his ever yielding. The perpetual elaboration of the story corresponds to the inward steeling of the Herculean hero, whose "trials" fail to crush his inner strength. Multiplicity of "adventures," unity of character—this is the principle at the heart of the adventure novel.

(Is it this fact that you have in mind when you assert that "nothing survives except a sort of vaporous memory of all that has happened. And it is that sort of time along the length of which the novels of Marivaux end by evaporating" (*ID*, p. 27). Do you think that Marivaux himself grew weary of the "indefinite motion" of his novel, and that his own "memory" of the adventures of Marianne "evaporated"?) In the very subject of Marianne an artistic pitfall exists that must have sobered the novelist: Marianne, the "heart," whose precocious intuition anticipates her years, is an essentially *young* protagonist. It is her youth that makes her a genius. Thirty or forty years later (at the time when the old Marianne writes), her reasonable decisions would no longer have had any *éclat*. Genius anticipates; the child prodigy grown old is no longer prodigious. The genius of life, victor over time, would have gained nothing being submitted to the great leveler, Death's brother, to Time . . .

I have demonstrated, dear friend, the difference between our two methods, and consequently between our results, in relation to a single Marivaudian work. But I believe that the same disparity would have arisen had I treated other works. Thus my eye falls on one of your first quotations, which you use to establish the principle of existence according to Marivaux: "primitive inertia," the "preliminary state," "state of emptiness and indolence," "the state, in short, of Adam before the Creator had breathed into him" (*ID*, p. 3), out of which only the "surprise of love" can draw him. And you cite, from the play *La Surprise de l'amour*, this admirably precise descriptive phrase:

Sans l'aiguillon de l'amour et du plaisir, notre cœur, à nous autres, est un vrai paralytique; nous restons là comme des eaux dormantes, qui attendent qu'on les remue pour les remuer. (act 1, sc. 2)

[Without the spur of love and of pleasure, our heart is a veritable paralytic: we remain here like dormant waters that wait to be stirred in order to stir them.]

But you do not tell us that Lélio, who pronounces these words, understands them as pertaining only to the masculine portion of humanity, and that he opposes to this state of uncreated Adam that of eternal Eve, whom one can imagine only as created, and well created at that, complete with all her feminine resources. Lélio continues:

Le cœur d'une femme se donne sa secousse à lui-même; il part sur un mot qu'on dit, sur un mot qu'on ne dit pas, sur une contenance . . . c'est de la jalousie, du calme, de l'inquiétude, de la joie, du babil, et du silence de toutes couleurs. (act 1, sc. 2)

[A woman's heart sets itself aflutter: it quickens at a word that is spoken, at a word that is not spoken, at a look . . . it is jealousy, calm, anxiety, joy, lighthearted chatter, and many-hued silence.]

Hadn't Lélio, enamored of the "self-engendering movement" that he sees personified in woman, used a bit earlier these words that remind us of *La Vie de Marianne*?

Que de vivacité! quelles expressions! que de *naïveté*! L'homme a le bon sens en partage; mais, ma foi, *l'esprit n'appartient qu'à la femme* . . . nous faisons l'amour réglément comme on fait une charge. Nous nous faisons des méthodes de tendresse. . . . Une femme ne veut être ni tendre, ni délicate, ni

fâchée, ni bien aise; elle est tout cela *sans le savoir*, et cela est charmant. (act
1, sc. 2)

[What vivacity! what expressions! what *naïveté*! Man is endowed with
common sense; but, my faith, *spirit belongs only to woman* . . . we make
love systematically as one undertakes a commission. We create methods of
tenderness for ourselves. . . . A woman wants to be neither tender, nor delicate, nor angry, nor at ease; she is all that *without knowing it*, and that is
what is charming.]

As for Marianne, wasn't she able to be "many women in one,"
didn't she possess this feminine intuition, naively adapting herself to
every situation without method or calculation, but not without continuity? And Mme Dorsin—wasn't she the incarnation of "wit,"
uniting a man's common sense with feminine charm? We touch here
upon Marivaux's principal idea of the perfection of woman, who
unites in her spirit the qualities of both sexes, and of the incompleteness of the masculine being, an incompleteness that the artist, Marivaux, escapes by creating an ideal "ambisexual" type. Why have
you suppressed the second tableau of the diptych that features Lélio,
transforming what he says exclusively of the masculine sex into an
existentialist description of the human condition? Our passage concerns the inherent lassitude of man-*vir*, not man-*homo*. And if man-
vir can in effect be compared to stagnant water, what good fortune
for him that he shares his world with woman, who alone is capable
of moving those waters! However, Marivaudian existence is not "as
sad as all that."*

---

*Another case of quotation arbitrarily removing a passage from its con-
text: in support of your description of Marivaudian consciousness as lacking interior continuity ("it knows neither why nor how it is," *ID*, p. 7), you
cite *La Seconde Surprise de l'amour*:

Ah! je ne sais où j'en suis; respirons. D'où vient que je soupire? Les larmes
me coulent des yeux; je me sens saisi de la tristesse la plus profonde, et je ne
sais pourquoi. (act 3, sc. 11)

[Ah! I do not know where I am; let's take a breath. Whence comes that sigh?
Tears run from my eyes; I feel seized by the most profound sadness, and I do
not know why.]

The words in question are located in the Marquise's monologue just before the end of the play: caught between a cavalier whom she considered a
friend but with whom she was really in love and who decided to marry another woman, and a count who loves her and who asks for her hand but
whom she doesn't love, the Marquise is disconcerted. The solution at the

end is that the cavalier-friend discovers in himself his love for the Marquise, and they marry. In this typical monologue, which permits two contrary emotions to confront each other and which conveys the confusion of a moment, I can see *absolutely no* evidence for the feeling of Marivaudian existence. By the same token, from verses like these from Auguste's monologue in Corneille's *Cinna*—

> Mais, que mon jugement au besoin m'abandonne!
>
> .   .   .
>
> O rigoureux combat d'un cœur irrésolu
> Qui fuit en même temps tout ce qu'il propose! (act 4, sc. 2)
>
> [But, how my judgment abandons me in time of need!
>
> .   .   .
>
> O rigorous combat of an irresolute heart
> Which simultaneously flies from that which it proposes!]

—one could ascribe a pessimistic philosophy to the poet, which would contradict all that is known about him. No, the "Where am I?" of Marivaux, like the "judgment [that] abandons me" and the "irresolute heart" of Corneille, is a *dramatic* element (an element of the Dialectic of Drama), and not an *existential* one.

You might object that expressions such as "paralytic heart" and "stagnant waters," much like the "Where am I?" that appears so frequently, point to Marivaux's profound pessimism and that, according to my own method, this original and intense expression must lead us directly to the heart of the writer's sensibility: Marivaux must have felt profoundly that which he expressed so intensely. And here we are in full accord: Marivaux was bound to have seen the profound void of human existence. However, he is absolutely not a baroque writer (as are Pascal, Quevedo, or Gracián) but a rococo writer who turns his gaze, as soon as it threatens to become anguished, toward the rosy side of human existence, to its resources and interior riches, to the steadfastness of the ideal character who, despite everything, can save us. *La Vie de Marianne* is still a *novela ejemplar* [exemplary novel], with an "exemplary" heroine at its center. This heroine no longer possesses the crystalline purity of Cervantes's classic Preciosa, but her intrepid virtue will suddenly burst forth beyond the temptations that destiny has prepared for her. The pessimistic philosophy of the eighteenth century had not yet terminated in the destruction of the personality (Proustian type). The thinking Reed that is man develops all his flexibility and his inner grace, which in turn exempts him from the fate of La Fontaine's

Oak.[15] I can well understand that you would find the real Marivaux, the original Marivaux, in the directionless being who says "Where am I?" while the rosy, rococo Marivaux seems to you insignificant and conventional, but I ask myself if we have the right, in studying the tree of human personality with its dense foliage, to cut it off from the profound roots that connect it to the tradition of the past. A past not repudiated is a present, an essential part of our being. You have discovered the negative "Where am I?" that makes Marivaux a predecessor of Proust and Kafka. But have you sufficiently accounted for the artistic realization of Marivaux's *je ne sais quoi* as an affirmation of his ideal of *exemplary* beauty?

The friendly reproach which I direct to your method is that it is philosophy applied to literature and that it involves the danger of sacrificing the latter to the former. Having applied your exquisite metaphysical sense of time and of interior space to thirty authors of the first order, you are possessed of a marvelous touch in the handling of these concepts. But the danger is that your philosophic intuition does not always coincide with the artistic intention of your authors, who in my opinion can fully reveal themselves only by means of an introspection—one that remains at first deliberately within the literary framework—of particular works. It is not only that, after having established the intimate sense of work *A*, then of work *B*, then of *C*, etc., of an author, I feel one can safely put forward a synthetic view of his œuvre and assign to it its place in the world of ideas. One must have been *within* (within many times) in order to get *beyond*. The a priori of the author is for the philologist only an a posteriori. On the contrary, the practice of imposing general (Kantian) philosophical categories (time, space, person, number, "What do I know?") from the outside to works of literary art risks doing violence to their meaning. Philosophical ideas have an inherent tendency to free themselves from the literary context, to group themselves into sovereign systems, to label themselves one or the other, and to engage in a fantastic dance (macabre?) beyond the characters supposed to represent them in works of art. Abstract ideas require air and must be in their own climates, beyond the contingency which would imprison them. But doesn't this game of philosophy and of chance risk deforming precisely that "literary concreteness" which is the proper domain—and the love—of the philological critic of works of literary art? The experienced and attentive philologist, reading a work without preconceived ideas and open to whatever strikes him, precisely because he is immersed in the concreteness that the work offers him, is more likely to discover the essence of a literary work of art that may not conform to any philosophical system or that develops aspects of a philosophy that a systematic philosopher would not have been able to foresee. The innate "chameleonism" of the philologist is better able to shape itself to the concreteness of the artistic work than is the "systematism" of the philosopher.[16]

A CENTRAL THEME AND ITS
STRUCTURAL EQUIVALENT
IN LOPE'S 'FUENTEOVEJUNA'

Lope de Vega's play *Fuenteovejuna* provided Spitzer with an ideal opportunity to display both his powers in interpreting poetic language and structure and the depth of his historical understanding. As a study of a successful peasant revolt against a tyrannical local ruling lord, the play had, since the late nineteenth century, served as a battleground for highly divergent and often politically motivated interpretations. Like several other Golden Age plays on similar themes, it attracted leftist critics because of its purportedly revolutionary sentiments. More conservative-minded interpreters stressed the play's metaphysical and moral meanings. Spitzer does not attempt to mediate among these interpretations, but rather demonstrates that a proper knowledge of the literary and intellectual traditions within which Lope was working demands an interpretation that is political and metaphysical at once—not, certainly, from a modern point of view, but within the framework of ancient, medieval, and Renaissance theories about the correspondence between celestial harmony and earthly communal relationships.

   In relating Lope's play to this framework of ideas, Spitzer here applies to an individual work one of his major intellectual preoccupations during the later part of his career, namely, the continuity and changes since antiquity of classical and Christian conceptions of world harmony. Although his formal study of these conceptions was never completed,[1] their application to *Fuenteovejuna* provides an exemplary model of how certain traditional notions about the world become embodied and transformed in a great literary work.

   As the title to this essay indicates, Spitzer believed that formal and thematic matters are "equivalent" to each other. Thus he shows how the emergence of group solidarity in the course of the play manifests itself in the play's ceremonial language and in Lope's imitation of themes and rhythms characteristic of Spanish folk songs. Indeed, for Spitzer the play's themes reveal themselves in even the most minute details of language, for example in the words "¡Los reyes . . . vivan!" in which the deviation from the expected word order ("¡Vivan los reyes!") suggests what he calls "an exceptional leap from the idea of lawlessness to the affirmation of loyalty to the Crown." To create that encompassing interpretation of the play which Spitzer finds lacking in the work of earlier critics, he shows how a multitude of earlier texts—drawn, for example, from pastoral poetry, musical theory, political theory, balladry, chronicle history—are brought together in Lope's play, fused, in fact, with a harmony that is itself an "equivalent," as it were, of the world harmony that the play seeks to voice.

This essay was first published in *Hispanic Review*, 23 (1955): 274–92. It was reprinted in Spitzer's *Romanische Literaturstudien: 1936–1956* (Tübingen, 1959), pp. 760–77.

A Central Theme and Its Structural Equivalent in Lope's 'Fuenteovejuna'

Thanks to Professor Joaquín Casalduero's article *"Fuenteovejuna,"* we know that this play of Lope de Vega's has no political (or "revolutionary") purpose, as Marcelino Menéndez y Pelayo thought—and as the Russians who revived the play in our days may still think—but treats a metaphysical or moral problem:

> Against the violent affirmation of instinct there rises, equally decisive, the affirmation of society. Against instinct's individualizing and destructive force, the power of society's total concert. The master cannot be, must not be, instinct; man, society, has the will to overcome this evil master and replace him with his true lord, reason, majestic and Catholic. Passion remains within the sphere of individuality; the institution of matrimony—now (in the seventeenth century) more than ever a religious and social institution—belongs to society.[1]

Recently Professor Alexander A. Parker has reaffirmed the unity of theme in the play "to be found in the moral conceptions governing the presentation of the theme—so common in the Spanish literature of the later Golden Age—of the rebellion of the individual against the social order. Treason and rape are dramatically unified in *Fuenteovejuna* because they are morally akin—aspects of an individual will to social disorder.[2] Geoffrey W. Ribbans has shown more specifically the coherence and basic unity of the two plots of the play (that of the Comendador's rebellion against the Catholic Kings [Ferdinand and Isabella] and that of the outrages perpetrated by him upon the women of the community): strangely enough, while quoting Casalduero's and Parker's judgments mentioned above with approval, he takes exception to most of the former's parallels between various passages in the play.[3]

In my opinion, both Casalduero and Ribbans have overlooked one aspect of the central theme that dominates the whole play: the relationship between love and musical harmony. The first indication of this theme is to be found in scene 2 of act 1 (discussed by both our critics, but without mention of its impact on the play), in which the debating contest between the rural people of Fuenteovejuna about courtesy ("the key to love") and love takes place.*

---

* Frondoso provokes the debate on courtesy (which will be logically followed by the debate on love since (ll. 13–14) "es llave la cortesía / para abrir la voluntad" [courtesy is the key to good will][4] by calling the *labradoras* [peasant girls] Laurencia and Pascuala *hermosas damas* [fair ladies]. Professor Casalduero thinks that the *labradoras* are "transformed"—a transformation he calls "typically baroque"—into "ladies" so that they may be able to sustain their roles as arbiters in the debate.[5] I believe that they *are*, to Lope's mind, true ladies while refusing to be so called (ll. 321–23: *Laurencia*. "*Allá en la ciudad*, Frondoso, / llámase por cortesía / de esa suerte" [*In the city*, Frondoso, such words are used in courtesy]). Indeed, the meaning of the debate of rustic characters on courtesy and love must be that true courtesy (neither hypocrisy, ll. 292–320, nor discourtesy, ll. 328–48) is found, not in the *ciudad* (or *corte* [court]) but only in the *aldea* [village], and that, similarly, true love is better known in the latter than in the former. The peasants also philosophize without any schooling in philosophy (ll. 371–72: *Mengo*. "Yo no sé filosofar; / leer, ¡ojalá supiera!" [I don't know how to philosophize; as for reading, I wish I could!]; ll. 427–30: *Pascuala* (to Barrildo). "En materia habéis entrado / que, por ventura, acrisola / los caletres de los sabios / en sus cademias y escuelas" [You have raised a question which the wise men in their schools and academies cannot solve]); they are also historians without being trained in this field (Mengo confesses, l. 1178: "que yo no entiendo de historia" [I don't know too much about history], yet knows the nature of the tyrant Heliogabalus whose name he mispronounces); they are also born poets, as we shall see later, and they are sometimes stylized poetic personages derived from poetry (the name *Frondoso* belongs to the climate of the Nemorosos and Silvanos of bucolic poetry). Fuenteovejuna itself is an idyllic island of Primitivism in which the values of the Golden Age are still miraculously preserved. In this ideology in which biblical (the shepherds first aware of religious truth, as in Lope's "Christmas novel" *Los pastores de Belén*) and classical themes (the poetic shepherds of bucolic poetry, as in Lope's pastoral novel *Arcadia*) are fused, how much belongs distinctively to the baroque? Karl Vossler has wittily characterized the shepherds in Lope's *Los pastores de Belén* in a manner reminiscent of our scene: they behave like a "Spanish academy or contestants for literary prizes, or else—and therewith humor makes its entrance into their conversation—like *an association of ladies and gentlemen* devoted to entertainment, play and wit. . . . Occasionally they act very sophisticated, dainty, encyclopedic in knowledge and with their simple souls

improvise the most abstrusely artificial speeches. Lope's own cultural heritage is entirely at their disposal: they are given, as it were, to mixing and stirring, with their native nimble wooden spoons, a dough that is composed of pastoral and scholastic, literary and popular, humanistic and theological traditions."[6]

In another passage Vossler describes Lope's habit of having his characters expand on general topics (such as love, rural life, etc.) in rhetorical-lyrical couplets in which the basic thought is varied as though it were a musical theme—a *melodramatischer Sprachzauber* [melodramatic linguistic magic] that often makes on us an impression as of "villagers' Sunday clothes."[7] This description fits Frondoso and Laurencia's "duet" (with variations on the theme of "courtesy") in our scene. Vossler seems to have sensed the relationship between such "music of words" and music, without, however, having recognized the thematic value of music for any of Lope's plays.

Anyone familiar with my study on the pagan and Christian concept of World Harmony (especially with the passages on world harmony in the literature of the Spanish Golden Age) will immediately recognize in that scene certain *topoi* connected with the Pythagorean-Platonic tradition.[8] In the debate which appears at this point as a dramatic hors d'oeuvre, the three peasants Frondoso, Barrildo, and Mengo submit their different opinions on love to the judgment of the two maidens Laurencia and Pascuala—a debate which is medieval in origin and, *pace* Casalduero, "baroque" only insofar as baroque literature, as has been demonstrated by Ernst Robert Curtius in many other cases, has preserved medieval devices. Since the characters of the villagers appear firmly delineated in their theoretical opinions on love, and since the integration of the contrasting opinions will take place in the course of the play, when the deeds of the debaters can be measured against their words, one must concede that this apparent hors d'oeuvre is, to the contrary, essential to the dramatic development of the play. In the debate we see Barrildo and Frondoso (the latter, however, remaining mainly silent because his own love must make him partial) pitted against Mengo. Barrildo represents the Platonic-Christian concept of musical world harmony (ll. 379–82):

> El mundo de acá y de allá,
> Mengo, todo es armonía.
> Armonía es puro amor,
> Porque el amor es concierto.

[The world here and beyond, Mengo, is perfect harmony. Harmony is pure love, for love is complete agreement.]

We recognize here the typical identification of love with musical harmony: *el mundo de allá* is the Pythagorean harmony of the spheres
which is reflected on this earth (*el mundo de acá*) in human friendship and love; and *concierto*, meaning *concordia discors*, loving
strife, rivalry in love, is the traditional term used at Lope's time for
the cause of the harmonious functioning of the laws of nature. And
Barrildo's subsequent reference to a recent sermon of the local parish
priest who quoted Plato's concept of love is meant to underline the
basic unity of Christian and Platonic thought. On the contrary, the
earthy Mengo, a philosopher *malgré lui*, the "natural man," purports to think rather in Aristotelian terms: for him "love" is mainly
"self-love," equal to "need." Nevertheless, this naturalistic philosopher still retains the ancient teaching about the well-tempered condition, or harmonious blend, of our temperaments (whether chol-
eric, melancholic, phlegmatic, or sanguine) as well as the corollary
belief that the love of each individual "corresponds" (= is harmoniously attuned) to his individual, permanent temperament (ll. 390–
92: "cada cual tiene amor / correspondiente a su humor / que le con-
serva en su estado" [each person has love proportionate to his humor, which preserves him in his condition]); he even admits the existence of the harmonious divine love and of the Platonic Idea (ll.
385–88: "Amor hay, y el que entre sí / gobierna todas las cosas, /
correspondencias forzosas / de cuanto se mira aquí [As far as the natural world goes, I do not deny it. There is love which rules all things
through an obligating interrelationship]), insisting only that on this
earth man's love is disharmoniously selfish—in the play, however, he
will be shown to be more idealistic in his practice than in his theory:
he will defend Laurencia with altruistic courage and the spirit of self-
sacrifice. Indeed, already in our scene, though Aristotle had paralleled love and hunger as the two main urges of mankind, Mengo proposes as parallel to love the somewhat nobler instinct of self-defense,
later to give a shining example for defense of others. In her tentative
arbitration of the debate (which is characterized as such by Pascuala,
ll. 441–43: "Laurencia no quiere bien, / yo tengo poca experiencia; /
¿cómo daremos sentencia?" [Laurencia does not love deeply, and as
for me, I have little experience. How are we to pass judgment?]),
Laurencia proposes a synthesis of Barrildo's idealistic and Mengo's
more naturalistic philosophy, a synthesis in which the desire for transcendent beauty (l. 410: "{amor} es un deseo de hermosura" [love is
a desire for beauty]) is fused with self-love in the more refined form

of love for one's own honor (ll. 435–36: "¿Amas tú?—Mi propio honor" [Are you in love?—I love my honor]), a solution which she, too, later in the play will transcend: while defending her honor against the Comendador, she will reach the harmony of true love with a noble fellow being, Frondoso, whose spirit of sacrifice will satisfy her desire for spiritual beauty and with whom she comes to identify herself completely.*

---

*This second stage in Laurencia's development is reflected by the sonnet in act 3 (ll. 2159–72), in which she gives expression to the suffering inflicted on her by the fear for her beloved's life: by this very suffering she has become the truly loving wife of Frondoso:

> Que no es, a firme fe, pena ligera
> ver llevar el temor, el bien robado. . . .
> *Al bien suyo se inclina mi deseo.*
>
> [For the heart is rare that does not bend or move
> When fear his threat on the belov'd has lain. . . .
> *His good is all the end of my desire.*][9]

Lope has not given to Frondoso any similar poem as a counterpart, for Frondoso, who from the start loved Laurencia altruistically and ideally, has not undergone any parallel inner development.

The motif of the musical harmony of love which was outspokenly mentioned in act 1, scene 2, by Barrildo will continue through the play in the form of delicate dramatic allusions: whenever *music* will be played (or a song sung by the *músicos*) we must infer also the presence of the motif of *love and harmony*. Thus, in the next scene, after Fernán Gómez's (the Comendador's) servant Flores has reported to the villagers the martial exploits of his master in company of his friend, the Maestre de Calatrava (their seizure of the city of Ciudad Real and the revenge taken by them on its inhabitants) and he hears the strains of music evidently in preparation for the reception of the conqueror, he bids them welcome the Comendador with all joy and *love* (love being taken here as feudal loyalty; ll. 525–28):

> Mas ya *la música* suena:
> recebilde alegremente,
> que al triunfo, *las voluntades* {=el amor}
> son los mejores laureles.

[But now the *music* sounds. Welcome him (the Comendador) with festivity, for *good will* is one of the most precious of a victor's laurels.]

And when the Comendador arrives and the *músicos* have sung by way of welcome their *coplas* [poems, songs], whose archaically simple language, the language of the folk song,* reflects the community's naive feelings of loyalty (ll. 529–30: "Sea bien venido / el Comendadore . . ." [Welcome, Comendador . . .]), the former acknowledges their friendliness by praising their *amor* (ll. 545–46):

> Villa, yo os agradezco justamente
> *el amor* que me habéis aquí mostrado.

[Citizens of Fuenteovejuna, I am most grateful to you for *the love* you show me.]

Then the Alcalde Esteban in his welcoming speech offers to Fernán Gómez the simple rural presents which are all that the *aldea* can offer to a nobleman who is a city-dweller (ll. 566–68):

> Acá no tienen armas ni caballos,
> no jaeces bordados de oro puro,
> si no es oro *el amor de los vasallos*.

[Here you will find no arms, no horses, no harnesses studded with pure gold. The only gold is the *love your vassals feel toward you*.]

(note again the feudalistic expression!), assuring him of the "voluntades {=amor} que tenéis ganadas" [literally, the wills you have won over—EDS.].

---

*Note the paragogic -*e* of *comendadore*, a feature suggesting popular epic or *romance* [ballad] poetry. Lope, who as we know through Ramón Menéndez Pidal has preserved for us so much of otherwise unattested authentic Spanish folk poetry, is here inventing a folk song—as Goethe and Heine will do again in the age of the systematic revival of folk poetry.

The scene is rounded out by the repeated singing of the stanza of welcome "Sea bien venido el Comendadore. . . ." In this song, in which the villagers have chosen, at this moment before the latent crisis has broken out into the open, to emphasize the *harmonious* nature of the conqueror of Ciudad Real (he is affable and soft-spoken in peace just as he is courageous in war (ll. 535–38): "Si en las paces blando, / dulce en las razones. / Venciendo moricos / fuertes como un roble" [In peacetime gracious, / Gentle his reasoning, / When fighting the Moors / Strong as an oak]),* we find the traditional *viva*'s characteristic of public expression of communal good feelings (ll. 533–34, 543–44):

¡*Vivan* los Guzmanes!
¡*Vivan* los Girones!
¡*Viva* muchos años,
viva Fernán Gómez!

[*Long live* the Guzmanes!
Long live the Girones!
May he live for many years,
Long live Fernán Gómez!]

These *viva*'s, these chanted pledges of loyalty (or love), will accompany us throughout the play—with them it is as though the concepts of "love" and "musical harmony" that had been brought into a relationship in act 1, scene 2, had now found durable artistic expression, and as though a musical superstructure† had been erected before the eyes of the mind of the spectator above the development of the plot on the stage.

---

*This is how the passage should be punctuated (no period after *razones!*). [Spitzer's view is contrary to that of many modern editors.—EDS.] We have to do here with the ancient and medieval *topos*, analyzed by Curtius, of the hero who is wise (eloquent) as well as brave (Odysseus, Olivier, etc.). It must be noted that in those *coplas* of welcome the villagers show their extraordinary candor and good will: although Fernán Gómez comes to them as the conqueror of Ciudad Real, they also see in him the conqueror of the Moors (ll. 537–40: "Venciendo moricos / fuertes como un roble, / de Ciudad Reale / viene vencedore" [From Ciudad Real he comes victorious]), and in the welcome is included the Maestre, the friend and comrade-in-arms of Fernán Gómez, although he does not appear together with him on the stage:

¡*Vivan los Guzmanes!*
¡*Vivan los Girones!*

†It is well known that in Renaissance paintings we find visual representations of such a musical superstructure: in the *supercoelum* of Lorenzo Bicci's "Coronation of the Virgin" or in the arches and vaults of Leonardo's "Last Supper" (in which Charles de Tolnay has recognized allusions to World Harmony).

The next *música* with *viva*'s we will hear ushers in the scene of the wedding of Laurencia and Frondoso in act 2, scene 15: it is Mengo* who sings the *coplas* which, if not too successful poetically, render the feelings of the community as well as they define the total absence of disharmony in an ideal marriage (ll. 1472–74, 1503–6):

¡Vivan muchos años
los desposados!
¡Vivan muchos años! . . .
¡Vivan muchos años juntos
los novios, ruego a los cielos,
y por envidias ni celos
ni riñan ni anden en puntos!

[Long live the bride and groom!
Many long and happy years to them. . . .
God grant the bride and groom long life
Free from envy and jealous strife.]

---

*He is blamed by other characters for the prosaic quality of his verse (ll. 1477–80, 1510–11: *Barrildo*. "¿Supiéraslo tú trovar / mejor que él está trovado?" —*Frondoso*. "Mejor entiende de azotes, / Mengo, que de versos ya. . . . ¡Maldiga el cielo el poeta, / que tal coplón arrojó! [*Barrildo*. You could have done better (singing) yourself, couldn't you? —*Frondoso*. Mengo knows more about whippings now than songs. . . . Heaven curse the poet who conceived such a poem!], but Mengo exculpates himself by comparing the poet—obviously an improvising poet *à la* Lope himself—with a pastrycook who throws his verse at random, as if it were dough, into the "cauldron of paper," confident that its sweetness will overcome its comic effect, only to be forced perhaps in default of customers to eat the cake himself. Why does Lope here, as if in an interlude, present Mengo as a miscast troubador? Obviously because he wishes to present Mengo as the "natural man," of no poetic talent, but endowed with good will, the right insight into the harmony of marriage—and an untamable urge to sing out of the fulness of his heart. Lope saw in Mengo the raw material of himself, the poet Lope.

But already the Comendador approaches—who will disturb the ceremony and transform it into "mourning" (l. 1642: "Volvióse en luto la boda" [The wedding has become a mourning]). He too is introduced by *música* (= a song sung by the *músicos*), but not by any *viva*'s, rather by a *romance* (broken down by the refrain into two stanzas) which treats of lust (ll. 1554–57):

¿Para qué te escondes,
niña gallarda?
Que mis linces deseos
paredes pasan.

[Why are you hiding, fair maiden,
Know you not that my keen (literally, lynx—EDS.) desire
Can pierce the thickest wall?]

The musical superstructure above the action on the stage serves this time to foreshadow the threat of disharmony: the "lynxes of desire" may overcome any obstacle (ll. 1558–65: "ramas-celosías-paredes-los mares y las montañas" [branches, curtains, walls, sea and mountain]) in a parody of true love (ll. 1562–64: "quien tiene amor, / los mares y las montañas / atraviesa fácilmente" [love passes sea and mountain]). This *romance*, which describes the victory of lust over modesty, decency, and (we must infer) social order, is a foil to the picture of harmonious marital love as unfolded in Mengo's previous *coplas*. It is, however, not a part of the action of the play by which the villagers take a stand (as in the *viva*'s) but rather one of those warnings to the protagonists,* customary in Lope's plays, issued by a chorus voicing popular opinion and therefore presented in the objective, lyrical form of a folk song.

---

* The protagonists of our play and the place where its action takes place appear here suddenly transformed and stylized into the typical figures and the setting of a *romance* that relates historical events (ll. 1546–49):

> *Al val* de Fuenteovejuna
> *la niña en cabellos* baja;
> *el caballero* la sigue
> *de la Cruz de Calatrava*
>
> [*To the valley* of Fuenteovejuna
> Came *the maid with the flowing hair.*
> *A knight of Calatrava*
> Followed her to the valley here.]

A similar transposition occurs in Lope's play *El caballero de Olmedo* when a *labrador* sings to the protagonists a song of warning in which the murder appears as already having taken place:

> *Que* de noche lo mataron
> al caballero
> la gala de Medina,
> la flor de Olmedo.
>
> [By night they killed him
> The knight
> The splendor of Medina,
> The flower of Olmedo.]

Treating of the "narrative *que*" in popular texts that indicate rumors, or hearsay, I wrote about the stanzas of *El caballero de Olmedo*, "Lope presents the song, so anchored in the plot of the work, as emanating from the anonymous popular patrimony."[10] The difference between the folk song of warning in *El caballero de Olmedo* and that of *Fuenteovejuna* is that in the former the warning is not heeded by the protagonist while it is in the latter. Franz Grillparzer remarked that such poetic warnings (for instance in *El duque de Viseo*) issued choruslike by the anonymous soul of the people go generally unheeded by the protagonists of Lope's plays, and Walter Naumann, in an article on Grillparzer and the Spanish drama,[11] builds a general theory of Lope's drama on Grillparzer's remarks (exemplifying with *El caballero de Olmedo* and *Las paces de los reyes y Judía de Toledo*): according to him the unity of the play consists only in that religious and national collective consciousness (*Bewusstsein der Gemeinschaft*) which finds its expression both in the "warnings" given to the characters and in the deeds of the latter (the connection between warnings and deeds not being of a moral nature). But this generalization fails to count with plays such as *Peribáñez* and *Fuenteovejuna* in which the communal conscience is itself a protagonist. In such a type of play the "warning" by the communal spirit must necessarily be heeded.

One might still ask why the maiden's submission to lust is presented in the lyric in so artistic a form, for the two stanzas show beautiful patterns of visual design and an enchanting dance-rhythm, as was pointed out by Dr. Carmen P. Fernández-Cerra: "In the dance of the souls the *seguidilla* joins the figures of knight and maiden, painted by the ballad in a simulation of movement."[12] It is as though Lope at this point took the part of the "tyrant" and wished his enterprise well. The answer must be that the musical superstructure corresponds here, not to the actual expression of the townspeople's moral feelings (as do the *viva*'s), but indeed to that collective timeless Mneme, characterized by Naumann, for which the story of the seduction of a beautiful Maiden by a handsome Knight has become a historically remote, objective *aesthetic* subject. Many folk songs have a manner of treating heartrending events of individual human lives as if nature itself, in her cruel, unalterable and impressive beauty, had willed them.

To the mind of the people the victory of evil appears here as having already happened, as though the age-old communal experience fatalistically admitted the possibility of that event and had already an age-old musical-poetic pattern ready for its description. The subsequent moral victory of Laurencia (for she will not succumb to the Comendador) will appear all the greater precisely because *vox populi* [the voice of the people] had already anticipated her defeat.

Coming back now to the more direct intervention of the communal spirit as embodied in the *viva*'s, we shall find these again, but this time counterbalanced by as many *muera*'s [Death to . . .], in the first scene of act 3 in which the village council decides to kill the "tyrant," but to uphold royalty, the ultimate guarantor of justice. Here emphasis is placed on the breach of order to which the villagers see themselves forced to resort in order to reestablish the order ("gobernar en paz esta república" [govern this republic in peace], as one of the Regidors formulates it)[13] that had been disrupted by the tyrant. For this disorderly reestablishment of order to take place, one element of harmony at least is necessary—the unanimity of the public opinion of Fuenteovejuna (l. 1806): "juntad el pueblo a una voz" [to rally the whole town, or, literally, to unite the people in one voice—EDS.] is a requirement not only dictated by "democratic procedure," but related to the idea of harmony and social order as such (we may be reminded of the term *unisonus,* coined without any political implication by the Platonist Boethius; ll. 1801–14):

Regidor.	Muramos todos.
Barrildo.	. . . mueran estos {the rulers who have transgressed the "norm" = the "tyrants"}.
Juan Rojo.	¿Qué *orden* pensáis tener?
Mengo.	Ir a matarle *sin orden.*
	Juntad el pueblo a una voz,
	que todos están conformes
	en que los tiranos mueran. . . .
	¡Los reyes nuestros señores
	vivan!
Todos.	*¡Vivan muchos años!*
Mengo.	*¡Mueran tiranos traidores!*
Todos.	*¡Traidores tiranos mueran!*
[*Councilman.*	We shall die together.
Barrildo.	. . . death to the traitors.
Juan Rojo.	What shall our *orders* be?
Mengo.	To kill the Comendador *without order.*
	To rally the whole town around us:
	let us all agree to kill the tyrants. . . .
	Long live the Kings, our lords!
All.	*Long live the Kings!*
Mengo.	*Death to the traitor tyrants!*
All.	*Death to the traitor tyrants!*]

Later, Laurencia decides that the women of Fuenteovejuna, as modern Amazons acting in exemplary fashion, shall take part in the uprising, but (as Casalduero has seen) "with preservation of order," that is, of the limitations that "order" imposes on the feminine sex (ll. 1829–31):

Que puestas *todas en orden,*
acometamos un hecho
que dé espanto a todo el orbe.

[I propose that *we all band together* and (literally, arranged in order, let us—EDS.) perform a deed that will shake the world.]

What interests us here mainly is the manner in which the decision of the villagers to shift their allegiance from the "tyrant" to "the Kings" adopts the form of shouted *viva*'s, no longer set to music, from which, however, they were generated in the scenes of the welcome of Fernán Gómez and of the marriage of Laurencia and Frondoso. Since the villagers who in this moment are violating the order of love and harmony have ultimately not ceased to act in the name of those principles, it is only fitting that the expression of their attitude should reflect the same ambiguity: the *viva*'s now *come* from "music" but *are* no longer music, but shouts of passion. The principle of order is even present in that primitive mind Mengo, who had proclaimed the rule of disorder and murder (*matarle sin orden*): it would have been logical that he would have proceeded from his statement (ll. 1807–8), *todos están conformes / en que los tiranos mueran*, to a wild shout: *¡Muera el tirano!* [Death to the tyrant!] or *¡Fernán Gómez muera!* [Death to Fernán Gómez!] (which will indeed be the battle cry in the later scene of the actual murder, l. 1887). Instead, his mind leaps in our scene to a first affirmation of order (l. 1811): *¡Los reyes, nuestros señores, vivan!* which will precede the negative wish (l. 1813): *¡Mueran tiranos traidores!**

---

* Notice the plural *tiranos* by which, even in the outburst of popular passion, the principle is put before the individual case of Fernán Gómez. After the murder of the latter the Alcalde will formulate the same idea even more abstractly (l. 2078): *muera la tiranía* [death to tyranny]. The assertion by Mengo first of the principle of order, then of that of "disorder," has an analogy in Lope's own way of thinking: the title of his play *Las paces de los reyes y Judía de Toledo*, at first glance puzzling because of its hysteron proteron (for there must first have existed the attraction of the Jewess of Toledo to the King for the reconciliation of the King with the Queen to take place), must be explained by the same emphasis on order first, disorder later.

In this moment of a desperate decision "the Kings," the only principle of order left, must come first. The syntactical form of the two passionate outcries (*¡Los reyes . . . vivan! ¡Mueran tiranos traidores!*) is also interesting: as Professor Anna Hatcher has pointed out to me, we would expect in the first sentence the inversion of the subject regular in the syntactical pattern of the wish: *¡vivan los reyes!* (as we find it indeed in the previous *viva*-scenes: *¡Viva Fernán Gómez! ¡Vivan los desposados!*), but in Mengo's mind the exceptional leap from the idea of lawlessness to the affirmation of loyalty to the Crown entailed also a breaking away from the pattern of inversion usual in wishes, so that an "inversion of the inversion" took place: therefore *¡Los reyes . . . vivan!*, only later to be followed, in the curse of the tyrants which grows out of the blessing of the sovereigns, by the regular inverted form of the sentence (l. 1813): *¡Mueran tiranos traidores!**

---

* The subsequent line (l. 1814) given to the chorus (*todos*), *¡Traidores tiranos mueran!*, shows in its "inversion of the inversion" (the order: subject-verb contrary to the previous pattern: verb-subject) the typical syntax of an "echo-speech."

Thus *orden, paz, armonía, amor* [order, peace, harmony, love] are not totally absent in this turbulent scene which is somehow "unmusical" and "musical" at the same time. That I am right in the assumption of the presence of the motif of "love and harmony" even in the worst moments of the uprising seems to me to be borne out by l. 1864 (when the Comendador, freeing Frondoso from his chains, asks him to pacify the leaders of the revolutionary crowd, Frondoso answers): "Yo voy, señor, que *amor les ha movido*" [I'm going, sir— *love has spurred them to action*]—this verse, left unexplained by the editions I have seen, must mean that the rebellion was ultimately an act of love, an attempt to reestablish harmony.

In the process of the rebellion the *viva*-motif will be further expanded: now it is the name of the village as such that will enter the pattern. The village that had already repeatedly been presented as a unit (in ll. 545, 1237, etc.) is now shown us in united activity (l. 1806: *a una voz*). After Mengo has repeated (l. 1865) the original cry, *¡Vivan Fernando e Isabel, y mueran los traidores!*, Frondoso calls out (l. 1874) *¡Viva Fuenteovejuna!*, and this new battle cry will from now on be fused with the previous variations; it comes at the time when the group spirit of the community has become fully articulate, when Fuenteovejuna becomes the true antagonist of the tyrant and must act autonomously; at the same time the cry *¡Viva Fuenteovejuna!* reminds us of the relative smallness of the now constituted cell of resistance (for it obviously represents a brave attempt to imitate the model of such national battle cries as *¡Viva España!*):

Esteban. *¡Fuenteovejuna, y los tiranos mueran!* (l. 1878)
Todos.   *¡Fuenteovejuna! ¡Viva el rey Fernando!*
            ¡Mueran malos cristianos, y traidores! (ll. 1882–83)
Todos.   *¡Fuenteovejuna, y Fernán Gómez muera!* (l. 1887) {Note the
            progression from "the tyrants" to the individual "tyrant."}
Todos.   *¡Fuenteovejuna, y viva el rey Fernando!* (l. 1919)

Música will return to the stage again [in scene 10] at the moment
when the villagers celebrate their liberation from the tyrant and
when violent collective passion has subsided (ll. 2028–30):

Músicos (cantan). ¡Muchos años vivan
                     Isabel y Fernando,
                     y mueran los tiranos!

At this celebration each one of the three *labradores* whom we already know improvises *coplas* as required by rural etiquette. (We remember that the parallel singing of *coplas* has been interrupted in
act 2 by the appearance of Fernán Gómez.) In the three *coplas* the
tone of love for the sovereigns has increased, the expressions of
hatred for the "tyrants" (now no longer the one tyrant Fernán
Gómez) having dwindled. The three *coplas*, bound together by the
viva's of the refrain and, perhaps, by the single melody to which they
were sung, reflect the individual frame of mind of the three improvis-
ers: Christian, classical, and burlesque-popular. Frondoso, the pious
Christian lad* who has won the hand of Laurencia, focuses his attention on the faithfulness of the regal married couple who on a
higher level reflect the union of love between himself and Laurencia
(note the return of the expression *para en uno son* [freely translated,
they are made for each other—EDS.] that had been applied previously {l. 738} to the rural couple)—indeed, we have the impression
that the marriage of the Catholic Kings is celebrated before us, at
that moment (ll. 2035–42):

                    ¡Vivan la bella Isabel
                    y Fernando de Aragón
                    pues que para en uno son,
                    él con ella, ella con él!
                    A los cielos San Miguel
                    lleve a los dos de las manos.
                    ¡Vivan muchos años,
                    y mueran los tiranos!

[Long live fair Isabella
and Ferdinand of Aragon.
*He is made for her
And she is meant for him.*
May Saint Michael guide them
To Heaven by the hand.
Long live Isabella and Ferdinand
And death to the tyrants!]

---

* It is now the more cultured Frondoso who, when improvising his *copla*, expresses a modest *sit pro ratione voluntas* [let will take the place of reason], just as the uncultured Mengo had done before (compare l. 2059 with ll. 2035–42)—the unglorious Miltons of Lope's Arcadia, whether cultured or not, are endowed with equal modesty.

Barrildo the Platonist thinks rather in terms of ancient *fama* and ancient heroes (ll. 2047–49, 2051–53):

> ¡Vivan los reyes *famosos*
> muchos años, pues que tienen
> *la vitoria* . . .
> ¡Salgan siempre *vitoriosos*
> *de gigantes y de enanos,*
> y mueran los tiranos!

> [Long live the *famous* kings
> For they are *victorious* . . .
> May they conquer always (literally,
>   may they always emerge
>   *victorious* over—EDS.)
> *All giants and dwarfs* . . .
> And death to the tyrants!]

Finally Mengo, the proponent of natural self-love, who has still not forgotten his flogging, deals in his *copla* with his personal ordeal, only at the end echoing the *viva*'s of the others in a comical manner that betrays his ignorance of the right words even when his feelings are right (ll. 2064–65):

> ¡vivan los Reyes *Cristiánigos,*
> y mueran los *tiránigos!**

(It is characteristic of him to use, so to speak, hypercorrect forms, the proparoxytonal suffixes having for him a more learned flavor.)

*The formations in *-igo* belong to a pattern familiar in burlesque popular poetry: compare the Asturian *copla* quoted by Menéndez Pidal, "Axudádeme aquí meus óyigos / A faguéregue esta comídiga, / Que esta gárabugarabuyádiga / Non la podo ver encendídiga" [loosely translated, My eyes, help me to make this dinner (meal), for I cannot see that this torch is aglimmer (lit)—EDS.].[14] Mengo is showing in his willful alteration of traditional language the anarchic "natural man" that is in him and that, even when bowing to social order (in rallying to the *viva*'s), is tempted to go his own capricious way—which however implies a recognition of higher standards.

After the lyrical *coplas* have been recited the Alcalde Esteban brings home to the villagers (and to the spectators) the dramatic situation in which they are caught now, after the murder of Fernán Gómez: they will have to undergo an investigation by the Crown. The Alcalde's speech will begin with the pattern of the *coplas* (the type *¡vivan los reyes y mueran los tiranos!*), only modified by him to the more official or impersonal wording (ll. 2076–78):

> ¡Vivan Castilla y León,
> y las barras de Aragón,
> y muera la tiranía!

> [Long live Castile and Leon
> And the bars of Aragon.
> Down with tyranny!]

then to return to the idea of the unity as it had crystallized in the battle cry *¡(viva) Fuenteovejuna!*—unanimity, he admonishes his listeners, is again required from the villagers (ll. 2079, 2087–88: "Advertid, Fuenteovejuna . . ." {compare the same *ad sensum* construction in l. 545}; "Concertaos todos a una / en lo que habéis de decir" [People of Fuenteovejuna, listen . . . agree now among yourselves on what to say]) and it is this very unanimity which should be affirmed in their answers to the royal investigator: "it is {no single person, but the whole of} Fuenteovejuna that murdered Fernán Gómez"—to which proposal the villagers give indeed their unanimous consent (ll. 2089–94):

Frondoso. ¿Qué es tu consejo?
Esteban.   Morir
          diciendo ¡Fuenteovejuna!
          Y a nadie saquen de aquí.
Frondoso. Es el camino derecho:
          ¡Fuenteovejuna lo ha hecho!

Esteban.   ¿Queréis responder así?
Todos.   ¡Sí!

[*Frondoso.* What is your advice?
Esteban.   To die saying *Fuenteovejuna* and nothing else.
Frondoso. That's fine! *Fuenteovejuna did it!*
Esteban.   Do you want to answer in that way?
All.   *Yes!*]

Thus the affirmation of group solidarity after the collective murder grows out of the expression of group solidarity that preceded it: *Fuenteovejuna* (*lo ha hecho*) is, as it were, the past tense of *¡(viva) Fuenteovejuna!* that at the moment when it was pronounced was a future tense heralding action yet to be taken. And this unanimity crystallized in *Fuenteovejuna* (*lo ha hecho*) will carry over into the dress-rehearsal trial scene with Mengo by which the villagers prepare themselves for the investigation and into the actual scene of the trial before the royal *pesquisidor* [investigator] in which four representatives of the citizenry give under torture the stereotyped answer, *Fuenteovejuna*, Mengo again capping his answer by a burlesque word-coinage of his own (ll. 2246–47):

Juez.   ¿Quién le mató?
Mengo. Señor, *Fuenteovejunica.*

[*Judge.* Who killed him?
Mengo. Sir, *Fuenteovejunica* (literally, Little Fuenteovejuna—EDS.).]

As is so often true in Spanish classical drama, it is left to the *figura del donaire* [the jesting figure] to formulate deepest insights: Mengo's diminutive in *-ico*, one of those superb linguistic finds of Lope, not only characterizes the former's personal attachment to his home town and his personal whimsicality in treating the common language (compare the coinages *tiránigos-cristiánigos* mentioned above), but also serves to emphasize the objective smallness of the township, that smallest social cell in the texture of a country or civilization which however functions, thanks to its Golden-Age-like "primitivism," with a cohesion and firmness reminiscent of the Roman republic.

To the harassed judge there is nothing left but to report to the sovereigns that he is unable to make any report, since there was only one version in existence among the villagers (ll. 2364–67):

porque *conformes a una,*
con un valeroso pecho,

en pidiendo quién lo ha hecho
responden: "*Fuenteovejuna*."

[when asked who had done it, the people answered bravely *with one accord*: "*Fuenteovejuna*."]

Another reflection of the group spirit will occur in the last scene of the play when the Alcalde Esteban pays homage to the sovereigns in their presence (ll. 2388–91):

Isabel.   ¿Los agresores son éstos?
Esteban.   *Fuenteovejuna*, señora,
               que humildes llegan ahora
               para serviros dispuestos.

[*Isabella.* Are these the aggressors?
Esteban.   *Fuenteovejuna*, Your Majesty, who humbly kneel before you,
               ready to serve you.]

(Note again the sense-construction serving to affirm the plurality-that-is-one.) Finally, when we hear in the last lines of the play its title repeated, as was customary in the drama of the Spanish Golden Age (ll. 2450–55),

       Y aquí, discreto senado,
       Fuenteovejuna da fin.

[And at this point, worthy audience, ends the play *Fuenteovejuna*.]

we realize that this title expresses the essence of the play (the solidarity of the village in its own group spirit as it grew before us during the play) to a degree we could hardly have anticipated at the beginning. What Vossler says of the "emphatic" usage in such recapitulations of titles at the end of Lope's plays obtains surely here: the words of the title have at the end become filled with deeper content (they have become *erfüllte Worte* [realized words]). Here—and this is different from the titles quoted by Vossler,[15] for instance, *Sangre inocente* [Innocent Blood], or *¡Mirad a quién alabáis!* [Be Careful of Whom You Praise!], which sum up meaningfully the action of the play—the word *Fuenteovejuna* as it was spoken on the stage has undergone a long and meaningful development during the play: from the *música* of the *viva*'s representative of peace, harmony, and order, an uninterrupted line has led to the battle cry of the villagers united in the attempt at reestablishment of harmony, *¡Viva Fuenteovejuna!* Once this cry had been abridged to *¡Fuenteovejuna!*, it could also serve as a communal confession, *Fuenteovejuna (lo ha hecho)*, in which the guilt is shared by the community, which thus is able to reenter the world of order and peace (and order and peace were present even during the disorder of the uprising in cries of the type *¡vivan los Reyes!*).

Up to this point our study has been concerned with the organic development of our theme and its reflection in a structural element of the play, within the play itself. But since in the case of *Fuenteovejuna* we are in the happy position of knowing exactly its immediate source—the *Chronicle of the Three Orders of the Knights of Santiago, Calatrava, and Alcántara* [*Crónica de las Tres Órdenes y Caballerías de Santiago, Calatrava y Alcántara*], by the member of the latter order Fray Francisco de Rades y Andrada (Toledo 1572)—we may *now* attempt to define—and only now has come the time for such investigation of things extraneous to the play—to what degree our motif was preconditioned by the text of the source. In the about three and a half pages of the chronicle concerning the revolt of Fuenteovejuna we find the following passages parallel to passages of the play:

... determinaron todos *de un consentimiento y voluntad* alzarse contra él {Fernán Gómez} y matarle. Con esta determinacion y furor de pueblo ayrado, con voz de *Fuenteovejuna*, se juntaron. ... {They entered the Comendador's house.} Todos apellidaron: "*Fuente-Ovejuna*," "*Fuente-Ovejuna*," y dezian: "*vivan los reyes don Fernando y doña Isabel, y mueran los traidores y malos christanos.*"* {They did not answer the Comendador's questions about the motives of their rebellion;} antes con grande impetu, *apellidando "Fuente-Ovejuna"* combatieron la pieza. ... Antes que diesse el ánima a Dios, tomaron su cuerpo con grande y regocijado alarido, diziendo "*vivan los Reyes y mueran los traidores ...*" {in the scene of the investigation by the *Pesquisidor*,} preguntavales el Juez: "quién mató al Comendador mayor?" Respondian ellos: "*¡Fuente-Ovejuna!*" Preguntavales: "*¿*Quién es Fuente-Ovejuna?" Respondian "todos los vecinos desta villa."

[*With unanimous consent and one will* they all decided to rise up against him {Fernán Gómez} and kill him. Having thus resolved, in a fury, the enraged people united, shouting "*Fuenteovejuna!*" {They entered the Comendador's house.} They all cried out: "*Fuenteovejuna! Fuenteovejuna!*" and "*Long live the Monarchs Ferdinand and Isabella! Death to traitors and bad Christians!*" {They did not answer the Comendador's questions about the motives of their rebellion;} instead, with great and violent force, *crying "Fuenteovejuna!"* they fought their way into his house. ... Before he gave up his soul to God, they took his body with great and joyous cries of "*Long live the King and Queen!*" and "*Death to traitors!*" ... {In the scene of the investigation by the *Pesquisidor*,} the Judge asked them: "Who killed the Comendador?" They replied: "*Fuenteovejuna!*" He asked them: "Who is Fuenteovejuna?" They replied: "All the people of this town."]

---

*The comparison of the play with its source allows us to state that the particular wording (with no inversion of the subject) of this battle cry at its first appearance is due, as was to be expected, to Lope (the chronicle shows the normal inversion). Lope has then carefully reworded the historically given cry (with inversion) so as to suggest to us the working of the brain of the *gracioso* at the moment when he was coining it before us.[16] It is, of course, Lope who introduced into the cry as preserved by the chronicle (which referred only to *traidores* and *malos cristianos*) the learned ancient concept of *tiranos*, which had been redefined by the Spanish *tratadistas* Suárez, Vitoria, Mariana, who advocated tyrannicide.[17] At one point in the play a comparison of the Comendador with the "Roman Heliogabalus" is suggested by a Mengo who "no entiende de historia" (l. 1178) and, as we said before, while mispronouncing his name, knows exactly his nature.

Thus the idea of the group personality and group responsibility as represented in the battle cry *¡Fuenteovejuna!* in the unanimous answer *Fuenteovejuna* given to the investigating judge, and also in the shouts proclaiming a new regime (*¡vivan los Reyes y mueran los traidores!*)—all this belongs to the source. Lope, reading the text, dramatic in itself, of this chronicle, must already have heard in his ears the echoes of the lines of the play he was to write, and the repetition of the cries in the chronicle must have suggested to him a flow of action punctuated by such ejaculations. But whereas in the chronicle these are only symptoms of rebellion and violence, it was Lope's genius to see them as emanating ultimately from a musical harmony denotative of love, order, and peace (which we find expressed in act 1, scene 2). Lope worked, as it were, from the historical battle cries backward to their metaphysical source. By means of this projection he was able to lift the original village of Fuenteovejuna out of time and space as an island of metaphysical peace, the realization of the Golden Age in the midst of our age of iron, the locus of cosmic harmony in the midst of our world of chaos, at the same time an Arcadia and a Utopia. Thus the "political action" to which the villagers are forced to resort (and with which the drama is mainly concerned) is due only to a temporary and local invasion of that idyllic, timeless peace that is the principle of *any* "Fuenteovejuna" by transient dark forces of disorder. Fernán Gómez, as Casalduero defines him—"the barbarous, instinctive man, this is the man who has lost the purity of heart, the man of the city (city means modern)"[18]—he whose role does not allow him to take part in any of the "music," is also the unmusical man depicted by Shakespeare:

> The man that hath no music in himself
> Nor is not moved with concord of sweet sounds,
> Is fit for treasons, stratagems and spoils.[19]

In contrast, the ideal seat of harmony Fuenteovejuna created by Lope might be described in terms of the same theme of musical harmony that we find with Jonathan Edwards (1747):

The best, most beautiful and most perfect way that we have of expressing a sweet concord of mind to each other is by music. When I would form in my mind ideas of a society in the highest degree happy, I think of them as expressing their love, their joy and the inward concord, and harmony, and spiritual beauty of their souls, by sweetly singing to each other.[20]

The play, starting with harmony and ending in harmony, is throughout informed by that nostalgia for the primitivistic dream of peace which Nietzsche (in his *Birth of Tragedy*) has recognized as the characteristic feature of the "Renaissance Opera," and indeed, the musical superstructure of our play is of an operatic nature. According to Nietzsche, the opera, in contradistinction to Greek tragedy born out of Dionysiac music, shows us an idyllic and optimistic picture of life in which the Ideal appears as attainable and Nature not as lost:

According to this belief there existed once a primeval age of mankind in which man lay at the bosom of Nature and thus was able, in a quite natural way, to enjoy the ideal state of both paradisiac goodness and artistry. And, so the reasoning goes, it is from this primeval man that we all still today are descended and as his descendants still reflect that picture of man. In order better to recognize ourselves in that picture we must only abandon certain features which we have acquired: superfluous learning and the excess of civilization. The civilized man of the Renaissance allowed himself to be led back, by means of imitation of Greek tragedy in his operas, to such a harmony of Nature and Ideal. . . . What pious kindly sentiments must have been the source of such bold endeavors in the midst of a rational civilization—explainable only by the consoling belief that man is at heart indeed the eternally virtuous protagonist of the opera, the eternal shepherd singing to his flute who for all his wayward wanderings can always in the end find his way back to that primeval state. . . . Among the features of the Renaissance Opera there is lacking any note of elegiac grief over the loss {of the Ideal and of Nature}, rather is there to be found the note of serenity which comes from the assurance of possible reconquest.[21]

However satirical may have been Nietzsche's intent in his portrayal of the timeless, unrealistic, primitivistic, pastoral dream underlying the Opera, it is this naive dream of a Christian World Harmony, cherished by the Spanish poet of the Golden Age Lope (the "poet of a poetically innocent age," as Grillparzer* called him), which informs the operatic superstructure in *Fuenteovejuna*.

---

*Our analysis of *Fuenteovejuna* has, however, shown that the further statements of Grillparzer are not correct: "Lope is innocent of concepts and intentions. He creates out of poetic imagination and visualization" (*Vorstellung und Anschauung*). [22] Our play is the consistent realization of a poetic intention centered around a concept ("harmony"). What makes him a poet of what we may call a naive age is his firm belief in the *reality* of this concept.

———————— • ————————

[The comment that follows, originally written in Spanish, appears to have been added by Spitzer sometime after he finished the rest of the essay.—EDS.]

The equation love = musical harmony is also found in Lope's *Dorotea*,[23] which quotes Marsilio Ficino on Plato's *Symposium*:

Fernando. Music is a divine art.
Cesar (the Astrologer). Some say Mercury invented it, others say Aristotle, but what is certain is that the inventor was love. Because harmony is concert, concert is the concord of grave and sharp sounds, and concord was instituted of love; so with that reciprocal benevolence the effect of music, which is delight, continues.

See also Bruce Wardropper's study of *Fuenteovejuna*.[24]

DEVELOPMENT OF A METHOD

Spitzer presented this essay as a talk at the University of Rome on May 23, 1960, only four months before his death at age 73. It reads in every way as his intellectual last will and testament. Like his earlier autobiographical essay, "Linguistics and Literary History," published twelve years before (and reprinted in this volume), this essay recapitulates what Spitzer saw as some of the high points of his career—his dissertation on Rabelais, which combined literary and linguistic methods of investigation to challenge the positivistic assumptions of his teachers; his study of Charles-Louis Philippe, which brought together the new stylistic analysis of narrative with a Freudian attempt to link a writer's verbal habits with his psyche; his essays in what he called "historical semantics," a method that sought to ground the tracing of etymologies within the history of culture.

Yet this later essay is also considerably more self-critical than "Linguistics and Literary History." For one thing, it offers a more detailed history of the stages in his career, including the immensely productive years between the two essays. Thus he explains his turning away from Freud to stress what he calls "structural" analysis, by which he does not of course mean the structuralist mode that was to dominate French criticism during the succeeding decade, but rather an approach that sought to illuminate the various formal and thematic relationships that structure an individual literary work. As in all phases of his career, Spitzer insists on placing his formal insights within a historical framework.

Indeed, Spitzer's belief in the need for such a historical framework motivates his critique, in the last third of this essay, of two critical movements, the New Criticism in America and existentialist criticism on the Continent, both of which had become dominant within their respective geographical domains since the earlier essay. Similar though these movements are for Spitzer in their lack of an adequate historical dimension, they arouse his ire on quite separate grounds. The New Critical emphasis on the ambiguous effects of individual words and syntactical units and its consequent theory of a work's multiplicity of meanings comes into direct conflict with Spitzer's long-held belief that a critic with both historical erudition and sensitivity to language can establish the meaning of a literary work. The existentialist emphasis on the consciousness of the writer, exemplified for Spitzer in the work of his colleague Georges Poulet, in turn violates Spitzer's belief in the integrity and individuality of particular literary works.

In the quarter century since Spitzer's death, the various movements that have crossed the critical scene—structuralism and its aftermath, the study of reception and of the individual reader's response, the view of literature from a feminist perspective and from various ethnic focal points, the attempt to place literary study within the larger framework of the history of institutions—may well have made certain of the values that Spitzer proclaims here seem obsolete. Among these values one might cite his faith in the autonomy of the individual work of art, his refusal to pursue a single line of inquiry to the exclusion of all other lines, his belief that great literature is different in kind from other forms of writing, and his insistence (voiced with particular fervor at the end of this essay) on the critical act as a display of love for a particular poem and for the language in which it was written. Yet Spitzer's faith in a work's coherence and in the recoverability of its meaning is also consonant, as John Freccero points out in the foreword to this volume, with some new views about interpretation that are emerging today. Still, Spitzer's humanistic faith—above all, his faith in that harmonious balance of opposites which he advocates in the final paragraph of this essay (a view consonant with those ideas of world harmony whose history he had traced for many years)—will doubtless seem archaic and idealistic to readers of the late 1980's; indeed, as he reminds us early in the essay, his values were shaped in a stable and seemingly changeless late nineteenth-century Central-European world that few if any of his listeners would have remembered even in 1960.

For inclusion in this volume, the essay was translated by Eileen Reeves from the Italian "Sviluppo di un metodo," which was published in *Cultura neolatina*, 20 (1960): 109–28. To preserve the tone of Spitzer's original lecture, first names have been added in editorial brackets.

Development of a Method

I am grateful to you for having invited me to discuss the development of a method for creating poetic texts—a method called, I believe, the "Spitzerian." Though the development of this method has already been described by several perceptive Italian critics such as [Alfredo] Schiaffini, [Pietro] Citati, and [Emerico] Giachery, and has even been politely criticized by eminent writers such as [Mario] Fubini and [Pier Paolo] Pasolini,[1] I would suppose that the victim of even such friendly treatment might be allowed to express his own doubts about certain aspects of his thought and to point out what he now sees to have been real errors in his work. Permit me, then, to explain how I journeyed from linguistics, which was my field when I began writing around 1910, to literary criticism, now virtually my sole occupation.

I hope that you will pardon this autobiographical touch; it is meant to show how a certain type of criticism originated from a particular chain of factors and influences, not necessarily present in the development of other critics whose work may be as valid as or more valid than my own. *Methode ist Erlebnis*, said the great German literary critic [Friedrich] Gundolf: "method is lived experience."[2] The methods of different literary critics should be different because their experience of life is necessarily different. The radical difference among human beings explains how new discoveries concerning works known for centuries can still be made even by relatively young critics who bring a new sensitivity all their own, their uniqueness as individuals, to an ancient text. Of course, individual temperament may also lead to interpretative errors, such as those I have often committed myself and have had to acknowledge in my later work.

Born and raised in the Vienna that existed before World War I, I studied at the so-called Humanistic Gymnasium, where I was taught the existence of a *poësis perennis*, that is, an ancient classical poetry forever valid as a model or measure for all poetry. In that era, one of a peace such as very few of you will have ever known, values seemed established for all time: Horace and Sophocles, Tacitus and Demosthenes were unchallenged models of artistic perfection. Modern education differs from the one I received, for today, in the absence of stable values, the student is forced to determine for himself a standard for the highest poetry. That is, he does not begin from the experience of an already constituted aesthetic that is beyond his grasp.

In any case, from that early contact with classical poetry I developed the idea that any text could be intelligible, even after millennia, and the conviction that a single explanation of a passage is in all instances the best: in other words, I was protected from the modern anarchy of the multiplicity of intended meanings.

I was cruelly banished from the world of pure and univalent aesthetic forms, however, when I began studying at the university, where the great linguist [Wilhelm] Meyer-Lübke treated language in the manner of a scientist, that is, as a historical sequence of developments conditioned only by intralinguistic factors, and not as an aesthetic product. But his sober and technical instruction familiarized me with the facts of ordinary speech, consisting of well-defined and carefully limited phenomena, along with an exact discipline that enabled me to distinguish the true from the hypothetical with a rigor and a precision that could serve as a prerequisite for any study, even a literary one.

Like all great scientists, Meyer-Lübke could see beyond what he knew how to do so well in his own field. I felt something like relief the day he remarked, during his lecture, that it might be important for the history of Old Italian to determine the verb forms used in Dante's *Rime*, but that "perhaps Dante is too beautiful for this." He was also magnanimous enough to accept my thesis on a subject that he would never have examined himself and that was for me a compromise between linguistic and literary interests: "The Formation of Neologisms as a Stylistic Device Exemplified by Rabelais."[3]

Today, it is self-evident that a poet, particularly a humorist, can obtain extraordinary stylistic effects by the use of neologisms; but around 1910 this was a novel idea, at least in philological circles. At the same time, in Vienna a man outside the discipline of philology—outside, in fact, the academic world—had already intuited the importance of the neologisms that occur unconsciously in dreams, in *lapsus linguae* [linguistic slips], and in conscious forms of self-expression such as jokes and puns. Needless to say, this man was Sigmund Freud, who in his examination of all human deviations from the norm pointed out not so much their aberrant aspect as their functional necessity and productive potential. The fantastic element in a newly coined word gives it an unreal quality, but at the same time such a word has a false reality: if well-formed, it reproduces various determined linguistic paradigms.

Rabelais, whose art of the grotesque had impressed me so profoundly because of its incessant movement between reality and unreality (or nonreality), seemed to me to be the ideal subject for a stylistic analysis of neologisms. In the famous phrase that he used to characterize the professors of the Sorbonne as "sophistes, sorbillans, sorbonagres, sorbonigenes, sorbonicoles, sorboniformes, sorboniseques, niborcisans, sorbonisans, saniborsans," I could see not only an obvious satirical intention but also a desire to create new words capable of generating a new reality. The basis of all these word-formations and the object of Rabelais's assault, the word *Sorbonne*, represents something real, as do the various suffixes, since they are found in other words as well. *Sorboniforme*, too, through its similarity to *multiforme* and *uniforme*, evokes a certain reality. Yet the entire series, and not just the fantastic words *niborcisans* and *saniborsans*, borders on chaos—a chaos bursting with monsters recently given life, which we find amusing only after an instant of fright. (That mixture of sentiments is characteristic of the grotesque.) As if before our very eyes, Rabelais's neologisms depict the infinite number of forms assumed by the monster *Sorbonne*. In Freudian terms, Rabelais frees us from the obsession that he and his fellow humanists must have felt was personified by that medieval institution, and we, though modern readers, experience both the fear and his liberation from it.

Not for twenty years did I discover that the Rabelaisian art of the grotesque is generally characterized by its extraordinary ability to confer reality upon the nonreal, as in the allegorical myth of Antiphysis, who walks head down and feet in the air—by analogy with trees in medieval allegory, whose roots, corresponding to hair, are in

Development of a Method

the earth—or in the myth of the frozen words from the arctic region, which can be thawed and thrown like solid objects onto the bridge of Pantagruel's ship. However, the thesis I had written two decades earlier merely classified, in pedantic fashion, Rabelais's neologisms according to rather insipid literary categories such as "farcical," "burlesque," and "grotesque." Yet at the very least I had treated a prominent linguistic feature of Rabelais's work as if it arose from a creative need that mirrors our own.

After this work on Rabelais, I wrote a stylistic analysis whose title, *Syntactical Innovations of the French Symbolists*, masked its true subject. Though I now consider it an immature work, this piece has recently reappeared in a book published by Einaudi, *Marcel Proust ed altri saggi di letteratura francese moderna*.[4] The editor, [Pietro] Citati, did well to discern in this early study the hesitant first steps of what was to become my method for reading poetic texts, in spite of the experimental and unsteady nature of my categories at that time.

Grammarians like [Ferdinand] Brunot, in his history of the French language, and men of letters like André Barre objected—in the name of the linguistic tradition and in a "sorbonicale" manner that would amaze us today—to the syntactic-stylistic innovations of the Symbolist school. When Brunot, for example, discussed certain Symbolists' use of prepositions, he made this pronouncement: "*De* cannot replace *avec* as [the poet] might wish in this line: '[la tour] devient plus grave et sonore des heures'; and would it work to restore *dans* in place of *en*? 'Et la cloche du soir appelle en le vallon.'"[5] Here we have the rhetoricians' old theory of substitution: *avec* is substituted for *de*, *dans* for *en le*, when in fact, with the phrase "grave et sonore des heures" the poet did not mean "the tower became more solemn and sonorous with the passing hours," but rather "*because of* the passing of the hours, *because of* the hourly chiming of the bell," although even this translation is too heavy-handed, since the original suggests a rather vague relationship between the tower and the sounding of the hours. Certainly "en le vallon" [in the dale] is even more vague, even less circumscribed by space, than the material or ponderous *dans*, and uncertainty, obscurity, and lack of contour were among the aims of the Symbolists. The critic can, of course, disagree with this tendency, but he must identify it before condemning it, and in this "apologetic" stance I see none of the dangers of "divismo" feared by [Giacomo] Devoto.[6]

In that study of Symbolism, I arranged the so-called syntactical in-

novations in a lengthy catalogue according to grammatical categories: prepositions, conjunctions, adverbs, verbs. As an example of
the new strength imparted to existential verbs by Symbolist poetry, I
cited enumerative or anaphoric poetry in which the prosaic *il y a*
(which Racine would have avoided because of the hiatus) was em-
phatically repeated. [Francis] Jammes, for instance, wrote:

> Il y a une armoire à peine luisante
> qui a entendu les voix de mes grand'tantes,
> qui a entendu la voix de mon grand'père,
> qui a entendu la voix de mon père . . .
> Il y a aussi un coucou en bois . . .
> Il y a aussi un vieux buffet . . .
>
> [There is a (dark) cupboard:
> it has heard the voices
> of my great-aunts and my grandfather
> and the voice of my father . . .
> There is also a wooden cuckoo-clock . . .
> There is also an old sideboard . . .]

The last strophe brings us to a conclusion that might by present-
day standards seem poetically superfluous:

> Il est venu chez nous bien des hommes et des femmes
> qui n'ont pas cru à ces petites âmes.
> Et je souris que l'on me pense seul vivant
> quand un visiteur me dit en entrant:
> —Comment allez-vous, Monsieur Jammes?
>
> [Many people come to call on me
> who do not believe in these little souls.
> I smile when I hear a visitor coming in
> and asking, "Alone here, Mister Jammes?"][7]

Yet in the repetition of these *il y a* I saw a movement toward the
unadorned simplicity of everyday life, a discovery of the existence of
those humble and familiar objects which are overlooked in the normal course of things. In those days, one could not have foreseen that
it would be precisely the bare list of things as such, whether poetic or
prosaic, rather than any attempt to give them symbolic import, that
would constitute the innovation foreshadowing our present poetic
tastes. Thus the vague label "Symbolism" in fact designates contradictory characteristics.

As I noted, that article on the Symbolists' style was conceived as a
polemic against the opinions of other critics. I have remained faithful

to that polemical habit in spite of the hostility it sometimes arouses in those whose opinions I attack and the consternation it causes among those who write without addressing the views of their fellow critics. In my case, the tendency toward controversy in literary criticism is not, I hope, a sign of a malevolent temperament, but a consequence of my background in linguistics; it is in fact standard procedure for the linguist, in his treatment of a particular problem, to present first the opinions of his predecessors, then to demonstrate their untenability, and finally to offer his own views. For instance, in examining the splendid new Spanish etymological dictionary of [Juan] Corominas, one finds under the word *trovar* that the author cites the curious opinion of [Hugo] Schuchardt, who saw a relationship between this word and one drawn from fishing—namely, *turbare*, the clouding of waters in this operation—hence "to fish," "to capture," "to find." The opinion of Gaston Paris follows: he refuted this naturalistic etymology and considered instead the Greco-Latin *tropos*, whose first meaning would have been "to modulate" in music, then "to compose poetry," and finally "to invent" or "to find." A view which modifies that of Gaston Paris follows, and then it in turn is modified by Corominas.[8]

In matters of taste it is obviously not as easy to determine the sole correct hypothesis (*de gustibus* . . .): yet even in the aesthetic domain the *consensus omnium* is always the ideal. Closest to the truth is that interpretation of a poetic text which countenances all possible objections and which explains each detail in the most satisfying fashion, just as a correct etymology must account for all the forms and all the attested meanings of the word in question. Had all etymologists proceeded in the fashion of so many literary critics—that is to say, writing nothing but monologues of their own, avoiding what is in Greek called συμφιλολογεῖν (to do philology together), and not conversing with their colleagues—a critical compilation as great as that of Corominas would scarcely have come into existence. Naturally, however, the day is far off when some superhuman critic will publish a critical dictionary with all the various comments that the individual great works of Western literature have received.

In those years after 1920 there was perhaps a greater need for polemics than there is today, because at that time the positivist school, in no way shaken by anti-positivists like [Benedetto] Croce and [Karl] Vossler, continued to dominate the academic profession in Germany. Thus it happened that, in an article on [François de] Malherbe's "Consolation à Monsieur du Périer" published by a philologist of the old school, the aesthetic beauty of only these two famous lines was acknowledged:

> Et rose elle a vécu ce que vivent les roses,
> L'espace d'un matin.[9]
>
> [And like a rose, she lived what roses live,
> The space of a morning.]

But even these lines were not, in the critic's opinion, beyond reproach, because they recall previous poets who had compared a young girl to a rose, and, once a source is found, according to positivist logic, the originality of a passage is destroyed. This is the fallacy of "source study," in which poetry is reduced to content and its form is neglected. I showed at that time that the two verses, one rather long and the other rather short, correspond, so to speak, to a diastole and a systole, to an outbreak of grief followed by a contraction of the spirit: a rhythmic version of Stoic self-control.[10] Here, for the first time, I was treating the structure of a poem that through its sounds approximated the rhythm of existence—in this case philosophical existence. Here Stoic philosophy found its poetic equivalent. I called my procedure "immanent," in contrast to those methods that transcend the poetic realm, for example, source studies and the search for biographical clues.

Studies such as this one came to the attention of a famous student of German literature, Oskar Walzel of the University of Bonn, where I had transferred after World War I. In those days he was the only specialist of Germanic literature in Germany interested in the artistic form of poetry, since it was then customary in that country to study German literature only from a positivist or from a philosophical perspective. In Germany, as you may know, philosophy and not the aesthetic sense reigns supreme, and Walzel, a Viennese, was a commendable exception to this. At this time he was in fact writing a book about literary methods, called *Gehalt und Gestalt* [Content and Form],[11] with the emphasis on form, and he was happy to learn a thing or two from his colleague in Romance languages for whom aesthetic form was a *conditio sine qua non* of the work of art. But I learned from him as well: he had developed, for example, the category of *klassische Dämpfung* [classical "muting" or "smoothing out"] in the course of his studies of German eighteenth-century classicism, and I was able to apply this category to the study of Racine's style, about which very little was then known.[12] It is certainly true that the best-known poets, those studied by millions of French schoolchildren, are for this very reason the least known for their stylistic innovations. Permit me to use a couplet from *Phèdre* as an example of Racinian *klassische Dämpfung*: the horses of Hippolytus have been frightened by the monster sent by Neptune:

> On dit qu'on a vu même, *en ce désordre affreux,*
> Un dieu qui d'aiguillons pressait leur flanc poudreux.[13]

> [Some even say they saw, *in this frightful disorder,*
> A god who pricked with spurs their dusty flanks.]

The terrible event leading to the death of Hippolytus is seen and expressed poetically: "on a vu" the god who spurs on the horses, but the hemistich "en ce désordre affreux" contains a judgment, a rational diagnosis. It adds an element of prosaic reflection that serves to diminish the emotional force of the couplet. It is as if the poet had withdrawn the empathy he owes to his character and were observing him from the outside. We have therefore to do here with an interpretation that the classical poet wanted to introduce into a description of pathetic situations, an element of rationality or normality by which that particular event or situation might be judged.

In appropriating terms such as *klassische Dämpfung* that had previously been used by other critics, I exposed myself to the oft-repeated charge of eclecticism. In response to this I contend that the only important issue is whether the category used by the critic really suits the phenomenon in question, and not whether it is original. It certainly would be ridiculous if a physicist, in his analysis of the forces that act upon an object, refrained from considering the law of gravity just because it was discovered not by him but by Newton. In the field of literary criticism there are in fact too few rather than too many categories that might help us describe the phenomena that we examine.

Although these descriptive studies of style followed the principles of Croce, who disdained what he called *allotria* [hodgepodge], I might add that I was not influenced by him in my concrete analysis of poetry, since his entire theory of language, in which intuition and expression are seen as a unity, would not have allowed me to undertake the analysis of linguistic particularities in poetry. I am all the more indebted to the great philosopher inasmuch as he encouraged studies of mine whose inspiration was so different from his own—yet another example of that innate magnanimity that is characteristic of the greatest men. It is also true that I did not limit myself to "imma-nent" descriptions of the literary product but worked in ways that were closer to those of Freud, who, by treating the unconscious as a motivating force in all human behavior, including that of the artist, breathed new life into [Wilhelm] Dilthey's theory of *Erlebnis*.

With the work of Dilthey, as with that of Freud, one passes from the work of art to the person, which is to say, to the personal expe-rience of the artist; and this is true whether one classifies that expe-rience [*Erlebnis*] in terms of a general psychological typology, as does Dilthey,[14] or more specifically in terms of repressed complexes, as does Freud.

In 1918 my friend Hans Sperber and I published a study called *Motiv und Wort*—that is, "Literary Motive and Verbal Expres-sion"[15]—in which he demonstrated, with the aid of many examples drawn from the work of the Austrian writer Gustav Meyrink, that certain well-defined complexes color this author's imaginative world: obsessed by the fear of strangulation, this writer saw ties as serpents around the necks of those who wore them. The nearly reg-ular repetition of such images finds a parallel in the regularity of cer-tain nervous tics or errors, both consequences of complexes that Freud had outlined in his research on the unconscious. Later, Sper-ber elaborated this idea with the intention of demonstrating, in the semantic development of words during a given period, a relatively regular appearance not of symptomatic manifestations but of the principle preoccupations or emotions of the given period: an abun-dance of musical imagery will be found in the literature of an era drawn to music, whereas terms borrowed from architecture will pre-vail in the literature of an age similarly obsessed. I used this orienta-tion, combining it with the history of ideas, many years later in my *Essays in Historical Semantics*,[16] in which I proved that our modern words *ambiente, ambiance, environment,* and *Umwelt* ultimately derive from the Greek concept of the space or air surrounding us, περιέχον—a concept later put to use by the Renaissance, by New-ton (*circumambient medium*), and by Goethe, who coined the word *Umwelt*, translated in turn as *environment* by Carlyle; or that the Pythagorean concept of the music of the spheres reappeared in the Renaissance and in the baroque period, with the result that the Ger-man word *Stimmung*, originally meaning "harmony," "the world's musical concord," became a rather common word signifying "state of mind," and one shorn of the emotional overtones it possessed in the baroque era.

In other words, a concept inherited from a preceding period is revived when it is capable of expressing a particular impression of life, as in the case of the Leibnizian harmony of the world. (At this point, however, we have strayed far from literary criticism.) Developing Sperber's assertion about the recurrence of a writer's expressions whose regularity follows that of his *Erlebnis*, in the years following 1920 I sought examples in French literature, where the basic *Erlebnis* of the author was reflected in his style. Thus, for instance, I found that in a novel about thugs and prostitutes, *Bubu de Montparnasse*, Charles-Louis Philippe demonstrated a sense of social sympathy for these amoral types, and that a particular linguistic trait corresponds to this personal identification with them.[17] Of one pimp and his way of enjoying women, Philippe writes,

[Il aimait] sa volupté particulière, quand elle appliquait son corps contre le sien et qu'elle se pliait pour qu'il la pénétrât. Il aimait cela qui la distinguait de toutes les femmes qu'il avait connues parce que c'était plus doux, parce que c'était plus fin et parce que c'était sa femme, à lui, qu'il avait eue vierge.[18]

[He loved her special voluptuousness when she pressed her body to his, bending it so he could penetrate her. He loved what distinguished her from all the women he had known, because it was sweeter, because it was more delicate, and because this was his woman, his own, whom he had had as a virgin.]

It is evident that we have to do here with that form of transposed discourse which we call *style indirect libre* or *erlebte Rede*, in which the characters' actual utterances are put into the past tense as if they were part of the narrative. The pimp had certainly said, "J'aime cela . . . parce que c'est plus doux, parce que c'est plus fin" [I love that . . . because it is sweeter, because it is more delicate].

I offer another example that uses the conjunction *car* [for]: of a pimp who also steals, Philippe writes in a tone of pseudo-objectivity:

Les femmes l'entouraient d'amour comme des oiseaux qui chantent le soleil et la force. Il était un de ceux que nul ne peut assujettir, car leur vie, plus noble et plus belle, comporte l'amour du danger.

[The women surrounded him with love, like birds singing the praises of the sun and power. He was one of those who cannot be subjugated by anything, for their life, more noble and beautiful, includes the love of danger.]

The dangerous life of such a low character seems attractive to women, and their idealization of him is approved, albeit somewhat ironically, by the author.

Once we have found pity for his characters expressed linguistically in Philippe's irony, we can also discern this same attitude in the way the author handles the plot. In the case of Rabelais, likewise, the linguistic detail brings us to the psychological root of his writings so that we may recognize this same basic element elsewhere in his art—for example, in his treatment of ideas, in the plot, and so forth. I call this method, following the lead of [Friedrich] Schleiermacher and Dilthey, a circular process. By this I mean not a vicious circle but rather a legitimate means available to the humanist or to the historian, whether his background is linguistic or literary, who wants to understand a human phenomenon. When he notices a peculiarity—and it may or may not be linguistic—he assumes its origin to be psychological and verifies his hypothesis against other such peculiarities: his path is a continual movement between induction and deduction, a coming and going from detail to essence and back from essence to detail. Naturally, in order to describe a literary phenomenon that is offered to us as a global entity, we need a handle with which to grasp it. This handle is provided us by the observation of the detail, which, I repeat, may be of linguistic or of nonlinguistic nature. In the case of Philippe, I had made a linguistic observation about the author's way of expressing a pseudo-objective causality; in other cases, I adopted the positions of other literary critics, furnishing only linguistic proofs for their hypotheses. Thus the French essayist [René] Johannet had asserted that [Charles] Péguy possessed the style that [Henri] Bergson should have possessed but didn't; his so-called rhetorical repetition is in fact an ascent, motivated by his *élan vital*, toward higher and higher regions, a continual self-correction of the writer who is never satisfied with his own manner of portraying the flow of life.[19] In the case of Proust, by following up an article written by [Ernst Robert] Curtius, I tried to show how the rhythm of a sentence corresponds to the author's conception of that multifaceted, multilayered reality which the author must render: the novel-river is mirrored by the sentence-river.[20]

In accepting the judgments of other critics, of course, one runs the risk of assuming their prejudices as well. On the other hand, a great danger exists for the critic who uses his own observations as his sole basis: he may confuse the ease with which he discriminates certain aspects of a writer's style with the absolute aesthetic value that these aspects imply. Not all that may be observed in an author's work is of literary value. In the case of Péguy and Proust, their particular style is an integral part of these authors' literary excellence and uniqueness; with other authors, the style may be extraneous to the work or a facile formula that lends itself to imitation. Such is the case, it seems to me, with the *Unanimisme* of Jules Romains, which I probably overvalued thirty years ago when I wrote an essay on his work.[21] Romains, in an effort to describe the collective entities of individuals (a barracks, a home, a factory) at the moment they withdraw from life in general and merge with it once more, uses terms such as "birth," "evacuation," "secretion," and "vomiting." In examining passages such as these that describe people leaving rooms or houses—"La salle le pondit comme un œuf" [He emerged from the room like an egg from a hen], or "Les maisons . . . se vidèrent. . . . Les portes faisaient un à un des hommes vêtus de noir, *comme une chèvre fait ses crottes* et jusqu'à l'épuisement. Cette espèce d'envie gagna les maisons de proche en proche. À quatre heures toutes s'étaient soulagées"[22] [The houses . . . were emptying out. . . . Men dressed in black came through the doors one by one *like turds from a she-goat* until there were none left. This sort of need passed from house to house. At four o'clock all had relieved themselves]—I am no longer certain if the metaphors, given their physical and mechanical aspect, succeed in lending aesthetic expression to the phenomenon of group solidarity. I now judge them this way not because they are so unappealing but because once such a metaphor is used, the others seem to follow automatically; and where lies the merit of a critical judgment that merely records what the author has laid out in such a conspicuous, indiscreet, and repetitive fashion? For this reason an evaluation of the literary value of the particular work (the answer, that is, to the eternal Crocean question, "Is it poetry?") must always precede the critic's analysis. Peculiarities in works of art are not always aesthetic qualities.

My last essay in the Freudian mode, in which the critic seeks out the stylistic details that recur regularly in an author's work and that are motivated by an inner impulse comparable, but not identical, to Freudian complexes, was my study on [Denis] Diderot in *Linguistics and Literary History*, in which I tried to prove that an impulse—fundamentally erotic—to transcend oneself and to unite with another, can be found in many of the author's writings.[23] This attitude, typical of Diderot, finds expression in one of his aphorisms: "L'art d'écrire n'est que l'art d'allonger les bras" [The art of writing is nothing more than the art of extending one's arms].

When Diderot, in an article in the *Encyclopédie*, wrote about the *jouissance* [enjoyment] experienced in an erotic encounter,

l'être qui pense & sent comme vous, qui a les mêmes idées, qui éprouve la même chaleur, les mêmes transports, qui porte ses bras tendres & délicats vers les vôtres, qui vous enlace, & dont les caresses seront suivies de l'existence d'un nouvel être . . . [24]

[the being who thinks and feels as you do, who shares the same ideas, the same warmth, the same passions, who brings her tender and delicate arms toward yours, who embraces you and whose caresses will be followed by the existence of a new being . . .]

the reader feels, in the rhythm of the entire sentence, the increasing sentiment of the author himself in the happy memory of the *étreinte* [embrace]. This is a characteristic trait of Diderot's style, one that is found in many other works, whether didactic or narrative.

In the meantime, I concluded that the Freudian procedure could not always be applied to those earlier literary periods in which the individual writer had not yet been permitted to give in to his own idiosyncrasies and phobias; when the cult of originality, which began in the eighteenth century, did not even exist; and when works tended to have a more impersonal and objective character. One of my students who was working on *Les Tragiques* of Agrippa d'Aubigné was struck when examining that poetry by what an American critic of Freudian inspiration had called *emotional clusters* such as "milk" opposed to "poison" or "mother" to "serpent" or "wolf" to "lamb"—antithetical pairs representing for d'Aubigné the natural attitude of French Protestants of the sixteenth century against the Catholic party of Catherine de Medici. Having just finished reading James Joyce, my student believed he could find particular associative types like those of Joyce in the work of the Renaissance poet, and I had to explain to him that all those antithetical pairs had been suggested by scriptural tradition. D'Aubigné surely must have relived these biblical models, for the expressive force of his sentiments is so great that the Catholics are for him the ravenous wolf and the Protestants the gentle lamb, but in contrast to Joyce, no personal complex of the author can be found in these images.

Professor Fubini, in a critique of the volume of my essays published by Laterza, showed the two different sources of inspiration in my work, the one Freudian and the other, which he seemed to prefer, structural.[25] I am in partial agreement with him, and in fact I was increasingly aware that the method of describing an author according to *Erlebnis* [lived experience] must be limited to those literary periods and genres in which *Erlebnis* is really the author's goal. This discovery had two consequences for me. On the one hand, I was even more attracted to the pre-*Erlebnis* poetry—that is, the poetry of the Middle Ages, of the Renaissance, of the baroque period, or of a modern poet such as [Paul] Claudel, who speaks not for himself but for humanity in general. On the other hand, with the analysis of structure, I was concerned more with the *Gestalt* [formal] element of the poetic product, be it old or new, as I had been even before beginning the study on the "Consolation" of Malherbe, from which followed essays on the "Ballade des dames du temps jadis" of [François] Villon,[26] on [Luis de] Góngora, and on others. In the essay on Góngora,[27] I coined a slogan modifying the original *Motiv und Wort*— that is, *Werk und Wort*, "work and word"—in order to express the necessary nexus linking the whole of a poetic work with its verbal components.

Let it be said, parenthetically, that when Pasolini and other critics glorying in their youth define me, probably because of the authors I chose to study, as a "champion of European Decadence" (p. 55), they commit a grave error; even if the volume published by Einaudi gave them this impression (though Claudel can only with difficulty be called "decadent"), it is shattered by the German volume, which included the articles I wrote in America from 1936 to 1956.[28] Of its forty-nine essays, thirty are concerned with works from the Middle Ages, eleven with those of the Renaissance and the baroque period, and only seven with poetry of the nineteenth and twentieth centuries. The only significance of this statistical computation is that I have worked on Romance poetry from all centuries except the eighteenth century and the Romantic era. (The only poem of Victor Hugo treated in this volume is of Parnassian character: "Le Rouet d'Omphale.")[29] My having begun in 1919 with the nearly contemporary French Symbolists can be justified even today by the fact that their use of language represented the most violent revolution that ever took place in French poetry, a revolution that prepared the terrain for the still more daring innovations in today's lyric poetry. The fact that, in the years after 1930, I drew away from psychoanalysis and turned toward the study of poetic structure is probably due not to a study of *Gestalt* psychology but to a growing distrust of the rather cloudy concept of *Erlebnis*, as well as to a predilection for a clear formal contour and to a personal impulse toward health and rationality, an impulse natural in a man no longer young.

The critic who turns from a mysterious *che* [what] intuited by him in the poet to the *hic et nunc* [here and now] of the objective work becomes himself more rational. Further, the "cold, scientific rationalism" (p. 54) that to my great delight Pasolini discerns in me, corresponds of course to a similar disposition in that artist of the word, the poet and artificer, who makes us weep with his verses but who has not forgotten to count the syllables. (It is not, incidentally, a matter of mere chance that the two critical schools with which I had no direct contact when I turned toward the study of structure—namely, the Russian Formalists and the American New Critics—agreed on this idea of the artist as artificer.)

At the same time I was also aware that many literary works, particularly those of the Middle Ages, had not been analyzed in their structure and therefore had not been clearly understood. For instance, in the *Lai du Chievrefueil* of Marie de France, the central motif had not been adequately defined by critics; after the publication of an article of mine and one by my successor at Johns Hopkins, Professor Anna Hatcher, however, it seems evident to me that this *lai* is concerned with a miracle of love, that of Yseult, who miraculously understands the message hidden in the name "Tristan," the only word carved on the hazel rod that Tristan puts in her path.[30] The hazel rod will evoke for the queen its complementary plant, the honeysuckle, and the two are compelled to die apart from each other: "Bele amie, si est de nos: / ne vos sanz moi, ne moi sanz vos!"[31] [Fair friend, thus it is with us: / neither you without me, nor I without you]. This, the tale of the inseparable hazel tree and honeysuckle vine, is the central motif of that poem, which celebrates the miraculous power of passionate love to understand and to accept one's inevitable destiny, death. It seems incredible to me that so many critics failed to discover this theme over the course of sixty years. No particular method should be necessary to understand so simple a truth.

Similarly, in the Old Spanish poem "Razón de Amor" we find a voluptuous love scene in a paradisal garden tied to a debate between Water and Wine;[32] not one critic, not even [Ramón] Menéndez Pidal, could find a nexus between these two scenes drawn from entirely different genres. Yet in fact the connection between the love scene, with its sharp contrast of spiritual and physical love, and the debate, in which Water is the spiritual, Wine the physical principle of Life, is brilliantly defined, and the moral that derives from the two positions taken together is simply that the union of these two principles makes our universe complete and perfect.

One further example of my studies of the structure of medieval works can be found in the "Cantico delle creature" of Saint Francis.[33] Italian critics from [Alfredo] Casella to [Giovanni] Getto have not perceived what I call the combination of an *Alleluia* with a *Dies Irae*, the blending of the praise of God and of His creatures with a severe moral admonition to man to imitate Christ and to avoid sin in order to be worthy of the Creator. In studying these examples drawn from medieval literature, the critic must be endowed with a sense of logical exactitude in his explanation of a mysterious symbol; he must be able to feel the central symbol with its imaginative force and structural importance, and he should be capable of following it in the details of the poem built around this symbol. Thus we find ourselves confronted by Dilthey's circular procedure, applied, however, to the understanding of a concrete poetic unity. Only the reader who remains inside the poem—he, that is, who considers the poem in an immanent manner, excluding all the elements that lie outside the work—can feel its structural cohesion.

Lately, however, I have become convinced that it is not easy for a man of letters to neglect a text's sources altogether, even though the American New Critical school may be trying, in its dogmatic fashion, to do just that. When I define the "Cantico" of Saint Francis as an *Alleluia* complemented by a *Dies Irae*, I have already indicated two sources or forms of inspiration: it is clear, in fact, that the praise of the Brother Sun or of the Sister Mother Earth could not be conceived except in the manner of the Psalms of David and the Book of Daniel, which praise the Creation and God's creatures in a similar fashion. To draw an analogy, the "Cantico" cannot be understood outside of its tradition any more than a Madonna of Raphael could be if it were severed from the genre of Madonna portraits to which the artist added his own contribution.

For this reason I had to revise my previous, too radical and too antihistorical stance against the examination of sources. This new line of reasoning was buttressed by another consideration: it is worth noting that a truly great literary work will appear even greater when compared to its models. I realized this when examining the "Consolation" of Malherbe, in which the rhythmic design that serves to explain the Stoic philosophical stance was in fact an invention of the author; it is not to be found in the old *consolationes* of Plutarch and Seneca, Malherbe's sources. It is the same with the famous "Sonnet de l'Idée" [Joachim] Du Bellay: thirty years ago I discovered a rhythm that, when read aloud, forces our voice to rise continuously until the end, when the Platonic idea, "l'idée de la Beauté," appears like the epiphany of a goddess, and this vocal design seemed to me characteristic of the Platonic idea that raises us above the earth to an unearthly level of adoration.[34] In examining the sources of the sonnet, in Bernardino Daniello, Petrarch, Boethius, and Plato, I found that none of these had discovered the particular acoustic design that makes Du Bellay's poem so convincing. It is not of course a question of dissolving a poem into its various sources, as did Pio Rajna with the *Orlando furioso*,[35] and as does Curtius with his *topoi* in his justly famous book,[36] in which all the poems that treat a definite *topos* are reduced to the same level, out of which an indistinct historical continuity emerges. An investigation of sources does not damage great poetry if it is made after one has read and understood the beauty immanent within the work; if I had begun, however, with the sources of the "Sonnet de l'Idée," I would never have arrived at its characteristic vocal design. Thus a source study has its proper place at a certain stage in the analysis of a poem, and it is at this juncture that I depart from the goals of the American New Critics, with whom I have so often been in agreement.

You are perhaps aware that in recent years, in opposition to the positivism that has dominated American universities, a school of criticism, composed in large part of high-school teachers, has been formed. These critics, realizing that their students did not know how to read poetry, waged and eventually won a campaign in defense of poetry through books of criticism and anthologies used in secondary schools. It was therefore through this upheaval in American high schools—a movement from below to above, in contrast to the Crocean reform in Italy—that the study of literature, and not just of English and American literature, in which the movement began, has been completely renewed, and a new critical literature born.[37]

I believe that the New Critics have done a great service to America in making the principal task of the student of literature a sensitive reading of the work itself, considered in its visible, structural aspects.

A book by one of these critics bears the title *The Well Wrought Urn*, an expression borrowed from the poetry of John Donne.[38] In their anti-Romanticism the New Critics agree with the Russian school of Formalists who preceded them by twenty years but who—as Victor Erlich has shown in his excellent book[39]—were suppressed by the Soviet bureaucracy at exactly the moment (1930) when the New Critics came to the fore. Both schools display extremist positions—above all, a faith in the purity necessary to the reading of poetic texts. The New Critics sometimes speak of "heresies" in reading, and they do so with a nearly religious fanaticism that makes one want to subscribe to this or that heresy worthy of excommunication. I would even say that their radical stance of twenty years ago, though somewhat softened today, of pitting aesthetic criticism against historical erudition, seems mistaken to me: it means that the critic cannot be simply a critic, whereas all the great critics of the past—[Gotthold Ephraim] Lessing, the German Romantics, [Charles-Augustin] Sainte-Beuve, Albert Thibaudet, [Francesco] De Sanctis, [Benedetto] Croce, and [José] Ortega [y Gasset]—were in fact erudite men.

Shortly before he died, Erich Auerbach wrote:

Friedrich Schlegel, the greatest modern critic, claimed that the best theory of art was its own history, and that one could not pursue the reading of philosophy or poetry alone without the help of philology. . . . A Copernican revolution took place in the later eighteenth century: historical perspectivism. Thanks to this revolution critics have abandoned the method of judging literature according to absolute criteria outside of history and have learned instead to adopt elastic, flexible, historic criteria.[40]

If I do not share Auerbach's thoroughgoing historicism, I am even more opposed to the normative, Aristotelian criticism that the so-called Chicago school of criticism has been trying to revive. I believe, in the final analysis, that good criticism must be above all descriptive in character, and also to a degree historical. If I believe that I have discovered a poetic translation of Stoicism or of Platonism in Malherbe or Du Bellay, these very terms are of a historical nature, and the critic would only degrade himself if he avoided them in order to be faithful to a fetish of our own time.

Another point of disagreement with the New Critics is their tendency, following [William] Empson's lead,[41] to allow the presence of multiple meanings, even in the writings of poets who do not belong to the Metaphysical school. A person with classicizing tastes as strong as mine cannot admit such semantic flexibility, thanks to which the meanings that a word possesses in general discourse or in the dictionary would be only half present in the poetic passage, simply because in everyday language, as in poetry, the theoretical ambiguity of one word is generally limited, or eliminated, by the other words in context. How would any verbal communication whatsoever be possible, if the sentence did not define the precise meaning exacted by the words that compose it? I think in fact that the hypothesis of polysemy in poetic language is an illegitimate extension of the daily experiences created by those ambiguous slogans in politics and advertising that we now recognize as so destructive. ("Semantics" has become a pejorative term in America.)

One variety of polysemous interpretation is the allegorical explanation favored by the New Critics. It seems to me that the particular importance that Dante had for T. S. Eliot, and consequently for the New Critics, has encouraged to a certain degree a reading of all medieval and Renaissance literature as if it were allegorical and contained a moral or religious message; it may even be that this trend complements the religious tendencies—at times hesitant, at times blatant, even clericalist—in America today. Since I believe that the university is not a church and that the university searches not for faith but for truth, I tend to accept the moral or religious message of a text only when it can truly be demonstrated that it is contained in that particular work, as in the *Commedia*. Some critics maintain instead that the allegorico-religious interpretation of a poem is an act of piety and thus in itself better than a nonallegorical or secular interpretation. It seems to me, however, that the truth lies elsewhere: an explanation, allegorical or otherwise, will be good only if it takes into account the general tone and the particularities of the poetry in question. After my study of the "Razón de Amor," a certain Mr. Jacob published an article in which the child that appears singing in the Garden of Venus, with a hat, gloves, and a cape that she drops immediately in order to kiss the poet in silent fervor (all details given in the text), was deemed an allegory of the Blessed Virgin.[42] I challenge anyone to show me a medieval text in which the Virgin is portrayed wearing a hat and gloves and dropping her cloak to kiss the poet. In this instance the critic has wholly abandoned philological precision as well as the careful examination of details such as the tone of the whole work. When all is reduced to allegory, a poem loses its individual spell in favor of some moralizing simplification. The most intensely literary and picturesque works, if they are read merely as allegories, take on a patina of greyish sameness. Chapman's allegorization of the *Odyssey*, thoroughly approved by one modern critic, transforms the epic into the spiritual quest of a man, Ulysses, toward Ithaca, the final goal of the pilgrimage being Heaven; in such an analysis, it seems to me, all the specific elements of the *Odyssey* evaporate and only an insipid and anachronistic *topos* remains. I believe that the moralizing hyperallegorizing common within modern Anglo-Saxon criticism corresponds to a tendency to introduce elements willfully into the reading of poetic texts and to deduce from these elements precepts for the active life in place of the disinterested contemplation of poetry that old Kant taught us.

Now that I have defined my attitude toward psychoanalysis, source studies, and allegory, permit me to express my opinion about recent existential critics such as [Albert] Béguin, [Gaston] Bachelard, and [Georges] Poulet, who transport us, it seems to me, from the work of art to the *Erlebnis* of the artist—an *Erlebnis* that consists of experiencing the existential givens of human life: space, time, dreams, and physical elements such as earth, water, fire, and air. My friend Georges Poulet confessed to me that not only is his method without applicability to writers such as Molière and Rabelais (as if these great artists of the comic were exempt from *le temps humain*), but also that it tends for the most part to destroy the work of art.

The existential critic does not stop to consider the things that make a work of art what it is—that is, the marriage of form to content; he is forced to demolish the work of art and to fragment it into texts that reveal the author's psychological attitude, that are used as instruments on the same level as letters, conversations, and diaries, and that thus remain prime materials not yet sublimated into art. His ideal writer is [Henri-Frédéric] Amiel, who gives free rein to his confessions without, however, the artistic form we find in a Rousseau. M. Poulet is now himself working on Amiel: it can even happen that a critic may falsely interpret artistic elements of a poetic text in his search for *new* psychological data on his hero. Thus, in his study of Marivaux, M. Poulet insists that *La Vie de Marianne* is composed of separate moments, without connection, in which the protagonist would wonder, "Où en suis-je?" [Where am I?] and that this is the stance of the author. I have been able to show, however, that those single moments are adjoined to each other by means of a line of constancy and strength of spirit that inform the character of Marianne.[43] The frequent use in this novel of the words *cœur* and *courage* in the sense of "strength of spirit" reveals a fundamental toughness in Marianne's soul that enables her to overcome her moments of hesitation. Extrapolating from this particular case of erroneous interpretation, I deduced that the critic who wishes to establish constant elements in the psyche of his author must first firmly *establish* the *meaning* of each of his works and *only then* proceed to the explanation of constant elements in his psyche.

The danger that an existential critic will arrive at false interpretations increases in the case of works from the past, works isolated within their own time and written by authors about whom we know little. The famous Spanish tragicomedy *La Celestina* appeared to such philological critics of the older generation as [Marcel] Bataillon to be of a didactic nature, a warning against the imprudence and the passion that make sensual lovers into the slaves of bawds like Celestina and their cynical servants. According to a young scholar from Harvard, Stephen Gilman, the *Celestina* is instead an existential drama that reveals to man his cosmic position of being suspended in that extreme element, space.[44] (As a matter of fact, the young and imprudent protagonist Calisto does slip from a ladder that he had climbed to reach his beloved Melibea, and such a fall is indeed a fall through a spatial element without sympathy for the man who happens to fall.)

I have perhaps talked too much about my opposition to current American critical tendencies, which may not be of particular interest to you, and I am eager to end by defining my attitude toward post-Crocean Italian criticism. As you will have noticed from my preceding observations, the most important question, in my view as a critic, is no longer the Crocean one, "Is it or is it not poetry?"—a question that the critic must have already decided for himself at the inception of his task—but rather a structural one, "Does this particular part of the poem fit in or not?"

There are times when the Crocean question and mine are in conflict; in a *Festschrift* for Helmut Hatzfeld I shall publish a study of [Giacomo] Leopardi's "Aspasia," similar in method to the magisterial study of [Angelo] Monteverdi on the "Passero solitario";[45] there I will show how, like some Italian critics who followed Croce (rather than the great maestro himself, who wrote a brilliant and exhaustive sentence on that poem, which he labeled "dramatic"), by not taking account of its structure we have condemned passages of this incomparable work, passages justified not by their sensuality, nor by resentment, nor by their untamed polemical spirit (all sentiments for which those fastidious critics show very little sympathy), but by structural considerations, correspondences, and parallels between the various verse paragraphs. The initial "vision superba" of the divinely beautiful and alluring courtesan as she kisses her children in the presence of the poet reveals a duplicity or duality in the character of Aspasia; it is this double element that informs the four verse paragraphs (2×2) or structural units of this poem in its description of the *two* years during which the poet was incapable of distinguishing the *two* natures of Aspasia—the "amorosa idea" of the ideal woman and her sordid actual existence.

I would also like to voice certain reservations about the expression "stylistic criticism," by which my method of criticism was defined in the title of the Laterza volume:[46] while it is true that I often analyze stylistic devices, I do not believe that aesthetic criticism can be exhausted through stylistic considerations. It is, rather, a question of aesthetics in the plot, in the fabulation of a poetic work. Thus I have become increasingly hesitant to call collections of my analyses "stylistic studies" (the title of my first collection, some thirty years ago). Since then, one collection was called *Romanische Stil- und Literaturstudien* and the most recent one, published last year, *Romanische Literaturstudien*. As you will have noticed, the structural element, the architecture of the thought reflected in the poems, has increasingly occupied my attention. If it is merely a question of mental gymnastics for an aesthetic reading, stylistics can be at best ancillary to artistic perception. I think I can in good faith recommend today what I believe I have always practiced, the direct observation of a concrete literary work from every angle—an act of observation, both direct and thorough, that respects the unity of the poem and does not extract the particular from its context. I have had occasion to notice that the direct observation of concrete works helps us to discover characteristics of a poet that must remain hidden when whole works are treated in a general and summary fashion. No matter what the approach to the text, be it that of the history of ideas, stylistics, structural analysis, metrics, psychology, or sociology—this last exemplified by Auerbach's *Mimesis*, which is not, as [Aurelio] Roncaglia so clearly saw, "stylistic criticism"[47]—the results will always be new, provided that the critic does not wander too far from the work in question, and provided that he reads the text, as should all readers, with full attention. My studies of Marivaux or of the *Lettres portu-*

gaises[48] have nothing whatsoever to do with style, unless you would choose to call "stylistics" the attention accorded the recurrence of motives in the plot, that element which Formalists call "architectonic tautology," distinguishing it from "verbal tautology," the recurrence of words or of sounds, which is truly stylistic and linguistic since the first could be filmed in a silent movie, whereas the second could not.

In an article soon to be published, I will try to prove that the two protagonists of Calderón's *El príncipe constante*, Don Fernando, the Christian hero, and Fénix, the melancholy daughter of the Moorish king, are not, as some have asserted, figures without nexus incarnating "constancy" and "beauty," but rather characters who love each other and who, in the moment they become aware of this, are thrust in opposite directions (he toward death, she toward a loveless marriage), because of Fernando's spirit of sacrifice and Fénix's selfish nature.[49] Stylistic analysis does not permit the critic to make such an evaluation (though Calderón uses varied and interesting stylistic devices): the author assumed that his audience would recognize what is important—namely, the tone and the psychological stance of the two protagonists, the design of the various scenes that first bring them together, then separate them, and the contour of the whole plot. Such results, if correct, do not seem to me representations of any particular method but a simple reading based on the good sense that every reader should exercise. I arrive at the conclusion, therefore, that there is no specifically "Spitzerian" method. Good sense is a critic's only guide. By means of his good sense he discerns the method of reading suggested by the work itself, one whose imperative he must obey without superimposing extraneous categories on the text. It is thus vain to look for interesting similes in the *Lettres portugaises* where none exist, or, if we find majestic similes in *El príncipe constante*, we must not neglect their functional value in the tragedy as a whole. Further, this empiricism, whereby every text is considered a unique and unrepeatable experience, can perhaps excuse what has been pointed out by so many critics: the absence in my work of an aesthetic philosophy capable of organizing my various experiences. A rather cynical king once said that to conquer a foreign country he had first to send out his generals and troops and then to follow up with his philosophers and historians, who would supply justifications for the whole venture. Similarly, I think that, as critics standing before the still numerous *terre incognite* of poetry, we must begin by mobilizing our perceptive forces (the soldiers of our expedition) and leave to the philosophers the task of justifying, or perhaps disapproving, post factum, our tactics from their global perspective.

I shall finish by telling my Italian audience that over the years an evolution in the focus of my studies has become evident: I began my *explication de texte* with French authors, convinced that I could observe stylistic deviations in them better than in others, for French was a language that I had known since my Austrian childhood. Later, especially in America, I turned to Spanish texts, mainly for thematic reasons; their religious content, for a certain period, proved fascinating to a mind not indifferent to religious values, to the point of making it mistake religious sensitivity for true religion. Having discerned this confusion, I turned to Italian poetry, or rather I returned to it, given that during my youth I had discovered the very real poetry that exists in letters written by Italian prisoners of war; what I most liked, particularly in the Italian poetry of the medieval period, as in those humble letters of World War I, is what I would call *offenen Weltsinn* in German—the propensity to love life, the wise temper that governs this propensity, the judicious avoidance of the extremes of altruism and egotism, the spirituality balanced by a sense of reality—in short, all that is attractive to a man of my age. This personal change of interests is different from that of Vossler, who began with Italian poetry, went to French, and finished with Spanish; or from that of Curtius, who began with French, later turned to Spanish, and was never quite able truly to appreciate Italian poetry except for that of Dante, whom he transformed into a Stefan George; or from that of Auerbach, who moved from Italian to French and never came to Spanish poetry except to write a single chapter on the *Quijote*. What does this change have to do with the methods of literary criticism, the sole focus of this address? Nothing at all; it serves only to remind us that no method can substitute for the basic sympathy that a critic has for a field of study; philology is the *love* for works written in a particular *language*. And if the methods of a critic must be applicable to works in all languages in order that the criticism be convincing, the critic, at least at the moment when he is discussing the poem, must love *that* language and *that* poem more than anything else in the world. In the final analysis, the critic, beneath the cold rationality of the professional, is not an automaton or a robot but a sentient being, with his own contradictions and spontaneous impulses.

Notes

Notes

Foreword

1. Leo Spitzer, "A New Book on the Art of *The Celestina*," *Hispanic Review*, 25 (1957): 19.
2. Stephen Gilman, "A Rejoinder to Leo Spitzer," *Hispanic Review*, 25 (1957): 112.
3. See Spitzer, *Essays in Historical Semantics* (New York, 1948), pp. 171–78.
4. Pier Paolo Pasolini, "Nota su Spitzer," *Palatina*, 3, no. 10 (Apr.–June 1959): 55.

Linguistics and Literary History

1. Friedrich Gundolf, *Shakespeare und der deutsche Geist* (Berlin, 1914), p. viii. [The phrase used by Gundolf here reads "Methode ist Erlebnisart" (method is a type of experience).—EDS.]
2. The *Pèlerinage de Charlemagne* is a twelfth-century French *chanson de geste*.—EDS.
3. Leo Spitzer, "Mes souvenirs sur Meyer-Lübke," *Le Français moderne*, 6 (1938): 213–24.
4. Here Spitzer refers to Wilhelm Meyer-Lübke's *Romanisches etymologisches Wörterbuch* (Heidelberg, 1911–20).—EDS.
5. These etymologies have appeared in Spitzer, "Conundrum-Quandary," *Journal of English and Germanic Philology*, 42 (1943): 405–9; there I suggested also the possibility of a **calembourdon* as etymon, but today I prefer *calembredaine* to that unattested formation.
6. See Spitzer, "Estudios etimológicos," *Anales del Instituto de Lingüística*, 1 (1941): 30–70. [These annals were published by the Universidad Nacional de Cuyo (Mendoza, Argentina, 1942).—EDS.]
7. See Yakov Malkiel, "Review of V. Šišmarev. *Očerki po istorii äzykov Ispanii*," *Language*, 20 (1944): 155–60.
8. Here Spitzer refers to works such as Karl Vossler's *Die göttliche Komödie*, 2d rev. ed. (Heidelberg, 1925).—EDS.

9. Spitzer, " 'Fait accompli'—Darstellung im Spanischen," in his *Stilstu-dien*, 1 (Munich, 1928), pp. 258–94.

10. Spitzer's essay "Pseudo-objective Motivation in Charles-Louis Phi-lippe" follows the present essay in this volume.—EDS.

11. Spitzer, *Die Wortbildung als stilistisches Mittel exemplifiziert an Ra-belais* (Halle, 1910).

12. Johann Nestroy was an early nineteenth-century Viennese comic ac-tor and dramatist.—EDS.

13. All translations from Rabelais are taken from the Penguin edition, *Gargantua and Pantagruel*, trans. J. M. Cohen (Harmondsworth, Eng., 1955). All French quotations were checked against the Pléiade edition, *Œuvres complètes*, ed. Jacques Boulenger (Paris, 1951).—EDS.

14. Here Spitzer refers to the extensively annotated critical edition of Rabelais's *Œuvres complètes*, ed. Abel Lefranc et al. (Paris, Geneva, and Lille, 1912–55). The notes on the coinages of the word *Sorbonne* are in 4 (1922): 217.—EDS.

15. Here Spitzer refers to a school of poets that flourished in the late fif-teenth and early sixteenth centuries and in whose work linguistic and rhe-torical forms achieved a high degree of autonomy.—EDS.

16. Gustave Lanson and Paul Tuffrau, *Manuel d'histoire de la littérature française*, 5th ed. (Paris, 1938), p. 119.

17. Johann Wolfgang von Goethe, *Die Wahlverwandtschaften*, 2:2. [Spitzer quotes the text in an English translation, most likely his own.—EDS.]

18. Kenneth Burke, *Philosophy of Literary Form: Studies in Symbolic Action* (Baton Rouge, La., 1941).

19. Compare Spitzer, "Why Does Language Change?" *Modern Lan-guage Quarterly*, 4, no. 4 (Dec. 1943): 413–32; see especially p. 430, n. 29, and the polemics resulting therefrom in *Language*, 20 (1944): Leonard Bloomfield, "Secondary and Tertiary Responses to Language," pp. 45–55, and Spitzer, "Answer to Mr. Bloomfield," pp. 245–51.

20. Spitzer, "Die klassische Dämpfung in Racines Stil" in his *Roma-nische Stil- und Literaturstudien*, 1 (Marburg, 1931), pp. 135–268; and in the same work, his "Saint-Simons Porträt Ludwigs XIV," 2: 1–47; and "Zur Kunst Quevedos in seinem 'Buscón,' " 2: 48–125.

21. See Friedrich Schleiermacher, "Ueber den Begriff der Hermeneutik mit Bezug auf F. A. Wolfs Andeutungen und Arts Lehrbuch" (a speech deliv-ered in 1829), in his *Philosophische und Vermischte Schriften*, 2 (1838): 344–86, especially pp. 360–66.

22. Erich Frank, *Philosophical Understanding and Religious Truth* (London, 1945).

23. Harold Cherniss, "The Biographical Fashion in Literary Criticism," *University of California Publications in Classical Philology*, 12, no. 15 (1943): 279–92. Quotation is on p. 288.

24. Martin Heidegger, *Sein und Zeit* (Frankfurt, 1977), pp. 199–204. English translation from *Being and Time*, trans. John Macquarrie and Ed-ward Robinson (New York, 1962), pp. 191–95.—EDS.

25. Franz Rosenzweig, "Das neue Denken," *Kleinere Schriften* (Berlin,

1937), pp. 375–76. As Spitzer notes, he finds this quotation in Kurt H. Wolff, "The Sociology of Knowledge: Emphasis on an Empirical Attitude," *Philosophy of Science*, 10, no. 2 (1943): 104–23.—EDS.

26. Wolff, "The Sociology of Knowledge," p. 113.

27. Gustav Gröber, *Grundriss der romanischen Philologie*, 1 (Strassburg, 1888), p. 3.

28. Ernst Zupitza, "Miscellen," *Zeitschrift für vergleichende Sprachforschung*, 37, no. 3 (1901): 387.

29. Robert A. Hall, "Progress and Reaction in Modern Language Teaching," *Bulletin of the American Association of University Professors*, 31, no. 2 (Summer 1945): 220–30. Quotation is on pp. 224–25.

30. Luigi Pulci (1432–84) was a Florentine poet whose comic *Morgante Maggiore* presented a burlesque of the Charlemagne and Roland epic material and later influenced writers such as Rabelais and Byron.—EDS.

31. This point has been entirely overlooked in the treatment of the passage by an antimentalist; see Spitzer, "Crai e Poscrai o Poscrilla e Posquacchera Again, or the Crisis in Modern Linguistics," *Italica*, 21, no. 4 (1944): 154–69, especially p. 154.

32. Turoldus (or Turold) is thought to have been the author of the eleventh-century epic poem *La Chanson de Roland*. The name appears in the final line of the poem, "Ci falt la geste que Turoldus declinet." W. S. Merwin renders it in English as "The story which Turoldus set down ends here" (*The Song of Roland*, New York, 1963). Some critics maintain that Turoldus was not the author but the scribe who wrote the poem down.—EDS.

33. André Gide, "Le Juif, Céline et Maritain," *Nouvelle Revue française*, no. 295 (Apr. 1938): 630–36.

34. Ferdinand Céline, *Bagatelles pour un massacre* (Paris, 1937), p. 76.

35. Goethe, "Einleitung in die Propylaen," (Darmstadt, 1964), p. xxx.

36. George Santayana, *The Middle Span* (New York, 1945), pp. 154–55.

37. According to Gundolf, "Schleiermacher," in his *Romantiker* (Berlin, 1930), pp. 141–275. According to Alfred Götze, "Weltanschauung," *Euphorion*, 25 (1924): 42–51, however, the word was not previously coined by him but is a creation of his period.

38. William J. Entwistle, "Remarks on the Idealistic Extensions of Linguistic Science," *Miscel.lània Fabra* (Buenos Aires, 1943), pp. 133–42.

39. Ibid., p. 142.

40. In context, Buffon's phrase, which occurs in a speech on style delivered upon his entrance to the French Academy in 1753, suggests that by means of a good writing style man achieves his essential humanity and assures his immortality. The phrase has often been misinterpreted to suggest that what marks an individual author's style defines his individuality.—EDS.

41. André Lalande, "Méthode," *Vocabulaire technique et critique de la philosophie* (Paris, 1926); 10th rev. ed. (Paris, 1968), pp. 623–25.

42. René Descartes, *Œuvres de Descartes*, ed. Charles Adam and Paul Tannery, 1 (Paris, 1897), p. 324.

43. Here Spitzer refers to "The Style of Diderot," *Linguistics and Literary History: Essays in Stylistics* (Princeton, N.J., 1948), pp. 135–91.—EDS.

44. Musset used this proverb as the title of his one-act comedy, which was published in 1845.—EDS.

45. The so-called *récit de Théramène* [Théramène's narrative] is the subject of one of Spitzer's essays. See "The 'Récit de Théramène,'" in his *Linguistics and Literary History: Essays in Stylistics* (Princeton, N.J., 1948), pp. 87–134.—EDS.

Pseudo-objective Motivation in Charles-Louis Philippe

Headnote

1. See Charles Bally, "Le Style indirect libre en français moderne," *Germanisch-Romanische Monatsschrift*, 4 (1912): 549–56, 597–606.

2. See Eugen Lerch, "Die stilistische Bedeutung des Imperfectums der Rede ('style indirect libre')," *Germanisch-Romanische Monatsschrift*, 6 (1914): 470–89, and Jean Etienne Lorck, "Passé défini, Imparfait, Passé indéfini, III," ibid., pp. 177–91.

3. See M. M. Bakhtin, *The Dialogic Imagination*, trans. Caryl Emerson and Michael Holquist (Austin, Tex., 1981), pp. 42n, 305–8, 337.

Text

1. The phonetic spelling of *menschlich* (human) is slightly altered.—EDS.

2. Thomas Mann, *Der Zauberberg*, ed. Peter de Mendelssohn (Frankfurt, 1981), ch. 7, p. 839.

3. Ibid., pp. 794–96.

4. Leo Spitzer, *Motiv und Wort* (Leipzig, 1918), and *Studien zu Henri Barbusse* (Bonn, 1920).

5. Charles-Louis Philippe, *Bubu de Montparnasse* (Paris, 1905). All quotations are from this edition. Specific page references are included in the text.—EDS.

6. Spitzer here illustrates the problems that a translation of *à cause de* can present. He draws his examples from Camill Hoffmann's translation of the novel into German, *Bubu vom Montparnasse* (Munich, 1920). After having pointed out what was lost in the translation, he offers his own translation, which tries to rescue some of the French nuances. The translation into English by Laurence Vail, *Bubu of Montparnasse* (London, 1952), similarly tends to lose the nuances of *à cause de* and other causal connections that are important for Spitzer's argument. Although we have relied heavily on Vail's work for this translation, we had to make changes in almost every case in order not to obscure Spitzer's point. For instance, "Ils n'étaient heureux ni l'un ni l'autre à cause de l'amour qui remue les hommes à vingt ans, et à cause de Paris, qui est dur aux pauvres" (p. 110) has been translated by Vail as "They were not happy, neither of them, because love disturbs young men of twenty, and because Paris is hard on the poor" (p. 47). To preserve the stylistic nuances of the parallel construction with *à cause de*, the trans-

lation should rather read: "They were not happy, neither of them, because of love, which disturbs young men of twenty, and because of Paris, which is hard on the poor." One further example: "C'est ainsi que Pierre rencontra Berthe, le soir du quinze juillet. Il souriait à cause de sa gentillesse et de ses bandeaux" (p. 35). This has been translated by Vail as "It was like this that Pierre met Berthe on the night of the fifteenth of July. He smiled because she was nice and because she wore a black ribbon in her hair" (p. 13). More precise would be the following: "He smiled because of her engaging manner and because of her ribbons."—EDS.

7. Spitzer refers to the rhapsodic style of Emile Verhaeren (1855–1916), the Belgian Symbolist poet.—EDS.

8. Kurt Glaser, "Zum Bedeutungswandel im Französischen," *Die neueren Sprachen*, 29 (1921): 360–61.

9. From Gustave Flaubert, *Madame Bovary*, in his *Œuvres complètes* (Paris, 1951), pt. I, sec. 1, p. 334, quoted in Glaser, p. 361. Compare also Ferdinand Brunot, *La Pensée et le langage* (Paris, 1922), p. 611 and p. 810, on *à cause de*.

10. Marguerite Lips, "Le Style indirect libre chez Flaubert," *Journal de psychologie*, 18 (1921): 644–53.

11. Compare Eugen Lerch's review of books on Flaubert in *Literaturblatt für germanische und romanische Philologie*, nos. 11–12 (1917): 393.

12. Spitzer, "Persona pro re," in his *Aufsätze zur romanischen Syntax und Stilistik* (Halle, 1918), pp. 232–46.

13. Friedrich Gundolf, *Goethe* (Berlin, 1922), p. 144.

14. *Leur* can also have the pejorative meaning of a pronoun displacing the omitted noun, as in, for example, *leur "Kultur,"* referring to the Germans, or *Leur Etymologies*, as Gilliéron labels his study mocking the etymologies of conventional linguists; see Jules Gilliéron, *Les Etymologies des etymologistes et celles du peuple* (Paris, 1922). Although the word *leur* does not actually appear in this title, it is implied by the words *des etymologistes*, and this is what Spitzer probably remembered.—EDS.

15. Compare "Ueber 'Rahmenstellung' im Romanischen" in Spitzer, *Aufsätze*, pp. 265–73.

16. Jean Etienne Lorck, *Die "Erlebte Rede"* (Heidelberg, 1921).

17. Honoré de Balzac, *La Muse du département*, in *La Comédie humaine*, ed. Marcel Bouteron, 4 (Paris, 1952), p. 160.

18. Lorck, *Die "Erlebte Rede,"* p. 38.

19. Emile Zola, *Lourdes* (Paris, 1898), p. 466.

20. Lorck, *Die "Erlebte Rede,"* p. 35.

21. Ibid., p. 59.

22. Mann, *Buddenbrooks* (Berlin, 1930), pt. 11, ch. 2, p. 697.

23. Lorck, *Die "Erlebte Rede,"* p. 59.

24. Prosper Mérimée, *Colomba*, ch. 1, in *Théâtre de Clara Gazul, Romans et nouvelles* (Paris, 1978), p. 762.

25. Charles Bally discusses this passage from *Colomba* in "Le Style indirect libre en français moderne," *Germanisch-Romanische Monatsschrift*, 4 (1912): 552, 600–601, but we have been unable to find the remark about the author showing "the tip of his nose" in this essay.—EDS.

26. Lorck, *Die "Erlebte Rede,"* p. 33.

27. René Benjamin, *Grandgoujon* (Paris, 1919), p. 7.

28. See Lerch, *Germanisch-Romanische Monatsschrift*, 6 (1914): 470–89.

29. Lorck, *Die "Erlebte Rede,"* p. 66.

30. Ibid., p. 57.

31. Spitzer, *Aufsätze*, p. 77.

32. José María de Pereda, *Sotileza* (Madrid, 1906), p. 16.

33. Eduard Wechssler, philologist, famous for his work on national character.—EDS.

34. Alice Berend, *Jungfrau Binchen und die Junggesellen* (Munich, 1920).

35. Ibid., p. 5.

36. Oskar Walzel, "Objektive Erzählung," *Germanisch-Romanische Monatsschrift*, 7 (1915–19): 161–77.

37. Berend, *Jungfrau Binchen*, p. 5.

38. Ibid., p. 8.

39. Ibid., pp. 10–11.

40. Karl Kraus, *Die Fackel*, nos. 546–60 (July 1920): 20.

41. Ibid., p. 19.

42. For an extended analysis of Alfred Kerr's habit of mixing different linguistic levels, see Spitzer's article, "Sprachmittel als Stilmittel und als Ausdruck der Klangphantasie," *Germanisch-Romanische Monatsschrift*, 11 (1923): 193–216.—EDS.

43. André Suarès, *Portraits* (Paris, 1914), pp. 119–20.

44. Ernst Robert Curtius, *Die literarischen Wegbereiter des neuen Frankreich*, 3d ed. (Potsdam, 1923), pp. 19–20.

Two Essays on Góngora's *Soledades*

Headnote

1. Erich Auerbach, "Leo Spitzer: *Romanische Stil- und Literaturstudien*," in *Gesammelte Aufsätze zur romanischen Philologie* (Bern, 1967), pp. 342–44.

2. See Dámaso Alonso, "El toro celeste," *Obras completas*, 6 (Madrid, 1982), pp. 289–301.

On Góngora's *Soledades*

1. Luis de Góngora, *Soledades*, ed. Dámaso Alonso (Madrid, 1927; reprinted Madrid, 1982). [The English verse translation is from E. M. Wilson, *The Solitudes of Don Luis de Góngora* (1931; reprinted Cambridge, Eng., 1965), pp. 3, 5.—EDS.]

2. Dámaso Alonso, ed., *Soledades*, p. 181.

3. See Alfred Morel-Fatio, "Histoire de deux sonnets," *Etudes sur l'Espagne*, 3 (Paris, 1904), pp. 141–64.

4. Dámaso Alonso, "Góngora y la censura de Pedro de Valencia," *Revista de filología española*, 14 (1927): 366, n. 2.

5. See Dámaso Alonso, ed., *Soledades*, p. 110.

6. See Albert Wellek, "Renaissance- und Barock-Synästhesie," *Deutsche Vierteljahrsschrift*, 9 (1931): 534–84.

7. See Dámaso Alonso, ed., *Soledades*, p. 31.

8. See Hermann Pongs, *Das Bild in der Dichtung* (Marburg, 1937).

9. Dámaso Alonso, ed., *Soledades*, p. 16.

10. Oskar Walzel, "Barockstil bei Klopstock," in *Festschrift für Max H. Jellinek* (Vienna, 1928), p. 187.

11. Victor Klemperer, "'Victorieusement fui . . .': Zur Bewertung Mallarmés," *Germanisch-Romanische Monatsschrift*, 15 (1927): 300.

12. Wilhelm Michels, *Barockstil bei Shakespeare und Calderón* (Paris, 1929), p. 20.

13. Printed in Georges Duhamel's *Anthologie de la poésie lyrique française* (Leipzig, 1923), pp. 113–14.

14. See Leo Spitzer, *Romanische Literatur- und Stilstudien*, 1 (Marburg, 1931), pp. 17–25.

15. For Spanish examples of "longing," see Carolina Michaëlis de Vasconcellos, *A saudade portuguesa* (Porto, 1922), p. 67.

16. Ludwig Pfandl, *Spanische Nationalliteratur* (Freiburg im Breisgau, 1929), p. 234.

17. See Ramón Menéndez Pidal, *L'épopée castillane* (Paris, 1910), p. 118.

18. See Eugenio d'Ors, *Tres horas en el Museo del Prado* (Madrid, n.d.), p. 99.

19. See José Ortega y Gasset, *Espíritu de la letra* (Madrid, 1927), p. 21.

20. See Karl Vossler's review in *Deutsche Literaturzeitung*, 52 (1931): 16–18.

21. See Walther Pabst, "Góngoras Schöpfung in seinen Gedichten *Polifemo* und *Soledades*," *Revue hispanique*, 80 (1930): 1–229.

22. See Julius Schmidt, "Ein Beitrag zur sinnvollen Gestaltung der mündlichen Reifeprüfung," *Neuphilologische Monatschriften*, 2 (1931): 355–61.

23. Ulrich Leo, "Historie und Stilmonographie," *Deutsche Vierteljahrsschrift*, 9 (1931): 472–503.

Selections from Góngora's First *Soledad*

1. Luis de Góngora, *Soledades*, ed. Dámaso Alonso (Madrid, 1927; reprinted 1982), and *Soledades* (Madrid, 1936).

2. E. M. Wilson's verse translation, *The Solitudes of Don Luis de Góngora* (1931; reprinted Cambridge, Eng., 1965) has been used throughout as the basis of translation, but has been modified whenever a more literal rendering was necessary.—EDS.

3. Hermann Brunn, *Die Soledades des Don Luis de Góngora y Argote* (Munich, 1934), pp. 174–75.

4. Karl Vossler, *Poesie der Einsamkeit in Spanien*, 1 (Munich, 1935), p. 148.

5. Dámaso Alonso, *La lengua poética de Góngora* (Madrid, 1935), p. 124.

6. Ibid., p. 68.

7. Here, as in other citations from these works, the Loeb translations of Ovid's *Metamorphoses*, trans. Frank Justus Miller (1916) and of Horace's *Odes and Epodes*, trans. C. E. Bennett (1914) and *Satires*, trans. H. Rushton Fairclough (1929) are used.—EDS.

8. Walther Pabst, "Góngoras Schöpfung in seinen Gedichten *Polifemo* und *Soledades*," *Revue hispanique*, 80 (1930): 1–229. See p. 163.

9. Dámaso Alonso, *Lengua*, p. 341.

10. Bernardo Alemany y Selfa, *Vocabulario de las obras de don Luis de Góngora* (Madrid, 1930), p. 411.

11. L. P. Thomas, *Góngora et le gongorisme* (Paris, 1911), p. 101.

12. Góngora, *Obras completas*, ed. Juan Millé (Madrid, 1932), p. 258. English translation from *Renaissance and Baroque Poetry of Spain*, ed. and trans. Elias L. Rivers (New York, 1966), p. 161.

13. Benedetto Croce, "Góngora," *Critica*, 37 (1939): 334–49, quotation on p. 345.

14. For the study of *fortuna* in the sense of "storm" in Spanish, Catalan, and Portuguese, compare O. J. Tallgren, "*Fortuna* 'tempête," *Neuphilologische Mitteillungen*, 22 (1921): 53–58 (in the sixteenth century, "corrió fortuna en el golfo de Marsella" [there was a storm in the gulf of Marseille]); then Rudolph Schevill, *The Dramatic Art of Lope de Vega* (Berkeley, 1918), p. 294, in his note to line 1164 of Lope's *La dama boba* (". . . is common in the writers of the Renascence"); and lastly H. R. Lang, "The Spanish *Estribote*, *Estrambote*, and Related Poetic Forms," *Romania*, 45 (1918–19): 406: in the *Cancionero de Baena* and the *Crónica de don Juan II* (1434), and therefore, probably, the oldest example known at present: "comenzó tan grande fortuna de aguas y nieve" [such a great storm of rain and snow began], which is paralleled in the Old Provençal by the "fortuna d'aura, de vent, de temporal, de mar" and in the Italian by the "fortuna di mare, di tempo, di vento" and the *fortunale* cited in the *Dizionario della Marina*.

15. Ernst Robert Curtius, "Flieder-Studie," in *Französischer Geist im neuen Europa* (Stuttgart, 1925), pp. 59–62.

16. Leo Spitzer, "Kenning und Calderóns Begriffsspielerei," *Zeitschrift für romanische Philologie*, 56 (1936): 100–102.

17. All translations of Virgil are from the Loeb edition: *Eclogues, Georgics, Aeneid*, trans. H. Rushton Fairclough (1916); rev. ed. (1935). —EDS.

18. See Spitzer, "Zeitschriftenschau," *Zeitschrift für romanische Philologie*, 59 (1939): 405, concerning [the conservation of the boxwood spoon] in the Vió valley in upper Aragon. See "Span. *dibujar* 'zeichnen' = afrz. *deboissier*," *Zeitschrift für französische Sprache und Literatur*, 45 (1918–19): 375–79, and *Lexikalisches aus dem Katalanischen* (Geneva, 1921), p. 43. See also Wilhelm Meyer-Lübke, *Romanisches etymologisches Wörterbuch* (Heidelberg, 1935), p. 132, and Walther von Wartburg, *Französisches etymologisches Wörterbuch* 1 (Bonn, 1928), pp. 666–67, s.v. *buxus*.

19. Brunn, p. 48.

20. Werner Krauss, "Das neue Góngorabild," *Romanische Forschungen*, 51 (1937), 80.

21. Santorre Debenedetti, *Flamenca* (Turin, 1921), p. 20.

22. S. Eugene Scalia, "Diamond or Loadstone: A Note on Guinizelli," *Romanic Review*, 27 (1936): 278.

23. This is a genuine influence that modern scholarship does not deny. See, for example, the *Enciclopedia italiana* 8 (Milan and Rome, 1930), pp. 163–71, s.v. *bussola*.

24. Eunice Joiner Gates, "Góngora's Indebtedness to Claudian," *Romanic Review*, 28 (1937): 26–31.

25. See Meyer-Lübke, *Romanisches etymologisches Wörterbuch*, p. 12, s.v. *adamas*.

26. English translation from the Loeb edition of the *Phaedo*, trans. Harold North Fowler (1914).—EDS.

27. See Frank Dornseiff on *Gibraltar y la leyenda antiqua*, reviewed in *Revista de filología hispánica*, 1 (1939): 282–83.

28. Elise Richter, "Luis de Camões," *Germanisch-Romanische Monatsschrift*, 13 (1925): 295–306.

29. English translation from Dante's *Inferno*, trans. Charles S. Singleton (Princeton, N.J., 1970–75).—EDS.

30. Brunn, *Die Soledades*, p. 60.

31. Pabst, "Góngoras Schöpfung," p. 52.

32. Margit Sahlin, *Etude sur la carole médiévale* (Uppsala, 1940), p. 168.

33. Johan Huizinga, *Ueber die Verknüpfung des poetischen mit dem theologischen bei Alanus de Insulis*, Mededeelingen der Koninklijke Akademie van Wetenschapen (Amsterdam, 1932), vol. 74, ser. B, p. 64. English translation from *The Complaint of Nature*, trans. Douglas M. Moffatt (1908; reprinted Hamden, Conn., 1972), p. 87.—EDS.

34. Sahlin, *Etude*, pp. 171, 181.

35. English translation from the Loeb *Tibullus*, trans. J. P. Postgate (1913).—EDS.

36. In a passage of this essay not included here, Spitzer identified Father Owen as an auditor in his course on Góngora at Johns Hopkins University.—EDS.

The Spanish Baroque

Explanatory endnotes, none of which are included in the original, have been provided by the editors.

1. Heinrich Wölfflin, *Kunstgeschichtliche Grundbegriffe* (Munich, 1915); and Wölfflin, *Principles of Art History*, trans. M. D. Hottinger (London, 1932).

2. Here Spitzer refers to Fritz Strich, *Deutsche Klassik und Romantik* (Munich, 1922); and Oskar Walzel, *Wechselseitige Erhellung der Künste* (Berlin, 1917).

3. Wilhelm Worringer's major ideas were first suggested in his disserta-

tion, *Abstraktion und Einfühlung* (Berlin, 1908), and were developed in later essays.

4. Eugenio d'Ors presented his controversial theory of an "eternal baroque," manifesting itself in over twenty distinct styles, in *Las ideas y las formas* (Madrid, 1928), and *Lo Barroco* (Madrid, n.d.).

5. See Josef Nadler, *Geschichte der deutschen Literatur* (Vienna, 1951).

6. Here Spitzer refers to Julius Meier-Gräfe, *Spanische Reise* (Berlin, 1923), and Werner Weisbach, *Der Barock als Kunst der Gegenreformation* (Berlin, 1921).

7. Karl Vossler's "Spanischer Brief an Hugo von Hofmannsthal" appeared in *Eranos. Festschrift für Hugo von Hofmannsthal* (Munich, 1924), pp. 123–53; Ernst Robert Curtius's "Spanische Kulturprobleme der Gegenwart" appeared in *Hochland*, 23 (1926): 678–91.

8. Ludwig Pfandl, *Geschichte der spanischen Nationalliteratur in ihrer Blütezeit* (Freiburg im Breisgau, 1929).

9. Maurice Barrès, *Le Greco ou le secret de Tolède* (Paris, 1912).

10. Here Spitzer adapts, rather freely, Count Hermann Keyserling's anecdote about an encounter with the Spanish philosopher Miguel de Unamuno. See Keyserling, *Das Spektrum Europas* (Heidelberg, 1928), p. 99.

11. Spitzer's sentence incorporates the sentiments and the specific phrases of the final lines of Segismundo's famous soliloquy that concludes act 2 of *La vida es sueño*.

12. Spitzer's critical essay "Die Literarisierung des Lebens in Lope's *Dorotea*" (Bonn, 1932) is one of the few fundamental studies of Lope's complex baroque masterpiece (1632).

13. Spitzer's two studies of Luis de Góngora's major work, *Las soledades*, appear in this volume.

14. The "fantastic hero" is, of course, Don Quijote.

15. Baltasar Gracián, *El Criticón* III, xi; see ed. E. Correa Calderón (Madrid, 1971), III, 265.

16. Spitzer's study of Quevedo's dark, picaresque novel is "Zur Kunst Quevedos in seinem *Buscón*," *Archivum romanicum*, 11 (1927): 511–80.

17. Helmut Hatzfeld's theory that Spain was the radiating center of baroque culture throughout Europe is set forth in "El predominio del espíritu español en las literaturas del siglo XVII," *Revista de filología hispánica*, 3 (1941): 9–23, and *Estudios sobre el barroco* (Madrid, 1966).

18. Spitzer is referring to a lively scholarly debate among Hispanists which was touched off by Victor Klemperer's *Weltstellung der spanischen Sprache und Literatur* (Leipzig, 1922). Klemperer subsequently clarified his views in a long article: "Gibt es eine Spanische Renaissance?" *Logos*, 16 (1927). Américo Castro's most influential argument for the presence of the European Renaissance in Spain appeared in his *El pensamiento de Cervantes* (Madrid, 1925). Marcel Bataillon's *Erasme et l'Espagne* (Paris, 1937), to which Spitzer refers below, is another of the most important studies of the Renaissance in Spain.

19. Vossler's views on Spain's resistance to the European Renaissance are set forth in his *Spanien und Europa* (Munich, 1952).

20. The quotation is from the introduction to *Los Milagros de Nuestra*

Señora, written by the clerkly poet Gonzalo de Berceo in the thirteenth century. Manrique's elegy on the death of his father, the knight Rodrigo Manrique, dates from the late fifteenth century. Calderón's *La vida es sueño* was written in 1635.

21. Benedetto Croce's hostile view of the contemporary reevaluation of the baroque is expressed in many of his writings. Probably his most influential statement on the matter is his *Storia della età barocca in Italia* (Bari, 1929).

22. Spitzer interjected these words in English within an essay published in Spanish. He may have been thinking of these lines spoken by Shakespeare's Richard II just before his murder (*Richard II*, act 5, sc. 5, ll. 32–34): "Sometimes am I king, / Then treasons make me wish myself a beggar, / And so I am."

23. Jean Rousset, *La Littérature de l'âge baroque en France* (Paris, 1953).

Three Essays on Dante's *Commedia*

Speech and Language in *Inferno* XIII

1. Dante Alighieri, *La Divina Commedia*, ed. Charles H. Grandgent, 3 vols. (Boston, 1909–13); rev. ed., 1 vol. (Boston, 1933), pp. 116–17. I consulted also Erich Auerbach, *Dante als Dichter der irdischen Welt* (Berlin, 1929); Karl Vossler, *Die göttliche Komödie*, 2d ed. (Heidelberg, 1925); Benedetto Croce, *Dantes Dichtung*, trans. Julius Schlosser (Zurich, 1921); *La Divina Commedia*, ed. Francesco Torraca (Rome, 1905); Francesco De Sanctis, "Pier delle Vigne," in *Quattro saggi Danteschi* (Naples, 1903), pp. 57–72; Francesco Novati, "Pier della Vigna," in *Con Dante e per Dante* (Milan, 1898), pp. 1–36; Leonard Olschki, "Dante and Peter de Vinea," *Romanic Review*, 31, no. 2 (Apr. 1940): 105–11; and Francesco D'Ovidio, "Il canto di Pier della Vigna," in his *Nuovi studii Danteschi* (Milan, 1907), pp. 143–333. I am indebted for various suggestions to my pupils with whom I read the canto in class: A. Bianchini, E. Fenimore, and Perry J. Powers. [The translation of Virgil is taken from the Loeb edition of *Eclogues, Georgics, Aeneid*, trans. H. Rushton Fairclough (1916); rev. ed. (1935). —EDS.]

2. The translation of Ovid is taken from the Loeb edition of *Metamorphoses*, trans. Frank Justus Miller (1916). This passage is from bk. 3, ll. 237–39.—EDS.

3. D'Ovidio, "Il canto," p. 160.

4. De Sanctis, "Pier delle Vigne," p. 66.

5. *La Divina Commedia di Dante Alighieri*, ed. Tommaso Casini (Florence, 1892). The quotation from Venturi may be found on p. 85.—EDS.

6. Torraca, ed., *La Divina Commedia*, p. 98.

7. Vossler, *Die göttliche Komödie*, 2: 682.

8. Hermann Ammann, *Die menschliche Rede. Sprachphilosophische Untersuchungen*, 2 (Lahr, 1928), p. 103.

9. The first passage cited is from Americ de Bellinoi, "Al prim pres," in

Friedrich Diez, *Die Poesie der Troubadours,* 2d ed. (Leipzig, 1883), p. 88. The second passage may be found in Emil Levy, *Provenzalisches Supplement-Wörterbuch,* 1 (1894), p. 139, s.v. *benc.* Compare also Dimitri Scheludko, "Beiträge zur Entstehungsgeschichte der altprovenzalischen Lyrik," *Archivum romanicum,* 15, no. 2 (1931): 137–206, especially p. 159.

10. Giuseppe Antonio Borgese, "The Wrath of Dante," *Speculum,* 13, no. 2 (Apr. 1938): 183–93. See p. 190n.

11. Alfredo Schiaffini, *Tradizione e poesia nella prosa d'arte italiana dalla latinatà medievale a G. Boccaccio* (Geneva, 1934); 2d rev. ed. (Rome, 1943).

12. See ibid., p. 67.

13. Ibid.

14. D'Ovidio, "Il canto," pp. 257–58. The Latin quotation may be found in a note on p. 258. In the pun *Orsini—orsatti,* the proper name *Orsini* is linked to *orsa* [she-bear] in l. 70 and to *orsatti* [bear cubs] in l. 71. Grandgent, ed., *La Divina Commedia,* in a note on p. 172, comments on this wordplay as follows: "Giovanni Gaetano Orsini, Pope Nicholas III from 1277 to 1280, was notorious for his nepotism. Because of the fact that the she-bear, *orsa,* was the cognizance in his family arms, Dante refers to his relatives as *orsatti,* or 'cubs.'"—EDS.

15. Vossler, *Die göttliche Komödie,* 2: 681–82. [Our translation from the German. For Novati's response to De Sanctis's approach to Piero's language as caricature, see his "Pier della Vigna," especially pp. 28–31.—EDS.]

16. Ibid.

17. D'Ovidio, "Il canto," p. 237.

18. These words are spoken by Hippolyte in *Phèdre,* act 4, sc. 2, l. 1112.—EDS.

19. This particular repetition, the repetition of a finite verb in the form of a past participle, is a device with a long past in Latin (and especially in late Latin) poetry and prose writing; compare the *Stolz-Schmalz Lateinische Grammatik,* 5th ed., ed. Manu Leumann and Johann B. Hofmann (Munich, 1928). Ovid (p. 831): "Mars videt hanc visamque cupit potiturque cupita" [Mars saw her who was seen and he wished and acquired what he wished for]; Orosius (p. 830): "Croesum cepit captumque . . . donavit" [He captured the captive Croesus . . . and he sacrificed].

20. D'Ovidio, "Il canto," p. 202.

21. Grandgent, ed., *La Divina Commedia,* p. 117.

22. For quotations, see the Torraca edition of *La Divina Commedia, Inferno* XV, 43, cited in n. 1; see also ll. 121–23.

23. Grandgent, ed., *La Divina Commedia,* pp. 116–17.

24. This line is from François de Malherbe's "Consolation à Monsieur du Périer . . . sur la mort de sa fille" in his *Œuvres,* ed. Antoine Adam (Paris, 1971), p. 41.—EDS.

25. This line is from Suetonius, *The Twelve Caesars,* bk. 12, sec. 7.—EDS.

26. See Helmut Hatzfeld, "Einige Stilwesenszuge der altfranzösischen religiösen Reimdichtung," *Zeitschrift für romanische Philologie,* 52 (1932): 707–9.

27. For complete bibliographical information, see n. 1.—EDS.
28. D'Ovidio, "Il canto," p. 331.
29. Ibid.
30. Vossler, *Die göttliche Komödie*, 2: 682.
31. Arpad Steiner, "An Unnoticed Evidence of French Argot in the Early Thirteenth Century," *Modern Language Notes*, 58 (1943): 121–25.
32. Compare also Torraca, ed., *La Divina Commedia*, on *drappo* in *Inferno* XV, 112 (see n. 1).
33. Olschki, "Dante and Peter de Vinea," pp. 110–11.
34. Ibid., p. 111.
35. Ibid., p. 110.

The Farcical Elements in *Inferno* XXI–XXIII

1. Karl Vossler, *Die göttliche Komödie*, 2d ed. (Heidelberg, 1925), 2: 695–96.
2. *Le Garçon et l'aveugle* is an anonymous *fabliau dramatique* of the thirteenth century. *La Farce de maître Pathelin* is a fifteenth-century farce.—EDS.
3. Dante Alighieri, *La Divina Commedia*, ed. Charles H. Grandgent, 3 vols. (Boston, 1909–13); rev. ed., 1 vol. (Boston, 1933), p. 195.
4. Ibid., p. 203.
5. See my article "Die Branche VIII des *Romans de Renart*," in my *Romanische Literaturstudien, 1936–1956* (Tübingen, 1959), pp. 64–94.
6. Grandgent, ed., *La Divina Commedia*, p. 186.
7. See Gustave Lanson, *Esquisse d'une histoire de la tragédie française* (New York, 1920); rev. ed. (Paris, 1927).
8. On the well-devised farcical names of the devils, see my article "Two Dante Notes," *Romanic Review*, 34, no. 3 (Oct. 1943): 243–62, especially pp. 256–62.

The Addresses to the Reader in the *Commedia*

1. Ernst Robert Curtius, *European Literature and the Latin Middle Ages*, trans. Willard R. Trask (Princeton, N.J., 1953), pp. 238–39.
2. Hermann Gmelin, "Die Anrede an den Leser in Dantes *Göttlicher Komödie*," *Deutsches Dante-Jahrbuch*, 29–30 (1951): 130–40.
3. Giovanni Andrea Scartazzini, *Saggio del commento al Paradiso di Dante Alighieri* (Florence, 1880).
4. Erich Auerbach, "Dante's Addresses to the Reader," *Romance Philology*, 7 (1954): 268–78.
5. Dante Alighieri, *La Divina Commedia*, ed. Giovanni Andrea Scartazzini (Leipzig, 1882), p. 601.
6. See "Ritmo cassinesse" in Lucio de Palma, *Poesia arcaica italiana. Buon umore a Monte Cassino* (Bari, 1946), p. 255. The second quotation is from ch. 28 of *Le Romant de Jehan de Paris Roy de France*, a late fifteenth-century tale. It may be found on p. 62 of Anatole de Montaiglon's edition, published in Paris in 1874.—EDS.
7. T. S. Eliot, "Dante," in his *Selected Essays*, 3d ed. (London, 1951), p. 243.

464 *Notes to Pages 191–212*

8. Ibid., p. 244.

9. Auerbach, "Dante's Addresses," p. 273n.

10. Giuliano Bonfante, "The Romance Desiderative 'se,'" *PMLA*, 57 (1942): 930–50.

11. Thomas B. W. Reid, "Old French Formulas of Asseveration and Adjuration in Comparative Form," *French Studies*, 8, no. 3 (July 1954): 193–206.

12. Leo Spitzer, "La Conjonction romane 'si' vient-elle du Latin 'sit'?" *Romania*, 65 (1939): 289–311.

13. Reid, "Old French Formulas," p. 201.

14. Ibid.

15. Boethius, *The Consolation of Philosophy*, trans. V. E. Watts (Harmondsworth, Eng., 1969), p. 97.—EDS.

16. Auerbach, *Dante: Poet of the Secular World*, trans. Ralph Manheim (Chicago, 1961); Auerbach, *Mimesis*, trans. Willard R. Trask (Princeton, N.J., 1953).

17. Quoted by Auerbach, "Dante's Addresses," p. 277.

18. Werner Jaeger, "Review of Georg Misch's *A History of Autobiography in Antiquity*," *Speculum*, 28 (1953): 406.

19. Spitzer, "Note on the Poetic and the Empirical 'I' in Medieval Authors," *Traditio*, 4 (1946): 416.

20. Ibid., pp. 416–17.

21. Charles Singleton, "Justice in Eden," *Annual Reports of the Dante Society with Accompanying Papers* (Cambridge, Mass., 1954), pp. 3–33.

22. Isaiah Berlin, *The Hedgehog and the Fox: An Essay on Tolstoy's View of History* (London, 1953).

23. Eliot, "Dante," p. 242.

24. George Santayana, *Three Philosophical Poets* (Cambridge, Mass., 1910), p. 77.

25. Auerbach, *Literary Language and Its Public in Late Latin Antiquity and in the Middle Ages*, trans. Ralph Manheim (New York, 1965), pp. 297–317.

Geistesgeschichte vs. History of Ideas as Applied to Hitlerism

Headnote

1. Arthur O. Lovejoy, "On the Discrimination of Romanticisms," *PMLA*, 39 (1924): 229–53.

Text

1. Arthur O. Lovejoy, "The Meaning of Romanticism for the Historian of Ideas," *Journal of the History of Ideas*, 2, no. 3 (June 1941): 257–78.

2. Karl Mannheim, *Man and Society in an Age of Reconstruction: Studies in Modern Social Structure* (London, 1940), pp. 10–11. Spitzer finds this quotation in John Herman Randall, Jr.'s review of Mannheim's book published in the *Journal of the History of Ideas*, 2, no. 3 (June 1941): 377.

3. Spitzer is varying the terms he and Lovejoy used earlier by adding the

phrase "into the infinite" to the idea of striving, which he defines earlier as "dynamism or voluntarism."—EDS.

4. Lovejoy, "Meaning of Romanticism," pp. 270–71.

5. Thomas Mann, *Deutsche Ansprache* (Berlin, 1930), pp. 17–18.

6. Eric Vögelin, "Some Problems of German Hegemony," *The Journal of Politics*, 3 (May 1941): 164.

7. Lovejoy, "Meaning of Romanticism," pp. 272–73.

8. Lovejoy, *The Great Chain of Being* (Cambridge, Mass., 1936).

Linguistic Perspectivism in the *Don Quijote*

1. Américo Castro, *El pensamiento de Cervantes* (Madrid, 1925).

2. Joaquín Casalduero, "La Composición de 'El ingenioso hidalgo Don Quijote de la Mancha,'" *Revista de filología hispánica*, 2 (1940): 323–69.

3. Helmut Hatzfeld, *Don Quijote als Wortkunstwerk* (Leipzig, 1927).

4. Miguel de Cervantes, *The Adventures of Don Quixote*, trans. J. M. Cohen (Harmondsworth, Eng., 1981), has been used for translations throughout this essay. We have occasionally altered Cohen's translation to make clear the elements necessary to Spitzer's argument. All Spanish quotations were checked against the Aguilar edition, *El ingenioso hidalgo Don Quijote de la Mancha*, eds. Justo García Soriano and Justo García Morales (Madrid, 1968).—EDS.

5. Spitzer has evidently confused the appearance of Merlin in II, 35 with that of Trifaldi in II, 38.—EDS.

6. Cervantes, *El ingenioso hidalgo Don Quijote de la Mancha*, ed. Antonio Rodríguez Marín, 7 (Madrid, 1913), pp. 29–30.

7. Leo Spitzer, "Dieu et ses noms (Francs les cumandent a Deu a ses nuns, Roland, 3694)," *PMLA*, 56, no. 1 (March 1941): 13–32.

8. Spitzer, "Eng. 'dismal' = O. F. *dism-al,'" *Modern Language Notes*, 57, no. 7 (Nov. 1942): 602–13.

9. Nicolo Tommaseo and Bernardo Bellini, *Dizionario della lingua italiana*, 9 (Turin, 1865), p. 716.

10. Rabelais, *Gargantua and Pantagruel*, trans. J. M. Cohen (Harmondsworth, Eng., 1955), bk. 1, ch. 16.

11. Stephen Gilman, "El falso 'Quijote': Versión barroca del 'Quijote' de Cervantes," *Revista de filología hispánica*, 5 (1943): 148–57.

12. Yakov Malkiel, "The Etymology of Hispanic *que(i)xar*," *Language*, 21 (1945): 156.

13. It should be noted that in some of these examples Cohen (see n. 4) translates freely in order to capture the effects of Sancho's humorous misuse of Castilian.—EDS.

14. Alfred Morel-Fatio, "Periodiques," *Romania*, 26 (1897): 476. [Summary of an article by R. Foulché-Delbosc, "Yogar, Yoguer, Yoguir," *Revue hispanique*, 4, (1897): 113–19.—EDS.]

15. Giuseppe Antonio Borgese, 'Il senso della letteratura italiana," *Domani*, 1, no. 2 (1943): 111.

16. See Spitzer, "Español y portugués *decorar*: 'Aprender, recitar de memoria,'" *Revista de filología hispánica*, 6 (1944): 176–86. See especially pp. 176 and 183.

17. Spitzer, "Muttersprache," *Monatshefte für deutschen Unterricht*, 36, no. 3 (March 1944): 113–30. See especially p. 120.

18. Castro, *El pensamiento*, p. 147.

19. Ibid.

20. One of the legends that explains the Muslim invasion of Spain in 711 is "that King Roderick had dishonored a Visigothic lady, Caba [*La Cava*]; her father, Count Julian, invited the Muslims to invade, as a means for avenging Caba's honor." See Jaime Vicens Vives, *Approaches to the History of Spain*, 2d rev. ed., trans. Joan Connelly Ullman (Berkeley, 1972), p. 27n. It is to this legend that Cervantes (and Spitzer) refer.—EDS.

21. Oskar Seidlin, "Laurence Sterne's *Tristram Shandy* and Thomas Mann's *Joseph the Provider*," *Modern Language Quarterly*, 8 (1947): 101–18.

22. From Thomas Mann, *The Theme of the Joseph Novels* (Washington, D.C., 1942), p. 16. Cited in Seidlin, "Laurence Sterne's *Tristram Shandy*," p. 102.—EDS.

23. Mann, "Meerfahrt mit Don Quijote," in his *Leiden und Grösse der Meister* (Berlin, 1935), pp. 209–70.

24. Mann, *Joseph the Provider*. Spitzer quotes from H. T. Lowe-Porter's translation, *Joseph and His Brothers* (New York, 1948), p. 1056.—EDS.

25. E. M. Forster, *Howards End* (London, 1910); reprint (New York, 1955), p. 3.

26. Lionel Trilling, *E. M. Forster* (London, 1944; new and rev. ed., London, 1967), p. 11.

27. See Edgar Zilsel, *Die Entstehung des Geniebegriffes* (Tübingen, 1926), pp. 115–16, 123.

28. Mann, "Meerfahrt mit Don Quijote," p. 230.

29. Ludwig Edelstein, "Sydenham and Cervantes," in *Essays in the History of Medicine Presented to Professor Arthur Castiglione . . .*, Supplements to the Bulletin of the History of Medicine, no. 3 (Baltimore, Md., 1944), pp. 55–61.

30. Erich Auerbach, *Mimesis* (Bern, 1946), p. 319.

Interpretation of an Ode by Paul Claudel

Headnote

1. See Leo Spitzer, *Classical and Christian Ideas of World Harmony: Prolegomena to an Interpretation of the Word "Stimmung,"* ed. Anna Granville Hatcher (Baltimore, Md., 1963); Spitzer, "La enumeración caótica en la poesía moderna," in his *Lingüística e historia literaria* (Madrid, 1961), pp. 295–346; and Spitzer, "*Explication de Texte* Applied to Walt Whitman's Poem 'Out of the Cradle Endlessly Rocking,'" in his *Essays on English and American Literature*, ed. Anna Granville Hatcher (Princeton, N.J., 1962), pp. 14–36.

Text

1. Paul Claudel, *Cinq Grandes Odes suivies d'un processional pour saluer le siècle nouveau* (Paris, 1913). [For inclusion in this volume, all quotations were checked against the Gallimard edition, published in Paris in 1936.—EDS.]

2. All translations of the odes are taken from Claudel, *Five Great Odes*, trans. Edward Lucie-Smith (London, 1967). We have occasionally modified this translation in order to make clear the elements necessary to Spitzer's argument.—EDS.

3. The article Spitzer refers to is entitled "A Linguistic and Literary Interpretation of Claudel's *Ballade.*" It appeared in *French Studies*, 16, no. 2 (Dec. 1942): 134–43.—EDS.

4. See Alfredo Schiaffini, *Tradizione e poesia nella prosa d'arte italiana dalla latinatà medievale a G. Boccaccio* (Geneva, 1934); 2d rev. ed. (Rome, 1943).

5. Claudel, "Reflexions et propositions sur le vers français," in *Positions et propositions, I. Œuvres complètes de Paul Claudel*, 15 (Paris, 1959), p. 15.

6. Jacques-Paul Migne, *Patrologie cursus completus. Series latina*, 22 (Paris, 1887), p. 627.

7. For these oppositions, compare Dag Norberg, *L'Olympionique, le poète et leur renom éternel: Contribution a l'étude de l'ode I.1 d'Horace* (Uppsala, 1945).

8. Ambrose, *De Isaac et Anima*, ch. 7, sec. 57, in *Patrologia Latina*, ed. J.-P. Migne, 14 (Paris, 1882), p. 550. Augustine, *Confessions*, bk. 6, ch. 5. Spitzer here cites the quotation as it appeared in an article by Erich Auerbach that was later reprinted in the latter's *Literary Language and Its Public in Late Latin Antiquity and in the Middle Ages*, trans. Ralph Manheim (New York, 1965), pp. 48–49. Manheim cites the F. J. Sheed translation. The translation we give translates more of the Latin than Spitzer chose to include.—EDS.

9. See Leo Spitzer, "La enumeración caótica en la poesía moderna," in his *Lingüística e historia literaria* (Madrid, 1961), pp. 295–346.

10. The translation of Lucretius is taken from the Loeb edition of *De rerum natura*, trans. W. H. D. Rouse, 3d rev. ed. (London, 1937), pp. 170–71.—EDS.

11. Paul Friedländer, "The Epicurean Theology in Lucretius' First Prooemium (Lucr. I. 44–49)," *Transactions of the American Philological Association*, 70 (1939): 373.

12. See Etienne Gilson, *Le Thomisme, Introduction au système de Saint Thomas D'Aquin*, 3d ed. rev. and expanded (Paris, 1927), p. 201.

13. Rudolf Allers, "Intellectual Cognition," in *Essays in Thomism*, ed. Robert E. Brennan, O.P. (New York, 1942).

14. Claudel, "Connaissance du temps," in his *Art poétique* (Poitiers, 1907). English translation from *Poetic Art*, trans. Renée Spodheim (New York, 1948), p. 25.—EDS.

15. Gilson, *Le Thomisme*, p. 176.

16. Jean Giraudoux, *Juliette au pays des hommes* (Paris, 1924).
17. Karl Viëtor, *Geschichte der deutschen Ode* (Munich, 1923).
18. See Claudel, "Reflexions," in *Positions et propositions, I*, pp. 9–56.

American Advertising Explained as Popular Art

1. I have used in this connection: Henry Foster Adams, *Advertising and Its Mental Laws* (New York, 1916); Arthur Judson Brewster and Herbert Hall Palmer, *Introduction to Advertising* (New York, 1947); and Harold Ernest Burtt, *Psychology of Advertising* (Boston, 1938).
2. Burtt, *Psychology of Advertising*, p. 8.
3. Ibid., p. 50.
4. Leo Spitzer, *Linguistics and Literary History: Essays in Stylistics* (Princeton, N.J., 1948), pp. 1–39. [This piece, "Linguistics and Literary History," is reprinted as the first essay in the present volume.—EDS.]
5. Pedro Salinas, *Aprecio y defensa del lenguaje* (San Juan, Puerto Rico, 1948), p. 64.
6. S. I. Hayakawa, "Poetry and Advertising," *Etc.: A Review of General Semantics*, 3, no. 2 (Winter 1946): 116–20.
7. Gustav Theodor Fechner, *Vorschule der Aesthetik*, 1 (Leipzig, 1876), p. 89.
8. Philip Wylie, *Generation of Vipers* (New York, 1942), p. 220.
9. See Paul Friedländer, *Documents of Dying Paganism: Textiles of Late Antiquity in Washington, New York and Leningrad* (Berkeley, 1945), and Richard Hamann, *Geschichte der Kunst von der altchristlichen Zeit bis zur Gegenwart* (Berlin, 1933).
10. The only attestation [to the expression "sun-kissed"], according to the *New English Dictionary*, is from a certain E. Brannan: 1873. For passages of Shakespeare referring to the kiss of the sun, see John E. Hankins, "Hamlet's 'god-kissing carrion': A Theory of the Generation of Life," *PMLA*, 64 (June 1949): 514.
11. Anna Granville Hatcher, "Twilight Splendor, Shoe Colors, Bolero Brilliance," *Modern Language Notes*, 61, no. 6 (June 1946): 442–47.
12. Hatcher, "'Mr. Howard Amuses Easy,'" *Modern Language Notes*, 58, no. 1 (Jan. 1943): 8–17.
13. Burtt, *Psychology of Advertising*, p. 373.
14. Brewster and Palmer, *Introduction to Advertising*, p. 124.
15. Burtt, *Psychology of Advertising*, p. 437.
16. Spitzer is not entirely accurate here. Disparaging statements about competitors' goods were never prohibited by law, but rather by means of an informal convention agreed upon by advertisers. This convention broke down during the last decade.—EDS.
17. E. K. Sheldon, "The Rise of the Incomplete Comparative," *American Speech*, 20 (1945): 161–67.
18. Dennis William Brogan, *The American Character* (New York, 1944), p. 131.
19. Ibid.
20. Alexander Rüstow, "Der moderne Pflicht- und Arbeitsmensch," *Re-*

vue de la Faculté des Sciences Economiques de l'Université d'Istanbul, 5
(1944): 107–46.

Apropos of *La Vie de Marianne*

Explanatory endnotes have been provided by the editors, with the exception
of Spitzer's note 16.

1. Georges Poulet's *La Distance intérieure*, the second volume of *Etudes
sur le temps humain*, appeared in Paris in 1952. References to this edition
are identified by page number within the text after the abbreviation *DI*.
References to the English translation of this volume, *The Interior Distance*,
trans. Elliott Coleman (Baltimore, Md., 1959), are identified by page number after the abbreviation *ID*.

2. Benedetto Croce, *La poesia di Dante*, 2d ed. (Bari, 1921), p. 10. Croce
coined the word *allotria* (hodgepodge) to refer to those heterogeneous materials from history and philosophy that scholars of his time customarily
employed as a means of interpreting Dante. What Croce complained of is
what later came to be called the "extrinsic" mode of interpretation, in contrast with Croce's own "aesthetic" mode.

3. The phrase is from Stendhal, *Le Rouge et le noir*. Translation is
quoted from *The Red and the Black*, trans. C. K. Scott-Moncrieff, 2 (New
York, 1926), p. 166.

4. Spitzer drew his quotations for this essay from Marivaux, *La Vie de
Marianne* (Paris, 1947). The italicizations that he indicated within these
quotations will be retained here. Page numbers from this volume are cited
within the text.

5. Spitzer alludes here to the following lines of the ninth-century poem
"La Séquence de Sainte Eulalie": "Melz *sostendreiet* le empedementz, /
Qu'elle perdesse sa virginitet" [It would be better to *sustain* the obstacles /
Than to lose her virginity]. See Karl Bartsch, *Chrestomathie de l'ancien
français*, 8th ed. (Leipzig, 1904), pp. 5–6 (italics ours).

6. These are the words with which Preciosa, the heroine of *La Gitanilla*,
depicts herself. See Cervantes, *Novelas ejemplares*, ed. Francisco Rodríguez
Marín, 1 (Madrid, 1969), p. 38.

7. See Ernst Robert Curtius's discussion of *puer senex* in his *European
Literature and the Latin Middle Ages*, trans. Willard R. Trask (Princeton,
N.J., 1967), pp. 98–101.

8. Marcel Arland, *Marivaux* (Paris, 1950), pp. 51–52.

9. See Gustave Larroumet, *Marivaux: Sa Vie et ses œuvres* (Paris, 1894),
pp. 327–30. Larroumet's "list of errors" appears as a long footnote on pp.
329–30.

10. Spitzer here refers to the chapter on French realism in Erich Auerbach, *Mimesis*, trans. Willard R. Trask (Princeton, N.J., 1953), pp. 454–
92.

11. Quoted by Spitzer from Charles-Augustin Sainte-Beuve in a *causerie*
on Marivaux (Jan. 16, 1854). In *Causeries du lundi*, 3d ed., 9 (Paris, n.d.),
p. 351.

12. A phrase used (though with qualifications) by Arland in his intro-

duction (p. 19) to the edition (Paris, 1947) of *La Vie de Marianne* from which Spitzer drew his quotations.

13. Spitzer, who did not identify his source for this quotation, was actually conflating at least three passages. Two of these, drawn from the correspondence of Frédéric-Melchior Grimm, report Voltaire's judgment that Marivaux was wont to "peser des riens dans des balances de toiles d'araignée" [weigh mere nothings in the scales of spider webs]; see *Correspondance littéraire, philosophique et critique par Grimm, Diderot, Raynal, Meister, etc.*, ed. Maurice Tourneux, 4, 5 (Paris, 1878), pp. 179 and 236, respectively. The third passage, which does not refer to Marivaux but instead displays Voltaire making fun of himself, includes the image of the eggs of a fly ("pesant gravement des œufs de mouche dans des balances de toile d'araignée" [gravely weighing the eggs of a fly in the scales of a spider web]) and is thus closer to the words quoted by Spitzer in this essay; see *Voltaire's Correspondence*, ed. Theodore Besterman, 45 (Geneva, 1959), p. 313 (letter of Apr. 27, 1761).

14. Arland, *Marivaux*, pp. 51–52.

15. Spitzer here refers to La Fontaine's fable "Le Chêne et le roseau."

16. [Spitzer's note:] My article has not yet been considered in the introduction to the recent edition of *La Vie de Marianne* by Frédéric Deloffre (Paris, 1957). The glossary is very useful; for example, Marivaux's attestations of *heart* in the sense of "dignity," "pride."

A Central Theme and Its Structural Equivalent in Lope's *Fuenteovejuna*

Headnote

1. Those parts of his project on world harmony that Spitzer completed were published posthumously as *Classical and Christian Ideas of World Harmony: Prolegomena to an Interpretation of the Word "Stimmung,"* ed. Anna Granville Hatcher (Baltimore, Md., 1963).

Text

1. Joaquín Casalduero, "*Fuenteovejuna,*" *Revista de filología hispánica*, 5 (1943): 22–44. See p. 31.

2. Alexander A. Parker, "Reflections on a New Definition of 'Baroque' Drama," *Bulletin of Hispanic Studies*, 30 (1953): 145–46.

3. Geoffrey W. Ribbans, "The Meaning and Structure of Lope's *Fuenteovejuna,*" *Bulletin of Hispanic Studies*, 31 (1954): 150–70.

4. Here, and in all other citations from *Fuenteovejuna*, the translation used is by Angel Flores and Muriel Kittel. See *Masterpieces of the Spanish Golden Age*, ed. Angel Flores (New York, 1957), pp. 33–80. Because this translation sometimes takes liberties with the text, we have modified it when necessary to make clear the elements essential to Spitzer's argument. We also consulted the translation by Jill Booty in *Lope de Vega (Five Plays)*, ed. R. D. F. Pring-Mill (New York, 1961), pp. 57–108. Spitzer notes that he has quoted the Spanish text according to the *Biblioteca romanica* edition,

vol. 319–24 (1952), prepared by Eugen Kohler and published in Strassburg by Heitz. We have been unable to locate this edition. All quotations from *Fuenteovejuna* were checked against the edition prepared by Jesús Cañas Murillo and published in Barcelona by Plaza and Janes in 1984.

5. Casalduero, "*Fuenteovejuna*," p. 25.

6. Karl Vossler, *Lope de Vega und sein Zeitalter* (Munich, 1932), p. 149.

7. Ibid., p. 301.

8. Here Spitzer refers to his treatise *Classical and Christian Ideas of World Harmony: Prolegomena to an Interpretation of the Word "Stimmung,"* which was originally published in two parts in the journal *Traditio.* Part I appeared in *Traditio*, 2 (1944): 409–64; Part II appeared in *Traditio*, 3 (1945): 307–64. After Spitzer's death, the study was revised and considerably expanded by Anna Granville Hatcher and republished in book form under the same title in Baltimore by the Johns Hopkins University Press in 1963.—EDS.

9. Here Flores and Kittel (see n. 4) translate freely to maintain sonnet form and rhyme and to capture Laurencia's suffering and fear.—EDS.

10. Leo Spitzer, "Notas sintáctico-estilísticas a propósito del español *que*," *Revista de filología hispánica*, 4 (1942): 105–26. See p. 116.

11. Walter Naumann, "Grillparzer und das spanische Drama," *Deutsche Vierteljahrsschrift fur Literaturwissenschaft und Geistgeschichte*, 28 (1954): 345–72.

12. Carmen P. Fernández-Cerra, "El lirismo en los argumentos históricos de Lope," Ph.D. diss., Johns Hopkins University, 1952, p. 211.

13. The phrase "gobernar en paz esta república" does not occur in this scene. Perhaps Spitzer was thinking of the similar line spoken by Juan Rojo, "en paz tienen los reyes a Castilla" [the Kings (Ferdinand and Isabella) hold Castile in peace].—EDS.

14. Ramón Menéndez Pidal, "Sufíjos átonos en español," *Bausteine zur romanischen philologie* (Halle, 1905), p. 400.

15. Vossler, *Geist und Kultur in der Sprache* (Heidelberg, 1925), p. 214.

16. The *gracioso* is a standard character in the Spanish Golden Age *comedia*. Often a servant, the *gracioso* is both jesting and witty. Here Spitzer refers to Mengo. Although many critics do not consider Mengo to be a true *gracioso*, he has some of the attributes of the type, most notably the wit.—EDS.

17. See Perry J. Powers, "The Concept of the City-State in the Dramas of Lope de Vega," Ph.D. diss., Johns Hopkins University, 1947.

18. Casalduero, "*Fuenteovejuna*," p. 44.

19. These lines are from Shakespeare's *The Merchant of Venice*, act 5, sc. 1, ll. 83–85.—EDS.

20. The quotation is from Jonathan Edwards, "Theological Miscellanies" notebook, no. 188.—EDS.

21. From Friedrich Wilhelm Nietzsche, *The Birth of Tragedy*, sec. 19, quoted by Spitzer in an English translation, most likely his own.—EDS.

22. Naumann, "Grillparzer," p. 361.

23. Lope de Vega, *La Dorotea*, ed. Edwin S. Morby (Berkeley, 1958), p. 397.

24. Bruce Wardropper, "*Fuente Ovejuna*: El Gusto and Lo Justo," *Studies in Philology*, 53, no. 2 (Apr. 1956): 159–71.

Development of a Method

Explanatory endnotes, none of which are included in the original, have been provided by the editors.

1. See Alfredo Schiaffini's introduction to his edition of selected Spitzer essays, *Critica stilistica e storia del linguaggio* (Bari, 1954), pp. 1–26; Pietro Citati's introduction to another selection, *Marcel Proust ed altri saggi di letteratura francese moderna* (Turin, 1959), pp. ix–xxix; Mario Fubini's review of the first of these volumes, "Ragioni storiche e ragioni teoriche della critica stilistica," *Giornale storico della letteratura italiana*, 133 (1956): 489–500, 502–5; and Pier Paolo Pasolini's "Nota su Spitzer," *Palatina*, 3, no. 10 (Apr.–June 1959): 53–55. Later references to Pasolini's note will be cited in parentheses in the text. We have been unable to trace the references to Emerico Giachery.

2. Friedrich Gundolf, *Shakespeare und der deutsche Geist* (Berlin, 1914), p. viii. The phrase used by Gundolf in the original German is *Methode ist Erlebnisart.*

3. See Leo Spitzer, *Die Wortbildung als stilistisches Mittel exemplifiziert an Rabelais* (Halle, 1910). The discussion of Rabelais's wordplay on *Sorbonne*, mentioned below, occurs on pp. 30–31, 67, of the book.

4. For the former, see Spitzer, "Die syntaktischen Errungenschaften der Symbolisten," in his *Aufsätze zur romanischen Syntax und Stylistik* (Halle, 1918), pp. 281–339; for the latter, see n. 1.

5. The quotation from Ferdinand Brunot comes from his contribution to Louis Petit de Julleville's *Histoire de la langue et de la littérature française*, 8 (Paris, 1899), p. 802. The passage from André Barre to which Spitzer refers is from *Le Symbolisme* (Paris, 1912), pp. 395–96. Spitzer takes specific issue with these writers in "Die syntaktischen Errungenschaften der Symbolisten," pp. 283–88.

6. By "divismo" Giacomo Devoto meant the type of hero-worship extended in modern times to film and sports stars. See the definition in Devoto and Gian Carlo Oli, *Vocabulario illustrato della lingua italiana* (New York, 1967).

7. Francis Jammes, "La Salle à manger," in his *De l'Angelus de l'aube à l'Angelus du soir* (Paris, 1971), pp. 62–63. The English translation is by Teo Savory, in *Jammes* (Santa Barbara, Calif., 1967), p. 17.

8. Juan Corominas, *Diccionario crítico etimológico de la lengua castellana*, 4 (Berne, 1954), pp. 608–11.

9. François de Malherbe, *Œuvres*, ed. Antoine Adam (Paris, 1971), p. 41.

10. See Spitzer, "Ehrenrettung von Malherbe's 'Consolation à Monsieur du Périer,'" in his *Stilstudien*, 2 (Munich, 1928), pp. 18–29.

11. Oskar Walzel, *Gehalt und Gestalt im Kunstwerk des Dichters* (Potsdam, 1923).

12. See Spitzer, "Die klassische Dämpfung in Racines Stil," in his *Romanische Stil- und Literaturstudien*, 1 (Marburg, 1931), pp. 135–268.

13. *Phèdre*, act 5, sc. 6, in Jean Racine, *Théâtre complet*, ed. Jacques Morel and Alain Viala (Paris, 1980), p. 628.

14. See Wilhelm Dilthey, *Das Erlebnis und die Dichtung* (Leipzig, 1905).

15. Hans Sperber and Leo Spitzer, *Motiv und Wort: Studien zur Literatur- und Sprachpsychologie* (Leipzig, 1918).

16. Spitzer, *Essays in Historical Semantics* (New York, 1948). The investigations that Spitzer describes were continued in his unfinished, posthumously published *Classical and Christian Ideas of World Harmony: Prolegomena to an Interpretation of the Word "Stimmung,"* ed. Anna Granville Hatcher (Baltimore, Md., 1963).

17. This essay, "Pseudo-objective Motivation in Charles-Louis Philippe," is included in the present volume.

18. Charles-Louis Philippe, *Bubu de Montparnasse* (Paris, 1905), pp. 57–58. Another quotation, from p. 53, is cited in the next extract in the text.

19. See Spitzer, "Zu Charles Péguy's Stil," in his *Stilstudien*, 2 (Munich, 1928), pp. 301–64.

20. See Spitzer, "Zum Stil Marcel Proust's" *Stilstudien*, 2, pp. 365–497.

21. See Spitzer, "Der Unanismus Jules Romains' im Spiegel seiner Sprache," *Stilstudien*, 2, pp. 208–300.

22. Jules Romains, *Les Copains* (Paris, 1922), pp. 18, 215.

23. See Spitzer, "The Style of Diderot," in his *Linguistics and Literary History: Essays in Stylistics* (Princeton, N.J., 1948), pp. 135–91.

24. Denis Diderot, "Jouissance," in *Encyclopédie*, ed. John Lough and Jacques Proust, 3 (Paris, 1976), p. 576.

25. See Fubini, "Ragioni storiche," cited in n. 1.

26. See Spitzer, "Etude a-historique d'un texte: Ballade des dames du temps jadis," in his *Romanische Literaturstudien, 1936–1956* (Tübingen, 1959), pp. 113–29.

27. This essay, "On Góngora's *Soledades*," is included in the present volume.

28. The two volumes to which Spitzer here refers are, respectively, *Marcel Proust ed altri saggi di letteratura moderna*, cited in n. 1, and *Romanische Literaturstudien*, cited in n. 26.

29. See Spitzer, "Zu Victor Hugo's 'Le Rouet d'Omphale,'" in his *Romanische Literaturstudien*, pp. 277–85.

30. See, respectively, Spitzer, "La 'Lettre sur la baguette de Coudrier' dans le lai du Chievrefueil," *Romanische Literaturstudien*, pp. 15–25, and Anna Granville Hatcher, "Le Lai du Chievrefueil, 61–78, 107–13," *Romania*, 71 (1950): 330–44.

31. *Poètes et romanciers du moyen age*, ed. Albert Pauphilet (Paris, 1952), p. 340.

32. See Spitzer, "Razón de Amor," in his *Romanische Literaturstudien*, pp. 664–82.

33. See Spitzer, "Nuove considerazioni sul 'Cantico di frate Sole,'" *Romanische Literaturstudien*, pp. 464–87.

34. See Spitzer, "The Poetic Treatment of a Platonic-Christian Theme," *Romanische Literaturstudien*, pp. 130–59.

35. Pio Rajna, *Le fonti dell'Orlando furioso* (Florence, 1876).

36. Ernst Robert Curtius, *European Literature and the Latin Middle Ages*, trans. Willard R. Trask (Princeton, N.J., 1953).

37. Spitzer's attempt to trace the origins of the New Criticism to secondary-school instruction does not stand up to scrutiny; the New Criticism began as a method designed to teach literature to undergraduate college students.

38. Cleanth Brooks, *The Well Wrought Urn* (New York, 1947).

39. Victor Erlich, *Russian Formalism* (The Hague, 1955).

40. Erich Auerbach, *Gesammelte Aufsätze zur romanischen Philologie* (Berne, 1967), pp. 356, 357, 261, respectively. Spitzer, who did not provide footnotes to his citations in this essay, is here apparently quoting from three separate passages by Auerbach.

41. See William Empson, *Seven Types of Ambiguity* (London, 1930).

42. Alfred Jacob, "The 'Razón de Amor' as Christian Symbolism," *Hispanic Review*, 20 (1952): 282–301.

43. Spitzer's essay taking issue with Georges Poulet on Marivaux's novel *La Vie de Marianne* is included in the present volume.

44. Stephen Gilman, *The Art of La Celestina* (Madison, Wis., 1956). See Spitzer's review-article taking issue with Gilman's approach, "A New Book on the Art of *The Celestina*," *Hispanic Review*, 25 (1957): 1–25.

45. Spitzer's essay on "Aspasia" did not appear in the Hatzfeld *Festschrift* but was published posthumously in *Cultura neolatina*, 23 (1963): 114–35. The Monteverdi essay he refers to is Angelo Monteverdi, "La Data del 'Passero solitario,'" reprinted in Monteverdi, *Frammenti critici leopardiani* (Naples, 1967), pp. 67–101.

46. *Critica stilistica e storia del linguaggio*, cited in n. 1.

47. Auerbach, *Mimesis* (Princeton, N.J., 1953). For Aurelio Roncaglia's refusal to call Auerbach's book "stylistic criticism," see his introduction to the Italian translation, *Mimesis: Il realismo nella letteratura occidentale*, trans. Alberto Romagnoli and Hans Hinterhäuser (Turin, 1956), pp. xvii, xxviii–xxx, xxxii.

48. See Spitzer, "Les 'Lettres portugaises,'" in his *Romanische Literaturstudien*, pp. 210–47.

49. See Spitzer, "Die Figur der Fénix in Calderón's *Standhaften Prinzen*," *Romanistisches Jahrbuch*, 10 (1959): 305–35.

Index

In this index an "f" after a number indicates a separate reference on the next page, and an "ff" indicates separate references on the next two pages. A continuous discussion over two or more pages is indicated by a span of page numbers, e.g., "pp. 57–58." *Passim* is used for a cluster of references in close but not consecutive sequence. References to literary works have been included under the author's name.

Library of Congress Cataloging-in-Publication Data

Spitzer, Leo, 1887–1960.
Representative essays.

Contents: Linguistics and literary history (1948)—Pseudo-objective motivation in
Charles-Louis Philippe (1923)—Two essays on Góngora's Soledades (1930, 1940)—
The Spanish baroque (1944)—Three essays on Dante's Commedia (1942, 1944,
1955)—Geistesgeschichte vs. history of ideas as applied to Hitlerism (1944)—Lin-
guistic perspectivism in the Don Quijote (1948)—Interpretation of an ode by Paul
Claudel (1948)—American advertising explained as popular art (1949)—Apropos of
La vie de Marianne (letter to Georges Poulet) (1953)—A central theme and its struc-
tural equivalent in Lope's Fuenteovejuna (1955)—Development of a method (1960).
   Bibliography: p.
   Includes index.
   1. Literature—History and criticism.
I. Forcione, Alban K., 1938–   . II. Lindenberger, Herbert Samuel, 1929–
III. Sutherland, Madeline, 1952–   . IV. Title.
PN37.S65   1988   809   87-10100
ISBN 0-8047-1367-7 (alk. paper)